Designing Instructional Strategies

The Prevention of Academic Learning Problems

Edward J. Kameenui
University of Oregon

Deborah C. Simmons
Vanderbilt University

Merrill Publishing Company

Cover Image: Marko Spalatin

Published by Merrill Publishing Company
Columbus, Ohio 43216

This book was set in Quorum and Helvetica

Administrative Editor: Anne Castel
Developmental Editor: Linda James Scharp
Production Editors: Linda Kauffman Peterson, Peg Connelly Gluntz
Art Coordinator: Vincent A. Smith
Cover Designer: Russ Maselli
Photo Editor: Terry L. Tietz

Photo Credits: pp. 3, 7, 57, 99, 133, 144, 199, 359, 367, 375, Linda Duncan Malone; pp. 21, 147, 210, Kay Cozad; pp. 34, 431, Andy Brunk/Merrill; p. 35, Alan Cliburn/Merrill; pp. 63, 249, Jean Greenwald/Merrill; pp. 79, 91, 119, 181, 254, Cynthia Griffin; pp. 87, 150, 467, Edwina Lee; p. 305, Billy Barnes/Merrill; p. 319, Karen Van Horn; p. 419, Bruce Johnson/Merrill; p. 480, Gail Tompkins.

Library of Congress Catalog Card Number: 89-62848
International Standard Book Number: 0-675-21004-9
Printed in the United States of America
1 2 3 4 5 6 7 8 9—94 93 92 91 90

Preface

Designing Instructional Strategies: The Prevention of Academic Learning Problems is about designing and delivering instruction to students with academic learning problems. These students are identified as learning disabled, mildly handicapped, or emotionally disturbed who receive services in special education or general education settings. They are also nonhandicapped students in general education classrooms who are referred to as low performers, academically at-risk, or culturally disadvantaged, as well as students "prereferred" for academic assistance. Although these students may differ with respect to intelligence, social–emotional development, or educational placement, they are the same in at least one respect—they have significant difficulties successfully performing academic tasks in reading, mathematics, language, or expressive writing. For some students, these difficulties create a cycle of failure. In order to break the cycle, instruction must be intensive, direct, sustained, carefully designed, and passionately delivered.

We developed this book for both special education and general education advanced undergraduate and graduate courses designated for training teachers of students with academic learning problems. In our own teaching, we found many "methods" texts too cursory in their treatment of the teaching of academic skills. These texts, for a variety of reasons, often fail to provide teachers with a clear framework or "way of thinking" about instruction—how it should be systematically designed and consistently delivered.

In this text, we establish an instructional framework (the *Before, During,* and *After* phases of instruction) and an instructional template (the *Generic Instruction Set* [GIST]) as pedagogical anchoring points. These features are constants throughout the instructional tasks—constants that teachers can rely on when teaching everything from simple facts to complex cognitive operations. Examples of specific instructional strategies in language, decoding, reading comprehension, mathematics, expressive writing, and classroom management are developed utilizing this instructional set and framework. Because it is not possible to describe instructional strategies for every academic skill, we have designed the Generic Instructional Set so that it can be adapted by teachers when developing other teaching sequences.

ORGANIZATION OF THE TEXT

The text is divided into four parts. Part I is an introduction to the design of instruction. Chapter 1 describes a set of assumptions about the teacher, learner, and skill or content to be taught. The premise of this chapter is that the beliefs a teacher brings to the instructional context influence the design and delivery of the instruction. Chapter 2 examines the relationship between instruction and assessment, describing the critical task dimensions, response requirements, and instructional assessment procedures that interact with learner performance.

Part II discusses the principles of designing instruction. Chapter 3 describes the different forms of knowledge that make up a curriculum. These knowledge forms range from simple associations and facts in mathematics to complex cognitive strategies in reading comprehension. Chapter 4, a pivotal chapter, discusses the *Generic Instructional Set* (GIST) that is used as the basic design of instruction framework in Chapters 5 through 11. In addition, we introduce and describe the *Before, During,* and *After* phases of instruction.

In Part III, the design of instruction principles are applied to the teaching of simple facts, discriminations, concepts, rule relationships, decoding, reading comprehension of narrative and content area texts, mathematics, and expressive writing. In Chapters 5 through 11, the Generic Instructional Set is used as the framework for describing the details of specific instructional strategies. In each Generic Instructional Set, the form of knowledge, range of examples, sequence of examples, test examples, and practice examples are described. Each chapters also includes instructional formats that incorporate the *Before, During,* and *After* phases of instruction.

Part IV, Chapter 12, deals with designing classroom management strategies. The management of behavior problems within the context of instruction, rather than in the context of behavior management, is discussed. Five assumptions for guiding classroom management and decision making are proposed and several general procedures for preventing, rather than reacting to, management problems are described.

TEXT FEATURES

This text includes several organizational features to assist the reader.

- □ **Chapter Objectives.** Each chapter opens with a set of objectives alerting the reader to the critical content of the chapter. The objectives also serve as statements of what the reader can reasonably expect to have accomplished after reading each chapter.

□ **Application Items.** At the end of each chapter, we provide a set of application items to assess the reader's understanding of important information in the chapter. The application items require students to analyze and apply the principles described to actual instructional situations.

□ **Instructional Formats.** Chapters 5 through 11 include instructional formats that describe and apply the Generic Instructional Set to the details of teaching selected skills. These details include teacher wording, a sequence of examples, test examples, practice examples, and guidelines for correcting mistakes. In addition, the instructional formats are developed within each of the three phases of instruction— *Before, During,* and *After.* These three phases and the Generic Instructional Set establish a consistent framework from chapter to chapter and serve as critical anchoring points of the text.

□ **Graphic Organizers.** The text discussion and instructional formats are supplemented by graphic organizers that summarize and highlight the chapter's main points through visual displays.

□ **Chapter Summaries.** Each chapter ends with a summary.

In addition, references are found at the end of each chapter. Several chapters include appendixes with extended examples of instructional formats, and both an author index and a subject index are included at the end of the book.

ACKNOWLEDGMENTS

We collaborated on this text from great distances and in varied settings—Purdue University, Bowling Green State University, United States Department of Education, Vanderbilt University, and University of Oregon. In each setting, many people helped us, directly or indirectly, with the text preparation. Eric Jones, Bowling Green State University, co-authored Chapter 10, "Designing Instructional Strategies for Teaching Mathematics: Facts, Concepts, and Operations." We also thank Sharon Allen and Diane Adams, secretaries at Purdue University, who assisted us in the very beginning. We appreciate the contributions of graduate students at Purdue who shared their ideas with us and unknowingly field-tested many of the instructional pieces proposed in the text: Karen Becker, Teresa Bowers, Adele Brown, Dawn Cartwright, Mary Eisert, Kim Foster, Robin Gilman, Julia Gilstrap, Debbie Glick, Vickie Hibbert, Cheryl Lundsford, Donna McIlwrath, Meg McNamara, Georgia Patrick, Julie Raymond, Diana Stewart, Karen Van Horn, and Cindy Watts. We are especially grateful to the following people for their quiet support and friendship: Kay Cozad, Craig Darch, Lyle Lloyd, Linda Duncan Malone, Ed Fiscus, Cyndy Griffin, Asha Jitendra, Edwina Lee, Tricia Mathes, Janice Pate, and Susan and Randy Woodson. Our editors at Merrill Publishing Company, Ann Castel, Linda James Scharp, Linda Peterson, and Peg Gluntz were gracious and encouraging with their assistance. We extend a special thanks to our former editor, Vickie Knight, who suggested the idea for the text, then stuck with us during its long development.

We have learned from the teaching and research efforts of many colleagues who influenced our thinking about instruction. We extend thanks to Jim Baumann, Wes Becker,

Ted Coladarci, Geoff Colvin, Bob Dixon, Zig Engelmann, Doug Fuchs, Lynn Fuchs, Russell Gersten, Mary Gleason, Joe Jenkins, Eric Jones, Marty Kaufman, David Majsterek, Stan Paine, Pat Shannon, Janet Spector, Jerry Silbert, Randy Sprick, Marcy Stein, and Rich Wilson.

The two people who worked on preparing the indexes and references for this text deserve special mention—Jean Estepp (University of Oregon) and Meg Couch (Vanderbilt University).

The following reviewers contributed valuable insights during preparation of the text: Jeanne Bauwens, Boise State University; Nikki Murdick, University of Arkansas; Sara G. Tarver, University of Wisconsin—Madison; Bill Bursuck, Northern Illinois University; Laura Jordan, University of Illinois; Elliott Lesson, Northern Illinois University; Rena Lewis, San Diego State University; and Eric Jones, Bowling Green State University.

Finally, our deepest thanks and gratitude to our families:

Barb and Dick Baldwin
Brenda and Bree and Ani—E. J. K.
John, Gean, and Leslie—D. C. S.

Contents

PART I
INTRODUCTION TO DESIGNING INSTRUCTION   **1**

ONE   **Academic Learning Problems and the Design of Instruction**   **2**

The Transformation of Special Education   4
The Teacher/Learner/Content Interaction   7
Summary   17

TWO   **Instructional Assessment of Academic Learning Problems**   **20**

Instructional Assessment: Accounting for Failure to Learn   22
Purposes and Limitations of Assessment   24
Dimensions of Instructional Assessment   27
Techniques to Link Assessment and Instruction   36
The Degree of Instructional Assessment   42
Implementing Instructional Assessment   44
Applications of Instructional Assessment   44
Withdrawing Instructional Assessment   52
Summary   52

PART II
PRINCIPLES OF INSTRUCTIONAL DESIGN   **55**

THREE   **A Taxonomy of Knowledge Forms
and Instructional Requirements**   **56**

The Universe of Knowledge: A Structural Analysis   58
Types of Knowledge Forms: From Simple to Complex   67
Categories of Knowledge Forms: Instructional Dimensions
      and Requirements   72
Summary   82

FOUR   **Principles of Designing Instruction: The Three Phases
of Instruction and the Generic Instructional Set**   **86**

The Requirements of an Instructional Cycle   88
The Phases of Instruction: Before/During/After   88
Requirements of an Instructional Sequence   105
Summary   114

PART III
INSTRUCTIONAL STRATEGIES FOR ACADEMIC SKILLS   **117**

FIVE   **Designing Instructional Strategies for Teaching
Verbal Associations: Teaching Simple Facts,
Verbal Chains, and Discriminations**   **118**

Bundles of Knowledge   120
Teaching Simple Facts   122
Teaching Verbal Chains   128
Teaching Discriminations   136
Summary   145

SIX   **Designing Instructional Strategies for
Teaching Concepts and Rule Relationships**   **146**

Teaching Concepts   148
Teaching Rule Relationships   180
Summary   194

SEVEN   **Designing Instructional Strategies for
Teaching Reading: Decoding**   **198**

Introduction   200
A Review of Beginning Reading Instruction   200
Primary Reading Methods   201
Defining Decoding Skills   204

Phase I: Phonics Instruction   206
Phase II: Structural Analysis   215
Phase III: Contextual Analysis   216
Summary of Decoding Phases   218
Integrating Design and Delivery in Beginning Reading Instruction:
     Applying the Generic Instructional Set   218
Summary   244

EIGHT Designing Instructional Strategies for Teaching Reading Comprehension: Narrative Prose   248

The Components of Reading Comprehension Instruction   250
Instructional Strategies   263
Instructional Formats for Teaching Selected Reading
     Comprehension Skills   281
Summary   300

NINE Designing Instructional Strategies for Teaching Reading Comprehension: Content Area Textbook Prose   304

Content Area Learning: The Problem   306
Analyzing Textbook Prose: Factors That Contribute to
     Comprehension Failure   306
Instructional Strategies to Enhance Textbook Prose Learning   316
Designing Comprehension Instruction: Applying the Generic
     Instructional Set   324
Instructional Formats for Teaching Selected Informational Prose
     Comprehension Skills   338
Summary   349
Appendix A: Comprehension Tasks Classified by Response Form,
     Response Modality, and Comprehension Type   352
Appendix B: Classification of Content Area Text Comprehension Skills
     by Knowledge Form   353
Appendix C: Range of Examples for Content Area Prose   354
Appendix D: Sequence of Examples for Content Area
     Textbook Prose   355
Appendix E: Text for Graphic Organizer   356

TEN Designing Instructional Strategies for Teaching Mathematics: Facts, Concepts, and Operations   358

Approaches to Mathematics Learning   360
Developing Mathematics Curricula for Students with Learning
     Problems   362
Designing Math Instruction: Applying the Generic
     Instructional Set   365
Instructional Formats for Mathematics Skills   380

Curriculum-Based Deficiencies and Predictable Problems of Students
    with Academic Learning Problems   393
Modifying Mathematics Curriculum Programs   404
Summary   410
Appendix A: Hierarchies of Numeration, Computation, and Problem-
    Solving Skills   414

**ELEVEN   Designing Instructional Strategies for
            Teaching Expressive Writing**   **418**

Expressive Writing: The Problem   420
Theoretical Models of Writing   425
A Skills Analysis of Expressive Writing   430
Using the Generic Instructional Set in Expressive Writing   438
Examples of Beginning Expressive Writing Skills   446
Summary   461
Appendix A: Sentence Completion Examples   463
Appendix B: Sentence Generation Examples   464

**PART IV
STRATEGIES FOR CLASSROOM MANAGEMENT**   **465**

**TWELVE   Designing Classroom Management Strategies
            Within the Context of Instruction**   **466**

Conceptualizing Classroom Management as Instruction   468
General Procedures for Preventing Management Problems   475
Summary   487

NAME INDEX   **489**
SUBJECT INDEX   **494**

PART I

Introduction to Designing Instruction

C H A P T E R

ONE

Academic Learning Problems and the Design of Instruction

Chapter Objectives

Upon successful completion of this chapter, you will be able to:

1. DESCRIBE a framework upon which the instructional strategies identified in the text are based.

2. IDENTIFY the problems inherent in the transition of learning between general and special education.

3. DESCRIBE a set of assumptions about the teacher, learner, and skill that are essential to break the cycle of failure that children with academic learning problems face in the classroom.

THE TRANSFORMATION OF SPECIAL EDUCATION

In the last two decades, the field of special education has undergone evolutionary changes in its purpose, structure, and character, as well as its spirit. What are the nature and basis of these changes? To what extent do they reflect substantive and structural changes? How does this transformation of structure, purpose, and character change the way the general public thinks about special education and in particular about a disability? How have these changes transformed what takes place in the face-to-face instruction that unfolds in general and special education classrooms? We begin our examination of the answers to these questions with a look at some legal and technological changes that have affected the field of special education.

Legal and Technological Changes

Significant changes have unquestionably taken place in how special education now fits into the bigger scheme of providing *all* children with access to an "appropriate" public education. This new fit was brought about by radical changes in the federal laws that prescribed who was to be educated in the public schools. The most well-known legal change in education was in the form of two federal laws—Section 504 of the Rehabilitation Act of 1973 (Public Law 93–112) and the Education for All Handicapped Children Act of 1975, commonly known as Public Law 94–142. Because of these two major pieces of federal legislation and an established but ever-expanding body of case law, schools were no longer free to systematically or capriciously turn away children who were deemed "incapable of benefiting substantially from further instruction" (*Cuyahoga County Association for Retarded Children and Adults v. Essex*, 1976).

Public Law 94–142, in a sense, gave schools a new purpose and at the same time transformed their very structure and character. Public schools were now charged with the responsibility of educating not only "regular," nonhandicapped students, but handicapped students as well. Nonhandicapped students, teachers, and school officials were required to change how they thought about the class of citizens typically housed somewhere else in noneducational and institutional settings. The "problem"—the presence of handicapped students—was rightly placed in full view of the educational community and made a structural part of public schools.

The legal changes initiated by the well-known case of *PARC*, or *Pennsylvania Association for Retarded Children v. Commonwealth of Pennsylvania* (1971), were indeed profound. The changes were formally established into federal and state laws by Public Laws 93–112 and 94–142 and other subsequent federal legislation. But other changes were taking place at the same time—changes not only in law but in the *instructional technology* of special education. These technological changes were the result of advances in our knowledge of techniques, methods, procedures, and approaches that made a difference in how handicapped children and adults performed on specific tasks under instructional conditions that were made *exceptional* (Throne, 1970). Advances in the applied research conducted at the time provided a factual basis for the legal argument in the *PARC* case. The argument was straightforward: Handicapped children could indeed benefit from an education. As Thomas K. Gilhool (1973), attorney for the *Pennsylvania Association for Retarded Children*, eloquently noted:

> The factual argument for right to education was equally straightforward. It rested on the now clear proposition that without exception, every child, every exceptional child, every retarded child is capable of benefiting from an education. There is no such thing as an uneducable and untrainable child. To put it another way, for example, for every 30 retarded children with a proper program of education and training, 29 of them are capable of achieving self sufficiency, 25 of them in the ordinary way on the marketplace and 4 of them in a sheltered environment. The remaining 1 of every 30 retarded children is capable with a proper program of education and training of achieving a significant degree of self care. (p. 603)

The technical facts presented by numerous special education experts in the *PARC* case were essential to the case's successful legal decision. Without these facts, the significant changes in the federal laws affecting the education of handicapped students probably would not have taken place (Bateman & Herr, 1981).

Sweeping changes in the laws governing school districts prompted or accelerated significant changes in the technology of instruction. In a sense, the basic rights of handicapped citizens changed not only because society's view of what was just changed, but also because the basic "essentials of teaching" (Bateman, 1971) were validated. Today they serve as the foundation of a technology of instruction (Algozzine & Maheady, 1986; Bickel & Bickel, 1986; Gersten, Woodward, & Carnine, 1987; Reith, Polsgrove, & Semmel, 1982).

Our premise in this text is also straightforward: A technology of instruction is available, and when applied with care, it makes a positive difference in children's academic performance. The fields of education, both special and regular, now have access to more than 20 years of research on the success of effective instruction (Becker, 1977; Englert, 1984; Gersten, 1985; Gersten, Woodward, & Darch, 1986; Rosenshine, 1983) in teaching reading (Carnine, Silbert, & Kameenui, 1990; Williams, 1985), reading comprehension (Kameenui, 1985), mathematics (Kameenui, Carnine, Stein, & Darch, 1986; Kelly, Carnine, Gersten, & Grossen, 1987), expressive writing (Engelmann & Silbert, 1983), spelling, logical reasoning (Fielding, Kameenui, & Gersten, 1983; Simmons & Kameenui, 1988), content area reading (Adams, Carnine, & Gersten, 1982), and computer applications (Woodward & Carnine, 1988). We argue that the success of this instruction is, in part, a result of how the instruction is "designed" (Engelmann & Carnine, 1982; Gersten, Woodward, & Darch, 1986; Kameenui, 1985). The purpose of this text is to show how instruction should be designed in teaching language, reading, mathematics, expressive writing, and content area subjects to students with academic learning problems.

The Design of Instruction

Hallahan and Kauffman (1978) argue that the study of exceptional children is the "study of differences" (p. 2). Exceptional children, they note, are "markedly different from most children" in ways that require special education. Special education is defined in Public Law 94–142 as "specially designed instruction which meets the unique needs of an exceptional child." In other words, specially designed instruction is *required* to address the differences that exceptional students bring to the instructional context. The design of the instruction allows handicapped students to acquire the skills they need to compete with their nonhandicapped peers. We address this design of instruction directly in this text.

We will not explore the psychological, psychodynamic, or sociological dimensions of academic learning problems. Although these topics are important, they are beyond the scope of this text. We are concerned with identifying the *instructional dimensions* that create the conditions of failure for students with academic learning problems. By understanding these, we can design (or redesign) the instruction to meet the needs of students. We do not offer simple solutions to the complex problems facing general and special education classroom teachers. If the problems were simple, "special" education would be unjustifiable and this text unnecessary. The problems of teaching are indeed complex and require complex solutions. However, the problems and solutions are not beyond our reach—we argue that they are well within our grasp.

The study of exceptional children is the study of differences within a context that makes them unique. In the language of special education, we refer to the differences of exceptional children as *disabilities*. We rely on H. Prehm's (personal communication, March 20, 1975) definition of a disability:

> Disability: a deviation (actual or objectively measured) in body or functioning that results in a functional inadequacy in view of environmental demands.

By examining this definition closely, we begin to appreciate what is involved in studying the differences of exceptional students and to see how the design of instruction attempts to diminish those differences. According to Prehm, a disability is a deviation that can be observed either in the physical part of a person or in the way a person acts, behaves, or performs. However, this deviation in body or functioning constitutes a disability *only* when it fails to meet the demands of the environment. This is an important point, because it casts a disability as a dynamic, interactive set of conditions. According to Prehm, a disability is not a static condition. A person restricted to a wheelchair is not disabled by virtue of being confined to a wheelchair. In the same vein, a child who has been identified as developmentally delayed because of an inability to discriminate between the basic language concepts of *yes* and *no* or *up* and *down* is not automatically disabled by virtue of those deficits. A difference becomes a disability only when the learner *fails* to meet the demands of the immediate environment. This difference then becomes a deviation "that results in a functional inadequacy." In this definition, a child's failure to respond adequately to the demands of the environment is referred to as a "functional inadequacy."

Prehm's definition of a disability breaks the historical tradition in special education by recasting a disability as a dynamic interaction of the learner with the environment. It moves away from the medical characterization of a disability as a fixed, unalterable condition that resides within the individual, thereby casting the individual as disabled (Ross, 1977). Instead, it holds the individual up as a potentially dynamic force in the environment; that is, a driving force capable of shaping one's own environment rather than merely reacting to it. With this view of a disability in mind, we can readily appreciate the "marked differences" of exceptional children and the way in which "specially designed instruction" can and must be developed to break the cycle of failure that many of these children and youth face.

THE TEACHER/LEARNER/CONTENT INTERACTION

By conceptualizing a disability as a dynamic interplay of the learner and the environment, we can begin to identify and understand the variables in this interaction that can make a significant difference in how we teach, what we teach, when material is taught or retaught, and under what classroom conditions material is taught. In any interaction, whether it be a chemical, social, or statistical interaction, the total interaction is always more than the sum of its individual parts. The teacher, like the chemist or statistician, is faced with "unpacking" this instructional interaction to identify the cause of the disability, functional inadequacy, or failure. The teacher faces the difficult task of trying to sort out what is responsible for the problem in the interaction. The difficulty of the task is compounded by the many elements to examine. The *learner* must be considered (e.g., "Maybe the learner simply isn't trying hard enough?"); the *teacher* must be considered (e.g., "Maybe the teacher is assuming the learner already knows the skill?"); and the *skill* being taught must be considered (e.g., "Perhaps too much is being taught too fast?"). When looking at the variables that could explain why a student is failing on a particular task, the teacher cannot escape making judgments about these variables and

The learner, the teacher, and the skill being taught must all be considered in the total interaction and in identifying the variables that contribute to a disability.

their interaction. After all, teachers make judgments all the time that range from administrative to academic placement decisions, and it is important to determine what guides these judgments. Furthermore, it is of even greater importance for teachers to determine what will serve to guide their judgments in teaching children who require specially designed instruction.

In the next section of this chapter, we detail a set of assumptions that are essential to guiding the judgments and decisions the teacher will make about a student who is unable to respond to the demands of the environment (i.e., a functional inadequacy). These assumptions are specific to the three prominent variables that are a part of almost every instructional episode: the *teacher,* the *learner,* and the *skill* to be taught. By describing a set of assumptions for each of these variables, we hope to offer teachers a kind of "personal charter" to prevent them from losing the focus of buttressing against student failure. In Figure 1–1, the three variables (learner, teacher, content/skill) are illustrated separately and then in interaction with one another. To understand the interaction of these three variables, teachers must be clear about the assumptions they make for each variable.

The assumptions delineated in the next section of this text will serve as the foundation for instructional strategies we recommend throughout the text. These are not intended to be exhaustive or absolute. They are intended to guide our thinking and problem solving when faced with student failure.

The Teacher: Assumptions

> **Assumption 1:** The teaching process is complex. Consequently, the solutions to problems in the teaching process are complex.

The complexity of the teaching process should not be underestimated. The teacher is but one individual who is responsible for orchestrating a chorus of learners within a system driven by many forces—cultural, social, political, economical, ethical, moral, professional, intellectual, historical, legal, and, of course, personal. Even if we choose to ignore events outside the classroom and focus only on events within the walls of the classroom, the teaching process is no less complex.

To appreciate the complexity of this process, all we need do is observe a teacher *before, during,* and *after* teaching a small reading group of 6 "poor readers" while managing the independent seatwork of 12 other children, most of whom are at different skill levels on basic and content-area skills, and directing the flow of traffic in and out of the classroom for a period of 40 minutes. The abilities required of a teacher to manage successfully a small group engaged in reading instruction are no less demanding than those of a highly skilled technician: The teacher watches eyes and mouths as children read orally; stops to make a correction or to praise a child's fluent reading while also attending to those who are following along; looks up to praise a child who appears to be working diligently at seatwork; points to the clock, indicating that it is time for a student to make the transition to speech.

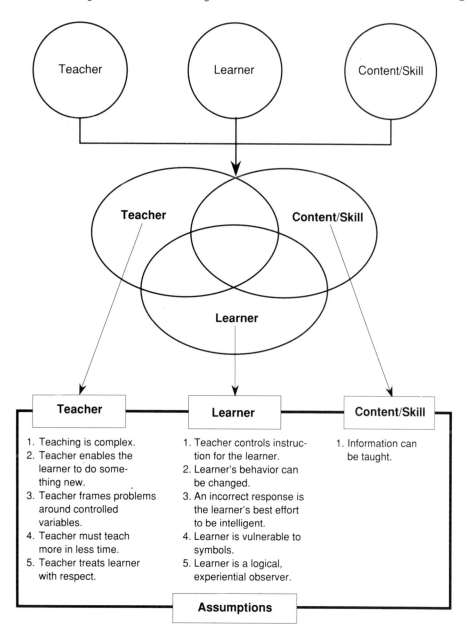

FIGURE 1-1
The teacher, learner, content/skill interaction

To address complex academic learning problems, we must take care to attend not only to the teacher's actions during small group instruction, but also to what the teacher teaches. That is, we must attend to the curriculum, the individual teaching sequences and lessons that comprise that curriculum, and when and under what conditions the instruction occurs. In essence, to begin to address complex learning problems intelligently, we must attend to the *details of the instruction* and to what Gage (1978) refers to as the "intricate requirements" of complex academic tasks. The complexity of the teaching process need not be paralyzing. However, it should alert teachers to the importance of sound instructional assessment, programming, and implementation.

Assumption 2: Teaching involves enabling the learner to do things that could not be done before.

The purpose of this assumption is to recognize the often unacknowledged and unspoken power and influence a teacher holds in the teaching context. Christa McAuliffe, the teacher killed in the *Challenger* disaster, captured this power when she said, "I touch the future, I teach." Teachers "touch the future" by teaching in a way that allows children to learn things they haven't known before. Teachers are ultimately responsible for taking a child from a state of "unknowing" to a state of "knowing;" that is, a state in which a child can read basic CVC (consonant, vowel, consonant) words (e.g., *cat, cot, sit*) or interpret the fourth soliloquy of *Hamlet* in ways that weren't possible before. The teaching process should involve more than merely providing children with an opportunity to demonstrate what they already know. It must involve the integration of new knowledge with old knowledge in ways that allow the learner to go beyond the immediate demands of the task at hand.

For students with academic learning problems, this assumption holds a unique challenge, for it will require the teacher to design teaching in such a way that basic preskills or "old" knowledge and skills are systematically reviewed while new skills are also taught, applied, and reviewed. Balancing the need to review old skills while forging ahead to cover new skills is an important challenge for teachers.

Assumption 3: Teaching involves framing problems in terms of variables that the teacher controls.

Holding to this assumption when a problem surfaces means that the teacher must examine every possible instructional detail that affects how ideas, concepts, facts, rules, and operations are communicated to the learner. In the face of a problem, the teacher must first scrutinize these instructional details. This assumption really addresses the teacher's professional frame of mind during instruction. The teacher should ask: "When a problem surfaces during instruction (e.g., the student responds incorrectly or isn't attending to the lesson), what is my instinctive response? Do I immediately become frustrated by finding fault with the learner? Or do I examine my own instruction?"

This assumption doesn't preclude the teacher from becoming frustrated by failure. It simply requires teachers to be more effective problem solvers by compelling them to examine those features of their profession that they directly control— the features of their instruction. To appreciate this assumption, we need only to reflect on working with computers. When a problem occurs during an interaction with a computer, the user's first response typically is to ask: "What did I do wrong to create the error?" Unless the hardware is smoking or on fire, the user's instinct is to assume that the problem is with the user.

The teacher should consider the input (i.e., the details of the instruction) in the face of a problem in much the same way that a user would first consider the problem to be with the information fed to the computer. It would make no sense for the computer user to sneer, kick, or curse the computer as a means of solving the problem.

Assumption 4: Teaching children with academic learning problems involves teaching more in less time.

Much attention has been drawn in the last decade to the issue of time and how it is spent in the classroom (Carroll, 1966; Rosenshine, 1979). The research on teacher effects (Brophy & Good, 1986; Rosenshine & Stevens, 1986) appears unequivocal in supporting a significant relationship between the amount of time children spend on academic tasks and their subsequent achievement. The more children are engaged in studying academically related tasks, the more likely they are to improve their achievement. For children with significant skill deficiencies, the relationship between engaged time and achievement is no different. What *is* different is the way in which that time is spread between working on deficits and keeping up with the pace of the mainstream. We have characterized this unfortunate dilemma as **curriculum compression.**

As we see it, securing enough instructional time and protecting it is the teacher's most important administrative responsibility. Effective instructional strategies, well-designed curriculum programs, enthusiastic teacher presentation skills, insightful correction procedures, and dynamic instructional assessment techniques are essentially moot if we don't have adequate time to use them. As noted previously, for children who are behind to catch up, they simply must be taught more in less time. There is no way around this scenario. If the teacher doesn't attempt to teach more in less time and everything remains at the same pace of instruction, the gap in general knowledge between a normal and a mildly handicapped student becomes even greater.

The gap between low performers and high performers is real. For example, Biemiller (1977–1978) found that first-grade readers in the "least able" groups read substantially fewer words per reading session than children in the "most able" groups. For example, in October, students in the most able groups read a mean of 12.2 words per child per reading lesson, the students in the average ability groups read 11.9 words per child per reading lesson, and the students in the least able groups were not reading. By January, the mean for the most able groups was 51.9, for the average ability groups, 25.8, and for the least able groups, 11.5. By the month of April, the respective means were 81.4, 72.3, and 31.6. This trend in favor of children who are most able appears to haunt first-grade classrooms even today. Allington (1984) found that the average skilled reader read approximately three times as many words during group reading as the average less skilled reader. Finally, Nagy and Anderson (1984) estimated that "the least motivated children in the middle grades might read 100,000 words a year while the average children at this level might read 1,000,000. The figure for the voracious middle grade reader might be 10,000,000 or even as high as 50,000,000. If these guesses are anywhere near the mark, these are staggering individual differences in the volume of language experience, and therefore, opportunity to learn new words" (p. 328).

Stanovich (1986) resurrected an old characterization of these chilling statistics that he refers to as "Matthew effects." Stanovich states, "The very children who are reading well and who have good vocabularies will read more, learn more word meanings, and hence read even better. Children with inadequate vocabularies—who read slowly and without enjoyment—read less, and as a result have slower development of vocabulary knowledge, which inhibits further growth in reading ability" (p. 381). In light of this research, it is absolutely imperative that more is taught in less time.

Assumption 5: Teaching involves treating the learner with respect, dignity, and compassion—always.

Teaching students who have academic and social skill deficiencies day in and day out for 180 days or more is demanding. This kind of teaching creates a fatigue that can wear a teacher down physically, psychologically, and emotionally. In light of this fatigue, or when faced with a threatening situation (e.g., an aggressive adolescent having a tantrum), it would be natural for a teacher to respond in a manner that doesn't treat the learner with respect. For example, if an angry and distraught student took a swing at a teacher, the teacher might wrestle the student to the ground. Although such a response is understandable, it is still unacceptable.

Teachers cannot treat students with anything less than respect and integrity, regardless of the circumstances. In many cases, students carefully examine these moments of crisis to "test" the responses of adults. In these moments students tacitly grope for role models who maintain a sense of individual integrity and professional equilibrium.

The Learner: Assumptions

Assumption 1: If the learner fails, the failure must be framed in terms of the instruction the teacher controls.

This assumption is similar to Assumption 3 posed earlier in the teaching context. It serves as a critical guide for thinking about errors that occur within an instructional episode, whether the error is a decoding error (e.g., the child says *buh* for the letter *d*), a fact error (e.g., the child says that 7×8 is 65), or an error in general knowledge (e.g., the child doesn't know that the month of December is in the winter season). It is important for teachers first to view all these errors as errors of instruction or information; that is, the child does not have the correct information or the instruction did not unambiguously communicate the information to the learner. It would be inappropriate to dismiss the failure as simply a result of the child's "learning disability" or laziness.

By embracing this assumption, the teacher is positioned to examine the numerous features of instruction. This allows the teacher to be an active agent of change. To assume the problem is inherent in the learner leaves the teacher without any influence, because the problem is framed as being outside the teacher's province of control (i.e., in the learner's head). Conversely, the teacher should automatically examine the instructional sequence when the learner gives an incorrect response. As Algozzine and Maheady (1986) suggest, "When all else fails, teach!"

Assumption 2: A learner's behavior can be changed by controlling environmental events.

Disability and failure can be explained in many different ways (e.g., abnormal behavior = presence of disease; normal behavior = absence of disease). We could examine numerous conceptual and theoretical models for explaining the origin and nature of a problem, be it learning disabilities, emotional disturbance, or mental retardation. For example, one model could approach the problem from a biological perspective in which genetic, neurological, and biochemical factors are identified as the basis for academic learning problems. Another model might approach the problem from a psychoanalytic perspective, in which the deep-rooted, underlying aspects of the psyche are explored as the basis of the problem. Each conceptual model would bring its own way of interpreting the problem. Assumption 2 is derived from a behavioral approach for practical reasons.

The assumption acknowledges that the teacher's province is the classroom. Within this context the teacher will have the most significant impact on a student. The teacher is responsible for ensuring that a student progresses from a state of unknowing—not knowing a skill (Ross, 1977)—to a state of knowing. To be effective, the teacher must assume that teaching can be arranged to bring about this change in a student's state of knowing. Moreover, the teacher must also assume that a student's behavior on a day-to-day basis will be predictable; that is, what Dr. Jekyll learned one day will not be undone by Mr. Hyde the next day. The student's behavior occurs with some regularity, and teaching can make a difference. As Schwartz and Lacey (1982) point out, "There are regularities to human action which are universal, which are a part of the essential nature of man. When these regularities are discovered . . . they will account for human action in the past and predict human action in the future" (p. 12). To assume that there are no regularities to human action leaves the teacher in a hopeless position with only chaos as a constant. By embracing the second assumption that the teacher has control, the teacher can hope to make a difference in breaking the cycle of failure of students with academic learning problems.

Assumption 3: A learner's incorrect, inappropriate, or inadequate response to a task is the learner's best effort to be intelligent.

If we hold to the assumption that students tend to rely on their experiences in making sense of information a teacher presents, we must also assume that their responses to the world around them are based on genuine efforts to understand the events of this world. This assumption states that no matter how ridiculous, stupid, or hostile a response may seem, the teacher must view it as a student's *best effort to be intelligent* (Sprick, 1981). This is not an easy assumption to embrace or to hold to in the day-to-day work with students over the course of a school year.

Some teachers view this assumption as naive and perhaps irresponsible, especially after being struck by a student with a history of aggressive behavior or after waiting out a 30-minute screaming, scratching tantrum by a 12-year-old in a treatment center. But the assumption that learners are putting forth their best effort to be intelligent, even in the face of these gut-wrenching incidents, is not naive. It *is* naive to think that these behaviors are incidental or "not smart" for the learner, even though the learner ends up in the "quiet room" and loses privileges and reinforcers. The fact is that these tantrums and incidents of noncompliance end up being "intelligent" for the learner in the long run. As Engelmann and Colvin (1984) have noted, incidents of noncompliance are students' best efforts to be intelligent, because they learn in time that the more they hit, bite, soil, or swear, the more they will be left alone. In essence, what appears to be "stupid" ends up being "smart" for the learner.

The danger in not embracing our assumption is obvious. We are certainly free to view incorrect or inappropriate behaviors as stupid or unintelligent, or even as violations against our personal dignity as professionals. The risk we take in holding to such a viewpoint is that it makes it easy to see the learner as stupid, unintelligent, and abusive. Once a teacher arrives at this opinion, the entire teaching process is short-circuited and is in serious jeopardy.

> **Assumption 4:** The learner is vulnerable to the world of symbols.

Students with academic learning problems, whether they are labeled learning disabled, mildly handicapped, educable mentally retarded, mildly mentally handicapped, or emotionally disturbed, experience difficulty with symbolic operations. Much of the information about the world and the different knowledge sources that allow learners to negotiate their way in the world successfully are communicated through symbols. Symbolic operations refer to a process in which a learner operates with symbols, as is the case with most academic or cognitive tasks. Nonsymbolic tasks, on the other hand, consist of physical, motor tasks such as picking up a cup, kicking a soccer ball, or buttoning a coat. Nonsymbolic tasks do not require the learner to decode, interpret, or read symbols.

Students with academic learning problems require an instructional system that is sensitive to their inadequacy with complex symbolic operations. A student who is required to interpret the following passage from *Hamlet*, in the absence of some direct guidance and instruction from the teacher, is completely vulnerable to the complexity of this symbolic soliloquy:

> For who would bear the whips and scorns of time,
> Th' oppressor's wrong, the proud man's contumely,

The pangs of despised love, the law's delay,
The insolence of office, and the spurns
That patient merit of th' unworthy takes,
When he himself might his quietus make
With a bare bodkin?

However, we need not invoke *Hamlet* and a piece of the "To be, or not to be" soliloquy to point out the vulnerability that all learners universally feel in certain learning situations. Unless the environment, or in most instances the teacher, gives the learner feedback on the interpretation of a symbol, the learner could easily interpret the symbol incorrectly. Nothing prevents the learner from pointing to the word *cat* and reading it as *cot*, or from insisting that *Hamlet* is simply a play about a spoiled, fatherless son who is jealous of his mother's new acquaintance. Because symbols can be arbitrarily interpreted to represent what a learner may mistakenly think they represent, the teacher must guide this interpretation. The teacher is in the position to lead the learner through the correct decoding of the word "cat" and of a reasonable interpretation of the tragedy *Hamlet*.

Assumption 5: The learner is a logical, experiential observer.

D. W. Carnine (personal communication, September 18, 1982) once noted that children, especially low-performing learners, tend to be tenacious in their interpretation of what they see happening around them. In the context of an instructional episode, students rely on their experiences, however undeveloped, in making sense of the information (i.e., the concept, fact, rule, or operation) being presented to them. Carnine characterized this insistent tendency of children to report what they see by noting that children are sometimes "merciless empiricists;" that is, they generally operate on the information presented to them without going much beyond what they see and know from past experience. Schwartz and Lacey (1982) refer to children's reliance on past experience as an "associative bias." A child's response to a current set of events, as the child sees them, is strongly influenced by experience with similar past events.

For example, if the teacher presents the learner with a picture of a red, well-polished McIntosh apple and asks, "What is this?" it would not be unreasonable or unintelligent for the learner to respond by identifying the apple as an "orange" (because apples and oranges are fruits and are frequently paired), or a "tomato" (because apples and tomatoes are both red), or even a "ball" (because apples and ball are of similar shape).

The learner is simply making logical observations of the information presented and squaring those observations with individual experience. More specifically, the learner is attempting to key in on one of the many attributes of "apple" (i.e., red, a fruit, round, shiny, has a stem) to determine the *one* attribute that makes an apple an "apple." It is unlikely that the learner would point to the picture and respond by calling it an "elephant" (unless, of course, the learner has experienced only red elephants or elephants the size of an apple). These responses are logically plausible, but highly improbable because they are not likely to be part of the learner's experience. By holding to the assumption that learners rely on experience, the teacher is able to see students as logical decoders of the world around them (Campbell, 1982). The teacher consequently views the student's responses as reasonable, sensible, and based on some attribute or feature of the information being presented that is also linked to experience.

The Content or Skill: Assumptions

Specifying the assumptions about the content or skill to be taught and clearly communicating those assumptions are not easy tasks. First of all, it is difficult to identify a starting point of a skill, because skills come in many different shapes, sizes, colors, and packages. Moreover, to make intelligent assumptions about the skills to be taught, teachers must specify the various dimensions of those skills and how they fit in the broader scheme of knowledge. The assumptions teachers make will affect how the skills are taught. In the face of these disclaimers, and to avoid the detailing of skills that is to be given in following chapters, we offer the following assumption.

> **Assumption 1:** Information, whether in the form of a skill, concept, fact, rule, operation, algorithm, or a set of relationships and facts in a content area, can be taught.

This is a cumbersome assumption, but its clumsiness is perhaps representative of the nature and diversity of what teachers are responsible for teaching—information. This assumption acknowledges that information comes in many different forms (Engelmann & Carnine, 1982; Gagne, 1985; Tennyson & Cochiarella, 1986). Information comes in the form of reading skills, language concepts, mathematics operations, social studies, and so on. Every reading skill or language concept is a piece of information. Sometimes that piece is part of a bigger package of skills and concepts that is composed of many little-connected and unconnected pieces. By holding to this assumption, teachers are deemed responsible for breaking down information in a way that facilitates a learner's acquisition, storage, and later retrieval. Like the other assumptions we have described so far, this assumption places the teacher in a frame of mind to say, "I can design the instruction to make it more effective."

The Teacher/Learner/Content Interaction: Assumptions and Action

We have described the assumptions that should direct and drive the teacher's actions in attempting to prevent, buttress against, and account for failure. These assumptions are intended to guide the teacher's thinking and decision making when faced with a "functional inadequacy," or disability, or, in real terms, failure. As illustrated in Figure 1–2, when a functional inadequacy or failure occurs within the context of these three variables and their interaction, the need to hold to the assumptions we have delineated is even more important. By holding to them, the teacher takes on the primary responsibility of breaking the cycle of failure that many students face in school.

FIGURE 1–2
A functional inadequacy and the
teacher/learner/content interaction

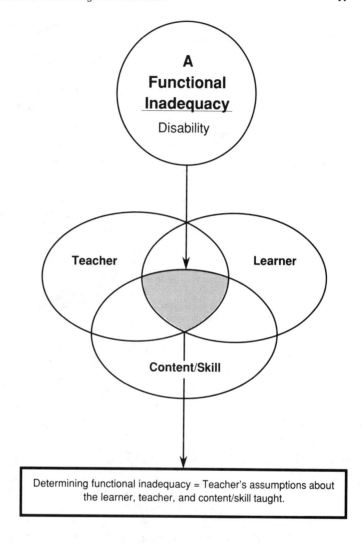

SUMMARY

The primary purpose of this chapter was to introduce and frame a way of thinking about teaching and learning in general and academic learning problems in particular. We proposed a set of assumptions for the teacher to embrace. These assumptions are specific to the three prominent variables in the instructional episode: the teacher, the learner, and the content or skill to be taught. The assumptions are intended to serve as guidelines for the teacher to follow in breaking the context and cycle of failure that children with academic learning problems experience.

APPLICATION ITEMS

1. Write the definition of a disability provided by Prehm on p. 6. Find another definition of a disability (e.g., introductory text to special education; World Health Organization definition;

federal or state statutory definition) and compare them. Describe how the definitions are the same and how they are different. Discuss the implications each definition carries for instruction.

2. Select one assumption from each of the teacher and learner contexts described in the chapter. Discuss your agreement or disagreement with each assumption. Describe at least one additional assumption you would add to both the teacher and learner contexts.

3. Describe what is meant by the design of instruction. Specify how the transformation of special education influenced this feature.

REFERENCES

Adams, A., Carnine, D., & Gersten, R. (1982). Instructional strategies for studying content area texts in the intermediate grades. *Reading Research Quarterly, 17*(1), 27–55.

Algozzine, B., & Maheady, L. (1986). When all else fails, teach! Editorial in *Exceptional Children, 52*(6), 487–488.

Allington, R. L. (1984). Content coverage and contextual reading in reading groups. *Journal of Reading Behavior, 16,* 85–96.

Bateman, B. D. (1971). *The essentials of teaching.* Sioux Falls, SD: Dimensions Publishing.

Bateman, B. D., & Herr, C. (1981). Legislation and litigation in special education. In D. Hallahan & J. Kauffman (Eds.), *The handbook of special education* (pp. 330–360). Englewood Cliffs, NJ: Prentice-Hall.

Becker, W. C. (1977). Teaching reading and language to the disadvantaged—what we have learned from field research. *Harvard Educational Review, 47,* 518–543.

Bickel, W. E., & Bickel, D. D. (1986). Effective schools, classrooms, and instruction: Implications for special education. *Exceptional Children, 52,* 489–500.

Biemiller, A. (1977–1978). Relationships between oral reading rates for letters, words, and simple text in the development of reading achievement. *Reading Research Quarterly, 13,* 223–253.

Brophy, J., & Good, T. L. (1986). Teacher behavior and student achievement. In M. Wittrock (Ed.), *Third handbook of research on teaching* (pp. 328–375). Chicago: Rand McNally.

Campbell, J. (1982). *Grammatical man: Information entropy, language, and life.* New York: Simon & Schuster.

Carnine, D. W., Silbert, J., & Kameenui, E. J. (1990). *Direct instruction reading* (2nd ed.). Columbus, OH: Merrill Publishing Company.

Carroll, J. B. (1966). Words, meanings, and concepts. *Harvard Educational Review, 34,* 178–202.

Cuyahoga County Association for Retarded Children and Adults v. Essex, 411 F. Supp. 46 (N.D. Ohio, 1976).

Engelmann, S., & Carnine, D. (1982). *Theory of instruction; Principles and applications.* New York: Irvington.

Engelmann, S., & Carnine, D. (1982). *Theory of instruction: Principles and applications.* New York: Irvington.

Engelmann, S., & Silbert, J. (1983). *Expressive writing I.* Tigard, OR: C. C. Publications.

Englert, C. S. (1984). Examining effective direct instruction practices in special education settings. *Remedial and Special Education, 5,* 38–47.

Fielding, G. D., Kameenui, E. J., Gersten, R. (1983). A comparison of an inquiry and a direct instruction approach to teaching legal concepts and applications to secondary school students. *Journal of Educational Research, 76*(5), 287–293.

Gage, N. L. (1978). *The scientific basis of the art of teaching.* New York: Teachers College Press.

Gagne, R. M. (1985). *The conditions of learning and theory of instruction* (4th ed.). New York: Holt, Rinehart & Winston.

Gersten, R. (1985). Direct instruction with special education students: A review of evaluation research. *Journal of Special Education, 19*(1), 41–50.

Gersten, R., Woodward, J., & Carnine, D. W. (1987). Direct instruction research: The third decade. *Remedial and Special Education, 8*(6), 48–56.

Gersten, R., Woodward, J., & Darch, C. (1986). Direct instruction: A research-based approach to curriculum design and teaching. *Exceptional Children, 53*(1), 17–31.

Gilhool, T. K. (1973). Education: An inalienable right. *Exceptional Children, 89,* 597–610.

Hallahan, D. P., & Kauffman, J. M. (1978). *Exceptional children: Introduction to special education.* Englewood Cliffs, NJ: Prentice-Hall.

Kameenui, E. J. (1985). Direct instruction of reading comprehension: Beyond teacher performance variables to the design-of-instruction. In J. Niles & R. Lalik (Eds.), *Thirty-fourth yearbook of the National Reading Conference, Issues in literacy: A research perspective* (pp. 257–262). Rochester, NY: National Reading Conference.

Kameenui, E. J., Carnine, D. W., Stein, M., & Darch, C. (1986). Two approaches to the development phase of mathematics instruction. *Elementary School Journal, 86*(5), 633–650.

Kelly, B., Carnine, D., Gersten, R., & Grossen, B. (1987). The effectiveness of videodisc instruction in teaching fractions to learning handicapped and remedial high school students. *Journal of Special Education Technology, 8*(2), 5–17.

Nagy, W. E., & Anderson, R. C. (1984). How many words are there in printed school English? *Reading Research Quarterly, 19*(3), 304–330.

Pennsylvania Association for Retarded Children v. Commonwealth of Pennsylvania, 334 F. Supp. 1257 (E.D. Pa., 1971).

Reith, H. L., Polsgrove, L., & Semmel, M. I. (1982). Instructional variables that make a difference: Attention to task and beyond. *Exception Educational Quarterly, 2,* 61–71.

Rosenshine, B. V. (1979). Content, time, and direct instruction. In P. L. Peterson & H. J. Walberg (Eds.), *Research on teaching: Concepts, findings and implications* (pp. 28–56). Berkeley, CA: McCuthan.

Rosenshine, B. V. (1983). Teaching functions in instructional programs. *Elementary School Journal, 83,* 335–351.

Rosenshine, B., & Stevens, R. (1986). Teaching functions. In M. C. Wittrock (Ed.), *Handbook of research on teaching* (3rd ed., pp. 376–391). New York: Macmillan.

Ross, A. O. (1977). *Learning disability: The unrealized potential.* New York: McGraw-Hill.

Schwartz, B., & Lacey, H. (1982). *Behaviorism, science, and human nature.* New York: Norton.

Simmons, D. C., & Kameenui, E. J. (1988). Ten and twelve-year-old learning disabled and normal achievers' vocabulary knowledge: A quantitative and qualitative analysis. In J. R. Readence & S. Baldwin (Eds.), *Dialogues in literacy research: Thirty-seventh yearbook of the National Reading Conference* (pp. 133–140). Chicago: National Reading Conference.

Sprick, R. S. (1981). *The solution book.* Chicago: Science Research Associates.

Stanovich, K. (1986). Matthew effects in reading: Some consequences of individual differences in the acquisition of literacy. *Reading Research Quarterly, 21*(4), 360–407.

Tennyson, R. D., & Cochiarella, M. J. (1986). An empirically based instructional design theory for teaching concepts. *Review of Educational Research, 56,* 40–71.

Throne, J. M. (1970). A radical behaviorist approach to diagnosis in mental retardation. *Mental Retardation, 8*(3), 2–5.

Williams, J. P. (1985). The case for explicit decoding instruction. In J. Osborn, P. T. Wilson, & R. C. Anderson (Eds.), *Reading education: Foundations for a literate America* (pp. 205–213). Lexington: Heath.

Woodward, J. P., & Carnine, D. W. (1988). Antecedent knowledge and intelligent computer assisted instruction. *Journal of Learning Disabilities, 21*(3), 131–139.

CHAPTER

Instructional Assessment of Academic Learning Problems

Chapter Objectives

Upon successful completion of this chapter, you will be able to:

1. DESCRIBE the relationship between instruction and assessment.
2. LIST the multiple contexts that influence learning.
3. CONTRAST the purposes and limitations of traditional, curriculum-based, and instructional assessment.
4. NAME the critical dimensions of tasks, responses, and instruction that interact with learner performance.
5. INTERPRET a learner's performance in relation to the tasks, responses, and instruction used during assessment.
6. APPLY the instructional assessment procedures to mainstream academic curricula.

INSTRUCTIONAL ASSESSMENT: ACCOUNTING FOR FAILURE TO LEARN

Assessment is the process of collecting information. This information is needed to document disability, to verify the need for special education services, to monitor academic progress, and to plan instruction for students with learning problems. Just as there are many reasons for assessment, there are many means of gathering this information. The measures and procedures used depend on the purpose of assessment. Special education assessment procedures must vary with the objective of assessment.

This chapter introduces the **instructional assessment approach**, an approach that examines disability in relation to environmental demands. Specifically, instructional assessment attempts to define academic disability according to instructional influences on a learner's opportunity to succeed. Such factors include the task and response requirements, assessment materials, or even the instructional assistance available during assessment.

The explicit purpose of this model is to derive information that leads to the design and delivery of effective instruction. As such, our proposed approach to assessment does not involve administering standardized batteries of tests. Instructional assessment entails a systematic and selective analysis of elements within the instructional environment that teachers can draw on for instructional planning. To derive this informational data base requires that we expand assessment beyond the traditional focus on the learner to factors within the instructional setting.

Expanding the Focus of Assessment

We pass through this world but once. Few tragedies can be more extensive than the stunting of life, few injustices deeper than the denial of opportunity to serve or even hope, by a limit imposed from without, but falsely identified as lying within.

Stephen J. Gould, 1981
The Mismeasure of Man, pp. 28–29

Academic disability, like Gould's characterization of intellectual ability, is often considered a condition that lies within the child and is not attributable to outside factors. When a learner fails, it is only natural to assume the learner lacks the ability to complete the task. This traditional analysis of academic learning problems is founded in the "germ theory" paradigm (Gallagher, 1986). The procedure of searching for the "germ," or hypothesized cognitive, perceptual, linguistic, or motor deficit of learners, unfortunately diverts our attention from the role outside factors—such as tasks, teachers, and materials—play in learning.

An analysis of failure that recognizes the effect of external environmental factors in no way discounts that learners vary in biological, neurological, and psychological makeup. Learners enter classrooms with different chemistries and histories. However, a multicontextual analysis recognizes the limited control teachers have over these preexisting, internal variables and emphasizes the role of alterable, external components on student performance.

Analyzing learners' disabilities has been the state of the art in special education. Nonetheless, emerging evidence shows that this traditional assessment approach is lacking. Researchers and educators suggest that standardized tests are deficient in both technical adequacy and instructional relevance (Algozzine & Ysseldyke, 1986). To address these instructional inadequacies, more inclusive examinations that recognize the multiple contexts of learning must replace traditional assessment procedures that focus principally on the learner.

The Multiple Contexts of Learning/Failure

Children's failure to learn cannot be ascribed solely to bad genes or unalterable factors. Endorsing this genetic position indicts the learner and absolves the educator of responsibility for change. A more comprehensive and instructionally oriented approach emphasizes that many variables are responsible for a learner's success or failure. To obtain this comprehensive and more accurate picture of failure requires us to look at the problem through a broader lens. Rather than focusing on the learner, assessment must consider additional factors. To analyze academic failure, we must examine the multiple interacting variables that come into play in instructional situations.

In a contextual pyramid, Mosenthal (1982) defined five general factors (contexts) that influence learning. Figure 2–1 depicts the contexts of learner, task, situation organizer (teacher), setting, and materials.

Any one of these variables can influence learning. Obviously, we cannot consider all the contexts in the learning environment. Realistically, an assessment of learning can only focus on a select group of variables. These factors are determined by the information needed; that is, *what* is assessed and *how* it is assessed depend on the purpose of assessment.

FIGURE 2–1
The context pyramid of learning

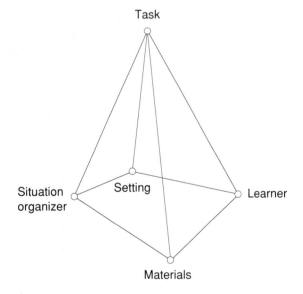

PURPOSES AND LIMITATIONS OF ASSESSMENT

In this section, we review three approaches to assessment and discuss the strengths and limitations of each in relation to the purpose of assessment and the contexts examined.

Traditional Assessment

The most traditional approach to special education assessment is normative-referenced testing. Performance on a standardized measure or norm-referenced test indicates where a student is compared to where a student "ought to be." We derive this achievement goal or "ought to be" by comparing the performance of the learner to that of peers who are administered identical test items in similar conditions.

The purpose of traditional assessment in special education is to determine a learner's degree of deviation from the norm group. This information is then used to determine a student's eligibility for special services. The use of normative-referenced tests to document differences and assign categorical labels is an integral step in the identification process of special education. Although the information gathered through traditional assessment measures may document the discrepancy between average and low-performing students, the standardized diagnostic measures are often insensitive to the demands and task requirements of the mainstream where academic problems originate and exist. As Valencia and Pearson (1988) noted:

> We have been so seductively drawn to the so-called objectivity, reliability, and validity of standardized norm-referenced tests that we have forgotten that they may only be minimally useful for making instructional decisions about individual students. (p. 27)

Simply stated, traditional measures are limited because they analyze failure through measures, tasks, response forms, and content that do not parallel the features of the instructional context. Additionally, they provide an incomplete and limited picture of a learner's knowledge because they are learner focused. The primary factor examined in traditional measures is the learner. Because of this narrow focus, traditional assessment only partly meets the needs of the students experiencing academic learning problems and the teachers attempting to remediate these deficits. Traditional standardized measures identify who to teach but define a learner's knowledge in a rigid manner that fails to recognize the effects of instructional factors.

Curriculum-based Measurement

Curriculum-based measurement (CBM) is an alternative assessment approach that has gained substantial support among researchers and practitioners. It attempts to measure whether students can perform tasks typical of the instructional curriculum—the materials used and tasks performed on a day-to-day basis. To date, curriculum-based measures are used primarily to measure student progress and evaluate the effectiveness of instruction. However, ongoing research studies the feasibility of using curriculum-based procedures to determine eligibility for special education and related services. A curriculum-based approach to assessment stresses that the child's performance or progress on classroom tasks is the most important element for gauging that child's academic progress. When contrasted to traditional, standardized tests, curriculum-based measures offer several advantages.

First, the CBM method emphasizes a close connection between what is tested and what is taught (Deno & Fuchs, 1987). The data are instructionally useful because they describe student performance in reference to the classroom curriculum. Curriculum-based measurement tasks may include (1) reading aloud passages selected from the school's basal reading series, (2) reading aloud passages selected from the class content-area texts, (3) writing words or letter sequences dictated from a level of the school's spelling curriculum, (4) writing words or letters in stories in response to a story starter or topic sentence, or (5) computing solutions to operational problems selected from a specified grade level of the mathematics curriculum. As such, CBM tasks represent exercises learners encounter day to day.

CBM evaluates student performance by charting progress toward a long-term objective from the classroom curriculum. The objective is a performance level determined by the teacher and represents an ambitious expectation of where the student "ought to be." In contrast to traditional measures, the objective is not defined solely by normal achieving peers' performance but by the student's current level of functioning and reasonable expectations of the progress that can be made through instruction and practice. For example, a sample objective might be: "The student will be able to read passages randomly selected from the third-grade reading text at a rate of 80 correct words per minute." Objectives for other students in the class may vary. However, the student's instructional goal remains constant across assessment periods, and progress is assessed by calculating the change in discrepancy between the learner's current level of functioning and the goal.

An additional advantage is that curriculum-based tasks can be administered frequently and routinely to obtain an ongoing measure of student progress. Normative-referenced tests can only be administered a limited number of times (annually or at the beginning and end of the school year) because there are limited versions of the text. However, CBM tasks use standard procedures but different content for each administration, thus allowing multiple, frequent samples of academic progress. This data base allows teachers to evaluate continuously the effectiveness of instructional interventions and to determine more immediately the need for instructional changes.

Another advantage of CBM is the relative ease of collecting and charting data. Classroom aides and other students can be taught to collect curriculum-based data. This information is then analyzed through special computer software that scores and plots the results in graphic form. This reduces the teacher's responsibility yet concurrently supplies a visual summary of information needed to evaluate student progress.

The primary usefulness of curriculum-based measures is in monitoring student progress and evaluating the effectiveness of instructional interventions. Because the focus is on tasks and materials common to the curriculum, this simplifies the process of determining what to teach.

Instructional Assessment

Traditional assessment uses annually administered, standardized measures to identify *who* is failing or at risk and provides a general index of areas of deficit. Curriculum-based measures refine our understanding of student performance by defining *what* to teach. Instructional assessment broadens the scope of assessment by providing information on *how* to teach. It accomplishes this by examining the effect of task features and instruction on student performance. The purpose of instructional assessment is to define what a learner knows in relation to the types of questions asked, the responses made, and the instructional assistance provided. It defines the conditions necessary for a learner to succeed and in that sense provides information critical for instruction.

Before we discuss the specifics of instructional assessment, we must keep in mind the distinctions between traditional, curriculum-based, and instructional assessment. Table 2–1 contrasts these three models according to the contexts, time, measures, and purpose of assessment.

Instructional assessment differs from traditional and curriculum-based measurement in a number of dimensions. These differences stem largely from the purpose of instructional assessment. The proposed method examines a learner's performance not in comparison to other learners' performance on standardized measures but rather as a response to the tasks and instruction of the instructional setting. The following questions illustrate the types of features examined and information gathered through instructional assessment:

1. Does the order of tasks make a difference in student performance?
2. Does allowing the student to answer orally rather than in writing affect performance?
3. Can the student correct an incorrect response when provided instructional prompts?
4. How does the number of tasks presented influence student performance?
5. If the student cannot orally state the correct answer, can the student select the correct response from a set of options?

TABLE 2–1
Comparison of assessment models

	Norm-Referenced	CBM	Instructional
Contexts	Learner	Learner Materials Tasks	Learner Materials Tasks Instruction
Time	Annually, biannually	Frequently (preferably twice weekly)	Whenever information is needed to evaluate learner understanding
Measures	Standardized tasks	Tasks from curriculum	Tasks introduced in instruction
Purpose	Identify who to teach by comparing student performance on standard academic categories	Specify what to teach and monitor progress and effectiveness of instruction	Identify how to teach in response to tasks and instruction

Traditional special education assessment methods address none of these questions and provide limited information about a learner's knowledge. They provide even less prescriptive information for designing instruction. The objective of instructional assessment is to specify the connection between *what we ask, how we ask it,* and *how students perform.* Through this process, we learn more about the types of tasks and instructional support students need to succeed as well as the procedures teachers need to employ during instruction.

Limitations and Benefits of Instructional Assessment

The primary disadvantage of instructional assessment is the complexity of the process. Instructional assessment is not a circumscribed approach to information collection. It does not offer the psychometric properties or standards of more traditional measures. Determining what, when, and how to assess is not a fixed process defined on a checklist or record sheet.

Because no one prescription applies in every case, teachers may be wary of experimenting. Instructional assessment places the burden on the teacher to determine the best means of collecting information for instruction. It requires the teacher to make smarter decisions regarding what to ask, how to ask it, and how to interpret information.

Despite the apparent complexities, instructional assessment offers several advantages for instructional planning. It provides the opportunity to assess students' knowledge in instructional settings, to integrate instructional techniques such as reteaching and prompting, and to modify probes to fit the proficiencies of the learner. To this end, it specifies the conditions under which children can perform successfully.

Instructional assessment evolved from a need for information that could enhance teachers' ability to teach low-performing students. It complements traditional and curriculum-based approaches by refining our knowledge of failure. Analyzing failure is a complex process. We believe that academic failure is a function of many factors, some over which we have control and others over which we do not. In the next section, we discuss the alterable factors and specific dimensions of each type that form the basis of instructional assessment.

DIMENSIONS OF INSTRUCTIONAL ASSESSMENT

Failure is a complex process, and its causes are often difficult to unravel. Our premise is that learners do not fail independently but rather as they interact with extra-child factors such as materials, tasks, response requirements, and instructional methods. Therefore, educators should specify those instructional factors that limit a learner from acquiring and demonstrating knowledge. When we speak of instructional factors, we speak of those conditions within teachers' control, conditions teachers can adapt to improve learner performance.

We limit our analysis to two general influences on student performance: tasks and responses. These items are targeted for discussion and exploration because they are amenable to change. Within each of these general factors are multiple dimensions that can be manipulated, adapted, and examined to determine their impact on student performance. Figure 2–2 diagrams these general factors as well as specific dimensions of each that will be discussed in the next section. In the final portion of this discussion of instructional dimensions, we recommend means of adapting these instructional dimensions to bridge instruction and assessment.

Task Dimensions

When thinking of task dimensions that influence learner performance, it is useful to consider those properties or features that are common to the majority of assessment tasks. What general features of tasks affect learners' overall performance? Clearly, there are many. However, in designing assessment sequences we examine three task dimensions of competency, domain, and schedule. Figure 2–3 specifies these task dimensions and examples of each.

Task Competency

Task competency refers to the learner's proficiency with the task. This dimension is critical to assessment and instructional sequences because a learner's success on tasks often sets the stage for subsequent performance. Task competency can be classified according to level of mastery. For assessment purposes, we identify three levels of task competency: mastery, practice, and new learning. As a general rule, we recommend that

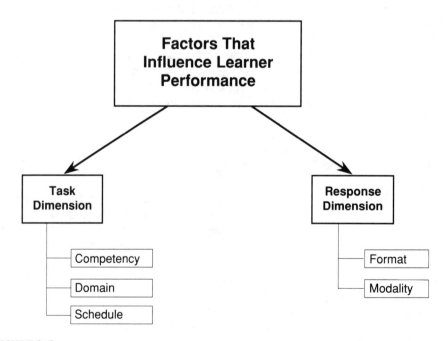

FIGURE 2–2
Task and response dimensions that influence learner performance

FIGURE 2–3
Competency, domain, and schedule
dimensions of tasks

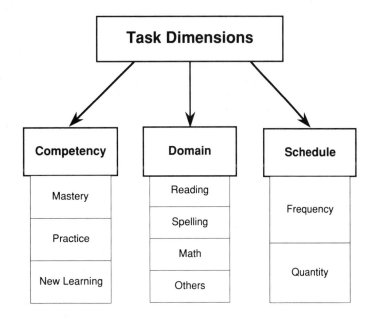

initial tasks in any assessment sequence are those the learner can perform with high rates of success. These are sometimes referred to as mastery-level tasks.

Mastery-level tasks require the least cognitive effort because the learner has had extensive practice with the task and performs the task accurately and fluently. Typically, after students reach criterion, mastery-level tasks are often not routinely tested because they are presumably "learned." Nevertheless, mastery-level tasks in assessment sequences serve strategic functions. First, they represent success opportunities for the learner and can be systematically sequenced among more difficult tasks to provide the learner an academic reprieve. Not only can mastered tasks be introduced first in assessment sequences, they can also be interspersed between difficult tasks. Second, periodically assessing mastery-level tasks provides a measure of the learner's ability to retain information over time. If a learner fails tasks that were previously mastered, this indicates a need for more frequent review and instruction.

Practice-level tasks are tasks learners should perform with relative competence and consistency. As a general rule, practice-level tasks should be performed with 75–80% accuracy. Although learners have had moderate exposure, experience, and success with practice-level tasks, they are not performed automatically. Therefore, we suggest that approximately 50% of the tasks assessed be at the practice level. This provides learners the additional exposure and feedback necessary to convert practice-level to mastery-level tasks.

The third competency level is **new-learning tasks.** Tasks in this stage of learning are predictably the most difficult because the learner has had limited or no instruction with the task requirements. New-learning tasks must be carefully sequenced to avoid early and prolonged failure. Nevertheless, in assessment it is important to administer a sufficient number of new-learning tasks to obtain an accurate reading of student competency.

Task Domain

A second task feature that influences learner performance is domain. In traditional assessment, students are tested in domains or major skill categories such as arithmetic computation or word study skills. Assessment in the specific academic domain continues until the time limit expires or the learner either completes or fails to solve a designated number of tasks. Once the domain assessment is complete, another skill area is tested. At least two problems evolve in testing low-performing students in this manner.

First, even the most naive of us recognizes that basic skills such as word recognition, reading comprehension, and basic computational skills are integral parts of social studies, science, and word-problem solving. Nevertheless, testing in academic domains fails to consider this influence. The impact of poor word recognition or deficit reading comprehension skills on learners' performance in content areas such as social studies or science cannot be extracted from standard measures. Therefore, poor performance in one area is likely to result in depressed scores in other areas requiring the base skills. The second problem of domain testing is even more subtle but crucial when assessing low performers. Testing within the same domain often creates an aversive condition for low-performing students who must endure a difficult task for a prolonged period. In these unfavorable situations, learners often surpass their tolerance level for failure and shut down. For example, if decoding is particularly troublesome for the learner, the successive presentation of decoding tasks (e.g., CVC words, CVCC words, CVCe words, r-control words) may be an unnecessary, if not punishing, procedure. In instructional assessment, a learner's frustrations may be reduced by alternating tasks from different domains. This task variation allows the learner a time to rest and recapture self-esteem that is often deflated by continuous sequences of failure.

Task Schedule

The assessment schedule refers to the frequency and quantity of testing.

Tasks at the new-learning stage should be assessed with greater *frequency* than practice-level and mastery-level tasks. Through frequent assessment probes, teachers may check learners' understanding early in the instructional sequence and preempt opportunities the learners may have to practice errors. Frequent assessments also structure opportunities for teachers to provide feedback to learners. Once learners reach practice or mastery levels, task checks are less frequent but periodically scheduled to evaluate skill maintenance.

Assessment *quantity* involves both the time (i.e., 5 minutes, 30 minutes) and amount of tasks (i.e., five problems, three paragraphs) assessed. The quantity of time and tasks assessed should vary with the requirements of the task and the competency of the learner. For younger and lower performers, the time and tasks should be partitioned in relatively small segments. More mature and higher performers will be able to handle larger segments of time and materials.

The quantity of information assessed also depends on learners' competency with the task. New-learning tasks often require more effort; therefore, the number of tasks assessed should be aligned with learner competency. For instance, five practice-level word problem-solving tasks may be challenging but manageable for one learner, but that same set of problems may overload another learner, resulting in extreme frustration and failure.

An instructional approach to assessment radically differs from traditional one-sitting assessment periods. A luxury of instructional assessment is that teachers are free to alter, restructure, and schedule assessment tasks according to learner performance. For example, consider learners who progress through the primer, first, and second levels of the Dolch sight words in a 5-minute period while others require 5 minutes to labor through 10 words. Rather than require that the learner struggle through the entire word list in one uninterrupted sitting, teachers may subdivide the list into sets of five to seven words and alternate sets with tasks from another domain. As the learner becomes more proficient on a task, task duration and quantity increase.

Table 2–2 illustrates possible variations in assessment sequences derived by incorporating task dimensions. In studying this example, it is important to remember that the individual learner determines the task competency and domain difficulty. Mastery-level tasks for one learner may still be at the new-learning stage for another.

Response Dimensions

Learners demonstrate their knowledge by responding to a task. There are a variety of response types and, not coincidentally, the response required by the task directly influences whether a learner can perform the task. Like the task, a response contains multiple dimensions, each contributing to the ease or difficulty of the task for the individual learner. For instructional assessment, we examine two modifiable response factors: format and modality. Figure 2–4 depicts the features of format and modality while simultaneously illustrating the options and complexity of response requirements.

Response Format

Response format refers to the structure of the task and to the subsequent demands of the learner. Tasks can provide minimal or extensive amounts of information; therefore, the response format directly impacts learner performance.

TABLE 2–2
Assessment schedule with variation in task dimensions:
Global assessment of primary academic tasks

Task Schedule	Task Domain and Description	Task Competency
9:00–9:02	Language (positional concepts)	Mastery level
9:03–9:08	Reading (15 CVC words)	Practice level
9:09–9:14	Math (numeral writing)	New learning
9:15–9:17	Language (comparative concepts)	Mastery level
9:18–9:23	Reading (5 CVCC words)	New learning
9:24–9:28	Math (addition facts)	Practice level
9:29–9:30	Review of errors on difficult tasks	

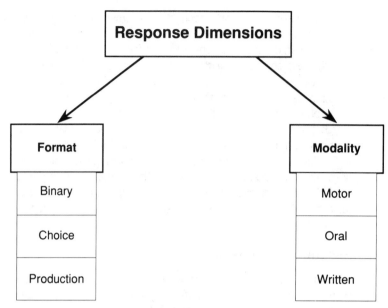

FIGURE 2–4
Format and modality dimensions of responses

Three primary response formats are used to assess learner knowledge: binary, choice, and production. These response formats are sequenced along a hierarchical continuum, with discrimination responses representing the easiest form within the hierarchy and production responses the most difficult. Table 2–3 provides definitions of response formats and example tasks.

The response format should parallel the response format of assessment tasks required during instruction. That is, if the instructional task requires the learner to select synonyms of vocabulary words from a set of response options, so should the assessment tasks. Less difficult response formats such as binary or choice responses should be used in introductory lessons. As learner competency develops, more difficult response structures should be introduced.

Selecting the appropriate response format is not as complex as it may appear. Table 2–4 categorizes tasks typically used to assess academic performance as either production, choice, or discrimination response formats. By surveying these tasks and becoming familiar with response demands, teachers can ensure a better alignment between instruction, assessment, and learner competency. Note in the table how task modifications alter the response form.

Knowing how and when to reduce the response demands of the learner is a skill. Like any other skill, it will require practice, but once it is mastered, teachers can vary response demands to access information not obtainable through standardized response forms. By changing the response form teachers can determine the optimal information a learner has on a particular task. Rather than indicating that a student knows or doesn't know, task modifications can better specify a student's actual level of information.

TABLE 2–3
Tasks classified by response format

Binary: Binary tasks require learners to show or say whether information is correct or incorrect. Either yes/no or, in more advanced situations, true/false formats are used. The information required of the learner is minimal; nevertheless, failure on binary tasks generally indicates the need for further instruction.

Teacher	Student
Tell me, is the ball red?	(Yes or no.)
Coal is a fossil fuel. True or false.	(True or false.)
Men is a singular noun. True or false?	(True or false.)
Is 32 less than 35?	(Yes or no.)
Water contains two molecules of hydrogen. True or false.	(True or false.)

Choice response: The learner selects the correct response from a set of supplied options.

Circle the number that is less than 32.
Response set: (a) 37   (b) 23   (c) 32   (d) 43.
Tell me the action verb in the following sentence.
Response set: The loaded bus stopped at the corner.
Put your finger on the *red* box.
Response set: (a) blue box   (b) red box   (c) yellow box.
Select the capital of Tennessee.
Response set: (a) Memphis   (b) Nashville   (c) Lexington.
Write the first word. After it, write the word that is its synonym.
Response set: *infuriate*—anger, calm, confuse, sadden.

Production: Production tasks require the learner to generate a solution. No prompts, options, or cues are provided other than those structured in the task itself.

Write a number that is less than 32.
Tell me the plural form of *man.*
Fill the missing action word in the following sentence.
The loaded bus _____ at the corner.
Tell me the color of the ball.
Write the chemical formula for water.
Write a synonym for *infuriate.*

Response Modality

Learners can use several basic modalities to respond to tasks. Depending on the task, the learner may answer with a motor, oral, or written response. The difficulty of the response modality again varies with the learner; however, written responses are often quite difficult because they require learners to derive the correct solution and to express that solution in grammatically and mechanically correct written form.

TABLE 2-4

Assessment tasks categorized by response format

Production Tasks

Essay tests/short answer: Discuss the reasons dinosaurs became extinct.

Listing: List in order the reasons dinosaurs became extinct.

Fill-in-the-blank: Dinosaurs became extinct because the climate was _____ and the _____ was inadequate.

Choice-Response Tasks

Multiple-choice: Select the main reason dinosaurs became extinct. (a) frigid temperatures (b) lack of food   (c) people.

Binary

True/false: Dinosaurs became extinct because the temperature was too hot. True or false?

Variations in response modes may involve the learner in motor, oral, or written task responses.

Using strategic variation in response modes prevents overuse of specific modalities and facilitates learner success.

When scheduling assessment tasks, educators should consider the skills of the learner and *strategically* vary response modalities (e.g., oral responses for 2–3 minutes, written responses for 3–4 minutes, motor responses for 1–2 minutes) accordingly. By alternating response modes, teachers can prevent overuse of a particular response form (e.g., all written responses for a 40-minute period), increase learner attention to task, and actually minimize failure by attending to features of the response mode.

The assessment sequence in Table 2–5 illustrates the task/response variations discussed thus far. Most likely, this sequence represents a marked deviation from the procedures typically used to assess student knowledge. It is not always necessary to vary every task/response feature. Some students will require extensive alterations while others may achieve success by simply modifying the response mode from written to oral tasks. Learner performance and the teacher's prior knowledge of learner competencies determine the task variation. As a general rule of thumb, tasks/responses should be modified only to the degree necessary to achieve success. When learners are successful, the information needed to design instruction should be available.

In this section, we reviewed two factors that influence learner performance: task dimensions and response dimensions. Clearly, these are not the only factors teachers must examine when analyzing student performance. However, they do provide a frame-work for focusing on variables that teachers can change. Once these alterable and influential variables are identified, teachers can begin to experiment with adaptations and methods that generate data relevant for instruction. In the following section, we

TABLE 2–5
Assessment sequence with variation of task/response dimensions:
Global assessment of elementary academic tasks

Task Schedule	Domain and Description of Assessment Task	Response Modality	Response Format
8:30–8:36	Expressive writing (using capitalization and punctuation in sentences)	Written	Production (choice)*
8:37–8:46	Passage reading (comprehension)	Oral	Production (choice)*
8:47–8:49	Count by series (fives and twos)	Motor	Production
8:50–8:57	Addition and subtraction facts (5–9)	Written	Production (choice)*
8:58–9:00	Reassess comprehension of passage (8:37)	Oral	Production

*Production responses provide the most comprehensive measure of knowledge; therefore, in this sequence they were used as the primary response format. In the event learners are unsuccessful on production response, use alternate choice-responses as follow-up probes.

introduce some of the procedures teachers can employ to adapt the task and response dimensions in response to learner performance.

TECHNIQUES TO LINK ASSESSMENT AND INSTRUCTION

Throughout this chapter, we acknowledge the importance of outside-the-learner variables and emphasize the need to adapt traditional assessment procedures. An outside-the-learner variable that is critical to the usefulness of instructional assessment is the teacher and more specifically the procedures the teacher uses to assess knowledge. In contrast to standard assessment measures where the teacher's role is to administer the tasks as prescribed by the manual, the teacher activates and actually defines the instructional assessment process. The proposed task and response variations at the heart of instructional assessment depend on the teacher's skill in selecting tasks and instruction that enhance the learner's ability to succeed and the understanding of failure. In this section, we introduce four procedures teachers can employ to aid the analysis of academic failure. Figure 2–5 lists these generic procedures that teachers can apply to most content, task, or assessment contexts.

The degree to which each technique functions effectively depends on the learner's needs and the teacher's skill at extracting instructional information from assessment. No patented formula exists prescribing how much or how little of a particular technique to use. Instructional assessment is an experimental process defined by the learner and the learner's interaction with the assessment contexts. Next, we define the critical features of each technique and prescribe methods of implementing these procedures in assessment settings.

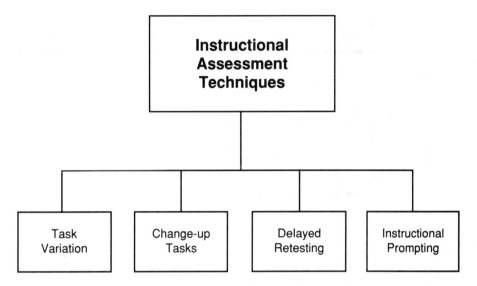

FIGURE 2–5
Generic instructional assessment procedures

Task Variation and Sequencing

One fundamental tool of instructional assessment is the variation and sequencing of tasks. Task variation involves the strategic arrangement of tasks within the assessment/ instruction sequence. Tasks may be varied and sequenced according to a number of dimensions, including the learner's competency with the task, task domain, task frequency and quantity, response format, and response mode. When used in instructional settings, task variation maximizes learner motivation, and when applied to the assessment setting, the separation of difficult tasks minimizes the negative feelings often prompted by testing and repeated failure.

One application of the task variation process involves alternating the presentation of both mastered and unmastered tasks in the assessment sequence. Mastered tasks are interspersed among new, less-established tasks to foster positive feelings and success in the learner. We recommend a one-to-one ratio of mastered/practice to new tasks; however, the amount of variation depends on the learner and the task. The sequence in Table 2–6 illustrates how tasks from other content areas are varied with reading tasks.

This assessment sequence introduces a nonreading task (i.e., addition facts) first because of the learner's prior history of reading difficulty. This eases the learner into the assessment context and structures an opportunity for success. Reading tasks of relatively short duration are alternated with presumably less difficult math and language tasks to create a more reinforcing and manageable task sequence for the learner.

Change-Up Task

Instructional assessment allows teachers to intervene when learners are besieged by a series of difficult tasks. The change-up task is a technique teachers may use to break up

TABLE 2–6
Assessment sequence with tasks varied according to learner competency

Task Sequence and Description	Competency	Approximate Time
Orally answering addition facts (sums to 10)	M	2 minutes
Reading CVC words (e.g., cat, run, red)	N	2 minutes
Writing numerals 1–20	P	5 minutes
Reading CVCC words (e.g., rest, back, belt)	N	3 minutes
Naming days of the week	M	1 minute
Reading CCVC words (e.g., clap, drip, sled)	N	2 minutes

M = mastered tasks.
P = practice tasks.
N = new tasks.

lengthy task sequences. The change-up procedure introduces a task that differs from the previously administered tasks in difficulty, content, or response requirements. This activity provides a change from previous assessment tasks in pace, response form, or cognitive demand. Although intended to provide the learner with a break from the rigor of the assessment sequence, change-up tasks should also provide information that is useful for instructional planning. Change-up tasks are not simply "fillers" in the assessment sequence. In Table 2–6, naming the days of the week functioned as a change-up activity because it was a task that could be completed quickly and with relative ease, and it tapped a different skill area from preceding tasks. No prescribed placement exists regarding when and where to insert change-up tasks in the assessment sequence. However, they are typically scheduled between highly similar tasks or following a series of difficult activities.

The effectiveness of change-up tasks depends on the learner's needs as well as the teacher's selection and timing of such activities. What serves as a change-up task for one learner may not serve the same function for another. Nevertheless, particular categories of tasks such as sequences of verbal information are particularly suitable for change-up activities. The change-up task can be selected from a range of academic tasks. Table 2–7 lists activities teachers may deploy to change the intensity and pace of assessment sequences.

Note that all these activities are short-answer tasks learners can complete in relatively brief periods. If change-up tasks are not at the student's practice level or mastery level, they consume too much time and cognitive effort, thereby defeating the purpose of the change-up task.

Delayed Retesting

In simple terms, delayed retesting is a test-teach-retest process designed to provide learners additional instruction and repeated trials on problematic tasks. It is a technique used to reevaluate a learner's knowledge on a task that was either inconsistently or inaccurately performed in the previous assessment sequence. Two basic components

TABLE 2–7

Possible change-up tasks for assessment sequences

Task Category	Example
Sequences of verbal information	1. Name the days of the week. 2. Name the months of the year. 3. Counting a specified sequence of numbers: Count by twos, beginning at 2 and stopping at 20. 4. Name the planets in order. 5. Rehearse a series of multiplication facts.
Auditory tasks	1. Statement repetition and inference: Light-colored clothing is cooler than dark clothing. What color clothing is cooler? 2. Definitions: *Migrate* means *move to a distant place.* What does *migrate* mean? 3. Oral discriminations: Tell me if this is a compound or a complex sentence.
Factual information	1. Name three forms of water transportation. 2. Tell me three holidays that are in winter. 3. Name the four types of animals. 4. Name the state capitals. 5. Write the symbols for these chemical compounds.
Multistep motor sequences	1. Write your name on the line and put an X in the circle. 2. Give me the red crayon and put the blue crayon in the box. 3. Open your book to chapter 3, locate the first word in the second paragraph, and find the meaning of the word in the glossary.

comprise the delayed retesting procedure: (1) the reteaching of tasks in error and (2) the systematic re-presentation of probes within and across assessment/instructional sessions. Delayed retesting is not only an assessment tool but also functions as an instructional reinforcer. Three sequences in Table 2–8 illustrate the delayed retest procedure.

In Table 2–9, the delayed retest procedure focuses on a specific class of errors demonstrated in the initial primary assessment sequence.

Table 2–10 depicts the retesting procedure when applied to the specific language task of forming plurals.

When using delayed retests, reteaching should immediately follow any error and the original task should then be re-presented to the learner. This cycle of teach-retest continues until the learner responds correctly and without hesitation. Distributing retest probes throughout the assessment sequence allows the teacher to assess the learner's retention of the problematic tasks. When scheduling tasks, the number of delayed probes should decrease as the learner approaches mastery of a particular skill. If learners fail a number of tasks, teachers should not attempt to reteach and retest every error. Instead, delayed retest procedures should be used on simpler tasks and separate reteaching/retesting sequences should be scheduled for more complex and persistent errors.

TABLE 2–8
Assessment sequence with competency variations and delayed retesting:
Global assessment of primary academic activities

Task Sequence and Description	Competency	Approximate Time
Orally answering addition facts (sums to 10)	M	2 minutes
Reading CVC words (e.g., cat, run, red)	N	3 minutes
(Teach word in error: *run*.)		
(Retest *run*.)		
Writing numerals 1–20	P	6 minutes
(Teach numeral in error: 9.)		
(Retest.)		
Delayed retest of incorrect tasks (*run* and 9)	N	10 seconds
Reading CVCC words (e.g., *rest, belt*)	P	3 minutes
Delayed retest of incorrect tasks (*run* and 9)	?	8 seconds
Naming days of the week (change-up task)	M	1 minute
Reading CCVC words (clap, drip, sled)	N	3 minutes
(Error on *clap, drip, sled*.)		
(Teach CCVC soundblending.)		
(Retest.)		
(Error on *clap*.)**		
Delayed retest of tasks in error (*run* and 9).	?	5 seconds
Cumulative review and delayed retest of erred tasks	?	2 minutes

 * M = mastered tasks.
  P = practice tasks.
  N = new tasks.
  ? = competency unknown.
** When persistent errors occur even after retesting, the task requires more extensive analysis.

Instructional Prompting

Instructional prompting characterizes the distinction between instructional and traditional assessment. In traditional measures, a task is administered once, the learner's response is recorded, and the next task in the sequence is presented. Instructional prompting uses the learner's response and the task to determine the next task to present. If the response is correct, the next task is assessed in sequence. However, for incorrect responses, the teacher uses prompts derived from the task to assist the learner. The idea of using the task as the basis of the prompt requires that teachers be quite familiar with task solution procedures. For example, if a student omits a step in an arithmetic algorithm, the appropriate prompt directs the learner to the correct process. This may require having the student "think aloud" when solving the task, verbally explaining the steps and computations necessary. If the error stems from an inaccurate application of a rule, the teacher's prompt may simply be to restate the rule.

Through instructional prompts, teachers determine how much information students have and how much additional information they need to satisfy task requirements.

TABLE 2–9
Assessment sequence with delayed retesting: CCVC words

TASK 2–1

TEACHER: Tell me the word as I point to it. (Stimulus—*slip.*)
STUDENT: Uh . . . , *si* . . . *slll* . . . I don't know.
TEACHER: OK, listen and watch as I sound out the word. *Sssllliiip.* Now it's your turn to sound it out with me. *Sssllliiip.*
TEACHER: Great. Now sound it out in your head. (Pauses for 2–3 seconds.) What word?
STUDENT: (Hesitates for 3–4 seconds.) *Slip.*
TEACHER: Nice job of sounding it out in your head.

TASK 2–2

TEACHER: Watch as I sound out this word in my head and then read the whole word. (Stimulus— *trap.*)
(Teacher slides finger under sounds in word.)
Trap. You sound it out in your head and get ready to read the whole word. What word?
STUDENT: *Trap.*
TEACHER: Right, the word is *trap.*

TASK 2–3

(Delayed Retest)

TEACHER: What word? (Stimulus—*slip.*)
STUDENT: (Hesitates.) *Slip.*
TEACHER: The word is *slip.* Good for you.

TASK 2–4

TEACHER: What word? (Stimulus—*blot.*)
STUDENT: *Blot.*
TEACHER: That's right.

TASK 2–5

TEACHER: What word? (Stimulus—*slot.*)
STUDENT: Slot.
TEACHER: Great.

TASK 2–6

(Delayed Retest)

TEACHER: What word? (Stimulus—*slip.*)
STUDENT: Slip.
TEACHER: Wonderful reading.

TABLE 2–10
Assessment sequence with competency variations and delayed retesting:
Assessment of specific language skill—Elementary Level

Task Sequence and Description	Competency	Approximate Time
Orally answering multiplication facts (1–5)	M	2 minutes
Writing plurals of regular and irregular nouns (error on *leaves*)	N	5 minutes
Reteach rule for forming plurals. Retest *leaf* and other nouns ending in *f*.	?	2 minutes
Oral passage reading	P	3 minutes
Oral retelling of passage	N	2 minutes
Retest of plural rule	?	1 minute
Written solution to subtraction problems using two-digit numbers	P	5 minutes
Written response to comprehension questions	N	5 minutes
Delayed retest of plural rule	?	1–2 minutes

M = mastered tasks.
P = practice tasks.
N = new tasks.
? = competency unknown.

In some cases, the prompt may simply focus the learner's attention to a particular feature of the task such as the prefix at the beginning of the word or the zero in the ones column. In other instances, the prompt may be more extensive, leading the learner through all the steps of a complex strategy. The amount and type of prompting provided will necessarily depend on the task and the learner. In all cases, teachers should be cautious not to provide more information than the learner needs. Overprompting may encourage learners to become teacher-dependent. To illustrate the relationship between instructional prompts and tasks, consider the examples in Tables 2–11 and 2–12.

In these examples, prompts directed the learner's attention to critical task features. This form of corrective feedback is effective if students have the basic skill knowledge. We again caution teachers to consider the interaction of the task and learner competency when selecting prompting procedures. The information students have should be used to shape their responses, but teachers must be careful not to badger learners when information is not easily accessible.

THE DEGREE OF INSTRUCTIONAL ASSESSMENT

Which techniques of instructional assessment should be used? Our best advice is to match the technique with the information needed about the learner. Delayed retesting measures the learner's ability to retain information. Task variation and change-up tasks indicate the amount of information that can be successfully processed in one sitting. Instructional prompting reveals the amount of information the learner has on that particular skill and the learner's ability to access that information when cues are offered.

TABLE 2–11
Instructional Prompting of decoding skills

TASK 2–7

TEACHER: Tell me the word as I point to it. (Stimulus—*cat*.)
STUDENT: *Cot.*
TEACHER: (Points to the letter *a*.) What sound?
STUDENT: *A* (ă).
TEACHER: So what word?
STUDENT: *Cat.*
TEACHER: Exactly right!

TASK 2–8

TEACHER: Tell me the word as I point to it. (Stimulus—*made*.)
STUDENT: *Mad.*
TEACHER: (Points to the end of the word.) Is there an *e* at the end?
STUDENT: Yes.
TEACHER: (Points to the *a*.) So what sound does this letter make?
STUDENT: A (ā).
TEACHER: So what word?
STUDENT: *Made.*
TEACHER: Very nice reading.

TABLE 2–12
Instructional prompting of alphabetizing task

TASK 2–9

Put the names of these cities in alphabetical order:

| Denver | Seattle | Cleveland | Omaha |
| Oak Ridge | Des Moines | San Francisco | Detroit |

Learner's response:

| 1. Cleveland | 2. Detroit | 3. Des Moines | 4. Denver |
| 5. Oak Ridge | 6. Omaha | 7. Seattle | 8. San Francisco |

TEACHER: When you alphabetize words what is the first thing you do?
STUDENT: You put the words in order. You look at the first letter and put them in the order of the alphabet.
TEACHER: That's right. You look at the first letter. But what is the rule if more than one word begins with the same letter?
STUDENT: Oh, that's right. You have to look at the next letter.
TEACHER: Look at your answers. Are there any cities that begin with the same letter?
STUDENT: There are a lot.
TEACHER: Remember the rule. If more than one word begins with the same letter, you have to look at the next letter. Now, I want you to use that rule and try this again.

Generally, the lower the performer and the more complex the task and response, the greater the need to modify assessment. Task and response variations as well as instructional prompts, change-up tasks, and delayed retesting procedures can be overused just like traditional assessment measures. Only extreme cases require comprehensive adjustments in assessment procedures.

In most cases, the cause of academic failure is unknown. Instructional assessment techniques shift the emphasis from searching for learner-based causes to identifying the tasks, responses, and instruction necessary for the learner to succeed. The instructional assessment techniques proposed are a first step toward acquiring this information.

IMPLEMENTING INSTRUCTIONAL ASSESSMENT

Instructional assessment is not a global assessment procedure that will document a learner's general reading comprehension level or generate a percentile ranking. Instructional assessment is designed to be instructionally specific. Its purpose is to analyze failure not in generic terms but rather in specific task-related, response-related, and instructionally related terms.

How then does one start the process of analyzing academic failure through instructional assessment? The flowchart in Figure 2–6 depicts the general sequence of events that would occur in the implementation of instructional assessment. To determine the learner's skill levels, the teacher defines the tasks by considering the instructional objectives and the learner's prior performance on similar tasks. Next, the tasks typical of the instructional setting and instructional curriculum are administered. If the learner meets the specified criterion, performance can be assessed on a more difficult objective. However, if the learner fails to meet the criterion, instructional assessment procedures should be incorporated. Focusing on the specific skill, the teacher should use multiple examples and a variety of probe and task variations to disclose the circumstances in which the learner is able to demonstrate task knowledge.

After employing instructional assessment procedures, the teacher analyzes the learner's response to these adaptations. Was the learner able to satisfy task demands with minimal changes, or were extensive adaptations required? Instructional assessment should also determine whether the learner's deficiencies can be addressed in the mainstream instructional materials or if special materials will be necessary. Based on the information assembled during instructional assessment, instructional plans that accommodate the existing skills of the learner can be designed.

APPLICATIONS OF INSTRUCTIONAL ASSESSMENT

The following examples present hypothetical but typical applications of instructional assessment procedures in academic content in general education classes. Each example includes the following instructional information: learning outcome, materials, response modality, response format, and task competency. Each example includes a brief summary of the learner's prior academic performance to demonstrate how the instructional assessment tasks and sequences were selected and developed. In each example, first we assess a student's skill in a general area such as reading comprehension or basic computation skills to identify the starting point for instructional assessment.

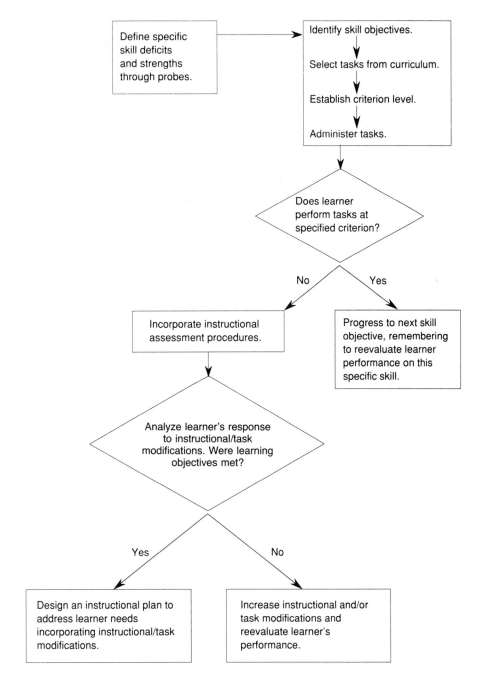

FIGURE 2–6
Flowchart of instructional assessment procedures

EXAMPLE 1
Beginning Decoding Skills

Learner   A 7-year-old student repeating first grade. Academic records indicate below grade level reading skills (third percentile on word study skills on group achievement test; third percentile on reading comprehension). A more recent assessment on words selected from level one of the first-grade basal reader revealed the learner recognized 3 words from a list of 30. Given the lack of word recognition skills, the learner's knowledge of sounds in isolation was deemed an appropriate beginning instructional assessment task.

Learning Outcome   The learner will orally produce all letter-sound correspondences with 100% accuracy.

Materials   Chart with randomly ordered letter-sound correspondences and consonant blends.

Response Modality   Oral.

Response Format   Production.

Competency   Unknown.

Assessment Sequence

TEACHER: Every letter makes a sound. This letter says *a* (ă). When I touch a letter, you tell me the sound the letter makes.
TEACHER: (Points to *m*.) What sound?
STUDENT: *M*. (Immediate response.)
TEACHER: (Points to *t*.) What sound?
STUDENT: *T*. (Immediate response.)
TEACHER: (Points to *s*.) What sound?
STUDENT: *S*. (Immediate response.)
TEACHER: (Points to *a*.) What sound?
STUDENT: *E* (ĕ).
TEACHER: Listen, this says *a* (ă). What sound? (Prompt.)
STUDENT: *A* (ă). (Retest.)
TEACHER: Nice job.
TEACHER: (Points to *r*.) What sound?
STUDENT: *R*. (Immediate response.)
TEACHER: (Points to *a*.) What sound? (Delayed retest.)
STUDENT: (No response.)
TEACHER: This says *a* (ă). What sound? (Prompt.)
STUDENT: *A* (ă). (Retest.)
TEACHER: Very good.
TEACHER: (Points to *l*.) What sound?
STUDENT: *L*. (Delayed response.)
TEACHER: (Points to *a*.) What sound? (Delayed retest.)
STUDENT: *A* (ă).
TEACHER: Good remembering, *a* (ă).

Assessment continues until 6–8 letter-sound correspondences have been evaluated. A language task is then introduced as a change-up activity. Letter-sound assessment is continued and distributed across the session. No more than 6–8 sounds are assessed at a time. The *a* sound is systematically assessed throughout the session.

Error Analysis   a, i, e, u, o, x, q, y, k

Instructional Assessment Procedures

In addition to prompting (teaching erred letter-sound correspondence) and delayed retests, task quantity was also varied. Because letter-sound recognition was found to be a difficult task, the original set of tasks was divided into smaller chunks (sets of four to six letter correspondences). The chunks were then distributed across the session and assessed separately (i.e., on the second, fifth, seventh, and tenth task in the sequence a new set of letter-sound correspondences was assessed).

EXAMPLE 2
Arithmetic Computational Skills (second–third grade level)

Learner   A 10-year-old student; average reading skills; 2.5 grade-equivalent score on computational skills as measured by group achievement test.

Learning Outcome   Given a set of 30 computation problems (10 each of addition, subtraction, and multiplication) from the third-grade mathematics text, the learner will perform the computation and write the answers to the problems with 80% accuracy.

Materials   Survey instrument containing 2–3 examples from various third-grade computational skill areas.

Assessment Sequence

TASK 2–10

TEACHER: Try to answer all the problems on this page. Look carefully at the signs. If you can't answer a problem, answer as much as you can and go on the the next one. Remember to try your best.

15 − 8 7	9 + 4 =13	368 + 21 389	461 +370 831	25 30 +38 93
249 − 15 234	586 −332 254	50 −20 30	8 × 6 =48	0 ×5 0
9 × 6 =54	682 + 38 720	963 −272 691	473 +388 861	408 − 59 349
800 −436 364	9 × 9 =81	845 −243 602	953 +469 1422	3708 +1916 5624

(Entire task set not displayed.)

Error Analysis   Addition problems that require regrouping from the tens to the hundreds column; subtraction problems that require regrouping; subtraction problems with zeros in the tens place, basic multiplication facts. (Multiplication facts should be assessed in a separate assessment to reduce cognitive demands on the learner.)

Instructional Assessment Phase   Three-digit addition and subtraction problems with or without regrouping.

Learning Outcome   When presented 15 addition and 15 subtraction problems containing up to three digits with or without regrouping, the student will write the sums or differences with 80% accuracy.

Materials   Worksheet with randomly ordered addition and subtraction problems with numbers up to three digits with or without regrouping.

Response Modality   Written.

Response Format   Production.

Competency   Established preskills on two-digit addition and subtraction problems.

Assessment Sequence

TASK 2–11

TEACHER: Write the answer to each of the problems on the worksheet. Remember to look at the signs carefully. If you can't answer the whole problem, answer any part that you can. Try your best.

259	695	107	977	267	885
+ 140	− 503	− 93	+ 366	+ 22	− 391
399	192	14	1343	289	494

(Entire task set not displayed.)

Instructional Assessment Procedures

In the abbreviated mathematics assessment set just presented, the easy/hard task variation should be noted. Easy tasks (e.g., addition and subtraction problems without regrouping) were interspersed among more difficult tasks in the assessment sequence to structure opportunities for the learner to succeed and thereby increase motivation. In addition, the following assessment techniques were implemented (though they are not discernible through the examples):

1. **Variation of response modality:** On selected items that were in error, the student was stopped and asked to explain orally the addition or subtraction process while solving the item.
2. **Prompting with rule (subtraction problems):** What must you do if the bottom number (points to number) is bigger than the top number (points)? What must you do when there is a zero in the tens place?

3. **Prompting with rule (addition problems):** What must you do when you have ~~more~~ than nine tens in this column (points) and there are numbers in the hundreds column (points to number)?
4. **Delayed retesting of prompted tasks.**

Assessment Alternatives   According to the individual's performance, the following options could have been incorporated in the assessment sequence:

1. **Vary task quantity:** If the number of problems was considered excessive, schedule problems into smaller sets.
2. **Vary task domain:** Separate addition and subtraction problems.

EXAMPLE 3
Reading Comprehension—Intermediate Level

Learner   A 13-year-old student with a history of word recognition and comprehension deficits. Current level of functioning in reading comprehension: 3–4th grade.

Learning Outcome   Given a multiple-paragraph passage (approximately 200 words) from the fourth-grade reading text, the learner will orally answer passage-dependent literal comprehension questions with 80% accuracy.

Materials   Passages selected and reproduced from end of third-grade level reader and beginning and middle of fourth-grade text.

Response Modality   Silent reading, oral responses.

Response Form   Production.

Competency   New learning.

Assessment Sequence

TASK 2–12

TEACHER: Read the story to yourself. Remember to read carefully because I will ask you to tell me about the story when you are finished. Try to remember what you read. (Teacher will select appropriate passage.)

TASK 2–13

(Following Silent Reading)

TEACHER: I want you to tell me the main things that happened in this story. Try to tell them to me in the order they happened in the story. (Oral production task.)
STUDENT: (Provides partially correct information.)
TEACHER: Can you remember anything else?
STUDENT: (Fails to supply any additional information.)

TASK 2–14

(Following Oral Production Task with Passage-Dependent Literal Comprehension Questions)

TEACHER: What was the main thing this story was about?
STUDENT: (Provides descriptive terms, but fails to identify main theme of the passage.)
TEACHER: Who was the story about?
STUDENT: (Provides correct response.)
TEACHER: What were the characters trying to do?
STUDENT: (Fails to provide correct response.)
TEACHER: What happens at the end of the story?
STUDENT: (Fails to provide correct response.)
TEACHER: What does the word (select critical vocabulary term) mean?
STUDENT: (Provides partially correct information.)

Error Analysis   The learner provided generally sparse but correct information on oral production tasks. The learner was unable to answer probes assessing specific details. Additional information is needed to assess the learner's knowledge of passage vocabulary.

Instructional Assessment Phase

Learning Outcome   After reading a selection of several paragraphs, the learner will orally answer passage-dependent literal comprehension questions including main idea, characters, supporting details, story problem, and vocabulary with 80% accuracy.

Materials   Same passage used in previous assessment. Supplement with additional passages from basal text.

Response Modality   Oral.

Response Form   Production.

Competency   New learning.

Assessment Sequence

TASK 2–15

TEACHER: (Presents passage.) I want you to read the story again. But this time I want you to read it out loud. Remember to read carefully because I'm going to stop you now and then and ask you questions about the story. If there are words you don't know, try to read the word, then I will help you. (Teacher records miscues.)

TASK 2–16

TEACHER: (After reading first paragraph.) Tell me about what you just read. What was the most important idea in the paragraph?

If the student is unable to recall the main information of the paragraph, provide specific prompts: (1) What was the main thing that happened? (2) Who was the paragraph about? (3) What was that person doing? If the learner is unable to produce information about the paragraph, an alternative is to provide choice responses from which the reader can select the best answer.

TASK 2–17

Teacher: Who was the story about?
Student: (Student supplies incorrect response.)
Teacher: Were they going (provision of choice responses):
    (a) away from the equator (b) toward the equator (c) near the ocean.
    Teacher provides choice responses including the correct answers plus at least 2 distractors.
Student: Toward the equator. (Student selects correct response.)
Teacher: Very good.
Teacher: (Continues probing on paragraph.) What were the characters trying to do?

If answers are correct, proceed to next paragraph; if answers are incorrect, have student reread a sentence at a time, probing after each sentence.

TASK 2–18

Teacher: Now I want you to read the next paragraph. (After reading.) Now tell me about this part of the story. (If correct, ask for recall of both paragraphs; if incorrect, use the prompting procedure, followed by rereading if answers to prompts are incorrect.)

TASK 2–19

To assess summary skills of an entire story or selection for a student who has difficulty producing answers, provide summary statements or titles and have the student select and evaluate the statements. Valencia and Pearson (1988) suggested the following techniques:

1. Which summary provides the most support for the main conclusion?
2. Which summary is filled with too many unimportant ideas?
3. Which statement would best help someone else get a picture of what the selection was about?

Instructional Assessment Procedure

In these instructional assessments of reading comprehension, the following assessment procedures were employed:

1. **Modified reading modality:** Student read passage orally rather than silently.
2. **Varied quantity of information assessed:** Rather than having student read entire passage before assessing comprehension, information was chunked into paragraphs

(or reasonable amount for student) and comprehension assessed immediately after each segment.

3. **Modified position of assessment probe:** Probing of critical information (e.g., key vocabulary, main ideas) occurred immediately after the information was encountered in the passage.

4. **Altered response format:** Production responses that were in error were followed with choice response tasks.

Assessment Alternatives

Following are additional variations that may be incorporated in the assessment sequence in response to the learner's performance on prior tasks:

1. **Prompt reading strategies:** Is there anything in the story that might help you find the meaning of that word?

2. **Modify complexity of directions:** Ask for only one piece of information rather than multiple.

3. **Vary materials:** Assess comprehension in another story.

4. **Structure prompting and delay retesting of oral miscues.**

5. **Reduce reading segments to one to three sentences.**

WITHDRAWING INSTRUCTIONAL ASSESSMENT

Instructional assessment defines a learner's level of knowledge according to the tasks, materials, and instruction used in the information-gathering process. The types of prompts, degree of task modification, or changes in response form needed to achieve success during assessment translate directly into instructional programming. Teachers should initiate instruction with the most complex task, response form, or instructional prompt the learner was able to accomplish successfully in assessment.

If instructional adaptations enhance performance in assessment sequences, they should be incorporated in instructional sessions. However, as the learner progresses and moves closer to criterion on the instructional objective, assistance *must* be systematically withdrawn. Prompts, variations, and manipulations of assessment materials, tasks, and instruction are means to gather information and to structure success for the learner. As the student masters the skill with assistance (e.g., with modifications in task quantity, response modality, and task domain), prompts should be reduced. The goals of instructional assessment are to measure skills in the conditions that are most like those of the mainstream instructional context and to provide information on how to teach that information. To this end, instructional assessment can be viewed as an intermediate step between instruction and assessment.

SUMMARY

This chapter introduced the instructional assessment model, an assessment prototype designed to enhance our understanding and analysis of academic failure. Instructional assessments describe and explain learner performance in relation to the tasks, response requirements, and instruction learners encounter on a day-to-day basis. It supplements the information gained through traditional and curriculum-based measures by more carefully scrutinizing the instructional factors that influence learner performance.

Instructional assessment merges the process of collecting information about student performance with the procedures of instruction. This tack to "unpacking academic failure" creates conditions where learners can succeed and where teachers can gather information useful for instruction. This model uses instruction not simply as a follow-up to assessment but as an integral feature of the assessment process. Accordingly, assessment was portrayed as an ongoing process that takes place whenever learners are presented academic tasks.

Advantages of the assessment model were described in relation to its multicontextual basis. Because of this multifaceted and experimental approach to information gathering, instructional assessment was described as a procedure that places heavy responsibility on the teacher to identify and alter those factors that impact learner performance. To assist teachers in this identification process, the chapter detailed selected instructional factors and specific dimensions of each. In addition, procedures for developing, initiating, and adapting instructional assessments were detailed and applied to academic content typical of the general education classroom.

APPLICATION ITEMS

1. Label each of the following tasks as a binary (b), choice (c), or production (p) response:

$$\frac{56}{-37}$$

_____ Spelling a word dictated orally
_____ Circle the correct synonym of the word *boisterous*.
    (a) quiet (b) careful (c) noisy (d) tardy
_____ Write a sentence using each of your spelling words.
_____ Water freezes at 212 degrees. True or false.

2. Adapt each of the preceding items to demonstrate a different response format.

3. The learner has mastered addition facts 1–5 and performs addition facts 5–9 with 80% accuracy. The new task to be introduced is 2-digit addition without regrouping. Design a set of 20 problems that would assess the learner's skills in these areas. Remember to sequence tasks according to competency.

4. Select a passage from an elementary basal reading text. The passage should have accompanying comprehension questions. Assume the learner is unable to answer the comprehension questions correctly when presented in this format. Based on the comprehension questions provided with the passage, respond to the following items.

   a. Analyze the comprehension questions according to the task and response dimensions and recommend adaptations to improve student performance.

5. A new student has been assigned to your classroom. Cumulative academic records are forthcoming; however, at present you have no information on the student's current levels of functioning.

   a. Specify the grade level of your classroom.

b. Design a sequence of tasks that would allow you to identify general levels of functioning in reading, spelling, and math. Keep task and response dimensions in mind when designing these tasks.

c. Select one academic area and design a task sequence that will allow you to determine specific strengths and weaknesses of the student.

d. Suggest methods you would use to gather information useful for planning instruction.

REFERENCES

Algozzine, B., & Ysseldyke, J. (1986). The future of the LD field: Screening and diagnosis. *Journal of Learning Disabilities, 19*(7), 394–398.

Deno, S. L., & Fuchs, L. S. (1987). Curriculum-based measurement systems. *Focus on Exceptional Children, 19,* 1–16.

Gallagher, J. J. (1986). Learning disabilities and special education: A critique. *Journal of Learning Disabilities, 19*(10), 595–601.

Gould, S. J. (1981). *The mismeasure of man.* New York: Norton.

Mosenthal, P. (1982). Designing training programs for learning disabled children: An ideological perspective. *Topics in Learning and Learning Disabilities, 2*(1), 97–107.

Valencia, S. W., & Pearson, P. D. (1988). Principles for classroom comprehension assessment. *Remedial and Special Education, 9,* 26–35.

PART II

Principles of
Instructional Design

C H A P T E R

THREE

A Taxonomy of Knowledge Forms and Instructional Requirements

Chapter Objectives

Upon successful completion of this chapter, you will be able to:

1. IDENTIFY the different forms of knowledge and describe how they differ, from simple facts to complex cognitive strategies.
2. PROVIDE a rationale for examining the different forms of knowledge and their relationship to instruction.
3. DISTINGUISH between symbolic operations such as reading and nonsymbolic operations such as kicking a ball.
4. PROPOSE a taxonomy of knowledge forms and describe each in detail.
5. EXAMINE the essential instructional features of each knowledge form and discuss the implications for designing teaching sequences.

THE UNIVERSE OF KNOWLEDGE: A STRUCTURAL ANALYSIS

Whenever teachers instruct, direct, explain, describe, communicate, define, or otherwise "teach," these actions involve the giving of information. The information could be a message, an idea, a name, a number, a concept, an operation, a fact, a group of facts, a rule, and so on. When teachers teach, they teach about "something"—something that the learner doesn't yet know or is only beginning to understand. We generally think about that "something" as comprising the academic domains of language, reading, mathematics, writing, and the content areas (e.g., social studies, earth science). For example, that "something" could involve a language concept like the locational concept of *over,* or facts about the state of California, its population, state bird, state flower, and history. In a sense, teachers' actions are designed to make the information clear to the learner. This chapter is concerned with identifying, describing, and classifying the pieces of information that teachers teach in the academic skill areas. This information is generally referred to as **knowledge**. Similarly, the classification of this knowledge is referred to as a **taxonomy of knowledge**.

When we teach reading, language, mathematics, and other academic skills, we teach specific pieces of information. We teach concepts, facts, operations, algorithms, rules, routines, and procedures. In fact, it is not possible to teach a curriculum without teaching individual pieces of information that comprise that general curriculum. These pieces vary not only in their subject matter (e.g., language, mathematics, social studies), but also in their structure. For instance, we know that a factual piece of information, such as "Helena is the capital of the state of Montana," or "The pituitary gland or hypophysis is considered the master gland of the human body," are much different pieces of knowledge than the locational language concepts of *on, between,* or *over.* Similarly, the concept *over* is a much different piece of knowledge with a different form than the concept *parallelogram.* *Parallelogram* is much different in knowledge form than a rule that specifies a relationship between two events, facts, or entities (e.g., "The faster you run, the more oxygen you use"). What the teacher teaches and the flow of information to the student are depicted in Figure 3–1.

The *What* That Shapes the *How* of Teaching

What teachers teach is just as important as how it is taught. In this chapter we argue that having a clear understanding of what is taught ultimately helps the teacher decide how it should be taught. What is taught is part of a larger group or universe of concepts, facts, rules, definitions, operations, and other general information. No piece of knowledge is discrete. A piece of knowledge is part of a larger family of knowledge. Its membership in that family is based on its similarity in form to the other members in that family. A fact, rule, concept, or operation belongs to a larger group of facts, rules, concepts, or operations that are similar to one another. This grouping of knowledge into categories is not unlike the classification of objects (e.g., big objects, heavy objects, tall objects, ugly objects), animals (e.g., mammals, reptiles, birds, fish), events (e.g., a party, a graduation), people (e.g., Native Americans, Black Americans, Pacific Islanders), or music (e.g., jazz, rock 'n' roll, country, gospel).

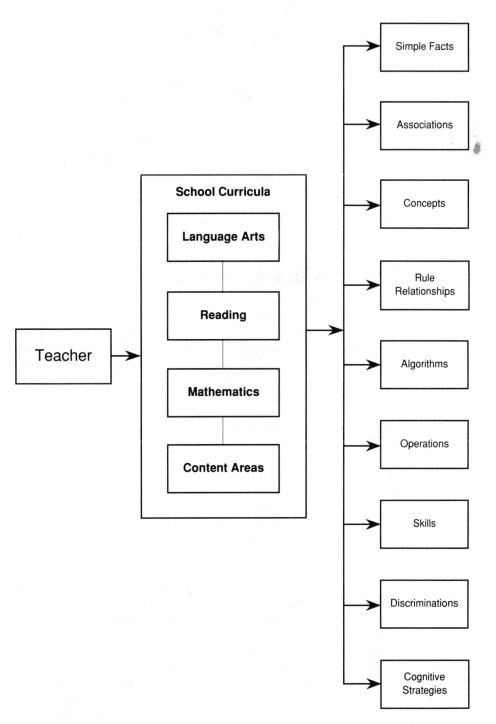

FIGURE 3–1
What the teacher teaches

By knowing the form of what is to be taught, the teacher should have a clear idea of how that piece of knowledge (i.e., concept, rule, fact) will be taught. In a sense, the teacher engages in the same thinking process as a medical doctor faced with treating a patient after diagnosing a problem. The medical practitioner determines how to treat the problem on the basis of what the problem appears to be. Unless the problem is rare, the physician's diagnosis is one of determining the class, family, or group of diseases to which the problem belongs. By knowing this, the doctor is alerted to ways of treating the problem. In the same manner, a teacher who knows the class to which a piece of knowledge belongs will probably be alerted to the best ways of teaching or communicating that piece of knowledge. For example, a teacher who knows a piece of knowledge is a fact wouldn't attempt to teach that fact as if it were a rule. Similarly, the teacher wouldn't teach a rule as if it were a fact, or a cognitive strategy as if it were a simple concept. How something is taught depends largely on the form or structure of that piece of knowledge.

Delivering vs. Designing Instruction

One of the most serious misconceptions about teaching is that teachers merely "teach"; that is, that teachers merely impart knowledge to students by means of lessons. This implies that the teacher's primary responsibility is one of simply dispensing information in the same way a nurse dispenses medication to patients or a mail carrier delivers the mail. The act of dispensing something, as the misconception goes, really doesn't require any critical analysis, because the teacher's role is simply to deliver a product (i.e., the lesson) that has already been prepared and packaged. One can easily get the impression that the "packaged" information or knowledge is transferred directly from the commercial curriculum to the students, without passing through the brain of the teacher. The packaging of skills and knowledge, after all, has been done elsewhere by curriculum experts and promoted by publishers with the latest technological resources at their fingertips. The curriculum materials are presumed to be acceptable for daily use in the classroom.

These conceptions of teaching and curricular materials are mistaken on at least two serious counts. First, students with academic learning problems have, for all practical purposes, already failed partly *because* of the mainstream curriculum materials. Using the same curriculum materials *without some significant adaptations* only serves to promote further failure. Consequently, teachers must have the skills to modify these materials. These skills require knowing how to design instruction. Second, ample descriptive research raises serious concerns about the adequacy of curriculum materials, not only for children with academic learning problems but for other children, as well (Armbruster & Gudbrandsen, 1986; Beck, McKeown, McCaslin, & Burkes, 1979; Beck, Omanson, & McKeown, 1982; DuncanMalone & Kameenui, 1987; Durkin, 1978–1979, 1981; Jitendra & Kameenui, 1988; also see *Elementary School Journal*, 1987, vol. 87).

Teaching involves more than simply delivering knowledge or information as prescribed in a curriculum lesson. It also involves knowing enough about the universe of knowledge and its different forms, and how each form should be taught. By understanding the different forms of knowledge, we can begin to hold to the assumption we made back in Chapter 1 regarding the content or skill—information or knowledge can be analyzed in ways to be taught.

Symbolic and Nonsymbolic Operations: An Instructional Distinction

Before we take a detailed look at how the universe of knowledge can be divided into different categories of knowledge, it is important to appreciate the distinction between the world of symbols or symbolic operations and that of nonsymbolic operations or physical tasks (Becker, 1986). According to Gagne's (1985) main categories of "learned capabilities," symbolic operations comprise intellectual skills, cognitive strategies, and verbal information. In contrast, nonsymbolic operations are similar to motor skills in Gagne's analysis of knowledge. Simply put, symbolic operations refer to any instructional task that requires the learner to interpret a symbol system, as discussed earlier in Chapter 1 (see Assumption 4: The learner is vulnerable to the world of symbols, p. 14). Nonsymbolic operations, on the other hand, refer to physical tasks such as holding a pencil, picking up a fork, or kicking a ball.

The purpose of examining the distinctions between symbolic and nonsymbolic operations is to understand the complexities of symbolic tasks, especially those that have many different steps and require the mastery of prerequisite skills. These distinctions will also be used to frame this text's orientation to instruction. As indicated in Table 3–1, symbolic and nonsymbolic tasks differ along three dimensions: (1) observability of the component processes, (2) identification of the component skills, and (3) feedback from the environment. Each of these differences is described in the following section.

Observable vs. Nonobservable Steps

An interesting distinction between a symbolic task, such as reading a multisyllabic word like *chattering* (selected from a second grade basal reading workbook), and a nonsymbolic task, such as kicking a ball (another favored second grade activity), is that the intermediate steps can be observed in one but not the other. For example, during oral reading, a second grader could mistakenly read the word *chattering* as "chatting." In observing this error, we do not observe the intermediate steps that lead to the mistake. In fact, all we observe is the word that the learner finally reads, *chatting*. We cannot step into the child's head to observe the component learning processes that brought about the incorrect response, only the final outcome of that hidden process.

TABLE 3–1
Distinction between symbolic and nonsymbolic operations

Symbolic Operations	Nonsymbolic Operations
All component learning processes are covert and can't be seen. Only a final product can be observed.	All component learning processes are overt and remain overt and observable.
The component skills of an operation or task are difficult to identify and demonstrate.	The component skills of a task are easy to identify and demonstrate.
Feedback from the environment is unpredictable and not inherent in the execution of the task.	Feedback from the environment is predictable, instantaneous and inherent in the task.

In contrast to the symbolic task, the nonsymbolic or physical task of kicking a ball is entirely open to public scrutiny. The observer can see the steps required for a successful or unsuccessful kick. The learner's behavior of kicking and the events that preceded the kicking are overt and observable. The steps the learner takes in kicking the ball or in coiling the leg in its swing toward the ball are all observable. Unlike the performance of a symbolic task, in which the intermediate steps are not observed, the performance of a nonsymbolic task allows not only the final outcome to be public, but also the entire performance of the task, from beginning to end.

Identifying Component Skills

Because a symbolic operation takes place in the learner's head and is hidden from view, identifying the component skills that comprise a complex symbolic operation is impossible. In contrast, identifying the component skills that comprise a nonsymbolic task should be straightforward because the task is physical in nature and can be observed in its entirety.

Much of the controversy surrounding the teaching of academic skills centers on this very issue of breaking down complex symbolic operations (e.g., reading in general, decoding in particular, solving mathematics word problems, literacy skills in language and expressive writing). Some educators argue that the attempt to break down and identify the intermediate, component skills of complex tasks in effect trivializes the learning process (Goodman, 1986; Shannon, 1988). Others note that when component skills are not identified as a means to simplify complex tasks, students with academic learning problems are left without strategies for successfully working complex symbolic operations (Becker & Carnine, 1980; Kameenui, 1988).

In kicking a ball, the required component skills are obvious and can be immediately tested by simply executing them and observing the results. The case is not so clear-cut with symbolic operations. The identification of component skills can vary, depending on *who* does the identifying (e.g., a linguist, a behaviorist, a whole language specialist) and *what* component skills need to be identified to accommodate the skill level of the learner. Furthermore, the partitioning of a complex task into smaller pieces may also require extensive experimental teaching to determine the utility and validity of the component or prerequisite skills.

Feedback from the Environment

Another important distinction between symbolic and nonsymbolic tasks involves the feedback each task is likely to prompt. With nonsymbolic (motor) tasks, feedback from the environment is likely to be immediate, predictable, and easily associated with the task itself. For example, preparing to kick the ball a learner coils her foot back and momentarily takes her eyes off the ball, and as a result she misses the ball and lands on her back. In this instance, the environment gives the learner instant feedback about her performance. If the learner continued to kick the ball in the same manner, the feedback would be predictable. In effect, the environment tells the learner, "Something is wrong with your performance." In most cases, the learner heeds the feedback and modifies future kicking behavior.

In the case of symbolic tasks, the environment is not likely to provide the learner with instant feedback about performance. The feedback ultimately depends on the conditions of the environment at the time of the learner's performance. A learner could silently read an entire book and make erroneous observations about the text. Unless someone else (e.g., teacher, parent, or peer who has read the same book) is in the environment to provide feedback at the time, the learner could hold firmly to some incorrect interpretations.

In contrast, no one needs to be present to give a clumsy child or adult feedback when he walks, nose first, into a door without first grasping the doorknob and opening the door. The environment, namely the door, is likely to give this well-bruised individual the instant feedback necessary to correct his performance. This distinction should remind the reader of the assumption that was made of the learner in Chapter 1—the learner is vulnerable to the world of symbols. Unless the teacher structures teaching in ways that provide learners with systematic feedback about performance, learners are left to their own imagination about the correctness or adequacy of a performance on a symbolic task.

Designing Symbolic Tasks: What Kicking a Ball Can Teach Us

By understanding the distinctions between symbolic and nonsymbolic tasks and operations, we can begin to appreciate the importance of these distinctions from an instructional standpoint. What we notice is that nonsymbolic, motor tasks are easier to teach than symbolic, cognitive tasks. The component parts of physical tasks are always public, observable, and more easily identified than those of symbolic tasks. Moreover, providing

Reading aloud provides a forum for feedback and requires the reader native product—the spoken word.

a learner with feedback on a physical task is more manageable than providing feedback on a symbolic task. The features of nonsymbolic tasks make them more amenable to teaching, and it is reasonable to capitalize on those features when teaching symbolic tasks. In other words, it seems logical to design symbolic tasks in ways that make them more like nonsymbolic, or physical, tasks. This means that we should initially design symbolic tasks in ways that make the component skills more overt instead of covert. In so doing, we provide the learner with immediate practice and feedback on a skill.

For example, a task such as silent reading of a paragraph could be modeled after a nonsymbolic task. Instead of requiring a learner to provide only a final product of the reading task (e.g., answering comprehension questions about the paragraph), much of the reading process and its intermediate steps should be made public to the teacher. The reader would be required to read aloud what was once read silently. By requiring the reader to make silent reading public or to paraphrase important ideas verbally, the teacher is able to give the reader feedback about accuracy, fluency, and expression in reading and comprehending the text.

An important qualification is necessary at this point. Designing tasks in which component, intermediate skills are made overt for both the teacher and learner to observe is *not* an adequate teaching outcome. Making covert complex skills more public and observable is a necessary phase of initial instruction to provide the learner with instant information about performance. But it is certainly not the *final* phase of instruction; that is, instruction for the purpose of bringing a learner to mastery level performance on a skill should not end with the normally covert tasks or operation being overt; rather, instruction must be designed to allow the learner to internalize the skill. The once overt and publicly displayed skill must, in a sense, go "underground" (Baer, 1979) and become unobservable. The assumption is that adequate overt practice of a skill will bring the learner to a level of fluency or automaticity (LaBerge & Samuels, 1976) that makes further practice unnecessary. In fact, once a skill reaches an acceptable level of mastery, the overt practice could disrupt the fluency of a student's performance.

By examining the distinction between symbolic and nonsymbolic tasks, we can begin to think about how to design or redesign complex symbolic tasks to make them more manageable for children with academic learning problems. We can break down complex tasks such as reading into component skills in much the same way we would in ~~ching a child to ride a bicycle. We can break down the reading of CVCe (consonant/ ~~onsonant/small *e*) words such as *rate, gate,* and *late* by teaching students a ~~ for decoding these word types (e.g., "When there's an *e* at the end of word, ~~ of the vowel"). The teacher would require students to apply the rule ~~. *rate, rat, hope, hop:* "Look at the first word. Is there an *e* at the ~~say the name of the vowel? What's the name of the vowel? ~~ient practice and monitoring, students would read CVCe ~~ying the rule to identify the individual letters. ~~n a complex comprehension task, such as reading Jack ~~During the reading of the story, the teacher would require ~~tory grammar" components, such as the characters (e.g., the ~~e problem (e.g., building a fire under a snow-covered tree), the ~~problem (e.g., the old man runs to warm himself), the resolution ~~entually dies), and the theme of the story (e.g., the struggle for

survival in an unknown environment). After identifying th
student retells or summarizes the entire story and the au

After component skills of a complex task are identifi
more complex chunks as the learner becomes fluent in ex
The distinctions between symbolic and nonsymbolic oper;
tional strategies we design in this text.

Knowledge Forms

In the introduction to this chapter, we noted that symbolic k   ... ... different
forms. This idea is not a new one. We can point to many significant contributions,
beginning with the taxonomy of educational objectives for the cognitive domain developed
by Benjamin Bloom (1956) and his colleagues. This taxonomy consists of six levels of
cognitive knowledge: knowledge, comprehension, application, analysis, synthesis, and
evaluation. The levels of the taxonomy are stacked hierarchically from bottom to top,
with the recall of factual information (Level 1—Knowledge) serving as the first tier of
objectives for the cognitive domain and representing the least complex level of knowledge.
The top of the taxonomy is concerned with a learner's appraisal or judgment about the
value of something (Level 6—Evaluation). The hierarchical features of this taxonomy are
depicted in Figure 3–2.

Although Bloom's taxonomy focuses much attention on the different levels of
knowledge, it does not, as Becker (1986) points out, specify the different forms of
knowledge. Instead, it describes "how the learner acts on the communications" (p. 175)
or knowledge. That is, the learner acts on the knowledge presented by recalling it,
comprehending its meaning, applying it to new situations, and judging its value.

The examination of different forms of knowledge and the concern for developing
an efficient means of communicating knowledge were established almost simultaneously
by Bruner (1966) and Gagne (1965). In his essay "Notes on a Theory of Instruction,"
Bruner calls for a theory of instruction that would "specify ways in which a body of
knowledge should be structured so that it can be most readily grasped by the learner"
(p. 41). The optimal structure of knowledge, as Bruner characterized it, would provide
practitioners with a "set of propositions from which a larger body of knowledge can be
generated" (p. 41).

Gagne's (1965) work provided perhaps the first comprehensive effort at prescribing a set of propositions for how knowledge is structured. In the most recent edition of
The Conditions of Learning and Theory of Instruction, Gagne (1985) describes five
categories of "learned capabilities" (p. 47). In his analysis, individuals have the capacity
to learn or to change in a way that "persists over a period of time and is not simply
ascribable to processes of growth" (p. 2). According to Gagne, these "learned capabilities . . . must be observed as human performances" (p. 47). Gagne's five major categories
of learned capabilities, therefore, are based on characteristics of the way a learner carries
out or performs "what is learned" (p. 47). These capabilities as presented in Table 3–2
include (1) intellectual skills (comprising discriminations, concrete concepts, defined
concepts, rules, and higher-order rules); (2) cognitive strategies; (3) verbal information;
(4) motor skills; and (5) attitudes. Gagne views these "five main categories of capabilities
that human beings learn" as "comprehensive" (p. 48), so that *any* learning outcome
could be classified into one of these categories.

Prir

FIGURE 3–2
Bloom's ta
From TA
cation
Ben

66

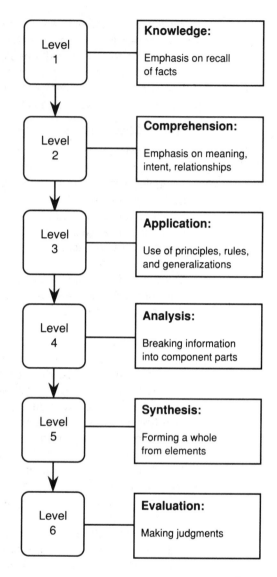

Apart from Bruner's (1966) and Gagne's (1965; 1985; Gagne & Briggs, 1979) contributions to the analysis of different types of knowledge, the efforts of Markle (1975; 1978) and her colleagues (Markle & Tiemann, 1969), Tennyson and his colleagues (Tennyson & Christensen, 1986; Tennyson & Cochiarella, 1986; Tennyson & Park, 1980), and others (Bourne, Goldstein, & Link, 1964; Clark, 1971; Engelmann & Carnine, 1982; Klausmeier, 1976; Klausmeier, Ghatala, & Frayer, 1974; Merrill, 1971) have established a broad and substantial research base for potentially linking what is taught (i.e., knowledge) to how it should be taught.

Examining Forms of Knowledge Within the Context of Instruction

Identifying what Bruner (1966) refers to as an "optimal structure" of knowledge and engaging in a description of knowledge structures directly benefit the design and imple-

TABLE 3–2
Gagne's five major categories of learned capabilities

Learned Capability	Examples of Performance
Intellectual skill	Manipulating symbolic information such as:
Discrimination	Distinguishing between phonemes *i* and *e*
Concrete concept	Identifying an object as a ball
Defined concept	Defining constant equilibrium
Rule	Demonstrating relationship between the movement of air and temperature
Higher-order rule	Predicting the relationship between a character's apparent motive in a story and the character's true motive to the outcome of events in a story
Cognitive strategy	Implementing a five-step procedure for estimating the velocity of an object
Verbal information	Naming the months of the year
Motor skill	Picking up a pencil
Attitude	Preferring to avoid loud people

Source: Adaptation of Table 3–1 from *The Conditions of Learning and Theory of Instruction*, Fourth Edition by R. M. Gagne, copyright © 1985 by Holt, Rinehart and Winston, Inc., Reprinted by permission of the publisher.

mentation of teaching sequences. What teachers gain from knowing about different types of knowledge forms is likely to serve them not only in the daily, face-to-face instruction of specific skills but also before instruction takes place (i.e., in the planning of how something should be taught). What is gained with this knowledge is a feel for whether a teaching sequence is designed properly, similar to how an architect appraises the structural features of a building at first glance. By knowing about the structure of knowledge, teachers should know whether a teaching sequence is structurally adequate. Furthermore, teachers will also be ready to make structural changes in the teaching sequence if necessary—changes that require considerable thought and experimentation.

TYPES OF KNOWLEDGE FORMS: FROM SIMPLE TO COMPLEX

In the next section of this chapter, we specify the different types of knowledge forms that are likely to comprise school-based curricula at the primary, elementary, and intermediate grade levels. We do not intend to describe the intricate details of how these different classes of knowledge should be taught; the details of designing and constructing teaching sequences for different knowledge forms will be provided in later chapters.

A Taxonomy: From Plants to Pedagogy

A taxonomy of knowledge is not unlike a taxonomy of plants that consists of the classification of plants into different groups depending on certain features. Classification is usually based on a cluster of features that the plant possesses, rather than a single property of the plant. Obviously, plants could be classified along numerous dimensions.

r instance, we could classify plants by size, leaf patterns, color, or geographic location. t surprisingly, the sophistication of a taxonomy depends to a great extent on the ∪plexity of what is being classified and on the purpose of the taxonomy. Most taxon-∪mes, as in the case of plants, comprise many classification schemes that are hierarchically arranged, beginning with gross, observable distinctions between selected features of things (e.g., leaf configuration and venation patterns) and progressing to highly refined distinctions discerned only by a microscope (e.g., DNA and RNA structure of plant cells.).

The universe of knowledge can benefit from an analysis similar to that applied to the universe of plants. We can select a group of features specific to each kind of knowledge, as we would select features of plants, and arrange the classes of knowledge hierarchically. The taxonomy of knowledge that we propose in this text is derived primarily from Gagne's (1985) analysis of learned capabilities, described earlier in this chapter. We have made several changes in the number, type, and hierarchy of Gagne's categories. Before describing each category of knowledge, we present an overview of the entire taxonomy.

Four different categories of knowledge forms are listed with definitions and examples of each. In the sections that follow, we discuss the rationale for this taxonomy and provide a fuller description of each category. An illustration of these is given in Figure 3–3.

Categories of Knowledge

Category 1: Verbal Associations

A verbal association is defined as the connection of a set of specific responses with specific stimuli. Verbal associations consist of three different types: simple facts, verbal chains, and discriminations. Definitions and examples of each follow.

a. **Simple facts:** The association of a specific response with a specific stimulus; a question that has only one answer.

   Examples: The learner is required to name a specific person (e.g., the name of the teacher), name the capital of a particular state, or tell the number of ounces in a pound.

b. **Verbal chains:** A sequence of successive related simple facts.

   Examples: The learner is required to state the days of the week beginning with Monday and stopping at Thursday, to count by fives beginning at 15 and stopping at 50, or to name the months of the year in order.

c. **Discriminations:** The recognition of a difference between two stimuli in which the association of a specific response to a stimulus is made in the context of another stimulus.

   Examples: The learner is required to distinguish between the letter names of p and q when they are presented together on the blackboard (e.g., "When I point to a letter, I want you to say its name"), or the learner is required to differentiate a heavy object from a light object after lifting them.

FIGURE 3–3
Taxonomy of knowledge forms

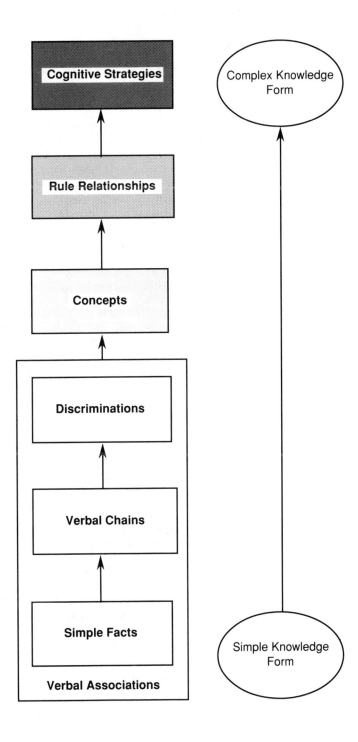

Category 2: Concepts

A concept is defined as an object, event, action, or situation that is part of a class of objects, events, actions, or situations that are the same, based on a feature or a set of features that are the same. Examples of concepts follow.

> *Examples:* The learner is required to observe and label the spatial relation of an object when presented a range of novel examples representing various locations in a classroom (e.g., "Watch me and tell me if I place the ball *on, under, behind, in front of,* or *farther away from* the desk"). Or the learner is required to state the name of a class to which an object, event, or action belongs (e.g., "I'm going to point to some objects and I want you first to name the object and then tell me another class in which that object belongs." Teacher points to a desk, the learner names the object correctly, then states the class—furniture).

Category 3: Rule Relationships

A rule relationship is a proposition that specifies a connection between at least two facts, discriminations, or concepts. Examples of rule relationships follow.

> *Examples:* The teacher presents the learner with the following rule: "The faster you run, the more oxygen you use." The teacher also presents several novel examples of the rule and requires the learner to apply the rule by predicting the relationship between running faster and oxygen usage (e.g., "Look at the video of these two runners and tell me which runner is using more oxygen." Or in a less prompted fashion, the teacher states, "Look at the video of the runners and tell me about the rule").

Category 4: Cognitive Strategies

We define a cognitive strategy as a series of multi-step associations and procedures that may involve facts, verbal chains, discriminations, concepts, and rules designed to bring about a response or a set of responses to a specified problem. Examples of cognitive strategies follow.

> *Examples:* A learner is required to solve the analogy dog: lungs:: fish: _____ , or the arithmetic problem 305 × 177, or answer a literal comprehension question specific to a clause construction in a narrative passage.

Figure 3–4 provides a visual summary of the six different types of knowledge forms in which the definition and an example of each form is given.

We have modified Gagne's analysis in three fundamental ways. First, we have arranged the taxonomy hierarchically in such a way that categories of knowledge are listed in order of their increasing cognitive complexity, beginning with simple verbal associations and ending with complex cognitive strategies. This is in contrast to Gagne's "arbitrarily ordered" (1985, p. 66) categories. We think this hierarchical feature makes it easier for teachers to think about knowledge as having a continuous quality, from knowledge forms that are least complex to those that are most complex. If teachers are able to identify where a particular category of knowledge fits into the hierarchy, they are alerted to the complexity of the teaching requirements of the category.

The hierarchical nature of the taxonomy is represented not only by the ranking of categories from least complex to most complex, but also by the connections between

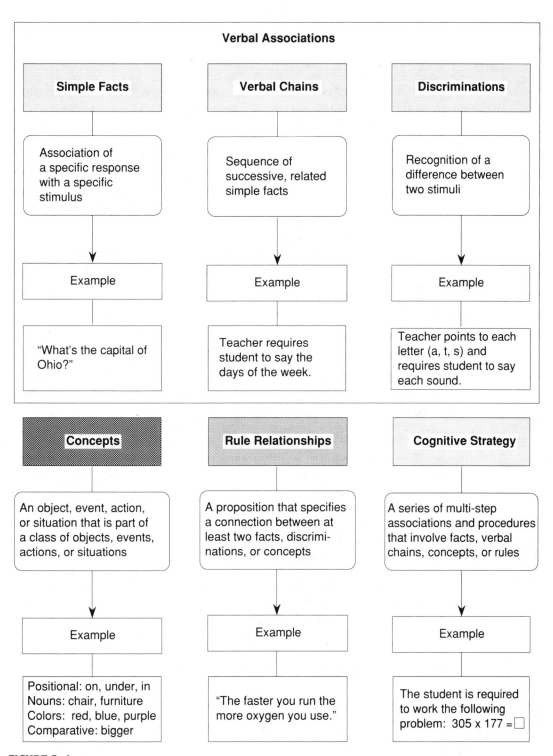

Verbal Associations

Simple Facts	**Verbal Chains**	**Discriminations**
Association of a specific response with a specific stimulus	Sequence of successive, related simple facts	Recognition of a difference between two stimuli
Example	Example	Example
"What's the capital of Ohio?"	Teacher requires student to say the days of the week.	Teacher points to each letter (a, t, s) and requires student to say each sound.

Concepts	**Rule Relationships**	**Cognitive Strategy**
An object, event, action, or situation that is part of a class of objects, events, actions, or situations	A proposition that specifies a connection between at least two facts, discriminations, or concepts	A series of multi-step associations and procedures that involve facts, verbal chains, concepts, or rules
Example	Example	Example
Positional: on, under, in Nouns: chair, furniture Colors: red, blue, purple Comparative: bigger	"The faster you run the more oxygen you use."	The student is required to work the following problem: 305 x 177 =☐

FIGURE 3–4
Summary of knowledge forms

categories of knowledge. In a sense, the taxonomy represents a knowledge chain in which the links between the different categories of knowledge are critical. Obviously, complex categories of knowledge, such as rule relationships, comprise previously established categories of knowledge that are lower in the taxonomy. This interdependence of categories of knowledge is most readily reflected in the terms used to define the categories. For example, verbal chains are defined in reference to simple facts. Similarly, rule relationships are defined in reference to simple facts, discriminations, or concepts, and cognitive strategies are defined in reference to simple facts, verbal chains, discriminations, concepts, or rule relationships. The categories of knowledge are defined in terms of one another. This consistency in terminology provides the taxonomy with a lexical coherence that links all the categories of knowledge while diminishing the often cumbersome vocabulary that makes taxonomies easily forgettable.

The second change we have made is specific to Gagne's category of intellectual skills, which comprises five subordinate categories. We have broken that general category of intellectual skills into three major categories (verbal associations, concepts, rule relationships). We consider the subordinate categories of intellectual skills identified by Gagne to be major learning outcomes in school. These intellectual skills (discrimination, concrete concepts, defined concepts, rules, higher-order rules), as conceptualized by Gagne, are some of the more pivotal academic tasks in the primary and elementary grade levels and can be considered the building blocks for later, more sophisticated cognitive functioning, such as cognitive strategies (Klix, 1983; Tennyson & Christensen, 1986). In light of the academic significance of these subordinate intellectual skills, we decided to assign them a major role in the taxonomy of knowledge.

The final change made in Gagne's analysis of learned capabilities is the omission of the major categories of motor skills and attitudes. These omissions do not imply that motor skills and attitudes (i.e., "internal states that influence the individual's *choices of personal action,*" Gagne, 1985, p. 219) are unimportant. Obviously, motor skills are essential to the execution of numerous cognitive tasks. As we pointed out earlier in this chapter, understanding the requirements of physical tasks is critical to appreciating the complexities of designing symbolic tasks. Similarly, attitudes and their relationship to learning and the contexts of failure as sketched in Chapter 1 are very important. However, a competent and worthy analysis of motor skills and attitudes is beyond the scope of this text.

Our proposed taxonomy is not exhaustive, nor are its categories absolute in specifying where one class of knowledge ends and another begins. Our purpose is to provide teachers with a manageable framework for thinking about different forms of knowledge. As is often the case, managing something as complex as the universe of knowledge requires reducing one's field of vision. In keeping with the focus of this text, we have chosen to concentrate on academically related forms of knowledge (e.g., basic skills).

CATEGORIES OF KNOWLEDGE FORMS: INSTRUCTIONAL DIMENSIONS AND REQUIREMENTS

In this section, we elaborate each of the categories of knowledge identified earlier by embellishing the definitions and examples. We show how the different categories of knowledge are embedded in the broader context of instruction by discussing the instructional dimensions of each knowledge form. We have relied heavily on Engelmann and Carnine's (1982) text, *Theory of Instruction: Principles and Applications*, for the instructional details specific to each category of knowledge.

Verbal Associations

We have defined verbal associations as the connection of a set of specific responses with specific stimuli. In this sense, a learner is required to name or state a specific label in the presence of a specific stimulus. The essential feature of all verbal tasks is that the question asked has only one answer. Here is a sequence of task examples:

TASK 3–1

TEACHER: Tell me your first name.   LEARNER: Ted.

TASK 3–2

TEACHER: Write the name of the day of the week today.   LEARNER: Thursday.

TASK 3–3

TEACHER: Write the number of months in a year.   LEARNER: Twelve.

TASK 3–4

TEACHER: I want you to name all the months of the year.   LEARNER: January, February, March, April, . . . December.

TASK 3–5

TEACHER: Tell me the capital of Hawaii.   LEARNER: Honolulu.

In each example, the question posed can be correctly answered with only one response. Other convergent responses are plausible but not likely to be correct, given the nature of the question. For example, if a teacher asked a learner in Task 3–2, "What day is it today?" and the learner responded, "It's the day after Wednesday," the learner's response would be correct, because the teacher did not ask the learner to state the *name* of the day, as requested in Task 3–2.

Verbal associations are analogous to the nuts and bolts of learning. A specific 3/8-inch bolt is likely to be useless unless matched with a 3/8-inch nut. Attempting to thread a 3/8-inch bolt with anything else will be futile. Verbal associations serve as the hardware for the large body of information that children begin to acquire in the formative years before school. However, for many primary and elementary age children, this general knowledge base is not well established. In our taxonomy, verbal associations serve as the foundation for higher-level knowledge forms. The three different forms of verbal associations (simple facts, verbal chains, discriminations) are not necessarily isolated bits and pieces of knowledge, but networks of information that are associated in some way or another.

The structure of verbal associations is simple, because they have as their pivotal point a connection between only two elements, words, things, and events. In a verbal association, the learner is required to communicate knowledge of this association by producing a verbal response.

Instructional Implications

Because a verbal association is the connection of two elements in which the learner is required to retrieve one element from memory when presented with the appropriate stimulus, such a task is unlikely to command a complex teaching sequence of multiple steps. The instructional dimensions of verbal associations based on their structure (i.e., the association of two elements) should make it an easy task to teach. After all, there are not many ways to teach a verbal chain like the days of the week, months of the year, or the simple fact that a year has 12 months. The teaching presentation will follow a model, lead, and check or test sequence (Carnine, Silbert, & Kameenui, 1990) in which the teacher *models* the information (e.g., "Listen to me while I say the months of the year"), *leads* the learner in repeating the information (e.g., "Now I want you to say the months with me"), then finally *checks* or tests the learner on the information (e.g., "You say the months of the year all by yourself").

What is important to teaching verbal associations is scheduling *how many to teach* in one lesson and *when to teach them.* Because verbal associations require the retrieval of information from storage (i.e., either working memory or long-term memory), the teacher must design the teaching sequence so that the information is stored adequately. To facilitate adequate storage of newly taught information, the teacher must schedule the practice of that information intelligently (and perhaps frequently) during initial instruction. In the case of verbal associations, presenting information adequately isn't difficult, because the learner is required only to recall a specific response in the presence of a specific stimulus. The real issue is in getting the information stored adequately so that it can be retrieved quickly over time. Consequently, determining how big a chunk of information to teach and how frequently it should be reviewed daily or weekly is *most* critical to teaching verbal associations. The details for designing instructional strategies for teaching verbal associations are described in Chapter 5.

Concepts

The next category of knowledge is that of concepts. We view concepts as more complex than verbal associations, and it is reasonable to assume that concepts require more than merely retrieving the association of two elements. A concept is an object, event, action, or situation that is part of a class of objects, events, actions, or situations that are the same based on the same feature or set of features. Here are some examples of concepts:

Positional concepts: under, on, between, over, in front of

Color concepts: red, purple, light blue, navy blue, burgundy

Polar concepts: full/empty, hot/cold, high/low, up/down

Class concepts: furniture, dogs, food, appliances, people

Comparative concepts: bigger, brighter, faster, deeper

As the definition implies, merely identifying and labeling an object (e.g., "This is a dog") does not constitute concept learning. To demonstrate knowledge of a concept, a learner must be able to identify "novel" instances (i.e., newly encountered, never before seen examples) of an object or event as belonging to a particular class of objects or events. This process of acquiring new concepts requires the learner to observe, manipulate, or somehow interact with selected examples of a concept and then identify novel examples of the same concept. These leaps and inferences are typically referred to as the processes of generalization. As Gagne (1985) and others (Markle & Tiemann, 1969; Tennyson & Park, 1980) have pointed out, the process of generalization is essential to the learning of concepts. However, describing the process of generalization is not the same as designing teaching sequences to bring about the generalization. Designing teaching sequences that allow low performers with serious academic learning problems to generalize from taught examples of a concept to untaught examples of the same concept must be undertaken with care.

Engelmann and Carnine (1982) provide an insightful analysis that makes the elusive process of generalization more amenable to instruction. They argue that when the learner is presented examples of a particular concept, the learner in effect "makes up a rule" (p. 4). This doesn't mean that the learner actually articulates a formal rule. It means that the learner is aware that something systematic is going on in the examples presented. This rule is not arbitrary but is based on the examples presented to the learner and, more importantly, on the features or qualities of those examples. The rule indicates to the learner what the "sameness of quality" is in all the examples presented to the learner. As Engelmann and Carnine state:

> Once the mechanism "has determined" what is the same about the examples of a particular concept, generalization occurs. The only possible basis for generalization is sameness of quality. If the example to which the learner is to generalize is not the same as the earlier examples with respect to specific qualities, it is impossible for generalization to occur unless the learning mechanism is empowered with magical properties. (p. 4)

Concepts as a knowledge form are structurally different from verbal associations that involve a link between only two elements. Concepts require the learner to identify a quality that is the same in a set of examples. Unfortunately for the learner, this identification process doesn't happen instantly or flawlessly. The learner must note all the qualities in an example, then decide which quality or qualities are the same with each successive example that is presented. In effect, the learner must hold numerous qualities in mind and systematically discard or ignore those that are not the same across examples.

After a series of examples has been presented and labeled for the learner, the learner is able to make a generalization—the process of detecting the same quality in all examples of a particular concept.

The "sameness of quality" principle identified by Engelmann and Carnine (1982) should not be construed as meaning any quality or feature that is *similar*. As noted in our definition of a concept, the recognition of a novel example of an object, event, action, or situation is based on a feature or set of features that are the same. The quality or feature that allows the learner to recognize an example as belonging to a concept class must be the *same* (not similar) in all examples of the concept.

Instructional Implications

This analysis of concepts doesn't make the instructional dimensions of concepts readily obvious. We do know, however, that examples of concepts (i.e., objects, events, actions, situations) are necessary to the teaching of concepts. We also know that these examples must be carefully selected to make obvious the "sameness of quality" they all have. However, what we don't know from this analysis and discussion of concepts is what kind of examples to present, how many examples to present, how the examples should be sequenced, and what to label the examples in a teaching presentation of concepts. The details for designing instructional strategies for teaching concepts are described in Chapter 6.

Rule Relationships

To this point, we have described verbal tasks and concepts that comprise the first two categories of knowledge forms in our taxonomy. The next level of knowledge in this hierarchy is that of rule relationships. We have defined a rule relationship as a proposition that specifies a connection between at least two facts, discriminations, or concepts. As this definition suggests, a rule is a verbal statement that specifies a relationship between two other knowledge forms. In the following series of rule relationships the component parts of the rules are identified:

Examples of Rule Relationships	Component Knowledge Forms

TASK 3–6

Just because you know about a part doesn't mean you know about the whole thing.	**Discrimination:** Distinguishing between a part of something and the whole of the same thing.
	Concepts: Recognizing the parts of things; recognizing when something is a whole.

TASK 3–7

The bigger the fire, the more oxygen it uses.	**Concepts:** Recognizing a fire; recognizing concept of *bigger.*

TASK 3-8

When the long hand is on the 12, it is o'clock.

Discrimination: Distinguishing between the long and short hand on a clock. Distinguishing numbers on the face of the clock from one another.

Concepts: Recognizing the numbers on the face of a clock and the hands of the clock.

TASK 3-9

Products that are ready to use cost more.

Concepts: Recognizing products by name; recognizing when the same product is prepared or unprepared for immediate use; recognizing costs of products; recognizing concept of *more.*

The essential feature of rule relationships is the connection or linkage between two other component forms of knowledge. Although a rule is composed of several facts, discriminations, or concepts, the feature that distinguishes a rule from a concept or a verbal association is not the concept itself, but the connection or relationship it specifies between already known facts, concepts, and discriminations.

The learner may know the component concepts or elements of the rule but not know how the component pieces of information are related to create a new piece of information. For example, a learner could understand the component parts of the rule in Task 3–6 ("Just because you know about a part doesn't mean you know about the whole thing"), but not the relationship communicated in the rule. Understanding this relationship requires that the learner make judgments about situations (e.g., "Mary is very messy in the kitchen. Do you think she is a messy person in general?").

Understanding and applying rule relationships should not be confused with merely stating or verbalizing rules. A learner's ability to state a rule does not necessarily indicate that the learner has learned the rule and understands the new relationship specified by it. After all, a rule is not a verbal association that requires linking a specific response with a specific stimulus, as in "Name the capital of Hawaii." Although a rule does involve a linking of elements as in a verbal association, the elements in a rule relationship are more complex categories of information that are associated in some way. That association allows the learner to respond to many different examples of the concepts specified in the rule statement. In fact, a rule relationship is a very efficient knowledge form, because it can be used to link an association between different classes of information. Once the learner knows the key association, the learner unlocks answers to many questions. For example, if a learner understands the rule "Prime numbers have only one and themselves as factors," the learner should be able to determine whether *any* number is a prime number. Obviously, the learner must understand the concept of factors and the strategies associated with factoring a number. Nonetheless, the rule relationship allows the learner to provide a correct response to a range of examples, not just one example of a concept.

Instructional Implications

Because the essential feature of a rule relationship is the connection it makes between known concepts, the instructional dimensions of rule relationships hinge on communicating that connection to the learner. Although teaching the "relationship" part of the rule is perhaps most important to teaching rules, it is not the only consideration in designing a teaching sequence. A rule is a complex proposition of facts, concepts, and discriminations. The teacher must either have accurate information that the learner already knows the concepts embedded in the rule or must teach them in separate teaching sequences. Once the components of the rule are taught and known, the teaching of the rule relationship can proceed.

The advantage of teaching a rule relationship is that the learner knows the component concepts, facts, or discriminations that comprise the rule. The learner has partial knowledge of the rule and its component parts, and it is appropriate to use that knowledge about the rule to teach the rule. Teaching the learner the relationship specified in the rule, then, depends on already known concepts in the rule, which will make the teaching more manageable. In light of these parts in a rule, Engelmann and Carnine (1982) provide another clever design of instruction analysis in teaching rule relationships (p. 93). They recommend requiring learners to make a *prediction* about the relationship the rule specifies based on the known parts of the rule. For instance, in the previous example of prime numbers, the following interactions would take place:

TEACHER: (Points to the number 13 on the blackboard.) Tell me, John, is this number a prime number?
JOHN: Yes, it is. (Prediction.)
TEACHER: How do you know it's a prime number?
JOHN: Because it's a number that has only one and itself as factors. (Verification statement.)

In this sequence, John uses his knowledge of factoring (i.e., the known concepts in the rule, "only one and itself as factors") to make a prediction about the unknown relationship that the rule specifies, which is the connection between numbers that have "only one and themselves as factors" and the label of "prime numbers." After making a prediction, the learner must then verify it by connecting the parts of the rule together (e.g., "It's a prime number because it has only one and itself as factors").

The instructional dimensions of teaching rule relationships, like concepts, involve the use of examples. In Chapter 6, we provide the instructional details for designing teaching sequences to teach rule relationships.

Cognitive Strategies

We have identified cognitive strategies as the most complex knowledge form in the taxonomy. Cognitive strategies are defined as a "series of multi-step associations and procedures that involve facts, verbal chains, discriminations, concepts, or rules designed to bring about a response or a set of responses to a specified problem." A strategy by definition is "skillful planning or management of anything" (Webster's Dictionary). A cognitive strategy therefore involves the skillful planning and management of those activities involved with thinking, remembering, and interpreting symbolic operations. A cognitive strategy allows the learner to purposefully use information in ways to manage or solve a problem that demands understanding symbols. A learner who applies a cognitive strategy "planfully" orchestrates numerous pieces of information to solve a problem. The actual execution of the strategy and the sequence in which the facts, discriminations, concepts, or rules are brought to bear on a problem depend largely on the requirements of the problem. For example, applying a cognitive strategy to identify the judicial test or standard in a court case involving the Fourteenth Amendment equal protection clause is likely to involve a different sequence of steps and activities than solving an analogy such as dog: bark:: cat: _____ . Certainly, what the learner knows and the learner's facility with the knowledge forms of the strategy also influence the application of the strategy.

Cognitive strategies have three essential features. First, they require the learner to engage in more than two distinct and successive activities that involve verbal associations, concepts, and rule relationships. Second, they require the learner to have complete knowledge of the component skills or knowledge forms that comprise the strategy. Third, they are planful orchestrations of knowledge designed to solve a problem efficiently. All these features are important to learning academic skills. In the context of the general education classroom, learners with academic learning problems must use cognitive strategies very efficiently.

However, cognitive strategies need not be "planful" or "efficient" to be complex and useful forms of knowledge. Many contributions to the history of knowledge were not a result of efficient or planful cognitive strategies but were instead a result of laborious calibrations and grinding factual associations. In some cases, these contributions were unplanned leaps of insight that some would characterize as nothing less than providential in nature (Kuhn, 1970; Watson, 1965). Gagne (1985) argues that "effective cognitive strategies that are truly general may take a long time to learn" (p. 152).

Applying cognitive strategies facilitates problem-solving, and learners with disabilities must use these strategies efficiently.

Cognitive strategies are as varied as the learning experiences a child faces in the schooling (or, for that matter, nonschooling) process. Moreover, what passes as a cognitive strategy will also vary, depending on who does the defining and the problem context in which the strategy is used. For example, what Gagne (1985) refers to as "cognitive strategies of thinking" (p. 143), or a learner's ability to exercise control over a way of thinking, some would consider metacognitive strategies (Brown, 1978). At this point, the research on metacognition is far from definitive (Palincsar & Brown, 1984; Paris, Wasik, & Van der Westhuizen, 1988; Tharp & Gallimore, 1985). This issue notwithstanding, cognitive strategies are both specific and tailored, as in mathematics, or general and flexible, as in logical reasoning. Because the concern in this text is with academic learning problems, we have limited our analysis of cognitive strategies to academic tasks. Examples of cognitive strategies, the component skills that comprise each strategy, and the steps that would be involved in executing each strategy are given here.

| **Examples of Cognitive Strategies** | **Component Knowledge Forms** |

TASK 3–10

Reading words that end in VCe (e.g., *ate*) by naming the first vowel.	**Discrimination:** Words that do or do not end in VCe.
	Simple fact: Names of vowels.
	Rule relationship: Connecting fact and discrimination.

Steps of Strategy:

1. *Determine* if the word ends in VCe (e.g., "Does this word end with an *e*?").
2. *Determine* if the name of the first vowel is to be said (e.g., Teacher points to first vowel, "So are you going to say the name of this letter?").
3. *Identify* the name of the first vowel (e.g., "What is the name of this letter?").
4. *Read* the word (e.g., "What is this word?").

TASK 3–11

| Comprehending clause constructions in text (e.g., Alice, who is stronger than George, loves to lift weights). | **Concepts:** Recognizing pronouns in clause constructions (e.g., who, what, that, those). |
| | **Rule relationships:** Connecting pronouns and antecedents in a clause. |

Steps of Strategy:

1. *Read* the sentence.
2. *Identify* the pronoun in the clause construction.
3. *Link* the pronoun with the antecedent in sentence (e.g., "*Who* stands for *Alice* in this sentence?").
4. *Answer* the comprehension questions specific to the clause construction (e.g., "Who loves to lift weights?")

TASK 3–12

Working a simple subtraction problem that includes renaming (e.g., 32 − 18).

Simple Facts: Reading symbols (e.g., 32, 18, subtraction sign).

Concepts: Recognizing value of numbers (e.g., ones, tens); recognizing mathematical operations (addition, subtraction); recognizing when borrowing or renaming is necessary.

Steps of Strategy:

1. *Read* the entire problem.
2. *Read* the numbers in the ones column only.
3. *Determine* if the minuend needs to be renamed.
4. *Rename* the minuend.
5. *Subtract* the entire problem.
6. *Read* the entire problem to check for understanding and correctness.

Instructional Implications

The examples of cognitive strategies are intended to demonstrate the network of parts and procedures that comprise this complex knowledge form. These examples are by no means exhaustive, but they do indicate the multiple sets of features and requirements of complex strategies. The examples will alert the teacher to some of the instructional requirements of cognitive strategies: (1) to identify the component pieces of knowledge that comprise the strategy, (2) to assess learners on their knowledge of these component pieces, (3) to teach or reteach the component pieces of knowledge that are not well established, (4) to select examples for demonstrating the application of the entire cognitive strategy, (5) to assess learners' ability to apply the strategy, and (6) to provide sufficient practice on the cognitive strategy. The teacher's role in designing the instruction of cognitive strategies is critical to the learner's successful execution of a strategy.

The instructional requirements of cognitive strategies are based on three essential features we described earlier. First, we know that cognitive strategies involve more than two distinct successive steps, and the identification of the component parts of a cognitive strategy is an essential first step to its application. The decision rules for engaging in this process of identifying the component parts of a complex cognitive routine are varied but logical and experimental. For some skills, as in Task 3–11, the starting point of the subtraction operation and its component steps is simple. For other skills, as in reading comprehension, the starting point is less obvious and the teacher may need to experiment with several procedures before deciding on a teaching sequence for the cognitive strategy.

The second feature of cognitive strategies requires that learners have a firm grasp of the component skills identified in the strategy. Once a teacher has identified the component parts of a strategy, then the teacher must bring the learner to an acceptable criterion level of performance on each component skill before the entire cognitive strategy is taught. A learner's failure to master one of the component parts of a strategy may end up short-circuiting the execution of the entire cognitive strategy. The teacher's role in monitoring the learner's mastery of each component skill and scheduling extra instruction when necessary before introducing the cognitive strategy is critical to its acquisition.

The third feature of cognitive strategies is their efficient execution. To be effective in using cognitive strategies, the learner must become anticipatory and fluent in their execution. Bringing a naive learner to a high criterion level of using a strategy is no easy task. The teacher must schedule the appropriate amount of practice on the entire cognitive strategy and also make certain that the practice is neither too easy nor too difficult. Maintaining mastery of component skills, selecting a range of new examples, and retesting previously taught examples contribute to the complexity of teaching cognitive strategies. Unless students with academic deficits receive adequate practice and feedback on the use of cognitive strategies, they are not likely to reach the level of flexibility and fluency that is necessary to maintain their use.

SUMMARY

In this chapter, we have drawn a clear distinction between symbolic and nonsymbolic operations. Observing nonsymbolic or physical operations can help us design teaching sequences for symbolic tasks. Within the universe of symbolic tasks, we offered a way of classifying knowledge into different categories, based on the significant precedents established by Gagne (1985), Bruner (1966), and Engelmann and Carnine (1982). The taxonomy of knowledge that we proposed comprises four categories of knowledge forms: verbal associations, concepts, rule relationships, and cognitive strategies. We noted that the taxonomy is hierarchical and academically focused. Within the taxonomy, each knowledge form is defined, examples are given, and instructional implications are drawn. This chapter is based on the premise that it is important to know the different forms of knowledge that comprise the universe of knowledge.

By knowing about the structure of knowledge, the teacher will be in a position to make important decisions about how a piece of knowledge should be taught. A teacher who knows that a piece of information is a verbal association or a concept or a rule will be more aware of the instructional requirements for teaching verbal associations, concepts, and rules. This is not to say that the teacher will be completely knowledgeable about how a piece of information should be taught, but the teacher will know enough to determine what is needed next to develop an adequate teaching sequence.

In this chapter we noted that the teacher not only delivers information, but must also make critical decisions about the quality of the information that is passed on to students. When children with academic learning problems are considered, the teacher's responsibility to scrutinize how the information is packaged before its delivery is even more pronounced. The teacher must examine the structure of knowledge to ensure that the "structural" requirements of different knowledge forms are correctly considered in the design of teaching sequences, in much the same way that the structural requirements of a car, house, or space shuttle are considered in their design and construction.

We summarize the essential features of each knowledge form and their respective instructional requirements in Table 3–3.

APPLICATION ITEMS

1. Why is it important for a teacher to understand different forms of knowledge? How does a hierarchical taxonomy of knowledge inform a teacher about instruction? Explain your answers and give examples.

TABLE 3–3
Summary of knowledge forms and instructional requirements

Knowledge Form	Requirements of Instruction
Verbal associations A connection between a specific stimulus and a specific response.	Use model-lead-test procedure. Primary concerns are scheduling how much and when to teach.
Concepts An object, event, action, or situation that is a part of a class of objects, events, actions, or situations that are the same, based on a feature or set of features that are the same.	Use concrete examples that have a feature or set of features that are the same. Determine what kinds of examples, how many examples, and sequence of examples.
Rule relationships A proposition that specifies a connection between at least two facts, discriminations, or concepts.	Use learner's knowledge of known concepts to teach an unknown relationship. Use concrete examples and require learner to make a prediction about relationship.
Cognitive strategies A series of multi-step associations and procedures that involve facts, verbal chains, discriminations, concepts, rules, or rule relationships designed to bring about a response or a set of responses to a problem.	Use learner's knowledge of component verbal associations, concepts, and rule relationships to teach overall strategy. Use examples to apply strategy in planful and efficient manner.

2. Examine each of the following items and classify each according to the taxonomy (e.g., simple facts, verbal chains, discriminations, concepts) described in the readings.
   a. A person's birthdate.
   b. A group of six objects.
   c. Counting by sixes (6, 12, 18).
   d. Locating a word in a dictionary.
   e. Rounding numbers with decimals to whole numbers.
   f. Identifying the letters *b, r, j, a.*

3. Explain how the procedure for correcting errors in simple facts differs from the procedure for correcting errors involving concepts. Explain how the correction procedures differ for a concept and a rule relationship.

REFERENCES

Armbruster, B. B., & Gudbrandsen, B. (1986). Reading comprehension instruction in social studies programs. *Reading Research Quarterly, 21*(1), 36–48.

Baer, D. (1979). *Is attribution the square root of modification?* Paper presented at the annual meeting of the Association for the Advancement of Behavior Therapy, San Francisco, CA.

Beck, J., McKeown, G., McCaslin, E., & Burkes, A. (1979). *Instructional dimensions that may affect reading comprehension: Examples from two commercial reading programs* (LRDC Publication 1979/20). Pittsburgh: University of Pittsburgh, Learning Research and Development Center.

Beck, I. L., Omanson, R. C., & McKeown, M. G. (1982). An instructional redesign of reading lessons: Effects on comprehension. *Reading Research Quarterly, 17*(4), 462–481.

Becker, W. C. (1986). *Applied psychology for teachers* (rev. ed.). Chicago: Science Research Association.

Becker, W. C., & Carnine, D. W. (1980). Direct instruction as an effective approach to educational intervention with disadvantaged and low performers. In B. Lahey & A. Kazdin (Eds.), *Advances in clinical child psychology* (vol. 3, pp. 429–473). New York: Plenum.

Bloom, B. S., (Ed.) (1956). *Taxonomy of educational objectives: The classification of educational goals. Handbook I—cognitive domain.* New York: McKay.

Bourne, Jr., L. E., Goldstein, S., & Link, W. E. (1964). Concept learning as a function of availability of previously presented information. *Journal of Experimental Psychology, 76,* 439–448.

Brown, A. L. (1978). Knowing when, where, and how to remember: A problem of metacognition. In R. Glaser (Ed.), *Advances in instructional psychology* (pp. 77–163). Hillsdale, NJ: Erlbaum.

Bruner, J. S. (1966). *Toward a theory of instruction.* Cambridge, MA: Belknap Press of Harvard University.

Carnine, D. W., Silbert, J., & Kameenui, E. J. (1990). *Direct instruction reading* (2nd ed.). Columbus: Merrill Publishing Company.

Clark, D. C. (1971). Teaching concepts in the classroom: A set of teaching prescriptions derived from experimental research. *Journal of Education Psychology Monograph, 62,* 253–278.

DuncanMalone, L., & Kameenui, E. J. (1987). *Social studies text analysis.* Unpublished manuscript.

Durkin, D. (1978–1979). What classroom observations reveal about reading comprehension instruction. *Reading Research Quarterly, 14*(4), 481–533.

Durkin, D. (1981). Reading comprehension instruction in five basal reader series. *Reading Research Quarterly, 26,* 515–544.

Engelmann, S., & Carnine, D. W. (1982). *Theory of instruction: Principles and applications.* New York: Irvington.

Elementary School Journal (1987), vol. 87.

Gagne, R. M. (1965). *The conditions of learning and theory of instruction.* New York: Holt, Rinehart & Winston.

Gagne, R. M. (1985). *The conditions of learning and theory of instruction* (4th ed.). New York: Holt, Rinehart & Winston.

Gagne, R. M., & Briggs, L. J. (1979). *Principles of instructional design* (2nd ed.). New York: Holt, Rinehart & Winston.

Goodman, K. (1986, December). *Examining our assumption about the relationship between teaching and learning.* Special discussion session presented at the annual meeting of the National Reading Conference, Austin, TX.

Jitendra, A., & Kameenui, E. J. (1988). A design-of-instruction analysis of concept teaching in five basal language programs: Violations from the bottom up. *Journal of Special Education, 22*(2), 199–219.

Kameenui, E. J. (1988). Direct instruction and the great twitch: Why DI or di is not the issue. In J. E. Readence and R. S. Baldwin (Eds.), *Thirty-seventh Yearbook of the National Reading Conference,* (pp. 39–41). Chicago: National Reading Conference.

Klausmeier, H. J. (1976). Instructional design and the teaching of concepts. In J. R. Levin & V. L. Allen (Eds.), *Cognitive learning in children* (pp. 191–217). New York: Academic Press.

Klausmeier, H. J., Ghatala, E. S., & Frayer, D. A. (1974). *Conceptual learning and development: A cognitive view.* New York: Academic Press.

Klix, F. (1983). An evolutionary approach to cognitive processes and creativity in human beings. In R. Groner, M. Groner, & W. F. Bischop (Eds.), *Methods of heuristics* (pp. 19–36). Hillsdale, NJ: Erlbaum.

Kuhn, T. S. (1970). *The structure of scientific revolutions* (2nd ed.). Chicago: University of Chicago Press.

LaBerge, D., & Samuels, S. J. (1976). Toward a theory of automatic information processing in reading. In H. Singer and R. B. Ruddell (Eds.), *Theoretical models and processes of reading* (pp. 548–579). Newark, NJ: International Reading Association.

Markle, S. M. (1975). They teach concepts, don't they? *Educational Researcher, 4,* 3–9.

Markle, S. (1978). Teaching conceptual networks. *NSPI Journal, 17*(1), 4–7.

Markle, S. M., & Tiemann, P. W. (1969). *Really understanding concepts: Or in frumious pursuit of the jabberwock.* Champaign, IL: Stipes.

Merrill, P. F. (1971). *Task analysis: An information processing approach (Report No. 27).* Tallahassee, FL: Florida State University.

Palincsar, A., & Brown, A. (1984). Reciprocal teaching of comprehension-fostering and comprehension-monitoring activities. *Cognition and Instruction, 1,* 117–125.

Paris, S. G., Wasik, B. A., & Van der Westhuizen, G. (1988). *Meta-metacognition: A review of research on metacognition and reading.* Paper presented as the annual review of research at the National Reading Conference, St. Petersburg, FL.

Shannon, P. (1988). Can we directly instruct students to be independent in reading? In J. E. Readence and R. S. Baldwin (Eds.), *Thirty-seventh Yearbook of the National Reading Conference* (pp. 36–39). Chicago: National Reading Conference.

Tennyson, R., & Christensen, D. L. (1986). *Memory theory and design of intelligent learning systems.* AERA Paper, San Francisco.

Tennyson, R. D., & Cochiarella, M. J. (1986). An empirically based instructional design theory for teaching concepts. *Review of Educational Research, 56,* 40–71.

Tennyson, R. D., & Park, O. (1980, Spring). The teaching of concepts: A review of instructional design research literature. *Review of Educational Research, 50*(1), 55–70.

Tharp, R. G., & Gallimore, R. (1985). The logical status of metacognitive training. *Journal of Abnormal Child Psychology, 13*(3), 455–466.

Watson, J. D. (1965). *The double helix.* New York: New American Library.

Principles of Designing Instruction: The Three Phases of Instruction and the Generic Instructional Set

Chapter Objectives

Upon successful completion of this chapter, you will be able to:

1. DESCRIBE the three phases of the instructional cycle—before, during, and after instruction.

2. DESCRIBE the 15 instructional features of each of the three phases of instruction.

3. IDENTIFY the five generic design-of-instruction features that serve as the basic framework for designing and constructing teaching sequences in language, beginning reading, reading comprehension, mathematics, and written expression.

4. APPLY the generic instructional set to designing a cognitive task.

5. APPLY the three phases of instruction to the development of a teaching sequence.

THE REQUIREMENTS OF AN INSTRUCTIONAL CYCLE

The functions of teaching take place in time and are partly determined by the complexities of the learning and teaching process. It wouldn't make sense to describe a set of teaching functions without considering how they vary with time. Too often, teaching is viewed narrowly as the face-to-face interaction between teacher and student, with little consideration for what happens before and after the interaction. We argue that for face-to-face instruction to be successful, the entire instructional cycle (i.e., what the teacher does *before, during,* and *after* instruction) must be examined carefully. Figure 4–1 illustrates the three phases of the instructional cycle.

It is easy to consider what the teacher does during instruction as the most important part of the instructional cycle, because the teacher then is most visibly engaged with students. It is, after all, during this time that the teacher gives "shape to the shapeless" (Campbell, 1982, p. 113) by teaching verbal associations, presenting examples and non-examples of concepts, stating rule relationships, and probing a learner's knowledge of the component skills of a cognitive strategy. During instruction, the teacher takes a student from a state of unknowing to a state of knowing.

The success of what happens during instruction is determined largely by what takes place before and after instruction. To make a significant break in the cycle of failure experienced by students with academic learning problems, instructional details of the before, during, and after phases of instruction must be considered. In the following section we name the critical features of each of these phases.

THE PHASES OF INSTRUCTION: BEFORE/DURING/AFTER

The process of instruction has a beginning, middle, and end, which we have characterized as an instructional cycle with three distinct phases of instruction. The activities that the teacher develops and initiates **before, during,** and **after** instruction will be similar for a variety of learning outcomes. This doesn't mean that the teacher repeats the same activities for each teaching presentation, but it does mean that the teacher's actions within each phase of instruction will be similar for a variety of learning outcomes. What the teacher does before teaching a verbal association will be much like what the teacher does to prepare to teach a concept, rule relationship, or cognitive strategy. The before and after phases of instruction are likely to be more connected than their separation in time suggests. As depicted by the arrows in Figure 4–2, the instructional objectives, outcomes, and features of each of the three temporal phases of instruction are closely linked. Furthermore, the objectives, outcomes, and features for the after phase of instruction should ultimately determine the instructional objectives, outcomes, and features of the first two phases of instruction—the before and during instruction phases.

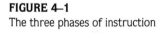

FIGURE 4–1
The three phases of instruction

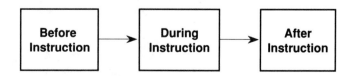

FIGURE 4–2
Phases of the instructional cycle

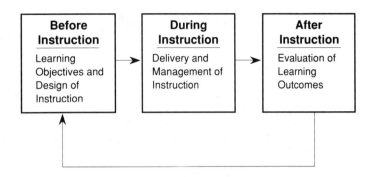

In other words, what learners are capable of doing after instruction should direct the instructional objectives, learning outcomes, and instructional features for the first two phases of instruction.

If the teacher has taken the learner from a state of unknowing in the during phase of instruction to a state of full and complete knowing after instruction is completed, then the instructional objectives and learning outcomes have been met. New instructional objectives and learning outcomes can now be designed to accommodate this new knowledge. It becomes obvious that all three phases of instruction *must* be considered separately and collectively if instruction is to make a difference in breaking the cycle of failure. As noted in previous chapters, teachers must offer nothing short of full attention to the details of instruction in each of the three phases to make a significant difference in student performance. The critical features comprising each phase of instruction will be detailed next.

Critical Features: Before Instruction Phase

The features of instruction that we identify as critical are not absolute or exhaustive. They are, however, derived from the research on effective instruction and practices (Brophy & Good, 1986; Englert, 1984; Rosenshine & Stevens, 1984; Stevens & Rosenshine, 1981; Ysseldyke & Christenson, 1987). These features provide the practitioner with a cohesive model of instruction that can be used as a starting point for teaching. They can also be modified or expanded as a teacher sees fit. In the following section, we identify and describe 15 features of the before phase of instruction and cluster them into four categories of instructional activities. A rationale for the features comprising each category of instructional activities is provided after the list.

PHASE 1

BEFORE INSTRUCTION ▬▬▬▬▬▬▬▬▬▬▬▬▬▬▬▬▬▬▬▬▬▬

Defining Instruction

1. Use assessment that is instructionally based and translates into specific instructional objectives and learning outcomes.

2. Select examples of specific knowledge forms and skills that are appropriate to the instructional objectives and learning outcomes of the learner.

Designing Instruction

3. Place examples of a skill in an appropriate sequence within a lesson.
4. Place tasks within a particular lesson in an appropriate sequence.
5. Schedule the appropriate amount of time for each task within a lesson.
6. Specify the kind of practice for new and well-established tasks.
7. Select and schedule independent seatwork appropriately.
8. Identify and preteach potentially difficult tasks.
9. Establish a firming cycle of periodic reviews of newly taught tasks.

Managing Instruction

10. Specify the rules and expectations of how students are to behave during instruction.
11. Specify the reinforcement activities the teacher will use to increase appropriate behaviors during instruction.
12. Detail a plan for responding to potential management problems during instruction.

Adapting/Modifying Instruction

13. Establish a plan for recording errors during instruction.
14. Establish a plan for responding to academic errors during instruction.
15. Establish a plan for responding to chronic academic errors during instruction.

Rationale

Defining Instruction

Assessment.   What the teacher does before instruction should set the occasion for a successful second phase of instruction, when the teacher begins to work directly with students. We suggest that the first phase of instruction should begin with assessment that is instructionally based. As discussed in Chapter 2, instructional assessment should lead directly to instruction. Through instructional assessment, the teacher can gauge a child's performance on skills and tasks in the context of failure, the general education classroom. Instructional assessment allows the teacher to isolate not only the specific skill deficiency, but also the various dimensions of the tasks (e.g., familiarity, competency, domain, schedule) and the learner's responses (e.g., production, choice, yes/no, written, oral, motor) by "exceptionalizing" the assessment conditions (e.g., using change-up tasks, delayed retesting, prompting, and probing).

Selecting examples.   Many categories of knowledge, such as concepts, rule relationships, and cognitive strategies, are best communicated through examples. The second feature of instruction in this phase is the selection of examples to communicate the particular form of knowledge to the learner. The guidelines for selecting appropriate examples depend on many considerations, including (1) knowledge form being taught, (2) learner's prior performance on the skill, (3) dimensions of the task and required learner response, and (4) examples used in previous teaching sequences. Guidelines and criteria for selecting examples across a range of skill areas (e.g., language concepts, decoding procedures, mathematics strategies) are detailed in the chapters on instructional strategies (Chapters 5–11).

The importance of correctly selecting examples of a particular skill cannot be overlooked. The selected examples "define" a learner's state of knowing. If a teacher selects examples of only white dogs under 20 pounds to teach the concept of *dog,* then the learner's knowledge of dogs will be limited. A teaching sequence that incorporates examples that are inadequate will communicate information that is spurious or incomplete (Engelmann & Carnine, 1982).

Designing Instruction

Sequencing examples.   The primary emphasis in this phase of instruction is on designing instruction to be delivered. As a result, 7 of the 15 features important to this phase have been categorized as design features. These are primarily concerned with the construction of the teaching sequence. By attending to these features, the teacher literally designs how the teaching sequence will unfold, the amount of time that will be spent on each activity, and the nature of the practice the learner is to receive.

The third feature of instruction is concerned with the sequence of examples selected to teach a specific knowledge form (e.g., verbal association, concept, rule relationship). The manner in which concrete examples are placed back to back in a presentation is critical to the successful communication of knowledge. For example, there is ample research available (as well as ample logic) to suggest that if stimuli with highly similar visual and auditory characteristics (e.g., *b/d, i/e, m/n*) are presented successively, they are likely to be confused (Carnine, 1981). Although the problem of confusing *b* and *d*

Designing instruction requires a detailed construction of the teaching sequence.

has been characterized as strephosymbolia (twisted symbols) or dyslexia, it is also the result of teaching similar letters in close sequence.

Sequencing tasks.   Apart from the sequencing of examples within a particular teaching sequence, the sequencing of different tasks derived from teaching different skills within a lesson must also be considered. This feature is predicated on the assumption that a lesson will comprise teaching activities involving different knowledge domains (e.g., reading, language, mathematics), task dimensions, and learner responses.

We must make three considerations in sequencing tasks within a lesson. First, to what extent do the tasks place similar demands upon the learner? Tasks that are highly similar in knowledge form or response requirements may be confused. Second, what is the learner's competency on the tasks? It would be inappropriate for a learner to face a series of new "difficult" tasks back to back within a lesson. Sequencing easy (established) tasks with hard (new) tasks, as suggested in Chapter 2, will contribute to a more successful and motivating lesson for the naive learner. Third, are new tasks introduced within a lesson reviewed within the same lesson? The lesson must build in frequent opportunities to review newly introduced skills.

Scheduling tasks.   In Chapter 1, we discussed the need to teach more in less time. Teachers should approximate the amount of time that will be spent on each task within a lesson. By detailing the amount of time on each task within a particular instructional session, the teacher creates a temporal blueprint of what is to be taught, when it is to be taught, and for how long it will be taught. The time assignments also force the teacher to evaluate if sufficient time is allotted to new "difficult" tasks or to the review of old, yet-to-be-established tasks. This feature of instruction requires teachers to be sensitive to how instructional time is spent.

Independent seatwork.   Arguably, the real test of effective instruction is not how the learner does in the teacher-led instruction but how that learning is transferred to independent seatwork practice after instruction. This practice is critical to assessing the learner's state of knowing, and proper scheduling and monitoring are essential. In addition, the independent seatwork assigned to a learner must correspond with the responses required of the learner during instruction, as well as the complexity of the task itself and the learner's competency on the task.

Preteaching.   Although preteaching is frequently overlooked, it is important that potentially difficult tasks be identified before instruction is initiated. This can be done by examining the learner's prior performance on the tasks or by considering the logical requirements the tasks will put on the learner. Preteaching requires the teacher to alert the learner to select dimensions of previously introduced tasks that proved difficult. The following are examples of a "preteaching strategy" that a teacher might use to alert the learner to potentially difficult tasks.

TASK 4–1

TEACHER: (Points to a letter on the chalkboard.) Now be careful. I want you to tell me the sound of this letter.

TASK 4–2

TEACHER: (Points to subtraction problem.) Look at this problem. I want you to read the problem and decide if you'll need to rename.

TASK 4–3

TEACHER: (Points to expository passage.) Remember that after you read this passage, I'm going to ask you questions about the big vocabulary words that tell about friction. It's important that you remember what the words mean.

The preteaching strategy should provide the learner with minimum information necessary to work a task independently.

Firming cycle. The final design feature of this phase of instruction is establishing a firming cycle for newly introduced tasks. The purpose of the firming cycle is to structure opportunities for the learner to practice further on newly introduced tasks. This feature requires the teacher to schedule periodic review of the targeted skill within a lesson.

Managing Instruction

Rules and reinforcement. This set of features is explicitly concerned with the teacher's preparation for managing students' behavior (social, academic, affective) during instruction. These features require the teacher to decide before instruction takes place how students are to behave during instruction. What behaviors are acceptable or unacceptable during instruction? By establishing exactly what is expected of students during instruction, the teacher can indicate in advance how those expectations will be communicated. The teacher can also detail how to respond to students when expectations are not met during instruction. By specifying expectations ahead of time and preparing to reinforce them, the teacher is in a proactive position ready to prevent disruptive behavior problems during instruction.

A framework for thinking about behavior management within the context of instruction is described in Chapter 12. The procedures for preventing and responding to behavior problems before, during, and after instruction are discussed in greater detail in this chapter.

Adapting/Modifying Instruction

Recording errors. The last three features of the before phase deal with the teacher's response to academic errors. The errors students make during instruction provide the teacher with critical information about the learner and the instruction. It is important for the teacher systematically to record errors during instruction.

Correction procedures. The teacher should also prepare strategies for responding to errors that surface during instruction. These correction procedures will vary with the different errors and the knowledge form taught. Although the teacher is not expected to anticipate every error response the learner will make, the teacher is in a position to prevent chronic error patterns by thinking about correction procedures ahead of time. The teacher must also decide how chronic errors will be handled in the course of instruction. Will the teacher simply repeat the task and require the learner to respond again? Or will the teacher terminate the task and introduce an established one? By planning for academic errors, the teacher can prevent errors from cycling to other naive learners while also ensuring that teaching will not become punishing for the learner.

A summary of the critical features for the before phase of instruction is given graphically in Figure 4–3.

Critical Features: During Instruction Phase

Most features in this phase are the same ones identified in the before instruction phase. It seems reasonable that efforts made in preparing the instruction now be "actualized" in this phase. Instruction in this phase will follow naturally and successfully from the

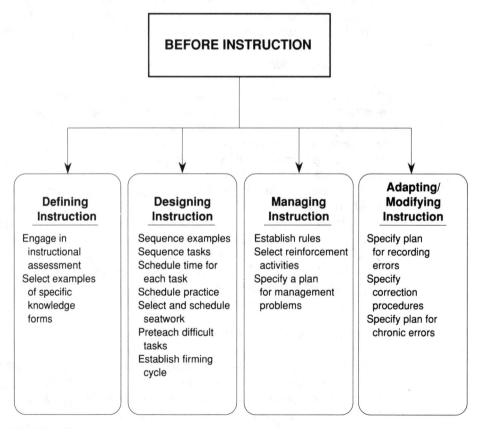

FIGURE 4–3
Before instruction phase

activities of the before instruction phase, because the teacher has set the stage for successful instruction.

The 15 features of instruction are again arranged by different categories of instructional activities. Rationales for each of the categories of instructional features are then given.

PHASE 2

DURING INSTRUCTION

Managing Instruction

1. Present and reinforce the rules of how students are to behave during instruction at the beginning of the session.
2. Reinforce the rules throughout the entire instructional session.
3. Preteach the task requirements throughout the lesson.
4. Reinforce correct academic responses throughout the lesson.
5. Monitor students constantly either through verbal or physical prompts.
6. Monitor and provide feedback on independent seatwork.
7. Record academic and nonacademic errors throughout the session.

Delivering Instruction

8. Present the instruction (i.e., teacher verbalizations, verbal and physical transitions between tasks) at a brisk pace.
9. Present clear, consistent signals for group or individual responses.
10. Provide students with adequate thinking time before requiring them to respond.
11. Present the information in an enthusiastic manner.

Modifying Instruction

12. Implement correction procedures accurately and consistently throughout the session.
13. Present preteaching strategies consistently and appropriately with difficult tasks.
14. Implement a firming cycle consisting of periodic reviews of newly taught tasks.
15. Monitor and adjust when necessary the number and quality of student responses to tasks.

Rationale

Managing Instruction

Rules and reinforcement. We have identified management features that are important to the instructional activities designed in the first phase. For the most part, these features are the same as those identified in the before instruction phase. First of all, the teacher must make expectations of how students are to behave clear and unambiguous. This requires that the teacher teach rules in the same manner as a complex cognitive strategy, rather than simply state expectations and move on. The teacher should teach these behavior rules through positive and negative examples, require students to practice the rules, and finally assess students' knowledge of the rules. The rules are then reinforced throughout the session by the teacher acknowledging when a learner is following the rules. By noting what is expected of students, the teacher is in a position to reinforce expectations, and students have the necessary information to succeed during the instructional session.

Monitoring responses.   Another important management feature is monitoring of students throughout the session. During instruction the teacher can monitor students in at least three ways: visually, verbally, and physically. By visually scanning the instructional setting, the teacher can gauge how instruction is going. The teacher can also give students feedback about performance through facial (e.g., a wink, frown, or "evil eye"), verbal (e.g., oral words of praise, written smiley faces, oral reprimands), and physical (e.g., touching, turning a child's head, holding a hand) cues. The cue used depends on the learner's response and the demands of the context.

Framing.   The purpose of framing is to make certain the learner understands the requirements of a task before instruction is initiated. The teacher avoids the dilemma of determining if an error is the result of a learner not understanding the requirements of the task or the task itself. See Table 4–1.

Independent seatwork.   As noted in the before phase of instruction, independent seatwork is essential to determining a learner's acquisition and retention of information presented during instruction. Seatwork should not be viewed as a "filler" activity in which a learner is given instructionally trivial or too-difficult worksheets. Nor should this time be viewed simply as a break from the face-to-face work of small- or large-group instruction. It should be viewed as the real test of whether the information during instruction was presented clearly and effectively. It is important for the teacher to provide learners with feedback about their performance during this seatwork time, for this communicates the importance of independent seatwork to the learner.

Recording errors.   Recording errors during instruction is critical, for without this, the teacher has no valid basis for making further instructional decisions. Errors might be specific to the nature of the academic task, or they can be procedural, nonacademic errors, such as attending or following a group signal to respond. Often the difficulty in consistently recording errors is one of orchestrating a number of activities at once, and the teacher doesn't have enough hands to monitor group response, attend to the low performers, reinforce responses, and record errors. However, these demands should not dissuade the teacher from recording errors during instruction but should indicate the importance of working out a recording system before instruction.

TABLE 4–1
Procedures for framing tasks

Instructional Procedures

Step 1. Elicit attention by establishing how students are to attend to the task.

Step 2. Identify the knowledge form (i.e., verbal association, concept, rule relationship, or cognitive strategy).

Step 3. Require the learner to identify the task with a production response.

Step 4. Determine how the learner is to respond.

Step 5. Use a yes/no discrimination response and a production response to assess the learner's understanding of the task requirements.

Step 6. Provide a preview (if appropriate) of the series of tasks or activities to follow the teaching sequence.

Example of Framing a Task: Teacher Wording

Step 1. Everyone, eyes on me. Eyes on me, Burt. All eyes are on me, that's great.

Step 2. We're going to count by 10.

Step 3. What are we going to do, Albert?

Step 4. Yes, Albert. We're going to count by 10, and I want you to remember what I say. I also want you to keep your eyes on me.

Step 5. What are you going to do when we're counting by 10, Beulah? And what are we going to count by, Julius?

Step 6. After we count by 10, you're going to count by yourself, and then we'll get back to reading our story.

Range of Tasks

Framing can be used with the following tasks:

All cognitive tasks (e.g., verbal chains, simple facts, concepts, cognitive strategies).

All physical motor tasks (e.g., using scissors, picking up a cup, hanging up a coat, kicking a soccer ball).

Tasks related to behavior management (e.g., walking into a room quietly, keeping hands quiet, cooperating on project assignments).

Delivering Instruction

Pacing.   This phase deals with the actual delivery of instruction, and it is appropriate to delineate a set of features that names the qualities of presenting information. The first feature is concerned with the pace of activities during instruction, which is set by the rate of the teacher's verbalizations, solicitations, and physical movements within and between teaching sequences. The optimal pace of instruction will vary for different types of instructional activities. The pacing in teaching verbal associations will be faster than for teaching a cognitive strategy. Although Brophy and Good (1986) note that further research is needed on pacing, one needs only the aid of a metronome to appreciate the importance of pacing. A teacher's rate of verbalizations can obviously be very low, characterized on a metronome as slow (i.e., *largo* or 40–60 beats per minute), or fast (i.e., *moderato* or 108–120 beats per minute) to very fast (i.e., *prestissimo* or 200–208 beats per minute). A *largo* teaching presentation may be too slow. In contrast, a *prestissimo* teaching presentation may leave learners in a frenzy.

Enthusiasm.   Another feature of delivering instruction has to do with a quality that is difficult to quantify and, some would argue, difficult to teach—enthusiasm. The absence of enthusiasm in a teaching presentation is easy to notice. Enthusiasm refers to the eager interest or zeal displayed in teaching. A presentation in which a teacher demonstrates little interest will stimulate little interest in return. For students who have experienced significant academic difficulties, a teacher's lack of enthusiasm in teaching may be construed as a lack of interest in them. This may be interpreted as more evidence that those with learning difficulties don't deserve the best instruction available.

Signals.   The use of signals in teaching is an interesting feature that sends up red flags for many teachers. The use of a signal to prompt a choral response from a group is often viewed as a "control" feature of instruction; that is, its use reduces all students to a chorus of faceless voices who echo one response and are not allowed to express their individuality. In this context, the teacher is also viewed as "in control," intolerant of deviation from the group response, and concerned primarily with the form and not the substance of the response.

The purpose for using signals to prompt either a group or individual response is simple. First, signals are typically used in conjunction with group and choral responses that provide learners with more opportunities to practice the information presented. It is obvious that when one learner gives a response, the only learner who we know is receiving practice on that skill is the one responding. By requiring a group response, we extend the practice to more than one learner. If 10 voices are asked to respond, it is likely that 10 minds have had another chance to get the information into storage for future retrieval. As a means of orchestrating the mechanics of group responses in which 5, 10, or more voices, eyes, lips, and minds are required to respond, a signal is used. Without some visual cue to learners about when to respond, the orchestra of voices, like an orchestra of instruments, will loose its rhythm and harmony at the same time. This leaves low performers not knowing when to respond, "piggybacking" (mimicking), or simply mouthing the responses provided by higher performers. It is important to note that after a choral response is given, the teacher should provide many opportunities for students to respond individually. We refer to this feature of instruction simply as an individual check or test. The individual check/test specifies for the teacher whether the learner has the information that was taught and practiced with the group.

Thinking time.   Sometimes a signal is used when working with an individual child. In this instance, the signal structures the child's response by providing the learner with "thinking time" before a response, which preempts impulsive responding. Once the skill is brought to a high criterion level of performance, the signal can be eliminated. A signal can also be used to provide thinking time for a group, which will help them prepare to

Group responses provide practice for many learners at one time, yet they require visual cues supplied by the teacher.

respond to a task. It is typically used with tasks that are new or have a history of being difficult for a learner.

Adapting/Modifying Instruction

Correction procedures.   The spontaneous and unpredictable nature of interactions during instruction makes it necessary for the teacher to be flexible, yet prepared. This seems counterintuitive, and perhaps it is, but it reflects the nature of active, face-to-face instruction with students. In essence, a teacher must be both flexible and unyielding, zealous and calm, prepared and spontaneous, structured and unstructured. A proactive approach to teaching requires that a teacher both anticipate problems and respond to unanticipated problems. The teacher must be in a mental state of expecting the unexpected.

During instruction, the teacher should consistently implement the correction procedures chosen before instruction. Implementing correction procedures consistently provides the learner with more opportunities to acquire the information in a clear way.

Inconsistent correction procedures may result in muddying the very information that the learner is already having difficulty understanding. In some cases, it may be necessary for the teacher to modify the preselected correction procedure or select a new one altogether.

Preteaching.   In the previous section, we noted the importance of the preteaching strategy as a means of precorrecting potential errors of a learner on a new or difficult task.

Firming cycle.   We have noted on numerous occasions the importance of reviewing information that is newly taught or troublesome for students. During instruction, this systematic review is a firming cycle in which the teacher literally cycles through this information offering frequent opportunities for the learner to practice the unestablished skill. These periodic reviews are brief and should last no more than 1 or 2 minutes. In some cases, these reviews can be used as "change-up" activities after lengthy, dissimilar tasks.

Quality of responses.   The final feature of modifying instruction during this phase is concerned with the quantity and quality of learners' responses. During instruction, the teacher must attend to students' responses, because this is the basis upon which the teacher makes instructional decisions. The number and quality of responses solicited during instruction should also vary with the dimensions of the task, the characteristics of the learner, and the specified learning outcome. If the learning outcome demands response accuracy and the task is new, then the number and quality of responses for a naive learner may be low during initial instruction. If the learning outcome is to increase the response rate of an established task, the number and quality of responses for a naive learner will probably be high. The teacher must monitor students' responses carefully during instruction and make the necessary instructional adjustments.

The essential features of the during phase of instruction are summarized in Figure 4–4.

Critical Features: After Instruction Phase

The final phase of instruction can be characterized as a reflective phase in which the teacher takes time to review and reflect upon the instructional lesson. This can be a brief, "targeted" reflection that examines select features of the session, or it can be a study of every aspect of the instructional session. As in the first two phases of instruction, we identify and describe 15 features of instruction for the after phase. Not surprisingly, these features are similar to those of the previous phases. However, because the purpose of this phase is to get teachers to reflect on their teaching, we have phrased the features of instruction in a question format.

The 15 features of instruction are arranged into categories of instructional activities. A rationale for each of the categories follows the entire list.

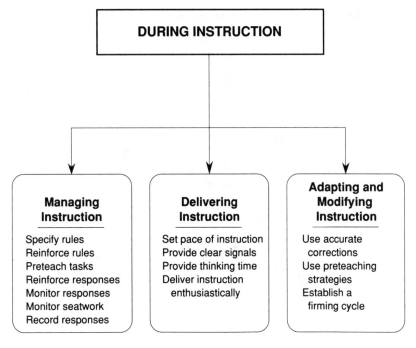

FIGURE 4–4
During instruction phase

PHASE 3

AFTER INSTRUCTION

Assessing Instruction

1. Were students able to perform a task at the end of the session that they couldn't perform before the session began? If not, why not?
2. What learning objectives and outcomes specified for the lesson were students able to accomplish?
3. Will the learning objectives and outcomes need to be revised? If yes, which? Why?
4. Which students should be placed at a higher or lower level in the instructional program?
5. Were students held to a high criterion level of performance throughout the lesson? If yes, is it time to raise the criterion level of performance for the task? If no, was the problem one of management, teacher presentation, or program design?

Adapting/Modifying Instruction

6. Will newly introduced skills require more instructional time than was scheduled in the lesson? If yes, how much time and how should it be scheduled?
7. Do the recorded errors indicate a pattern that will require either intensive remediation or additional instruction and practice for the entire group? For individual learners?
8. Should the firming cycle be adjusted to reflect students' mastery of skills? If yes, should longer chunks of time be scheduled for certain tasks?
9. Should the curriculum materials for the next lesson be adapted, modified, or adjusted in any way? If yes, does the teacher need to model more examples? Are more practice examples needed? Does a complex strategy need to be simplified?

Managing Instruction

10. Were there any management problems during instruction that will require a planned, systematic response? If yes, were the problems specific to a particular part of the instruction? Were they specific to a student?
11. Did the students appear to be motivated, responsive, and involved in the instructional lesson? If not, why not?

Transferring Instruction

12. Can newly taught skills be placed in a different context to facilitate generalization?
13. Was the criterion level of performance on independent seatwork met? If yes, should the criterion be raised to a higher level? Should the difficulty of the task be increased?
14. How should the schedule and nature of independent skills practice be adjusted?

Reflecting on Instruction

15. How do you feel about the lesson in general and your teaching in particular?

Rationale

Assessing Instruction

Learning objective. In this phase, the teacher must decide whether the learning objectives and outcomes specified in the before phase of instruction were met at the conclusion of instruction. New objectives must be specified or old objectives revised, depending on the learner's performance at the end of instruction.

Program placement. The teacher must also determine if more can be taught in less time by placing students in a more advanced part of the instructional program. For students with academic learning problems, the instructional decisions the teacher makes at this point are critical, for they will directly shape the child's academic future. If the teacher incorrectly assumes that a learner has mastered the necessary skills to advance to a more complex skill, the learner could end up in a punishing situation. On the other hand, if the teacher requires a learner to review skills already mastered, precious instructional time is lost. This also communicates to the learner that it doesn't pay to be smart!

Criterion level of performance.   An important feature of instruction in this set is holding students to a high criterion level of performance. This feature is strictly teacher controlled, for only the teacher can make judgments about the quality of student performance. In so doing, teachers sometimes "fudge" by reinforcing answers that are partly correct, incomplete, or simply "close enough" to the correct answer. We characterize this as the "fudge factor" in instruction. Teachers generally don't do this knowingly, but it is a natural consequence of the fatigue of facing students day in and day out, especially those who never seem to get things right the first time. Either because of the eagerness to see students succeed on difficult tasks or because of the physical fatigue of instruction, teachers often accept responses that do not meet the necessary criterion level of performance. This is especially noticeable with students who have a history of "sloppy responding." Sloppy responders simply wear teachers down to the point that they give up and accept sloppy responses.

To buttress against this problem, a teacher must be aware of it and make a systematic effort to hold students to a high criterion level of performance. Sloppy responses cannot be accepted, and a systematic correction procedure (e.g., repeating task) must be used.

Adapting/Modifying Instruction

Schedule of instruction.   After instruction has been assessed, the teacher may also want to adapt or modify the instruction. First, the teacher must determine whether newly taught skills will require more instructional time than originally scheduled. The teacher may decide to schedule a larger block of instructional time or hold two instructional sessions in which the new skill is taught on two separate occasions in one day. The teacher may also decide to include more opportunities for the learner to review the skill in the firming cycle.

Recording errors.   The errors recorded during instruction must also be examined in this phase. The teacher must determine if the errors reflect a pattern of responses in which the learner is consistently demonstrating incorrect knowledge of a fact, rule, or strategy. Once this pattern is identified, steps can be taken to correct the error through further instruction.

Adapting/modifying materials.   The teacher must also examine the next lesson scheduled to determine if modifications in the design of the lesson are necessary. If the lesson is from a commercial program, modifications in a number of features (e.g., number of examples, sequence of examples, amount of practice, explicitness of strategy, knowledge of prerequisite skills) may be necessary.

Managing Instruction

Management problems.   In the previous phases of instruction, we called for clear and unambiguous rules that communicate to learners the teacher's expectations. In this phase, the teacher will determine the extent to which those expectations were consistently met. The teacher must decide whether the problems that surfaced during instruction were "can't" problems (the learner simply couldn't perform tasks adequately because of a lack of information) or "won't" problems (the learner has the information but deliberately chooses not to perform adequately). This can't/won't dilemma is a particularly troublesome one, because the teacher could treat a problem as a "won't" problem when it is actually a "can't" problem. By mistakenly punishing students for not having the skills to perform a task, the teacher risks losing students' respect. Although we discuss this dilemma in detail in Chapter 12, it is important to note now that the teacher must be certain to teach behavior rules and review them adequately.

Motivation.   The teacher must determine if students were engaged in the instruction. Unmotivated students are often sloppy in their responses, quick to disagree or argue, evasive in their eye contact with the teacher, unwilling to do more than the assigned task, and off task during independent seatwork. If students regularly appear unmotivated and lethargic, the teacher must begin by examining the features of instruction. For example, the material could be too easy or the pacing too slow. Other noninstructional features of the setting should also be examined (e.g., room temperature, time of instruction). If motivation is a serious concern, the teacher should consider a planned system of reinforcement in which students earn access to a range of reinforcers based on academic performance. However, these systems consume a great deal of teacher time, monitoring, record keeping, and so forth. Reinforcement systems can be powerful in changing student behaviors, but they can also take away from valuable instructional time if not carefully managed.

Transferring Instruction

Generalization.   One of the most important features of effective instruction is enabling students to transfer newly acquired skills to novel contexts. The teacher's task is to communicate a skill clearly, so that it will be learned, and to communicate it in a way that will generalize to untaught situations. To this end, the teacher must consider the various dimensions of each task and how they can be expanded. For example, one dimension of a task is the required learner response to a task. As noted in Chapter 2, response forms range from oral yes/no responses to written production responses. The teacher can manipulate the response form of a task (e.g., oral yes/no choice response) to place the newly taught task in a new untaught context (e.g., written multiple choice responses). In summary, after an instructional session, the teacher must explore ways to expand or stretch the newly taught task to new and untaught contexts.

Independent seatwork.   Independent seatwork is one way newly taught skills are transferred in small but important ways, because here students must apply the new skills independent of the teacher. However, independent practice of a skill can be structured in many ways. The teacher structure can be high, with the teacher directing almost every step of the independent practice, or it can be low, with the teacher prompting only select parts of the practice (Silbert, Carnine, & Stein, 1990). After instruction, the teacher must determine if the criterion level of performance specified before instruction for independent seatwork was met. At this time, the teacher may want to change the structure of independent practice (e.g., high/medium/low teacher structure), as well as the criterion level of performance.

Reflecting on Instruction

How do you feel?   Experienced teachers know too well the fast and often frenetic pace of classroom life. A teacher engages in literally hundreds of interactions during a school day that run the gamut of social and emotional experiences. When students with academic learning problems are drawn into the instructional province, the teacher's responsibilities are intensified, as is scrutiny of the teacher's performance. To suggest that teachers take time to "reflect" on their teaching while being overworked seems a bit idealistic, if not downright daffy; but at one point it was daffy to consider that mentally retarded students could benefit from an education!

We think it is important for teachers to reflect on their teaching after an instructional session. This reflection can be brief and targeted to a particular task, or it can be lengthy and general. It allows time for teachers to examine their feelings about the instructional session and may lead to adjustments.

Finally, by reflecting on the instructional session, the teacher may determine that something doesn't seem right, but may be unable to account for this unsettling feeling. To clarify and define the problem, Sprick (1983) recommends that the teacher audiotape the part of the session in which the problem occurs. The audiotape can be examined along several dimensions (e.g., number of positive or negative statements to learners, the number of opportunities for high/middle/low performers to respond) to identify the problem. A videotape of the session would be even more informative than an audiotape.

In Figure 4–5, the essential features of the after phase of instruction are depicted.

REQUIREMENTS OF AN INSTRUCTIONAL SEQUENCE

Dunkin and Biddle (1974) noted in discussing the effects of teacher behavior on student outcome that "the largest shortcoming concerning these findings is the lack of an integrative theory of teaching to make sense out of them. It is quite impossible to keep findings for seventy-five different variables in one's head" (pp. 409–410). Since that plaintive call for a lucid and simple theory of teaching more than a decade ago, many models of teaching have surfaced (Becker, 1977; Berliner, 1984; Brophy & Good, 1986; Hunter, 1984; Joyce & Weil, 1980; Murphy, Weil, & McGreal, 1986; Rosenshine, 1983; Rosenshine & Stevens, 1986; Squires, Huitt, & Segars, 1983). The extent to which these models have heeded Dunkin and Biddle's call for simplicity is open to debate. It is also questionable whether a theory or model of teaching can integrate and simplify a complex process of interactions for teacher training purposes without jeopardizing the quality and integrity of that information.

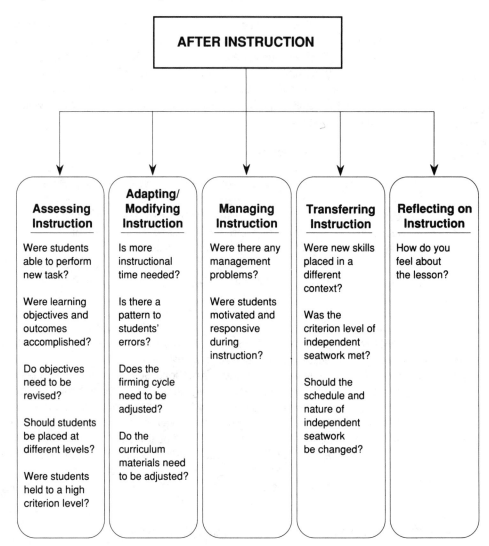

FIGURE 4–5
After instruction phase

The cycle of instruction that we have presented is necessarily complex. Its complexity is a function of the numerous instructional details that must be attended to if teachers are to make a difference in the lives of students who are failing. We believe it is nothing less than the careful attention to the tedious details of instruction that will make this difference. At this time, an easier way of breaking the cycle of failure just doesn't exist.

Active and Static Features of Instruction

We have identified, described, and discussed three phases of an instructional cycle and the 15 intricate features that make up each phase of instruction. By placing these 45 instructional features in the context of a cycle, we want to emphasize the active process of teaching—a process in which the teacher plays a primary role in effective instruction. After all, the teacher activates instructional assessment, records errors, reinforces correct responses, frames and firms a fragile verbal chain, and paces a small reading group's responses. In short, the communication of information takes place in a dynamic cycle of instruction in which the components of the teacher, learner, and content or skill, as noted in Chapter 1, interact in sometimes powerful ways.

In contrast to the active teacher-driven features of instruction, static instructional features are essentially passive dimensions of an instructional lesson. In other words, these features are already built into a curriculum program and are a part of the fabric of the lesson. Static features include, for instance, the kinds, number, and sequence of examples used to communicate a concept, fact, or rule. These features were described to some extent in Chapter 3 when we discussed the forms of knowledge (e.g., verbal associations, concepts, rule relationships, and cognitive strategies) and their arrangement in a taxonomy.

In the next section of this chapter, we examine closely the static design features of an instructional lesson. These are the real anchor points of a lesson, and if they are well grounded, the lesson will be sufficient in its design, and the "active" features of instruction noted earlier will make the lesson effective. If the anchor points are not well grounded, the lesson is likely to be ineffective, irrespective of how well the teacher is activating features of the instructional cycle. In other words, if the examples used in a lesson to communicate a piece of information are inadequate in number or wrong in sequence, then how the teacher acts on that information will not change the misinformation. In some cases, the teacher could actively promote a misrule or reinforce a chronic error pattern unless the design of the instructional lesson is corrected. The active and static features of instruction are depicted in Figure 4–6.

FIGURE 4–6
Active and static instructional features

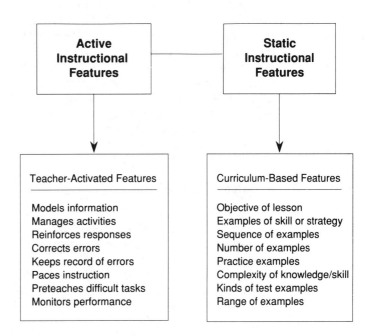

Active Instructional Features	Static Instructional Features

Teacher-Activated Features	Curriculum-Based Features
Models information	Objective of lesson
Manages activities	Examples of skill or strategy
Reinforces responses	Sequence of examples
Corrects errors	Number of examples
Keeps record of errors	Practice examples
Paces instruction	Complexity of knowledge/skill
Preteaches difficult tasks	Kinds of test examples
Monitors performance	Range of examples

Generic Design of Instruction Features

All teaching sequences in which the teacher's objective is to communicate a concept, rule, strategy, or piece of information to take the learner from a state of unknowing to a state of knowing have a set of design features that are necessary. Without them, the teaching sequence would be inadequate. The purpose of the teaching sequence is to communicate a message that must contain the proper elements for the communication to be received and understood. Likewise, for a teaching sequence to be effective, it too must contain the proper elements that we refer to as design features. We have identified five features that we consider essential to design a sequence to teach any knowledge form (i.e., verbal association, concept, rule relationship, cognitive strategy). Unless a teaching sequence incorporates these five design features, it is likely to be inadequate. The five design features listed should serve as the generic anchor points of any teaching lesson:

1. **Knowledge form:** The teaching sequence must be designed to communicate information correctly. The form of the knowledge to be communicated must be correctly identified; that is, a concept must be taught as a concept and not as a verbal fact. The teaching sequence must be designed to represent correctly the knowledge form.
2. **Range of examples:** Teaching sequences are made up of concrete examples that are selected to represent the range of the concept, rule, or strategy (i.e., knowledge form) being taught.
3. **Sequence of examples:** The selected examples must be placed in a proper sequence.
4. **Test examples:** The examples used to assess the learner's knowledge of what was taught must be carefully selected and sequenced.
5. **Practice examples:** The examples used to bring a learner to a high criterion level of performance must be carefully selected and sequenced.

These five generic features represent the *minimum* set of static design features that should be a part of any teaching sequence. Obviously, many other features could be included. However, we wanted to delineate the minimum requirements for designing a teaching sequence for students with academic learning problems. These were extrapolated from the instructional design research alluded to in Chapter 3 (Bruner, 1966; Gagne, 1965; 1985; Markle, 1975; Tennyson & Christensen, 1986; Tennyson & Cochiarella, 1986; Tennyson & Park, 1980), but were drawn in particular from the work of Engelmann and Carnine (1982). Each of these design features will be detailed and discussed in the following section.

Knowledge Form

In Chapter 3, we argued that by knowing about the structure of knowledge, the teacher could make important decisions about how a piece of knowledge should be taught. If a teacher knows that a piece of information is a verbal association, concept, or rule relationship, then the teacher can be informed about the instructional requirements for teaching verbal associations, concepts, rules, and cognitive strategies. By understanding the form of knowledge, the teacher at least knows not to teach a simple fact as a concept or a concept as a simple fact.

The knowledge form certainly doesn't specify for the teacher the necessary details for designing a teaching sequence; the details for designing teaching sequences in language, decoding, reading comprehension, mathematics, and expressive writing are complex and will be given in Chapters 6–11. However, by determining that a form of knowledge is a verbal association, concept, rule relationship, or cognitive strategy, the teacher is immediately alerted to the complexity of the instructional requirements.

Range of Examples

As we have frequently noted throughout the first part of this text, knowledge is generally transformed into action through concrete examples. When the teacher teaches, actions and verbalizations are usually examples that refer the learner to a world of actual objects and situations, as well as to the learner's prior knowledge and experiences. A teaching sequence literally comes to life through examples. For instance, in teaching a language concept such as *over,* the teacher could use a pencil and a table to demonstrate examples of the concept. In teaching main idea comprehension, the teacher could use brief, teacher-prepared narrative passages that clearly specify a main idea. The teacher could also use lengthy narrative passages selected from a basal reader that contain multiple main ideas. In teaching the concept of renaming in subtraction, the teacher could spontaneously generate the subtraction problems and demonstrate the concept of renaming on a chalkboard. On the other hand, the teacher could use the lessons in the regular classroom basal mathematics program to teach the concept of renaming. The teacher's examples serve as the heart of the teaching sequence.

When selecting examples, the teacher must be careful to choose those that represent the range of the verbal association, concept, rule relationship, or cognitive strategy to be taught. In other words, some forms of knowledge are expansive and include a wide range of real world referents that denote the meaning of the knowledge form. For example, the concept of *dog* is a wide-range concept that refers to many types of dogs. According to the American Kennel Club, 125 registered breeds of dogs have been classified into six groups: toy dogs, sporting dogs, hounds, nonsporting dogs, working dogs, and terriers. To represent accurately the complete concept of *dog,* the selected examples would have to show the range of "dogness" from toy dogs, like the miniature Pinscher and Chihuahua, to working dogs, like the Newfoundland and Border collie. In other words, for a learner to appreciate fully the concept of *dog,* the teacher should present a range of examples (e.g., using color pictures) of dogs that vary in size, color, fur, and facial features. With the presentation of each pictured example, the teacher simply notes, "This is a dog."

In contrast to the wide-range concept of *dog,* some forms of knowledge have a very narrow range of meanings or real world referents. For example, learning about the letter *m* within the context of learning to read is likely to involve little variation. The learner can be informed of its alphabetic name (e.g., "The name of this letter is *m*") and its sound (e.g., "The sound we say for this letter is /*mmm*/"). Even the form of the letter (e.g., upper case and lower case handwritten, roman, or gothic) will not vary greatly. The letter *m* certainly does not have the same range of examples as the concept *dog,* unless the teacher intends to inform the learner of the lexicographic dimensions of *m* (e.g., the Greeks called *m mu,* and the Semites, *mem;* it ranks as the 14th most frequently used letter; it is the 7th letter of the Hawaiian alphabet).

By knowing about this design feature, the teacher can decide how much of the range to teach in a teaching sequence. For simple knowledge forms such as discriminations (e.g., letter *m*) and facts (e.g., there are 16 ounces in a pound), the entire range can be taught in one teaching sequence. For more complex forms of knowledge such as concepts (e.g., first-, second-, and third-class levers), rule relationships (e.g., knowing about a part doesn't tell you about the whole thing) or cognitive strategies (e.g., identifying main ideas in narrative texts), the teacher may be required to design several teaching sequences to teach the entire range of the concept, rule, or strategy. If the teacher chooses to teach the complete range of a concept (e.g., *dog*) in one teaching sequence with many different examples, the learner may simply be overwhelmed with information and not see what we referred to in Chapter 3 as the "qualitative sameness" across the examples. On the other hand, if the teacher failed to present the entire range of a concept, a learner may end up thinking that only Chihuahuas are dogs and Great Danes are mysterious aberrations of the animal kingdom, neither horse, cat, nor dog.

In summary, when designing a teaching sequence, the teacher must ascertain the extent to which the range of a concept, rule, or strategy will be taught. Wide, expanded range forms of knowledge may require further development of several teaching sequences presented in successive order (e.g., small dogs first, medium-size dogs next, small and medium-size dogs together, large dogs next, then various size dogs last). As stated before, knowledge forms with a narrow or limited range could be taught in one or two successive teaching sequences. The details for selecting the range of examples across the various forms of knowledge will be given in Chapters 5–11.

Sequence of Examples

By using a range of examples in a teaching sequence, examples naturally fall into a sequence. The information communicated to the learner is as much a function of the order in which the examples are presented as of the range of examples presented. Of course, the range of examples selected determines, in part, the potential sequences in which the examples can be ordered. For instance, when teaching letter-sound correspondences in beginning reading, letters that are highly similar visually and auditorily (e.g., *m/n, i/e, b/d, p/q*) are known to cause problems. If "like" letter pairs are not also chosen for the teaching sequence, the order the letters, *m, i, b,* are taught is not likely to be an issue.

When designing or evaluating a teaching sequence, the teacher may need to adjust the order in which the examples follow one another. In some cases, the similarity between examples of a concept (e.g., angiosperms and gymnosperms), fact (e.g., number identification of 6 and 7), rule (e.g., relationship of supply and demand in the marketplace), or strategy (e.g., renaming in subtraction and addition) should serve as a basis for adjusting the sequence of examples. In other cases, the learner's prior knowledge and competence on prerequisite skills may influence the sequence in which examples are ordered.

Test Examples

Teaching sequences must be designed not only to convey information but also to assess the degree to which the information was adequately communicated. The testing of this knowledge must occur within the same context as the teaching. In other words, the testing should not take place an hour or day later but should follow the teaching immediately. In some cases, the examples used to teach a concept or skill may in turn be used as test examples (e.g., math facts and computations). In general, however, using already "taught" examples as the *only* test examples would be inappropriate, because the learner could memorize the examples. Untaught examples should also be included in the testing sequence to assess the learner's ability to generalize.

However, the nature of the testing sequence depends, in part, on the learning objective, the learner, and the form of knowledge taught. In some cases, the testing sequence may consist of assessing the learner's ability to retain the information presented. For example, after teaching a simple fact (e.g., "Today is Friday"), the teacher may be interested only in assessing the learner's ability to remember what day it is.

Teaching Sequence
TEACHER: Listen, Betsy, today is Friday. What day is it today?
STUDENT: Friday.
TEACHER: Yes, today is Friday. Very good remembering.

Testing Sequence
1. TEACHER: What day is it today?
   STUDENT: Friday.
2. TEACHER: What's your name?
   STUDENT: Betsy.
3. TEACHER: (Points to a book.) Betsy, what is this?
   STUDENT: A book.
4. TEACHER: Betsy, what day is it today?
   STUDENT: Friday.

This testing sequence comprises four test examples that represent both *immediate* acquisition tests and *delayed* retention tests of the information taught at the beginning of the teaching sequence. Test example 1 provides the learner with an immediate retest of the information, while example 4 represents a delayed retest of the same information. By adding other test examples, the retest of this simple fact could be delayed even further. In this testing sequence, the teacher requires the learner to discriminate the fact ("Today is Friday") from other facts (e.g., "What is your name?") and concepts (e.g., object identification of a book). The discrimination examples in the testing sequence also serve to delay and test the learner's recall of what day it is. In this testing sequence, requiring the learner to generalize by identifying an untaught example of a fact is not possible. Because a simple fact was taught ("Today is Friday"), there is no basis for a generalization unless the learner already knows all the days of the week and the concepts of *yesterday, tomorrow, the day after, the day before.*

The teaching of more complex forms of knowledge, such as concepts, rule relationships, and cognitive strategies, will obviously include more complex testing sequences than will the teaching of simple facts. The testing of these knowledge forms will be less concerned with retention (i.e., determining if the learner can recall the information) than with independent and spontaneous application, discrimination, and transfer of the information to novel, untaught contexts (i.e., generalization). For example, in the teaching sequence for the concept *dog* described earlier, numerous objectives for the testing sequence are possible, depending on the examples presented in the teaching sequence. It would be impossible (and unnecessary) for the teacher to present an example of every breed of dog, and the teacher must select a few examples that represent either a limited range of dogness, as we alluded to earlier, or the entire range of dogness. Examples for the limited range could include just small dogs such as a Maltese, pug, bulldog, Boston terrier, and Shih Tzu. The teacher would present these examples in the teaching sequence and later test the learner's knowledge of dogness by presenting some of the same examples.

The teacher should also include in the testing sequence examples of *known* similar concepts that look like a dog, such as varieties of large cats, or known concepts that are dissimilar (e.g., furniture). By including examples of cats in the testing sequence, the teacher tests the learner's ability to discriminate a known but similar concept (*cat*) from an unknown concept (*dog*). Finally, the teacher could include in the testing sequence an example of a dog that was *not* presented in the teaching sequence. For example, the teacher could present an example of a Pekingese or a Lhasa Apso. If the learner correctly identifies these as dogs, the learner will have demonstrated the ability to generalize the concept of *dog*. Once several types of dogs are taught through a series of teaching sequences, a testing sequence could consist of a cumulative retest of different examples of dogs previously presented. The details for designing teaching sequences for concepts will be presented in Chapter 6.

In summary, the purpose of the testing sequence is to determine if the learner can recognize (acquisition test), remember (retention test) and discriminate (discrimination test) the information from other pieces of similar and dissimilar information and generalize (generalization test) the information to novel and untaught contexts.

Practice Examples

Following the immediate, delayed, and cumulative testing of taught and untaught examples within the context of the teaching sequence, the teacher must structure opportunities for the learner to practice applying the information. These practice opportunities, like the testing examples, vary with the learner, the knowledge form, and the learning objectives and outcomes. Practice can vary in *length* (e.g., brief periodic review episodes to long, sustained independent worksheet sessions), *supervision* (e.g., highly structured guided practice to independent practice), *schedule* (e.g., frequent to infrequent practice), and *form* (e.g., written production responses to oral choice responses). Practice might consist of brief, frequently scheduled, highly structured sessions in which the learner is asked to discriminate different examples of the concept *dog* from well-established concepts. Practice might also be one 25-minute independent worksheet session.

As expected, the instructional dimensions of the practice session are in part determined by the learner's competence, the learning objectives, the form of knowledge, and the administrative constraints of the instructional context at the time. However, the practice dimensions should be aligned with the instructional dimensions of the teaching sequence. The length, schedule, form, and supervision of practice should be similar to the requirements placed upon the learner during instruction. More importantly, the scheduled practice should *not* be radically different from the instruction, unless the teacher plans to walk the learner through the practice session.

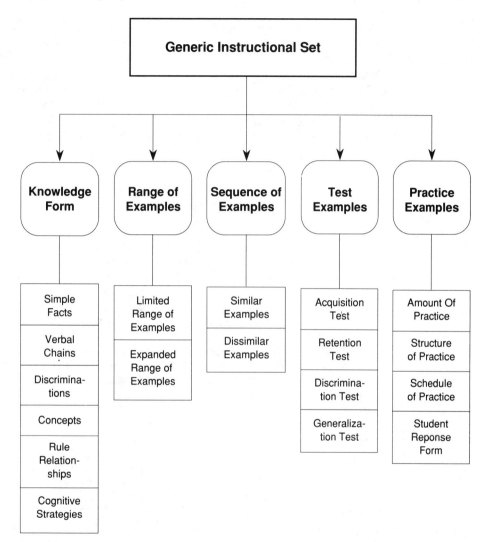

FIGURE 4–7
The generic instructional set

For students with academic learning problems, practice, especially in the form of independent worksheets, is sometimes perceived negatively—a time when the learner is left alone to puzzle through unfamiliar and difficult information without assistance. We recommend using a preteaching strategy before independent practice that alerts the learner to the kinds of responses the worksheet requires, as well as the potentially difficult tasks of the worksheet. Once the worksheet is "pretaught" to the learner, the teacher can be more confident that the responses reflect the learner's actual knowledge.

We have identified and described five static design features. These features are the *minimum* set of requirements necessary to designing and constructing *any* teaching sequence. At minimum, an adequate teaching sequence will represent some knowledge form, include a range of examples properly sequenced, and include a set of test and practice examples. These generic features will serve as the basic framework for the instructional strategies in language, reading, mathematics, and expressive writing proposed in this text. The teaching sequences we propose will include more than these minimum features. As discussed earlier, an effective instructional sequence is part of a cycle that consists of "active" and "static" instructional features. The interaction of these features in the execution of a teaching sequence is the teacher's best bet at breaking the cycle of failure we have alluded to throughout the text. An illustration of the generic instructional set is given in Figure 4–7.

SUMMARY

This chapter is based on the premise that a set of general teaching functions (Brophy & Good, 1986; Rosenshine & Stevens, 1986) have been identified in the teacher effects literature. From this we have derived a set of 45 instructional features that we placed in an instructional cycle of three phases. We have described the active and static features of instruction that make up the before, during, and after phases of instruction. The relationships between the phases, as well as the interdependence of instructional features within and between phases, were drawn. Every teaching sequence must be designed to include five generic design features (i.e., knowledge form, range of examples, sequence of examples, test examples, and practice examples) that serve as the minimum features necessary to design and construct teaching sequences. By attending to the instructional requirements presented in this chapter, teachers will take a significant step toward diminishing the problems faced by students in schools.

APPLICATION ITEMS

1. Describe the step-by-step procedures for framing a task involving a verbal chain (e.g., orally stating the months of the year). Specify the teacher wording and student responses. Explain how the framing for the verbal chain is different than for a simple fact (e.g., 1 year = 12 months).

2. Identify the management features of the before, during, and after phases of instruction. List three specific management features and describe how the features change from phase to phase.

3. Identify and describe each component of the generic instructional set. Explain the purpose of using a generic set of instructional components. Describe the advantages and disadvantages of the generic instructional set.

4. Explain the purpose of preteaching a task. Describe when this strategy is or is not appropriate.

REFERENCES

Becker, W. C. (1977). Teaching reading and language to the disadvantaged—what we have learned from field research. *Harvard Educational Review, 47,* 518–543.

Berliner, D. (1984). The half-full glass: A review of research on teaching. In P. Hosford (Ed.), *Using what we know about teaching* (pp. 61–77). Alexandria, VA: Association for Supervision and Curriculum Development.

Brophy, J., & Good, T. L. (1986). Teacher behavior and student achievement. In M. Wittrock (Ed.), *Third handbook of research on teaching* (pp. 328–375). Chicago: Rand McNally.

Bruner, J. S. (1966). *Toward of theory of instruction.* Cambridge, MA: Belknap Press of Harvard University.

Campbell, J. (1982). *Grammatical man: Information entrophy, language, and life.* New York: Simon & Schuster.

Carnine, D. W. (1981). Reducing training problems associated with visually and auditorily similar correspondences. *Journal of Learning Disabilities, 14,* 276–279.

Dunkin, M. J., & Biddle, B. J. (1974). *The study of teaching.* New York: Holt, Rinehart & Winston.

Engelmann, S., & Carnine, D. W. (1982). *Theory of instruction: Principles and applications.* New York: Irvington.

Englert, C. S. (1984). Effective direct instruction practices in special education settings. *Remedial and Special Education, 5,* 38–47.

Gagne, R. M. (1965). *The conditions of learning and theory of instruction.* New York: Holt, Rinehart & Winston.

Gagne, R. M. (1985). *The conditions of learning and theory of instruction* (4th ed.). New York: Holt, Rinehart & Winston.

Hunter, M. (1984). Knowing, teaching, and supervising. In P. Hosford (Ed.), *Increasing your teaching effectiveness* (pp. 9–31). Palo Alto, CA: Learning Institute.

Joyce, B. R., & Weil, M. (1980). *Models of teaching* (2nd ed.). Englewood Cliffs, NJ: Prentice-Hall.

Markle, S. M. (1975). They teach concepts, don't they? *Educational Researcher, 4,* 3–9.

Murphy, J., Weil, M., & McGreal, T. L. (1986). The basic practice model of instruction. *Elementary School Journal, 87*(1), 83–95.

Rosenshine, B. V. (1983). Teaching functions in instructional programs. *Elementary School Journal, 83,* 335–351.

Rosenshine, B., & Stevens, R. (1984). Classroom instruction in reading. In D. Pearson (Ed.), *Handbook of research on reading* (pp. 745–798). New York: Longman.

Rosenshine, B., & Stevens, R. (1986). Teaching functions. In M. C. Wittrock (Ed.), *Handbook of research on teaching* (3rd ed., pp. 376–391). New York: Macmillan.

Silbert, J., Carnine, D., & Stein, M. (1990). *Direct instruction mathematics* (2nd ed.). Columbus, OH: Merrill Publishing Company.

Sprick, R. (1983). *The solution book.* Chicago: Science Research Associates.

Squires, D., Huitt, W., & Segars, J. (1983). *Effective schools and classrooms: A research-based perspective.* Alexandria, VA: Association for Supervision and Curriculum Development.

Stevens, R., & Rosenshine, B. (1981). Advances in research on teaching. *Exceptional Education Quarterly, 2,* 1–9.

Tennyson, R., & Christensen, D. L. (1986). *Memory theory and design of intelligent learning systems.* AERA Paper, San Francisco.

Tennyson, R. D., & Cochiarella, M. J. (1986). An empirically based instructional design theory for teaching concepts. *Review of Educational Research, 56,* 40–71.

Tennyson, R. D., & Park, O. (1980, Spring). The teaching of concepts: A review of instructional design research literature. *Review of Educational Research, 50*(1), 55–70.

Ysseldyke, J. E., & Christenson, S. L. (1987). Evaluating student's instructional environments. *Remedial and Special Education, 8*(3), 17–24.

PART III

Instructional Strategies for Academic Skills

C H A P T E R

FIVE

Designing Instructional Strategies for Teaching Verbal Associations: Teaching Simple Facts, Verbal Chains, and Discriminations

Chapter Objectives

Upon successful completion of this chapter, you will be able to:

1. RECALL the details for designing teaching sequences for simple facts, verbal chains, and discriminations.

2. IDENTIFY the five components of the generic instructional set that are to be used as the basic framework for designing teaching sequences.

3. DESCRIBE detailed examples of teaching sequences for simple facts, verbal chains, and discriminations.

4. DESCRIBE the design-of-instruction requirements for teaching simple facts in the before, during, and after phases of instruction.

5. DESCRIBE the design-of-instruction requirements for teaching verbal chains in the before, during, and after phases of instruction.

6. DESCRIBE the design-of-instruction requirements for teaching discriminations in the before, during, and after phases of instruction.

BUNDLES OF KNOWLEDGE

In Chapter 3 we discussed how the universe of knowledge can be bundled into the following forms: (1) verbal associations (e.g., simple facts, verbal chains, and discriminations), (2) concepts, (3) rule relationships, and (4) cognitive strategies. These forms are depicted in Figure 5–1.

The organization of knowledge is based on the features of knowledge and the memory and cognitive requirements these features impose on the learner. Specifically, pieces of knowledge that require the learner to code, transform, and recall the symbolic information in the same way are placed into the same category. For example, verbal associations require the learner to make connections between stimuli for which there is only one answer to a specific question (e.g., "Tell me the number of months in a year"). In contrast, cognitive strategies involve a series of multi-step associations and procedures that involve facts, verbal chains, discriminations, concepts, and rule relationships designed to bring about a response or a set of responses to a specific problem. When compared to cognitive strategies, verbal associations are simple in form and function. Designing teaching sequences for these forms of knowledge requires a great deal of attention to the smallest details of instruction.

In designing the teaching sequence for simple facts, we will rely on the five design features described in Chapter 4. These generic design features include:

1. Knowledge form. The form of the knowledge to be communicated must be correctly identified. The teacher must decide whether the form of knowledge falls into one of the following categories:

    Verbal associations (simple facts, verbal chains, discriminations).

    Concepts.

    Rule relationships.

    Cognitive strategies.

2. Range of examples. A teaching sequence must include numerous concrete examples that reveal the various intended meanings of a piece of knowledge that is being communicated. The range of examples in a teaching sequence can be placed in either one of the following sets:

    Limited set. Examples are primarily of one kind or type.

    Expanded set. Examples are varied and differ along more than one feature.

3. Sequence of examples. The examples selected in a teaching sequence must be placed in an appropriate order. The examples in a teaching sequence can be sequenced according to the similarity of their attributes. Specifically, the examples can be placed in the following sequences:

    Sequence of similar examples.

    Sequence of dissimilar examples.

4. Test examples. A teaching sequence must contain examples that are used to assess the learner's ability to remember and recall the information that was presented.

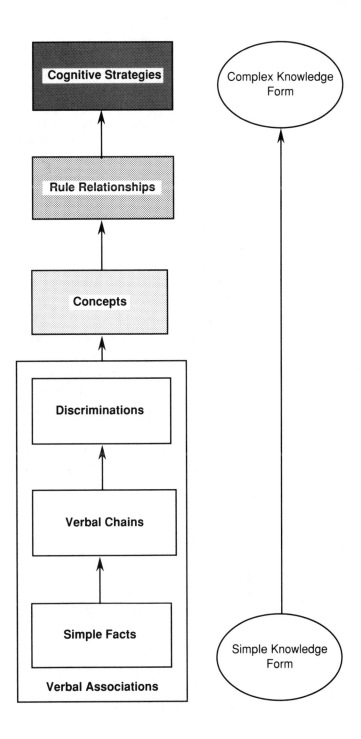

FIGURE 5–1
Taxonomy of knowledge forms

Cognitive Strategies

Complex Knowledge Form

Rule Relationships

Concepts

Discriminations

Verbal Chains

Simple Facts

Verbal Associations

Simple Knowledge Form

These must be carefully selected and sequenced in one or more of the following test sequences:

Acquisition set. Examples are selected to assess the learner's ability to acquire the information immediately following instruction.

Retention set. Examples are selected to assess the learner's ability to recall the information at a later time after instruction.

Discrimination set. Examples are selected to assess the learner's ability to recognize the difference between examples that are similar.

Generalization set. Examples not previously seen by the learner are selected to assess the learner's ability to identify novel instances of the information taught in the teaching sequence.

5. Practice examples. A teaching sequence must contain examples used to provide the learner with opportunities to reach a high criterion level of performance in mastering the information. In selecting and sequencing these examples, the following dimensions should be considered:

Quantity or length of practice. The number of examples or the amount of time scheduled for practice can be either brief or extensive.

Structure of practice. The kind of support required from the teacher can also vary. Practice opportunities can be guided by the teacher, independent of the teacher, structured in a cooperative learning context, or computer assisted.

Schedule of practice. Opportunities for practice can be scheduled in massed practice or distributed practice.

These five generic design features provide the teacher with the *minimum* requirements of a teaching sequence. In designing teaching sequences for teaching simple facts, we will use this generic instructional set as the basic framework. A summary of the generic instructional set is given in Figure 5–2.

TEACHING SIMPLE FACTS

In this section, we describe the procedures for designing teaching sequences to teach simple facts. In subsequent sections, we will also describe the details for designing teaching sequences to teach verbal chains and discriminations.

Determining the Knowledge Form

Before instruction begins, the first task facing the teacher is to determine the kind of knowledge form to be taught. In this case, we've already noted that simple facts are to be taught. A simple fact specifies a connection between two elements, words, events, or actions. A simple fact posed in the form of a question has only one answer (e.g., "Tell me the number of months in a year"). Because simple facts require the learner to retrieve one element (e.g., 12 months = 1 year) from memory when presented with the appro-

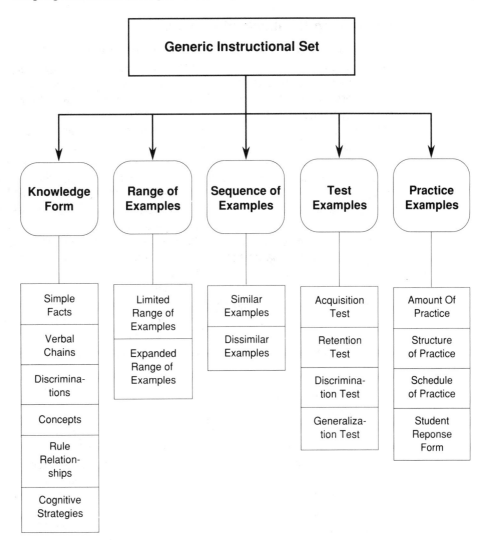

FIGURE 5–2
The generic instructional set

priate stimulus, the teaching sequence is straightforward. Simple facts are unique, because no two facts are the same, which means that knowing one fact doesn't provide the learner with information about another fact. By knowing that a piece of knowledge is a simple fact, the teacher readily knows that the actual teaching of a fact is not likely to require a great deal of instructional time. The teacher also knows that the primary instructional requirement of simple facts is not in how to teach them, but in scheduling how many facts to teach and how often they should be rehearsed until mastery. As noted previously, the teacher must design the teaching sequence in ways that allow the information to be stored and retrieved adequately.

Determining the Range of Examples

Teaching sequences are made up of concrete examples selected for the purpose of clearly presenting the most salient features of the information to be taught. Depending on the form of knowledge to be taught, the examples can be either varied or limited. As noted before, verbal associations tend to have a limited range of examples, which means the teaching sequences are likely to be short. Therefore, the teacher need not worry about designing multiple teaching sequences that cover the entire range of a simple fact.

Because each simple fact communicates a different piece of information, the range of examples is limited. In some cases, there is only *one example* to a simple fact, as the fact and the example are one and the same. For instance, Millard Fillmore was the 13th President of the United States. This piece of information is both a simple fact and the only example of that fact. No other examples could be contrived to assist the teacher in communicating this piece of information. The teacher could embed the presentation of this fact. For example, the teacher could place the number 13 written in black on a piece of 15 × 15-inch cardboard below President Fillmore's picture to accentuate the fact, or the teacher could require all children to wear the number 13 on their shirts for a week to remind them of this fact. However, this does not assist the learner in understanding the fact, but merely in remembering it.

Because simple facts have but one example, namely themselves, there can be no actual range of examples. Therefore, the teacher need not worry about identifying or generating numerous concrete examples to demonstrate the range of a fact to the learner.

Sequencing Examples

Because there is no range of examples to teaching facts, it follows that there are no examples to place in proper sequence. Like the previous generic design feature, the teacher need not worry about sequencing similar or dissimilar examples, because there is only one example to be used in teaching a simple fact. In the after instruction phase of teaching facts, the teacher may need to attend to the sequencing of facts when the primary purpose of a lesson is to discriminate newly taught facts from known facts. In a teaching sequence designed to review old and new facts, the old facts would be separated from the new facts in a distributed manner (e.g., new fact-N; old fact-O: N, O, O, N, O, N, O, O, N). This sequence requires the learner to discriminate the new fact from the known facts. The sequencing of the new fact with the old facts serves to delay and test the learner's recall of the new information.

Selecting Test Examples

The purpose of this generic design feature is to evaluate the learner's performance. Typically, the testing sequence consists of different examples of the knowledge form to be taught. In the case of simple facts, the testing sequence consists of one primary example, the fact itself. Once the fact has been presented, the teacher is left to assess the learner's ability to remember and recall the fact. A test of the immediate acquisition of the fact is straightforward (e.g., "Millard Fillmore was the 13th President of the United States. Who was the 13th President of the United States? What number President of the United States was Millard Fillmore?"). Testing the learner's immediate recall (i.e., acquisition test) of simple facts is not the most important test the teacher should design. Instead, the primary test is the retention test. This test is designed to evaluate the learner's ability to recall the fact from memory after a specified amount of time has elapsed since the fact was first taught. Example testing sequences for simple facts follow.

TASK 5–1
Testing sequence for simple facts

Simple fact: 7 times 8 is 56.

Model

Step 1. Listen, 7 times 8 equals 56.
Step 2. Listen again, 7 times 8 is 56.

Acquisition Test

Step 3. What does 7 times 8 equal?

Discrimination Test

Step 4. (Old fact) What is 7 times 2? (Or an easier old fact: 5 times 1)
Step 5. (Old fact) What is 8 times 5?

Immediate Retention Test

Step 6. (New fact) What is 7 times 8?
Step 7. (Old fact) What is 6 times 7?
Step 8. (New fact) What is 7 times 8?

Delayed Retention Test (5–10 minutes later)

Step 9. (New fact) What is 7 times 8?

The following schedule provides a general framework for designing these tests:

1. The first test of the new fact is given 5–10 minutes following instruction.

   This test is a brief presentation of the new fact and an old fact, as described above in steps 6–8 of the discrimination and retention test. This abbreviated test should take no more than 30 seconds to conduct and can be done unobtrusively when the learner is engaged in independent seatwork.
2. The second test of the new fact can be given 20 to 30 minutes later, if the classroom schedule is appropriate. The same format as described previously can be followed.
3. The remaining delayed retention test should be given periodically through the remainder of the classroom period or school day. The teacher should make an effort to retest the new fact at the end of the day and the beginning of the next school day.

Correction Procedures

All fact errors should be corrected by the teacher, who first repeats the test question (e.g., "What is 7 times 8?") following an incorrect response and then models the correct answer for the learner (e.g., "Listen, 7 times 8 is 56"). If errors persist, the teacher should refrain from any further testing and reteach the fact. This reteaching should be accompanied by a carefully designed schedule of practice, in which old mastered facts are juxtaposed with the new fact.

A testing sequence can be made difficult (1) by increasing the amount of time between the initial teaching of a fact and the testing of that fact, (2) by introducing previously taught facts that are highly similar to the new fact, or (3) by doing both (1) and (2). In the acquisition test described, neither of these features is present. There is no delay between the teaching and testing of the fact, nor are known facts interspersed with the new fact in the testing sequence. For these reasons, the acquisition test is not a very robust test of a learner's knowledge. However, both these features are present in the discrimination and retention test described. Specifically, the new fact is taught in steps 1 and 2, then immediately retested in step 3, followed by a delayed retest in steps 6 and 8. Between steps 3 and 6, known facts are included, which extends the memory requirements placed on the learner. First, the learner must retain the new fact in memory before retrieving it again at a later time; second, the learner must also attend to and recall other facts that are similar (e.g., 8 times 5; 7 times 2; facts that include the numbers 7 and 8) to the new fact. These known facts require the learner to discriminate similar items in a set (e.g., 6 times 7; 8 times 5; 7 times 8). Other known facts that are dissimilar to the new fact could have been included in the testing sequence to make the sequence easier. For example, the known facts of 2 times 5, 6 times 0, 4 times 4 are not similar to the new fact of 7 times 8, because they do not involve the numbers 7 or 8. The inclusion of these dissimilar facts in the testing sequence comprises a discrimination testing sequence. The more similar the known facts are to the newly taught fact, the more difficult the testing sequence is likely to be. The more dissimilar the known facts are from the new fact, the easier the testing sequence will be.

In summary, the testing sequence can be easy or difficult, depending on the introduction of similar facts or the increase in the time that separates the initial teaching and testing of the new fact. In testing simple facts, the primary objective should be to assess a learner's ability to retain and recall the fact, not merely remember the fact immediately after the teaching sequence.

Designing and Scheduling Practice Sessions

Because the primary concern with the teaching of facts is their retention over time, the feature of instruction that will require the greatest attention is scheduling practice sessions. These sessions should provide the learner with ample opportunity to rehearse the information presented during the initial teaching sequence. Practice sessions for simple facts should be brief and reinforcing. Because facts require making only one connection between a specific stimulus and a response and do not involve a series of cognitive connections, long blocks of practice time are not necessary. Instead, practice opportunities should be brief (1–3 minutes) and scheduled frequently through the day and week. We recommend that simple facts be placed in a firming cycle that provides the learner with frequent opportunities to rehearse and recall the facts. The requirements of the firming cycle are shown in Table 5–1.

In addition to the brief and repeated practice sessions that should be scheduled for facts, these sessions should be conducted at a brisk pace and be reinforcing to the learner.

Instructional Format for Teaching Simple Facts

Once the five generic design features have been identified and their requirements for teaching simple facts determined, the details for designing teaching sequences for facts become clear. For example, we know that there will be only one example of the fact, rather than a range of examples, and the testing sequence is limited. As a result, teaching sequences for simple facts are likely to be short and require little instructional time. The teaching sequence for simple facts consists of three parts: (1) model, (2) lead, and (3) check/test. This model-lead-check/test format is straightforward and easy to employ as described in the following task.

TABLE 5–1
Firming cycle: Features and requirements

1. Initial instruction on facts is provided.

    Example: Lesson is taught from 9 to 9:05 one day.

2. Repeated practice is provided on facts initially taught.

    Example: Quick "booster" review sessions are provided at 9:15, 11:45, 1, and 2:30 or end of day.

3. A brief review of the facts taught on the first day is provided at the beginning of the next day.

    Example: The facts that were taught on the first day are reviewed quickly on the second morning between 8:30 and 8:35.

4. A systematic cumulative review of previously taught facts should be scheduled for the week. The simple facts to include in this cumulative review are:
    a. Facts introduced or taught most recently.
    b. Facts missed most frequently during the previous reviews.
    c. Facts presented least frequently during the last three or four review sessions.
    d. The cumulative review set should not contain more than six facts.
    e. Facts that are most similar to the new fact should be included in the review set. However, this similar fact should only be included if the teacher is confident that the learner is firm on the previously taught fact (Engelmann & Carnine, 1982).

TASK 5–2

Fact: The capital of Indiana is Indianapolis.

Model: The teacher presents the information by stating the fact.

TEACHER: Listen, the capital of Indiana is Indianapolis.
          Listen again. The capital of Indiana is Indianapolis.

Lead: The learner states the fact in concert with the teacher.

TEACHER: Say that fact with me. (Teacher pauses for a second)
          The capital of Indiana is Indianapolis. (Repeat if necessary)

Check/Test: The teacher evaluates the learner's ability to recall the fact in response to a specific question.

TEACHER: Name the capital of Indiana.

The model-lead-check/test format for presenting one fact should take no more than 30 seconds of instructional time. It is not a very powerful teaching sequence and isn't intended to be. The model-lead-check/test format simply reflects the structure of facts—a knowledge form that is simple and designed to communicate one basic association between two labels or elements (e.g., 12 inches = 1 foot). This format merely requires the learner to imitate the teacher by repeating a label. As we noted earlier, the real issue with teaching facts is not in their presentation, but in their practice and rehearsal.

The teacher may want to vary the use of the lead part of model-lead-check/test format. Some learners may not require the additional practice of restating the fact provided by the lead portion of the format. Depending on the skill level of the learner, it may also be inappropriate and unnecessary to require learners to restate orally a cumbersome fact. The lead portion of the format provides the learner with another opportunity to rehearse the fact and gives the teacher another chance to evaluate the learner's ability to attend to the task and hold the fact in memory.

TEACHING VERBAL CHAINS

Verbal chains, like simple facts, are a form of verbal association. Verbal chains are a succession of related facts. For example, the days of the week and the months of the year are verbal chains. Math facts such as counting by twos, fives, or tens are also verbal chains, as is the alphabet. Although a verbal chain comprises numerous individual facts, the chain itself is a piece of information separate from these facts. A learner could know the individual facts that make up a chain but not know the verbal chain itself. Similarly, a student could recite an entire verbal chain, such as the months of the year, and not be able to answer questions related to specific individual facts that make up the chain. For example, a child could fail to name the first month of the year as a result of not understanding the ordinal concept *first*.

The requirements for teaching verbal chains are similar to those for teaching simple facts. Like simple facts, the primary concern when teaching verbal chains is their retention over time. Therefore, the scheduling of practice sessions and the establishment of a firming cycle are the most important instructional features. Verbal chains can also be taught using the model-lead-check/test format. However, unlike simple facts, verbal chains require more modeling and leading to ensure their acquisition. Because the learner is required to learn a "chain" of associations and not just one association, it's reasonable to assume that the teaching of verbal chains requires more instructional time.

Using the Generic Instructional Set to Teach Verbal Chains

In designing the teaching sequence for verbal chains, we will rely again on the five generic design features. Because verbal chains are similar to simple facts, our task of identifying the requirements of each of the five design features is made easy. In fact, as shown in Table 5–2, designing a teaching sequence for verbal chains is virtually identical to designing one for simple facts.

A quick glance at the table reveals the similarity between the teaching of verbal chains and the teaching of simple facts. The teaching of a specific verbal chain results in the learner acquiring only that specific chain and nothing else. The teaching sequence doesn't provide the learner with information about any other aspect of the universe of knowledge. With other forms of knowledge, an example of a concept (e.g., truck as an example of a vehicle) could provide the learner with information about other categories of knowledge not presented in the teaching sequence (e.g., large trucks = vehicles). However, a verbal chain, like a simple fact, provides information only about itself.

A review of the generic design requirements suggests that the teaching of verbal chains involves designing a teaching sequence to communicate the specific verbal chain and only that chain. Furthermore, the design feature of concern is the scheduling of

TABLE 5–2
Teaching verbal chains

Design Feature	Requirements for Designing Verbal Chains
Knowledge form	Verbal chains: sequence of related successive facts involving a string of associations.
Range of examples	None. There are no examples other than the specific chain itself.
Sequence of examples	None. Because there is only one example to each verbal chain, there are no other examples to include in a sequence.
Test examples	Only the specific verbal chain itself.
Practice examples	Only the specific verbal chain itself. The primary concern is not with selecting the number of practice examples but with the schedule for practicing verbal chains.

practice opportunities. As with simple facts, the primary mechanism for facilitating practice on verbal chains is the firming cycle. The details for developing a firming cycle are the same as those described in Table 5–1.

Instructional Format for Teaching Verbal Chains

We will use the model-lead-check/test format for teaching verbal chains. As in the teaching of simple facts, the use of this format is straightforward. However, because verbal chains involve multiple associations, the teacher must decide whether to present the entire chain or just a part of it at one time. The decision should be based on several factors, including the length of the chain, the length and familiarity of the individual links (associations) in the chain, the purpose for learning the chain, as well as the learner's language skills, memory capacity, and attention to task. In most cases, the teacher will have the necessary information to make this decision before teaching a verbal chain. However, determining how much of a verbal chain to teach shouldn't require too much time or effort, for the teacher needs merely to ask the learner to orally recite the verbal chain. After a few trials (e.g., the learner tries again after an incorrect response) and some minimal teacher prompting (i.e., the teacher leads a difficult response), the teacher should have the information necessary to determine where to start teaching. This brief but dynamic assessment shouldn't take more than 3–4 minutes.

The following tasks detail a model-lead-check/test format for teaching verbal chains in small chunks. This chunking of knowledge requires the teacher to observe carefully the learner's responses to determine whether to move ahead with a new chunk, provide further practice on the same chunk, or even reduce the chunk to a smaller, more manageable piece of information. It's especially important for the teacher to pay close attention to the errors that the learner makes. If errors are successive (e.g., three to four incorrect responses) or are random and inconsistent in nature, the teacher may need to end the lesson or make adjustments in some aspect of the instruction (e.g., pacing, reinforcement). Stopping the lesson eliminates the learner's opportunities to "practice" or repeat the errors. At the same time, the teacher buys time to rethink the design of the teaching sequence and to make adjustments in the format by switching to a change-up task or a completely different instructional activity.

TASK 5–3
Verbal Chain: Teaching Months of the Year

BEFORE INSTRUCTION

Task Status: New.

Preskills

1. Purpose for knowing months of year.
2. Knowledge that there are 12 months in a calendar year.

Instructional Design Guidelines

1. Only one example of verbal association to present.
2. Identify chunk or piece of chain that will be taught first (e.g., first three months only).
3. Identify appropriate reinforcers (social, material, activity) to use both during and after instruction to encourage student performance.
4. Set pace or rate of verbal presentation of task before actual presentation.
5. Decide on a visual or auditory signal/cue to use during instruction to prompt and reinforce pace of presentation (e.g., clapping or hand signal for each month).
6. Set instruction and practice for brief time intervals of approximately 3–5 minutes. Juxtapose verbal chain with another dissimilar task (e.g., oral or silent group reading; independent worksheet on mathematics).
7. Prepare a familiar task to use if performance on verbal chain results in frequent and persistent errors. The task should not be another verbal association but should involve a different knowledge form (e.g., concepts, rule relationship, or cognitive strategy).

Introductory Set: Introduce the first three months (January-February-March). The entire task should be oral.

Expanded Set

Present the next three months once students reach a criterion of orally saying the first three months correctly on successive trials. Continue in the same manner with the following six months.

Generalization Set

None, because there is only one example of the verbal chain for months of the year. Students could be taught to generalize to new settings.

TASK 5–4

DURING INSTRUCTION

Instructional Delivery Guidelines

1. Frame task carefully because it is new. The framing should be brief.
2. Be certain all students are attending (eyes on teacher, hands and feet quiet) before beginning instruction.
3. The pacing of the verbal chain should be brisk but appropriate to learner (e.g., slower for less competent learners).
4. Errors should be corrected immediately. Upon detecting the error, the teacher states the correct month.
5. Task should be kept highly reinforcing by praising students frequently. However, reinforcement should always be contingent on student performance.

TASK 5–5
Teaching Procedure for Verbal Chain

Framing

TEACHER: We're going to say the months of the year. What are we going to say?
STUDENTS: Months of the year.
TEACHER: And when we say the months of the year, where are you going to have your eyes?
STUDENTS: On you.

Model

TEACHER: Exactly. I'll say the beginning months. Listen big.
    January-February-March. Listen again.
    January-February-March. Say those months with me.
    (Pause.) Get ready.

Lead

TEACHER AND STUDENTS: (Teacher claps as each month is said.) January-February-March.
TEACHER: Good, one more time. (Pause.) Get ready.
TEACHER AND STUDENTS: (Teacher claps.) January-February-March.

Test

TEACHER: Very nice. Now I want you to say the months all by yourself. (Pause.) Get ready.
STUDENTS (Teacher claps as students say each month): January-February-March.
TEACHER: Good. One more time. (Pause.) Get ready.
STUDENTS (Teacher claps again for each month): January-February-March.
TEACHER: Excellent job. One more time.

It may be necessary to repeat this piece of the chain many times, depending on the learners. The teacher claps to keep the students together and to keep the pacing brisk.

The teacher should follow the same procedures when teaching the remaining months of the year. However, the primary concern will be the transition and linkage between the previously mastered part of the chain (e.g., January-February-March) and the newly taught part of the chain (e.g., April-May-June) as the teacher attempts to combine both chunks into a verbal chain. These points of transition in which the learner must weave old and new learning require much practice and teacher guidance. An example of teaching this transition follows. In this teaching sequence, the teacher has just completed teaching the months April-May-June. The children have already mastered the first three months, January-February-March. Linking the second three months to the first three months shouldn't be too difficult as the transition involves linking multisyllabic words (January-February) with one and two syllable words (April-May-June).

Visual or auditory cues help prompt students and reinforce the pace of the presentation of task sequences.

TASK 5–6
Linking Old and New Chunks in a Verbal Chain

Model

TEACHER: Now we're going to add more months. Listen. (Pause.) April-May-June. Listen again, April-May-June. Get ready to say it with me. (Pause.) Get ready.

Lead

TEACHER AND STUDENTS: (Teacher claps for each month.) April-May-June.
TEACHER: Great, one more time. (Pause.) Get ready.
TEACHER AND STUDENTS: (Teacher claps.) April-May-June.
TEACHER: One more time for good luck. (Pause.) Get ready.
TEACHER AND STUDENTS: (Teacher claps.) April-May-June.

Test

TEACHER: Wonderful. Now all by yourself. (Pause.) Get ready.
STUDENTS: (Teacher claps for each month.) April-May-June.
TEACHER: Great. One more time, and this time you're on your own. I'm not going to clap. Eyes up here, everyone. (Pause.) Get ready.
STUDENTS: April-May-June.

TEACHER: One more time. (Pause.) Get ready.
STUDENTS: April-May-June.

Framing

TEACHER: Excellent, excellent. Now let's say all of the months from the very beginning. We're saying the months from the very beginning. What are we going to do, Philip?
PHILIP: Say the months from the very beginning.
TEACHER: Yes, we're going to say the months from the very beginning. Can someone tell me the first month we say when we say the months from the very beginning?
JEAN: April?

Correction Procedure

TEACHER: No. When we say the months from the beginning we start with the very first month of the year. What's the first month of the year?
JACK: January.
TEACHER: Excellent, Jack. What's the first month of the year, everyone? (Pause.)
STUDENTS: January.

Error Retest

TEACHER: What's the first month of the year, Jean?
JEAN: January.
TEACHER: So what month are we going to say when we start from the beginning, Jean?
JEAN: January.

Lead

TEACHER: Yes, excellent, Jean. OK, everyone. We're going to say the months from the beginning. (Pause.) Get ready.
TEACHER AND STUDENTS: (Teacher claps for each month.) January-February-March-April-May-June.

The teacher repeats the procedures as often as necessary until students have mastered this part of the verbal chain. To correct any errors, the teacher uses the model-lead-check/test format. Before ending the session, the teacher should briefly retest all errors.

Several important instructional features to the procedures described require elaboration. First, the teacher doesn't engage in lengthy explanations. A quick model of the task will inform students more effectively than a lengthy verbal explanation. Excessive verbalizations waste much valued instructional time.

In the first part of the teaching sequence described, the teacher employs the model-lead-check/test format on the transition part (e.g., April-May-June) of the verbal chain. This is followed by the teacher framing the second part of the transition, which involves the learner saying the months from the beginning. This framing is important because it allows the teacher to assess if students understand the requirements of the new task (i.e., starting the chain with January and not April). During the framing, the teacher corrects an error by Jean, who thinks that the first month is April. Such an error is predictable, as April was the first month in the second chain recited by the students. In the correction procedure, the teacher obtains the correct answer and immediately retests Jean on the error. In the final section of the teaching sequence, the teacher models the entire chain. This is followed by a lead and test of the chain.

One final concern involves the use of the "lead" part of the format, in which the teacher responds with students. It is important for the teacher to eventually eliminate or fade this particular part of the format. In the teaching sequence, the teacher omits clapping for students after they state the chain. By eliminating the clapping, the teacher is free to attend to the performance of individual students. The lead part of the format serves to prime students to respond. It is not likely to be a factor in assisting students to make sustained and accurate responses.

TASK 5–7

AFTER INSTRUCTION

Following instruction on the verbal chain, the teacher should concentrate on the errors made during the session and on the fluency and accuracy of students' performance. The teacher should reflect on these concerns:

1. Were students attentive during instruction? If not, adjust the pacing of the lesson and reexamine the level, type, and schedule of reinforcement. If the lesson was especially disruptive, determine if the problem was specific to a particular child or seating arrangement. A structured management plan may be required before the next lesson.
2. Were students accurate and fluent 90 to 100% of the time? If not, determine if the difficulty was specific to a particular part of the chain or to the entire chain. Isolate the difficult part and schedule more individual practice time with selected students. Provide these students with more opportunities to practice the chain.
3. Did students receive adequate practice? If not, establish a firming cycle that provides successive and frequent retesting of the verbal chain. Low performers should be given more practice opportunities than high performers. This firming cycle should be similar to the one described on facts (see Table 5–1).
4. Was a record of students' performance kept? If not, set up a record-keeping system. This record is critical to determining the kind and amount of practice and the retesting individual students will require.
5. Were errors retested? If not, a delayed retest of all errors should be given after the end of the instructional session. Special attention must be given to these errors.
6. Could the learner retain the skill? If not, following the initial teaching of this verbal chain, the teacher should consider juxtaposing this verbal chain with other tasks that are dissimilar (e.g., concept lesson or cognitive strategy). This juxtaposition of dissimilar tasks will assist in building retention of the verbal chain.

TEACHING DISCRIMINATIONS

The final knowledge form that we have identified as a verbal association is that of discriminations. A discrimination is defined as the recognition of a difference between two stimuli in which the association of a specific response to a particular stimulus is made in the context of other stimuli. Discriminations are critical forms of knowledge that can be found in more complex forms of knowledge (e.g., cognitive strategies, concepts, and rule relationships). Discriminations require the learner to observe and tell the difference between two stimuli, which can obviously occur in many different contexts. The learner can be required to indicate the difference between two concepts, two rules, two facts, or two cognitive strategies. Discriminations must be taught within the context of skill areas such as reading, language, mathematics, and so on.

Because discriminations require the learner to make associations within a particular skill area, designing teaching sequences for discriminations involves carefully selecting those associations. The teacher must have the appropriate assessment information within each of these basic skill areas to select the right associations to teach. Discriminations can be made difficult or easy, depending on the associations that are included in a particular teaching sequence and the knowledge the learner brings to the instructional session. As a general rule, the more similar the stimuli are, the more difficult the discrimination will be for the learner. For example, in teaching decoding skills, the letter-sound associations of *d* and *b* are well known for the confusion they cause learners because of their similarity both visually and auditorily. We recommend separating the introduction of stimuli that are visually (e.g., *d, b*), auditorily (e.g., *e, i*), or conceptually (e.g., *more, less*) similar. In fact, the primary concern when teaching discriminations is the selection and sequencing of examples. If the examples are highly similar, the teaching sequence is likely to cause difficulty for some low performers.

Using the Generic Instructional Set to Teach Discriminations

Because discriminations require more than the recall of a specific response to a specific question, as with simple facts and verbal chains, designing and teaching discriminations will require more sophistication and attention to detail. We will use the generic instructional set to guide the teaching of discriminations. We should note an important but elusive difference between the teaching of discriminations and the teaching of verbal chains and simple facts. Simple facts and verbal chains can be taught independent of a specific skill area. We could teach a verbal chain (e.g., months of the year) as an independent piece of information. We could also teach a simple fact by itself and not connect it with any other information. For example, a learner could be taught that the capital of Hawaii is Honolulu and acquire that information without having to learn anything else about Hawaii. The learner would know that fact and not have to recall from memory any other information to appreciate the fact. While knowing more about Hawaii would enhance the meaning of the fact, that knowledge is not necessary to appreciate that Honolulu is the capital of Hawaii. The same is true if a learner was taught days of the week as a verbal chain. A learner could orally state the days of the week without reference to any other source of information. In contrast, discriminations are not taught for the sake of simply teaching them. Discriminations are not stand-alone

TABLE 5–3
Teaching discriminations

Design Feature	Requirements for Designing Discriminations
Knowledge form	Discrimination. The recognition of a difference between two stimuli in which the association of a specific response to a particular stimulus is made in the context of another stimulus.
Range of examples	Varied. The range of examples depends on the specific skill area being taught. This range can involve a very broad range of examples, or it can be narrow and involve a limited range of examples.
Sequence of examples	Systematic and controlled. The sequence of examples will consist of selecting and ordering examples that are dissimilar and similar. The decision rules for sequencing will vary depending on the specific skill area to be taught.
Test examples	Varied. The test examples will be determined in part by the range of examples included in the teaching sequence. Test examples will include those to evaluate the learner's ability to acquire, retain, and generalize the specific skills taught.
Practice examples	Varied. These examples will be limited initially to those in the range of examples presented in the teaching sequence. The primary concern is with the selection of examples that require the learner to tell the difference between similar examples.

pieces of information but must be taught within the context of other specific skills. We will use the generic instructional set to assist in specifying the best context for teaching discriminations. In Table 5–3, we review each of the five generic design features and requirements.

An analysis of the generic instructional design requirements given in Table 5–3 makes clear the significant differences between the teaching of simple facts and verbal chains and the teaching of discriminations. Unlike verbal chains and facts, discriminations involve a range of examples that must be selected and sequenced with care and purpose. Because we are dealing with more than one example in teaching a discrimination, the teaching sequence must consist of numerous demonstration, test, and practice examples.

A review of the generic design requirements for teaching discriminations suggests that a teaching sequence must include a range of examples. Therefore, the primary concern in designing these teaching sequences resides in the selection and sequencing of these examples rather than in the teacher delivery and presentation requirements.

Instructional Format for Teaching Discriminations

We will rely on the model-lead-check/test-retest format for teaching discriminations. As we have seen with the teaching of facts and verbal chains, this format is simple. The teacher models the information, guides the learner in responding, evaluates the learner's ability to identify or produce the correct responses, and retests the learner at a later time. What is not obvious in designing these teaching sequences is the selection and sequencing of the examples. Because discriminations require the learner to make a choice between different kinds of examples, that choice depends on the set of examples offered. The rules for selecting and sequencing these examples vary, depending on the information taught (e.g., concept learning, reading, mathematics).

The following tasks detail a model-lead-check/test-retest format for teaching discriminations. The modeling part of this format is limited, because the teacher need only demonstrate the information once or twice. However, the testing sequence is important, as it is the part that will require the learner to make discriminations.

TASK 5–8
Discriminations: Orally Producing Letter-Sound Associations

BEFORE INSTRUCTION

Task Status: New (first letter-sound correspondence to be taught).

Target Skill: s.

Preskills

1. Able to blend sounds auditorily (auditory blending).
2. Understands purpose of reading.

Introductory Set: s, S (lower and upper case).

Discrimination Set: s, individual pictures of a hat, a dog, and a chair.

Sequence for Discrimination Set: s, hat, S, dog, chair, s, S, hat, dog, s, chair, hat, dog, chair, S, hat, s.

Generalization Set: None.

Instructional Design Guidelines

1. Only one letter-sound correspondence is being taught. The learner doesn't know any other letter-sound correspondences at this point, so the discrimination set includes examples of stimuli that the learner does know. The teacher must identify and select these examples.
2. Specify the sequence in which the examples will be presented (see recommended sequence).
3. Set pace or rate of presentation prior to actual presentation.
4. Decide on a signal to use during instruction to cue learners when to respond.
5. Decide on a correction procedure to use before actual presentation.

TASK 5–9

DURING INSTRUCTION

Instructional Delivery Guidelines

1. Frame task carefully because it is new. The framing should be brief, and extensive verbalizations should be avoided.
2. Be sure all students are attending (e.g., eyes on teacher, hands and feet quiet).
3. The teacher should watch the learners' eyes and mouths during their responding.
4. The pacing should be brisk but appropriate to learners' performance.
5. Errors should be corrected immediately and retested periodically throughout the teaching sequence.
6. The teacher should model the target sound for 1–2 seconds.

TASK 5–10
Teaching Procedure for Discriminations

Introductory Set: Model

TEACHER: We will learn to say the sound for this letter. (Points to letter on the board.) Listen again to what we will do. We will say the sound for this letter. I need everybody's eyes on me. I'll point to the letter and say the sound. My turn. (Teacher places finger right below the letter *s* on the board.)

This letter says the sound */sssssss/*. Listen again. This letter says the sound */sssssssss/*. Say the sound with me. (Pause—teacher checks to make sure learners are attending.) Get ready; what sound?

Lead

TEACHER AND STUDENTS: */sssssssssss/*.
TEACHER: Once more. (Pause.) Get ready, what sound?
TEACHER AND STUDENTS: */sssssssssss/*.

Test

TEACHER: All by yourselves. (Pause.) Get ready, what sound?
STUDENTS: */sssssssss/*.
TEACHER: One more time. (Pause.) Get ready, what sound?
STUDENTS: */sssssssss/*.

Individual Test of Students

TEACHER: Very nice work. Jennifer, your turn to say the sound. (Teacher points to letter.)
JENNIFER: /sssssssss/.
TEACHER: Good job. Carlos, your turn. What sound is this?
CARLOS: /s/.

Correction Procedure

TEACHER: /sssssssssssss/. Say the sound again, Carlos. Get ready, what sound?
CARLOS: /sssssssss/.

Discrimination Testing Sequence

TEACHER: (Teacher has an easel with the examples for the discrimination set on it. The examples include: s, S, individual pictures of a hat, a chair, and a dog. The examples are not placed in any particular order on the easel. However, the teacher will point to them in a specific order.)

I need everyone's eyes and ears up here. Watch my finger. (Teacher points to the letter s.) Everyone, what sound does this say?
STUDENTS: /sssssss/. (Teacher removes finger from under the letter and students stop responding.)
TEACHER: (Points to picture of the hat.) What is this?
STUDENTS: A hat.
TEACHER: Good. (Teacher points to S on easel.) What sound does this say?
STUDENTS: /sssssssssss/.
TEACHER: Good job. (Teacher points to picture of the dog.) What is this?

The teacher repeats the same set of procedures following the discrimination set sequence described in the before instruction phase given earlier.

Several instructional features of the teaching sequence require elaboration. The introductory set involves only one letter-sound correspondence, and the teaching is simple. Following the model-lead-check/test parts of the introductory set, the teacher initiates a testing sequence designed to assess the learner's acquisition of the sound /s/. This individual test allows the teacher to determine if selected learners, especially low performers, have the information. If the teacher were to test students by requiring only a group choral response, it would not be possible to determine whether individual students know the taught sound. Only by conducting an individual test of students will the teacher be able to ascertain individual students' knowledge.

The correction procedure used in the teaching sequence follows a simple model-test procedure. However, in this instance, the teacher makes the correction immediately upon hearing the error. The teacher doesn't stop the learner and provide an explanation of the error. Instead, upon hearing the error, the teacher responds immediately by modeling the correct response, even if it involves interrupting. In fact, in some cases, this interruption is necessary to provide the learner with "instant" information about the correct response. In these cases, the teacher may need to "roll over" the learner's incorrect response by modeling the correct response immediately and loudly (i.e., the teacher says the correct sound a little louder than normal).

Once the model-lead-check/test format is completed, the teacher can assume that the learner has acquired the new information. The next critical step in the teaching sequence is the discrimination test. Up to this point in the teaching sequence, the only information that the teacher has is that the learner is able to make the association between the symbol *s* or *S* and the production of the sound /*sssssssss*/. Because the teaching sequence requires the learner merely to repeat what the teacher says (e.g., "This letter says the sound /*sssssss*/. What sound does this letter say?"), we can't be too impressed with the power and stability of the learner's responses. The first important test of the learner's ability to recall and apply this new knowledge is in the discrimination testing sequence, wherein the learner must recognize the difference between a newly learned stimulus-response association (e.g., *s/S*) and other previously learned associations (e.g., hat). It is the first real test of the learner's ability to recognize the similarities and differences between new and old learning.

The examples selected to assess the learner's ability to recognize the letter-sound correspondence *s/S* in the discrimination testing sequence described previously are unusual. First of all, no other letter-sound correspondences are included in the teaching sequence, because the learner doesn't know any other associations. The letter *s* is the first sound to be taught, and it is not possible to design a discrimination sequence that consists of other examples of letter-sound correspondences. The teacher is faced with the dilemma of not having any "real" discrimination examples (i.e., other letter-sound correspondences) to test the learner's ability to recognize the difference between *s/S* and other sounds. However, although the teacher may not have any discrimination examples that are similar to the newly taught letter-sound correspondence, the teacher does have access to dissimilar examples that can be used to test the learner's ability to discriminate the newly taught sound from something else. The dilemma is temporarily resolved by requiring the learner to discriminate the target sound from the pictures of a hat, a dog, and a chair. These examples may not assess the learner's ability to make subtle discriminations of highly similar stimuli (e.g., *s* vs. *z* or *b* vs. *d*), but the learner is nevertheless required to make a discrimination. This initial discrimination test is by no means the last test of the learner's decoding abilities. It is simply the first of many discrimination testing sequences that the learner will face. As the learner acquires more knowledge of letter-sound correspondences, the discrimination testing becomes more difficult as similar examples are included in the sequence.

In the following task we describe a discrimination testing sequence for an advanced session in which the learner has knowledge of many letter-sound associations. The model-lead-check/test-retest format for this teaching sequence is the same as described above. The teacher models the new sound (e.g., *m/M*), then provides a test and retest for the new skill. The correction procedure is the same as described previously. However, because the learner knows more than one sound, the discrimination testing sequence is different. In this case, the selection and sequencing of known and new sounds require careful consideration.

TASK 5–11
Discrimination Testing Sequence:
Orally Producing Letter-sound Associations

Target Skill: m/M.

Introductory Set: m/M.

Preskills: Firm knowledge of following sounds: t, a, s/S, b, r.

Discrimination Set: m/M, t, a, s/S, b, r.

Sequence for Discrimination Set: m, s, m, t, a, M, r, S, b, m, t, a, s, r, M, m.

Discrimination Testing Sequence

Step 1
TEACHER: (The discrimination set of letter sounds is written on the chalkboard or transparency for use with an overhead projector. The letters are written in an unordered fashion. The teacher has a small group of children sitting in chairs in front of the board.)

I like how you all watched me and said the new sound we just learned. Now you're going to say the new sound along with some sounds you already know. So, I need eyes and ears up here. Be sure to watch my finger. By watching my finger, you'll know the sound to say.

(Teacher places finger right below the letter *m*.) Look at this letter and get ready to tell me the sound. (Pause.) What sound is this? (Teacher lifts finger and touches under the letter.)

STUDENTS: /mmmmmmmmmmm/.

Step 2
TEACHER: (Teacher lifts finger from under the letter *m*, and students stop responding. The teacher moves finger to the letter *s* and places finger under the letter.)

Good, look at this letter. (Pause.) What sound?

STUDENTS: /ssssssssss/.

Step 3
TEACHER: (Teacher lifts finger from under the letter *s* and students stop responding. The teacher moves finger to the letter *m* again and places finger under the letter. The teacher raises finger quickly, then touches and holds finger under the letter.)

What sound is this?

STUDENTS: /mmmmmmm/.

Step 4

TEACHER: (Teacher moves finger to the letter *t*. The teacher holds finger slightly above the board but under the letter *t*.)

Good. Now look at this letter and get ready to tell me its sound. (Pause.) What sound?

(The teacher quickly taps under the letter *t* to indicate it is a stop sound.)
STUDENTS: /t/.

Step 5 The teacher repeats steps 1–5 with the remaining sounds. All errors are corrected immediately and retested at the end of the sequence.

The discrimination testing sequence described here contains several important instructional features. The sequence of the discrimination set is systematically controlled to provide the learner with successive opportunities to make a discrimination between the newly taught sound (*m*) and previously mastered sounds (*s/S, t, r, b, a*). In the process of the teacher going back and forth between the various sounds, the time interval between the new sound and the mastered sounds gradually increases. For example, the new sound is presented first in the sequence, then later as the third, sixth, tenth, and fifteenth sound. This increase is deliberately built into the design of the teaching sequence, for it requires the learner to develop greater retention of the new sound over time.

The other features of the discrimination testing sequence are specific to the teaching of letter-sound correspondences, such as the movement of the teacher's finger pointing to the letters. Because some sounds can be produced continuously (e.g., *s, m, r*), the teacher holds a finger under those letters to signal the continuous production of the sound. Other letters (e.g., *t, b*) require a quick, abrupt stop sound which the teacher indicates with a quick in-and-out tap of the finger. Finally, the upper and lower case letter *s* are introduced together because they are graphically similar. Graphically dissimilar letters (e.g., *r* and *R*) would be separated in a teaching sequence. These conditions related to the teaching of decoding will be discussed in greater detail in Chapter 7.

This discrimination testing sequence contains the necessary design features (e.g., range, sequence, and testing of examples) to serve as an adequate model for its application to other basic skill areas. We would use the same basic format for designing a teaching sequence for specific language concepts. For example, we would use a model-test-retest format to demonstrate the concept *more* (meaning to a greater degree). Following that part of the teaching sequence, we would then design a discrimination testing sequence that would require the learner to discriminate the newly taught concept of *more* with other previously mastered similar concepts, such as *many, none, few*, and *less* and dissimilar concepts, such as *together, between, above*, and *farther away*. We could also use the same teaching sequence for teaching numeral identification, where the learner is required to discriminate a newly taught number (e.g., 5) from already known dissimilar (e.g., 1, 8) and similar (auditory, 4; visual, 3, 6, 7) numbers.

In summary, if the teacher's primary objective is to require a learner to recognize the difference between stimuli within a particular skill area, then it is important for the

Movement of the teacher's finger, and pointing to letters, are vital to the sequence of teaching letter-sound correspondences.

teacher to design a discrimination testing sequence that will require the learner to recognize the differences between similar and dissimilar pieces of information. This sequence is critical to the acquisition of new information in the presence of known information. In a sense, the discrimination sequence is the instructional mechanism that allows the teacher to integrate new learning with old learning to ensure further learning of basic skills. These are some general guidelines for designing these discrimination testing sequences:

1. The introductory set should include only the new target skill (e.g., letter-sound association *m;* language concept *more;* a group of word types like those that follow a CVCe pattern, such as *rate, gate, name, sane*).
2. The introductory set should be taught using a model-lead-check/test-retest format.
3. The discrimination set should include only those examples that the learner has mastered. If the teacher is unsure, examples that are most dissimilar to the newly taught skill should be included in the set. A second discrimination set could then be introduced that included similar examples.
4. The sequence of examples in the discrimination set should be ordered to provide the learner with more opportunities to practice the newly taught skill than the already mastered examples.
5. The order of examples in the discrimination set should be such that the newly taught skill is presented 1st, 3rd, 6th, 10th, 14th and so on in the teaching sequence. If the student's performance requires, the new skill should be presented more frequently (e.g., on every second or third trial).

6. A model-test-retest correction procedure should be used, but emphasis should be on the delayed retesting of all errors committed during the teaching sequence. The final procedure in the teaching sequence should involve a retest of all errors.

SUMMARY

In this chapter, we specified the details for designing teaching sequences for verbal associations—simple facts, verbal chains, and discriminations. In each case, the five components of the generic instructional set are described and applied to the design of the teaching sequences. Teaching formats for each type of verbal association are detailed. These formats describe the knowledge form, range of examples, sequence of examples, test examples, and practice examples of each verbal association.

APPLICATION ITEMS

1. As a teacher, you've decided to teach students how to use the dictionary. An important component skill is identifying the section of the alphabet in which a word occurs. Design a teaching sequence to teach "chunking" the alphabet into parts (e.g., a–g, h–p, etc.). Specify the teacher wording and the student responses for the teaching sequence. Describe a correction procedure for a typical error in the verbal chain (e.g., The child says, "a, b, c, f, g").

2. Design a teaching sequence to teach a simple fact. First, identify a fact to teach (do not teach a fact for which there is a format in the text). Then describe the examples, teacher wording, and student responses that comprise the teaching sequence. Describe a correction procedure for a typical error.

3. In the teaching sequences below, the students are unable to make the correct discriminations. Explain the design problems with the teaching sequences and describe what you would do to correct each problem. Your analysis and explanation should focus on the selection and sequence of examples.

Color Identification Task

Teacher	Student
(The teacher presents the colors *red, orange, brown*. The colors are on the same size paper. The teacher points to *red*.) "What color is this?"	"Orange."
"No, this color is red." (The teacher then points to the color orange.) "What color is this?"	"Brown."

Numeral Identification Task

Teacher	Student
(The teacher writes the numbers 6, 7, 8, 9 on the board. The teacher points to the 6.) "What number is this?"	"7."
(The teacher points to 8.) "What number?"	"9."

REFERENCE

Engelmann, S., & Carnine, D. W. (1982). *Theory of instruction: Principles and applications.* New York: Irvington.

C H A P T E R

SIX

Designing Instructional Strategies for Teaching Concepts and Rule Relationships

Chapter Objectives

Upon successful completion of this chapter, you will be able to:

1. RECALL the details for designing teaching sequences for concepts and rule relationships.

2. USE the five components of the generic instructional set as the basic framework for designing teaching sequences.

3. PROVIDE detailed examples of teaching sequences for concepts and rule relationships.

4. DESCRIBE the design-of-instruction requirements that are specific to the before, during, and after phases of instruction.

5. EXPAND the generic instructional set to include criteria for selecting nonexamples of concepts and concise teacher wording.

TEACHING CONCEPTS

Basic language concepts are important to facilitating cognitive development and later learning (Gagne, 1985; Tennyson & Christensen, 1986). Stanovich (1986) states that "children with inadequate vocabularies—who read slowly and without enjoyment—read less, and as a result have slower development of vocabulary knowledge, which inhibits growth in reading ability" (p. 381). Children who begin their school experience with deficits in language and general knowledge are likely to fall farther behind in academic development unless this cycle of failure is broken.

Earlier in the text, we defined **concept learning** as the recognition of an object, event, action, or situation as part of a class of objects, events, actions, or situations that are the same, based on a feature or a set of features that are the same. Unlike simple facts, verbal chains, and discriminations, which are limited in scope, concepts are sweeping in range of meaning and in the examples tied to their use. A fact basically has one example—itself (e.g., Millard Fillmore was the 13th President of the United States). If a fact is part of a set of facts or fact family, the family is clearly related in a specific way (e.g., Presidents of the United States). On the other hand, concepts are not one-way mirrors but always involve examples that reflect many meanings and qualities. For example, the concept *dog* can refer to tiny dogs, white dogs, and large dogs, as well as the idiomatic meaning of lowly and contemptible. It can also mean a comparatively long time (e.g., a dog's age), or connote elegance (e.g., to put on the dog). To control the numerous meanings of a concept, the number of examples must be controlled. To expand the meaning of a concept, the examples are likewise expanded.

Expanding the Generic Instructional Set

Adding More Examples

As we have with the teaching of verbal associations, we rely on the generic instructional set as the basic framework to use in designing concept teaching sequences. Because concepts are more complex than verbal associations, we include additional requirements that are important to the design of concept teaching sequences. However, before we discuss these additional requirements, we must pause a moment to realign our thinking. An essential first step to thinking about the teaching of concepts is that they should be thought of as a set of examples. This thinking is important to making the transition from one example (e.g., simple fact), one chain of responses (e.g., verbal chain), or one pair of examples (e.g., discrimination) to a set of examples that must communicate a particular meaning. If a concept has multiple meanings or attributes that convey one meaning (e.g., *dog*), then it is necessary to use more than one set of 8–10 examples (e.g., four to five sets of 8–10 examples) to convey the information to the learner. However, the different sets of examples must be carefully selected, arranged, and scheduled. The procedures for doing this are often complex.

Adding Nonexamples

Another important change to make in our thinking when teaching concepts is related to the examples we use to teach them. When teaching concepts, we rely on concrete examples of the concept, be it an object, event, action, or situation. To teach the concept *getting bigger* (e.g., a balloon getting bigger), we use either a series of pictures of a balloon getting bigger or a balloon being blown up and increasing in size. However, we would also use *nonexamples,* or negative examples of the concept. These nonexamples are actual examples, but rather than communicate to the learner what the concept actually is (e.g., the balloon increasing in size and getting bigger), these nonexamples demonstrate to the learner what the concept *isn't* (e.g., the balloon isn't increasing in size and isn't getting bigger). In Chapter 5, we noted that teaching discriminations requires the inclusion of previously taught letter-sound correspondences (e.g., *t, a, s/S, b, c*) in the discrimination testing sequence, as well as the newly taught skill (e.g., *m/M*). These previously taught skills, for all practical purposes, served as nonexamples of the newly taught letter-sound correspondence, *m/M.* The letter-sound correspondence *t* is a nonexample of the newly taught letter-sound correspondence, *m;* that is, *t* is not *m,* just as an elephant is not a car and is therefore a nonexample of a car. Nonexamples or negative examples are essential to the teaching of most concepts. The clear communication of a concept will often hinge on the teacher's ability to select and sequence appropriate examples and nonexamples.

Controlling Teacher Wording

In addition to expanding the kinds of examples we use in teaching concepts (i.e., introducing sets of examples and the use of nonexamples), we will also take greater care in the actual words we use to talk about these concepts when teaching them. In short, we will control the teacher wording so that the learner doesn't become distracted or confused by what the teacher says. Instead, we want the learner's full attention on the examples we use to teach the concepts. What the teacher says should merely alert the learner to the important features of the concept. The teacher wording should not be used as a substitute for examples designed to teach the concept; that is, the teacher wording shouldn't attempt to explain the concept being taught.

Selecting Materials

The final addition we will make to the generic instructional set has to do with the actual teaching materials that will be used to teach concepts. Because this requires actual concrete examples and nonexamples of the target concept, teachers will need to select materials necessary in developing these concrete examples. We will discuss this particular requirement in detail later in this chapter. In Table 6–1, we review the five generic design requirements, as well as the additional requirements for designing concept teaching sequences.

Why Concrete Examples Instead of Abstract Words?

We noted in Chapter 3 that the process of learning a new concept through the presentation of examples requires the learner to observe and interact with these examples. But what is it that the learner observes and what is the nature of this interaction? Why present concrete examples to teach concepts? Why not use words to describe and teach these concepts? What kind of information do concrete examples provide that can't be readily provided in words?

Teacher wording should focus on examples, not on explaining the concept being taught.

Concepts are peculiar creatures. They are generally experiential and require the learner to draw on specific experiences to appreciate their meaning. Although it is possible to define certain concepts with words, it is often easier, more efficient, and more meaningful to use concrete examples. On occasion, the words we use to describe a particular concept are beyond the vocabulary level and cognitive development of the learner. We could define the concept *up* in the following manner: "When an object is in the upper projectile of another object, it is *up*." Or we could use a simpler definition: "When an object is *up*, it is in or on a higher position or level." In spite of these definitions, a learner who doesn't know this concept and must be taught the concept *up* is not likely to understand the definitions. Similarly, we could define the color *red* by noting that it is a primary color or a spread of colors at the lower end of the visible spectrum, varying in hue from bloodred to pale rose or pink. However, it's unlikely that a naive learner who doesn't know the color *red* will understand this definition. Abstract words are not apt to communicate the necessary information to the learner. Concrete examples are used to allow the learner to observe (e.g., by seeing, feeling, touching, holding, pushing) what can't be cognitively digested and processed by the use of abstract words. However, in cases where learners are sophisticated and the use of verbal explanations is appropriate, we would use definitions and rule relationships as part of the teaching strategy.

TABLE 6–1
Designing concept teaching sequences

Design Features	Requirements
Knowledge form	Concept learning. The recognition of an object, event, action, or situation as part of a class of objects, events, actions, or situations that are the same, based on a feature or set of features that are the same.
Materials	Varied. The materials used depend entirely on the concept taught and the sameness of quality to be communicated by the examples and nonexamples.
Range of examples	The examples will be of two kinds, positive and negative.
Positive examples	Varied. In some cases, a limited number of examples is needed to reveal the quality that is the same in all examples of a particular concept. In other cases, numerous examples are needed to reveal the features that are the same in examples of a concept.
Negative examples	Varied. These examples will be used in a limited fashion to indicate the borderline of a particular concept. Negative examples specify the quality that is *not* the same in the examples.
Sequence of examples	Systematic and controlled. The sequence of examples consists of positive and negative examples arranged in a particular order to reveal the most important quality or qualities of a concept. Sequencing guidelines are prescribed.
Test examples	Systematic and controlled. Test examples will be determined in part by the range of examples in the teaching sequence and will include ones that evaluate the learner's ability to acquire and generalize the specific concept.
Practice examples	Varied. These examples will be in the range of examples presented in the teaching sequence, as well as novel examples that are new to the learner.
Teacher wording	Systematic and controlled. The wording will be concise and will draw attention to the critical qualities of the concept.

Concrete examples serve the same function as words by presenting certain features of the concept to the learner. Each example that the teacher selects and arranges in a particular sequence is designed to communicate information about the concept. A learner presented with the first concrete example of a concept is free to make many observations and associations between the label (i.e., what the teacher says) and the example. For instance, the teacher holds up an object that is made of metal wire, 1 inch long, sturdy yet flexible, and used to hold loose sheets of paper together by pressure. The teacher calls attention to the object (e.g., "Look at this everyone") and says, "This is an *elip*." Following the presentation the teacher asks, "Can anyone tell me what an *elip* is?" To answer the question, the learner must make observations and judgments about the object. The observations involve the learner noting and recording various qualities of each example. In this case, the learner is limited to a visual inspection of the object. The learner is not free to taste, feel, or measure the object in any way but visually and draws inferences about the relationship between the label *elip* and the features observed in the example. Because only one example of *elip* was presented, there is nothing to prevent one learner from thinking that an *elip* is something made of metal, or another learner from thinking that an *elip* is a paper clip, or another learner from inferring that an *elip* is a curved object, and so on. Moreover, each answer is correct, based on the one (and only) example of *elip* presented by the teacher.

This may seem like a haphazard way to communicate information about concepts because the learner is left to extract passively any feature of the teacher's presentation. What if the learner keyed in on the wrong feature—perhaps the very feature the teacher hoped the learner would ignore? For example, if we teach the concept *on* by providing the learner with only one example of a block that is *on* a table, we cannot rule out the possibility that the learner will interpret *on* to mean a block, a table, the position of the block on the table, or the upright orientation of the block. The learner's mistake would be understandable if the teacher presented one and only one example of a concept. However, concepts are taught through a set of examples and not just one example. In fact, Engelmann and Carnine (1982) state: "It is impossible to teach a concept through the presentation of one example" (p. 37). Notice the word "impossible"—not "unlikely" or "improbable." In the example presented, *elip* could refer to any number of features (e.g., made of metal, a paper clip, a curved object). However, if the teacher presented another positive example of *elip*—an example that was different from the first example—then learners would be forced to adjust their answers. Through the careful presentation of positive and negative examples the learner discerns the meaning of the concept being taught.

Using the Generic Instructional Set to Teach Concepts

Understanding the Knowledge Form

Although we have defined concept learning, this definition still fails to represent what a concept looks like. Like the universe of knowledge, concepts can be separated into even smaller concept classes. Our intent is not to specify an airtight taxonomy of concept classes, but to provide teachers with a feel for the different kinds of concepts. Our assumption is similar to the one we made about knowledge forms; that is, by knowing the different classes of concepts, teachers can identify the instructional requirements of concepts. For example, the requirements for teaching *on* are slightly different than those for teaching the concept of *furniture*. However, the teaching of *on* is the same as the teaching of other positional concepts, such as *under, above,* and *below.*

Table 6–2 provides a framework for thinking about different concept classes. We have arranged these classes according to their general everyday use. Naturally, there are many ways to classify concepts. This framework is not absolute but provides teachers with a starting point for thinking about the similarities and differences between concepts.

To learn a concept such as *on, chair,* or *orange,* a student need not observe or experience every example of the concept *on,* or sit on every chair to learn the concept of *chair,* or rub, peel and eat every orange to identify a novel instance of the concept *orange.* Because the teacher cannot show the learner every possible example and nonexample of

TABLE 6–2

Concept classes and examples

Positional Concepts	Color Concepts
on, between, up, under, above, in, to the side, left, right, over, in front of, first, last, middle	red, blue, green, orange, yellow, chartreuse, puce, magenta, pink, red, lavender, black
Polar Concepts	**Action Concepts**
hot/cold, open/close, high/low, clean/dirty, big/little, full/empty, smooth/rough, up/down	run, push, lift, bounce, cut, fight, evade, play, jump, hit
Comparative Concepts	**Superlative Concepts**
wider, faster, brighter, bigger, deeper, heavier, harder, smoother, steeper	widest, fastest, brightest, biggest, deepest, heaviest, hardest, smoothest, steepest

Noun Concepts

General	Specific	Proper
food, fruit, plants, tools, vehicles, toys, people, pets, furniture, clothes, geometric shapes	meat, oranges, pliers, car, boy, chair, table, shirt, pants, circle, square	German shepherd, Albert, Chevrolet, *Newsweek*, Oshkosh B'Gosh, Polo

a concept, the general notion of teaching concepts is that by the teaching of a sufficient range of examples, the learner should be able to identify new examples of a concept. Given this understanding, a similar parallel exists in designing concept teaching sequences. If we are able to design a teaching sequence for a positional concept such as *between,* then we should be able to design teaching sequences for all positional concepts. We follow the same design and delivery requirements for teaching all positional concepts as we did for teaching *between.* We teach *up, on, over* and so forth, in the same way we teach *between.* Of course, we change the teacher wording and the materials, but we follow the same guidelines for selecting and sequencing the positive and negative examples in the demonstration, test, and practice portions of the teaching sequence. Therefore, by knowing that a concept is a positional concept, the teacher is alerted to the same design and delivery requirements for those concepts.

The general format we will use to teach all of the concept classes described in Table 6–2, with the exception of the noun concepts, is a variation of the model-lead-check/test format. This format involves the teacher presenting a range of positive examples of a concept, followed by negative examples and a testing sequence. The format can be altered so that negative examples of a concept are presented first, followed by positive examples, and ending with a testing sequence. To teach concepts of general and specific names, what Engelmann and Carnine (1982) refer to as "noun concepts," the format involves presenting a range of positive examples of the concept, followed by immediately testing the learner's ability to discriminate the newly taught concept from similar (or dissimilar) concepts the learner has mastered. The details for designing these teaching sequences are given later in the chapter.

Specifying the Instructional Objectives

The teaching of concepts revolves around the use of concrete examples and careful preparation, selection and sequencing of them. It is not surprising that most of the work in designing concept teaching sequences comes in the before instruction phase of teaching. In this phase, the teacher develops a new teaching sequence or modifies an existing sequence found in a basal reading or language program. To begin this endeavor, the teacher first decides on the instructional objective to be accomplished. In teaching concepts, the teacher decides on the meaning to be communicated in a teaching sequence. For example, if it is determined that a learner does not know the concept *on*, the teacher decides on the exact meaning of *on* that the learner doesn't know and the meaning that must then be taught through examples. For example:

1. In a position above, but in contact with, as the surface or upper part of a thing; placed or lying in contact with; as my book is *on* the table.
2. Toward and to; in the direction of; as the rain falls *on* the earth.
3. In contact with, as by touching or striking; as, to play *on* a harp, a violin, or a drum.
4. In addition to; besides; as heaps *on* heaps; loss *on* loss.
5. At or near; indicating situation, place or position; as a ship is *on* the coast.
6. With the relation of reliance or dependence; as to depend *on* a person for help; to rely *on*.

These six meanings are not exhaustive and represent about 20% of the meanings of *on*. Numerous definitions may overwhelm the teacher, who feels compelled to teach all of them all at once! But the strategy we recommend for teaching concepts is to teach one meaning at a time, especially when teaching low-performing students. In this way, we can be satisfied that the learner knows *one* meaning of the concept. However, we don't stop with one teaching sequence and communication of only one meaning, but we design teaching sequences to teach other meanings of *on*. By attempting to teach two or more meanings of a concept in one teaching sequence, we run the risk of the learner not acquiring even one meaning of the concept. Furthermore, we run the greater risk of the learner becoming confused by the various meanings communicated at the same time. It is not surprising to see students with chronic conceptual confusions about certain concepts (e.g., *more* and *less*; *greater than* and *less than*) because the concepts were taught at the same time. We can fall into the trap of thinking that because concepts are similar (e.g., *up/down; left/right; hot/cold; big/small*), they are more easily learned by being taught at the same time in the same teaching sequence. By learning one concept, some assume, it is easier to learn another similar or even opposite concept. This is faulty thinking because it fails to consider how concepts are learned, especially when they are taught through concrete examples. We note that most models of concept teaching state the need to teach one concept at a time (Clark, 1971; Engelmann & Carnine, 1982; Jitendra & Kameenui, 1988).

Once the teacher has decided on the meaning of the concept to be communicated in the teaching sequence, then the teacher can develop the materials that will be used in teaching the concept.

Developing and Selecting the Materials

As noted earlier, materials we select in designing the teaching sequence depend entirely on the meaning of the concept we want to convey. For example, to convey the concept *on* meaning "in contact with, as in the surface or upper part of a thing; placed or lying in contact with; as my book is *on* the table," the teacher is required to select materials that show something in contact with a surface. The teacher can use a table as the surface and a block as the object to demonstrate the contact. By placing the block on the table, the teacher demonstrates a positive example of the concept *on.* By holding the block above the table surface without any contact between the table and block, the teacher demonstrates a nonexample or negative example of the concept *on* (i.e., not on). Naturally, when teaching another meaning of *on* (e.g., meaning "in contact with") we would use a different set of physical materials (e.g., an object like a picture placed in various positions on the wall). Similarly, if we were to teach the concept *farther apart,* we would use a different set of materials (e.g., the teacher positions two hands to indicate the distances.)

Once the physical materials have been selected for the teaching sequence, they must be used for the entire concept teaching sequence. In teaching the concept *on* using a table and a block, we would use the same table and block to demonstrate all 8–12 examples of the concept *on* in the teaching sequence. We would *not* change these materials in the beginning or middle of the teaching sequence. If we wanted to teach another, or even the same meaning of the concept *on,* we would use another set of materials to design another teaching sequence.

In Table 6–3, we specify the materials and teacher wording that can be used in developing concept teaching sequences for a range of different concepts.

We don't have clear-cut and detailed criteria to assist teachers in selecting materials to develop a concept teaching sequence. Most of this knowledge is based on common sense and trial and error. The materials selected will be determined in part by the concept to be taught, the developmental level of the learner, the practical considerations of obtaining the materials in a classroom and school setting, and the information the teacher gains from simply trying out different materials. Here are some general guidelines to follow in developing materials to use in designing concept teaching sequences:

1. Select materials readily available in the classroom setting, if possible.
2. Select materials the learner is already familiar with. If a table and block are used to teach the concept *on,* the learner must know the names and functions of the materials, or they shouldn't be used.
3. Use the same materials to teach an entire sequence and do not change the materials during the teaching sequence.
4. Use the same materials to demonstrate both positive and negative examples. We could use a table and block to demonstrate both positive and negative examples of the concept *on.* However, if we teach the concept *chair* by using pictures of different kinds of chairs, we couldn't use a picture of a chair as a negative example of the concept *chair.* In this case, we would use examples of concepts the learner already knew (e.g., *couch, bench, dog, car*), much as we did in the discrimination testing sequences.
5. Do not require the learner to be part of the actual demonstration of the concept. In teaching the concept *under,* the teacher could require the learner to sit under a desk

TABLE 6–3
Teaching various concepts

Concept	Possible Materials, Actions	Teacher Wording
under He hid *under* the bed.	A block and a table: The teacher holds the block under the table in a number of different positions. A book and a chair: The teacher holds the book under the chair in a number of different positions.	Positive example: "The block is *under* the table." Negative example: "The block is *not under* the table."
getting farther apart The boys are getting *farther apart*.	Teacher's hands: With hands held out in front, the teacher moves them apart at varying distances. Two blocks of the same color and a table: The teacher places the blocks on the table and moves them away or toward each other at varying distances.	Positive example: "My hands are *getting farther apart*." Negative example: "My hands are *not getting farther apart*."
between The pencil is *between* the two books.	Two books of the same size and color and a cup: The books are flat on a table and placed about a foot apart. The teacher places the cup between the books in various positions. Teacher and two chairs: The two chairs are placed side by side and several feet apart. The teacher stands in the middle at various positions to indicate being between the chairs.	Positive example: "The cup is *between* the books." Negative example: "The cup is *not between* the books."

to experience the concept of *under*. However, by doing so, the teacher is not able to determine what the learner sitting under the desk is really attending to. The learner is required to observe a series of examples to extract the critical quality, and it would be difficult to assess if the learner is observing that specific quality.

6. Select materials that will allow the teacher to demonstrate the full range and scope of the meaning to be communicated in that particular teaching sequence. A paper clip and a cup could be used to teach the concept *under;* the teacher would place the paper clip in various positions under the cup, which is being held up. However, these materials restrict the meaning of under, and the examples of *under* may not be discernible to the learner.

7. Use materials that are greatly different in designing the second teaching sequence, the third teaching sequence, and so on.

TABLE 6–3
continued

Concept	Possible Materials, Actions	Teacher Wording
all Jack has *all* the marbles.	10 pencils of same size and color and a shoe box: The teacher places or removes pencils from the shoe box. Paper clip and a medium-size bowl: The teacher places or removes the paper clips from the bowl.	Positive example: "*All* the pencils are in the box." Negative example: "*Not all* the pencils are in the box."
some Jack has *some* of the marbles.	Use same materials as for teaching the concept *all*.	Positive example: "*Some* of the pencils are in the box." Negative example: "*Some* of the pencils are *not* in the box."
none Jack has *none* of the marbles.	Use same materials as for teaching the concept *all*.	Positive example: "*None* of the paper clips are in the bowl." Negative example: "*Some* (or *all*) of the paper clips are in the bowl."
(Concepts *all* and *some* should be taught and mastered before the teaching of *none*.)		
in front of Mark stood *in front of* the blackboard.	Teacher and desk: The teacher stands directly in front of the desk but in various positions. Block and two stacks of books: The teacher places the block in front of the stacks of books.	Positive example: "I am standing *in front of* the desk." "The block is *in front of* the books." Negative example: "The block is *not in front of* the books."

Materials and a Necessary Limitation

At this point, it's important to note a limitation to the selection and development of the materials for teaching concepts. If we examine some of the materials we described earlier for teaching concepts, such as a table and a block for teaching the concept *on*, we will note an inevitable limitation. If we use just a table and block to teach *on*, we run the risk that the learner will think that *on* has only to do with a table and a block. If the learner was presented with someone placing a ball on a chair and asked, "Is the ball *on* the chair?" we shouldn't be surprised by the learner's incorrect response or nonresponse. After all, the learner has been systematically "taught" that the concept *on* involves a table and block only. We have created what Engelmann and Carnine (1982) refer to as "stipulation." Others refer to this as "underextension" (Miller & Gildea, 1987). In a sense, we have intentionally restricted the learner's knowledge of the concept *on*. We have created a teaching condition that artificially allows the learner to gain a very limited understanding of a concept. However, this stipulation is a necessary evil and has both an advantage and a disadvantage. The advantage is that the learner will acquire a clear and unambiguous understanding of that one meaning communicated in that one teaching sequence. The disadvantage is that it is only one meaning, communicated under one set of limited instructional conditions.

Too often basal language programs attempt to teach too much (i.e., too many different meanings using different materials) too fast (Jitendra & Kameenui, 1988). This strategy runs the risk of not teaching any meaning correctly the first time around. Stipulation cannot be avoided. All new knowledge when initially taught and acquired is stipulated; that is, we learn to apply new information in a limited way. However, as more information is obtained, old and new knowledge expand and embellish one another. Although stipulation of new learning cannot be avoided, it can be corrected and expanded. The primary mechanism for this expansion is the teaching of the same concept with new materials, as described in item 7 of the list on p. 156. By teaching the same concept with different materials (e.g., teaching *on* using a basketball and a chair) in a new teaching sequence, we communicate to the learner that the materials are not the important feature of the concept *on*. Eventually, after three or four teaching sequences using different materials to teach the same concept, the learner sees the "sameness of quality" across all the teaching sequences; that is, the learner sees that *"on*-ness" has to do with an object in contact with a surface.

Specifying a Range of Positive Examples

Once the materials have been selected, they will be used to present the actual examples. Through these examples, the teacher will communicate to the learner the features, qualities, and essential characteristics that are representative of a particular concept. The meaning of a concept cannot be conveyed with just positive or negative examples, and both must be included in a teaching sequence as essential to communicating the concept unambiguously. Because both kinds of examples are essential, we should understand the role that each plays in a teaching sequence. Positive examples, like negative examples, have a specific, if not prescriptive, role to play in a teaching sequence.

We will use positive examples in a teaching sequence to communicate the essential quality of the concept. However, that quality varies from concept to concept, and in some that quality is narrow, while in others it is broad. The concept *vertical* (meaning a position perpendicular to the plane of the horizon; upright) has a quality (i.e., being upright) that is narrow. In contrast, the concept *on* (meaning in contact with a surface) has a quality (i.e., a book *on* the table) that is broad. If we use a pencil to demonstrate *vertical*, the pencil could be placed in only two different positions: (1) upright with the eraser facing up, or (2) upright with the eraser facing down. Of course, the teacher labels both these positive examples in the following manner, "The pencil is *vertical*." On the other hand, we could place a block in many different positions on a table to demonstrate the concept *on*. To determine the range of positive examples of the concept, the teacher must experiment with the materials selected to teach the concept.

In Table 6–4, we specify whether the selected concepts are likely to require a wide or narrow range of positive examples.

Once the range of a concept is established, the teacher can attend to the mechanics of how each positive example of the concept will be presented to the learner within the context of the materials selected for the teaching presentation. Specifically, the teacher must attend to the details of how and when each positive example will be physically presented in the teaching sequence. In teaching the concept *on* with a block on a table, the teacher must decide where to actually place the block on the table.

An important requirement when presenting these positive examples is that the teacher must demonstrate the full range of the concept. In teaching *on*, the teacher must place the block in various positions on the table (e.g., on the left edge of the table, the middle of the table, the right edge of the table, the back of the table). By presenting these positive examples at various places on the table, the teacher communicates to the learner that the quality of "*on*-ness" is not restricted to one spot on the table. In fact, it is important for the teacher to present positive examples that are very different from one another within the limits of the materials used to teach the concept (i.e., the table and block). An example of this is depicted in Figure 6–1, in which the block is placed on the back, right part of the table and close to the front, left edge of the table.

In summary, when selecting and presenting positive examples, the teacher must decide ahead of time how each will be presented and must present a full range of positive examples.

TABLE 6–4
Types of concepts

Wide-Range Concepts	Narrow-Range Concepts
Positional Concepts	
under, on, over, above, below, side, in front of, between	first, last, middle, end
Color Concepts	
red, blue, green, orange, yellow	cyan, chartreuse, puce, magenta
Polar Concepts	
hot/cold, open/close, up/down, high/low, clean/dirty, big/little, smooth/rough	empty close
Noun Concepts	
furniture, pets, dogs, cats, appliances, food, people, plants, tools, vehicles, toys	(none)
Comparative Concepts	
wider, faster, brighter, bigger, deeper, heavier, harder, smoother	(none)
Superlative Concepts	
(none)	widest, fastest, brightest, biggest, deepest, heaviest, hardest, smoothest

FIGURE 6–1
Greatly different positive examples of
the concept "On"

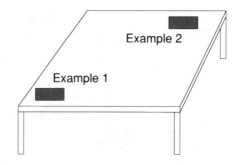

Example 2

Example 1

Selecting and Presenting Negative Examples

Negative examples are also designed to play a role in a teaching sequence. Positive examples are used to reveal the full range of a concept's particular meaning, but negative examples are designed to demonstrate when that range of meaning ends and no longer applies. By specifying the boundary of a positive example, the negative example also makes clear what the essential quality of a concept is. Negative examples, when placed in a sequence with positive examples, provide the learner with instant information about the critical quality of the concept being taught, but they must be carefully placed in relation to the positive examples.

Minimally Different Pairs of Examples

Not all negative and positive examples are the same. Some important negative and positive examples of a teaching sequence are those Engelmann and Carnine (1982) refer to as "minimally different" examples and Markle (1975) calls "close in" examples. These negative and positive examples differ *only slightly* from each other in the same teaching sequence. These minimally different examples are considered the most effective examples in concept attainment (Carnine, 1980; Engelmann & Carnine, 1982; Gagne, 1985; Klausmeier, 1976; Klausmeier, Ghatala, & Frayer, 1974; Markle & Tiemann, 1969; Merrill & Tennyson, 1977; Williams & Carnine, 1981). In teaching the concept *on* by using a block and table, a minimally different pair of examples of *on* would have the block *on* the table, followed immediately by a negative example that was slightly above the table. Of course, the teacher would label this example as *not on*. A minimally different pair of examples of *on* is presented in Figure 6–2.

Minimally different examples of *on* are labeled as such because only one feature changes (and only slightly) between a positive example and a negative example. In teaching *on*, the change is a matter of simply lifting the block slightly off the table. The orientation of the block is not changed at all. In fact, everything remains the same except for the slight change of off the table. The learner must only attend to this slight change to see the essential difference between *on* and *not on*. In a sense, we have made the learning of a concept rather easy for the learner. We have kept the materials the same from example to example. Although positive examples change, the label remains the same ("The block is *on* the table"), which allows the learner to focus on the actual physical changes in the examples without having to attend seriously to the label. Finally, when a negative example is presented, the learner must only key in on the slight physical

FIGURE 6–2
Minimally different examples of the
concept "On"

Positive Example of "On"

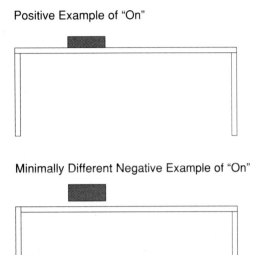

Minimally Different Negative Example of "On"

change in the presentation. The slight change is also immediately associated with the slight change in the teacher wording (e.g., "The block is *not on* the table").

To appreciate the power and importance of minimally different examples, we need only examine these positive and negative examples for teaching the nonsense concept of *plip* in Figure 6–3.

In this example, the learner must extract numerous differences from the presentation. *Plip* could mean (1) something on the bottom line, (2) an oval shape, (3) an oval speckled shape, (4) a horizontal shape, (5) a nonrectangular shaped object, (6) a smaller object, (7) an object that's closer to the ground. Compare the previous examples with the minimally different examples in Figure 6–4.

The negative example of *plip* is only different from the positive example in one slight but discernible way—it is not in contact with the bottom line. This minimally different negative example communicates to the learner the critical feature of "*plip*ness." Later in this chapter, we will detail how minimally different negative examples should be placed within a teaching sequence.

In addition to minimally different negative examples, other negative examples are used in concept teaching sequences. These are determined by the concepts themselves, as well as the concept knowledge the learner brings to the instructional session. For

FIGURE 6–3
Positive and negative examples of *plip*

This is *plip*.

This is not *plip*.

FIGURE 6–4

Minimally different examples of *plip*

example, when teaching noun concepts (e.g., *dogs, tools, appliances, furniture*), the negative examples are determined by what the learner knows. In fact, these are the same as the discrimination examples described in Chapter 5 on designing a discrimination testing sequence. These discrimination or negative examples are selected from what the learner knows. While teaching the concept *scissors,* we select concepts the learner knows as negative examples. Further, we select examples that are most similar to *scissors* in name (i.e., a concept that sounded like *scissors*) and feature (i.e., a concept that looked like a pair of *scissors*), such as the concept *pliers* (Engelmann & Carnine, 1982). However, we would use *pliers* only if the learner knew that concept and was firm in that knowledge. The more the learner knows, the more we can rely on the learner's knowledge to select negative examples for the concept teaching sequence.

Noun concepts such as *chair, car, vehicle, furniture,* and *shoe* present the teacher with a different instructional dilemma than positional concepts (e.g., *under, between, on*), comparative concepts (e.g., *wider, smaller, harder*), action concepts (e.g., *running, pushing, jumping*), and polar concepts (e.g., *hot/cold*). A noun concept is in contrast to a positional concept like *on* that has one quality that can be represented through minimally different positive and negative examples (e.g., contact with a surface vs. no contact with the same surface—see Figure 6–2). Concepts such as *shoe* have numerous qualities that in combination give the concept its meaning. Given these numerous qualities, it would be difficult to represent these qualities clearly with minimally different positive and negative examples. For instance, it would be difficult to identify or isolate just one feature that makes a shoe a shoe. If we removed the laces to the shoe, would it still be a shoe? If we cut the toe off the shoe, would it still be a shoe? If we removed the heel from the shoe, would it still be a shoe? One need only look at the variety of shoes in a store to appreciate the difficulty in pinpointing one feature that makes a shoe a shoe. We could run through the same questions with another concept like *chair* (e.g., if we broke a leg off of a chair, would it still be a chair?). Teaching sequence examples for noun concepts will be presented later.

Selecting and Presenting Testing Examples

We will use acquisition, discrimination, and generalization test examples in concept teaching sequences. As with other teaching sequences, the test examples will depend on the concept, the learner, and the instructional objective. Our primary concern following the demonstration of a concept is acquisition: Did the learner acquire the concept as presented through the positive and negative examples in the sequence? For most of the concepts, with the exception of noun concepts, we can answer this question by using the same examples we used to model the concept. For example, after presenting positive and negative examples of the concept *steeper* (e.g., "Watch the board. I'll tell you if it gets steeper. The board is *steeper.* The board is *not steeper.*"), using a 4-foot board held at different grades of steepness, we would use the same materials as test examples. The only change is in the teacher wording and sequencing of examples. The teacher presents positive and negative examples of the concept and asks the learner to indicate the appropriate label (e.g., "Yes, the board is *steeper*."). The teacher might ask, "Is the board getting *steeper*?" This choice response question requires the learner to give a "yes" or "no" response. Instead of requiring the learner merely to answer yes or no, the teacher might ask the learner to give a labeling response and name the concept. The teacher states, "I want you to watch the board. If it gets steeper, say it's steeper. If it's not steeper, say it's not steeper." The learner responds, "It's steeper" to positive test examples and "It's not steeper" to negative test examples. This response form is more demanding than the yes-no choice response form, because it requires the naive learner to remember and produce the concept labels (i.e., *steeper* and *not steeper*).

In addition to changing the teacher wording, we also vary the sequence of positive and negative test examples. We use a simple response form for labeling most concepts (e.g., *up/not up; steeper/not steeper, on/not on*) that involves only a two-choice response, which makes the testing sequence predictable. We could even sequence positive and negative examples one after another (e.g., positive/negative/positive/negative) so that the learner has no need to attend to the actual examples. The learner need only know the pattern to predict the next response, without even looking at the example. The final example of the following sequence can be predicted from the pattern of test examples:

Teacher and Test Examples	Student Response
"Tell me, is the block *on* the table?"	"Yes."
"Is the block *on* the table?"	"No."
"Is the block *on* the table?"	"Yes."
"Is the block *on* the table?"	"No."
"Is the block *on* the table?"	_____?

The final student response is "Yes," easily predicted given the previous sequence of four test examples. To counter this problem, the test examples must be sequenced in an unpredictable manner. Instead of a predictable sequence of P-N-P-N-P-N (P = positive example; N = negative example) test examples, a design with an unpredictable sequence, P-P-N-P-N-N, is preferred. When the test examples are in an unpredictable order, the learner is forced to attend to the features of the examples.

The testing of noun concepts will have an entirely different arrangement. In fact, we will use a discrimination testing sequence, as we used with verbal associations. This testing sequence involves the selection of previously mastered concepts. Following the presentation of only positive examples of the concept (e.g., a range of positive examples of the concept *chair*), we first assess the learner's ability to produce verbally the concept label (*chair*) and then present examples of familiar concepts juxtaposed with the newly taught concept. With the presentation of each example, the learner is required to name the actual examples (e.g., "That's a chair... bowl... table... chair"). The testing sequence involves more than a two-choice response (e.g., *on/not on*), and we need not be concerned with the predictability of the examples, as we were with the previous concept testing sequences. In this case, the learner will name each example instead of simply choosing between two responses.

To test the generalization of a noun concept, we would include an example of the target concept that was not presented previously in the teaching sequence. If we were teaching the concept *dog* using pictures of various kinds of small and medium-size dogs, we would also use a picture of a large dog that was not presented in the teaching sequence. This test example would be included with the other examples in the same testing sequence.

To assess generalization of other concepts (e.g., positional, color, action, polar, comparative, superlative concepts), we develop a teaching sequence using a new set of materials. If a board was used to teach *steeper* in the first teaching sequence, the teacher now places a hand in a slanted position to assess the learner's ability to generalize the new concept. By using a new set of materials to assess generalization, the teacher gains an indication of the learner's ability to discern the critical feature or features of a concept.

Designing and Scheduling Practice Sessions

The practice sessions for concepts will be significantly different than those designed for facts and verbal chains in which we were concerned primarily with retention of information. The primary concern when providing practice on concepts is with the expansion and generalization of the new concept to different and new situations. This typically involves demonstrating the concept with a different set of materials than those of the initial teaching sequence. Each successive demonstration of a concept with a new set of materials provides the learner a broader and deeper understanding. For example, if the learner was taught the concept *all* using pencils in a cup, the learner could be asked to demonstrate *all* by actually placing *all* (or *not all*) the pencils in the cup. In this case, the learner instead of the teacher would manipulate the pencils. A second teaching sequence could be developed using paper clips and a small container. The concept *all* is demonstrated by placing *all* the paper clips in the container. A few examples of the concept could be modeled for the learner, after which the learner again demonstrates the concept by placing the paper clips into (and taking them out of) the container. Following the two teaching sequences, the teacher might design a paper and pencil worksheet that requires the learner to discriminate *all* from instances of *not all* (e.g., *some, none, few*) using pictures of objects.

Instructional Format for Teaching Concepts

In the next section, we describe details for teaching concepts. Like previous instructional formats for teaching verbal associations, we will rely on the general model-lead-check/test format. In teaching concepts, however, we omit the "lead" part of that format, but the teacher will still model the concept through the presentation of positive and negative examples. The teacher will evaluate the learner's knowledge by using a testing sequence and will provide practice on the newly taught concept.

TASK 6–1
Concepts: Teaching the Comparative Concept farther apart

BEFORE INSTRUCTION

Task Status: New.

Preskills

1. Knowledge of body parts, especially recognition of hands.
2. Ability to follow directions.

Materials: Teacher uses hands to demonstrate the concept.

Teacher Wording

Positive examples: "My hands are farther apart."
Negative examples: "My hands are not farther apart."

Instructional Design Guidelines

1. All positive and negative examples of the concept are presented by the teacher moving hands either closer to or farther away from each other. Although the distance between the teacher's hands will change, the position and orientation of the teacher's hands will not change.
2. All examples are presented successively within one teaching presentation of 2 or 3 minutes.
3. Students are situated with an unobstructed view of the teacher.
4. The specific example-by-example sequence of positive and negative examples is prescribed, and the teacher must follow that sequence.

Expanded Set

Require individual students to demonstrate the concept by using their own hands. ("Tom, hold up your hands. I want you to show me *farther apart.* Get your hands ready. Now show me your hands getting farther apart. Show me your hands not getting farther apart.")

Generalization Set

Use two blocks of the same size and color and require students to demonstrate the concept *farther apart.*

TASK 6–2

DURING INSTRUCTION

Instructional Delivery Guidelines

1. Frame task carefully, because it is new. The framing is brief and extensive verbalizations are avoided.
2. Be certain all students are attending (eyes on teacher, hands and feet quiet) before beginning instruction.

3. Errors are corrected immediately. Upon detecting an error, the teacher repeats the test example. If the error persists, the teacher returns to the beginning of the teaching sequence to reteach the concept.
4. The pacing of the lesson is not too brisk. The presentation of each example is approximately 3–4 seconds, with a pause after each example.
5. The teacher monitors student on-task behavior during the lesson by watching students' eyes and oral responding.

TASK 6–3
Teaching Procedure for farther apart

Framing

TEACHER: (Holds hands in front in a vertical position so that they are 12 inches apart and the fingertips are perpendicular to the ceiling. The hands are held at the same vertical orientation and height throughout the teaching sequence.) "Watch my hands. I will tell you if they get farther apart. What are you going to watch?"
STUDENTS: "Your hands."
TEACHER: "What will I show you with my hands?"
STUDENTS: "If they get farther apart."
TEACHER: (Starting point: Holds hands 12 inches apart.)

Modeled Examples: Three Positive Examples to Demonstrate Range

TEACHER: (Example 1: Holds hands 16 inches apart from each other at the same vertical orientation and height.) "My hands are farther apart."
STUDENTS: (Observe teacher's actions.)
TEACHER: (Example 2: Holds hands 28 inches apart.) "My hands are farther apart."
TEACHER: (Example 3: Holds hands 36 inches apart.) "My hands are farther apart."

Minimally Different Example
TEACHER: (Example 4: Holds hands 34 inches apart.) "My hands are not farther apart."

Negative Example
TEACHER: (Example 5: Holds hands 28 inches apart.) "My hands are not farther apart. (Pause.) Now watch my hands and tell me if they get farther apart."

Testing Examples and Sequence

Minimally Different Example
TEACHER: (Example 6: Holds hands 30 inches apart.) "Tell me, did my hands get farther apart?"
STUDENTS: "Yes."
TEACHER: (Example 7: Holds hands 36 inches apart.) "Did my hands get farther apart?"
STUDENTS: "Yes."
TEACHER: (Example 8: Holds hands 12 inches apart.) "Did my hands get farther apart?"
STUDENTS: "No."

TEACHER: (Example 9: Holds hands 18 inches apart.) "Did my hands get farther apart?"
STUDENTS: "Yes."
TEACHER: (Example 10: Holds hands 24 inches apart.) "Did my hands get farther apart?"
STUDENTS: "Yes."
TEACHER: (Example 11: Holds hands 38 inches apart.) "Did my hands get farther apart?"
STUDENTS: "Yes."
TEACHER: (Example 12: Holds hands 10 inches apart.) "Did my hands get farther apart?"
STUDENTS: "No."

Correction Procedure

If the student responds incorrectly, the teacher first repeats the test example and question. If the error persists, the teacher returns to the starting point of the teaching sequence and presents the teaching sequence again (examples 1–5). Then the teacher tests the learner again, beginning with example 6.

TASK 6–4

AFTER INSTRUCTION

Analyze Errors and Make Instructional Decisions

The following instructional dimensions should be considered after the teaching sequence is completed:

1. The students may face the difficulty, on the above task, of seeing the difference between examples 4 and 5 when a positive example is followed by a minimally different negative example. The same transition to a minimally different positive example is shown in examples 5 and 6 in the testing sequence. The teacher must watch these points in the teaching sequence carefully, because the minimally different negative examples provide the learner with the critical information about the concept.
2. The teacher may consider modeling more than five examples in the next teaching sequence of *farther apart*. The teacher could model six to eight examples to provide the learner more information about the concept before the testing sequence.
3. The teacher prepares materials for the expanded and generalization sets.

Several instructional features of the teaching sequence require some explanation. First, the concept *farther apart* is a comparative concept, with examples of comparisons. Something is not "farther apart" by itself, for it is only farther apart in comparison to a previous example. Because of this requirement, comparative concepts must begin with a starting point that serves as a reference point for the first example. This should be in the midpoint range of the concept (e.g., teacher has hands 12 inches apart) and not at the extreme ends of the range of the concept (e.g., hands 1/2 inch apart or 50 inches apart). If the starting point is at the extreme ends, the teacher will have a difficult time showing the full range of examples. All comparative concepts (e.g., *higher, bigger, brighter*) will require the use of a starting point prior to modeling the first example.

Following the framing and starting point, the teacher presents three positive examples. These are designed to show the learner the range of *farther apart* within the context of the materials used (i.e., the teacher's hands). In this case, farther apart is represented by the teacher's hands moving from 12 inches to 36 inches apart. After the third example, the teacher presents a minimally different negative example that is only slightly different from the previous positive example. The teacher's hands move from 36 inches apart to 34 inches, a small but discernible 2-inch movement of the hands together. From the learner's perspective, everything remains the same, with the exception of the change in label (i.e., "My hands did not get farther apart") that is associated with the small change in the direction in which the teacher's hands move.

The minimally different negative example (example 4) is then followed by a negative example (example 5) that demonstrates "not getting farther apart." Once this has been modeled, the teacher prepares for the testing example sequence that begins with the next example (example 6). However, the first example of the testing sequence, example 6, is another minimally different example which is also accompanied by a change in teacher wording. For the entire testing sequence (examples 6–12), the student is required to respond with yes or no (e.g., "Did my hands get farther apart?"). The testing examples are also sequenced in an unpredictable order (i.e., P-P-N-P-P-P-N).

The teaching sequence for *farther apart* represents all of the necessary requirements needed to design a teaching sequence for other comparative concepts (e.g., *bigger, deeper, faster, wider, longer, harder*). In other words, we could follow the same basic structure of the *farther apart* teaching sequence to design other sequences for teaching comparative concepts. This basic structure is shown in Table 6–5.

TABLE 6–5
Basic structure for designing teaching sequences for comparative concepts

Kinds of Examples	Teacher Actions	Student Response
Starting point: This example is not a positive or negative example.		
Positive (range)	Models	Attends
Positive (range)	Models	Attends
Positive (range)	Models	Attends
Negative (minimal difference)	Models	Attends
Negative	Models	Attends
Positive (minimal difference)	Models	Attends
Positive	Tests learner	Responds orally
Negative	Tests learner	Responds orally
Positive	Tests learner	Responds orally
Positive	Tests learner	Responds orally
Positive	Tests learner	Responds orally
Negative	Tests learner	Responds orally

The basic rules for constructing teaching sequences for comparative concepts are these:

1. Begin with a starting point that serves as a reference for the first example. This is neither a positive nor a negative example and about a quarter of the way or halfway through the concept range.
2. Examples 1, 2, and 3 should be positives that differ from one another. The change between the starting point and example 1 should be a small change. The change from example 1 to 2 should be a large change, and the change from example 2 to 3 should be a medium physical change.
3. Example 4 should be a negative example that is minimally different from positive example 3.
4. Example 6 should be a positive example that is minimally different from negative example 5. Testing should begin with example 6.
5. Examples 6–12 should be a series of test examples that show no predictable order. These test examples should show some large physical differences and some small differences. The test examples should also assess the range of the concept.
6. Students' responses will always involve a binary response: "yes–no" or "farther apart–not farther apart" to the question, "Did my hands get farther apart?"

TASK 6–5
Concepts: Teaching the Positional Concept "On"

BEFORE INSTRUCTION

Task Status: New.

Preskills

1. Object knowledge of table and block.
2. Ability to follow directions.

Materials: The teacher uses a table and block to demonstrate the concept.

Teacher Wording

Positive example: "The block is on the table."
Negative example: "The block is not on the table."

Instructional Design Guidelines

1. All positive and negative examples of the concept are presented by the teacher placing a block in different positions on the table, but the orientation of the block will be the same.
2. See instructional design guidelines 2–4 of *farther apart* teaching sequence (p. 165).

Expanded Set

Require individual students to demonstrate the concept by placing the block either "on" or "not on" the table (e.g., "Take the block and show me *on*. Ready? Show me the block on the table. . . . Now show me the block not on the table").

Generalization Set

Use a pencil and a book. Require the learner to place the pencil on (or not on) the book to demonstrate the concept *on*.

TASK 6–6

DURING INSTRUCTION

Instructional Delivery Guidelines

These guidelines are the same as those specified for the concept teaching sequence on *farther apart*.

TASK 6–7
Teaching Procedure for "On"

TEACHER: (Stands at the back of the table and holds the block in hand 16–20 inches above the table. The block is held in a horizontal position for all examples. The orientation of the block is not changed at all.)

Figure 6–5 represents the side view of a table, and the numbers 1–12 represent the 12 examples consecutively presented in this teaching sequence. The plus (+) or minus (−) signs given in parentheses indicate whether the example (block) is a positive or negative example of the concept *on*.

Framing

TEACHER: "Everybody, I want you to watch the block. I'm going to show you the block *on* the table."
"Jim, what are you going to watch?"
JIM: "The block."
TEACHER: "Are you going to watch my eyes, Beatrice?"
BEATRICE: "No."
TEACHER: "What are you going to watch?"
BEATRICE: "The block."
TEACHER: "And what am I going to show you with the block, Leslie?"
LESLIE: "The block on the table."

FIGURE 6–5
Side view of table

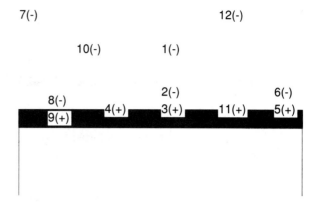

Modeled Examples: (two negative examples)

TEACHER: (Example 1: see Figure 6–5.) "The block is *not on* the table."
STUDENTS: (Observe teacher's actions.)
TEACHER: (Example 2.) "The block is *not on* the table."

Minimally Different Positive Example Followed by Two Positive Examples to Demonstrate the Range of the Concept

TEACHER: (Example 3.) "The block is *on* the table."
TEACHER: (Example 4.) "The block is *on* the table."
TEACHER: (Example 5.) "The block is *on* the table. (Pause.) Now I want you to get ready and tell me if the block is on the table."

Testing Examples and Sequence

Minimally Different Negative Example
TEACHER: (Example 6.) "Tell me what happened. Is the block *on* or *not on* the table?"
STUDENTS: "The block is not on the table."
TEACHER: (Example 7.) "Tell me what happened."
STUDENTS: "The block is not on the table."
TEACHER: (Example 8.) "What happened?"
STUDENTS: "The block is not on the table."
TEACHER: (Example 9.) "What happened?"
STUDENTS: "The block is on the table."
TEACHER: (Example 10.) "What happened?"
STUDENTS: "The block is not on the table."
TEACHER: (Example 11.) "What happened?"
STUDENT: "The block is on the table."
TEACHER: (Example 12.) "What happened?"
STUDENT: "The block is not on the table."

Correction Procedure

Follow the same correction procedure as described earlier for the concept teaching sequence of *farther apart*.

TASK 6–8

AFTER INSTRUCTION

Analyze Errors and Make Instructional Decisions

The considerations we raised for the *farther apart* teaching sequence apply here also.

The teaching sequence for *on*, unlike that for *farther apart*, begins with two negative examples instead of three positive ones. We could have easily begun teaching *on* by presenting three positive examples, and there's no reason not to do so. No particular advantage is found in presenting positive examples first, and we might have started the *farther apart* teaching sequence with two negative examples. However, if positive examples are used first, the teacher must present at least three of them to demonstrate the range of the concept.

The second and third examples of *on* are designed to show the minimal difference between *on* and *not on*. In this case, we moved from a negative example to a positive example to demonstrate minimal difference, as opposed to the teaching sequence for *farther apart*, in which we moved from a positive example to a minimally different negative example. Example 3 is also the first of three positive examples (examples 3, 4, and 5) used to demonstrate the range of *on*. These positive examples are placed in the middle and on the left and right edge of the table to show that *on* can be represented by various spots of the table and not just one spot.

Again, we begin the testing sequence with a minimally different negative example (example 6). The testing sequence is also unpredictable (N-N-N-P-N-P-N).

Like the teaching sequence for *farther apart*, the sequence for *on* contains all the necessary features for designing teaching sequences for other positional concepts (e.g., *between, over, under, in front of*). With the exception of changing materials and teacher wording, we follow the same basic structure of the *on* teaching sequence to design other sequences for *all* positional concepts, as shown in Table 6–6. We could even use the same basic structure described below to teach other concepts, such as action (e.g., *running, jumping, playing*), polar (e.g., *hot/cold, big/little, full/empty*), and superlative (e.g., *widest, farthest, hardest*).

These are the basic rules for constructing teaching sequences for positional concepts:

1. Begin with two negative examples. The second is placed to allow a minimal difference with the third positive example.
2. The second negative example must be minimally different from the first positive (example 3).
3. Positive examples 3, 4, and 5 should differ as much as possible from one another to demonstrate the range of the concept.

TABLE 6–6
Basic structure for designing teaching sequences for positional concepts

Kinds of Examples	Teacher Actions	Student Response
Negative	Models	Attends
Negative	Models	Attends
Positive (minimal difference)	Models	Attends
Positive (range)	Models	Attends
Positive (range)	Models	Attends
Negative (minimal difference)	Tests learner	Responds orally
Positive	Tests learner	Responds orally
Negative	Tests learner	Responds orally
Negative	Tests learner	Responds orally
Positive	Tests learner	Responds orally
Negative	Tests learner	Responds orally
Positive	Tests learner	Responds orally

4. Example 6 should be minimally different from the preceding positive example 5. These minimally different pairs should not demonstrate the same minimal difference between examples 2 and 3.
5. Testing should begin with example 6 and six to eight test examples presented in an unpredictable order.
6. Students' responses during the testing sequence will always be binary: yes or no in response to the question, "Is the block on the table?" Or "It is on" or "It's not on" in response to the question, "Tell me what happened."

TASK 6–9
Concepts: Teaching the Noun Concept bird

BEFORE INSTRUCTION

Task Status: New.

Preskills

1. Knowledge of other concepts that could be used as negative examples or discrimination examples for the newly taught concept *bird.*
2. Ability to follow directions.

Materials

Color 4 × 4-inch pictures of various birds. Most of the birds are perched on branches, but some are pictured in flight or on the ground. One bird is on each picture card.

Teacher Wording

Positive example: "This is a bird."

Negative example (discrimination examples): The student will name the specific object or animal depicted in the picture. These discrimination examples represent concepts that the learner has mastered. For example, if the learner knows *bat* then the learner would respond by saying, "That's a bat."

Instructional Design Guidelines

1. The teacher must decide on the range of the concept *bird* to be taught. *Bird* is a wide-range concept that consists of various types of birds, including birds of forests and woodlands (small birds), birds of grasslands (small to medium-size birds), birds of bushy areas (small to large birds), birds of inland waters and marshes, and so on.
2. The teacher might present examples of birds that represent the full range of birds, or the teacher presents a limited range in which just small birds are presented. Following mastery of small birds, a new teaching sequence with medium-size to large birds would be taught. Following this teaching sequence, a new teaching sequence integrating small and medium-large birds is presented.
3. The teaching sequence consists of the teacher first presenting approximately six to eight positive examples of *bird*. This demonstration part of the sequence can be longer or shorter, depending on the learner and the concept.
4. The primary consideration is with the selection of the negative or discrimination examples. These must be selected from concepts the learner already firmly knows. Partly mastered concepts should not be used.
5. Discrimination examples that are visually similar to the target concept should be included first in the testing part of the sequence. For example, if the target concept is *dog*, a visually similar discrimination example is *cat*. However, the learner must know the concept *cat* for it to be included in the task.
6. Discrimination examples that are auditorily similar to the target concept are included in the testing sequence. For example, *dog* is auditorily similar to *log*.
7. Discrimination examples that are visually and auditorily similar to the target concept are selected and included last in the testing sequence. A discrimination example both visually and auditorily similar to the target concept *dog* is *hog*.

Expanded Set

If the initial teaching sequence is a limited one with a small range of examples, then the expanded set should include another set of examples that exposes the learner to a wider range of the concept. If the initial teaching sequence has a wide range of examples, then the expanded set should include new examples that demonstrate the range of the concept.

Generalization Set

One or two novel examples (i.e., examples not seen before by the learner) are included in the testing sequence. If the learner fails to identify these examples correctly, then another teaching sequence will be designed to include examples like the generalization ones.

TASK 6–10

DURING INSTRUCTION

Instructional Delivery Guidelines

The five guidelines presented earlier for teaching *farther apart* should be reviewed. In addition, the following guidelines should be considered:

1. The demonstration portion of the teaching sequence is direct, and the teacher points to each picture and identifies it by name. ("This is a bird.")
2. The first test examples are of previously modeled positive examples of the concept. This is to evaluate the learner's ability to produce orally the name of the concept. The learner has been passive in merely observing the examples prior to the test examples, and this first test example is important in assessing the learner's attention to task and ability to produce the name of the concept.
3. Students' responses to the discrimination examples are monitored carefully. If the learner fails to identify the examples correctly the first time, the teacher may want to remove these examples from the teaching sequence and replace them with examples that are less similar to the target concept (*bird*).
4. The teacher should present one picture at a time and pause 3–5 seconds between pictures to allow students to study them.

TASK 6–11
Teaching Procedure for the Noun Concept bird

Framing

TEACHER: "I will show you some pictures of birds. I will need your eyes up here on the pictures so you can see what we're talking about. What will I show you, William?"
WILLIAM: "Pictures of birds."
TEACHER: "Excellent. And where should your eyes be, Eve?"
EVE: "On the pictures."
TEACHER: "Good. I'll show you the pictures one at a time, and all you need to do is listen and look at the pictures. Then I'm going to ask you some questions."

The teacher presents individual pictures of birds. The features of the birds, their color and size, as well as how they are depicted, are described in parentheses.

Modeled Examples

Examples	Teacher Wording	Student Responses
1. English sparrow (small, 5–6 inches, sitting on a branch, brown wings, gray-white breast)	"This is a bird."	Attends

2. American redstart (small, 4–5 inches, sitting on a pine branch, black, orange-white breast, black-orange wings)	"This is a bird."	Attends
3. Cardinal (small, 7–9 inches, perched on a maple tree branch, all red, black around beak)	"This is a bird."	Attends
4. Gambel's quail (small-medium, 10–12 inches, walking in brown grass, black face, gray-brown wings, black-red chest)	"This is a bird."	Attends
5. Robin (small, 9–11 inches, standing in grass, red-breasted, brown wings, gray-brown crest)	"This is a bird."	Attends
6. Western kingbird (small, 8–9 1/2 inches, sitting on branch with no leaves, white face, yellow breast, red top)	"This is a bird."	Attends
7. House wren (small, 4 1/2–5 1/4 inches, sitting on fence post, all brown)	"This is a bird."	Attends
8. Baltimore oriole (small, 7–8 inches, black head, orange breast, black-orange tail feathers, black-white wings)	"This is a bird."	Attends

Testing Sequence

Assessing Learner's Ability to Produce Concept Name

9. Teacher presents picture of example 5, robin.	"What is this?"	"A bird."
10. Teacher presents picture of example 2, American redstart.	"What is this?"	"A bird."

Visually Similar Example

11. Teacher presents picture of a small *dog*.	"What is this?"	"A dog."
12. Teacher presents picture of example 4, Gambel's quail.	"What is this?"	"A bird."

Auditorily Similar Example

13. Teacher presents picture of a *bear*.	"What is this?"	"A bear."
14. Teacher presents picture of example 1, English sparrow.	"What is this?"	"A bird."

Generalization Example

15. Teacher presents picture of bobwhite (small, robust bird, 9–11 inches, brown-white speckled breast, small beak).	"What is this?"	"A bird."
16. Teacher presents picture of example 6, western kingbird.	"What is this?"	"A bird."

Visually and Auditorily Similar Example

17. Teacher presents an enlarged picture of a   "What is this?"   "A bee."
    bee.

18. Teacher presents picture of example 3,   "What is this?"   "A bird."
    cardinal.

TASK 6–12

AFTER INSTRUCTION

Analyze Errors and Make Instructional Adjustments

The following instructional dimensions are to be considered after the teaching sequence is completed:

1. The students' performance on the discrimination examples is most important. If students weren't able to make the discriminations between the newly taught concept and previously mastered concepts, then the nature of the errors must be determined. It may be necessary for the teacher to use more "dissimilar" negative, or discrimination, examples.

2. If students had difficulty identifying the positive examples of *bird* in the testing sequence, then the teacher should consider limiting the range of positive examples even further, perhaps by presenting birds of one general color and size.

3. If students incorrectly identified the generalization example on the first trial, the teacher may repeat the example later in the testing sequence. If students still aren't able to identify the example, the error indicates that another teaching sequence consisting of examples like the generalization example are needed.

In the teaching sequence for *bird*, the range of examples presented to the learner was restricted to small birds instead of the entire range of the concept, including small birds, medium-size birds (e.g., greater prairie chicken, roadrunner), large birds (e.g., golden eagle, rhinoceros hornbill) and very large birds (e.g., secretary bird, shoebill). The decision to limit the range of examples is one the teacher must base partly on an assessment of the learner's capacity to absorb the varied pieces of information. With a wide range of examples, the teacher risks the learner not "seeing" the qualitative sameness of the examples (i.e., not seeing that no matter what the color, size, or position, all the examples are birds). However, this kind of teaching sequence is most efficient, because the teacher is teaching more about the concept by presenting a wide range of examples.

In contrast, a teaching sequence of a limited range of examples is designed to control the amount of information presented to the learner. In the teaching sequence presented, only small birds were used as examples, for size was controlled to limit the number of different features the learner had to attend to during the teaching sequence. However, this stipulated kind of teaching is costly in terms of time, because the teacher must construct other teaching sequences of medium, large, and very large birds. Therefore, by limiting the range of examples, we are likely to increase the probability of students acquiring the concept. However, much time will be spent in developing and teaching additional teaching sequences to show the full range of the concept. By presenting the entire range of examples of a concept in one teaching sequence, we will save much instructional time, but it's possible the learner will not acquire the concept on the first trial.

The discrimination examples selected for the teaching sequence of *bird* (e.g., *dog, bear, bee*) reflect what the learners know. The discrimination (negative) examples must be of concepts the learners have already mastered. In the teaching sequence presented, the concept *dog* was selected as the first discrimination example most similar visually to the new concept *bird*. We know that a dog and a bird are not similar, but in this case, *dog* was the only concept the learners knew that was at all similar in feature to *bird* (e.g., both are animals). If the learner knew other concepts more similar in features to *bird* (such as *mouse, bat, squirrel*), we would include them in the testing sequence. In this case we are restricted to *dog*, because the learner knows *dog*. By testing the learner's ability to discriminate a known concept that is similar in looks to the new concept, we gain information as to whether the learner is attending to the critical features of the examples. By testing this discrimination first, we can exclude subsequent errors related to the learner's ability to discriminate the features of the new concept from known concepts.

The second discrimination example of the testing sequence was *bear*. This was selected because of its auditory similarity to *bird*. If the learner knew another concept more similar in sound to *bird* than *bear*, then we would have included that example in the testing sequence. The primary concern is to assess the learner's ability to discriminate between the names of the new concept and known concepts.

The final discrimination example is a known concept similar both visually and auditorily to the new concept. This presents the most difficult discrimination the learner will face. In the teaching sequence presented earlier, the concept *bee* was selected from the learner's repertoire as most similar in name and feature to *bird*. *Bee* is similar to *bird* in sound because of the beginning /b/ sound and similar in features in having wings and living in a natural environment. Naturally, if the learner knew the concept *bat* (i.e., a mammal that flies), we would have included *bat* in the discrimination testing sequence.

The testing sequence also includes a generalization example to assess the learner's ability to identify a novel example that was not presented in the demonstration part of the teaching sequence. The generalization example is similar in size to the modeled examples of *bird*. We might have included a more varied example than those modeled, such as a canvasback (i.e., a duck, 19 to 24 inches in size) or even a shoebill (i.e., tropical African bird, 4 feet tall, peculiar bill). The decision of selection of generalization examples should be based on the learner, the modeled examples, and the instructional objectives of the lesson. However, the primary focus of the teaching sequence will be on the learner's ability to discriminate known concepts from the newly taught concept.

As noted earlier, the first two test examples were already modeled by the teacher. The purpose of presenting these first in the testing sequence is to assess the learner's ability to produce the name of the concept (i.e., *bird*). The teacher is interested only in learning if the learner can say the concept name *bird.* This test is important, because it rules out a subsequent error as the result of the learner's inability to say the concept name.

The basic structure of the teaching sequence we designed for *bird* contains all the ingredients needed to teach any noun concept. We could use the *bird* teaching sequence as a blueprint to teach concepts such as *table, chair, dog, cat, building, car,* and so on. We could use this teaching sequence to teach letter-sound correspondences (e.g., *m/p/a/e/sh*). The basic structure of a noun teaching sequence is described in Table 6–7.

The basic rules for constructing teaching sequences for noun concepts are:

1. Present positive examples in the teaching sequence. If the sequence is designed to teach the full range of the concept, present 8–12 examples. If the sequence is designed to teach a limited range, model 5–8 examples.
2. The teacher presents the positive examples and models the response for the learner.
3. The first examples to be tested are one or two positive examples previously modeled in the teaching sequence. This test is to assess the learner's ability to say the name of the concept.
4. All negative or discrimination examples are limited to ones mastered by the learner.
5. All negatives are minimally different from the positive examples but only with respect to what the learner knows. The first negative example in the testing sequence is similar in features to the new concept.

TABLE 6–7
Basic structure for designing teaching sequences for noun concepts

Kinds of Examples	Teacher	Student
Positive	Models	Attends
Positive	Models	Attends
Positive	Models	Attends
Positive	Models	Attends
Positive	Models	Attends
Positive	Models	Attends
Positive	Models	Attends
Positive	Models	Attends
Positive (already modeled)	Tests learner	Responds orally
Positive (already modeled)	Tests learner	Responds orally
Negative (similar in feature)	Tests learner	Responds orally
Positive	Tests learner	Responds orally
Negative (similar in name)	Tests learner	Responds orally
Positive	Tests learner	Responds orally
Positive	Tests learner	Responds orally
Negative (similar in feature and name)	Tests learner	Responds orally
Positive	Tests learner	Responds orally
Positive (generalization example)	Tests learner	Responds orally

6. The second negative example in the testing sequence is similar in name to the new concept.
7. The third negative example is similar in features and name to the new concept.
8. The learner says the name of both positive and negative examples.
9. Generalization examples are selected based upon the learner's performance on the discrimination examples and the range of examples modeled.

TEACHING RULE RELATIONSHIPS

Earlier, we defined a **rule relationship** as a proposition that specifies a connection between at least two facts, discriminations, or concepts. As noted in the previous chapter on knowledge forms, the essential feature of a rule is the "connectedness" it reveals about known concepts, facts, or discriminations. A learner might know the component forms of knowledge (e.g., a concept, simple fact) that comprise a rule relationship but not know the relationship communicated by the linkage of those component forms of knowledge.

By knowing the connectedness specified in a rule, the learner can detect that relationship in examples that contain the concepts or facts specified by the rule. For example, the rule for telling time, "When the long hand is on the 12, it is o'clock" (e.g., 1 o'clock, 12 o'clock, 5 o'clock), comprises at least two knowledge components—recognizing "the long hand" and the number 12 on the face of the clock. The rule specifies the conditions for determining when it is "o'clock," which require the learner to identify the long hand on the clock and determine if the long hand is on the 12. If these conditions are met, then the learner is safe to assume that it is "o'clock." If the conditions aren't met, the learner can assume that it is "not o'clock." In effect, the rule can be applied to any example of telling time. If it is 12:03, the learner will know it is "not o'clock." If it is 3, the learner will know it is "o'clock." This rule allows the learner to tell time if it is o'clock.

Rule relationships are prominent features of basic skill and content area instruction. Rules can be found in decoding skills (e.g., reading CVCe words: "When there's an *e* at the end of a word, you say the name of the first vowel"), math skills (e.g., "Prime numbers have only themselves and one as factors"), spelling skills (e.g., "*i* before *e* except after *c* as in *receive*"), reading comprehension (e.g., "If it's a main idea, it tells about the whole story"), critical reading skills (e.g., "Just because you know about the part doesn't mean you know about the whole thing") and content area instruction of the social studies and sciences. Example rule relationships in various content areas are given here:

1. In a first-class lever, the pivot point or fulcrum is between the effort and the resistance.
2. In a second-class lever, the pivot point is at one end of the lever, the effort force at the opposite end, and the resistance force is somewhere in between.
3. An acid is a chemical substance that dissolves metals, looks like water, has a sour taste, and turns blue litmus paper red.
4. If the dinosaur has a pelvic structure like a bird, the dinosaur is an ornithician dinosaur.

Learning a rule relationship, such as that for telling time, requires the learner to detect the *relationship* between concepts or facts associated with the rule, not just the concepts or facts in isolation.

5. The faster something moves, the more inertia it has.
6. When the demand is greater than the supply, prices go up.
7. A body moving with a constant velocity is in equilibrium.
8. Forces that break down rock but do not carry it away are called weathering agents.
9. Cold water is denser than warm water.
10. When the organism lives in an environment that has no free oxygen, it is called anaerobic.

Rule relationships are efficient procedures because they allow the learner to see the connectedness across a range of examples specified by the concepts in the rule. By learning a rule relationship, the learner gains access to a fixed principle or code that can be used to determine when an example is governed by the conditions of the rule. For example, to determine if something is a weathering agent, the learner must look at the example and determine if it meets the conditions specified in the rule. If the example is (1) a "force that breaks down rock," and (2) does not "carry it away," then the example can be labeled a *weathering agent*. The code can be applied to a wide range of examples. This efficiency of rule relationships contrasts to concept learning, which requires the learner to examine each example, one at a time, and determine the features of the examples that are the same. What the learner actually does in concept learning is extract and construct a rule internally, based on a series of concrete examples (e.g., positive and negative examples of the concept *on*). This rule construction in concept learning is not very efficient and depends on the teacher selecting the appropriate examples so that a clear and unambiguous rule is constructed. Once the rule is induced from the examples the teacher presents, it is internalized as a code that the learner uses to make judgments about new, unknown examples of the newly learned concept. In the final analysis, concept learning attempts to accomplish through a long process what rule relationships make explicit in the beginning. Given this contrast between concept learning and rule relationships, the efficiency of rules makes them of critical instructional importance.

Using the Generic Instructional Set to Teach Rule Relationships

We rely on the expanded generic instructional set for teaching rule relationships, as we did in teaching concepts. Because rule relationships are complex verbal statements, the design of their teaching sequences requires careful planning and execution. It is a mistake to treat rule relationships as mere verbal statements that need only be told in either oral or written form. This oral or written communication involves more than the mere statement of the rule relationship. We must determine if the learner knows the component facts, discriminations, or concepts within the rule relationship. If the learner hasn't mastered the component knowledge forms implied in the rule relationship, then they must be taught, practiced, and brought to a high criterion level of performance before the rule relationship is taught. As in the teaching of concepts, teaching rule relationships also involves demonstrating the application of the rule relationship through a series of appropriate positive and negative examples, which requires extensive practice. The teaching of rule relationships is a complex network of instructional decisions that touch on all of the generic design features we have discussed so far.

Because designing teaching sequences for rule relationships includes the same generic design features as that of concepts (e.g., selecting positive and negative examples, selecting materials, sequencing examples, selecting test examples, selecting and scheduling practice examples, and controlling teacher wording), we will omit a description of each of these features. In the next section we describe the instructional mechanics, decision rules, and assumptions of teaching rule relationships.

Breaking Rule Relationships into Chunks of Knowledge

The purpose of learning a rule relationship is to apply the rule to a set of examples. To simplify the complexity of learning rule relationships, we will teach rules by breaking them into two basic parts. Rule relationships are statements that specify a connection between at least two chunks of knowledge, and instruction should begin with the identification of these chunks. For example, the rule, "The hotter the liquid, the faster it evaporates," comprises the following two chunks of knowledge: (1) the temperature of the liquid ("the hotter the liquid"), and (2) the rate of evaporation ("the faster it evaporates").

We will use these chunks of knowledge as building blocks to learn the rule relationship. Our analysis of rule relationships goes something like this: If a rule specifies a connection between two chunks of knowledge, then it is logical that one chunk be used to predict the other chunk. We will build on one of the chunks and use it as a pivoting point for making predictions about the other chunk of knowledge specified in the rule relationship. In the example cited, we will use the first part of the rule relationship, "the hotter the liquid," as our building block and pivoting point to make predictions about the rate of evaporation (e.g., "Will the liquid evaporate faster?"). Given examples of liquids at different temperatures (e.g., a pot of water simmering, another lightly bubbling, and a third pot boiling rapidly), the learner will be asked to predict from which pot the liquid will evaporate fastest. Interestingly enough, to make the prediction, the only information the learner needs is in the first chunk of knowledge—"the hotter the liquid." In fact, all the learner actually observes is one chunk of knowledge (i.e., "the hotter the liquid"). The other ("the faster it evaporates") is not observed and needn't be. Obviously, the learner must know about liquids and how they react when heated (e.g., water that boils is hotter than water that simmers) and must use that background knowledge in conjunction with the first chunk of knowledge. The prediction is made possible by the mere fact that the two chunks of knowledge are connected, and this connectedness allows us to use one chunk of knowledge as a pivoting point for the other.

To gain a clear understanding of rules and their individual parts (i.e., what chunk is observed and what chunk should be predicted), we describe a set of rules in Table 6–8. For each rule relationship, we specify the part of the rule that will be observed, as well as the part that will be unobserved and predicted by the learner. We also specify the question that the learner will be asked in making a prediction.

TABLE 6–8
Rules and their parts

First Chunk of Knowledge Observed Part of Rule		Second Chunk of Knowledge Part of Rule to Be Predicted (Question to Learner)
The steeper the grade of the stream,	$\longrightarrow$	the faster the water flow. (Will the water flow faster?)
When the big hand is on 12,	$\longrightarrow$	it is o'clock. (Is it o'clock?)
If the pivot point or fulcrum is between the effort and resistance,	$\longrightarrow$	it is a first-class lever. (Is this a first-class lever?)
The faster something moves,	$\longrightarrow$	the more inertia it has. (Does it have more inertia?)
When the demand is greater than the supply,	$\longrightarrow$	prices go up. (Will the prices go up?)
Forces that break down rock but do not carry it away	$\longrightarrow$	are called weathering agents. (Is it a weathering agent?)
If an animal has six legs,	$\longrightarrow$	it is an insect. (Is it an insect?)
Products that are readier to use	$\longrightarrow$	cost more. (Will it cost more?)

We refer to the observed part of each rule as such because it is the part of the rule that the teacher will actually teach. Therefore, it is the part that the learner will observe the teacher teaching. For instance, in the rule, "If an animal has six legs, it is an insect," the teacher selects examples of the observed part of the rule, namely, "an animal with six legs." To teach this part of the rule, the teacher must first decide on the kind of knowledge form (e.g., a simple fact, verbal chain, discrimination, or concept) represented in the observed part of the rule. In this case, "an animal with six legs" is best taught as a noun sequence. It is not a positional concept, a comparative concept, a simple fact, or a basic discrimination. *Animal* is a noun that represents a class of objects that are the same in some way. The materials for teaching "an animal with six legs" include pictures of different animals of varying sizes, shapes, and colors. However, the critical feature for the learner to key on is the number of legs in each picture example. The teacher points to a picture of an animal and asks the learner to determine if it is an insect.

It should be clear by now that rule relationships are taught by building on the knowledge forms we have described throughout this chapter. In designing the teaching sequence, the teacher builds on the knowledge (i.e., facts, discriminations, and concepts) the learner brings to the instructional setting. The teaching of rule relationships doesn't differ much from the teaching of facts, discriminations, and concepts, which we have already detailed. In fact, we follow the same basic design of instruction principles to teach rule relationships as we did to teach these other knowledge forms.

However, teaching of rule relationships does require the teacher to make an important assumption about the learner: that the learner is firm on all of the component knowledge forms (i.e., simple facts, discriminations, concepts) specified in the rule.

To understand a rule relationship, the learner must understand the pieces of information (i.e., facts, discriminations, and concepts) that make up the entire rule. These must be taught and mastered before the rule relationship is taught. For example, the rule, "The steeper the grade of the stream, the faster the water flow," contains the following pieces of information and component knowledge forms:

Pieces of Information	Component Knowledge Forms
steeper	comparative concept
grade	noun concept
stream	noun concept
faster	comparative concept
water flow	noun concept

Almost all the words that make up the rule relationship can be taught as individual concepts. In fact, we could teach each concept by following the generic design of instruction requirements specified earlier in this chapter. We first select materials appropriate to each concept, select positive and negative examples to demonstrate and test each concept, determine the teacher wording, and finally schedule the expanded teaching and generalization sets. Once the component parts of the rule relationship are mastered, the rule itself can be taught. In fact, in most cases, the observed part of the rule relationship can be taught by using a teaching sequence constructed for teaching one of the component concepts, facts, or discriminations. For example, in the rule on steepness of grade and water flow, we use the teaching sequence designed for teaching the concept *steeper* to teach the observed part of the rule—"the steeper the grade of the stream." The concept *steeper* is pivotal in the observed part of the rule. We couldn't very well teach *grade* or *stream* to communicate the observed part of the rule, because those concepts aren't key to understanding the rule. The critical concept is *steeper,* because it's the rise or slope of the stream that causes the water to flow faster. Therefore, we use the same teaching sequence we used to teach *steeper* to teach the observed part of the rule relationship (i.e., "the steeper the grade of the stream"). The only significant modification in the teaching sequence is the teacher wording. We detail a teaching sequence for teaching the comparative concept *steeper* and follow it with another teaching sequence for teaching the rule relationship, "The steeper the grade of the stream, the faster the water flow."

TASK 6–13
Teaching Format for Steeper *(Comparative Concept)*

Materials

The teacher uses a 1 × 2-inch board painted brown that is 2 feet long. The board is positioned on a table to allow students a full view. The teacher holds the board at one end while the other end rests on the table. By raising the board up and down, the teacher demonstrates the slope and rise of a stream.

Framing

TEACHER: "I'm going to tell you about the concept *steeper.* I'm going to use this board to show you what I mean. I would like you to listen to what I say and watch what happens to the board. What are you going to do, J.B.?"

J.B.: "We're supposed to watch the board and listen to you."

Error and Correction Procedure

TEACHER: "Excellent, J.B. What am I going to tell you about, Alexis?"

ALEXIS: "About the board."

TEACHER: "Yes, I'm going to show you the board, but what am I going to tell you about while using the board?"

ALEXIS: "Uh . . . I don't know."

TEACHER: "Ken, what concept am I going to tell you about?"

KEN: "About steeper."

Retest of Error

TEACHER: "Good, Ken. What am I going to tell you about, Alexis?"

ALEXIS: "About steeper."

TEACHER: "Excellent, Alexis. OK, everyone watch the board. I'm going to tell you about steeper."

Example	Teacher Wording	Student Response
Starting Point		
Top of board held at 3 inches from table.	"Watch the board. I'll tell you if it gets steeper."	Attends
Range of Positive Examples		
1. Top of board moved up to 4 inches from table. (Positive example.)	"The board is steeper."	Attends
2. Top of board moved up to 7 inches from table. (Positive example.)	"The board is steeper."	Attends
3. Top of board moved up to 9 inches from table. (Positive example.)	"The board is steeper."	Attends
Minimally Different Example		
4. Top of board moved down to 8 inches from table. (Negative example.)	"The board is not steeper."	Attends
5. Top of board moved down to 3 inches from table. (Negative example.)	"The board is not steeper."	Attends
Testing Sequence		
Minimally Different Example		
6. Top of board moved up to 4 inches from table. (Positive example.)	"Everyone, tell me. Is the board steeper or not steeper?"	"Steeper."
7. Top of board moved up to 8 inches from table. (Positive example.)	"Tell me. Is it steeper or not steeper?"	"Steeper."
8. Top of board moved down to 2 inches from table. (Negative example.)	"Is it steeper or not steeper?"	"Not steeper."
9. Top of board moved up to 5 inches from table. (Positive example.)	"Tell me. What is it?"	"Steeper."
10. Top of board moved down to 1/2 inch from table. (Negative example.)	"Tell me."	"Not steeper."
Generalization Example		
11. Board laid flat on the table. (Negative example.)	"Tell me."	"Not steeper."

TASK 6–14
Teaching Format for the Rule Relationship:
"The steeper the grade of the stream, the faster the water flow."

Materials

The teacher will use the same materials as those used to teach the concept *steeper.*

TEACHER: Listen, we've been talking about nature and how rivers and streams change the land around them. Today I'm going to teach you a rule about streams. I'm going to use this board and I want you to pretend this board is a stream in the wilderness somewhere.

Now listen big. Here's the rule: "The steeper the grade of the stream, the faster the water flows." Listen again (repeats rule). Watch the stream (pointing to the board), and I'll show you how the rule works.

Example	Teacher Wording	Student Response
Starting Point: Same as in *steeper* sequence. (Board at 3 inches.)	"Watch the stream. I'll tell you if the water will flow faster."	Attends
1. Same as in *steeper* sequence. (Board at 5 inches.)	"Will the water flow faster? Yes. How do I know? Because the stream is steeper."	Attends
2. Same as in *steeper* sequence. (Board at 8 inches.)	"Will the water flow faster? Yes. How do I know? Because the stream is steeper."	Attends
3. Same as in *steeper* sequence. (Board at 9 inches.)	"Will the water flow faster? Yes. How do I know? Because the stream is steeper."	Attends
4. Same as in *steeper* sequence. (Board at 8 inches.)	"Will the water flow faster? No. How do I know? Because the stream is *not* steeper."	Attends
5. Same as in *steeper* sequence. (Board at 3 inches.)	"Will the water flow faster? No. How do I know? Because the stream is *not* steeper."	Attends
6. Same as in *steeper* sequence. (Board at 4 inches.)	"Your turn to tell me if the water will flow faster. Will the water flow faster?"	"Yes."
	"How do you know?"	"Because the stream is steeper."
7. Same as in *steeper* sequence. (Board at 8 inches.)	"Your turn again. Will the water flow faster?"	"Yes."
	"How do you know?"	"Because the stream is steeper."

8. Same as in *steeper* sequence. (Board at 2 inches.)	"Will the water flow faster?"	"No."
	"How do you know?"	"Because the stream is *not* steeper."
9. Same as in *steeper* sequence. (Board at 3 inches.)	"Will the water flow faster?"	"Yes."
	"How do you know?"	"Because the stream is steeper."
10. Same as in *steeper* sequence. (Board at 1/2 inch.)	"Will the water flow faster?"	"No."
	"How do you know?"	"Because the stream is *not* steeper."
11. Same as in *steeper* sequence. (Board flat on table.)	"Will the water flow faster?"	"No."
	"How do you know?"	"Because the stream is *not* steeper."

Describing the two teaching sequences back to back does not imply that they should be taught in successive order. In fact, the teacher will not need to teach the concept *steeper* if learners know the concept. By describing these formats in sequence, we are able to demonstrate how a concept teaching sequence is similar in design to the teaching sequence of a rule relationship. The materials, examples, and example sequence are all the same. The primary difference is the teacher wording, which becomes a little more complex when teaching rule relationships, because rules are verbal statements. Because these are complex, they must be presented one piece at a time. In our analysis of rule relationships, we model applying the rule to a set of examples and require the learner to make predictions based on what was demonstrated. The learner is also required to verify predictions. This prediction and verification format is important to rule learning, because it requires the learner to become actively involved by taking a risk and making a prediction (e.g., "Will the water flow faster?"). The learner is then asked to substantiate that prediction by verifying the answer (e.g., "How do you know?"). However, the risk the learner takes in making the prediction and verification is contrived by the teacher, because the teacher has demonstrated how the rule is to be applied to a range of examples, so that the learner is not making a blind prediction. The learner always has the option of adjusting the response based on the observed part of the rule being taught.

It is important to note that the teacher doesn't ask about the observed or taught part of the rule relationship (i.e., "the steeper the grade of the stream"). Instead, the teacher tests the learner immediately on the unobserved part of the rule, which seems rather peculiar at first. However, to answer the question (or make a prediction), the learner must rely on the observed or taught part of the rule relationship. This requirement demands more of learners, but it is also logically and instructionally acceptable, because the teaching sequence provides the learner with the information to answer the question or make the prediction in the first place.

In the teaching sequence cited earlier, the materials create an artificial physical setup for the rule. We know that a board is not a stream and that streams don't physically move up and down as part of the earth's surface. We might communicate a very peculiar picture of how the natural world works! However, the purpose of using such a teaching sequence on rule relationships is to provide the learner with an opportunity to grasp the relationship and connectedness between concepts that may otherwise remain abstract and unapproachable. This teaching sequence is not intended to approximate what happens in the real world, but it does provide low performers a framework for thinking about how concepts are related to each other to create new meaning.

Instructional Format for Teaching Rule Relationships

In the next section, we review and summarize the details for teaching rule relationships. The format, as we have already noted, is similar to that of teaching concepts. However, in this case, special care is given to the analysis of the rule relationship and how the rule is translated into teacher wording during the actual teaching sequence.

TASK 6-15
Teaching Format for the Rule Relationship:
"Products that are readier to use cost more"

BEFORE INSTRUCTION

Task Status: New.

Preskills

1. Must be firm on the noun concept of *products*, the comparative concept of *readier to use*, and the comparative concept of *more*. The concept *more* would be taught (if necessary) within the context of *more things*, such as more pencils, more paper, and so on, and not simply by itself.
2. Has a basic understanding of how goods and services are produced and distributed (e.g., how individuals and companies make money by making things that people buy).

Materials

Teacher will orally describe each example and use pictures of specific products.

Teacher Wording

Positive example: "This product will cost more. How do I know? It is readier to use."
Negative example: "This product won't cost more. How do I know? It's not readier to use."

Test example: "Which product will cost more? How do you know?"

Instructional Design Guidelines

1. The teacher must assess whether the learners are firm on the component concepts of the rule relationship.
2. Component concepts that are not mastered must be taught (or retaught) to a high criterion level of performance.
3. The two primary parts of the rule relationship (i.e., the observed part and the unobserved part) must be identified.
4. The part that will be observed by the learner (e.g., "the readier the product") must be taught by the teacher.
5. The part of the rule that remains unobserved by the learner is the part that the learner must predict (i.e., "costs more").
6. The pivotal feature or concept in the observed part of the rule must be identified. In this case, it is the comparative concept, *readier to use.*
7. Positive and negative examples will be presented by the teacher through oral descriptions of products.
8. All examples will be presented one after another in one teaching presentation of 8–12 minutes of instructional time.
9. The specific teaching sequence will be designed according to the details for teaching comparative concepts. However, in this case we need not use examples. Because of the nature of rules, we can get by with presenting fewer examples, because the learner has the rule to fall back on. In this sequence, we will present three examples, then start testing the learner, beginning with example 4. The teacher may use more examples if necessary.
10. The teacher wording must be carefully determined ahead of time.

Expanded Set

Present another similar teaching sequence with a different set of examples. After this teaching sequence, require students to collect examples of the rule relationship from the newspaper. Students should be asked to note in writing the nature of the products being compared and why one would cost more than another.

Generalization Set

Require students to find examples in which the rule relationship doesn't apply; that is, there are products that are readier to use but don't cost more.

TASK 6–16

DURING INSTRUCTION

Instructional Delivery Guidelines

1. Frame task carefully because it is new. Alert students to the fact that they will need to listen to each example carefully and make a choice.

2. Be sure all students are attending.
3. Errors are corrected by using the rule relationship. Restate the rule, then ask specific questions about the pivotal concept (e.g., "Is that product readier to use?") in the observed part of the rule. If this fails, the teacher should reteach the rule relationship beginning with the first example.
4. The pacing of the lesson should not be too brisk. The presentation of each example for the observed part of the rule should take only a few seconds. The teacher should pause after each example to allow learners time to absorb the examples.
5. The teacher must monitor student on-task behavior during the lesson by watching students' eyes and oral responding.

TASK 6–17
Teaching Format for the Rule Relationship:
"Products that are readier to use cost more."

The teaching sequence starts by the teacher framing the task as described in the previous teaching formats.

TEACHER: Listen to this rule about products. Products that are readier to use cost more. Listen again (repeats rule). I'm going to show you some products and tell you which product will cost more. When I'm done, I'll ask you to tell me which product will cost more.

Examples	Teacher Wording	Student Response
1. Picture of a pound of hamburger on a plate.	"Look at this picture. It's a pound of hamburger fresh from Safeway."	Attends
2. Picture of McDonald's hamburgers in wrappers piled on a plate.	"Look at this picture. It's a pound of cooked hamburger individually wrapped and fresh from McDonald's. I'm going to tell you which product will cost more. Which product costs more? The McDonald hamburgers." "How do I know? Because they are readier to use."	Attends
3. Picture of a box of brownies that lists all the ingredients to make a dozen brownies.	"Here's a picture of a brownie mix that will make a dozen brownies with frosting."	Attends
4. Picture of a plate of brownies purchased from a bakery.	"Here's a picture of a dozen brownies from a bakery." "The bakery brownies will cost more. How do I know? Because they are readier to use than the brownie mix."	Attends

5. Picture of ingredients for making brownies. Each ingredient is labeled and shown in a bowl on a kitchen table.	"Here's a picture of the ingredients needed to make brownies. These can be found in your kitchen."	Attends
6. Picture of a box of brownie mix as shown in example 2.	"Here's that box of brownie mix again." "Which product will cost more? The brownie mix. How do I know?" "It's all mixed and readier to use."	Attends

Test Examples

7. Picture of fabric, thread and buttons to make a dress.	"Here's a picture of some fabric and other items for making a dress."	Attends
8. Picture of a dress from a catalog.	"Here's a brand new dress you get from a catalog."	Attends
	"It's your turn. Tell me which product will cost more." (Teacher calls on an individual.)	"The dress from the catalog."
	"How do you know?"	"It's readier to wear. The other dress has to be made."

Error and Correction Procedure

9. Picture of noodles and sauce to make spaghetti for eight people.	"Here's a picture of the ingredients to make spaghetti for eight people."	Attends
10. Picture of eight cans of spaghetti.	"Here's spaghetti that you get from Giant Foods to feed eight people."	Attends
	"Will the ingredients cost more than the cans of spaghetti?"	Chris: "No."
	(The teacher repeats the same question.)	Chris: "No."
	"Look at each product, Chris. (Pause.) Which product is ready to use and ready to eat right now?"	Chris: "The spaghetti in the can."
	"Good. Listen, here's the rule: The product that's readier to use costs more. Chris, which product is readier to use?"	Chris: "The spaghetti in the can."
	"Yes. So which product is going to cost more?"	Chris: "The spaghetti in a can."

The teacher presents similar examples of products and tests the learner's knowledge of the rule relationship using similar teacher wording as described in example 7.

Generalization Example

| 11. Two individual pictures of comparable dresses from the same catalog. | "Which product will cost more?" | Hannah: "I don't know." |
| | "Why not?" | Hannah: "I don't know which one is readier to use." |

TASK 6–18

AFTER INSTRUCTION

Analyze Errors and Make Instructional Adjustments

The following instructional dimensions should be considered after the teaching sequence is completed:

1. This teaching sequence requires the learner to answer a question that has to do with a part of the rule that wasn't physically represented to the learner (i.e., the unobserved part of the rule). To answer this part of the rule, the learner must keep in mind the observed part of the rule. Holding in memory the part that was taught while providing an answer to a part that wasn't taught may be difficult for learners at first.
2. The teacher needs to determine if the errors are a result of the learner not being firm on some of the component pieces of knowledge contained in the rule relationship. If so, separate teaching sequences must be designed for these concepts.
3. The teacher may want to present a fuller teaching sequence the next time around, instead of the abbreviated sequence shown.
4. The teacher should prepare materials for the expanded and generalization sets.

The teaching sequence for the rule relationship "Products that are readier to use cost more" is an abbreviated sequence. Because we are teaching a more complex knowledge form, we can assume that the learner is capable of handling such a task. We can demand more of the learner than we ordinarily would, and we can cut the teaching sequence short because of the nature of rule relationships. Teaching rules requires fewer examples than the teaching of concepts. The rule explicitly informs the learner of the critical information that's needed to make a decision about a specific example. As noted earlier, concepts don't provide us with that luxury. By first stating the rule and then applying it to a few examples, the learner should be able to discern the critical features of the rule and examples. If the teacher is unsure of the learner's capabilities, then more examples of the rule relationship should be given.

SUMMARY

In this chapter, we specified the details for designing and constructing teaching sequences for concepts and rule relationships. We used the generic instructional set as the basic framework for designing these teaching sequences. However, we expanded the generic instructional set to accommodate the complexities of concepts and rule relationships. We noted that teachers must add more examples, nonexamples, and concise teacher wording to the generic instructional set. We also noted that the teacher must select the materials and determine the meaning of the concept to be taught.

Many different concepts were described, including positional concepts, polar concepts, action concepts, comparative concepts, noun concepts, and so forth. To design a concept teaching sequence, the teacher selects the materials to use, determines the range of positive examples, selects the type of negative examples, places the negative and positive examples in an appropriate sequence, selects and sequences the test examples, and selects the type of practice needed to master the concept. The teacher must also carefully select discrimination examples and minimally different negative examples. The design of concept teaching sequences requires careful attention to the principles of design of instruction.

We also specified the details for designing and constructing rule relationships. We noted that rule relationships require the teacher to identify and teach the component knowledge forms, such as facts and concepts. Teaching rule relationships requires the teacher to demonstrate the connection between the component forms of knowledge that comprise the rule. In doing so, the learner makes a prediction about an outcome specified by the rule. Designing teaching sequences for rule relationships also requires careful attention to the design-of-instruction principles.

APPLICATION ITEMS

Read each exercise carefully. Prepare your response to each item as if you were going to actually use the teaching sequence to teach the given concept. When selecting or evaluating materials for a particular setup, consider the real world constraints of the classroom. Be sure to *frame* each teaching sequence. Be certain also to attend to the design principles when constructing the teaching sequences.

1. Teach the concept *in,* meaning when an object is contained within the space of another object (not meaning chic or fashionable). For your setup, use a pencil and a container. Specify a series of 12 examples using simple drawings of a pencil and a container. The learner should be required to make a yes/no choice response in the testing portion of the teaching sequence. Identify a limitation of this teaching sequence.

2. Given the teaching sequence for the concept *in* as specified in Exercise 1, your task now is to design another teaching sequence to teach the same concept:
   a. Specify a new setup that is greatly different from the first setup. Describe the setup in detail. Use drawings for your examples (explain your drawings when necessary).
   b. Specify the learner's responses in the testing portion of the sequence. The learner's response should be more advanced than given in exercise 1.
   c. Specify the limitations of this new teaching sequence and the steps you would take to address them.
   d. Finally, briefly specify a correction procedure for an incorrect response on the first testing example.

3. Teach the concept *nearer,* meaning in closer physical proximity to something. Specify a setup and describe it in detail. Use drawings to depict your examples. If necessary, explain your drawings. Design a 12-example teaching sequence. The learner should be required to give a production response. Describe how the teaching sequence creates stipulation.

4. The following teaching presentation is attempting to teach the concept *getting deeper* (meaning extending far down as in the deep part of the sea, river, etc.). Examine the teaching sequence carefully. List and describe the possible problems with the teaching sequence. Be specific in describing the problems you identify. Briefly explain how you would remedy each problem.

Setup: The teacher sets an aquarium (14 inches × 24 inches) on a table and fills the aquarium with water. The teacher then chooses a child from the class and requires the child to place a hand into the aquarium. The teacher manipulates the child's hand and labels each movement. Each numbered circle in Figure 6–6 represents the sequence of examples (i.e., the child's hand

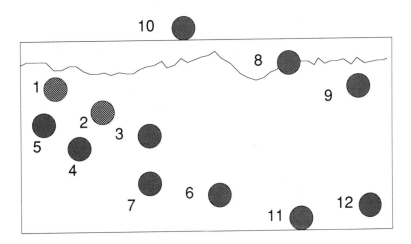

Examples		Teacher wording
#1	P	Listen to me. We're going to talk about "getting deeper." Are you ready? OK, watch Blossom's hand. Her hand is getting deeper.
#2	P	Her hand is getting deeper.
#3	P	Her hand is getting deeper. See it getting deeper?
#4	P	Now look at it. Blossom's hand is getting deeper.
#5	N	Her hand is not getting deeper.
#6	P	Now it's getting deeper. See?
#7	N	OK. You tell me about getting deeper. OK?
#8	N	Tell me.
#9	P	Tell me. Come on, Ralph, get with it. Tell me about the hand.
#10	N	The hand is getting deeper, right?
#11	P	Everybody, tell me about getting deeper.
#12	N	Well?

FIGURE 6–6
Side view of aquarium and examples of sequence

being manipulated in the water) the teacher presents to the learners. The teacher wording for each example is given following the illustration.

5. Construct a teaching sequence for teaching the concept *cereal*, meaning breakfast food. Treat this teaching sequence as an identification task—you merely want the learner to visually identify the food *cereal*. The learner has been taught the following concepts: *bowl, Jell-O, car, scissors, milk, sugar, spoon,* and *raisins.* The sequence should consist of 8–10 examples and appropriate teacher wording. Select the examples you need for the teaching sequence. Specify in detail what the features of the examples are. Provide a brief rationale for why you have chosen to juxtapose the examples you have in the testing sequence.

6. The following teaching presentation is attempting to teach the concept of *scissors.* The teacher wants the learner to identify different kinds of scissors. The learner is firm on the following concepts: *bowl, hammer, sugar, spoon, pliers, raisins,* and *book.* The learner has just been taught the concepts *knife, cereal,* and *shoes.* Examine the teaching sequence carefully. List and describe briefly the possible problems you identify. Design a teaching sequence to remedy the problems you have identified and described. Be sure to address problems with the learner's no responses and how you would respond to them. Briefly discuss whether the teaching sequence reveals a management problem, an instructional problem, or both.

Setup: The teacher sits across the table from George, a mentally handicapped learner, and places a pair of scissors (small size, rubberized yellow handles) on the table in front of George and proceeds with the following teaching sequence. George's responses are given in parentheses.

Examples Presented	Teacher Wording and Learner Responses
Small scissors, yellow handles are on the table.	"Hi, George. How are you today? (No response.) Good. I'm going to have you talk about scissors today. Have you ever worked with scissors, George? (No response.) OK. George, pick up the scissors." (George picks up the scissors.)
	"Great job, George! You picked up the scissors. Very nice. George, what are these (teacher points to the scissors) called?" (No response.)
	"George, these are scissors. Say *scissorsss.*" ("Scissorsss.")
	"Great, George!" Nice job." (Teacher pulls another pair of scissors from a box under the table.)
Large scissors, black handles, shear blades.	"George, what are these? (No response.) Here, George, take the scissors. (Teacher hands the black scissors to George.) Listen, you can cut with these scissors."
	"Here's some paper. Watch me. I can cut paper with these scissors." (Teacher cuts a piece of paper as George watches.)
	(Teacher points to the small, yellow-handled scissors being used.) "George, what are these called?" ("Scissorsss.")

"Great, George! Now touch your shoes,
George. (No response.) OK. George, go find
the picture of a hammer in the corner
(teacher points) over there."

(George gets up and goes to the corner.)

"Great, George!"

REFERENCES

Carnine, D. W. (1980). Three procedures for presenting minimally different positive and negative examples. *Journal of Educational Psychology, 72,* 452–456.

Clark, D. C. (1971). Teaching concepts in the classroom: A set of teaching prescriptions derived from experimental research. *Journal of Education Psychology Monograph, 62,* 253–278.

Engelmann, S., & Carnine, D. (1982). *Theory of instruction: Principles and applications.* New York: Irvington.

Gagne, R. M. (1985). *The conditions of learning and theory of instruction* (4th ed.). New York: Holt, Rinehart & Winston.

Jitendra, A., & Kameenui, E. J. (1988). A design-of-instruction analysis of concept teaching in five basal language programs: Violations from the bottom up. *Journal of Special Education, 22*(2), 199–219.

Klausmeier, H. J. (1976). Instructional design and the teaching of concepts. In J. R. Levin & V. L. Allen (Eds.), *Cognitive learning in children* (pp. 191–217). New York: Academic Press.

Klausmeier, H. J., Ghatala, E. S., & Frayer, D. A. (1974). *Conceptual learning and development: A cognitive view.* New York: Academic Press.

Markle, S. M. (1975). They teach concepts, don't they? *Educational Researcher, 4,* 3–9.

Markle, S. M., & Tiemann, P. W. (1969). *Really understanding concepts: Or in frumious pursuit of the jabberwock.* Champaign, IL: Stipes.

Merrill, M. D., & Tennyson, R. D. (1977). *Concept teaching: An instructional design guide.* Englewood Cliffs, NJ: Educational Technology.

Miller, G. A., & Gildea, P. M. (1987). How children learn words. *Scientific American, 257*(3), 94–99.

Stanovich, K. (1986). Matthew effects in reading: Some consequences of individual differences in the acquisition of literacy. *Reading Research Quarterly, 21*(4), 360–407.

Tennyson, R., & Christensen, D. L. (1986). *Memory theory and design of intelligent learning systems.* AERA paper, San Francisco.

Williams, P., & Carnine, D. W. (1981). Relationship between range of examples and of instructions and attention in concept attainment. *Journal of Educational Research, 74,* 144–188.

C H A P T E R

SEVEN

Designing Instructional Strategies for Teaching Reading: Decoding

Chapter Objectives

Upon successful completion of this chapter, you will be able to:

1. DESCRIBE the history of beginning reading instruction in special education.
2. COMPARE and CONTRAST the predominant methods of beginning reading instruction.
3. DESCRIBE the relationship between decoding and comprehension in low-performing readers.
4. LIST the hierarchy of skills for beginning reading instruction.
5. RECOGNIZE features of symbols and words that impact reading acquisition.
6. APPLY features of the generic instructional set in the design of beginning reading instruction.
7. USE the basic delivery features in reading instruction and provide explicit examples of beginning reading instruction.

INTRODUCTION

As educators of low-performing children, we are confronted daily with students who are unable to read age- or grade-appropriate material. These students are unable to function successfully in the regular classroom because their reading deficiencies typically cut across every aspect of the instructional curriculum. Low performers' reading problems are often related to decoding deficits or the inability to translate printed symbols into words.

Although controversies over the exact cause of reading problems and the "best" method for addressing these problems are far from resolved, a substantial body of knowledge serves as the foundation for the beginning reading instructional methods we prescribe in this chapter. These methods integrate findings from empirical studies of decoding with the phases and features of instructional design and delivery detailed thus far in the text. The proposed instructional procedures provide guidelines for determining *what* to teach and for detailing how to schedule, organize, and deliver reading instruction. The history of reading instruction for low-performing students sheds light on the changes that are generally shaping the field of reading education, particularly the area of how to begin instruction in decoding.

A REVIEW OF BEGINNING READING INSTRUCTION

In the developmental period of reading instruction, educators strongly believed that students who failed to learn to read required "special" methods of teaching. Reading deficits were linked to children's "within-the-head" problems, and remedial methods were prescribed to modify these presumed deficits. Reading disorders were characterized as problems of minimal brain dysfunction, cerebellar vestibular dysfunction (i.e., an inner-ear imbalance), and strephosymbolia, or "twisted symbols" (Simmons & Kameenui, 1986). Accordingly, assessment instruments and instructional programs were developed to measure and to treat these presumed deficits. Despite the intuitive appeal of these rather esoteric teaching methods, research within the last decade did not substantiate the effectiveness of such techniques, including training visual perception, teaching to the preferred modality, re-creating missing creeping and crawling stages, and establishing hemispheric dominance (Arter & Jenkins, 1977; Kavale & Forness, 1985; Lewis, 1983). Intensive attempts to develop students' abilities to walk balance beams and track visual objects have succeeded to the extent that the students could indeed walk balance beams and track visual objects more skillfully as a result of the training. Unfortunately, these improved skills have failed to translate into significantly improved reading abilities.

As Lewis (1983) noted, the view that reading disabilities can be cured through remediation of psychological processes lacks the necessary research evidence. Simply stated, the principles of specialized instruction intended to modify or compensate for internal deficits have been seriously questioned. A close look at this large body of research has spawned the rather simple and straightforward indictment: *If you want to improve reading ability, you must teach reading.* Perhaps because of this rather embarrassing, but informative, period of trial-and-error research, special educators have redirected their efforts to tasks more directly related to reading. Nevertheless, the issue of how to teach beginning reading still stirs controversy in both theory and practice.

From Jeanne Chall's (1967) formal acknowledgment of the conflict in her text, *Learning to Read: The Great Debate,* to present-day roundtable discussions at national reading conferences and in teachers' lounges, the issue of how to teach children to read remains an unresolved and oftentimes heated item on the instructional agenda. This issue assumes even greater importance when students are low-performing readers. No doubt, we will not resolve issues of the "great debate" within the confines of this chapter. However, it is important to discuss and sort through the various viewpoints to arrive at a manageable framework for designing and delivering reading instruction.

PRIMARY READING METHODS

The two basic theoretical positions within the reading discipline frame the two predominant approaches to teaching reading skills: code-based approaches and meaning-based approaches. As illustrated in Table 7–1, the terminology that surrounds the debate on beginning reading is as plentiful as the literature it labels.

The starting points and procedures for teaching low-performing readers fundamental reading skills differ markedly in the two approaches, as we will discuss in the following sections.

Code-based Programs

Code-based programs rely on intensive, systematic instruction of phonics skills. The code-based or bottom-up theory (Gough, 1972), as it is often characterized, focuses on the progression of skills beginning with small units such as sound-symbol associations, followed by larger units of text such as whole words. As students become proficient at identifying sound-symbol associations (e.g., teacher points to the letter *a* and says, "This letter says *aaa*"), this knowledge is applied to highly controlled, orthographically regular vocabulary, such as *ran* and *hats*. In the code-emphasis approach, students are initially taught to rely on the phonics properties of words exclusively; they are not encouraged to use surrounding words or contexts as word recognition strategies. Code-based enthusiasts believe a functional, phonics-based strategy for decoding words will enable

TABLE 7–1
Primary approaches to reading instruction

Code Emphasis	Meaning Emphasis
Bottom up	Top down
Associationist	Constructivist
Synthetic	Analytic
Phonics	Look-say
Sound it out	Whole word

students to attack a large proportion of words—even those they have not seen or heard before. They do recognize exceptions to words that can be accurately decoded in this manner. However, they first introduce words that follow the rules to communicate the usefulness of the approach. After students are skilled at breaking the code, supplemental methods are introduced for deciphering words that cannot be decoded through sound-symbol knowledge and soundblending skills. The following example represents a code-emphasis passage:

> Pam can dig.
>
> Pam can dig in sand.
>
> Pam will dig in mud.
>
> Pam and Pig dig and dig.
>
> Can Pam dig?
>
> Can Pig dig?

In this example, the words are relatively small units and contain only letters that represent their most common sound. Therefore, if a student knows the common sounds for letters, that knowledge can be applied in a soundblending procedure and result in the correct pronunciation of the word. Conversely, words such as *for* or *the* contain letters that would not allow the reader to employ the code-based strategy. In beginning reading exercises, code-based programs use highly controlled passages containing high concentrations of words that can be read by applying the code.

Meaning-based Programs

The major alternative to code-based reading programs is a meaning-based approach. In contrast to the small-to-large unit sequencing and decodable word selection criteria of code-based programs, meaning-based procedures teach children to identify words by examining meaning and position in context. Determining whether the word makes sense in the sentence is a major thrust of the meaning-based approach. Students identify the word by using the words around it rather than decoding letters into sounds and then into words. Additionally, students are repeatedly exposed to high-frequency words and are taught to use phonics as an adjunct instead of a primary word-identification strategy. Advocates of meaning-based programs stress the mechanical nature of code-based programs and warn of the potential hazards of code-based instruction on reading comprehension. The following excerpt illustrates a meaning-based reading selection:

> The boy will go.
>
> The girl will go too.
>
> The boy and girl will both go.
>
> Would you like to go too?

In this passage, note the inclusions of words such as *you, boy,* and *girl* that are common to children's vocabularies yet are difficult to decode because letters do not represent their most common sounds.

Which Method to Use

Although the pros and cons of each treatment abound, research within the last two decades favors early emphasis on decoding skills through a code-emphasis approach (Anderson, Hiebert, Scott, & Wilkinson, 1985; Bond & Dykstra, 1967; Williams, 1979). Data generally support the efficacy of phonics as a means of teaching word identification skills (Chall, 1989; Lesgold & Resnick, 1982). It is important to stress, however, that code- and meaning-emphasis programs share a common goal. The objective of both is to allow the reader to construct meaning from text. Both cohorts do agree on the importance of developing efficient, automatic decoding strategies that enable readers to focus on comprehension rather than words. The means each program takes to reach this goal distinguish the two primary reading methods. Code-emphasis approaches begin with sound-symbol association training and reserve the introduction of meaning-based strategies until the reader is adept at sounding out words. In contrast, meaning-based programs introduce reading skills in the reverse order. Here lies the principal difference between bottom-up and top-down reading approaches. As Carnine, Silbert and Kameenui (1990) suggested, the question of code vs. meaning is not an issue of *whether* but of *when.*

Decoding Instruction for Low Performers

When research is restricted to studies of low-performing (e.g., reading disabled, learning disabled, remedial) students, the instructional advantage of phonics-based programs becomes more pronounced, suggesting a strong relationship between decoding deficits and comprehension difficulties. Considerable evidence documents that less-skilled readers' comprehension difficulties originate from underlying bottom-up deficits (Spear & Sternberg, 1986). Juel's (1988) recent longitudinal study indicated that students who enter first grade with deficits in phonemic awareness and decoding skills in 9 out of 10 cases remain in the bottom quartile on decoding and comprehension measures 4 years later.

Specifically, students' reading skills are hampered by underdeveloped phonemic and decoding abilities that, as Stanovich (1986) theorized, have a reciprocal effect on future reading. In simpler terms, students who have limited decoding abilities also have limited successful experience with text, limited practice exercising newly taught decoding skills, limited opportunities interacting with text, and little motivation for engaging in sustained reading. As a result, the less able the individual, the greater the effect on subsequent reading achievement. Even students who eventually develop adequate decoding skills have lingering comprehension difficulties precipitated by early decoding deficits.

Many researchers who are actively studying the cause and treatment of reading failure express a common viewpoint regarding the direction of beginning reading instruction, as summarized in the following excerpts:

> Disabled readers' difficulties with reading comprehension and other higher level reading skills are a result . . . of original bottom-up processing deficits, namely, poor word decoding. (Spear & Sternberg, 1986, p. 25)

> Though not a cure-all, a phonic approach to reading still seems a logical course for the teacher to take in beginning reading instruction. (Spear & Sternberg, 1986, p. 25)

It has yet to be demonstrated that there are individuals who have comprehension strategy deficits without decoding fluency problems. (Perfetti, 1985, p. 244)

Children must be able to decode independently the many unknown words that will be encountered in the early stages of reading. (Stanovich, 1986, p. 363)

Why is it that there is so much resistance to the idea of teaching decoding skills? . . . I do not believe we can attribute it to the dearth of empirical evidence. (Williams, 1979, pp. 920–921)

The Need for Direct Decoding Instruction

The charge for reading instructors is obvious. Low performers have not incidentally inherited the ability to make the necessary correspondences between symbols and sounds; therefore, students need to be directly taught the phonics skills necessary to decode printed symbols accurately and fluently. The first step toward remediating and buttressing against reading failure is the process of teaching students how to translate systematically that code of printed symbols. Our qualifier in this chapter on decoding skills is the term *first*.

Decoding is a means to an end. In no case should teachers communicate to students that the final goal is to be fluent decoders. Yet research documents that we have stressed decoding to the extreme that children think of it as the *purpose* of reading. Obviously, our instructional priorities need close attention. Although there is no doubt that we must move beyond decoding instruction, we must first equip students with a reliable method of identifying words found in beginning reading vocabularies. Instruction and practice at the decoding level should develop word identification skills that are nondemanding, automatic, and attention-free (Perfetti, 1985). Once proficient at this basic strategy, readers may enhance their word recognition skills through interacting with text and applying more complex techniques. There is no interaction when phonics skills are nonfunctional. As Stanovich (1986) notes, "Comprehension fails not because of over-reliance on decoding, but because decoding is not developed enough" (p. 373).

The growing empirical support for the code-based approach serves as the basis for the decoding procedures detailed in this chapter. We emphasize, though, that instruction should not be *limited to* decoding. As early as learners master sufficient skills to read connected text (e.g., sentences, paragraphs, stories), teachers should initiate comprehension exercises. The next chapter discusses the interface of decoding and comprehension. Suffice it to say that we endorse a code-based approach because it allows teachers the necessary control over variables in reading curricula that are most difficult and unpredictable for beginning readers.

DEFINING DECODING SKILLS

Before we can design decoding instruction, we must clarify the comprehensive and critical skill of decoding. Decoding is the complex process of analyzing and synthesizing multiple pieces of information. Some researchers and practitioners would restrict decoding to the association and sounding out of letters and words. We embrace a broader view of decoding that includes the text-based factors a reader uses to identify words. These include letter-sound correspondences, phonics rules, and structural as well as contextual features.

We have partitioned decoding instruction into three basic phases: phonics analysis, structural analysis, and contextual analysis, as depicted in Table 7–2.

Within each of these three phases of Table 7–2 are hierarchies of skills that comprise the sequence of decoding instruction. As seen in Table 7–3, phonics is the basis of the proposed decoding sequence and subsequent instruction.

Although beginning reading instruction focuses on phonemic training and isolated sound-symbol associations, the goal of this sequence of skills is to move students as quickly as possible to the point where they are reading continuous text. Conceivably, a student could be working concurrently on more than one phase of decoding instruction. For example, if the student has mastered the sound-symbol associations *r, u, n, h, i, t, s, l, a,* and *m* (phase I, skill 2) and can fluently read words such as *run, sit, slam,* and *mop* (phase I, skill 3b), it is quite logical to extend that student's reading vocabulary by introducing the morpheme *-ing* and the accompanying words formed by the addition of that suffix (phase II, skills 1 and 2). Meanwhile, the student continues to receive training at the phonics phase on sound-symbol associations (phase I, skill 2) not yet introduced or particularly problematic for the learner. Moreover, students may also read continuous text containing sound-symbol associations, sight words, and morphemes that have been explicitly taught and mastered. The critical index of the feasibility of multiple-phase decoding instruction is the student's performance on instructional tasks. Given low performers' histories of decoding difficulties, we recommend introducing no new decoding skills until the student is proficient on specific skills within a particular phase. Nonetheless, we must not delay the introduction of new decoding skills simply because the student has not mastered every sound-symbol association. Teachers must be able to identify those skills that require prerequisite knowledge.

TABLE 7–2
Cumulative model of decoding instruction

	Phase I	**Phase II**	**Phase III**
Decoding Skill	Phonics plus analysis	Structural analysis	Contextual analysis
Skill Explanation	Exclusive use of sound-symbol associations	Integration of sound-symbol associations and word part strategy	Combination sound-symbol associations, word parts, and word's meaning/position in text.
Skill Context	Sound-symbol associations	Word reading	Text reading
Skill Application	Teacher points to *u* in *run.* "What sound does this letter say?" (*uuu*) "OK, let's sound out this word."	Teacher points to *turn* in *turning.* "You sound out this part (*turn*). "This part says *ing.* Now put the parts together."	Student identifies *nightly* as *nittly.* Teacher says, "Good try at sounding out the word. Now use the word in the sentence to see if it makes sense."

TABLE 7–3
Sequence of component skills of decoding instruction

Phase I: Phonics	Phase II: Structural	Phase III: Contextual

1. Phonemic training
  a. Auditory segmenting
  b. Auditory soundblending		

2. Sound-symbol associations		

3. Regular word reading
  a. Soundblending of words
  b. Whole-word reading		

4. Irregular word reading	1. Base words with suffixes or inflectional endings	
5. Letter combinations	2. Compound words	

6. Special rule words
  a. CVCe words
  b. Silent letter words
	3. Words with prefixes	1. Word meaning in a sentence

	4. Words with suffixes and prefixes	2. Position of word in sentence
	5. Multisyllabic words	

As a basic guideline, advanced decoding skills are supplements, not replacements, for phonics-based decoding. Upon the completion of this three-phase sequence of decoding instruction, students should gain a working knowledge of the strategies for identifying words and be able to select and deploy these strategies as required by the reading content.

Each of the component skills in Table 7–3 is part of a comprehensive model of decoding instruction. Although it is impossible fully to discuss each decoding skill within the confines of this chapter, we will briefly describe these skills and provide examples in the following sections. We will discuss the dimensions of specific decoding skills to develop your awareness of the many factors that impact decoding instruction and learning. Abbreviated teaching procedures accompany this descriptive information to acquaint you with selected decoding tasks. These examples only introduce the task and are not comprehensive instructional procedures. Explicit design and delivery procedures for representative tasks are presented later in the chapter.

PHASE I: PHONICS INSTRUCTION

As indicated in the sequence of component skills of decoding instruction (see Table 7–3), beginning decoding training emphasizes techniques and tasks that require and develop the use of a code. Proficiency in using the code is based on mastery of several component skills. Figure 7–1 diagrams the general skills and subskills of phonics analysis. Each of these skills is discussed in the following section.

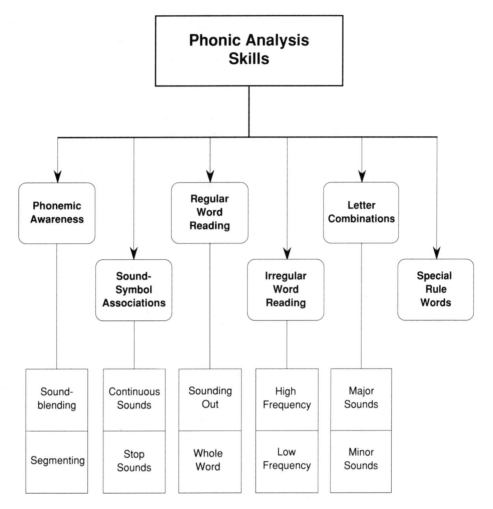

FIGURE 7–1
Phonics analysis skills

Phonemic Awareness Training

Results of studies consistently document the positive relationship between phonemic awareness skills and reading achievement in the early grades (Bradley & Bryant, 1983; Ehri, 1979; Juel, 1988). Phonemic awareness is the ability to recognize auditory features of words and to perform tasks using these auditory stimuli. Lewkowicz's (1980) review of phonemic awareness skills identified two tasks directly related to decoding ability: (1) segmenting and (2) soundblending words. Both segmenting and soundblending are auditory skills. That is, the skills are taught without visual stimuli to reduce the difficulty of processing both auditory and visual stimuli.

Auditory segmenting involves orally identifying and separating the individual phonemes within a word in the correct order. It is the slowed pronunciation of the word so the student can hear the individual sounds. In segmenting tasks, students slowly say or stretch out the sounds in the word *man,* "mmmaaannn."

Auditory soundblending entails recognizing, pronouncing, and combining isolated sounds into a whole word. In essence, this task teaches students how to put sounds together to form words. Because auditory soundblending focuses on joining sounds where no letters are present, it differs from the visual/verbal soundblending procedure used in beginning word reading.

The ability to segment is an effective way to improve soundblending ability (Fox & Routh, 1976). Lewkowicz (1980) noted that the easiest time to introduce soundblending seems to be when children have just got the hang of segmenting. In a soundblending exercise, the teacher would slowly pronounce the sounds in the word (e.g., "mmmmaaannn") and then ask students to say the whole word (e.g., *man*).

Sound-Symbol Association Training

Sound-symbol associations, sometimes referred to as letter-sound or grapheme-phoneme correspondences, are the student's first encounter with the printed code. In sound-symbol association tasks, the objective is to say a sound keyed to a particular letter or graphic symbol. The teacher presents a symbol and then asks the student to supply the corresponding sound (e.g., *m,* model the sound, "This letter says /*mmm*/"). This phase of phonics instruction is the foundation of subsequent decoding skills and critically important.

A common problem readers experience with sound-symbol associations is reversing letters that share common attributes. Every teacher knows at least one child who confuses *b* and *d* or *p* and *b*. A limited amount of research has been conducted on reducing problems associated with visually and auditorily similar correspondences.

Carnine (1981) used experimental figures and labels (e.g., *biff, diff*) that approximated the difficult discriminations of the letters *b* and *d* encountered by young children in school. He was interested in investigating different methods of introducing and scheduling a new symbol that was similar to previously taught symbols. His findings revealed that separating similar correspondences reduces possible confusion associated with these visually and auditorily similar letter-sound correspondences. A beginning sequence for introducing sound-symbol associations that would minimize reversals and expedite learning follows. The numbers in parentheses designate highly similar correspondences and those that need to be separated.

s   m(1)   e(2)   d(3)   r   a   i(2)   l   f   b(3)   t   o   n(1)

The sequence illustrates the distribution of similar letters such as *d* and *b, m* and *n, e* and *i.* This design allows the learner sufficient time to master the letter-sound correspondence before the introduction of a similar correspondence.

How sounds are pronounced is an additional attribute of sound-symbol associations that affects the ability to learn decoding skills. Sounds can be classified as either stop sounds such as *p* and *t* or continuous sounds such as *m* and *r.* Stop sounds are quick, almost explosive sounds, called plosive productions, that cannot be stretched. In contrast, continuous sounds allow for the prolonged stretching out of the sound. All vowels are continuous sounds. Table 7–4 categorizes all sound-symbol associations as either continuous or stop sounds. Note that the sequence of symbols does not suggest the particular order in which symbols within categories should be introduced.

Selecting words with easily produced sounds is particularly important. For beginning reading purposes, introduce continuous sounds first because they are easier to produce and use in soundblending activities than stop sounds.

Regular-Word Reading

Regular words are those in which letters represent their most common sounds (Carnine, Silbert & Kameenui, 1990). Words such as *red, blast,* and *stop* are examples of these regular words accurately decoded by translating symbols into sounds. Within the English language, many words conform to the common sound rule, and beginning word reading instruction should target these "reader-friendly" words. When initial reading is restricted to words that conform to the rules, students develop skill in decoding regular words and subsequently experience the usefulness and success of the sounding-out strategy and sound-symbol association knowledge. Introducing irregular words or words that do not follow the rules too early in reading instruction sends mixed signals to readers. That is, including words that can be sounded out with words that are not decodable through sound-symbol association knowledge forces the reader to practice *how* to sound out words as well as *when* to use a particular decoding strategy. Determining when to use sounding out vs. when to employ an alternate strategy is important; nonetheless, this is an advanced form of discrimination learning to be reserved until the learner is proficient at the sounding-out strategy. Once learners can distinguish that words are indeed regular, several additional decisions govern regular word reading.

Sounding Out vs. Whole-Word Reading

The goal of regular word reading is to teach the reader to recognize and produce words correctly and automatically. To accomplish this feat, we recommend a two-phase process of word reading instruction. In the first phase, students overtly pronounce each sound in the word; in the second phase, they produce only the whole word (Carnine, Silbert, & Kameenui, 1990).

The overt soundblending phase continues until the reader accurately and consistently decodes words at a rate of one letter per second. The process of attending to each letter-sound relation is sometimes referred to as "cipher reading" (Ehri & Wilce, 1987)

TABLE 7–4
Sound-symbol associations classified as stop or continuous sounds

Continuous	Stop
a e i o u	b c d g h
f l m n	j k p q t
r s v z	w x (ks) y

and differs from methods that encourage students to examine the first letter of the word or strings of letters (e.g., *ail*). Once proficient at sounding out, readers are instructed to internalize the sounding-out process; that is, they are asked to "sound it in your head" and combine the individual sounds into a whole word. At this phase of instruction, only the whole word is pronounced. Regular word reading is always initiated at the sounding-out phase because this practice affords instructors an audible model from which to monitor and analyze student performance. With this sounding-out/whole-word sequence serving as the general framework for regular word reading, regular word reading instruction must now focus specifically on words scheduled for beginning regular word reading exercises.

Word Complexity

A number of word dimensions contribute to the complexity of word types. The first feature addresses the pattern of consonants and vowels within the word along with the actual length of the word. Within the reading domain, words are frequently classified according to how consonants (C) and vowels (V) are ordered within the word. According to reading specialists, CVC or consonant-vowel-consonant word patterns such as *red* or *mat* are less complex than CVCC words (*best*) or CCVCC words (*blast*). This hierarchy of regular word types should be considered when designing word reading exercises. Along with this organizational feature, it should also be noted that the more units or letters within the task (or word), the more difficult the task (Golinkoff, 1978). Not surprisingly, words with fewer units or letters typically occur on the less difficult end of the consonant/vowel word type hierarchy. In Table 7–5, words are categorized according to word type

In the initial phase of regular word reading, students pronounce each sound in the word.

TABLE 7–5
Word types classified according to consonant/vowel arrangements

Word Type	Examples	Level of Difficulty
VC and CVC	am	easy
	sat	
	run	
CVCC	best	
	silk	
CCVC	slam	
	trip	
CCVCC	blast	
CCCVCC	splint	hard

and level of difficulty. Selected words are also included to illustrate these features of words.

Additional factors contributing to the complexity of regular words are specific to the sound-symbol correspondences within the word. Continuous sounds facilitate phonemic segmentation skills because they allow the reader more time to prolong the sound and make the transition from one sound to the next. Continuous sounds have similar advantages in regular word reading. In beginning sounding-out or soundblending instruction, words should begin with continuous sounds, such as *man* or *set*. As the learner becomes facile at sounding out this word type, introduce words beginning with stop sounds (*bat, tan*).

A final set of factors contributing to the success of regular word reading exercises involves the learner's preskills. To read regular words, learners must possess certain prerequisite skills. First, they must be intimately familiar with the sound-symbol associations of the word. Withhold words containing unfamiliar symbols until the sound-symbol relationship has been learned. Second, they must have a strategy for combining the parts into a whole. Phonemic training acquaints the learner with the blending process; however, low performers will require more concentrated direct instruction in the sound-blending strategy.

For soundblending of regular words, students should attend to each sound-symbol association and to the uninterrupted flow of sound from one symbol to the next. In an example lesson, the teacher would first model the visual/verbal soundblending procedure ("Listen while I soundblend the word /mmmaaannn/"), guide the students in soundblending the word ("Everyone, soundblend this word with me, /mmmaaannn/") and then have the students independently soundblend similar words. Once the learner is proficient at soundblending words presented in visual formats, schedule practice to read identical word types as whole words.

Irregular-Word Reading

Unfortunately, English orthography is plagued with many words that are exceptions to the rules. These words are referred to as irregular or sight words. Irregular words contain symbols that do not represent their common sound or that have not yet been taught in the skills sequence. For example, *the* and *was* are frequently encountered words that cannot be accurately decoded through the conventional application of sound-symbol relationships and soundblending. To teach these words, we recommend an alternate word identification strategy. This alternate instructional procedure is derived from the knowledge form of the skill. Irregular words are a form of verbal association—specifically, simple facts. As indicated in Chapter 3, simple facts are pieces of information that relate a particular stimulus (in this case, a word) with a specific response and cannot be broken down into smaller units that lead to the correct response. Words such as *night* or *two* are irregular words that cannot be read correctly by assembling the component sound-symbol associations. For example, a component skill approach to decoding the word *night* would result in the following pronunciation: /niguht/. Teach irregular words as facts, providing explicit teacher models and extensive practice on the word. Because facts require rote learning, careful attention must be paid to their order of introduction and review.

An additional guideline to consider when teaching irregular words is the frequency and usefulness of the words introduced. For example, words such as *the* and *was* occur frequently in beginning reading vocabularies and should be taught before words that are less common. Furthermore, irregular words are highly similar to sound-symbol associations in that similarities of features may pose problems for the learner. As *b* and *d* were separated in sound-symbol exercises, the strategic positioning of similar irregular words such as *they* and *them* or *was* and *saw* in instructional sequences should aid learning.

We propose teaching irregular words as simple facts using a model-lead-check/test format. In a sample instructional presentation, the teacher would first present the word to the student ("This word is *was*"), lead the student in producing the word *was* ("Say it with me . . . *was*"), and then request the student to produce the word independently.

Letter Combinations

Sometimes letters combine in ways that create sounds distinct from what they would be if they were sounded independently. We call these new creations **letter combinations**. Letter combinations (e.g., *sh, ea*) are odd creatures because even the same letter combination can represent more than one sound. Some letters combine to represent the same sound in the majority of words (e.g., *ai* as in *maid*). Others seem to surface almost by chance and occur less frequently. For example, the *ui* in *suit* occurs in approximately 6% of *ui* words while there are 16 word exceptions where *ui* takes on the pronunciation found in the word *build* (Clymer, 1963). Decide which letter combinations to teach and when to teach them by how consistently the letter combination represents the most frequent sound and how useful the letter combination is in word reading.

In the majority of words, consonant combinations such as *sh* and *ch* are pronounced consistently, although vowel combinations are more complex and unpredictable. A letter combination is a major sound if it is pronounced consistently over 50% of the time. For example, the *ai* in *rain* is a major sound. Letter combinations such as the *ai* in *villain* occur on a less frequent basis and are termed minor sounds (Schworm, 1979).

Given special educators' task to teach more in less time, such data have particular bearing on which letter combinations to teach and when they should be introduced.

Letter combinations that represent major sounds should receive priority over minor sounds as they are likely to be more useful to the reader in their early decoding efforts. Schworm (1979) identified 14 vowel-vowel (e.g., *ea*) or vowel-consonant combinations (e.g., *ar*) that represent their major sound over 70% of the time. These combinations should be first introduced in letter combination instruction. These letter combinations follow in Table 7–6.

Letter combination learning involves knowing the possible sounds as well as being able to discriminate which sound to use. When teaching students to decode words with letter combinations, the teacher should first model the sound most frequently associated with the letters ("These letters *sh* usually make the /sh/ sound"), apply that sound when soundblending the word (*shop*), and then verify the accuracy of the word and decoding strategy through pronouncing the word ("Yes, *shop* is the correct word"). If the letter combination represents its major sound, the learner's attempt to sound out the word will result in an acceptable pronunciation of the word. The discrimination exercise of determining an appropriate word from an inappropriate word is particularly important as it provides an external check to the accuracy of the response.

Special Rule Words

Rules specify patterns for learning that generalize across a range of examples. Decoding rules are patterned after the *if-then* contingency. In other words, *if* certain features are present in a word, *then* those features tell a reader how to pronounce the word. For example, in the rule "If there's an *e* at the end of the word, then the first vowel says its name," two pieces of information must be recognized and related. Learners must decide if there is an *e* at the end of the word. Then they must relate that piece of information to determine how it will influence the pronunciation of the first vowel in the word. In essence, the reader is asked to make a prediction about the pronunciation of the vowel, given the presence of the final *e.* The degree to which the rule works when applied to multiple examples determines its usefulness in decoding instruction. Unless the application of the rule consistently results in a correct response for the reader, the rule's generalizability and role are questionable.

In decoding, many rules or generalizations purportedly help readers read unfamiliar words. Unless a rule accurately assists the reader in a minimum of 50% of the instances,

TABLE 7–6
Vowel-vowel and vowel-consonant combinations: Major sounds

ai bait	*oa* coat
ea each	*ay* day
ee bleed	*ow* own/cow
ou ounce	*ir* bird
oo boot	*er* term
au cause	*ur* burn
oi coin	*ar* barn

we do not recommend introducing it as a rule. Instead, teachers may delay introducing words of that type and treat them as sight words or exceptions.

Many rules found in elementary reading programs fail to meet the 50% application criterion. For instance, when analyzed for its generalizability to a range of examples, the often quoted rule "When two vowels go walking the second one is silent and the first one does the talking" was useful in only 45% of the words examined. Clymer's (1963) research on phonic generalizations served as the basis for the rules selected in this section and should be consulted for more descriptive information. His extensive research in this area led to his conclusion that "many generalizations which are commonly taught are of limited value" (p. 258). Given the limited usefulness of these rules, teachers must scrutinize rules to determine their applicability, to establish priorities, and to design better methods of teaching word types that do not follow the rules.

The following rules meet the 50% application criterion. This subset of generalizations is not an exhaustive list but illustrates the rules that should be taught during beginning decoding instruction.

Phonics Rules

1. When there's an *e* at the end of a two-vowel word, the first vowel is long and the *e* is silent (*cake, time*).
2. When a vowel is in the middle of a one-syllable word, the vowel says its sound (*map, bun*).
3. If the only vowel is at the end of the word, the vowel says its name (*go, be*).
4. When a *c* is followed by *e* or *i*, it makes the *s* sound (*cent, city*).
5. When a *c* is followed by *o* or *a*, it makes the *k* sound (*cottage, cane*).
6. A vowel followed by an *r* produces a sound that is neither long nor short (*burn, girl*).

Phonics rule instruction must focus on the connections between the two components of the rule. An instructional sequence would involve the teacher stating the rule (e.g., "If the only vowel is at the end of the word, the vowel says its long sound"), confirming the "if" component by determining whether there is only one vowel, and then applying the information to decode the word (i.e., "Yes, there is only one vowel and it is at the end of the word so it must say its long sound. The word is *be*"). Students would then be led through a similar set of examples and then asked to apply the skill independently to a set of untaught words. It is this final application that establishes the generalizability of the decoding strategy to new instances and contexts.

Summary of Phase I Decoding

Up to this point, decoding strategies have focused exclusively on the code or sound-symbol associations as the means to identify unfamiliar words. In the next two phases, this code-based approach is not diminished but rather supplemented with additional sources to enrich the reacher's decoding strategies. In phase II, readers are taught to examine larger segments of words or morphemes, and in phase III students are exposed to a cumulative strategy that combines the components of sound-symbol associations, meaningful word parts, and context.

PHASE II: STRUCTURAL ANALYSIS

Structural analysis or morphological analysis is a more advanced form of decoding or word identification that involves breaking words into meaningful parts or morphemes (i.e., base words, affixes, inflectional endings). The primary skills within structural analysis instruction are illustrated in Figure 7–2.

We recommend reserving structural analysis until the student is able to read regular words accurately. After students demonstrate competency at decoding words through individual sound-symbol correspondences and phonics analysis, teachers may introduce the more advanced decoding technique of structural analysis. In essence, structural analysis is analogous to the segmenting-blending component of decoding only with larger linguistic units. Students are taught to identify chunks or pieces of words and then combine those pieces into wholes. Although it is a more efficient way of decoding, it assumes that learners are able to identify the parts of words. To know the parts, learners must either be proficient at decoding individual sound-symbol correspondences or be directly taught the separate parts of words. As with regular word types, certain features compound the difficulty of decoding through structural analysis.

Base Word

A factor that influences the success of structural analysis techniques is the base word. The base word is the word to which the prefix, suffix, or inflectional ending is added to

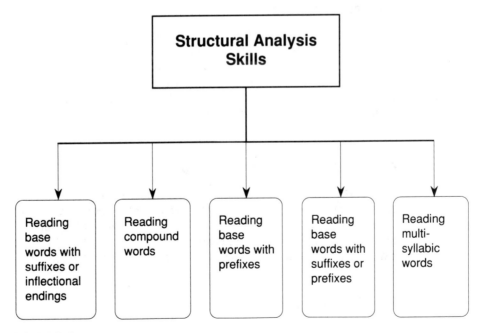

FIGURE 7–2
Structural analysis skills

From *Teaching new words through the word structure method* (p. 16) by E. Reid, 1978. Salt Lake City, UT: Cove Publishers. Copyright 1978 by Cove Publishers. Adapted by permission.

make a new word. If the base (e.g., *laugh* in *laughing*) is difficult to decode or requires modification (e.g., *wolf; wolves*), the strategy of decoding through using word structure is a more complicated task. Reid (1978) recommends introducing structural analysis tasks first in words where base words require no modification (e.g., *dangerous, missing, rented*). After students master base words plus affixes, base words that require changes to accommodate suffixes or inflectional endings (e.g., *puppies, running, happier*) may be introduced.

Affixes

An affix is the letter or letters added to the beginning or end of the word that changes the pronunciation or meaning of the word. The three types of affixes are suffixes (*-ous, -ion*), inflectional endings (*-ing, -ed, -s*), and prefixes (*re-, in-*). Beginning structural analysis tasks should include words with more familiar and serviceable affixes (*-s, -ed, un-*). Less frequently used affixes (*-ment, poly-, -ture*) may be introduced as learners develop proficiency with the word-part method.

The position of the affix further contributes to the difficulty of structural analysis strategies. Structural analysis strategy training should begin with words containing suffixes or inflectional endings only. In this sequence, students focus on the familiar base word first, then add the affix. Teachers may introduce words with prefixes next, followed by words containing both prefixes and suffixes.

Multisyllabic Words

Some words that contain multiple syllables are decoded more fluently by syllables than by identifying bases. This is particularly true when base words are unfamiliar or when there is no apparent base (manufacture, determine, orchestra). For this word type, we recommend teaching readers to read new words a syllable at a time. For word reading exercises, it is not critical that students adhere to syllabication rules. Rather, a strategy where they read parts based on how the word divides when it is pronounced is preferable (*re mem ber, de nom i na tor*).

General Structural Analysis Strategy

Three basic steps compose the strategy for decoding through structural analysis. First, teach students the affix through the model-lead-check/test procedure (e.g., "These letters say *ing*"). Once learners master the pronunciation of the affix, review the base word through a whole-word reading task ("What is this part?"). Finally, combine the two or more parts into one unit ("Put the parts together and read the word").

PHASE III: CONTEXTUAL ANALYSIS

In contextual analysis, both syntactic and semantic cues are used to identify words. Syntactic information refers to the grammatical structure of words in the sentence. That is, by recognizing that the word in the sentence should be a plural, a past tense verb form, or a possessive, the learner rules out other words that do not fit the grammatical criterion. On the other hand, semantics involves decoding the word through examining the word's meaning in the sentence or surrounding context. By determining how the word fits in the sentence, the reader has additional resources available to facilitate decoding.

A popular and influential theory is that skilled readers use context to aid word recognition more frequently and more skillfully than lower achieving students. Although research has found that better readers are more skilled at using context to facilitate comprehension, there is no clear distinction between less-skilled and more-skilled readers' ability to use context to facilitate word recognition (Stanovich, 1986). Actually, Perfetti, Goldman, and Hogaboam (1979) found that skilled readers are less likely to use context for word identification because they are less likely to need contextual assistance for word identification. In contrast, less-skilled readers' failure to use context to assist word identification can be traced to their poor decoding skills. Poor and laborious decoding skills render the surrounding context meaningless. That is, poorer readers would rely on context if they had the decoding skills to use the context. The primary skills within contextual analysis instruction are illustrated in Figure 7–3.

Whether you are teaching the learner to use the word's meaning in the sentence or focusing on the position of the word as the aid to word recognition, we stress using phonics, structural analysis, and contextual analysis skills. With many multisyllabic or less-familiar words, a single contextually based strategy may not suffice. Teaching students to rely solely on context is not advised. Contextual strategies alone may result in incorrect responses, but more important, the isolated use and early introduction of context encourages students to guess at words without examining their critical features.

FIGURE 7–3
Contextual analysis skills

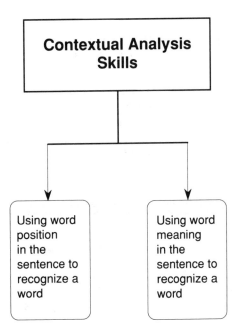

The generic contextual decoding strategy comprises three primary steps. First, the reader scrutinizes the word for familiar letter-sound correspondences and morphemes (*coughing*, "The first part says *k* and the last part says *ing*"). After delimiting the possible word choices through this procedure, the reader next puts the word in the surrounding context, either a phrase or sentence, to identify plausible acceptable responses ("The boy had a sore throat, he was c_____ing"). Finally, the learner combines information gathered in steps 1 and 2 to verify the appropriateness of the word identified ("Yes, *coughing*, that word makes sense"). As in previous instructional instances, the teacher models each step in the procedure, then students practice under teacher supervision and finally apply the skill independently to tasks of an appropriate instructional level.

SUMMARY OF DECODING PHASES

The goal of beginning reading instruction is to take the reader from the state of nonreader to the state of an automatic, fluent reader who not only identifies words independently, accurately, and automatically but also reads with understanding. To accomplish this, the reader cannot remain in the phonics analysis phase simply decoding words letter by letter. Students must learn to decode progressively larger units of words through applying knowledge of sound-symbol associations, using phonics rules, analyzing words structurally according to component parts, and verifying the word's pronunciation through its meaning or position in the text. It is necessary to make the transition from single-strategy decoding (i.e., phonics-based) to multiple-strategy decoding; however, these additional strategies cannot be introduced prematurely. The determination of *when* to introduce specific decoding strategies must be based on the learner's facility with basic code-based strategies.

INTEGRATING DESIGN AND DELIVERY IN BEGINNING READING INSTRUCTION: APPLYING THE GENERIC INSTRUCTIONAL SET

Having described and defined decoding subskills and the features of these tasks that impact word identification learning, how then does one translate these fragmented skills into a cohesive, effective decoding lesson? In the next sections, we implement the complementary procedures of designing and delivering instruction within the before, during, and after phases of instruction.

BEFORE INSTRUCTION

Step 1: Determining the Knowledge Form

The first task in designing decoding instruction is to determine whether the task is a verbal association, concept, rule relationship, or cognitive strategy. This classification specifies how information will be taught as well as how it will be corrected. The knowledge form also establishes the boundaries for the examples to be selected. To determine the knowledge form of a decoding skill, you must identify the component forms of the task and the requirements of the learner. Specifically, what does the task require of the learner? Is the reader required to make a connection between a symbol and the sound it typically makes? If so, sound-symbol association tasks would be classified as verbal associations. On the other hand, reading CVCe words such as *rate* and *like* requires applying a rule that indicates the relationship between how the *e* at the end of the word affects the vowel sound. Finally, using a procedure that involves searching out contextual cues to aid in identifying unfamiliar words is a more complex cognitive strategy comprising multiple sequential steps.

After the component forms within the skill are defined and the corresponding knowledge forms are selected, this information can be linked to essential features suggesting how the skill should be taught. For example, knowing that a letter-sound correspondence is a verbal association means that it should be taught through modeling, frequent practice, and review. In contrast, CVCe words require the application of a rule. Instruction entails using the learner's knowledge of the component form that an *e* appears at the end of the word and applying that skill to a range of words with similar features (i.e., words that end in *e*). In cognitive strategies, instruction must focus on each of the component forms and then systematically combine these separate pieces into a workable strategy.

Classifying decoding skills by knowledge form is not an absolute, fixed process. However, identifying the knowledge form is a first step toward designing instruction because it forces the designer (teacher) to examine components of the task. Identifying task components defines the beginning of instruction. Following are selected decoding tasks categorized by knowledge form, component parts, and essential instructional features to illustrate the information accessible in this first phase of instructional design.

Decoding Skills Classified by Knowledge Form

DECODING TASK 7–1
Orally Producing Consonant Sound-symbol Associations

Examples: m, s, t.

Knowledge Form: Verbal association.

Component Form: Simple facts.

Instructional Procedure

1. Model.
2. Lead.
3. Check/Test.
4. Practice.
5. Review.

DECODING TASK 7–2
Reading Irregular Words

> *Examples:*   *laugh, night, saw.*
>
> *Knowledge Form:*   Verbal association.
>
> *Component Form:*   Simple facts.

Instructional Procedure

1. Model.
2. Lead.
3. Check/Test.
4. Practice.
5. Review.

DECODING TASK 7–3
Reading Words Where the Only Vowel Is at the End of the Word

> *Examples:*   *we, my, go.*
>
> *Knowledge Form:*   Rule relationship.

Component Form

1. Discrimination: consonants from vowels.
2. Discrimination: words with one vowel or more than one vowel.
3. Discrimination: vowel at the end of the word or not at the end.
4. Simple fact: name of the vowel.

Instructional Procedure:

1. Discriminate vowel from consonants.
2. Determine placement of vowel in word.
3. Name the vowel.
4. Put parts of rule together and read word.

DECODING TASK 7–4
Reading Words with c Followed by e or i

> *Examples:*   *cent, city, cinnamon.*
>
> *Knowledge Form:*   Rule relationship.

Component Form

1. Discrimination: words with *c* followed or not followed by *e* or *i*.
2. Simple fact: *c* makes /*ssss*/ sound.

Instructional Procedure

1. Discriminate whether *c* is followed or not followed by *e* or *i*.
2. Determine if the *c* says *k* or *s*.
3. Put parts together and read word.

DECODING TASK 7–5
Reading Multisyllabic Words

> **Examples:**   *colorful, renew, international.*
>
> **Knowledge Form:**   Cognitive strategy.
>
> **Component Form**
>
> 1. Discrimination: determining base word from affixes.
> 2. Simple facts:
>   a. Reading root.
>   b. Reading affix or affixes.
>
> **Instructional Procedure**
>
> 1. Discriminate between base word and affixes.
> 2. Teach affix.
> 3. Review base.
> 4. Combine two or more parts.

Step 2: Determining the Range of Examples

In teaching decoding skills, it is important to make clear not only the components to be taught but also the range of examples that are needed to represent the skill accurately. Determining the knowledge form also indicates the range of examples. For example, by categorizing the letter-sound correspondence *m* as a verbal association or a task where there is a connection between a specific stimulus (*m*) and a specific response (/*mmm*/), the range of examples is delimited. In fact, the range consists of a very limited set including only the upper and lower case of the letter *m*. However, the decoding skill of reading CVC words represents a cognitive strategy requiring an expanded set of examples. These examples are restricted by the features of the (CVC) word and the sound-symbol associations familiar to the learner. More specifically, a CVC word is composed of a string of three successive letters. The range of examples is determined by the range of CVC words that can be constructed from the learner's repertoire of mastered sound-symbol relationships (e.g., *s, i, m, t*). Introductory sets or sets where skills are initially taught require strategic planning to convey adequately the features of the skill being introduced. Expanded sets complement introductory sets by providing additional examples and practice of the skill under study. By critically selecting a representative range of examples, students are more likely to transfer the taught skill to novel, never-taught-before examples. The range of examples communicates to the learner the extent of words to which the newly learned information can be applied.

As a general rule, verbal associations such as sound-symbol associations, letter combinations, and irregular words will have a limited range of examples. On the other hand, rule relationships and cognitive strategies will require a more extensive set of examples to communicate the information adequately and provide sufficient training for generalization. Sometimes referred to as general case programming, the instructional procedure of training on a range of examples increases the learner's ability to transfer that knowledge to new, untaught examples. In the following illustrations, decoding tasks are accompanied by limited introductory teaching sets or expanded sets, or both.

DECODING TASK 7–6
Orally Producing Consonant Sound-symbol Associations

> *Example:* m.
>
> *Knowledge Form:* Verbal association/simple fact.
>
> *Limited Set:* m, M.
>
> *Expanded Set:* None.

DECODING TASK 7–7
Reading Sight Words

> *Example:* the.
>
> *Knowledge Form:* Verbal association/simple fact.
>
> *Limited Set:* the.
>
> *Expanded Set:* Other mastered sight words.

DECODING TASK 7–8
Reading Words Where the Only Vowel Is at the End of the Word

> *Example:* we.

Knowledge Form: Rule relationship.

Limited Set: we, my, go.

Expanded Set

Include multiple examples of words containing each vowel (*we, my, go, be, no, by, so, he, hi, me*).

DECODING TASK 7–9
Reading Words with c *Followed by* e *or* i

Examples: cent, city.

Knowledge Form: Rule relationship.

Limited Set

Simple examples of words with *ce* and *ci* (*cent, city, cell*).

Expanded Set

Multiple examples (*cent, city, cinnamon, century, cement, civil, citrus*).

DECODING TASK 7–10
Reading Multisyllabic Words with Suffixes

Example: -ful suffix.

Knowledge Form: Cognitive strategy.

Limited Set

Only words containing familiar roots with known suffixes (*colorful, wonderful, joyful*).

Expanded Set

Multiple examples (*colorful, wonderful, painful, hopeful, joyful, truthful, spoonful, eventful*).

Having identified the knowledge form of the task and the range of examples, the next step pertains to how these examples will be sequenced within the instructional set.

Step 3: Sequencing Examples

By strategically sequencing examples with learning sets, you minimize potential problems of decoding. The sequence of examples should be determined by analyzing examples according to how they are the same and how they are different. This grouping factor of sameness or difference coupled with the knowledge form of the task determines how best to sequence examples. A crude yet helpful guidepost in sequencing examples is to separate similar examples of verbal associations and to cluster similar examples requiring the applications of rule relationships and cognitive strategies. An explanation of this sequencing principle follows.

Many sound-symbol correspondences such as *p* and *b* share common distinctive physical features. Likewise, many sounds have similar phonemic properties including *s* and *z*, *t* and *d*, *k* and *g*. In fact, some sound-symbol relationships are highly similar in both physical and phonemic characteristics (e.g., *p* and *b*, *d* and *b*). These pairs share multiple common features that often pose extreme difficulty for at-risk readers.

Because verbal associations have only one specific response for a specific stimulus, there is little benefit to be gained by successively sequencing similar sound-symbol associations (e.g., *p*, *b*, *d*, or *a*, *e*, *o*). In fact, recent research has indicated the potential confusion and the increased number of learning trials necessary when sound-symbol relationships sharing common features are initially taught in close proximity (Carnine, 1980). Similar sequencing guidelines apply to irregular words because they are also verbal associations. Sight words such as *was* and *saw* and *were* and *where* are examples that should likewise be separated in early instructional sequences to avoid potential confusion.

In contrast to the procedure of initially separating similar examples of verbal associations, words formed through the application of rules or strategies should be grouped or clustered according to sameness. For example, when teaching the use of context for decoding unfamiliar words, group words according to the contextual procedures required of the task. Specifically, practice would first be provided on multiple examples where the word's meaning in context would best supplement code-based word identification strategies. Example sentences where word meaning would facilitate word identification include:

> For supper, Ron ate salad and *lasagna*.
>
> Sam saw the bird sitting in the *cage*.
>
> It is too far to *walk* to the shop.

In these sentences, none of the italicized words can be accurately decoded through the application of sound-symbol relations only. Having the child *also* examine what makes sense in the sentence strengthens word identification procedures. Examples that necessitate using the word's meaning in context should be clustered and firmed before the introduction of other contextual strategies. After mastering one component of the strategy, students should then be introduced to using the position of the word in the sentence as a decoding aid.

An additional application of the sequencing guidelines involves the order of introducing word types. As illustrated earlier in the chapter, the organization of consonants and vowels in the word contributes to the difficulty of word learning. As such, the sequence in which words are introduced can minimize the amount of information to which the learner must attend. Knowing that CVC words (e.g., *red*) are less difficult than CCVCC words (e.g., *blast*) directs the sequence in which words are introduced.

Features within words affect the acquisition of reading. The position of stop and continuous sounds, the learner's facility with sound-symbol associations within the word, and the usefulness of the word itself must be considered when designing instructional sequences.

A set of decision rules for sequencing examples of beginning reading skills follows.

Based on knowledge form and similarity, determine whether to separate or cluster examples.

Separate according to similarity	Group according to similarity
1. Sound-symbol associations.	1. Regular words.
2. Letter combinations	2. Words that adhere to rules at least 50% of the time.
3. Irregular words.	3. Multisyllabic words according to affix.
	4. Contextual strategy applications.

Features of particular tasks should determine whether the teacher sequences similar examples in close proximity or separates similar items strategically. Each beginning reading skill encompasses multiple dimensions that must be considered along with the skills of the learner in designing the instructional sequence.

Design sequences according to task specific features.

Possible task specific features include:
1. Sound-symbol association knowledge.
2. Position of stop sounds within the word.
3. Difficulty of word type (CVC, CVCC).
4. Position of affix.
5. Number of components in strategy.

In the following applications, both knowledge form decisions and task specific factors have been considered. Each example outlines sequencing considerations as well as abbreviated task sequences.

DECODING TASK 7–11
Orally Producing Sound-symbol Associations

> ***Knowledge Form:***   Verbal association/simple fact.

Sequencing Considerations

1. Separate letters that are similar.
2. Separate sounds that are similar.
3. Include sound-symbol associations that are most useful.

Abbreviated Sequence of Introduction: m, s, e, t, r, a, l.

DECODING TASK 7–12
Reading Irregular Words

Knowledge Form: Verbal association/simple fact.

Sequencing Considerations

1. Separate words that are physically similar.
2. Separate words that are phonemically similar.
3. Include words of high frequency.

Possible Sequence of Introduction: the, saw, you, are, have.

DECODING TASK 7–13
Reading Words Where the Only Vowel Is at the End of the Word

Knowledge Form: Rule relationship.

Sequencing Considerations

1. Sound-symbol associations must be mastered.
2. Include words that are useful.
3. Include all mastered vowels.

Possible Sequence of Introduction: we, my, go, hi, be, no, by, so, he, me.

DECODING TASK 7–14
Reading Base Words with Affixes

Knowledge Form: Cognitive strategy.

Sequencing Considerations

1. Base words should be known.
2. Affix should first appear at the end of words.
3. Affix should be of high utility.
4. Base word should require minimal modification.

Possible Sequence of Introduction: -s, -ing, -ed.

DECODING TASK 7–15
Reading CVC Words

Knowledge Form: Cognitive strategy.

Sequencing Considerations

1. Learner must have knowledge of sound-symbol associations; e.g., *m, s, e, t, r, a, l, d, i.*
2. Stop sounds should occur at the end of the words.

Possible Sequence of Introduction of CVC Words

Set 1: *mat   sad*
       met   sit
       rid   let
       lit   red

After student is facile with CVC words beginning with continuous sounds, words with initial stop sounds may be introduced.

Set 2: *met   let*
       tim   rim
       sad   dim
       dam   sit

Step 4: Selecting Test Examples

As recommended in Chapter 2, test examples serve a variety of functions and provide varying types of information for both the teacher and learner. Within the decoding domain as well as other academic areas, test examples can be divided into four basic types:

1. Items that test immediate acquisition.
2. Items that test delayed retention.
3. Items that test discrimination.
4. Items that test generalization.

When designing test sequences, reading instructors must be aware of the purpose of the test and the information that can be derived from the exercise. For example, immediately after an irregular word is taught, it is important to assess the reader's knowledge of that newly taught word. However, it is equally important to measure that same student's retention of irregular words presented in previous sessions, as well as accuracy with words that have been particularly troublesome in earlier sessions. Such indices allow the teacher to assess whether the student has retained information and provides information for instructional decision making. For instance, if a student correctly pronounces irregular words introduced in the previous day's lesson but fails to produce words introduced in sessions 2 weeks earlier, the instructional remedy is to schedule more frequent practice and cumulative review. An example test set of sight words follows. Also indicated are the session in which the word was initially taught and the status of the task.

Example Test Set: Session #25

Words	Session Introduced	Status of Task
said	25	New
where	25	New
night	25	New
they	24	Previous session
about	18	Frequently missed
the	15	Frequently missed

Test examples should also measure the reader's ability to generalize the strategy to new, untaught instances of the skill. For example, if the CVC words *sat, man, red, rat, set,* and *ram* were introduced in the teaching format, a sample of these words, as well as other CVC words that were not presented during instruction, should be selected for inclusion in the test set. When designing test examples, it is important to consider the necessary prerequisite skills. For example, CVC words could only be composed of sound-symbol associations with which the learner is familiar.

Finally, a crucial test of knowledge is to sequence examples strategically to assess the reader's ability to discriminate between similar examples. Introductory sets contain only examples of the particular skill being taught. By restricting examples to one skill, the reader is able to focus on the critical dimensions of the skill under study. After the learner consistently demonstrates these skills under controlled contexts, discrimination items (items that are similar in many attributes but differ according to one critical dimension) are introduced as another index of learning. For example, after the student is firm on CVC and CVCe words when presented in separate sets, similar examples of these word types (e.g. *cap, cape*) are tested in a single test set to assess the learner's discrimination ability.

Introductory Set	Discrimination Set	Generalization Set
made	made	same
note	note	cone
bite	bit	name
same	mad	made
fine	bite	bone
	fin	dime
	Sam	note
	same	mole
	fine	
	not	

In the following instructional sets, the principles of designing test sequences are illustrated.

DECODING TASK 7–16
Orally Producing Sound-symbol Associations

>*New Target Skill:*   t.
>
>*Preskills:*   m, s, t (sounds already mastered).
>
>*Frequently Missed Skill:*   e.
>
>*Introductory Set:*   t.
>
>*Discrimination Set and Sequence:*   t, m, t, e, s, t, e, t
>The actual set contains only four symbols; however, the *t* is presented on multiple occasions to assess the student's ability to discriminate between the newly introduced symbol-sound relation and those previously taught. Additionally, more practice is scheduled for *e* because it has been identified as a tough skill for the learner.
>
>*Generalization Set:*   Use of letter in more complex tasks such as CVC word reading.

DECODING TASK 7–17
Reading Irregular Words

>*Target Skill:*   were.
>
>*Preskills:*   the, saw, you, are (words already mastered).
>
>*Frequently Missed Skill:*   have.
>
>*Introductory Set:*   were.
>
>*Discrimination Set:*   were, the, were, have, saw, you, were, have, were.
>
>*Generalization Set:*   Application of sight words in sentences.

DECODING TASK 7–18
Reading Words in Which the Only Vowel Is at the End of the Word

>*Preskills:*
>
>1. Knowledge of sound-symbol associations.
>2. Soundblending of words.
>
>*Introductory Set:*   we, my, go, be, hi.
>
>*Discrimination Set:*   we, my, wet, go, hit, be, bet, hi, got.
>
>*Generalization Set:*   no, by, hi, so, he, me, go, hi.

DECODING TASK 7–19
Reading Words with Suffixes (s)

Preskills:

1. Knowledge of base words.
2. Soundblending of words.

Introductory Set: cats, hits, runs, digs.

Discrimination Set: cats, cat, hits, run, dig, digs, runs.

Generalization Set 1:   cats, begs, hits, mats, digs.

Generalization Set 2:   Use of words with *s* suffix in sentences.

Step 5: Scheduling Practice

The fifth and final feature of the instructional design set addresses practice. Practice examples should be scheduled according to the difficulty and recency of the task. Particularly difficult tasks (i.e., tasks on which the learner makes consistent and frequent errors) should be scheduled for brief periods on multiple occasions within the initial teaching session. They should also be distributed across teaching sessions until the learner demonstrates mastery of the skill. Secondly, new tasks should receive extensive review with practice diminishing as the task is converted from a new to a familiar one. For example, if the learner had multiple errors on the sound-symbol association *o* when it was first introduced, the *o* would be practiced numerous times within the session and then routinely in subsequent sessions.

The structure of practice should likewise be considered. Initially, skills should be practiced under guided conditions where the teacher is available to monitor progress and provide immediate feedback. Group word list reading or flash card drill is a structure in which teachers are able to monitor performance and provide immediate corrective feedback. Once the reader is firm on the skill, independent practice activities should be scheduled. For instance, soundblending CVC words is a skill that will initially require an extensive period of overt practice under teacher-directed conditions. Once the learner skillfully decodes CVC words under guided conditions, the reader may apply CVC sound-blending skills on independent reading tasks.

Summary of Instructional Design Features As Applied to Decoding Tasks in Before Instruction Phase

A student's ability to learn information is directly linked to how information is designed and delivered. If examples of reading tasks are properly selected, well sequenced, routinely practiced, and systematically assessed, learning is more likely to occur. Through careful examination of the integral features of decoding instruction, teachers will not be required to make conceptual leaps of faith to explain why students *are* or *are not* learning to read. Progress can be in large part explained and facilitated through the design of instruction.

We have proposed the generic instructional set as a means of structuring beginning reading instruction. The majority of this design is conceived and mapped out before information is delivered to students. Modifications to the original design will necessarily depend on student performance. A lesson's effectiveness relies not only on how the information is structured for presentation but also on how that information is delivered. In the next section, delivery procedures for activating this plan for decoding instruction are detailed.

DURING INSTRUCTION

Delivering Decoding Instruction: Generic Procedures

In Chapter 4, procedures were detailed for delivering and modifying instruction. Because the delivery of instruction takes place in a public and oftentimes challenging context, it is necessary to have a repertoire of delivery procedures that can be automatically and consistently used. In the next section, we will apply seven such procedures to the delivery of decoding instruction. These delivery procedures include framing, preteaching, pacing, think time, signaling, corrective feedback, and firming.

This set of procedures is offered as a group of minimum requirements necessary to direct the delivery of academic instruction. Undoubtedly, numerous additional factors impact the successful delivery of decoding instruction. However, these procedures should generalize to all decoding skills and supply the needed direction effectively to transform information from an instructional design to an instructional episode. The features of each of these seven procedures are next illustrated in specific decoding tasks.

> **Framing:** Specifying the requirements of the task before the student's actual practice on the skill. This procedure readies the student for the task by outlining the critical behaviors necessary for task completion.

TEACHER: Class, I need your attention.
Thanks everyone for having eyes and ears on me.
Today we will learn how to soundblend words.
What are we going to learn? (Signal.)
STUDENTS: How to soundblend words.
TEACHER: Exactly right. Soundblending is important because you will use it when you read many words.

To soundblend words you must say the sound of the letter and stretch out the sound until you come to the next letter.

What's the first thing you must do when you soundblend? (Calls on individual.)

ANN: You must say the sound of the letter.

TEACHER: Right, you say the sound of the letter.

What's the other important thing you must do? (Calls on individual.)

EMILY: You must stretch out the sound until you come to the next letter.

TEACHER: Very nice; you must stretch out the sound until you come to the next letter.

Now let's practice soundblending.

My turn to soundblend this word.

Preteaching: The advance cueing of a potentially problematic task.

Example 1: Remember this letter (teacher points to *i* in word *bit*) and get ready to sound out the word.

Example 2: This passage has a number of words with multiple syllables. Think of how you break the word into parts to help figure it out.

Example 3: Some of the words in the list have an *e* at the end; others don't. Look carefully at the words as you read them in this list.

Pacing: The rate of instructional presentations and response solicitations.

As referenced in Chapter 1, a myth of special education is that teachers must slow the pace. Slowing the pace presumably gives students more time to labor over the task and derive the correct response. Although tasks must be regulated to allow adequate amounts of think time, when students require extended periods of time, it typically indicates the skill is not at the instructional or independent level of the student. Erroneously, teachers slow the pace instead of either breaking the task into smaller chunks or providing additional instruction on the skill.

Pacing is critical for low-performing students, given the need for curriculum compression (i.e., teaching more in less time). When tasks are presented at a brisk, regulated pace, three objectives are accomplished: (1) students are provided more information through exposure to additional trials and probes, (2) students are engaged in the instructional activity that results in higher academic achievement (Wilson & Wesson, 1986), and (3) behavior problems are minimized because students are on-task.

When pacing decoding activities, it is again important to consider the variation of the task and the learner's performance. Newly introduced words or sound-symbol associations will require a slower pace than will review tasks that can be presented at a faster rate. Additionally, the knowledge form of the task can be used as a criterion for setting the pace. Verbal associations that simply require readers to make a connection between a symbol and a sound or a printed word and its verbal counterpart will accommodate a faster pace than will decoding tasks such as decoding multisyllabic words or identifying a word through context.

Think time: The amount of time elapsed between the time a task is presented and the time a learner is asked to respond.

Think time must vary according to particular dimensions of the task. If a task is newly introduced, the amount of time allotted for formulating a response should be longer than if the task is reviewed. Furthermore, think time must vary with the knowledge form of the task. We suggest allowing longer think time or wait time when instruction deals with higher-level cognitive tasks. The length of pause or think time should vary directly with task difficulty level. A question calling for the production of a sound-symbol association would require less think time than a task requiring the application of contextual strategies. The following tasks reflect how think time should differ according to task familiarity and task demands.

TASK 7–20
Soundblending CVC Words

Status: Familiar.

Think Time: One second between word presentation and signal for response.

TASK 7–21
Sightreading CVC Words

Status: New.

Think Time: Three to five seconds between word presentation and signal.

Signaling: A visible or audible cue used to elicit responses.

To orchestrate responses, teachers will need to adapt and employ a signal. Signals such as clapping, snapping, hand-lowering, pointing, and voice inflections are possible means to coordinate and elicit responses. Signals serve an important function in early decoding exercises as they allow low performers the same amount of time to process information as other responders and, when used in conjunction with group responses, increase opportunities to practice.

> **Corrective Feedback:** The instructional procedure that directs the reader's attention to incorrect responses and provides correct information.

Our recommendation for providing corrective feedback is to use the knowledge form as the basis of the correction procedure. If the task in error is a simple fact, the correction procedure entails providing the fact and having the reader correctly apply the fact in the instructional context. For example, if the student incorrectly identified the irregular word *was* when presented in a list, the correction procedure would be for the teacher to supply the word *was* and have the student repeat the word. In addition, the teacher should alternate between subsequent words and the erred word to provide additional practice. A sample correction sequence follows.

TASK 7–22[1]

Stimulus	Response
said	STUDENT: (Error.) Sad.
said	TEACHER: This word is *said*. What's the word?
said	STUDENT: Said.
	TEACHER: Great, the word is *said*.
the	STUDENT: The.
said	STUDENT: Said.
	TEACHER: Nice job!
was	STUDENT: Was.
they	STUDENT: They.
said	STUDENT: Said.
night	STUDENT: Night.
where	STUDENT: Where.
look	STUDENT: Look.
said	STUDENT: Said.

When determining the appropriate correction procedure, it is critical to consider the interactive effect of the procedure and the word under correction. Future research may demonstrate that correction procedures should vary with dimensions of the task and the learner. Readers should be prompted to use the information they have to remediate

[1]Adapted, with permission, from Carnine & Silbert, *Direct instruction reading* (Columbus, OH: Merrill), 1979, p. 103.

errors. For example, if an error occurs at the rule level, teachers should target the particular subcomponent of the rule and proceed from the point. Consider the following example:[2]

TEACHER: (Points to word *rake*.) What word?
STUDENT: Rack.
TEACHER: Does this word have an *e* at the end?
STUDENT: Yes.
TEACHER: So, if there is an *e* at the end of the word, what does that tell you about the vowel?
STUDENT: It says its name.
TEACHER: Good. So what is the name of the vowel?
STUDENT: *A.*
TEACHER: Right. So what's the word?
STUDENT: Rake.
TEACHER: Exactly.

Firming Cycle: The repeated presentation of new and/or problematic tasks both throughout and at the end of a lesson to assure that students are firm on the information.

Englert's (1984) investigation of effective teaching procedures indicated a significant difference between the academic achievement of learning disabled students whose teachers implemented firm-up activities versus those who did not. The cumulative review of newly introduced decoding skills provides students additional exposure and practice with difficult tasks under guided conditions. In decoding instruction, new or frequently missed tasks would be presented in the session, documented, and reviewed throughout the session as well as intensively at the end of the session. A possible firming schedule for sound-symbol associations within a 30-minute session follows:

9:00–9:03	Introduce new sound-symbol association (*r*).
9:03–9:05	Review previously taught sound-symbol associations targeting *e* that were missed in the previous session.
9:05–9:06	Recheck *r*.
9:06–9:15	Group reading activity.
9:15–9:16	Review *r* and *e*.
9:16–9:25	Writing exercise.
9:25–9:26	Review *r* and *e*.
9:26–9:29	Assess delayed reading comprehension.
9:29–9:30	Review *r* and *e*.

---

[2]Adapted, with permission, from Carnine & Silbert, *Direct instruction reading* (Columbus, OH: Merrill), 1979, p. 200.

AFTER INSTRUCTION

Integrating Design and Delivery in Decoding Instruction

In the before phase of decoding instruction, the dimensions of decoding tasks and learner performance are merged to form an instructional plan. We propose that by attending to features of the generic instructional set, a plan for decoding instruction can be designed that acknowledges the complex attributes of decoding skills and is nevertheless sensitive to the skills of the learner. In the during phase of decoding instruction, this instructional plan is activated by a set of prescribed delivery procedures. These procedures are intended to alert the reader to upcoming task demands, to foster the acquisition of decoding skills, and to make concrete a new set of skills for identifying words. In the after phase of instruction, learner performance is analyzed and the design and delivery of decoding instruction are modified to accommodate the individual learner. These accommodations may necessitate scheduling extra practice on sound-symbol associations, adding generalization tasks to facilitate the transfer of CVCe word reading to sentences, or increasing the pace to establish automatic identification of irregular words. The following guidelines are offered to direct instructional decisions. After instruction, evaluate performance according to design and delivery features:

Learner Performance	Instructional Decision
Multiple errors	Reteach skill next day.
Inconsistent performance	Provide practice on additional examples.
Accurate performance	Increase pace to develop automaticity.
Fluent performance	Introduce more difficult examples.
	Apply task in context.

In unison, the design and delivery components of instruction interact to address plausible features of tasks that may impede the acquisition of decoding skills. In the following examples, we integrate features of instructional design and delivery in a select group of these skills. Each of these tasks is housed within the before, during, and after framework of instruction.

DECODING TASK 7–23
Auditory Segmenting

BEFORE INSTRUCTION

Task Status: New.

Preskills

1. Ability to follow oral directions.
2. Ability to follow visual cues.

Instructional Design Guidelines

1. Use words beginning with continuous sounds.
2. Begin with VC and CVC words.
3. Include words containing sounds to be introduced soon in sound-symbol association tasks.

Introductory Set: am, at, it, rat, sat, ram, sam, man.

Generalization Set: Any VC or CVC beginning with continuous sounds.

TASK 7–24

DURING INSTRUCTION

Instructional Delivery Guidelines

1. Frame task because it is new.
2. Maintain a moderate, consistent pace.
3. Prolong each sound 1–2 seconds.
4. Signal. Point to blank markers on board as each new sound is pronounced.
5. Firm any errors.

Teaching Procedure[3]

TEACHER: I'm going to say a word then I'll stretch out the sounds in the word. Stretching out sounds helps you hear all the sounds in the word.

As I say a sound I'll point to a marker on the board. Each marker stands for a sound.

As I stretch out the sounds, I need your eyes on the board.

Where do I need your eyes, Jeremy?

JEREMY: On the board.

TEACHER: Very good. That's right, on the board.

Listen and watch as I stretch out the sounds in the word *am.*

TEACHER: (Points to the first of two blank markers on the board.) *aaa* (Moves finger to next marker.) *mmm*

TEACHER: Your turn to stretch out the sounds with me. The word is *am.* Get ready. (Teacher positions finger in front of first marker, waits 1–2 seconds, then proceeds through task.)

TEACHER: Very nice. Your turn to stretch out sounds in the word *am* by yourself. Get ready.

---

[3]Adapted, with permission, from Carnine & Silbert, *Direct instruction reading* (Columbus, OH: Merrill), 1979, p. 67.

TASK 7–25

AFTER INSTRUCTION

Analyze Errors and Make Instructional Decisions

Determine whether error was a latency error where student could not keep up with the pace or whether the error was a general inability to follow directions and complete the task.

1. Latency error correction: Adjust time.
2. Procedural error: Model task again and provide more practice.

DECODING TASK 7–26
Soundblending of Regular CVC Words

BEFORE INSTRUCTION

Task Status: New.

Preskills

1. Ability to soundblend words presented auditorily.
2. Ability to follow visual cues.
3. Knowledge of sound-symbol associations.

Instructional Design Guidelines

1. Use words beginning with continuous sounds.
2. Begin with VC and CVC words.
3. Include words containing only mastered sound-symbol associations.

Introductory Set: am, at, it, rat, sat, ram, sam, man.

Generalization Set

Any VC or CVC beginning with continuous sounds and containing mastered sound-symbol associations (*mat, man, sat, sit, rim, at, ram, mit, rat*).

TASK 7–27

DURING INSTRUCTION

Instructional Delivery Guidelines

1. Frame task because it is new.
2. Maintain a moderate pace being careful to allow consistent think time.
3. Prolong each sound 1–2 seconds.
4. Signal. Point to letter on board as each new sound is pronounced.
5. Preteach any difficult sounds.
6. Firm any errors by correcting immediately and repeating the task.

Teaching Procedure[4]

TEACHER: Earlier we learned how to soundblend words without seeing the letters. Today we're going to learn to soundblend words when we do see the letters. This is very important because you will need to soundblend many words that you read.

When we soundblend words, it is important for you to watch my signal as I point to the letters on the board. Casey, when we soundblend words will you be watching my mouth or watching my finger?

CASEY: Your finger.

TEACHER: Right, Casey, you'll be watching my finger. Listen as I soundblend the first word. (Points to the *a* in the word *am*.) *aaa* (Moves finger to next letter.) *mmm*. Now I say the whole word. *Am.*

Your turn to soundblend the word with me. Get ready. (Teacher positions finger in front of first letter, waits 1–2 seconds, then proceeds through task.)

Nice soundblending. Your turn to soundblend the word by yourself. Get ready. (Teacher continues to signal by moving finger under letters but does not provide verbal cues. Teacher uses similar procedure for four to five more examples, then eliminates model and guided practice components and goes to check/test step only.

TASK 7–28

AFTER INSTRUCTION

Possible Error Types and Prescribed Actions

1. Latency error: Provide more think time.
2. Sound-symbol association error: Preteach specific sound-symbol association.
3. Blending error: Reteach procedure, provide more practice and examples.

---

[4]Adapted, with permission, from Carnine & Silbert, *Direct instruction reading* (Columbus, OH: Merrill), 1979, p. 97.

DECODING TASK 7–29
Irregular Word Reading

BEFORE INSTRUCTION

Task Status: New.

Preskill: Ability to follow visual cues.

Instructional Design Guidelines

1. Use high frequency words.
2. Limit number of examples in set according to learner competency.
3. Separate similar words.
4. Test for initial acquisition and retention.
5. Practice should be guided and of brief time periods.
6. Schedule distributed practice across sessions.
7. Discrimination tasks should be scheduled after learner is firm on new irregular words.

Introductory Set: the, was, I, see.

Discrimination Set: Any nonsimilar irregular words previously introduced.

TASK 7–30

DURING INSTRUCTION

Instructional Delivery Guidelines

1. Frame task because it is new, alerting readers that they will be reading whole words that do not soundblend.
2. Think time, 3–4 seconds.
3. Provide verbal cue and point to word on board.
4. Correct errors immediately.
5. Provide extra practice on inconsistent tasks.

Teaching Procedure

TEACHER: When you're reading, sometimes there are words that don't follow the rules. You can't soundblend them. Instead of reading the word letter by letter, you read it as a whole word.

How do you read a word that doesn't soundblend, Ollie?

OLLIE: As a whole word.

TEACHER: Right, you read it as a whole word. It is important that you learn and remember these words because you will see them often when you read.

I'm going to teach you some of these words and it is important that you look at the word carefully, try to remember what it looks like and how it sounds. Remember, you don't soundblend the words I'm going to show you.

Kirsten, will you soundblend the word I show you or will you read it as a whole word?

KIRSTEN: As a whole word.

TEACHER: Excellent job of remembering, Kirsten. Everyone listen and watch carefully as I teach you this word.

(MODEL): (Teacher readies hand under word and touches under word while pronouncing it.) This word is *the.*

(GUIDED PRACTICE): Everyone get ready. When I signal, say the word with me. (Signals.)

STUDENTS: The.

(Check/Test)

TEACHER: Great, OK, by yourselves. (Signals.)

STUDENTS: The.

TEACHER: Carey, by yourself.

CAREY: (Incorrect response.) *That.*

(Correction)

TEACHER: This word is *the.* What word, Carey?

CAREY: The.

TEACHER: Really nice, Carey.

Teacher presents new words and cycles back through all words, paying particular attention to words missed during session.

TASK 7–31

AFTER INSTRUCTION

Possible Error Types and Prescribed Actions

1. Latency error: Provide more time.
2. Word identification error: Demonstrate, prompt, and practice word again.

GENERALIZATION TASK 7–32

Reading irregular words in sentences (after learner is firm on reading words in isolation)

Preskills

1. Sound-symbol association knowledge.
2. Reads irregular words at a rate of 2–3 seconds.
3. Reads regular words at rate of 2–3 seconds.

Target Irregular Words: the, was, I, see.

Teacher Procedure

TEACHER: For the last few days, we've been learning to read words that don't soundblend. We read these words as whole words.

Today we're going to use these words along with words that do soundblend in sentences.

When you read the sentence, watch my finger. As my finger moves to the next word you say the word.

My turn to read this sentence.

The man was sad. (Teacher positions finger under each word and proceeds at a rate of one word per 3 seconds.)

(PRETEACHING AND GUIDED PRACTICE): Your turn to read it with me. Be sure to remember the words we just learned (points to *the* and *was*).

Session continues with sentences containing known irregular words. Modeling phase is dropped after one or two examples if students are accurately reading sentences.

DECODING TASK 7–33
Decoding Words Through Meaning in Context

BEFORE INSTRUCTION

Task Status: New.

Preskills:

1. Ability to read connected text accurately and fluently.
2. Knowledge of sound-symbol associations.
3. Knowledge of soundblending and regular whole-word reading procedure.
4. Knowledge of common irregular words.
5. Ability to use word-part strategy to decode multisyllabic words.

Instructional Design Guidelines

1. Select sentences with sufficient information to supply meaning.
2. Design sentences with only one target unfamiliar word.
3. Introduce strategy in easy context.

Introductory Set: Most fish will die if they are out of water.

Generalization Set: Sentences from text and other sources that comply with instructional design guidelines.

TASK 7–34

DURING INSTRUCTION

Instructional Delivery Guidelines

1. Frame task because it is new.
2. Preteach components of strategy and difficult irregular words.
3. Monitor pace, being careful not to rush the pace or let it drag.

Teaching Procedure

TEACHER: When you're reading, sometimes there are words that you don't know. These words don't sound out and you may not know them as whole words.

   If you come to a word you don't know in a sentence, there are three things you should do.

   First, see if you can figure out the word by soundblending and finding the parts you know.

   Next, read the word in the sentence to see if it makes sense.

   If it doesn't, use the way the word sounds in the sentence to help figure out a better word.

   Listen and watch while I try to figure out the word in this sentence.

   "Most fish will die if they are out of the (*water*)." (Teacher points to *water*.) This is the word I need to figure out.

   This part (*wat*) says *wat* and this part says *er*—*watter.*

   "Most fish will die if they are out of *watter.*" That doesn't make sense. Oh, the word is *water.* "Most fish will die if they are out of *water.*"

   Let's do this one together.

(PRETEACHING): Remember to use the way the word sounds as well as what it means to help figure out the right word.

Present multiple examples. First target a single word in each sentence for students to figure out through the combination strategy. As students become facile in identifying target words, expand the target set to a less controlled set.)

TASK 7–35

AFTER INSTRUCTION

Possible Error Types and Prescribed Actions

1. Failure to use components of strategy: Isolate strategy and reteach.
2. Failure to use strategy: Present objective of strategy again. Practice strategy in easy contexts.

GENERALIZATION TASK 7–36
Using Strategy in Connected Text (several days later)

Teaching Procedure

TEACHER: For the last few days, we've been learning to figure out words by combining how the word sounds and what it means in the sentence.

Today, we're going to use this plan in paragraphs from your social studies book.
(PRETEACHING): Remember, when you come to a word you don't know, what do you do?
(Teacher solicits responses from students in class.)
(GUIDED PRACTICE): Let's try this one together.

In the previous examples, we implemented the design and delivery components in selected decoding tasks. Because text is a static form of communication, it is difficult to convey the numerous interactions and instructional decisions that take place during a seemingly simple and straightforward session of decoding instruction. When determining *what* skills to teach beginning readers and *how* to teach those skills, it is important to position the design and delivery components of decoding instruction within the three primary phases of before, during, and after instruction.

SUMMARY

In this chapter, we addressed the controversial and complex issue of decoding instruction. Because of the documented phonics deficits of low-performing readers and the persistent effect of these skill deficiencies on higher-level comprehension, we proposed a code-based approach to beginning reading instruction. This direction allows teachers more control over variables that frequently impede reading acquisition. To initiate our approach to decoding instruction, features of a code-based decoding program were identified and analyzed according to how potentially problematic tasks can be minimized through strategic planning and skilled delivery. We proposed that a student's ability to acquire accurate and automatic decoding skills is directly linked to how information is packaged and presented. If examples of reading tasks are properly selected, carefully sequenced, routinely practiced, and systematically assessed, the likelihood of learning is increased. The before, during, and after model formed the framework for our approach to decoding instruction while the generic instructional set and delivery procedures supplied the details to structure and implement a decoding program for low-performing students. In the final section of the chapter, these design and delivery guidelines were applied to selected decoding tasks.

APPLICATION ITEMS

1. The learner knows the following sound-symbol associations: *s, a, m, t, e, n, r, l, i,* and *d.* Construct a list of words that would be appropriate for beginning word reading activities. Specify the criteria you used in selecting the words.

2. Specify the knowledge form for each of the following decoding tasks. Use the following code to answer:

   VA–Verbal association
     C–Concept
   RR–Rule Relationship
   CS–Cognitive Strategy

   a. _____ Reading the sight words *the, your, father.*
   b. _____ Pronouncing the sounds for the letter combinations: *sh, ch, ea,* and *oa.*
   c. _____ Determining the pronunciation of a word by using the meaning of the word in the sentence.
   d. _____ Decoding the words *go, be,* and *hi.*
   e. _____ Decoding the words *lovable, involuntary, irregular.*

3. For each of the preceding tasks (a–e), select the first word or letter combination in the list and specify the range of examples you would use during an initial teaching session.

4. For each of the words and letter combinations used in Exercise 3, design three test sequences. One test sequence should assess skill acquisition, the second should assess generalization, and the third discrimination skills. Note that not all items will have generalization items. Indicate those that do not. Also, in designing discrimination sets, indicate words or letter combinations that have been previously introduced.

5. Students have just been introduced to the strategy for decoding words using base words and affixes and successfully demonstrated their ability to decode base words with *-ing, -ed, -s, re-,* and *in-* affixes. Design an independent practice activity for words with these affixes.

REFERENCES

Anderson, R. C., Hiebert, E. H., Scott, J. A., & Wilkinson, I. A. G. (1985). *Becoming a nation of readers.* Washington, DC: National Institute of Education.

Arter, J. A., & Jenkins, J. R. (1977). Examining the benefits and prevalence of modality considerations in special education. *Journal of Special Education, 11,* 281–298.

Bond, G. & Dykstra, R. (1967). The first cooperative research program in first grade reading. *Reading Research Quarterly, 2,* 5–142.

Bradley, L. & Bryant, P. E. (1983). Categorizing sounds and learning to read: A causal connection. *Nature, 301,* 419–421.

Carnine, D. W. (1980). Three procedures for presenting minimally different positive and negative examples. *Journal of Educational Psychology, 72,* 452–456.

Carnine, D. W. (1981). Reducing training problems associated with visually and auditorily similar correspondences. *Journal of Learning Disabilities, 14,* 276–279.

Carnine, D. W. & Silbert, J. (1979). *Direct instruction reading.* Columbus, OH: Merrill Publishing Company.

Carnine, D. W., Silbert, J., & Kameenui, E. J. (1990). *Direct instruction reading* (2nd ed). Columbus, OH: Merrill Publishing Company.

Chall, J. S. (1967). *Learning to read: The great debate.* New York: McGraw-Hill.

Chall, J. S. (1989, March). Learning to read. The great debate 20 years later—A response to "Debunking the great phonics myth." *Phi Delta Kappan,* 521–537.

Clymer, T. (1963). The utility of phonic generalizations in the primary grades. *Reading Teacher, 16,* 252–258.

Ehri, L. C. (1979). Linguistic insight: Threshold of reading acquisition. In T. Waller & G. E. MacKinnon (Eds.), *Reading research: Advances in theory and practice* (vol. 1, pp. 63–111). New York: Academic Press.

Ehri, L. C., & Wilce, L. S. (1987). Cipher versus cue reading. *Journal of Educational Psychology, 79,* 3–13.

Englert, C. S. (1984). Examining effective direct instruction practices in special education settings. *Remedial and Special Education, 5,* 38–47.

Fox, B., & Routh, K. (1976). Phonemic analysis and synthesis as word-attack skills. *Journal of Educational Psychology, 68,* 70–74.

Golinkoff, R. M. (1978). Critique: Phonemic awareness skills and reading achievement. In F. B. Murray & A. J. Pikulski (Eds.), *The acquisition of reading: Cognitive, linguistic, and perceptual prerequisites* (pp. 23–41). Baltimore, MD: University Park Press.

Gough, P. B. (1972). One second of reading. In J. F. Kavanagh & I. G. Mattingly (Eds.), *Language by ear and by eye* (pp. 331–358). Cambridge, MA: MIT Press.

Juel, C. (1988, April). *Learning to read and write: A longitudinal study of fifty-four children from first through fourth grade.* Paper presented at the meeting of the American Educational Research Association, New Orleans, LA.

Kavale, K. A., & Forness, S. R. (1985). LD and the history of science. *Remedial and Special Education, 6,* 12–23.

Lesgold, A. M., & Resnick, L. (1982). How reading difficulties develop: Perspectives from a longitudinal study. In J. Das, R. Mulcahy, & A. Wall (Eds.), *Theory and research in learning disabilities* (pp. 155–187). New York: Plenum Press.

Lewis, R. B. (1983). Learning disabilities and reading: Instructional recommendations from current research. *Exceptional Children, 50,* 230–240.

Lewkowicz, N. K. (1980). Phonemic awareness training: What to teach and how to teach it. *Journal of Educational Psychology, 72,* 686–700.

Perfetti, C. A. (1985). *Reading ability.* New York: Oxford Press.

Perfetti, C. A., Goldman, S. R., & Hogaboam, T. W. (1979). Reading skill and the identification of words in discourse context. *Memory and Cognition, 7,* 273–282.

Reid, E. (1978). *Teaching new words through the word structure method.* Salt Lake City, UT: Cover Publishers.

Schworm, R. (1979). Word mediation and generalization in beginning readers. *Journal of Reading Behavior, 11,* 139–151.

Simmons, D. C., & Kameenui, E. J. (1986). Articulating learning disabilities for the public: A case of professional riddles. *Learning Disability Quarterly, 9,* 304–314.

Spear, L. D., & Sternberg, R. J. (1986). An information processing framework for understanding reading disability. In S. Ceci (Ed.), *Handbook of cognitive, social, and neuropsychological aspects of learning disabilities* (vol. 2, pp. 3–31). Hillsdale, NJ: Erlbaum.

Stanovich, K. E. (1986). Matthew effects in reading: Some consequences of individual differences in the acquisition of literacy. *Reading Research Quarterly, 31,* 360–406.

Williams, J. P. (1979). Reading Instruction Today. *American Psychologist, 34,* 917–922.

Wilson, R., & Wesson, C. (1986). Making every minute count: Academic learning time in LD classrooms. *Learning Disabilities Focus, 2,* 13–19.

C H A P T E R

EIGHT

Designing Instructional Strategies for Teaching Reading Comprehension: Narrative Prose

Chapter Objectives

Upon successful completion of this chapter, you will be able to:

1. IDENTIFY and DESCRIBE four components of the reading comprehension process: reader, text, task, and strategies.

2. IDENTIFY the features of each of the four components that influence the reading comprehension process.

3. EXPLAIN the features of each of the four components that may contribute to reading comprehension failure.

4. APPLY the generic instructional set to designing instructional formats for a range of reading comprehension skills.

5. DESCRIBE the instructional requirements for teaching specific reading comprehension skills within the before, during, and after phases of instruction.

THE COMPONENTS OF READING COMPREHENSION INSTRUCTION

The process of reading comprehension is not simply that of reading words. As Mason and Au (1986) state, "In fact, no matter how carefully the reader pays attention to the text, or how easy it is for him to say all the words in it, he may still fail to understand its message" (p. 131). The causes of comprehension failure are complex, and the instructional solutions to this failure are equally complex. Fortunately, in the last 10 years an explosion of research (Samuels & Pearson, 1980) in reading comprehension has taken place. This research allows us to understand some of the reasons for many comprehension problems. The research also provides numerous instructional strategies for preventing and remediating these comprehension problems.

We have identified the following four components as important to understanding the reading comprehension process: (1) the reader, (2) the text, (3) the task, and (4) the strategies. What makes the comprehension process so complex is that each of these components is a separate but interdependent part of the process (Mosenthal, 1984). These four independent and interdependent components are depicted in Figure 8–1. Each of these components is described and discussed briefly.

Reader

Although in this text readers with academic learning problems draw our primary attention, in this section we identify and discuss the essential knowledge that *any* reader must bring to the comprehension process. These essentials make up the reader's knowledge base, and this knowledge base will interact with the *text, task,* and *strategies* of the reading comprehension process. In the following section, we identify and describe three aspects of the reader's knowledge base. These include (1) *background knowledge,* (2) *component skill knowledge* (decoding skills, semantics, syntax, word parts, factual information, logic and reasoning, typographic features, literal skills), and (3) *motivation.*

Background Knowledge

One facet of the comprehension process that has received much attention in the research on reading comprehension is the reader's background knowledge (Anderson & Pearson, 1984). This refers to the knowledge the reader brings to the reading situation and comprises everything the reader knows, ranging from the knowledge obtained in school through instruction to the knowledge acquired incidentally or systematically outside school. This is both street knowledge and school knowledge. According to McNeil (1984), "The reader's prior knowledge interacts with text to create psychological meaning. Background knowledge determines the interpretations made from text" (p. 3).

Obviously, the reader does not bring every spark and trace of prior knowledge to bear on a text at any given time. Such a feat is neither possible nor necessary. Readers are selective in what prior knowledge they call up and use from memory. The background knowledge that is activated depends to a large extent on the demands of the topic and the text being read. To comprehend a text, the reader must activate and align prior knowledge with the text. Sometimes the text requires a reader to activate a great deal of background knowledge, because it does not give the reader much information. Some-

FIGURE 8–1

Reader/text/task/strategies
components of reading comprehension

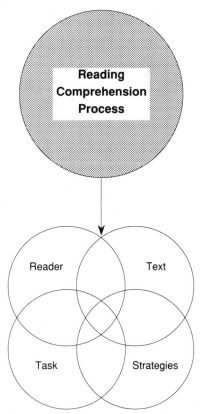

times the text gives the reader sufficient information, so that the reader need not rustle up much background knowledge to give meaning to the text.

Striking a balance between the right amount of prior knowledge a reader must have and the amount of explicit information the text should provide depends on the reader, the text, and the purpose for reading. If a text tells the reader too much, it could be boring. The reader may not be required to use prior knowledge to make many inferences, predictions, and connections. On the other hand, when the same text is approached by another reader, it may not tell enough. The reader may simply not have the necessary background knowledge to make the necessary inferences, predictions, and connections. In a case like this, where the fit between a reader's knowledge and the text is not very tight, the reader must work especially hard to remember and understand the text.

Much research has demonstrated the importance of prior knowledge to comprehension (Anderson, 1977; Rumelhart & Ortony, 1977; Schank & Abelson, 1977). For example, high school students with prior knowledge of sports and baseball were better able to remember texts about cricket matches, even though they had no background knowledge of cricket (Hayes & Tierney, 1982). In general, the research on prior knowledge seems to suggest that when a reader integrates and weaves knowledge from a new text with prior knowledge, the reader is better able to understand and remember this new knowledge (Anderson & Pearson, 1984; Au, 1979; Tierney & Cunningham, 1984; Wilson, 1983).

Component Skill Knowledge

To comprehend the text, the reader must have more than background knowledge. In the following section, we describe eight different component skills that are needed to comprehend various kinds of texts.

Decoding.   To comprehend texts, the reader must be a fluent decoder and not a laborious, word-by-word reader. In other words, a reader must be fairly automatic in translating printed symbols to meaningful thoughts. The process of comprehension is short-circuited if a reader devotes all or most of the effort to decoding each word of a text. By the time the word-by-word reader reaches the end of a sentence, comprehension is likely to be sparse or nonexistent. Some researchers refer to this phenomenon as the "bottle-neck hypothesis" (Perfetti, 1977). Specifically, the more cognitive processing a reader must devote to decoding words, the less is available for comprehension. Decoding and comprehension share a limited amount of "processing space" in the reader's head. Readers who are fluent decoders are in a position to devote most of that processing space to comprehension (Jenkins & Pany, 1979).

Component skill knowledge also consists of the reader's knowledge of semantics (word meanings), syntax (word order), anaphora such as pronouns, adverbs and their referents, factual information about the world, logic and reasoning, typographic features (punctuation) of written text (Durkin, 1987), and literal skills (Carnine, Silbert, & Kameenui, 1990) that involve scanning a text and identifying information to answer who, what, when, where, and how questions. An example of each type of skill knowledge follows.

Semantics.   Semantics refers to the meaning of words. Knowledge of word meanings is essential to reading comprehension (Anderson & Freebody, 1981; Baumann & Kameenui, in press; Kameenui, Dixon, & Carnine, 1987; Stahl, 1990). Although it's not necessary to know the meaning of every word in a text, it is important to know those words that are central to the author's message. Examine the sentences that follow:

> Joe and Ann went to school in Portland. They were antagonists. They saw each other often. They had lots of altercations. (Kameenui, Carnine, & Freschi, 1982, p. 373)

Without knowing the meanings of the words *antagonists* and *altercations*, the student would have a difficult time answering comprehension questions specific to these vocabulary words.

Syntax.   Syntax refers to the order in which the words and phrases of a sentence are arranged to show how they relate to each other. It describes the order of the subject and verb, the position of auxiliary words and objects, and the relation of modifiers to the words they modify. Word order is different in different languages. The meaning or semantics of a message can change by changing the syntax. As the noted educator and writer Frank Smith stated some time ago, "A blind Venetian is not the same as a Venetian blind."

Anaphora knowledge. Knowledge of word parts such as pronouns and adverbs is also important to comprehending texts. Pronouns, in particular, are known to account for some comprehension problems (Baumann, 1988; Kameenui & Carnine, 1982). Note the following passage:

> The Americans had no army or navy. They showed no signs that they could work together. Some Americans wanted to keep their ties with Britain and fought against the colonial army. Some escaped to Canada. Many other Americans did not care who won the war. *They* sold supplies to both sides.

In this passage, the pronoun *they* generally refers to "the Americans." However, in the last sentence, the referent changes. The pronoun *they* doesn't refer just to the Americans anymore but to the "many other Americans" who did not care who won the war. The referent for the pronoun *they* in this case is specific. If students were asked, "Who sold supplies to both sides?" they would be likely to answer, "The Americans." In fact, in a pilot study for a larger experiment, Kameenui and Carnine (1982) found that 83% of fourth-grade students responded incorrectly to this comprehension question. Much research has identified pronouns as an important feature of text comprehension (Baumann, 1988).

General factual knowledge. General factual information is also critical to the comprehension of texts. If a reader doesn't know basic facts about how the world works, comprehension is likely to suffer. If the reader doesn't know the seasons of the year (e.g., in the autumn, the leaves fall from trees), the time of day (e.g., the meaning of a.m. and p.m.), the direction in which the sun rises and sets, the location of body parts, or the nature of family relationships (e.g., siblings, grandparents, aunts, uncles), then it is difficult for the reader to comprehend texts requiring knowledge of that basic information.

Logic and reasoning. Logic and reasoning are concerned with making inferences about what is reasonably expected under certain conditions. If a student reads, "The cowboy rode his white horse east into the sunset," the sun setting in the east should cause the reader to question the validity of the sentence.

Typographic features. Typographic features refer to the punctuation conventions of written text. As Durkin (1987) points out, authors use these conventions as aids to convey the meaning of the text, and readers must be able to decode these signals. These typographic signals include periods, commas, question marks, exclamation marks, capitalization, semicolons, colons, and paragraph indentations (Durkin, 1987, pp. 382–383). Although many readers are able to respond to these signals without much instruction, naive readers will require direct instruction of the signals.

Literal skills. Literal skills are the skills that are important to understanding the words of a text in their exact and usual meaning, without exaggeration or imagination. A reader must be able to locate information in a text and answer basic *wh* questions: who, what, when, where, and how questions that are specific to the text.

Motivation

The tension between the child's ability to read and the child's desire to read can also create a dilemma for teachers. As Mason and Au (1986) state, "There is a big difference between *being able* to read and *wanting* to read or *enjoying* reading" (p. 164, original emphasis). For students with academic problems, the enjoyment of reading is generally lost in the difficulties that accompany reading. Stanovich (1986) speaks of the inevitable cascading effects that reading difficulties have on learning in general. As he states, "Children with inadequate vocabularies—who read slowly and without enjoyment—read less, and as a result have slower development of vocabulary knowledge, which inhibits further growth in reading ability" (p. 381). Students who begin their school experience with language and general knowledge deficits are naturally less motivated than their average peers. These basic skill deficits cause them to fall farther behind in their academic development.

To motivate students who, for whatever reason, have experienced more failure than success, the task facing teachers, parents, and schools is enormous. However, it is not impossible. We have learned much about motivating students to read on their own (Brophy & Good, 1986; Lapp & Flood, 1983; Spiegel, 1981). We know that parents play an important role in fostering students' reading interests and development. The connection between home and school in motivating students, especially low performers, is particularly important. However, establishing and sustaining connections with the home environment requires much work and skill. The greatest disadvantage to the teacher in working with the home environment is lack of control. The teacher has limited control over the quality of interactions between children and parents. The interactions can be positive and nurturing, or they can be punishing and counterproductive. Therefore, the teacher must be clear and supportive in aligning the parents' skills with the goals and requirements of a reading task. The teacher must be careful not to demand too much of

Motivating students to read on their own is a difficult, though not impossible, task.

parents. Parents should not be asked to tutor their children on skills that have been especially difficult for the students in school. The teacher should develop tasks for parents that are likely to result in positive interactions with children.

Figure 8–2 summarizes the various aspects of the reader's knowledge base.

Text

Unlike the reader component, the text component of the reading comprehension process can be more directly controlled and managed by the teacher. A teacher can choose a specific type, quality, and length of text to use when teaching comprehension. The teacher can even compose texts or stories as a way of controlling the vocabulary, sentence

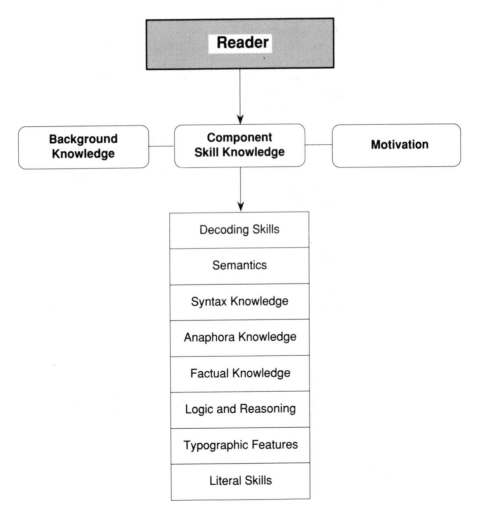

FIGURE 8–2
Three aspects of reader's knowledge base

structure, cohesiveness, and organization of the text. When we refer to the text, we refer to the printed reading materials that students are asked to read. These printed materials are of different types and have a range of features and characteristics that influence the reader's active construction of meaning. In fact, the text can determine the amount of work that both the teacher and reader must do to construct this meaning. Poorly organized texts with an abundance of technical terms inconsistent with the reader's interest and background knowledge will require more effort to comprehend than texts that are well organized and tap the reader's prior experience (Armbruster & Anderson, 1988; Idol, 1988). It is important to understand these text features to prevent, identify, and remediate some of the problems that the text creates for readers.

Text Types

We can divide texts into two basic types: narrative, storybook prose and expository, textbook prose. These differ in many ways, but most importantly they differ in their purposes. Because the purpose of each type of text is different, the expectations that readers have before and during reading are also different. The learning and comprehension outcomes that teachers have of these texts are also different. As a result, the instructional requirements and strategies for each type of text are different.

Narrative texts.   The purpose of narrative prose is to tell a story. Narrative, storybook prose has its own text structure, called story grammar, which has been researched extensively (Carnine & Kinder, 1985; Gurney, 1987; McConaughy, 1980; Shannon, Kameenui, & Baumann, 1988; Stein & Glenn, 1979). Story grammar refers to a system of rules that describes the organization of stories. Stories are generally formed around certain elements. Each of these elements in the story serves a different function. The ideal story would contain the following story grammar elements (Strickland, 1985, cited in Gurney, 1987):

1. Setting: Introduces the reader to the main characters, location, time, and context of the story.
2. Beginning: Serves as an "initiating event" that starts the action in the story.
3. Goal: The major objective of the story formed in reaction to the beginning or initiating event.
4. Attempt: The actions of the characters that are carried out in order to achieve the major goal.
5. Plot: The series of attempts and subgoals that the characters engage in to achieve the major goal.
6. Outcome: Also referred to as the consequence, which depicts the main character's success or failure at achieving the goal.
7. Internal response: The characters' thoughts and feelings that prompt the initiating events and actions in the story.
8. Ending: The final consequence of the story in which the characters make known their feelings about the outcome of the story.

Story grammar components provide the reader with important comprehension "hooks" to hang on to when reading the text. Two important hooks include the story characters and the problem or conflict they face. Another hook is the resolution of the conflict. Stories that contain these comprehension hooks readily prompt readers to draw on their background knowledge and experiences as they come eye to eye with a character's dilemma (i.e., goals, conflicts, internal responses) and as they walk the character through to the end or the resolution of the problem. The eight elements of story grammar establish the web of actions, events, and relationships that carry the reader from the beginning of the story to the end. These elements make clear the causal connections and relationships in the story that allow the reader to make inferences about the characters' goal-related actions.

The research on story grammar suggests that the more experience children have with stories, the more they are likely to develop an awareness of story structure that seems to influence their recall and comprehension. In fact, children in the fifth grade and above appear to recall and remember stories better than younger children. However, the specific elements of story grammar that children and adults remember most are not as clear-cut. McConaughy, Fitzhenry-Coor, and Howell (1983) found that children tended to remember actions in a story, while adults were most likely to recall character motives. Nezworski, Stein, and Trabasso (1982) found just the opposite effect. They found that primary grade children recalled character motives with great regularity.

Narrative texts also differ according to how the actions, events, and descriptions are related to a particular character's motivation for achieving a goal. The explicitness (or implicitness) of the goal in a story also varies. These variations in the linkage between the elements of the story grammar (e.g., the goal, internal responses, initiating events, outcomes) also influence comprehension. For example, some narrative texts require the reader to draw heavily on background knowledge. Other texts do not lean on the reader's prior knowledge and experience at all. Pearson and Johnson (1978) have identified three different types of texts: textually explicit, textually implicit, and scriptally implicit.

In *textually explicit* texts, the primary character's reasons for engaging in an action or series of actions to attain a goal are explicitly stated. The character's actions are also explicitly related to an explicit goal.

In *textually implicit* texts, the primary character's motivation is implied and not explicit. However, details of the character's actions and their relationship to obtaining a particular goal are made explicit in the story. Here is an example of a textually implicit text:

Clover and the King

Clover was a very clever rabbit who, along with other rabbits, loved lettuce. They lived outside the King's castle, and soon they had all the lettuce from nearby gardens except for the King's own garden.

The King loved his garden and grew the best lettuce in all the land. He did not want the rabbits to get any of his lettuce so his garden was well guarded. The rabbits didn't like the King either and just wanted his lettuce.

One day Clover got an idea. A rabbit could not sneak into the King's garden, but a rabbit could sneak into the King's kitchen. Clover sneaked into the King's kitchen every morning for several days. Each day the King's men brought in some lettuce for dinner, and each day Clover poisoned the lettuce. Soon, everyone in the King's palace was sick.

The King was very sad when he learned that his lettuce was making everyone sick. He ordered his soldiers to dig up the lettuce from his garden. Then he ordered the lettuce dumped outside the castle, near where the rabbits lived.

The King was very pleased with himself. He would solve two problems at once (Shannon, Kameenui, & Baumann, 1988, pp. 457–458).

In the fable "Clover and the King," Clover wants the lettuce, knows the king dislikes him, recognizes the king loves his subjects, and poisons the lettuce cut for royal consumption. To appreciate Clover's motivation for poisoning the cut lettuce, the reader must take the information about Clover's stated goal, the poisoning of the lettuce, and the King's response to the poisoned lettuce and make an inference about the relationship between those events. If the reader fails to make the connections between those events, actions, and intentions of the characters, then the reader will fail to understand why Clover the rabbit is so clever.

In *scriptally implicit* texts, the reader must depend heavily on background knowledge to detect the relationship between the primary character's motivation and a particular goal. Here is an example of a scriptally implicit text:

The Fox and the Grapes

One day a sly fox was running along a dry, dusty road and he was very hot and thirsty. After a long period, he saw a large bunch of purple grapes hanging from a tree on a vine in a garden by the side of the road. These grapes were large, ripe and very juicy looking. They looked especially good to the fox. "How I wish I could eat some of those beautiful grapes," said the fox as he licked his lips. The fox jumped high into the air to get the grapes, but he did not get them the first time he tried. He jumped again and again, but he still could not reach the grapes. He was still very thirsty, but he kept trying. After a while he became tired and at last he gave up. He said as he wandered away, "I am sure they are very sour grapes and I don't like sour grapes at all" (Shannon, Kameenui, & Baumann, 1988, pp. 459–460).

In the fable "The Fox and the Grapes," the relationship between the fox's stated goal of wanting to eat "some of those beautiful grapes" and the fox's observation that the grapes were sour is not explicit. To understand the fox's reasons for calling the grapes sour, the reader must bring to bear individual experiences that are similar to the fox's frustrated and unsuccessful efforts to reach a particular goal. The source of information that allows the reader to make the inference that the fox called the grapes sour to feel better about not reaching them is "in the reader's head, not on the page" (Pearson & Johnson, 1978, p. 162).

In summary, the purpose of narrative texts is to tell a story. These texts have their own structure called story grammar (e.g., characters, problems, goals, attempts). The story grammar components can be used as comprehension hooks for the reader to hold on to during comprehension.

Expository texts. In contrast to narrative texts that tell stories, the purpose of expository texts is to inform and to "teach" students (Allington & Strange, 1980; Schallert & Tierney, 1981). In fact, expository texts are considered a dominant feature of instruction in the content areas (e.g., social studies, history, health and the sciences). Until third grade, reading lessons in most basal reading programs consist of narrative or storybook reading passages. In fourth grade, students begin the transition from "learning to read" to "reading to learn." As Anderson, Heibert, Scott, and Wilkinson (1985) note, "subject matter textbooks pose the biggest challenge for young readers being weaned from a diet of stories" (p. 67). Strategies for comprehending expository, textbook prose are discussed in Chapter 9. A visual summary of the text features is given in Figure 8–3.

Task

Another important component of the comprehension process is the comprehension task. The task refers to the specific features, requirements, and activities that a reader must understand to produce a particular response. By responding correctly to specific task requirements, the reader displays comprehension of the text. For example, a reader may be asked to read a passage silently, then answer in writing the comprehension questions at the end of the passage. By completing this task successfully without any guidance from the teacher, the reader has demonstrated task knowledge. Task knowledge refers to the awareness and information the reader has about various features and requirements of tasks. This awareness allows the reader to produce an appropriate response to the task. Obviously, not all reading comprehension tasks are the same. Such tasks vary depending on the purpose for reading, the reader's level of reading, the specific learning outcomes desired, and the nature of the text. Naturally, tasks requiring different responses may also vary in difficulty. Tasks requiring a learner to *produce* spontaneously

FIGURE 8–3
Reading comprehension text features

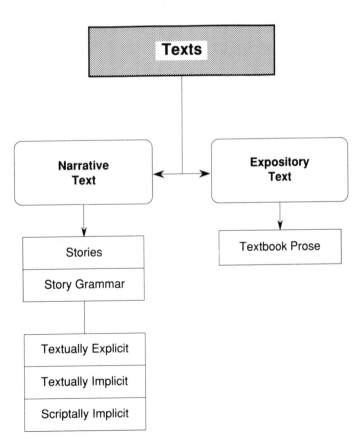

an oral response are more difficult than tasks requiring the learner to *select* a response from a set of choices (Simmons & Kameenui, 1987). It would be more difficult for a reader to state spontaneously the main idea of a story than to choose a correct answer from a series of choices.

In Chapter 2, we described a number of task dimensions that influence academic performance. These dimensions include (1) learner familiarity with the task (e.g., new task, practice task, review task), (2) learner competency on a task (e.g., new vs. mastered task), (3) task domain (e.g., reading, math, spelling), (4) schedule of instruction (e.g., extensive, moderate, minimal), (5) task modality (e.g., oral, written), and (6) form of response (e.g., choice response, production response). A reader's task knowledge is likely to be different for a review task than for a new task. The more familiar a reader is with the requirements of a task, the more successful the reader is likely to be. A learner may fail a task not because of the knowledge required, but because the learner doesn't know how to respond to the task requirements; the learner is unable to discern the kind of answer required or to provide the answer in the required format.

We have suggested several strategies in this text for buttressing against a learner's inadequate knowledge of task requirements. The primary strategy is that of framing; that is, specifying the requirements of the task before the student's actual completion of the task. By framing tasks, the teacher makes sure that learners have the information necessary to respond to requirements of the task.

Metacognition

The knowledge a reader has of task requirements is certainly important to the reading comprehension process. In fact, in the last decade much attention has been given to how readers respond to tasks, their features, and requirements. These processes and activities have been labeled metacognition, which refers to a learner's awareness and regulation of performance on a task (Brown, 1980; Flavell, 1976). Metacognition is evident when a reader engages in the process of monitoring and regulating ongoing performance on a task to accomplish a specific objective. During this process, the reader makes adjustments necessary to complete a task successfully. There seems to be some agreement that metacognition involves at least two major components: a reader's "cognitive self-appraisal" and "self-management" (Paris, Wasik, & Van der Westhuizen, 1988, p. 3). In effect, a reader must be self-watchful of performance as it unfolds. A reader must also be quick to make adjustments in performance when a problem is detected.

Armbruster, Echols, and Brown (1983) argue that metacognition in reading to learn involves the knowledge of four variables that include the text, task, strategies, and learner characteristics. The reader must also be able to regulate and orchestrate the interaction of these four variables. Specifically, the reader must be alert to "features of the to-be-learned materials that influence comprehension and memory" (Armbruster, Echols, & Brown, 1983, p. 2), the requirements of the task, the activities used to remember the text, and the personal attributes that influence performance (e.g., motivation, interest).

The research on metacognition suggests that younger and poorer readers tend to have deficits in both the self-appraisal and self-management of reading comprehension tasks. However, in their close analysis of the research on metacognition and reading,

Paris, Wasik, and Van der Westhuizen (1987) note that further research is needed, because "fundamental problems persist" (p. 30). The first problem they suggest is that of defining and agreeing on what is meant by metacognition. Although there is no consensus on what metacognition means, these researchers state, "Classroom instruction that promotes metacognition can encourage students to be better at appraising and managing their own cognitive resources while reading. They can become strategic and motivated by more thoroughly understanding the task at hand and the cognitive demands of reading different types of text in different types of situations" (p. 40). When we refer to metacognition throughout this text, we will rely on the definition provided by Paris and his colleagues. This definition refers to the reader's self-appraisal and self-management of the demands of the reading task at hand. Figure 8–4 summarizes task features.

Comprehension Strategies

The final component of our reading comprehension model consists of the strategies the reader must have to simplify, understand, and comprehend the text and task variables. In Chapter 3, we defined cognitive strategies as a series of multi-step associations and

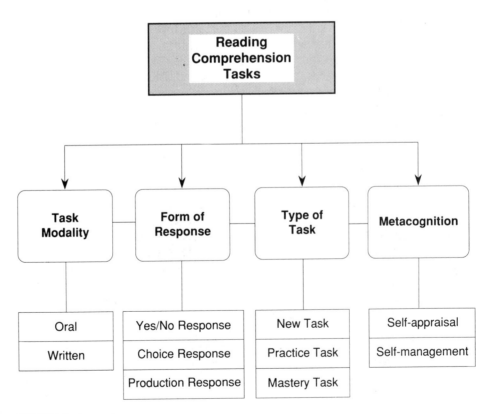

FIGURE 8–4
Reading comprehension tasks' features

procedures that involve simple facts, verbal chains, discriminations, concepts, and rules designed to bring about a response or a set of responses to a specified problem. We noted that a cognitive strategy involves the skillful planning and management of those activities that consist of thinking, remembering, and interpreting symbolic operations. A strategy allows the learner to planfully use information or knowledge in ways to manage or solve a particular problem that involves understanding symbols. Not surprisingly, we define reading comprehension strategies as the multi-step associations and procedures that allow the reader to use knowledge (e.g., background knowledge, semantic knowledge, factual world knowledge, syntactic knowledge, knowledge of typographic features) in both understanding the text and constructing meaning from the text.

Causes of Reading Comprehension Failure

To appreciate the causes of reading comprehension failure, we need to examine the complex interaction of the four components we have described. For example, if the reader lacks an adequate knowledge base (e.g., inadequate semantic, syntactic, factual, and reasoning knowledge), then the reader's comprehension of the text is likely to be fragmented. Moreover, if the same reader is required to read an expository text that is by all accounts "inconsiderate," meaning (1) it contains numerous low-frequency words and technical terms, (2) the overall text structure is unclear and not cohesive, and (3) the information in the text is quite dense, then reading comprehension failure is all but assured. In addition to the features of the reader and text, the misalignment between the task demands, the reader's skills, and the instructional objectives could also invite reading comprehension failure.

Numerous points and connections in the reading comprehension process, if short-circuited, could lead to some kind of failure. These points of failure can be considered deficits in the reader's knowledge base, component skills and strategies, or task knowledge. In other words, by identifying the reading comprehension problem as occurring within one or more of these components, we can design appropriate instructional strategies for solving the problem. For example, the teacher, as the center and anchor point of the reading comprehension process, is in a position to influence significantly each reader-based component. Specifically, the teacher can (1) provide the reader with background knowledge on a topic before text reading, (2) describe a situation that would readily activate a reader's appropriate prior knowledge or schemata, (3) preteach difficult vocabulary words, (4) provide further practice and review on selected word types for building decoding fluency, (5) frame the task requirements of a worksheet, (6) monitor a reader's logic and reasoning during the retell of a passage, and (7) select texts that are appropriate to the reader's interest and reading skill level.

A growing body of research chronicles why children fail to comprehend texts. This failure is attributed to a variety of factors, including inadequate reading comprehension instruction in the regular classroom (Durkin, 1978–1979), insufficient exposure and actual practice on reading (Allington, 1980, 1983, 1984), deficient word recognition skills (Spear & Sternberg, 1986), inadequate training in early phonics (Chall, 1983; Chall & Snow, 1988), deficient strategic memory capacity and functioning (Cohen, 1982), significant language deficiencies (Calfee, Spector, & Piontkowski, 1979; Jenkins, Stein, & Osborn, 1981), inadequate self-appraisal and self-monitoring of the reading comprehension process (Paris, Wasik, & Van der Westhuizen, 1988; Wong, 1980; Wong & Wong, 1986), unfamiliarity with text features and task demands (Jenkins & Pany, 1979), undeveloped attentional strategies (Jenkins & Pany, 1979), and the overall cascading effects of inadequate cognitive development and reading experiences that cause poor readers to become even poorer readers (Stanovich, 1986).

The teacher's task of preventing and responding to the problems of reading comprehension is an enormous one. Perhaps the most important consideration in a teacher's response to this failure is that of designing instructional strategies either to prevent or to correct reading comprehension failure.

INSTRUCTIONAL STRATEGIES

In the next two sections, we specify the procedures for designing and delivering reading comprehension instruction within the before, during, and after phases of instruction. Figure 8–5 provides a graphic overview of these comprehension strategies.

BEFORE INSTRUCTION

Applying the Generic Instructional Set

As in previous chapters, we will use the generic instructional set (i.e., knowledge form, range of examples, sequence of examples, test examples, and practice examples) as the basic framework for designing teaching sequences for reading comprehension strategies.

Determining the Knowledge Form

Because the first task facing the teacher is to determine the kind of knowledge form to be taught, it is fair to assume that in reading comprehension, most tasks will be either *rule relationships* or *cognitive strategies*. In general, reading comprehension tasks require the learner to rely heavily on memory for details, factual information, and general knowledge to make connections and inferences about the text, as well as to summarize and evaluate the information communicated by the text. These skills require the reader to engage in numerous associations that involve connecting facts, concepts, and rules against the background of the reader's general knowledge and life experiences. Because these rule relationships and cognitive strategies are complex and involve many pieces of knowledge, the best approach to teaching them is to break them down into more manageable parts.

In Table 8–1, several reading comprehension tasks are classified according to knowledge form. In addition, the tasks are broken down into component parts or skills (e.g., simple facts, discriminations, concepts, rules), and the essential instructional procedures for teaching these comprehension tasks are given. Naturally, each set of procedures for a particular comprehension task can be designed in many different ways to accommodate different learners of varied skill levels. In adapting these instructional procedures, the teacher could teach more component skills before teaching the cognitive

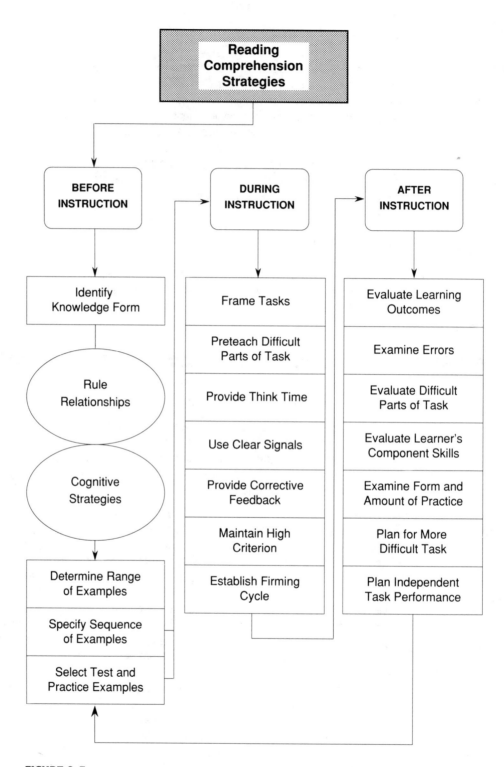

FIGURE 8–5

Instructional strategies for teaching reading comprehension

strategy or rule relationship. In cases of more advanced learners, the teacher would not need to teach these component skills. Instead, the teacher can assume that the learner will be capable of handling bigger, more complex chunks of information.

In the four examples shown, the comprehension skills were identified as either cognitive strategies or rule relationships. The instructional procedures of each skill involve multi-step strategies in which the reader must remember numerous pieces of information, make connections and associations between new and familiar knowledge, and maintain steadfast attention to the task at hand. As the examples indicate, the strategies are complex. They are not simple, one-step discriminations, nor are they verbal chains that can be memorized and stated by rote upon command.

Determining the range of examples.   The most difficult feature of designing teaching sequences for reading comprehension skills is example selection. Selecting the right examples of reading comprehension tasks is especially difficult because the examples must involve texts (e.g., phrases, paragraphs, passages, lengthy narrative or expository discourse). Unlike the examples we use in designing instructional sequences for teaching language concepts or math skills that involve smaller units of knowledge (e.g., single word concepts: *under, chair, red;* numerical operations: $27 \times 6 =$ _____ ; $5447 - 4501$ = _____), the examples for reading comprehension tasks are longer linguistic units of information. When we teach a comprehension skill like identifying the main idea, which requires the use of a passage or paragraph, each passage represents but *one* example of the skill. To demonstrate for the learner more than one example of identifying the main idea, we must use several passages. These longer examples naturally require more instructional time and teacher monitoring, because of the many intermediate steps in a cognitive strategy. Similarly, these examples also demand more cognitive processing time, sustained attention-to-task, and self-management and self-appraisal.

In contrast to decoding tasks (e.g., sound-symbol associations, letter combinations, irregular words) that have a limited range of examples, reading comprehension tasks have a wide range of examples. As a result, cognitive strategies and rule relationships will require extensive sets of examples if a reader is to acquire and master reading comprehension skills. Table 8–2 presents a series of comprehension tasks. In some cases, the actual examples are included in the table. In other cases, we provide brief descriptions of the features of examples that should be selected.

The criteria for determining what examples to include in a limited set and expanded set are determined in part by the skills the learner brings to the instructional situation. Advanced learners should be given more advanced examples of the strategy being taught. The alignment between the complexity of the examples selected and the learner's skills should vary together—complex examples that require the learner to focus on numerous features of the task for more advanced learners, and simple examples that require the learner to focus on the critical feature of the task for more naive learners. For example, for a naive reader who is not a facile decoder, the teacher may want to use selected pictures to teach the concept of identifying the main idea. Using pictures instead of written texts allows the reader to focus on a nonlinguistic piece of information before selecting from a group of sentences the one that represents the main idea. Following mastery of this task, the teacher may want to expand the teaching to include two- or three-sentence texts. At this point, the task should be manageable for the learner, because

TABLE 8–1
Reading comprehension skills classified by knowledge form

COMPREHENSION TASK 8–1

Identifying the Main Idea of a Passage

Knowledge Form: Rule Relationship
"If it's the main idea, it tells about the whole passage."

Component Skill: Concept knowledge of *whole* and *part* of something.

Instructional Procedures

1. Model rule relationship with one passage.
2. Lead learner in identifying main idea in another passage.
3. Model rule relationship with another passage.
4. Repeat step 2.
5. Repeat step 3.
6. Test learner on identifying main idea on at least three different passages.
7. Practice.

COMPREHENSION TASK 8–2

Answering who, what, where, when, *and* why *Literal Comprehension Questions*

Knowledge Form: Cognitive strategy.

Component Skills

1. Statement repetition.
2. Knowledge of concepts, *who, what, where, when,* and *why.*

Instructional Procedures

Facilitative questioning strategy.

1. Require child to read first sentence (or two or more sentences, depending on reader).
2. Alert child that a question will be asked.
3. Have child stop at end of sentence(s).
4. Ask a *wh* question specific to the sentence(s) just read.
5. If child is unable to answer, repeat the question and model the answer.
6. Physically point out how answer is derived from the text.
7. Repeat steps 1–4 with another sentence or two.
8. Test on another brief passage, holding learner to 100% criterion.
9. If task is too difficult, focus on only one type of question (e.g., *where* questions only) and repeat steps 1–8.
10. Practice on two passages, holding learner to 100% criterion.

COMPREHENSION TASK 8–3

Detecting the Correct Sequence of Events in a Story

Knowledge Form: Cognitive strategy.

Component Skills

1. Knowledge of ordinal concepts (e.g., *first, second*).
2. Knowledge of concepts *before, after.*
3. Knowledge of temporal signal words (e.g., *then, now, later*).

Instructional Procedures

Facilitative questioning strategy.

1. Repeat steps 1–3 of strategy for answering *wh* questions.
2. Ask child to identify first important event to take place in passage.
3. Require child to state orally the first event without looking at the passage.
4. Repeat steps 5–6 of *wh* questions strategy.
5. Require child to read next few sentences.
6. Ask child to identify next important event.
7. Repeat step 3.
8. Ask child to state orally the first two events that took place in passage.
9. Repeat steps 1–8 with new passage.
10. Test on two passages, holding child to 100% criterion.
11. Practice on one passage, holding to 100% criterion.

COMPREHENSION TASK 8–4
Using the Context to Understand Difficult Vocabulary Words

Knowledge Form: Rule Relationship
"When you don't know the meaning of a word, you need to look at other words around it to tell more about that word."

Component Skills

1. Self-appraisal knowledge.
2. Self-monitoring knowledge.

Instructional Procedures

1. State rule relationship and repeat it.
2. Require child to read a passage orally.
3. Ask child to identify any difficult words.
4. Continue reading if no difficult words are located.
5. Require child to identify and point to difficult word in sentence.
6. Require child to reread sentence containing difficult word.
7. State rule relationship again.
8. Ask discrimination questions for applying the rule.
9. Require child to scan surrounding sentences to identify clues to meaning of difficult word.
10. Repeat steps 7–8.
11. Continue reading and repeat appropriate steps as necessary.
12. Test child on at least two other difficult words.
13. Require child to apply strategy (steps 5–10) with 100% accuracy on two words.

TABLE 8–2
Range of examples of reading comprehension tasks

COMPREHENSION TASK 8–5

Identifying the Main Idea of a Passage (low performer and beginning reader)

>*Knowledge Form:* Rule Relationship.

>### Examples

>1. Pictures.
>2. Three to four sentences below each picture (only one sentence specifies the main idea in the picture).

>*Limited Set:* Only one picture frame with one clear choice of main idea from the sentences specific to each picture, as shown in Figure 8–6.[1]

>### Expanded Set

>Series of three to five pictures related to one main idea (see Figure 8–7). For some examples, the child chooses the main idea from a set of sentences. Minimally different examples of sentences are included, which makes the selection of the main idea more difficult. In other examples, the child must produce (orally or written) statements of the main idea.

COMPREHENSION TASK 8–6

Identifying the Main Idea of a Passage (naive learner but facile decoder)

>*Knowledge Form:* Rule relationship.

The man was scared.
The dog looked surprised.
The trap snapped the hunter's foot.
The hunter got caught in a trap.
The hunter found a trap.

Example 1

The cowboy ran into a snake.
The cowboy wore a hat.
The snake hissed at the horse.
The cowboy looked scared.

Example 2

A boy had a striped shirt on.
The boys were fighting.
The boys were on the floor.

Example 3

FIGURE 8–6
Choosing the main idea

The girl called for help.
A lifeguard was on duty at the beach.
A lifeguard rescues swimmers in trouble.
A swimmer was rescued by the lifeguard.
A lifeguard was running on the beach.

FIGURE 8–7
Choosing the main idea in a series of pictures

Examples

1. Selected narrative passages.
2. Four to five sentences given below some passages, with just one sentence specifying the main idea.

Limited Set: Brief 30–60 word passages with one sentence as clear choice of main idea.

Expanded Set

1. Passages of 60–150 words in length.
2. Some passages are followed by four to five sentences; main idea is not clear cut.
3. Some passages require child to produce (orally or written) the main idea of the passage.

TABLE 8–2
Continued

COMPREHENSION TASK 8–7
Making Inferences about Events in a Story

        Knowledge Form: Cognitive strategy.

        Examples: Selected sentences and passages (could use pictures if working with low performer, naive reader).

Limited Set

1. Two to four sentences depicting normal, everyday events (e.g., "It was late. John was mad. The bus was not on its way").
2. Series of questions specific to each set of sentences requiring reader to make an inference (e.g., "Why do you think John was mad?").

Expanded Set

1. Passages of 60–150 words in length
2. Series of questions that require reader to make inferences.
3. General (e.g., literal) comprehension questions specific to each passage.

COMPREHENSION TASK 8–8
Simplifying Passive Voice Constructions

        Knowledge Form: Cognitive strategy.

        Examples: Sentences, passages.

the concept of main idea was previously mastered with pictures and will require less cognitive processing when presented in sentence form.

    Once the knowledge form of a task and the range of examples have been identified, the next step in designing a lesson is the sequencing of the selected examples. The teacher must decide what examples to present first, second, and third.

Sequencing examples.   In Chapter 6 on teaching concepts and rule relationships, we noted that by selecting examples from the same set of materials (e.g., using a ball and table to demonstrate the concept *on*) and changing only one feature of the examples, the learner is required to detect only one change in the examples. In effect, the learner watches the examples and says, "Everything's the same. (Example 2 is presented.) That's the same. (Example 3 is presented.) That's the same. (Example 4 is presented.) That example is different because . . ." By carefully controlling the sequence of examples, the teacher can avoid assaulting the learner with too much information at one time.

Limited Set

1. Series of single sentences (e.g., "Joshua was hugged by Albert").
2. Questions specific to the passive voice constructions (e.g., "Who was hugged?" "Who did the hugging?").

Expanded Set

1. Passages of 30–60 words in length. Each passage should consist of one or two passive voice sentences.
2. Questions specific to the passive voice constructions.
3. General comprehension passages specific to each passage.

COMPREHENSION TASK 8–9

Literal Comprehension

Knowledge Form: Cognitive strategy.

Examples: Sentences, passages.

Limited Set

1. Individual sentences about familiar, everyday experiences.
2. *Wh* questions specific to sentences.

Expanded Set

1. Passages of 30–60 words in length.
2. *Wh* questions specific to each passage.
3. Child provides final oral retell of entire passage.

The examples of comprehension tasks a teacher selects can be greatly different or very similar, depending on the number of features that the teacher changes at one time. For example, in teaching a reader to comprehend pronoun constructions, a teacher could vary one, all, or a combination of the following features of the task:

1. *Linguistic unit:* phrase, sentence, sentences, paragraph, narrative text, expository texts, pages of a text, a chapter.
2. *Vocabulary:* easy vocabulary, difficult vocabulary with redundant information in text, difficult vocabulary with no redundant information in text.
3. *Sentence structure:* short, simple sentences, easy sentence structure to long, complex sentences, difficult sentence structure.
4. *Topic of text:* topic familiar to reader, topic unfamiliar and unknown to reader, topic only partially known to reader.
5. *Types of pronoun constructions:* personal, personal-plural, possessive, objective, object preposition, attributive, relative, contrast, and modifier.

These are not the only features of the comprehension task that the teacher must consider. There are other features (e.g., narrative or expository text, readability of text, learner response form), but we will consider the listed features as a starting point. In deciding to teach a reader how to comprehend pronoun constructions, many decisions face the teacher. The teacher must first determine whether the reader will be able to work with a single sentence, a group of sentences, a narrative passage of 60 or fewer words, or, a narrative passage of 60 or more words. Naturally, each of these examples would contain one or more pronoun constructions. Furthermore, each example, whether it is a single sentence or a narrative passage of 60 words, would serve as a *single* example of a text containing pronoun constructions. The teacher would be required to develop numerous examples (e.g., 6–10 single sentences containing pronouns, or 6–10 passages of 60 words or more containing pronouns) to provide the reader with a sufficient amount of practice on the skill of comprehending pronouns.

If the learner is a facile decoder and the teacher chooses to use 30–60 word passages for teaching pronoun comprehension, the teacher is also faced with the task of deciding whether to pull those passages from the reader's basal reading text or to create those passages. By writing the passages, the teacher can control the vocabulary difficulty of the passages, the topic familiarity, the complexity of the sentence structure, and the type of pronoun constructions in the passages. If the teacher decides to select those passages from the basal reading program, the teacher must be sure the passages aren't going to present the reader with too many different features at once.

A general guideline to follow when sequencing examples is to cluster examples that are similar. The examples a teacher uses in teaching a new cognitive strategy or rule relationship should be very similar. For example, it would be inappropriate for the teacher to present an example of a 15-word passage in which the topic is unknown to the reader, the vocabulary words are unfamiliar, and only three personal pronouns are included. It would also be inappropriate to present another example in which the passage is 300 words long, the types of pronouns are greatly varied, and the topic of the passage is uninteresting to the reader.

Because comprehension tasks are usually complex and can vary along many dimensions, the sequencing guidelines are not as straightforward as those for sequencing concepts. The primary guidelines for designing sequences according to features of cognitive strategies are:

1. Determine the number of task features of a cognitive strategy (e.g., type of linguistic unit—sentence, passages, texts; vocabulary difficulty; syntactic difficulty; topic familiarity).
2. Select the linguistic unit (e.g., two-sentence passages) the reader is most able to decode and comprehend.
3. Select the simplest form of the comprehension task and create numerous examples of that form only (e.g., one kind of personal pronoun embedded in two-sentence passages).
4. Create a teaching sequence using only examples developed in step 3.
5. Develop a new set of examples that is more complex; that is, the linguistic units are larger. Instead of two-sentence passages, the reader is now required to read four- to six-sentence passages. The passages may also include more than one type of personal pronoun.

6. Create a new teaching sequence using the examples developed in step 5.
7. Repeat steps 5–6 by developing more complex examples of the comprehension task.

For more advanced learners, the teacher should include both the examples specified in steps 3 and 5 within *one* teaching sequence, instead of two separate teaching sequences. For these learners, a teaching sequence could include a range of greatly different examples, instead of examples that are highly similar. In Table 8–3, we specify the knowledge form and example sequences of various comprehension tasks.

Selecting test examples.   In addition to specifying the form of knowledge to be taught, selecting the range of examples, and placing the examples in an acceptable order, the teacher must also choose a series of test examples. These test examples must be aligned with the intended outcomes of the lesson and the objectives of a learner's individual program. Test examples should be designed to assess a reader's immediate acquisition, delayed retention, discrimination, and generalization of a reading comprehension skill. A teacher may want to assess a reader's ability to remember and apply a comprehension skill immediately after it is taught. This immediate acquisition test provides the teacher with instant feedback about the effectiveness of the teaching sequence.

A teacher may also want to evaluate the reader's ability to retain information over time and then recall it to use in the context of a new example. In this case, a delayed retention and application test should be given. In another situation, the teacher might want to assess the reader's ability to discriminate one set of comprehension skills from another. For example, the teacher tests the reader's ability to simplify passive voice constructions that are embedded with clause constructions in a passage. In this case, the reader must discriminate when to apply the appropriate skills to the appropriate syntactical construction. This discrimination test will provide the teacher information about the reader's skill at simplifying both passive voice and clause constructions.

Finally, a reader's ability to apply a set of newly acquired comprehension skills to novel reading situations is a generalization test. This reveals the extent to which a reader understands the essential features of a comprehension strategy and knows when the requirements of a comprehension task call for the application of this strategy and not another.

Unlike the test examples for assessing a reader's ability to decode selected word types (e.g., CVC, CVCe, CVVC), the test examples for assessing a reader's comprehension ability are not as easy to prepare. In evaluating comprehension skills, often complex and lengthy passages must be used. After all, what is being assessed is not a reader's ability to read words, but to go beyond the words and allow the words to evoke images, old feelings, new emotions, and ideas. In every case, the test examples must be aligned with the intended objectives and outcomes of the lesson.

Table 8–4 delineates specific guidelines to follow in designing or selecting test examples.

Designing and scheduling practice sessions.   The final feature involved in designing a generic instructional set is providing practice. Practice should be scheduled according to the difficulty of the skill for the learner. Brief practice sessions on comprehension skills that are difficult for a reader should be scheduled periodically throughout the day. Instead of requiring a student to work 30–40 minutes on one comprehension skill, three

TABLE 8–3
Example sequences of reading comprehension skills

COMPREHENSION TASK 8–10

Identifying the Correct Sequence of Actions and Events in a Story

> **Knowledge Form:**   Cognitive strategy.

> ### Sequence of Examples

> 1. First teaching sequence: four 30–40 word passages that include two or three events given in clear, successive sequence.
> 2. Second teaching sequence: three 60–80 word passages that include four to five events given in sequence.
> 3. Third teaching sequence: three 60–80 word passages that include four to five events not given in successive sequence (e.g., the last event is mentioned first).

COMPREHENSION TASK 8–11

Comprehending Difficult Vocabulary Words in Context

> **Knowledge Form:**   Cognitive strategy.

> ### Sequence of Examples

> 1. First teaching sequence
>   Three 40–60 word passages that contain two or three unfamiliar words, familiar topic, context clues in close proximity to difficult words.
> 2. Second teaching sequence
>   Three 60–80 word passages that contain four to six unfamiliar words, familiar topic, context clues in close proximity to difficult words.
> 3. Third teaching sequence
>   Two 80–100 word passages that contain six to eight unfamiliar words, familiar topic, context clues in close proximity to difficult words.

or four 10-minute instructional sessions should be planned. Such a schedule sidesteps the cognitive fatigue that can occur when working on difficult and complex cognitive strategies. This practice schedule maximizes the learner's attention to task. Eventually, the length of the practice sessions should be lengthened to approximate the instructional sessions of the regular classroom.

Frequent practice sessions should be scheduled both for new comprehension skills and for those the learner has consistently missed. However, once the specified criterion levels of performance are reached, the length and frequency of the practice sessions should be scaled back. Likewise, the structure of practice sessions should vary according to the degree of assistance a reader requires. Beginning practice sessions may require the teacher to provide more instructional assistance and direction than later sessions.

COMPREHENSION TASK 8–12
Critical Reading Skills—Identifying Statements of Faulty Causality

> **Knowledge Form:** Rule Relationship
> "Just because two things happen at the same time doesn't mean that one causes the other."

Sequence of Examples

1. First teaching sequence
   Five 40–60 word passages, each passage with one example of the rule relationship.
2. Second teaching sequence
   Five 80–120 word passages, each passage with one example of the rule relationship.
3. Third teaching sequence
   One 160–220 word passage with two examples of the rule relationship.

COMPREHENSION TASK 8–13
Simplifying and Comprehending Clause Constructions

> **Knowledge Form:** Cognitive strategy.

Sequence of Examples

1. First teaching sequence
   Series of five single sentences of 7–12 words; each sentence contains the same type of clause construction.
2. Second teaching sequence
   Repeat similar kinds of examples as first sequence.
3. Third teaching sequence
   Series of five single sentences of 12–20 words; each sentence contains the same type of clause construction but is different from the first teaching sequence.
4. Fourth teaching sequence
   Three 80–120 word passages; each passage should contain at least four clause constructions of two different types.

Whenever possible, the teacher should provide as little assistance as necessary during practice sessions. Once the reader has mastered a skill, independent practice should be provided.

DURING INSTRUCTION

Delivering Reading Comprehension Instruction: Generic Procedures

In this phase of instruction, the main focus is on the delivery of the instruction designed in the before instruction phase. The primary instructional procedures used to commu-

TABLE 8–4
Guidelines for designing test examples

Immediate Acquisition

1. Use the same text format as in the teaching sequence. If the reader was required to read single sentences, the test examples should be single sentences.
2. Use the same learner response format as in the teaching sequence. If the reader was required to choose orally a correct response from a set of written responses, the test examples should require the same kind of choice-response.
3. Test immediately following the last teaching example and within the same teaching sequence.
4. Use the same degree of teacher prompting and instructional support during testing as provided during the teaching sequence.
5. If the reader fails on the first test example, present a previously taught example as the next test example. Follow this example with the test example that was missed initially. If the reader misses the test example again, stop testing and reteach.
6. The testing sequence should not introduce any new information, task requirement, or response form.
7. The testing sequence should not be very long. A series of three to four test examples is adequate for assessing immediate acquisition.
8. Testing for immediate acquisition is limited and doesn't indicate whether the reader will recall and apply the skill at later time and under new task conditions.

Delayed Retention Testing

1. Follow steps 1–7 of the immediate acquisition testing sequence.
2. At the end of the testing sequence, the teacher should retest any errors that were made *and corrected* during the testing sequence.
3. Selected test examples should be presented again on several occasions throughout the day.
4. Only one or two test examples should be presented at any given time. This distributed test should not be viewed as a full, complete test of a skill, but as a test of the learner's ability to retain and recall a comprehension skill.
5. If the learner fails the first delayed retest, the teacher should stop any further testing and schedule a session to reteach the skill.
6. The newly taught comprehension skill should be retested the next day and before the teaching of a new comprehension skill.

Discrimination Testing

1. This testing sequence should immediately follow the last teaching example.
2. The testing sequence should comprise examples of the newly taught skill and examples of a recently taught skill that are most similar in features.
   Example:
   a. Answering questions to textually implicit texts (new skill) and textually explicit texts (recently taught).

---

nicate the specific forms of knowledge (i.e., cognitive strategies and rule relationships) in reading comprehension are framing, preteaching, pacing, think time, signaling, corrective feedback, and firming. Because these instructional procedures have been described in previous chapters, in the following section we note only the specific adjustments of these procedures to reading comprehension tasks.

b. Reading three-sentence passages containing the pronoun *they* (new skill) and *he, she, I* (recently taught).

c. Reading 300-word passages containing statements of faulty causality (new skill) and faulty generalization (recently taught).

3. The testing sequence should not introduce a new response form or task requirement. If a written production response form is used, the teacher must be sure that the reader is facile at writing.

4. The teacher may provide guided prompting on the first test example until the learner understands the testing requirements. However, this support should not be used with the remaining test examples.

5. If the learner fails on the first test example, the teacher should walk the learner through this example by modeling the strategy. The learner should be tested immediately on a new example with little or no instructional support. If the learner fails again, the testing should stop and the teacher should assess the learner's knowledge of each skill separately. Reteaching both skills to a higher criterion level of performance may be necessary.

6. This testing sequence should be long enough to include in equal number all the skills being assessed.

7. Discrimination testing should be designed when the teacher is confident that the learner has reached an acceptable criterion level of performance on the similar skills. If discrimination testing is conducted too early, chronic errors may result.

Generalization Testing

1. This testing sequence should consist primarily of examples not previously seen by learner.

2. The teacher should frame this test before requiring the learner to respond. The framing should alert the learner to the purpose and response requirements of the test.

3. The instructional prompting should be minimal. Providing assistance on the task requirements and response forms is acceptable; assistance in the application of the strategy itself is not.

4. The first test of generalization should be conducted following an instructional session on the same set of skills. Subsequent testing sessions need not be "primed."

5. The first test example in the testing sequence should be most familiar to the learner in both format and task requirements. The second test example should be a novel application.

6. The first testing sequence should contain 60% novel examples and 40% familiar examples. Eighty percent or more of the second testing sequence should contain novel examples. The third testing sequence should consist of all novel examples of the comprehension skill.

7. A learner who fails the first test example should verbalize the strategy used to arrive at the answer. No feedback on the accuracy of the strategy should be given. If the strategy is correct, the testing should continue. If the strategy is incorrect, the testing should stop. If the strategy error is unclear, the testing should continue to provide the teacher with more information about the learner's knowledge of the strategy.

Framing

Because comprehension tasks are usually complex knowledge forms in which a single comprehension strategy consists of multiple steps, it is important for the teacher to alert the reader to this feature of comprehension strategies. For example, the following teacher wording could be used: "Listen, we're going to be working on a comprehension strategy that has many steps to it. So you'll need to follow along carefully. If you don't understand a part, stop me by raising your hand." Of course, the teacher would follow this statement with a series of discrimination questions to assess whether the information was acquired.

On some occasions, the teacher may need to frame a comprehension task more than once. A task could be framed before instruction, and then periodically throughout the teaching of the comprehension strategy. The purpose of framing is to alert learners to the requirements of the task; framing should not be overused. Too much framing could interfere with the application of the task in which the learner is required to attend more to the task requirements than to the task itself.

Preteaching

The purpose of preteaching is to prepare the learner for a potentially troublesome part of the task. In teaching complex comprehension skills, preteaching can be an effective strategy for "priming" learners. Like framing, preteaching can also be used periodically throughout the teaching of a complex comprehension strategy. In this case, the teacher should prime those spots in the task that were difficult for the learner when the task was first taught. However, like framing, too much preteaching can be disruptive. If a task requires too much preteaching, the teacher should return to an earlier step in the strategy and bring it to a higher criterion level of performance.

Pacing

Reading comprehension tasks require a great deal of instructional time. These tasks require much sustained attention and cognitive effort. Unlike decoding tasks that can be presented in a fast-paced manner, comprehension tasks are difficult to present at a brisk rate. Therefore, comprehension tasks should be scheduled before and after instructional activities that are fast-paced. They should also be initially scheduled in smaller chunks of time (e.g., 10–20–minute blocks of time), instead of the traditional 40–45–minute session. These brief time slots should eventually be increased until they approximate the traditional, regular classroom period.

Another procedure for breaking up the application of lengthy comprehension strategies is the use of change-up activities. Examples of change-up activities are verbal chains (e.g., multiplication facts) or simple facts (e.g., identifying the state capitals) that learners have mastered. These tasks also require the learner to produce nonsymbolic, motor responses (e.g., "Touch your head"). By inserting change-up activities into the teaching sequence of a comprehension strategy, the learner is provided with a quick (30 seconds to 1 minute) change of pace. This change of pace provides the learner with a break from the demands of the complex task at hand, as well as a shift to a task that can be successfully completed in a brief time. The sequencing of a quick, easy task with a complex, lengthy task should reestablish the learner's attention to the task. As we noted with both the framing and preteaching procedures, these change-up activities should also be used sparingly. The use of too many change-up activities will quickly diminish effectiveness of these activities.

Think Time

The amount of think time needed varies according to the learner and the dimensions of the task. Reading comprehension tasks will require longer thinking time than decoding tasks, multiplication facts, or saying the months of the year. The amount of think time should also be longer for new tasks than for familiar tasks, and for writing tasks than for oral tasks.

Corrective Feedback

The correction appropriate to a particular error is best determined by the knowledge form being taught. A verbal chain or fact will require a different kind of corrective feedback than a cognitive strategy. Moreover, a fact error is best corrected by a simple restatement. The learner either knows this fact and must retrieve it from memory or doesn't know it. In contrast, an error made in applying a cognitive strategy is best corrected by requiring the learner to back up and apply earlier, recognizable steps of the strategy.

The general corrective feedback strategy we recommend using with reading comprehension tasks is that of relying on the strategy. We recommend that teachers repeat a previous step of a cognitive strategy as a first step in providing corrective feedback. In correcting cognitive strategy errors, the teacher should rely on what the learner already knows about the strategy. This general strategy requires the teacher to take care in identifying the step of the strategy that is causing the learner the most difficulty.

In cases when the comprehension strategy is that of a rule relationship, the correction procedure should consist of requiring the learner to rely on the rule. If a learner makes an error in applying the rule, the teacher should prompt the learner to attend to the known parts of the rule relationship. An example of a correction procedure involving a rule relationship follows.

COMPREHENSION TASK 8–14
Correcting Errors in Identifying Faulty Relationships

The student has just completed reading the following passage that includes an example of a faulty relationship. The student has also been taught the rule relationship, "Just because you know about the part doesn't mean you know about the whole thing." Bree, the student, has answered the first three questions correctly.

Passage:

Nick drove a big, fast car. The car had a red stripe on the side. It also had new tires. Jack told everyone that Nick was rich and had lots of money. Nick liked to show off his new car.

Comprehension Questions

1. What do you know about Nick?
2. What do you know about Nick's car?
3. What did Jack say about Nick?
4. Is Nick rich? How do you know for sure?

Teaching Sequence

TEACHER: Bree, what did Jack say about Nick?
BREE: Jack said that Nick was rich and had lots of money.
TEACHER: Good job. Is Nick rich like Jack said?
BREE: I guess.
TEACHER: Well, what in the story made you think so? (Bree scans story.)
BREE: He had a new, fancy car.
TEACHER: Did Nick have a new car? Read the passage and find where it says that Nick had a new car. (Bree scans the passage and locates the appropriate sentences.)
BREE (READING SENTENCE): Nick drove a big fast car. The car had a red stripe on the side. It also had new tires. (Pause.)
TEACHER: So, did Nick have a new, fancy car?
BREE: No . . . His car just had new tires.
TEACHER: Yes, that's the part you know about for sure. If you know about a part, does that mean you know about the whole thing?
BREE: No.
TEACHER: What part do you know for sure?
BREE: I know about Nick's car. . . that it's big, fast . . . and has a red stripe on it.
TEACHER: What is being talked about?
BREE: Nick.
TEACHER: Does knowing about Nick's car tell you everything about Nick?
BREE: No.
TEACHER: So is Nick rich?
BREE: I don't know.
TEACHER: Why?
BREE: Because it just tells me about Nick's car. . . the part, and not about Nick.

Firming Cycle

Because a cognitive strategy comprises many component skills, these skills should be practiced periodically. In the firming cycle, the teacher schedules a number of brief 1–3–minute review sessions. These review sessions must be scheduled beginning with the very first day of instruction on a new skill. In fact, at least two firming sessions should be scheduled during the first day of instruction on a new skill. Firming of a new skill should be more frequent in the first few days of instruction and less frequent as the skill is mastered. The frequency with which a new skill is reviewed and placed in a firming cycle after the first 2 weeks of instruction should be determined by a learner's performance during the previous weeks of instruction.

INSTRUCTIONAL FORMATS FOR TEACHING SELECTED READING COMPREHENSION SKILLS

In the final section of this chapter, instructional formats for teaching reading comprehension skills are presented within the before, during, and after phases of instruction. In each format, we identify the reading comprehension skill being taught, the status of the skill (new or old), the prerequisite skill requirements (prior knowledge), guidelines for designing the instructional set, selected teaching and test examples, and teacher wording.

COMPREHENSION TASK 8–15
Identifying the Main Idea Using Pictures

BEFORE INSTRUCTION

Task Status: New.

Preskills

1. Ability to discriminate between whole and part of something.
2. Ability to read at first to second grade level.

Instructional Design Guidelines

1. Use single pictures that depict a clear-cut action, event, or situation.
2. Each picture represents only one positive example of a main idea.
3. Each picture is accompanied by a series of two to five statements. The incorrect statements should be clearly unrelated to the main idea of the picture.
4. Each teaching sequence should consist of at least seven pictures with accompanying statements (four modeled examples and three test examples).

Introductory Set: Use single pictures with accompanying statements that specify a clear main idea.

Generalization Sets

1. Use single pictures with a set of two to five statements that include a minimally different statement (i.e., the main idea is not clear-cut) of the main idea.
2. Use a sequence of three to four pictures to depict a main idea. The accompanying statements should specify one clear statement of the main idea.
3. Use a sequence of three to four pictures to depict a main idea. The accompanying statements should include a minimally different statement of the main idea.
4. Use a sequence of three to four pictures to depict a main idea. Require students to generate a main idea statement.

TASK 8–16

DURING INSTRUCTION

Instructional Delivery Guidelines

1. Frame the task because it is new.
2. Because the absence of a written text reduces the memory demands placed on the learner, the pacing can be moderately brisk.
3. Require learners to follow along with their fingers as the statements to each picture are read aloud.
4. Require learners orally to state the main idea once the correct statement has been selected from the accompanying set of statements.

Teaching Procedure[2]

Set-up: Modeled Example 1

FIGURE 8–8

The man was scared.
The dog looked surprised.
The trap snapped the hunter's foot.
The hunter got caught in a trap.
The hunter found a trap.

Illustration © 1983, the Stoelting Co., 620 Wheat Lane, Wood Dale, Illinois 60191. All rights reserved. Reproduced by permission.

Teacher Wording	Learner Response
1. Today we're going to learn about main ideas.	Observe teacher.
2. Look at the picture. (Monitor children to make sure they are looking at the picture.) I'll read all the sentences below the picture; you follow along. (Teacher reads all five sentences with children following along.)	Observe teacher, then look at picture. Look at picture then silently read sentences below picture.

---

[2]Text for Teaching Procedure Modeled Examples 1–5 reprinted with permission from the International Reading Association (IRA) (Kameenui, 1986, 477–482).

3. Now let's look at the sentences below the picture again. I'll read the first sentence; you follow with your finger. (Check children to see if their fingers are on the right sentence.)	Read sentences and follow along with finger.
4. "The man was scared." Is that the main idea of the picture? No. How do I know? Because it doesn't tell about the whole picture.	Read sentences and follow along with finger.
5. Put your finger on the next sentence. I'll read it; you follow along.	Read sentences and follow along with finger.
6. "The dog looked surprised." Is that the main idea of the picture? No. How do I know? Because it doesn't tell about the whole picture.	Read sentences and follow along with finger.
7. Put your finger on the next sentence. I'll read it; you follow along.	Read sentences and follow along with finger.
8. "The trap snapped the hunter's foot." Is that the main idea of the picture? No. How do I know? Because it doesn't tell about the whole picture.	Read sentences and follow along with finger.
9. I'll read the next sentence. "The hunter got caught in a trap." Is that the main idea of the picture? Yes. How do I know? Because it tells about the whole picture.	Read sentences and follow along with finger.
10. Next sentence. "The hunter found a trap." Is that the main idea of the picture? How do I know? Because it doesn't tell about the whole picture.	Read sentences and follow along with finger.

Set-up: Modeled Example 2 (new set of examples)

FIGURE 8–9

The cowboy ran into a snake.
The cowboy wore a hat.
The snake hissed at the horse.
The cowboy looked scared.

11. Now let's look at another picture. (Teacher presents the above picture and set of statements.) I'll read all the sentences below the picture; you follow along. (Teacher reads all sentences while children follow along.)
12. Teacher repeats steps 3–10 with the new picture and set of statements.

Set-up: Modeled Example 3 (new set of examples)

FIGURE 8–10

A boy had a striped shirt on.
The boys were fighting.
The boys were on the floor.

13. Teacher repeats steps 3–11 with the new picture and set of statements.

Set-up: Modeled Example 4 (new set of examples)

FIGURE 8–11

The creature was funny looking.
The spacecraft was broken.
The man was a farmer.
The man and the creature were
 working together.
The man and the creature were
 fixing the spacecraft.
The creature did not wear clothes.

14. Repeat step 13.

Set-up: Modeled Example 5 (new set of examples)

FIGURE 8–12

The man lost his canteen.
The man was thirsty.

Set-up: Testing Example 1

FIGURE 8–13

The frog sat on the river bank.
The frog had big eyes.
The frog had a long tongue.
The frog caught the dragonfly.

Teacher Wording	Learner Response
15. Look at this picture. (Monitor children's attention to picture.) I'll read all of the sentences below the picture. You follow along. (Teacher reads all four sentences with children following along.)	Observe teacher.

16. Now let's decide which sentence tells us the main idea of the picture. I'll read the first sentence, and you tell me if that's the main idea.	Observe teacher.
17. (Teacher reads the first sentence.) "The frog sat on the river bank." (Pauses and looks at children.) Listen, is that the main idea of the picture? (Teacher calls on a volunteer for a response.)	No.
18. How do you know that is not the main idea of the picture?	Because it doesn't tell about the whole picture.

Correction Procedure: If the child responds incorrectly, the teacher models the answer. Listen, that's not the main idea of the picture. How do I know? Because it doesn't tell about the whole picture. Now it is your turn again. Listen. "The frog sat on the river bank." Is that the main idea of the picture? (Child responds.) How do you know? (Child responds. The teacher may want to model a new set of examples for the learner before continuing with the testing sequence.)

19. I'll read the next sentence; you follow along. "The frog had big eyes." (Pauses and looks at children.) Is that the main idea of the picture? (Teacher calls on a volunteer for a response.)	No.
20. How do you know that's not the main idea?	Because it doesn't tell about the whole picture.
21. I'll read the next sentence. "The frog had a long tongue." (Pauses and looks at children.) Is that the main idea of the picture? (Teacher calls on a volunteer for a response.)	No.
22. How do you know?	Because it doesn't tell about the whole picture.
23. I'll read the next sentence. "The frog caught the dragonfly." (Pauses and looks at children.) Is that the main idea of the picture? (Teacher calls on a volunteer for a response.)	Yes.
24. How do you know?	Because it tells about the whole picture.

Set-up: Testing Example 2 (new set of examples)

25. Now let's look at another picture. (Teacher selects another picture and set of statements.)
26. (Teacher repeats steps 15–24 with new set up. The teacher may now require children to read the statements out loud or to themselves.)

The teacher should test children on a total of at least three new pictures before terminating the instruction.

Example picture series consisting of four pictures that could be used in a generalization set are given here:

The girl called for help.
A lifeguard was on duty at the beach.
A lifeguard rescues swimmers in trouble.
A swimmer was rescued by the lifeguard.
A lifeguard was running on the beach.

FIGURE 8–14

TASK 8–17

AFTER INSTRUCTION

Analyze Errors and Make Instructional Decisions

The teacher should examine the kinds of errors the student made during the lesson. These errors are likely to be either procedural or conceptual. Procedural errors are concerned with the learner's inability to follow the directions for the task (e.g., following along, focusing on the picture, sustaining attention to the picture and statements, producing the correct response form). To correct these errors, the teacher should make the following adjustments:

1. Increase or decrease the pace of instruction.
2. Break the task into smaller chunks of time and juxtapose the task with easier tasks (i.e., tasks already mastered and of short duration).
3. Reframe the task to clarify response requirements.
4. Reexamine the management strategies, expected outcomes, and specific contingencies for students.

Conceptual errors are related to the learner's inability to grasp and understand the symbolic associations being made. An example of a conceptual error is the learner not being able to grasp the meaning of main idea by linking the actions depicted in the picture with the statements below the picture. To correct this error, the teacher should use an example in which a picture is followed by only two statements. One statement (negative example of main idea) should be clearly unrelated to the picture. The other statement (positive example of main idea) should specify the main idea of the picture. The inclusion of two clearly contrasting statements provides the learner with an obvious and exaggerated example of the main idea. Subsequent picture examples should gradually include statements that are similar to each other in specifying the main idea.

The teacher should also establish a firming cycle schedule for the first 2 weeks of main idea instruction. This schedule should specify the number of times the skill is to be reviewed daily. It should also indicate the amount of time these review sessions will require.

COMPREHENSION TASK 8–18
Identifying the Main Idea of a Passage

BEFORE INSTRUCTION

Task Status: New.

Preskills: Same as for Comprehension Task 8–15.

Instructional Design Guidelines

1. Use brief passages that consist of a series of four to six sentences (approximately 25–60 words in length).
2. Each passage should depict one clear main idea.
3. Each passage should be accompanied by a series of two to six statements. Statements that are not the main idea should describe either one or two details of the text only and not the entire passage.
4. Each teaching sequence should consist of at least five passages with accompanying statements (two modeled examples and three test examples).

Introductory Set: Use 25–40 word passage (four to six sentences) with accompanying statements that specify a clear main idea.

Generalization Sets

1. Use longer passages (approximately 60–100 words; 6–10 sentences) with accompanying statements that specify a clear main idea.
2. Use longer passages [as in (1) above] with accompanying statements that include a minimally different, incorrect main idea statement.
3. Use longer passages. Require student to orally state main idea of passage.
4. Use longer passages. Require student to write main idea statement.

TASK 8–19

DURING INSTRUCTION

Instructional Delivery Guidelines

1. Frame task carefully because it is new and represents a shift from a nonsymbolic operation (main idea with pictures) to a symbolic operation.
2. Require students to read orally the passage and the accompanying statements.
3. Require naive learners to follow along with their fingers during text reading.
4. Correct oral reading errors either by prompting students to apply a mastered strategy for decoding a word, or by providing a whole word correction procedure in which the teacher tells the student the word (e.g., "That word is _____ ").
5. Require learners to state orally the main idea once the correct statement has been selected. Then require learners to justify why it is the main idea (e.g., "Because it tells about the whole passage").

Teaching Procedure[3]

Set-up: Modeled Example, Passage 1

Ann was excited. She had always wanted a puppy. She first heard it bark. Then she heard a scratch on her door. She jumped up from her bed and ran to open the door. Ann smiled and picked up her new puppy from out of the basket.

Underline the statement that tells the main idea.

1. Ann heard a scratch at her door.
2. Ann was excited.
3. The puppy lived in a basket.
4. Ann got a new puppy.
5. Ann got what she wanted.

---

[3]Text for Teaching Procedure Modeled Examples reprinted with permission from the International Reading Association (IRA) (Kameenui, 1986, 477–482).

Teacher Wording	Student Response
1. Today we're going to learn about main ideas. This time when we learn about the main idea we're not going to use pictures. From now on we're going to find the main idea of a passage.	Each student has a passage and statements as in the set up.
2. What are we going to find the main idea of?	STUDENTS: A passage.
3. Yes, we're going to find the main idea of a passage. Everyone, put your finger on the first word of the passage. (Monitor children to see if they've located the first word of the passage.)	Place finger on first word of passage.
4. I'll read the passage; you follow along with your finger. (Teacher reads the passage and monitors children.)	Children follow along.
5. Now I'll read all the statements below the passage. You follow along with your finger. (Teacher reads all of the statements.)	
6. Now let's go back and decide which statement tells us the main idea of the passage. I'll read the first statement; you follow along. (Teacher reads the first statement.) "Ann heard a scratch at her door."	
7. Listen, that's not the main idea of the passage. How do I know? Because it doesn't tell about the whole passage. So, am I going to underline it? No.	
8. I'll read the next statement. You follow along. (Teacher reads the next statement.) "Ann was excited."	
9. That's not the main idea of the passage. How do I know? Because it doesn't tell about the whole passage. So, am I going to underline it? No.	
10. I'll read the next statement; you follow along. (Teacher reads the next statement.) "The puppy lived in a basket."	
11. That's not the main idea of the passage. How do I know? Because it doesn't tell about the whole passage. So, am I going to underline it? No.	
12. I'll read the next statement. (Teacher reads the next statement.) "Ann got a new puppy."	
13. That's the main idea of the passage. How do I know? Because it tells about the whole passage. So, am I going to underline it? Yes.	

14. Listen to the next statement. (Teacher reads the last statement.) "Ann got what she wanted."

15. That's not the main idea of the passage. How do I know? Because it doesn't tell about the whole passage. So, am I going to underline it? No.

16. Look at all the statements. Let's review the main idea of the passage again. Who can read the statement that tells the main idea of the passage?

17. (Teacher calls on a volunteer who is raising a hand.)

STUDENT (reads the statement): "Ann got a new puppy."

18. (Teacher directs question to a child.) How do you know that is the main idea?

STUDENT: Because it tells about the whole passage.

19. (Teacher directs question to group.) If that's the main idea of the passage, what are you going to do to that statement?

STUDENTS: Underline it.

Set-up: Modeled Example, Passage 2

20. Now let's read another passage and find the main idea. (Teacher selects another passage and a set of statements.)

21. (Teacher repeats steps 4–19 with the new passage.)

Set-up: Modeled Example, Passage 3

22. (Teacher repeats steps 20–21 with a new passage and set of statements.)

Set-up: Modeled Example, Passage 4

23. Same as step 22.

Set-up: Test Example, Passage 1

Whales are like human beings in many ways. They are mammals like us. They have hair, they breathe air, they are born alive, and their babies take milk from their mothers. Whales are also warm-blooded animals like us.

Underline the statement that tells the main idea.

1. Whales are mammals like us.
2. Whales and human beings have many things in common.
3. Whales and human beings are common animals.

Teacher Wording	Student Response
24. Will someone please read the passage out loud? (Teacher calls on a volunteer.)	Child reads passage orally while others follow along.

25. Will someone please read the three statements below the passage? (Teacher calls on a volunteer.)

Child reads passage orally while others follow along.

26. Now let's go back and look at each statement. I'll read the first statement again; you follow along. "Whales are mammals like us." (Pauses and looks at children.) Listen, is that the main idea of the passage? (Teacher calls on a volunteer for a response.)

STUDENT: No.

(Correction Procedure) If the child responds incorrectly, the teacher models the answer: "Listen, that's not the main idea of the passage. How do I know? Because it doesn't tell about the whole passage. Now it's your turn again. Read the first sentence again." (Child reads, "Whales are mammals like us.") "Is that the main idea of the passage?" (Child responds.) "How do you know?" (Child responds.) The teacher may want to model a new set of examples for the learner before continuing in the testing sequence.

27. How do you know?

STUDENT: Because it doesn't tell about the whole passage.

28. So, will you underline it?

No.

29. I'll read the next sentence. "Whales and human beings have many things in common." (Pauses and looks at children.) Is that the main idea of the passage? (Teacher calls on a volunteer for a response.)

Yes.

30. How do you know?

Because it tells about the whole passage.

31. So will you underline it?

Yes.

32. Look at the next sentence. "Whales and human beings are common animals." (Pauses and looks at children.) Is that the main idea of the passage? (Teacher calls on a volunteer for a response.)

No.

33. How do you know?

Because it doesn't tell about the whole passage.

34. So, will you underline it?

No.

Set-up: Test Example, Passage 2

35. Now let's read another passage. (Teacher selects another passage and set of statements and presents it.)

36. Teacher repeats steps 24–34 with the new set up.

(The teacher should test children on a minimum of three new passages before terminating the instruction.)

Advanced strategy with extended expository text:

The first steamboat that worked was built in the United States in 1787. It had many paddles on the sides. The next year two men in Scotland made a steamboat, and it used wheels to move the paddles. This steamboat had a paddle wheel on each side. It could travel about 5 miles per hour. Soon other steamboats were built. One of these had a single paddle wheel at the back of the boat.

An American named Robert Fulton saw a paddle wheel steamboat in Scotland and decided to make one. He built a successful steamboat in France. When he went back home, he planned a bigger and better one than any that had been built. He thought such a steamboat would soon pay for itself. So he set about carrying out his plan. People told him the plan would not work. But he kept on trying.

At last Fulton's steamboat was finished. It was named the *Clermont.* It was ready for a trial on the Hudson River in New York State. The people who gathered on the banks of the Hudson made fun of it. They called it "Fulton's Folly." Soon the great paddle wheels on each side of the boat began to turn. The steamboat moved slowly up the Hudson River. The people on the river banks stopped laughing. They stared in wonder. The day of the steamboat had begun.[4]

STEP 1. TEACHER: I need a volunteer to begin reading. (Teacher calls on a volunteer.) Why don't you start reading the passage and I'll tell you when to stop.

LEARNER: (Reads the first three sentences out loud.)

STEP 2. TEACHER: Stop. Thank you. Can anyone tell me what those sentences were about? (Teacher calls on a volunteer.)

LEARNER: They were about steamboats.

(CORRECTION PROCEDURE) If the response is incorrect, the teacher may want to have a learner reread each sentence. After reading the first sentence the teacher would stop the child and ask, "What does that whole sentence tell about?" The child should respond, "It tells about the first steamboat." If the child responds incorrectly, the teacher may want to model the correct response. After reading the first sentence and identifying the main topic, the teacher should have a learner read the second sentence. After reading the second sentence, the teacher should prompt the learners about the main topic of the first sentence. For example, "Listen, what did the first sentence tell about?" (Child responds, "The first steamboat.") "Now, does the next sentence also tell about the first steamboat or something else?" (Child responds, "The first steamboat.") "So, what do the first two sentences tell about?" (Child responds, "The first steamboat.") After the third sentence is read, the teacher would continue prompting by asking, "Does the next sentence also tell about the first steamboat or about something else?" (Child responds, "Something else.") "Listen, the first sentence tells about a steamboat, the second sentence tells about a steamboat, and the third sentence tells about steamboats. What do all of those sentences tell about?" (Child responds, "Steamboats.")

STEP 3. TEACHER: Yes, they tell about steamboats. Now let's read the next three sentences and see if they continue to tell about steamboats. (Teacher calls on a volunteer to read.)

LEARNER: (Reads the next three sentences out loud.)

STEP 4. TEACHER: Stop. Thank you. Now let's see if those sentences still tell about steamboats.

(Steps 1–4 are repeated with remaining text.)

---

[4]Reprinted with permission of Macmillan Publishing Company from *Living in Our Country and Other Lands* by Mae Knight Clark (Macmillan Social Studies, Grade 4—Prudence Cutright & John Jarolimek, General Editors) Copyright © 1966 Macmillan Publishing Company.

TASK 8–20

AFTER INSTRUCTION

Analyze Errors and Make Instructional Decisions

Unlike the main idea teaching sequence using pictures, the inclusion of text in this format requires the teacher to take careful note of students' oral reading errors. The errors should be recorded to determine if there is a specific pattern to the oral reading errors. Specific word type error patterns (e.g., CVCe word types) should be noted. If the passage proves to be too difficult, another passage with an easier readability level should be selected. The teacher must discern whether the decoding errors are interfering with the student's ability to comprehend the passage.

If the problems appear related to the student's ability to comprehend the passage, then the following suggestions should be followed:

1. Determine if the passage is too long (i.e., the student is unable to remember critical information).
2. Require the students to reread the passage sentence by sentence. After each sentence is read aloud, the teacher requires the student to answer a literal comprehension question specific to each sentence. At the end of the passage, the student is required to retell the main actions and events in the passage. The student is then required to read each accompanying statement. After each statement, the teacher prompts the student to determine if the statement is the best main idea statement for the passage.
3. The teacher may be required to model the rule ("It's the main idea if it tells about the whole passage") with several more passages before testing the learner.

COMPREHENSION TASK 8–21
Literal Comprehension—Recalling Details

BEFORE INSTRUCTION

Task Status: New.

Preskills:

1. Ability to follow directions.
2. Ability to read with adequate fluency.

Instructional Design Guidelines

1. Use brief passages that consist of a series of six to eight sentences (approximately 60–100 words).

2. The sentences of the passage should be of simple syntactical construction.
3. The initial passages should not depict complex actions and events with numerous characters.
4. The readability of the passages should be aligned with the learner's reading skills.

Introductory Set

Use 60-word passages (six to eight sentences). Sentences should not be complex in syntactical construction. Events in the passage should occur successively.

Generalization Set

Passages should increase in length, syntactical complexity, number of characters, events, general story grammar features (e.g., problem resolution, goals, plot), and specific details over time as the student becomes more facile.

TASK 8–22

DURING INSTRUCTION

Instructional Delivery Guidelines

1. Frame task by alerting student to pay close attention to what is read. Inform students that they will be asked to read the passage a sentence at a time and to answer questions following the reading.
2. Require student to read each sentence orally.
3. Provide student with an immediate whole word correction on significant decoding errors (e.g., "Stop, the word is _____") then have student reread sentence.
4. The task should be kept highly reinforcing.

Teaching Procedure: Facilitative Questioning Strategy

TEACHER: I want you to read the first sentence. After you read, I'm going to ask you to answer some questions. What are you going to do after you read the first sentence, Joe?

JOE: Answer questions.

TEACHER: Exactly. Start reading please, Jack.

JACK: "It was dark outside and the . . . room was quit. . . ."

TEACHER: That word is *quiet*. Read the sentence again, please Jack.

JACK: "It was dark outside and the room was quiet for a long time."

TEACHER: Nice reading, Jack. I want everyone to turn your story over. Tell me about what you just read, Jack.

JACK: Well, I read about a room and . . . the room was dark . . . (long 3–4 second pause).

TEACHER: Was the room dark, Jack?

JACK: I think so.

TEACHER: How do we find out if the room was dark?

BETH: By looking back at what we read.

TEACHER: Right, by looking at the sentences we read. Read the first sentence again, Jack. (Jack reads the sentence.)

Was the room dark, Jack?

JACK: No, it said the room was quiet for a long time.

TEACHER: Good reading. Yes, the room was quiet for a long time. That's remembering the details of what you read, Jack. When you remember the details, you remember the little things in the story. So, let's see who can remember what was dark?

JOE: It was dark.

TEACHER: Yes, it was dark. But what is *it*?

LISA: Outside . . . was dark, I think.

TEACHER: Good, Lisa. It was dark outside. Very nice. Now, who can tell me everything we just read?

JACK: It was dark outside and the room was quiet for a long time.

TEACHER: Excellent remembering, Jack. You've got the details down. OK, Lisa, will you please read the next two sentences.

LISA: "Ben was sad. He was left alone all day with no water or food."

TEACHER: Good job, Lisa. Who was sad?

JOE: Ben.

TEACHER: What else do we know about Ben?

JACK: He was alone by himself all day and he didn't have much food.

TEACHER: Yes, he was alone all day. How much food did he have, though, Jack?

JACK: Not very much.

TEACHER: Look back at the sentence and reread it. (Jack reads the sentence aloud as the other students follow along). So how much food did Ben have, Jack?

JACK: He didn't have any food.

TEACHER: What else did you find out about Ben?

JACK: He didn't have any water either.

TEACHER: Right. Now, I'll ask some questions and I want you to answer by recalling the details of what you just read. Be sure you leave your stories turned over.

What was quiet for a long time?

LISA: The room.

TEACHER: Tell me two things you remember about Ben and his situation.

JOE: He was sad and he was by himself all day.

TEACHER: Excellent. I asked for two things and you told me two things about Ben—he was sad and alone all day. Nice job, Joe. How much water did Ben have? Jack, can you tell me?

JACK: Umm . . . he didn't have any water. . . and he didn't have any food.

The teacher continues following the same procedures previously described. Periodically, students should be required to read two to three sentences at a time before recalling the details of the story and answering comprehension questions.

TASK 8–23

AFTER INSTRUCTION

Analyze Errors and Make Instructional Decisions

Following literal comprehension tasks, the teacher should reflect on these concerns:

1. Were the students able to recall the information in the chunks they read, or will it be necessary to reduce the length of the text?
2. Did specific students appear to require more prompting and rereading? Were there students who failed to answer the comprehension questions correctly the first time they were asked? If so, the reading level of the text should be checked. It may be necessary for students to read and recall smaller chunks of the text (e.g., one sentence at a time).
3. Were there students who were unable to scan the text and locate the information being recalled? If so, provide these students with practice scanning and locating information in shorter texts. Students should be given selected words and asked to find them in the text. Students would not be required to read the text before scanning it for the target word or words.

COMPREHENSION TASK 8–24
Making Inferences Requiring Comparisons

BEFORE INSTRUCTION

Task Status: Familiar.

Preskills

1. Ability to identify supporting details of a particular fact.
2. Ability to identify the main idea that is not explicitly stated in a passage.
3. Ability to make inferences about the sequence of events in a story.
4. Ability to identify how things are the same and how they are different.

Instructional Design Guidelines

1. Use brief passages that consist of a series of 8–10 sentences (approximately 100–140 words).
2. The sentences should not be overly complex in their syntactical construction.
3. The initial passages should focus on two characters and their actions.

Introductory Set

Use brief passages of 100–140 words involving two characters with various similarities and differences.

Generalization Set

Passages should increase in length, syntactical complexity, number of characters, events, specific details, and general story grammar features (e.g., number of problems, nature of resolution, explicitness of goals, plot).

TASK 8–25

DURING INSTRUCTION

Instructional Delivery Guidelines

1. It may not be necessary to frame the task because it has been taught before. If there are any potential behavior management concerns (e.g., the session takes place immediately after recess), the task should be framed.
2. Require students to follow along with their fingers as the passage is being read, if appropriate.
3. Require students to read the passages aloud.
4. Provide students with an immediate whole word correction on decoding errors (e.g., "Stop, that word is _____"), then have students reread the sentence.
5. Keep task highly reinforcing.

Teaching Procedure

TEACHER: Alison, you start us out by reading. I'll tell you when to stop. As Alison is reading, I would like the rest of you to follow along with your fingers. That will help you keep up and help me know that everyone is together. OK? Go ahead and start, Alison.

ALISON: "One fine day a pig met a stork on the road and asked the stork to come to his home to eat dinner. The stork came the next night and the pig had fun serving the stork some soup in a shallow bowl. That is all the pig had for the stork to eat. The pig ate his soup very fast, but the stork could not eat any of her soup. Her long thin beak was not the right shape to eat soup in this way. The pig thought the dinner was very funny, but the stork went home hungry."

TEACHER: Let's stop there, Alison. Very nice reading. I also liked how every one of you followed along with your fingers. Let's think about what's going on in the story. Who can tell me what the story is about.

JANICE: It's about a pig and a stork . . . and how the pig is mean to the stork.

TEACHER: Very good. The story is about two characters, a pig and a stork. Sometimes stories tell us about two characters, in this case, two animals. Sometimes stories are about two different places, or two different people, or even two different times such as today and long ago when Abraham Lincoln was President of the United States.

When stories tell us about different people, places, and times, we can compare how things are the same or different. We can see how one person is similar to or different from another person. Let's think about our story. What kinds of comparisons can we make about the pig and the stork? How are they alike? How are they different?

VERN: Well, the pig is really a trickster. He likes to play tricks on the stork. He seemed kind at first by inviting the stork over for dinner. But that was just a trick to make fun of her.

TEACHER: Good. What do we know about the stork?

ALISON: The stork doesn't say much. The stork didn't get mad or anything. I would have been mad at that pig.

MARK: Yeah, the stork was too nice. She just went home hungry. I would have cooked that pig, good.

TEACHER: Sounds like we've decided that the pig was a trickster and the stork was too nice. So they seem like very different characters, don't they? Anyone want to make a prediction to see if our characters are going to stay the same? Yes, Janice.

JANICE: Yeah, I think the pig's going to get it in the end.

MARK: Yeah, the stork's going to peck his eyes out . . . you just watch.

TEACHER: Good predictions. Let's see if they hold true about our characters. Mark, will you please finish reading the story while we follow along?

MARK: Sure . . . "She said very little to the pig but later she asked him to come eat at her house the next day. The next day the pig came; he was very angry . . ." I mean . . . "he was very hungry and ready to eat a lot. The pig saw the food was served in a bottle with a long thin neck."

TEACHER: Excellent reading, Mark. OK. Were our predictions about the stork true? Did the stork get even with the pig?

ALISON: Yes, but she didn't peck his eyes out. She did the same thing to the pig that the pig did to her.

TEACHER: Good. So how are the pig and stork alike and how are they different?

The teacher completes the lesson by requiring students to list on a sheet of paper how the pig and stork are the same and different.

TASK 8–26

AFTER INSTRUCTION

Analyze Errors and Make Instructional Decisions

The following instructional dimensions should be considered after the teaching sequence is completed:

1. The primary difficulty students may face on this task is that of discerning how things are the same or different when events in time are being compared. For example, when a text refers to "here and there" or "then and now," students may have a difficult time recalling the events.

2. To correct errors involving comparisons of events in time, students may need to write things down during passage reading. Students could be given a work sheet with the categories to be compared listed in two separate columns. Students would list the features of each category as they read the passage.

SUMMARY

In this chapter we identified four components of the reading comprehension process: reader, text, task, and strategies. The features of each component were described. Specifically, the reader's background knowledge, component skill knowledge (e.g., decoding skills, semantics, syntax, factual information), and motivation were described and their interaction with the text, task, and strategies were discussed. Features of the text that include different types of text were also discussed. The various dimensions of reading comprehension tasks were identified and described. Finally, the generic instructional set was applied to a range of reading comprehension skills. In each case, the knowledge form, examples, sequence of examples, test examples and practice examples were specified.

APPLICATION ITEMS

1. For each item listed below, identify the component skill that is required of a reader's background knowledge (e.g., decoding, semantics, syntax, anaphora knowledge; see pp. 252–253) before reading comprehension can be successful.
   a. Does not know the meaning of a word.
   b. Fails to understand pronouns such as *they, it,* and *our.*
   c. Ignores commas, periods, and question marks when reading.
   d. Doesn't enjoy reading.

2. Identify the following story grammar components of the textually implicit story, "Clover and the King," on page 257: setting, characters, goals, attempts, outcome, and ending.

3. Write six comprehension questions for the scriptally implicit text, "The Fox and the Grapes," on page 258. Three of the questions should evaluate the reader's understanding of why the fox called the grapes sour. The other questions should be literal.

4. Explain how the instructional procedures of framing, preteaching, pacing, and think time are different for a reading comprehension task than for a simple fact (e.g., There are 12 months in 1 year).

5. Design a teaching strategy using the generic instructional set to teach a literal comprehension skill. Identify the knowledge form, the range of examples, the sequence of examples, the testing sequence, and the practice examples. Beginning examples should consist of brief passages consisting of three to five sentences and approximately 40 words.

REFERENCES

Allington, R. L. (1980). Teacher interruption behaviors during primary grade oral reading. *Journal of Educational Psychology, 72*, 371–377.

Allington, R. L. (1983). The reading instruction provided readers of differing abilities. *Elementary School Journal, 83*(5), 548–559.

Allington, R. L. (1984). Content coverage and contextual reading in reading groups. *Journal of Reading Behavior, 16*, 85–96.

Allington, R. L., & Strange, M. (1980). *Learning through reading: An introduction for content area teachers.* Lexington, MA: Heath.

Anderson, R. C. (1977). The notion of schemata and the educational enterprise. In R. C. Anderson, R. J. Spiro, & W. E. Montague (Eds.), *Schooling and the acquisition of knowledge* (pp. 415–433). Hillsdale, NJ: Erlbaum.

Anderson, R. C., & Freebody, P. (1981). Vocabulary knowledge. In J. T. Guthrie (Ed.), *Comprehension and teaching: Research reviews* (pp. 77–117). Newark, DE: International Reading Association.

Anderson, R. C., Heibert, E. M., Scott, J. A., & Wilkinson, I. A. G. (1985). *Becoming a nation of readers: The report of the commission on reading.* Urbana, IL: Center for the Study of Reading, University of Illinois.

Anderson, R. C., & Pearson, P. I. (1984). A schema-theoretic view of basic processes in reading. In P. D. Pearson (Ed.), *Handbook of reading research* (pp. 255–291). New York: Longman.

Armbruster, B. B., & Anderson, T. H. (1988). On selecting "considerate" content area textbooks. *Remedial and Special Education, 9*(1), 47–52.

Armbruster, B. B., Echols, C. H., & Brown, A. L. (1983). *The role of metacognition in reading to learn: A developmental perspective* (Reading Education Report No. 40). Urbana-Champaign, IL: University of Illinois. Center for the Study of Reading.

Au, K. H. (1979). Using the experience-text-relationship method with minority children. *Reading Teacher, 32*(6), 677–679.

Baumann, J. F. (1988). Teaching third-grade students to comprehend anaphoric relationships: The application of a direct instruction model. *Reading Research Quarterly, 21*(1), 70–90.

Baumann, J. F., & Kameenui, E. J. (in press). Vocabulary instruction. In J. Flood, J. Jensen, D. Lapp, & J. R. Squire (Eds.), *Handbook of research on teaching the English language arts.* New York: Macmillan.

Brophy, J., & Good, T. L. (1986). Teacher behavior and student achievement. In M. Wittrock (Ed.), *Handbook of research on teaching* (3rd ed.). (pp. 328–375). New York: Macmillan.

Brown, A. L. (1980). Metacognitive development and reading. In R. J. Spiro, B. C. Bruce, & W. F. Brewer (Eds.), *Theoretical issues in reading comprehension* (pp. 453–481). Hillsdale, NJ: Erlbaum.

Calfee, R., Spector, J., & Piontkowski, D. (1979). Assessing reading and language skills: An interactive system. *Bulletin of the Orton Society, 29*, 129–156.

Carnine, D., & Kinder, D. (1985). Teaching low-performing students to apply generative and schema strategies to narrative and expository material. *Remedial and Special Education, 6*(1), 20–30.

Carnine, D. W., Silbert, J., & Kameenui, E. J. (1990). *Direct instruction reading* (2nd ed.). Columbus, OH: Merrill Publishing Company.

Chall, J. S. (1983). *Stages of reading development.* New York: Academic Press.

Chall, J. S., & Snow, C. E. (1988). School influences on the reading development of low-income children. *Harvard Education Letter, 4*(1), 1–4.

Cohen, R. L. (1982). Individual differences in short-term memory. In N. Ellis (Ed.), *International review of research in mental retardation* (vol. 11, pp. 43–77). New York: Academic Press.

Durkin, D. (1978–1979). What classroom observations reveal about reading comprehension instruction. *Reading Research Quarterly, 14*(4), 481–533.

Durkin, D. (1987). *Teaching young children to read* (4th ed.). Newton, MA: Allyn & Bacon.

Flavell, J. H. (1976). Metacognitive aspects of problem solving. In L. B. Resnick (Ed.), *The nature of intelligence* (pp. 231–235). Hillsdale, NJ: Erlbaum.

Gurney, D. E. (1987). *Teaching mildly handicapped high-school students to understand short stories using a story-grammar-comprehension strategy.* Unpublished doctoral dissertation, University of Oregon.

Hayes, D. A., & Tierney, R. J. (1982). Developing readers' knowledge through analogy. *Reading Research Quarterly, 17*(2), 256–280.

Howe, D. E., & Kameenui, E. J. (1983). *Action express paragraph and story writers.* Wood Dale, IL: Stoelting Co., pp. 5–21.

Idol, L. (1988). Johnny can't read: Does the fault lie with the book, teacher, or Johnny? *Remedial and Special Education, 9*(1), 8–25.

Jenkins, J. R., & Pany, D. (1981). Instructional variables in reading comprehension. In J. Guthrie (Ed.), *Reading comprehension and education* (pp. 163–202). Newark, DE: International Reading Association.

Jenkins, J. R., Stein, M. L., & Osborn, J. R. (1981). What next after decoding? Instruction and research in reading comprehension. *Exceptional Education Quarterly, 2*(1), 27–39.

Kameenui, E. J. (1986). The iconicity of education: Thoughts on the transparency and intricacy of schooling. *Review of Education, 12*(2), 111–116.

Kameenui, E. J., & Carnine, D. W. (1982). Investigating the ecological validity of fourth grader's comprehension of pronoun constructions. *Reading Research Quarterly, 17*(4), 556–580.

Kameenui, E. J., Carnine, D. W., & Freschi, R. (1982). Effect of text construction and instructional procedures for teaching word meanings on comprehension of contrived passages. *Reading Research Quarterly, 17*(3), 367–388.

Kameenui, E. J., Dixon, R. C., & Carnine, D. W. (1987). Issues in the design of vocabulary instruction. In M. G. McKeown and M. B. Curtis (Eds.), *The nature of vocabulary acquisition* (pp. 129–145). Hillsdale, NJ: Erlbaum.

Lapp, D., & Flood, J. (1983). *Teaching reading to every child* (2nd ed.). New York: Macmillan.

Mason, J. M., & Au, K. H. (1986). *Reading instruction for today.* Glenview, IL: Scott, Foresman.

McConaughy, S. H. (1980). Using story structure in the classroom. *Language Arts, 57,* 157–164.

McConaughy, S., Fitzhenry-Coor, I., & Howell, D. (1983). Developmental differences in story schemata. In K. E. Nelson (Ed.), *Children's language* (vol. 4, pp. 385–421). Hillsdale, NJ: Erlbaum.

McNeil, J. D. (1984). *Reading comprehension: New directions for classroom practice.* Glenview, IL: Scott, Foresman.

Mosenthal, P. (1984). The problem of partial specification in translating reading research into practice. *Elementary School Journal, 85*(2), 2–28.

Nezworski, T., Stein, N., & Trabasso, T. (1982). Story structure versus content in children's recall. *Journal of Verbal Learning and Verbal Behavior, 21,* 196–206.

Paris, S. G., Wasik, B. A., & Van der Westhuizen, G. (1988). *Meta-metacognition: A review of research on metacognition and reading.* Paper presented as the annual review of research at the National Reading Conference, St. Petersburg, FL.

Pearson, P. D., & Johnson, D. D. (1978). *Teaching reading comprehension.* New York: Holt, Rinehart & Winston.

Perfetti, C. (1977). Language comprehension and fast decoding: Some psycholinguistic prerequisites for skilled reading comprehension. In J. Guthrie (Ed.), *Cognition, curriculum, and comprehension* (pp. 20–41). Newark, DE: International Reading Association.

Rumelhart, D., & Ortony, A. (1977). The representation of knowledge in memory. In R. C. Anderson, R. J. Spiro, & W. E. Montague (Eds.), *Schooling and the acquisition of knowledge* (pp. 99–136). Hillsdale, NJ: Erlbaum.

Samuels, S. J. & Pearson, P. D. (1980). Why comprehension? Editorial in *Reading Research Quarterly, 15*(2), 181–182.

Schallert, D. L., & Tierney, R. J. (1981). The nature of high school textbooks and learners: Overview and update. Paper presented at the annual meeting of the National Reading Conference, Dallas, TX.

Schank, R., & Abelson, R. (1977). *Scripts, plans, goals and understanding.* Hillsdale, NJ: Erlbaum.

Shannon, P., Kameenui, E. J., & Baumann, J. (1988). An investigation of children's ability to comprehend character motives. *American Educational Research Journal, 25*(3), 441–462.

Simmons, D., & Kameenui, E. J. (1987). Articulating learning disabilities for the public: A case of professional riddles. *Learning Disabilities Quarterly, 9*(4), 304–314.

Spear, L. D., & Sternberg, R. J. (1986). An information processing framework for understanding reading disability. In S. Ceci (Ed.), *Handbook of cognitive, social, and neuropsychological aspects of learning disabilities* (vol. 2, pp. 2–30). Hillsdale, NJ: Erlbaum.

Spiegel, D. L. (1981). *Reading for pleasure: Guidelines.* Newark, DE: International Reading Association.

Stahl, S. (1990). Research brief: Vocabulary instruction. In D. W. Carnine, J. Silbert, & E. J. Kameenui, *Direct instruction reading* (2nd ed.). Columbus, OH: Merrill Publishing Company.

Stanovich, K. (1986). Matthew effects in reading: Some consequences of individual differences in the acquisition of literacy. *Reading Research Quarterly, 21*(4), 360–407.

Stein, N. L., & Glenn, C. G. (1979). An analysis of story comprehension in elementary school children. In R. O. Freedle (Ed.), *Discourse processes: Advances in research and theory* (vol. 2, pp. 53–120). Norwood, NJ: Ablex.

Tierney, R. J. & Cunningham, J. W. (1984). Research on teaching reading comprehension. In P. D. Pearson (Ed.), *Handbook of reading research* (pp. 609–656). New York: Longman.

Wilson, C. R. (1983). Teaching reading comprehension by connecting the known to the new. *Reading Teacher, 36*(4), 382–390.

Wong, B. (1980). Increasing retention of main ideas through questioning strategies. *Learning Disabilities Quarterly, 2*, 42–47.

Wong, B. Y. L., & Wong, R. (1986). Study behavior as a function of metacognitive knowledge about critical task variables: An investigation of above average, average, & learning disabled readers. *Learning Disabilities Research, 1*, 101–111.

C H A P T E R

NINE

Designing Instructional Strategies for Teaching Reading Comprehension: Content Area Textbook Prose

Chapter Objectives

Upon successful completion of this chapter, you will be able to:

1. DESCRIBE the requirements of content area reading curricula and instruction for low-performing students.

2. SPECIFY the features of the reader, text, task, and strategies that influence textbook prose comprehension.

3. DESCRIBE how the generic instructional set can be used to simplify textbook prose learning.

4. DESIGN a set of instructional procedures for textbook prose learning using the before, during, and after instructional framework.

5. EVALUATE the adequacy of instructional procedures for teaching information from content area textbooks.

CONTENT AREA LEARNING: THE PROBLEM

Textbook prose is the primary medium used to inform students in content area classes such as social studies, history, health, and the sciences. In this chapter, we use the terms **textbook prose, content area prose, expository text,** and **informational text** interchangeably to refer to this text form that is the instructional staple of content area classes. Despite its widespread use in general education classes, there is little indication that this popular means of communicating information is appropriate or effective for low-achieving students. Nicholson (1984) describes some of the problems students with academic learning problems face when required to learn from content area text:

> They stumble and falter over words in the text, they misinterpret simple diagrams and overlook important task instructions. They are the "turned off" readers, sitting along the fringes of the classroom, seemingly unable to cope with the reading demands of their content area subjects. (p. 16)

Clearly, students who are "text-wise," have sufficient prior knowledge of the subject, decode words fluently, and show adequate comprehension skills may find informational text quite learnable. However, for those who have deficits in any of the component reading skills, learning from content area text is a most challenging if not defeating experience. To gain information from content area text, learners must have general decoding and comprehension skills as well as a firm understanding of the specific purposes, conventions, and requirements of informational prose.

Purpose of Textbook Prose

Students are introduced to textbook prose in the primary grades. Nevertheless, this text form assumes added importance and emphasis in the mid-elementary grades. In contrast to narrative texts that tell stories, expository or textbook prose teaches specific information. Textbook prose represents a "new script," a script that conveys factual information and places increasing responsibility on the reader.

According to Chall (1983), students make the transition from "learning to read" to "reading to learn" around the age of 8. Reading becomes a tool for exploring subject matter areas, a means for acquiring specific information. Low performers often do not possess the preskills to perform such a tedious and difficult task. For them, "reading to learn" from informational text is akin to entering an academic minefield. The obstacles camouflaged in content area texts are detonated by readers unable to maneuver their way skillfully through the unfamiliar headings and subheadings, technical terminology, and foreign concepts found in textbook prose. As a result, readers do not learn from reading but rather continue their cycle of failure.

ANALYZING TEXTBOOK PROSE: FACTORS THAT CONTRIBUTE TO COMPREHENSION FAILURE

When learners become so entrenched in a cycle of failure, trying to ferret out the source or sources of the problem seems an insurmountable task. As we have said throughout this text, any analysis of academic failure must be multicontextual, focusing on factors within the teacher's control. We begin our analysis of the problem by examining these variables.

A number of factors contribute to the difficulty of comprehending expository prose. To develop a plan for remediating and addressing low performers' comprehension difficulties, we will examine the same general components as explored when analyzing narrative prose comprehension: (1) text, (2) reader, (3) task, and (4) strategies. Although the basic components are common to both narrative and content area prose, the specific features within these general factors clearly distinguish the two prose formats.

When examining these elements, it is important to keep in mind that reading failure can result from one primary factor or, more probably, from the interaction of two or more of these factors. Attempting to determine the source of comprehension failure is a complex process because of the interdependence of text, task, reader, and strategies.

Explaining and addressing textbook prose comprehension difficulty requires investigative instinct. Identifying the major elements that interfere with comprehension is challenging. Isolating the details involves much more complex investigation. As Figure 9–1 illustrates, four general components and numerous features of each must be considered when analyzing failure and designing content area reading instruction.

Only by identifying the component parts of the process of reading comprehension can the teacher design a plan to remediate the problem.

Text

Expository prose has its own particular demands and nuances that make it particularly problematic for low performers. Consequently, in this chapter we will devote considerable attention to these features, some of which are shown in Figure 9–2.

Five categories of text features provide a framework for focusing and identifying text that is apt to be troublesome for low-achieving students. In the following section, we discuss each of these features and analyze the selected text excerpts in Figure 9–3 to illustrate the cause of the problem as well as to highlight sources that can be modified to enhance content area learning.

FIGURE 9–1
Factors that contribute to textbook prose comprehension difficulty

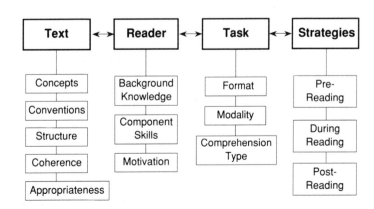

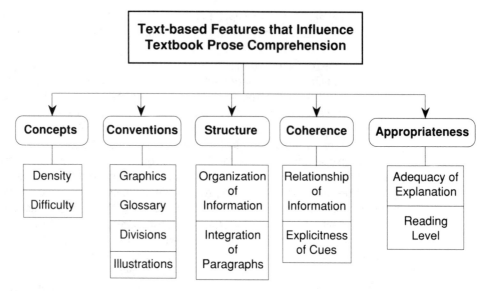

FIGURE 9–2
Text-based features that influence textbook prose comprehension

From B. B. Armbruster & T. H. Anderson, "On selecting 'considerate' content area textbooks," *Remedial and Special Education, 9*, pp. 47–52.

Concepts

First, examine the quantity and familiarity of information in each of the three paragraphs of the passage. Although the first paragraph contains only 80 words, each of the six sentences in the first paragraph communicates a new and complex piece of information. The new vocabulary terms (*friction, bearing, lubricants*) and the relationships between the new concepts and already familiar concepts represent this mass of information for which the learner is accountable. For example, the second sentence specifies a complicated rule relationship between the concepts of work and machines: "Compare the amount of work put into them with the amount of work they do." The relationship requires the reader first to think about the rather abstract concept of work, even though the nature and form of work is not defined. The text then asks the reader to make a comparison between the input and output of this undefined concept of work. Following this exercise in rule relationships, the next sentence introduces the reader to yet another new concept, *friction*, which hinges on the reader's understanding of the concept work. The passage informs the reader: "Because of friction, the amount of work a machine does is always less than the amount of work put into it." Next, the reader is told that work is changed to heat by friction. Up to this point (the fourth sentence), the text requires the reader to make connections between two new undefined concepts (*work, friction*) and an abstract rule relationship (work put into a machine and the amount of work done). Furthermore, the text requires the reader to link this quantity of information with the concepts of *more* and *less*. In addition to the conceptual density of the vocabulary, concepts, and relationships of information within textbook prose, the physical conventions of the text also have the potential to enhance or impede comprehension.

Machines and Friction

You can measure how well machines do work. Compare the amount of work put into them with the amount of work they do. Because of friction, the amount of work a machine does is always less than the amount of work put into it. Some of the work put into a machine is changed to heat by friction. This work is wasted because heat does not count as work done. The machine can do more work if there is less friction.

There are ways to make less friction between two surfaces. One way is to put a round object, or **bearing** (BER ing), between the surfaces. Then the surfaces will roll across each other. The wheels of cars and bicycles are like bearings. What are some things that have bearings?

Another way to make less friction is to use lubricants. **Lubricants** (LOO brih kuhnts) make surfaces smooth and slippery. Smooth surfaces make less friction than rough surfaces. Oil, grease, and soap are lubricants. How could bearings and lubricants be used to make less friction in machines? Where have you seen lubricants and bearings in machines?

FIGURE 9–3
Selected text excerpt

From *Accent on science*, Grade 5 (1980), p. 172, Columbus, OH: Merrill Publishing Company. Copyright 1980 by Merrill Publishing Company. Reprinted by permission.

Conventions

Informational text conventions refer to the mechanical tools content area texts use to clarify, embellish, and assist the reader's passage through the text. Table 9–1 presents a sample of the features a student may encounter in content area texts.

TABLE 9–1
Conventions of content area textbook prose

Headings	Italics
Subheadings	Table of contents
Graphic aids	Preview and summary statements
Boldface print	Pronunciation guides
	Glossary

In the following passage, selected textbook conventions assist the reader by cuing or explaining important information.[1]

Types of Permanent Teeth

You may have noticed that all your permanent teeth are not the same. They do not look the same, and they do not do exactly the same things. You probably realize that permanent teeth help break down food into smaller and smaller pieces. However, you may not realize that there are four types of permanent teeth, each type helping to break down food in a different way.

Incisors. The teeth found in the front of your mouth are called the *incisors* [ihn-SY-zurz]. Of the 32 permanent teeth, there are a total of 8 incisors—4 in the upper jaw and 4 in the lower jaw. Your incisors are the teeth that bite into foods. They have flat edges to cut food apart.

Cuspids. Next to the incisors are the *cuspids* [KUHS-puhdz]. There is a cuspid on each side of the incisors in the upper jaw and in the lower jaw, for a total of four cuspids. Cuspids are sharp and pointed so they can tear food apart.

Cuspids are sometimes called *canines* [KAY-NYNZ], or dog teeth. (Look at the picture)* Why, do you think, are cuspids sometimes called canines?

Bicuspids. After the food has been cut and torn into small pieces, the tongue pushes the food farther into the mouth. There the food is broken down by another type of teeth, called the *bicuspids* [by-KUHS-puhdz]. There are eight bicuspids. They are located next to the cuspids, as shown in the picture.* Bicuspids have two points. They also have a wider chewing surface than the cuspids do. Because of their shape, bicuspids can crush food.

Molars. In the back of the mouth are the 12 *molars.* Molars are the largest of the 4 types of permanent teeth. They have a wide chewing surface to grind food. Why, do you think, is it important that the molars grind food?

In the previous passage, the heading *Types of Permanent Teeth* earmarks the major topic of the section while subheadings highlight critical, but secondary, information. Italicized words signal key concepts as well as terms accompanied by pronunciation guides. Pivotal vocabulary terms such as *bicuspids* and *incisors* are also defined in context. Because these conventions are often unfamiliar to novice readers, the text-based features may require substantial and systematic instruction. A single exposure to these conventions will not provide the practice low-performing readers need to use the skills independently.

---

[1]Text selection is used by permission of Macmillan Publishing Company from *Good Health for You, Grade 5* by Fodor, Glass, and Gmur. Copyright © 1983 by Laidlaw Brothers. References marked with * are for a picture not reproduced here.

Structure, Coherence, and Audience Appropriateness

Analyzing text for these three criteria is perhaps a more subtle and difficult task. **Structure** involves the organization of ideas and paragraphs. **Coherence** refers to relationships between ideas and specifically the use of pronoun referents, connectives between sentences and paragraphs, and signal words that alert the reader to the progression or change in the flow of ideas in the passage (Armbruster, 1984). **Audience appropriateness** refers to the degree of agreement between text vocabulary, readability, topic, and the skills of the reader. Ideally, sufficient overlap between the content of the text and skills of the learner would allow comprehension to occur. If this level of agreement is inadequate or if the text fails to provide the necessary background knowledge and topic explanations, the text/reader interaction will result in comprehension failure.

Armbruster (1984) posited that the absence or inappropriate use of structure, coherence, and appropriateness often makes textbook prose highly "inconsiderate" for low-performing students. Based on her research, she reported that well-organized texts facilitate recall better than poorly organized texts. Texts that demonstrate relationships between ideas are particularly important for children less skilled in establishing these relationships. Empirical investigations indicate that poorer readers are significantly less able than better readers to identify important information in text (Smiley, Oakley, Worthen, Campione, & Brown, 1977) and to recognize poorly organized text (Wong & Wong, 1986). Generally, texts that contain main points and fewer intrusions of less important information are better recalled than passages containing extensive amounts of irrelevant information.

For example, Kameenui, Simmons, and Darch (1987) found that passages in which critical information is in close proximity aided learning disabled students' inferential comprehension. Furthermore, such texts prompted the use of more sophisticated comprehension strategies.

The following passages illustrate how the structure of passages can affect passage difficulty. The passages contain identical information; however, in the first example, the information necessary for comprehending the passage is dispersed amid irrelevant and distracting information. In the second passage, information critical to comprehension is collapsed in close proximity, allowing the reader to focus attention on the important text rather than the irrelevant text.

Dispersed Story Form

Don and Kathy want to buy a house. "We have been looking at houses for a long time, but we can't seem to find anything we like," Don said to the real estate agent. "All we really care about is living in a house that doesn't waste electricity. Do you know of any houses for sale?"

"This is a good time of year to buy a house. There are a lot of houses for sale right now. I'm sure we can find the right one for you," the real estate agent said. "Remember, the more windows in a house, the more energy is wasted.

"There is a house on Kelly Street that is for sale. It's an older house and it is in fair shape. The yard needs a lot of work and the house needs to be painted. The house is on a busy street so there is a lot of traffic noise. It has a small kitchen and bathroom. There is a window in the dining room that looks out on a big apartment building. The house has 10 windows in it.

"If you like new houses, there is one for sale on Oak Street. It has a beautiful view of the mountain and there is a nice park not too far away. The park has tennis courts and a swimming pool. There's room for a garden in the backyard. It is in a nice neighborhood and the house is on a dead end street. It has sliding glass doors that open onto the backyard. The kitchen has a built-in-dishwasher and microwave oven. The house has 24 windows in it."

Collapsed Story Form

Don and Kathy want to buy a house. "We have been looking at houses for a long time," Don said to the real estate agent. "We can't seem to find anything we like. Do you know of any houses for sale?"

"This is a good time of year to buy a house. There are a lot of houses for sale now. We have a beautiful house for sale that has a nice view of the mountains. We also have a house that is not too far away from a park with tennis courts and a swimming pool. Some of the newer houses even have built-in microwave ovens. If you like older houses, there is one for sale that is in a quiet neighborhood and has a big yard. It might need a little work, but it is worth it when you are finished."

"All we really care about is living in a house that doesn't waste electricity," Kathy said.

"You know, the more windows in a house, the more energy is wasted. The house for sale on Kelly Street has 10 windows in it. The house on Oak Street has 24 windows."

Textbook features do affect low-performing students' comprehension, and teachers may need to invest considerable time evaluating texts for features that influence learning. Armbruster and Anderson (1988) suggest the following guidelines for evaluating the "considerateness" of texts:[2]

I. Structure
   A. Make an outline of the headings and subheadings in a few chapters to evaluate the consistency and organization of the text.
   B. Look for clear signals, words, and phrases that identify the organizational patterns within the text.
II. Coherence
   A. Look for explicit connectives (*because, since, therefore*).
   B. Check for clear references.
   C. Examine text for transition statements that help the reader move from idea to idea.
   D. Make sure chronological sequences are easy to follow.
   E. Determine whether graphic aids are clearly related to the text.
III. Audience Appropriateness
   A. Consider the adequacy of topic explanations.
   B. Check for salience of main ideas. Is important information clearly presented through topic sentences, preview or summary statements, or highlight cues?

Reader

Comprehension failure is not attributable to a single, isolated factor, but is the result of the interaction of multiple components. Because we have previously discussed the im-

---

[2]Adapted from Armbruster & Anderson (1988), "On selecting 'considerate' content area textbooks," *Remedial and special education, 9*(1), pp. 49, 50, 51. Reprinted by permission.

portance of component skills, motivation, and background knowledge, we will only reiterate the need to consider these factors when analyzing comprehension failure.

Readers enter content area classes with varying levels of background knowledge, decoding fluency, vocabulary facility, and motivation. Because textbook content is often unfamiliar and tedious, low performers may require substantial instruction just getting ready to read. Learners who are unfamiliar with the concept *gravity* may require extensive development of conceptual knowledge, while more familiar concepts of *seasons* or *reptiles* may only require prompts to activate background knowledge. Likewise, students with a history of decoding problems may require pre-passage exposure to terms such as *metamorphosis* or *petroleum,* while more familiar terms will require minimal pre-teaching. If students have not been taught the conventions of headings and subheadings, these features may pose considerable barriers to comprehension, thus requiring extensive instruction.

Task

In addition to reader- and text-related variables, the type of task also affects a reader's ability to demonstrate information learned from content area text. As suggested in Chapter 2, the learner's proficiency with the modality (verbal or written), response format (choice or production), and task familiarity (new, practice, review) contributes to success or failure. Adding unfamiliar and densely concentrated content to task modalities that are difficult for learners compounds the problem of learning from informational prose.

In content area tasks, students are usually asked to demonstrate their knowledge through written formats that are often difficult for low performers. Therefore, teachers should be aware of the demands of written formats and the limited amount of information acquired by restricting assessment tasks to writing activities. For tasks to assess accurately the reader's ability to learn from content area text, the requirements should be familiar and doable by the learner.

In addition to these task features, the specific type of information requested in the task must be considered. Content area reading tasks may entail reading for details, for main ideas, to construct a summary, to locate specific information in graphs and maps, and so forth. Identifying the purpose of the task is a critical prerequisite if a reader is to perform successfully on content area assignments.

The task or type of questions asked also influences the information learned (Cook & Mayer, 1983; Valencia & Pearson, 1988). By focusing on literal questions that tap only the student's ability to select information from a passage, the task may limit the learner's ability to perform higher-level cognitive operations such as organization and integration activities. If the learning outcome is for students to select specific information from a passage, the following task form is appropriate:

Acquisition/Literal Task 9–1.   "List the three forms of fossil fuels."
However, if the learning outcome is for the learner to construct and make connections between information in the passage, consider the following task form.

Organization/Construction Task 9–2.   "Explain the process in which plants and animals become fuel."
Finally, a task that requires learners to integrate information from the passage with prior knowledge calls for a different task form.

Integration Task 9–3.   "Compare how fuel sources differ according to the location in which you live."
In Appendix A to this chapter are example comprehension tasks illustrating the features of format, modality, and type of comprehension. These features warrant serious consideration when designing tasks to assess content area text comprehension.

Low-performing students will often require extensive, direct instruction when learning content area tasks. Along with the instructional responsibilities of teaching text features and preparing the reader for upcoming text, teachers of content area subjects must be able to identify task requirements, to modify tasks to parallel learner abilities, and to teach task features.

Comprehension Strategies

A fourth factor that affects content area learning is strategies. A strategy is a plan for accomplishing a goal or objective. Learning from content area text requires a range of strategies because of the diverse skills required to comprehend this conceptually dense and often unfamiliar text form. Before we discuss specific strategies, the range of skills required to comprehend content area prose is summarized in Table 9–2, based on Armbruster and Gudbrandsen's (1986) review of basal social studies programs. General categories of comprehension skills are listed in the left column; the right column itemizes specific comprehension skills of the category.

All of these skills require strategic behavior. Undoubtedly, students who approach content area text with no apparent strategies for identifying unfamiliar words, defining unfamiliar vocabulary, relating background knowledge to new content, or locating specific information are apt to experience difficulty learning from textbook prose.

Research in cognitive psychology during the past two decades has produced rather consistent findings regarding the importance of strategic behavior. This research reveals that strategic behavior distinguishes skilled readers from less-skilled readers (Baker & Brown, 1984). In fact, multiple studies document that learning disabled and other less-successful readers often fail to deploy task-appropriate methods of approaching, reading, and evaluating reading performance.

This documentation of low performers' strategy deficits is not altogether unanticipated. Many of the strategic behaviors of more-skilled readers are never explicitly taught in either reading or content area curriculum. Although some students are able to acquire learning strategies incidentally, instructionally naive students require that skills be explicitly taught. Instruction is the missing piece of the puzzle.

Researchers have begun to identify instructional strategies that result in improved learning and retention. These strategies are known to induce students to apply and adapt the learning strategies independently and spontaneously (Jenkins, Heliotis, Stein, & Haynes, 1987). Although the goal is to equip students with strategies that can be accessed

TABLE 9–2
General and specific textbook prose comprehension skills

General Skill	Specific Skills
Using prior knowledge to facilitate comprehension	Drawing upon specific experiences
Defining new vocabulary	Defining words Determining meaning through context
Recognizing unfamiliar words	Using pronunciation guide Using context cues
Locating information	Using textbook features Using index, glossary, dictionaries, appendix, and table of contents Reading and interpreting captions
Using reference tools	Locating information in encyclopedias, newspapers and magazines
Comprehending	Reading to identify main idea Reading for details Paraphrasing and summarizing Distinguishing levels of importance
Reading different kinds of text	Distinguishing fact from opinion Understanding relationships Interpreting facts
Understanding purpose for reading	Skimming for information Reading to answer questions Reading to draw conclusions
Using text adjuncts	Outlining Note taking Constructing charts and graphs

independently, this does not mean the techniques must be learned independently. Because of the importance and breadth of this topic, we allocate an entire section to learning strategies in a subsequent section of this chapter.

Summary of Factors Contributing to Content Area Text Comprehension

A multitude of factors could presumably explain why low-performing students experience such problems learning from content area prose. In informational prose, the elements of reader, text characteristics, task requirements, and strategies all contribute to a single skill known as **reading to learn**. When a learner fails this task, any one of these factors could be the instructional culprit. To remediate low-performers' deficits, first teachers must identify the factor or factors that impede learning and address the deficits through instruction. Following our discussion of learning strategies, we discuss the details of designing content area instruction by applying the generic instructional set.

INSTRUCTIONAL STRATEGIES TO ENHANCE TEXTBOOK PROSE LEARNING

In recent years, reading researchers have identified a variety of instructional strategies or procedures teachers can employ to enhance students' comprehension of textbook prose. These procedures are often categorized as pre-reading, during-reading, and post-reading activities. These terms should not be confused with the before, during, and after instructional framework. The pre-, during-, and post- referents used to describe these comprehension strategies or procedures indicate where they are used in the actual reading sequence. It is impossible to review adequately the research literature relevant to pre-, during-, and after-reading instructional strategies. In this section, we sample these interventions designed to enhance readers' comprehension and recall of textbook prose.

Pre-Reading Instruction

Consistent with other areas of academic instruction, the bulk of the work in informational prose instruction is conducted upfront, before the student ever encounters the reading passage. Pre-reading interventions prepare the reader for passage reading by identifying and addressing those factors that could potentially interfere with comprehension during reading. The intent of pre-reading activities is to provide the knowledge and skill necessary for the reader to manage the new task. In essence, pre-reading instruction readies the reader for text reading.

Pre-reading instruction comprises multiple components. Table 9–3 outlines general areas of pre-reading instruction and offers selected methods to develop reading skills.

Two procedures that prepare the students for text reading by developing and activating their knowledge base are prediction generation and content framing.

Prediction Generation

Prediction generation motivates and prepares students by having them formulate questions about what they think will be revealed in upcoming text. Teachers will need to model explicitly the predictive questioning procedure, as demonstrated in the following example:

TEACHER: The title of this chapter is *Mexican-Americans in the West.*

What type of information do you think the authors tell you in the text?

What would you like to find out about Mexican-Americans?

Let's look at the first heading. *Territorial Rights.* Does anyone know what a territory is?

Right. A territory is an area of land or property. That's right, Josh, in school your desk is your territory.

What do you think the authors will tell you in this section?

(Teacher continues with other headings and subheadings and predictions.)

Let's read to find out if our predictions are correct.

TABLE 9–3
Pre-reading instructional procedures

Area of Pre-Reading Instruction	Instructional Procedure
Background Knowledge	Use facilitative questioning to determine students' current level of knowledge. Draw analogies between known and unknown information. Have students generate predictions about upcoming text based on title, headings, or pictures in text. Use advance organizers to overview content and organization of key concepts in the text.
Word Recognition	Preteach pronunciation of "difficult" words that are critical to comprehension of passage. Base instructional technique on knowledge form of word. 1. "Undecodable" words—teach as simple facts using sight word approach. 2. "Decodable" words—use sounding out strategy. 3. Multisyllabic words comprising known bases and affixes—use baseword strategy. 4. Compound words—break into base words. 5. Other difficult words—use context to facilitate word recognition. Teach use of pronunciation guides.
Vocabulary Knowledge	Teach words not defined in context by providing definition and relating word meaning to context. Teach contextual definition strategy for words defined in context.
Reading for Specific Purposes	Teach question answering strategy. Train to summarize paragraphs. Develop strategy for locating information. Teach strategy to identify main idea. Teach text sequencing skills.
Using Text Conventions	Teach purpose and location of chapter introductions and summaries. Provide practice in identifying headings and subheadings. Teach how to use glossary and index. Specify importance of boldface information.

The prediction generation activity is based on the premise that reading is a thinking process (Palinscar, 1986) and that both reading and thinking have to occur simultaneously. A corollary to prediction generation occurs in the during and after stages of reading when students gather information and either confirm or refute their predictions.

Content Framing

Cunningham and Cunningham (1987) suggested the feature matrix as a device for helping students gather, compare, and contrast information from text. The teacher prepares the matrix by identifying information in the text and categorizing the information according to critical features. Before text reading, the teacher displays the feature matrix and asks students to fill in the cells with information they already know. See Figure 9–4 for an example of a student completed pre-reading feature matrix.

In addition to organizing and prompting information, Cunningham and Cunningham propose the matrix as a device to evaluate text comprehension and structure writing activities or after text reading.

During-Reading Instruction

The next set of instructional activities includes techniques teachers and students use during text reading to enhance comprehension and learning. Even though the majority of these procedures are designed to be used independently by students, the teacher initially assumes responsibility for introducing and modeling the particular learning technique.

Initial skill lessons may appear particularly teacher-dominated. However, as learners become more proficient at comprehending and managing the comprehension process, many of the intrusive, overt, teacher-driven activities are assumed by learners. Initially, however, it is necessary that the procedures be made public to determine whether students are actually engaging in the activity and whether their comprehension is accu-

FIGURE 9–4
Prereading feature matrix as filled out by an individual student

Planets in Earth's solar system						
	Closer to sun than Earth	Larger than Earth	Has moon	Has rings	Orbits the sun	Inner planet
Earth	—	—	+	—	+	+
Jupiter	—	+	+	—		—
Mars	+	—	+	—	+	+
Mercury	+	—		—	+	+
Neptune	—	+		—		—
Pluto	—	+		—		—
Saturn	—	+		+		—
Uranus	—			—		—
Venus	+	—	+	—	+	

+ = student believes feature is true of that planet
— = student believes planet lacks that feature
Matrix items will later be checked against reading material.

From P. Cunningham and J. Cunningham (1987). *Reading Teacher, 40,* p. 509. Copyright 1987 by International Reading Association. Reprinted with permission of James Cunningham and the International Reading Association.

rate. In the following section, we reference and briefly describe selected learning strategies the teacher may initiate, and then later transfer to students to enhance content area text comprehension.

Adjunct Questions

Adjunct questioning involves the insertion of teacher-initiated questions within the reading passage. In this process, questions are added after short increments of the passage (a paragraph or less) are read as opposed to the traditional type of questioning that is generally reserved for the end of the passage. Procedures for adjunct questioning are:

1. Insert questions after short segments of text are read.
2. Increase length of text segments incrementally to parallel student comprehension.
3. Ask questions that require the reader to identify critical pieces of information, tie text together, or make predictions.
4. Ask questions to evaluate the reader's level of comprehension.

Although the technique of asking questions throughout the passage may seem commonplace, it may be of significant value for the instructionally naive learner who has difficulty comprehending lengthy passages (Carnine, Silbert, & Kameenui, 1990). Adjunct questions require the reader to attend to the task, to respond to inquiries, and to assess understanding of the passage.

Paragraph Restatements

In paragraph restatements, students generate summary sentences about what happened in the preceding section of text (e.g., paragraph). In essence, students translate a large

Adjunct questions, presented within reading passages, enhance comprehension and learning in the during-reading phase.

segment of the author's message into an abbreviated version in their own words. Variations of this procedure are found in Brown and Palinscar's (1982) reciprocal teaching method and Williams' (1986) procedure for teaching children to identify the main idea of expository texts. Jenkins et al. (1987) used similar procedures in teaching elementary-aged learning disabled students to summarize paragraphs of narrative text. Paragraph restatement procedures include the following:

1. Teach students to paraphrase paragraphs through modeling, practice, and corrective feedback. Teach students to paraphrase and restate the most important parts. Possible stimulus statements include:
   a. "Tell the most important parts."
   b. "Tell the major event that occurred in the paragraph."
   c. "What was the paragraph about?"
   d. "What is the general topic?"
2. Teach students to delimit their paragraph restatement. Example prompts include:
   a. "Was that the most important thing?"
   b. "Can you shorten that statement?"
   c. "What is the specific topic?"

Question Generation

Question generation is an exercise in which the student and teacher read sections of a passage and then take turns asking each other questions about the material just read. Questions may request factual information, summaries, vocabulary information, and so forth. Singer's (1978) preliminary work has shown that student-generated questions are more effective in promoting comprehension than teacher-generated questions, even for children in elementary school.

Constructing a question that accurately assesses the material one has read demands that the reader has a thorough understanding of the material, can identify the relevant information, and can determine components of the passage that are most significant. For the low performer, this task may be quite challenging. Therefore, practice in generating questions from simple reading material is recommended before introducing question generation exercises in the context of complex texts. Question generation procedures should involve these elements, adapted from Manzo (1970) and Palinscar (1986):

1. Model multiple demonstrations of question-generation procedure before transition to student-generated questions.
2. Read sections of text orally and ask students questions about what they have just read.
3. Ask questions that require factual information, understanding of cause-effect relationships, vocabulary knowledge, inferential reasoning, or predictions.
4. Shift reading responsibility to students. Students should read a section of the text and then generate the sort of questions that might occur on a test.

Self-Monitoring Procedure

The majority of the activities used during the reading activity fall under the rubric of comprehension monitoring skills. Comprehension monitoring is thought to be a way of breaking the students' passivity and involving them in the learning process. Comprehension monitoring involves keeping track of one's understanding and taking remedial action to ensure that the comprehension process is running smoothly. The following comprehension monitoring procedure was used by Graves (1986) with elementary-aged learning disabled students.

COMPREHENSION TASK 9–4
Direct Instruction Plus Mechanical Self-Monitoring Training—Reading Aloud[3]

	Teacher	Student
(Model)	Today, as you read, I want you to ask yourself if you understand what the whole story is about. I want you to stop twice during your reading, put your finger on our place, and ask yourself: "Do I understand what the whole story is about?"	
(Lead)	What will you ask yourself?	Do I understand what the whole story is about?
(Lead)	If you do not understand, start the story over again. If you do understand, keep reading.	
(Test)	What will you do if you do *not* understand?	Start the story over again.
(Test)	What will you do if you do understand?	Keep reading.
(Model)	Look at this card. It has the question, "Do I understand what the whole story is about?" printed on it. Make a checkmark on one of the lines each time you stop to ask yourself the question. (Teacher demonstrates making a checkmark.)	
(Test)	What will you do when you stop to ask yourself the question?	Make a checkmark.
	Read the story out loud. Ready. Begin.	

Cumulative Retell

A commonly reported method of involving the reader in the reading process is summarizing. This type of self-testing procedure can reveal the status of the reader's understanding. However, composing a summary is a complex task that may pose considerable difficulty for the low-performing reader.

Carnine, Silbert, and Kameenui (1990) attempted to make summarizing a more manageable task by using a cumulative retell technique. In this procedure, the reader completes a segment of the passage and is then instructed to "tell what has happened so far." This procedure is continued with the introduction of each new segment of the passage. By the end of the reading task, the reader has constructed a cumulative summary for the entire passage. Here is a list of items to help in teaching summarization of text:

[3]From Anne Graves, "Effects of Direct Instruction and Metacognition Theory" *Learning Disabilities Research, 1*(94), 1986. Reprinted by permission of the Division for Learning Disabilities.

1. Ask students to read a specified amount of text (in the early stages, it may be necessary to limit the amount of text to one or two sentences).
2. Ask students to tell what has happened so far. If students are unable to summarize the information, reread that section of text.
3. Ask students to read the next specified segment of the text and tell what just happened. If their summary is accurate, then ask students to tell what they have read about so far. If the summary is incomplete, review information from previous steps.
4. Repeat this procedure until the entire passage has been summarized.

Self-study Strategy

Recent research in reading comprehension indicates the importance of study skill instruction for the successful learning of expository prose (Adams, Carnine, & Gersten, 1982; Schumaker, Deshler, Alley, Warner, & Denton, 1982). Adams et al. (1982) found a modified version of the SQ3R (survey, question, read, recite, review) technique effective on a question measure of comprehension but not on retell tasks. Alexander (1985) modified Adams's study strategy, which resulted in learning disabled students' improved ability to retell expository prose passages. The study skill procedure includes seven steps:

1. Preview the passage by reading the paragraph headings.
2. Recite the paragraph heading without looking.
3. Ask questions about what might be important to learn.
4. Read the paragraph to find the important details.
5. Reread the paragraph heading and recite the important details.
6. Repeat steps 1 through 5 for each paragraph.
7. Rehearse by reading each paragraph heading and recall the important information.

Post-reading Instruction

A reader's comprehension is typically evaluated after reading. To determine whether learning has occurred, students are often asked to complete the exercises at the end of the text. In addition to assessing comprehension, post-reading exercises can also nurture comprehension and recall. In this section, we review activities for facilitating comprehension and recall.

Even though the most common method of assessing learning in content area classes is answering questions, it cannot be assumed that low-performing students know how to answer questions or evaluate their answers. Archer and Gleason (1989) proposed the following strategy to teach students how to complete chapter questions:

1. Read the question carefully.
2. Change the question into part of the answer.
3. Locate the section of the chapter that talks about the topic.
4. Read the section of the chapter until you find the answer.
5. Complete the answer.

The authors noted two steps of the strategy that are particularly difficult for low-achieving students: turning the question into a part of the answer and locating a section of the chapter that talks about a specific topic. In accord with accepted instructional design procedures, Archer and Gleason (1989) recommended teaching the steps in isolation before implementing the complete strategy.

For example, practice in changing a question into part of the answer should involve multiple opportunities to practice this skill. How would the following questions be modified into part of the answer?

1. What was Australia like before Europeans came?
   (Before the Europeans came Australia was like . . .)
2. Name the six major landforms of the United States.
   (The six major landforms of the United States are . . .)
3. What must meteorologists know to predict the weather?
   (To predict the weather, meteorologists must know . . .)

By restating the question into part of the answer, the task is framed and ready for the learner to complete.

In addition to evaluating comprehension, post-reading activities also provide opportunity for the reader to reencounter, organize, and synthesize information in the text, thereby strengthening the memory trace. Post-reading activities may involve students by having them confirm and extend pre-reading knowledge or highlight and draw relationships between critical information in the text.

Text Confirmation Activities

Post-reading exercises may actually serve as logical follow-ups to pre-reading activities. For example, after-reading activities may be designed for readers to confirm their pre-reading predictions as illustrated in the following example.

TEACHER: Before we read, we predicted the Mexican/American revolution was caused by these factors. (Teacher lists items on chalkboard.)

Now that you have read the passage, can you tell me what actually caused the conflict?

Let's look to determine how our reasons compare with those in the text.

Readers may also evaluate their level of knowledge by following up on pre-reading activities. In the pre-reading component of the feature matrix, students recorded what they believed was true of a particular topic (e.g., solar system, natural resources, Civil War). In the post-reading activity, the accuracy of prior knowledge is either verified or refuted and missing information is supplied. This procedure is illustrated as follows:

TEACHER: Before we read the text on the planets, we recorded that we knew Mars and Mercury were closer to the sun than Earth. Now let's see whether what we recorded was correct. Next let's find out what new information we have about the distance of planets from the sun.

Text Synthesis Activities

Restructuring or text synthesizing activities require the reader to integrate the critical segments of information to form a more cohesive picture of the text. Two standard procedures are outlining and summarizing. The additional exposure to the material necessary to complete the outline or summary as well as the amount of cognitive activity required to construct text outlines and summaries have been theorized to result in increased retention.

An alternative method for highlighting and signifying relationships between textual information is the graphic organizer. Graphic organizers are visual displays of key concepts in the text and have only been recently applied to special needs learners (Moore & Readence, 1980; 1984). With average and below-average achievers, graphic organizers have been used as pre-, during-, and post-reading activities; however, recent meta-analyses of graphic organizer literature (Moore & Readence, 1980; 1984) indicated they are most facilitory when used as a post-reading activity. The data regarding whether graphic organizers are more effective as pre-, during-, or post-reading activities is tentative at best; therefore, we do not suggest that these instructional tools be reserved for a particular position in the instructional sequence. Rather, additional research must supply the data for determining the most effective placement for these visual text adjuncts.

Graphic organizers serve two primary functions: (1) to introduce pivotal concepts and (2) to develop links between these concepts (Cook & Mayer, 1983). Because of the complexity of designing and delivering graphic organizers, teachers will spend considerable time constructing the displays and teaching students how to use the depicted information. As with previously introduced comprehension strategies, students will assume more responsibility in constructing and learning from graphic organizers as they develop proficiency under teacher-directed instruction. A sample graphic organizer and accompanying text may be found in Appendix E of the chapter as well as in the final section on integrating the generic instructional set.

Summary of Reading Instruction Activities

Figure 9–5 summarizes a range of pre-, during-, and post-reading instructional activities. Obviously, each technique cannot be incorporated in the daily lesson. The needs of the learner, complexity of the text, and requirements of the task will dictate which activities to include and the amount of instruction needed in each stage of reading.

The pre-, during-, and post-reading procedures previously identified are mechanisms for enhancing content area prose learning. Not inconsequentially, how these strategies are designed and delivered determines their effect on low-achieving students' content area comprehension. In the following section, we apply the generic instructional set as the structure for textbook prose comprehension instruction.

DESIGNING COMPREHENSION INSTRUCTION: APPLYING THE GENERIC INSTRUCTIONAL SET

Instructional studies indicate that teaching low-performing students comprehension skills and learning strategies often favorably impacts their comprehension and recall of textbook prose. The optimism behind such advances in pedagogical technology is encouraging. However, researchers caution that we must extend our investigation of learning strategies to determine which components are effective and which need to be taught. Many of the unresolved issues regarding how best to teach students with academic

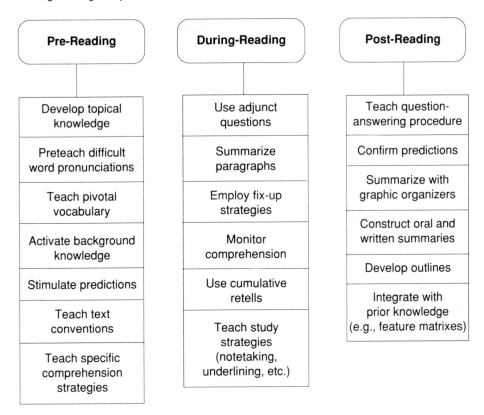

Pre-Reading	During-Reading	Post-Reading
Develop topical knowledge	Use adjunct questions	Teach question-answering procedure
Preteach difficult word pronunciations	Summarize paragraphs	Confirm predictions
Teach pivotal vocabulary	Employ fix-up strategies	Summarize with graphic organizers
Activate background knowledge	Monitor comprehension	Construct oral and written summaries
Stimulate predictions	Use cumulative retells	Develop outlines
Teach text conventions	Teach study strategies (notetaking, underlining, etc.)	Integrate with prior knowledge (e.g., feature matrixes)
Teach specific comprehension strategies		

FIGURE 9–5

Summary of pre-, during-, and post-reading activities

learning problems relate to the design of strategy instruction. In essence, how do we design instruction to make strategy training effective, durable and generalizable?

The principles we recommend for designing strategy instruction for content area text complement features of the generic instructional set. The selection, sequence, practice, and assessment features of instruction are as critical for expository text as they are for any other academic task. To increase students' likelihood of learning skills and strategies to comprehend textbook prose, we append the generic instructional set with the following guidelines for designing textbook prose instruction:

1. Progress from small units of text to larger units of text.
2. Teach skill in simple passages, then proceed to more complex.
3. Introduce skill in passages where critical information is explicitly presented.
4. Begin with teacher-directed instruction, gradually transferring responsibility to the learner.
5. Move from choice to production responses.
6. Model the skill overtly in initial teaching exercises. As the learner becomes proficient in performing the skill, make the skill covert (unobservable).

In the following section, we apply these guidelines along with the generic instructional set to selected examples of informational text.

BEFORE INSTRUCTION ▬▬▬▬▬▬▬▬▬▬▬▬▬▬▬▬▬▬▬

Step 1: Determining the Knowledge Form

Many of the skills necessary for comprehending informational text have been classified by knowledge form in preceding chapters. For example, irregular word reading (e.g., *algae*) was classified as a verbal association, multisyllabic word reading (e.g., *cardiopulmonary, rarefaction*) as a cognitive strategy, determining word meaning from context (e.g., *conservation*) as a cognitive strategy, and identifying the main idea of a passage as a rule relationship. Learning from informational prose often involves the merger of all these knowledge forms. In this section, we restrict our classification of textbook learning skills and strategies to a select group of skills specific to textbook prose. Additional examples may be found in Appendix B. The following tasks involve text comprehension skills classified by knowledge forms.

COMPREHENSION TASK 9-5
Identifying Topic Sentences of Paragraphs

Knowledge Form: Rule relationship:
"The topic tells what the paragraph is mainly about."

Component Skills

1. Discrimination of important vs. less important information.
2. Discrimination of sentence, paragraph, and passage.

Instructional Procedure:

1. Model identification of topic sentence explicitly stated in paragraph.
2. Repeat step 1.
3. Lead learner in identifying topic sentence in next paragraph.
4. Repeat step 3.
5. Test learner on identification of topic sentence in at least three different paragraphs.
6. Provide practice. Once child has mastered identifying explicitly stated topic sentences, begin the next phase of instruction.

Expanded Instruction

1. Review rule relationship regarding topics of paragraphs.
2. Present paragraph where topic sentence is explicitly stated.
3. Model paragraph where topic sentence is not explicitly stated and must be generated.
4. Model topic sentence generation in 3–4 additional paragraphs.
5. Lead learner in generating topic sentence in another paragraph.
6. Repeat step 5 with 2–3 paragraphs.

7. Test learner on generating topic sentences from additional paragraphs.
8. Practice topic generation on additional paragraphs.
9. Practice discriminating between explicit topic sentence identification and self-generated topic sentences.

COMPREHENSION TASK 9–6
Locating Specific Information from Text

Knowledge Form: Cognitive strategy.

Component Skills

1. Identification of key words.
2. Knowledge of subheadings concept.
3. Facility in answering literal comprehension questions.
4. Scanning strategy.

Instructional Procedure

1. Inform student that the objective of the lesson will be to find specific information in passages they read.
2. Introduce passage with only one paragraph. Require student to read paragraph orally.
3. Have student read question.
4. Review changing the question into part of the answer.[4]
5. Model locating the key words in the question.
6. Model locating key words in text.
7. Complete the answer.
8. Require student to read other one-paragraph passages and repeat procedure until student is proficient in locating information from one-paragraph passages.
9. Have student read question.
10. Lead student in changing question into part of answer.
11. Lead student in locating section of paragraph where answer is found (vary section of text from first example).
12. Have student complete the answer.
13. Practice answering questions from at least three additional paragraphs.

Once students consistently locate information from single parargraphs, present two or three paragraphs and use the same strategy. Strategy may be modified to introduce subheadings as cues for identifying specific information.

---

[4](Selected instructional procedure adapted from Archer & Gleason [1989], *Skills for School Success.* Boston: Curriculum Associates. For example: Question: Name three reasons for the Civil War. Question-changing Technique: Three reasons for the Civil War are:)

Even though the skills and strategies illustrated in the previous examples differ, they share inherent samenesses. Each skill involves multiple component skills and complex sequences of instructional procedures. Each was classified as either a rule relationship or a cognitive strategy. Recognizing the samenesses across tasks tells a great deal about teaching comprehension skills.

Because of their complexity, these skills command thoughtfully planned and delivered instruction. One of the primary factors that influence a student's acquisition and application of these skills is the set of examples used to illustrate and introduce the skill.

Step 2: Determining the Range of Examples

The examples for teaching a skill or strategy should satisfy at least two criteria. They should clearly communicate the critical information being taught and demonstrate the usefulness of the strategy. When determining the range of examples to meet these criteria, teachers must answer a fundamental question: "Can the skill be taught within the context of the instructional curriculum?" Teachers must determine whether the text contains sufficient examples for the student who is likely to require multiple exposures to the concept, simple fact, rule relationship, or cognitive strategy.

Unfortunately, general classroom content area materials often cater to the average-achieving student who "learns" with limited examples and through text that is not always reader-friendly. Content area text often creates aversive conditions for low performers and requires teachers to deviate from the instructional curriculum at least during the introductory period of skills instruction. Low-performing students will require many more examples than are found in content area teachers' guides or texts. This range of examples must consist of text selections simple yet substantive enough for learners to gain the critical information needed to use the skill.

As a general guideline, introduce skills within the context of the general education content area curriculum. This may require a great deal of textbook engineering when introducing the skills. However, because the learning objectives of content area classes are curriculum-bound, the larger the gap between the materials used to teach content area reading skills and the content on which the student will be actually evaluated, the more extensive the amount of instructional transitioning necessary. Teachers may need to introduce the skill in a simple passage and then make the transition to the text once students master the strategy. We illustrate the progression from simple to more complex skill applications by using a range of examples. Additional examples may be found in the chapter appendix.

COMPREHENSION TASK 9–7
Using Text Headings to Identify Important Information

Examples: Passages with chapter titles, section headings, and subheadings.

Knowledge Form: Rule relationship:
"Headings and subheadings show us important information to remember."

Limited Set

1. Passages with major headings only.
2. Major headings explicitly highlighted.
3. Text at student's reading level.

Expanded Set

1. Passage with a range of implicitly or explicitly stated headings and subheadings.
2. Passage of two or three pages in length.

COMPREHENSION TASK 9–8
Identifying Topic Sentences of Paragraphs

>*Knowledge Form:* Cognitive strategy.
>
>*Examples:* Paragraphs, multiple-paragraph passages.
>
>*Limited Set:* One-paragraph passage with explicitly stated topic sentence. For example:
> "Some of the important rivers of Europe start in the Alps. Among them are the Rhine and the Rhone rivers. They only start a few miles apart but they go in opposite directions."[5]

Expanded Set

1. Multiple-paragraph passages with explicitly stated topic sentences.
2. Single-paragraph passages with implicitly stated topic sentences.
3. Multiple-paragraph passages with implicitly stated topic sentences.
4. Multiple-paragraph passages, some with explicit and others with implicit topic sentences.

COMPREHENSION TASK 9–9
Comprehension Monitoring

>*Knowledge Form:* Cognitive strategy.

Examples

1. Selected expository passages at appropriate reading level.
2. Four to five sentences, only one of which is the best topic sentence.
3. Self-monitoring card with comprehension checks.

---

[5]Theodore Kaltsounis, *The world and its people: States and regions* (Morristown, NJ: Silver Burdett), 1984, 230.

Limited Set

1. Brief passages requiring student to discriminate between best topic sentence.
2. Two embedded self-monitoring checks.

Expanded Set

1. Longer passages requiring reader to select best topic sentence.
2. One embedded self-monitoring check per paragraph.
3. Longer passages requiring reader to produce topic sentence.
4. Reduced number of embedded self-monitoring checks.

Identifying passages that meet specified criteria is not an easy task. Optimal passages are not readily available, but they are critically important. When skills are introduced in text selections that reduce decoding and comprehension demands, the learner is able to focus attention on the new skill. Using a range of examples that originates with clear, precise segments of text and culminates in passages from the commercial curriculum is central to skill acquisition and generalization. As the learner becomes proficient with the skill, texts need not be as controlled as during initial instruction. Once text selections have been made, the next step in the generic instructional set is to determine the most advantageous sequence for introducing the passages.

Step 3: Sequencing Examples

The design sequence features offered in Chapter 8 are as applicable to expository prose selections as narrative passages. When sequencing informational passages, it is important first to analyze the text for conceptual density, unfamiliar conventions, inappropriate reading level, and textual explicitness. A salient guideline for sequencing examples of expository text is to reserve the introduction of lengthy passages, passages where critical information is not explicit, ambiguous passages, and passages laden with unfamiliar vocabulary until the learner masters the skill in simpler text.

When these potentially problematic features are controlled, learners should be able to demonstrate 80% or better comprehension accuracy on practice examples. If learners do not demonstrate this level of proficiency, the teacher must analyze the instructional sequence and make necessary adaptations.

The following summary of design features proposed in Chapter 8 reinforces the important sequencing considerations for informational text instruction:

1. Select the textual unit most manageable by the reader.
2. Design the simplest form of the comprehension task and create multiple examples.
3. Schedule textual units of increasing complexity (e.g., longer passages, passages with more examples of target skill, passages with less explicit information).
4. Increase difficulty of passages to parallel the proficiencies of reader.

A number of factors determine how materials should be sequenced. The bottom line is to schedule passages in an order that unambiguously communicates to the learner the skill under study and moves the learner through the skills sequence at the most expeditious rate. Obviously, the learner is the best barometer to gauge the appropriateness of the instructional sequence. The following examples specify the knowledge form and example sequences for selected expository prose comprehension skills. Additional examples are in Appendix D.

COMPREHENSION TASK 9–10
Using Text Headings to Identify Important Information

Knowledge Form: Rule relationship:
"Headings and subheadings show us important information to remember."

Sequence of Examples

First Teaching Sequence
1. Four passages with two or three major divisions.
2. Divisional headings explicitly presented.
3. Passage approximately 100 words in length.

Second Teaching Sequence
1. Three passages with four or five major divisional headings.

Third Teaching Sequence
1. Three passages with major divisional headings and subheadings.

COMPREHENSION TASK 9–11
Cumulative Retell

Knowledge Form: Cognitive strategy.

Sequence of Examples

First Teaching Sequence
1. Four passages of two or three paragraphs each (paragraphs of 20–40 words).
2. Familiar paragraph content.
3. Explicit topic sentences.

Second Teaching Sequence
1. Three passages of three to five paragraphs each (paragraphs of 20–40 words).
2. Familiar paragraph content.
3. Some topic sentences not explicitly stated.

Third Teaching Sequence
1. Three passages of four to six paragraphs each (paragraphs of 30–60 words).
2. Implicit topic statements.

The following text could be used in the second teaching sequence. Note that each paragraph is relatively short and the overall length of the passage is considered manageable for low performers.

> **Chlorophyll** (klôr′ ə fil) is the green coloring matter in plants. Chlorophyll is the chemical that traps light energy. Energy trapped by chlorophyll is used to make sugar.
>
> A plant must have more than energy to make sugar. It needs raw materials. One raw material is water. Another raw material is carbon dioxide.
>
> Carbon dioxide is a colorless gas. Most of the plants around you get carbon dioxide from air. Green plants are sometimes called food factories.
>
> A factory is a place that makes something from raw materials. What it makes is called its product. A factory must have a supply of energy to make its product.
>
> A green plant changes the raw materials of carbon dioxide and water into the product—sugar. This process is called **photosynthesis** (fō tə sin′ thə sis). Photosynthesis is the process by which green plants make food.[6]

After a skill is introduced, some students will require additional passages at the initial teaching sequence level. Other instructional sequences may be truncated if students are particularly competent. The previous sequencing guidelines illustrate the types of decisions teachers must make when designing content area instruction. Another instructional design consideration involves how to assess students' knowledge of content studied or read.

Step 4: Selecting Test Examples

Typically, we assess what students learn from content area text and instruction by asking them to complete questions at the end of chapters. As discussed in Chapter 2, low-performing students will need more frequent checks for understanding. Test examples should provide an on-line measure that (1) evaluates a student's progress immediately after skills are presented, (2) monitors skill retention over a period of time, and (3) evaluates the learner's ability to demonstrate the skill in complex and untaught contexts. If we only collect assessment data after several days of instruction, there is little opportunity to teach or provide additional practice in problematic areas. Instructional sessions must become assessment opportunities, times to receive feedback on learner performance and to make necessary modifications in instruction.

To assure a fair and accurate accounting of the learner's response to instruction, instruction and assessment tasks should share commonalities in a minimum of three areas: text format, response format, and task format. Specifically, the following parallels should exist in any assessment of informational prose learning:

1. *Test-text format* (length, structure, vocabulary) should parallel instructional text format.
2. *Test-response format* (production, identification) should parallel instructional response format.
3. *Test-task format* (literal, application, integration) should parallel instructional response format.

---

[6]From *Science: Understanding your environment* (1982), p. 9, by G. Mallinson, J. Mallinson, D. Brown, W. Smallwood, and J. Knapp, 1982. Morristown, NJ: Silver Burdett & Ginn. Copyright 1982 by Silver Burdett & Ginn. Reprinted by permission.

For more specific details on the procedures for assessing informational prose learning at the acquisition, delayed retention, discrimination, and generalization levels, see the guidelines offered in Chapter 8. There are a few specific points to reiterate related to assessment of informational prose learning.

First, assessment tasks, like instruction, should be progressive, designed to monitor students' comprehension as they move from entry level skills to the transfer of those skills to mainstream text assignments. Using a strategy for locating topic sentences in simple paragraphs is much more manageable than applying that skill to mainstream geography texts. Test examples must reflect what is expected in the general education setting. The tasks and text used to assess learning are only representative if they correspond with the tasks and text used during instruction. Furthermore, assessment should be cumulative. The skills and strategies introduced in previous lessons should be reviewed and assessed systematically.

Step 5: Designing and Scheduling Practice Sessions

Practice time lets learners develop proficiency and fluency in a skill. It is not the time for low performers to attempt to learn information independently. Learners with academic difficulties will often require more practice than teachers' manuals prescribe or teachers provide. This is particularly true if the content is densely concentrated and the skills are complex. Nevertheless, simply providing more practice is not a solution to the problems of low performers. The quality of instructional practice must be considered.

An overriding problem noted in Durkin's (1978–1979) observations of reading instruction in content area classes was the overuse of independent practice to the practical exclusion of guided practice and actual instruction. Certainly, the more-is-better mentality will not resolve the problems of low performers. To overcome the limitations of practice activities will involve alterations in the routine to which many students are accustomed (e.g., read the first half of the chapter on Monday, the second half on Tuesday, answer the questions at the end of the chapter on Wednesday, do the vocabulary exercises on Thursday, and take the test on Friday). In the acquisition stages of learning, the schedule of practice must be more frequent and the structure more teacher-directed. A less teacher-directed and more learner-based practice format can be instituted as the learner develops proficiencies in learning from informational prose.

A number of activities function quite successfully in guided practice conditions. Having students answer questions after reading short segments of text, completing group feature matrixes, and working through information on graphic organizers are all opportunities for the learner to practice strategies under teacher supervision.

Once students achieve an acceptable criterion in guided practice conditions, the teacher should introduce independent practice. However, it is ludicrous to assume that students will learn material that depends so greatly on established preskills and strategic behavior without explicit instruction and the opportunity to practice under teacher direction.

Having established the design for informational text instruction through classifying skills according to knowledge form, selecting the range and sequence of examples, and designing test and practice activities, now let us focus on the delivery of that information.

DURING INSTRUCTION

Delivering Textbook Prose Comprehension Instruction: Generic Procedures

By this time, you should be intimately familiar with the procedures used to deliver instruction: framing, preteaching, pacing, think time, signaling, corrective feedback, and firming cycle. We will not review the definitions or details of these delivery procedures provided in previous chapters but instead will apply each in selected examples of informational prose instruction.

Framing

TEACHER: Class, I need your attention.
  Today, we're going to learn about visual displays. Visual displays are a way to help learn information from your science book.
  What will we be using to help us learn?
  (Signals.)
STUDENTS: Visual displays.
TEACHER: Right, visual displays. Sometimes it is very hard to remember all the important information in the passages you read. Visual displays are pictures that help you remember the most important information.
  What are visual displays? (Calls on individual student.)
ELSA: Pictures about information.
TEACHER: That's good. Can anyone tell me what kind of information? (Calls on another student.)
JAY: The most important information.
TEACHER: Great listening. Visual displays are pictures of the most important information.
  Now I will show you a visual display on the overhead, then I will give you a copy.
  It is very important that you look at my visual display on the overhead.
  Now let's look at the visual display on matter (see Figure 9–6).

Preteaching

Example 1

TEACHER: Now it's your turn to remember what we've learned about matter by using the visual display. Remember, only the most important information is in the picture. When I point to the space, you tell me the important information about matter.

Example 2

TEACHER: When you read this chapter, try to use the two steps we practiced of the self-study strategy. What's the first step? (Calls on individual student.)
CLAIRE: Preview the paragraph headings.
TEACHER: Great, preview the paragraph headings.
  Everyone, what's the second step?

STUDENTS: Recite the paragraph heading without looking.

TEACHER: Fantastic. Now let's use these two steps with the passage you read about mammals.

Example 3

TEACHER: Some of the words in this passage you may not be able to read. If you can't pronounce a word, look for a pronunciation guide where you may find how to pronounce the word.

Pacing

Pacing is the rate at which you progress through a lesson, the rate at which you present information and solicit responses. Establishing the right pace where students are neither pushed nor pulled through the curriculum is a delicate maneuver. Often, curricular

FIGURE 9–6

Visual display of matter

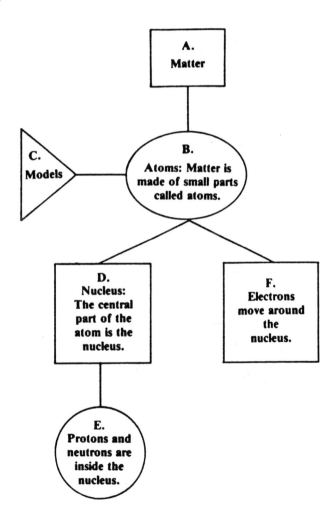

demands or the "I must get to World War II by March" syndrome places the teacher as well as the students in a footrace to see if they can reach the end of the text before June 1. The resolution to the problem is not to slow the pace, but rather to modify the schedule of instruction.

A technique used to maintain the appropriate pace in narrative comprehension exercises that is also appropriate for informational text involves dividing lengthy instructional periods into smaller segments and scheduling more frequent daily sessions. When lessons are partitioned into shorter time segments, students are more alert and not fatigued by the demands of comprehension tasks. Often, the divisions in texts logically lend themselves to shorter instructional time periods.

A final issue on pacing is dictated by student performance. Knowing when to accelerate or decelerate the pace of a lesson involves some practical intuition but, more important, it involves close monitoring of student performance. If students are responding incorrectly to more than 20% of the questions posed, it is time to examine the pace and content of the lesson.

Think Time

Informational prose assessment tasks often request highly detailed and technical information that normal achievers and low achievers alike have not committed to memory. For example, imagine that you are asked to name the three countries that once formed Indochina. Most likely, it has been a long time since you formally studied Southeast Asia. Therefore, the names of the countries of Vietnam, Laos, and Kampuchea may not have been immediately accessible, and answering this question may have involved going back into a text to locate the specific information.

The amount of think time allotted depends on the information requested. If the information is a basic fact all learners should recall without referring to a text (e.g., the first president of the United States, the chemical formula for water, how many bones are in the human body), a 3-second think time period is sufficient. However, if the task requires textual skimming or synthesizing of information, a longer time will be necessary. Rowe (1987) recommends a 3-second lag time between the time the teacher presents the task and the time a student is called on. This 3-second-period allows all readers a period to formulate answers.

Signaling

Coordinating group responses involving informational prose can be much more complex than orchestrating responses to sight words or math facts. Because answers to expository prose questions are often lengthy and quite diverse, teachers may need to structure the form of response by providing response options. Group responses may be solicited through a variety of student response forms. Consider the following examples.

Example 1

TEACHER: If you think Mars and Mercury are larger than the Earth, raise one finger. If you think Mars and Mercury are smaller than the Earth, raise two fingers.

Example 2

TEACHER (writes on board: A. Fish, B. Whales, C. Dogs):
Which of these animals is not a mammal?
Write the letter on your card and when I signal hold up your card.

Example 3

TEACHER: Find the main export of Mexico City in your text and when I signal, tell your neighbor.

Example 4

TEACHER: Row 1, tell me the name of the largest city in Italy.

Example 5

TEACHER: How many types of fossil fuels are there?
When I signal, hold up the correct number of fingers.

Corrective Feedback

The majority of tasks in informational text reading involve rule relationships or cognitive strategies. Whether the task is to construct a summary statement on a paragraph about mold and fungi or to answer a specific question about New Zealand's agriculture, multiple facts, rules, and concepts could cause comprehension failure. We propose using the rule or the strategy itself as the basis of the correction procedure. For instance, if the task is to identify the major types of landforms of the United States and the reader includes some landforms and neglects others, a correction procedure based on the importance of level headings would be initiated.

Correction Procedure Example

TEACHER: David, in your list you included the Atlantic and Gulf Coastal Plains, the Appalachian Mountains, the Central Lowland and Great Plains, prairies, and geographic regions. You're off to a good start, David. Can you tell me how you found your answer about landforms?

DAVID: I looked at the words that were bigger and the words that were darker than other words in the pages.

TEACHER: OK, I see. You're right, the words that are bigger and darker are important words. But sometimes they don't tell more about the topic.

Here's the rule: "Subheadings tell more information about major headings." "Landforms in the United States" is a major heading. So where will you look to find more information?

DAVID: In the subheadings.

TEACHER: Good, David. Let's look at this page. Can you tell me the first subheading of this section.

DAVID: The Atlantic and Gulf Coastal Plains.

TEACHER: Exactly. Why wouldn't prairies and geographic regions be landforms of the United States?

DAVID: Because they weren't subheadings under landforms.

TEACHER: Very nice, David. Let's try this one.

(Teacher continues with another example including emboldened terms as well as headings. Teacher continues firming the part until the learner consistently demonstrates proficiency, then presents the original task.)

Now let's try this one again. (Teacher returns to the original example.)

A final guideline for corrections is to use the information the learner has. By using what the learner knows, the teacher can tailor the correction procedure to address the specific deficit of the learner in the most efficient manner. Correction procedures should isolate the particular deficit component of the instructional strategy, firm that particular part, and then reintegrate that part in the whole cognitive strategy. For example, if the learner experienced difficulty delimiting a summary statement, the correction procedure would focus on that component of the strategy and then require the student to demonstrate that task first in isolated examples, then in the passage context.

Firming Cycle

Firming cycles reinforce emerging skills and strengthen old skills that may have deteriorated over time. Unlike precocious learners who seem to learn and maintain skills with relative ease, instructionally naive learners often require repeated exposure and practice with a skill before it is acquired and applied independently. Such repetition requires teachers to deviate from the prescriptions of teachers' manuals and to schedule additional examples and practice exercises for comprehension development.

For example, in initial skill development, teachers need to schedule multiple opportunities throughout the day for students to practice using pronunciation guides or study skills. They may also need to draw the lines explicitly between the application of those skills across content domains ("The strategy we learned for pronouncing words works in our health book just like it did in our science text"). Furthermore, in the case of previously taught skills, firming instruction may function as a refresher course, simply providing opportunities for students to brush up on skills central to informational prose learning that have not been the focus of recent instruction.

INSTRUCTIONAL FORMATS FOR TEACHING SELECTED INFORMATIONAL PROSE COMPREHENSION SKILLS

In this final section, we integrate the design and delivery features of informational prose instruction into teaching formats. Consistent with previous chapters on academic content, these formats are presented within the before, during, and after framework of instruction. Three formats illustrate procedures teachers can employ to simplify informational prose and enhance comprehension. Within each format, we identify the comprehension skill, the status of the skill (new or old), the prerequisite skill requirements (prior knowledge), guidelines for designing the instructional set, selected teaching and test examples, and teacher wording. In the formats, all the steps necessary for comprehension are not fully detailed. For example, some formats indicate the need to preteach pivotal vocabulary or to develop prior knowledge of the topic. In this section, we selectively review comprehension strategies. Our emphasis on a particular comprehension strategy in no way communicates that this is the only component of an instructional lesson. The formats focus on the "hard part" of teaching specific comprehension strategies related to the details of design and delivery.

COMPREHENSION TASK 9–12
Using Visual Displays to Facilitate Learning from Science Text

BEFORE INSTRUCTION

Task status: New.

Preskills

1. Ability to read at third to fourth grade level.
2. Ability to follow oral directions.

Instructional Design Guidelines

1. Introduce strategy in brief passages of 25–40 word paragraphs.
2. Select passages in which important concepts are easily identified.
3. Restrict passages to those in which relationships of concepts within the passage are explicitly stated.
4. Construct visual display and teaching script emphasizing superordinate, subordinate, and coordinate concepts.
5. Design visual displays that contain six to eight cells.
6. Progress to lengthier text.

Introductory Set

Begin with simple passages of 25–40 words, with easily identified concepts. Passages should be well-structured with clear organizational pattern and of appropriate reading level for learner.

Generalization Set

Introduce increasingly difficult passages. Paragraph length as well as number of paragraphs per passage should increase with learner proficiency. Paragraphs should be representative of mainstream content area text to facilitate generalization. Increase number of cells in visual display in accord with passage complexity.

TASK 9–13

DURING INSTRUCTION

Instructional Delivery Guidelines

1. Frame the task by directing students' attention to visual display.
2. Maintain conservative pace in initial examples because visual display and passage are new.
3. Maintain student attention to task through cues and directives to the visual display.
4. Monitor students carefully to ensure they are following along.
5. Solicit group responses as well as individual responses to evaluate comprehension and focus attention to task.
6. Use cumulative review to firm information presented in organizer.
7. Correct through model, check/test presentation of erred information.

Teaching Procedure: Post-Reading Activity

TEACHER: Today we are going to use a picture or display to help you remember important information that you read.

This picture is not like a photograph, but more like a group of shapes, lines, and words that show how information goes together.

How will the picture be different from a photograph? (Calls on individual student.)

TODD: It will have lines and words.

TEACHER: You're right, Todd. It will have lines and words. What else will it have? (Calls on another student.)

KATRINA: Shapes, I think.

TEACHER: Nice listening, Katrina. It will have lines, words, and shapes. These will help show how the information goes together.

TEACHER: From now on I will call these pictures displays. There are many parts to the display. It is important that you follow along carefully. Listen and watch carefully as I show you how to use it. (See Figure 9–7.)

TEACHER: Put your finger on A, Types of Permanent Teeth.

This whole display will tell us about types of permanent teeth.

What will the picture tell us about? (Signals.)

STUDENTS: Types of permanent teeth.

TEACHER: Great. Put your finger on B. This shape tells us there are four types of permanent teeth. How many types of permanent teeth? (Signals.)

STUDENTS: Four.

TEACHER: You're right, four types of permanent teeth. Now let's see what these four types are.

TEACHER: Touch C. Incisors. One type of permanent tooth is incisors.

What is the one type of permanent tooth? (Signals.)

STUDENTS: Incisors.

TEACHER: Correct, incisors.

TEACHER: Everyone, touch D.

TEACHER: Incisors have flat edges and help cut foods.

Who can tell me one thing about incisors? (Calls on student.)

ANTHONY: Incisors are one of the four kinds of permanent teeth.

TEACHER: Very good, Anthony. Who can tell me something else about incisors?

RACHEL: They have flat edges and help cut into foods.

TEACHER: Excellent remembering, Rachel.

Now let's review what we have learned about permanent teeth.

Review the part of the visual display introduced thus far and assess comprehension. If there are errors, reintroduce the particular cell on which the information was not firm. Once learners are firm on the information, proceed to next portion of the visual display. Use a cumulative review of the display after introducing each successive paragraph. A final review of all information should be conducted after the presentation of the final paragraph. Assess comprehension either through presenting a blank organizer and asking students to fill in missing information or through a regular paper and pencil test that taps information presented in the organizer.

FIGURE 9–7
Graphic organizer of types of permanent teeth

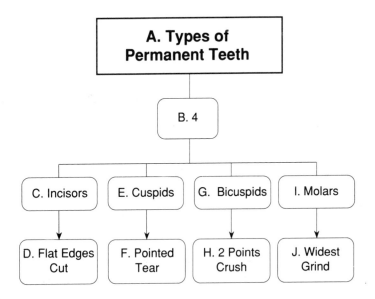

TASK 9–14

AFTER INSTRUCTION

Analyze Errors and Make Instructional Decisions

Possible error types are:

1. Latency responses: Students do not respond in unison with group.
   Instructional decision: Examine signaling procedure.
   Review particular spots in organizer where latency errors occur.
   Practice group responses.
2. General difficulty in supplying information upon signal.
   Instructional decision: Model response procedure.
   Decrease the amount of information presented before questioning.
   Examine teacher wording. Was it consistent?
   Re-present the part of the display where the error occurred and reassess students' knowledge.

Subsequent sessions would use passages and visual displays of comparable difficulty. As students become proficient in recalling information from displays based on shorter and less difficult passages, passage length and complexity may be increased.

COMPREHENSION TASK 9–15
Using Paragraph Restatements to Simplify Informational Prose Learning

BEFORE INSTRUCTION

Task Status: New.

Preskills:

1. Ability to read at second to third grade level.
2. Ability to formulate oral responses.
3. Knowledge of major topics or topic sentence.
4. Ability to discriminate between more important and less important information.

Instructional Design Guidelines

1. Use simple passages, four to five sentence paragraphs with explicit central topic.
2. Align reading level of passage with reading level of learner.
3. Select passage that contains minimal extraneous or irrelevant information.

Introductory Set

Use a range of four to five sentence paragraphs with explicit central topics or topic statements. Paragraphs should cover a variety of relevant contents (e.g., history, health).

Generalization Set

Schedule passages that increase in length, syntactical complexity, and degree of explicitness of major topics. Select paragraphs from mainstream texts.

TASK 9–16

DURING INSTRUCTION

Instructional Delivery Guidelines

1. Frame task alerting reader to remember the most important information.
2. Monitor pace closely because this is a new skill involving connected text. Allow sufficient time to read text.
3. Ask students to read initial passages orally to detect miscues or other factors that may contribute to comprehension difficulties.
4. Provide decoding assistance as needed on unfamiliar terms.
5. Allow adequate think time because students are required to synthesize information and construct summary statements.
6. Firm information within passages by reviewing previous paragraph restatements.
7. Correct paragraph restatement errors through reference to the rule: "A summary tells the most important information in the shortest way."

Teaching Procedure: Paragraph Restatement

TEACHER: Boys and girls, today we're going to use summaries to help us remember information we read.

(Shows the summaries at the end of science lessons.)
Remember the summaries at the end of the lessons in your science book?

Summaries retell the most important information in the shortest way.

What do summaries do?
(Calls on individual student.)

JULIE: Retell us things that are important.

TEACHER: That's right, Julie. Summaries retell the most important information in the shortest way.

Now, I will show you how to make a paragraph summary. You follow along as I read. Try to remember the most important information because you'll use that to make a paragraph summary. Terry, will you read for us? Everyone else needs to follow along.

Horseshoe Crabs

> Horseshoe crabs' bodies are in three main parts. They have a round front part, a flatter middle part, and a hard tail. The tail works like a lever. Sometimes the crab falls onto its back. Then the crab uses the tail to flip itself over.[7]

TEACHER: Listen, I'll summarize this paragraph. The main thing it talked about was horseshoe crabs. But it also told there were three parts and it told a little bit about those three parts.

Remember, a summary tells about the most important information in the shortest way.

Now, I'll underline the most important information.

OK, horseshoe crabs is important. (Teacher underlines.) The three main parts are important. (Underline front, middle, tail.) I don't think what the parts do is important enough to include. That's it.

My summary statement is: "Horseshoe crabs have three main parts. The parts are the front, a middle, and the tail."

I can shorten that. "The three main parts of the horseshoe crab are the front, middle, and tail."

First I found the most important information, then I put it together in the shortest way.

Let's try another.

(Teacher demonstrates procedure numerous times as needed, modeling the procedure and referring to the rule: "A summary tells the most important information in the shortest way." After modeling additional examples, teacher continues.)

TEACHER: OK, now it's your turn to make the summary statement with me.

Everybody, read the paragraph to yourself as Tim reads out loud. Remember to read for the most important information.

> Long, long ago, strange plants and animals lived on earth. Fossils are what is left of these animals and plants. There are several kinds of fossils. A fossil may be a tooth, a footprint, or a bone. It may be a whole animal.[8]

TEACHER: Thanks, Tim, for the nice reading.

TEACHER: Everyone, think to yourself, can you find one thing in this paragraph that you think is important? (Calls on individual student.)

JONI: That plants and animals were here on earth a long time ago.

TEACHER: Exactly, Joni. Plants and animals were here on earth long ago. That's an important part of this paragraph.

TEACHER: Josh, is there anything else that we should include in the summary?

JOSH: Uh, yes, maybe about the tooth.

TEACHER: OK, Josh. Let's look at the paragraph. Does the tooth tell about the most important information or about a part that's not quite as important?

---

[7]From *Teaching reading comprehension series,* Level D, DLM, Teaching Resources, 1983. Reprinted by permission.
[8]From *Teaching reading comprehension series,* Level D, DLM, Teaching Resources, 1983. Reprinted by permission.

JOSH: Just a part.

TEACHER: What's the rule about summary statements?

JOSH: They tell the most important information in the shortest way.

TEACHER: Right, so can you find any other information that's more important?

JOSH: Did anyone say the paragraph was about fossils?

TEACHER: No, they didn't, and fossils are an important part.

TEACHER: Let's look at what we have. "Plants and animals lived a long time ago. What's left of these plants and animals is called a fossil." Good.

Can anyone shorten that into a summary statement? (Calls on individual student.)

HYON: Fossils are what's left of plants and animals that lived a long time ago.

TEACHER: Everyone who thinks that is a good summary statement put one thumb up. If you think we need to change it, put two thumbs up.

TEACHER: Wow, Hyon, everyone agrees. That's a perfect summary statement. You retold the most important information in the shortest way.

Now let's try another.

Continue guided practice on single paragraphs until students construct accurate and succinct paragraph statements, then introduce paragraph restatements in context of two to three paragraph passages. Written statements may be juxtaposed with oral statements if students have sufficient written expression skills.

As students become proficient in generating paragraph restatements, introduce more complex texts. However, the abbreviated teaching sequence for paragraph summary statements does not communicate the complexity of the skill. Conducting summary statements is a complex cognitive task that will require extensive modeling, guided practice and feedback.

For low-performing students, it may be necessary to divide the summary strategy into two parts: (1) identifying the most important information, and (2) delimiting the topic statement. Once students consistently identify the important facts, then the shortening procedure can be introduced.

TASK 9–17

AFTER INSTRUCTION

Analyze Errors and Make Instructional Decisions

Possible error types are:

1. Unable to identify important information.
   Instructional decision: Reteach identifying important information skill.
2. Unable to condense important information into shortened statement.
   Instructional decision: Reteach information combination techniques.

3. General inability to perform task.

Instructional decision: Introduce skill in context of simpler passage.

Provide more modeling.

Subdivide task into component parts (decoding fluency, vocabulary knowledge, identifying important information, and sentence combination procedures) and assess proficiency on each part.

(This procedure was adapted from Jenkins, Heliotis, Stein, & Haynes, 1987.)

COMPREHENSION TASK 9–18
Locating Specific Information from Text

BEFORE INSTRUCTION

Task Status: New.

Preskills

1. Ability to read at second to third grade level.
2. Ability to answer literal comprehension questions.
3. Knowledge of level headings.
4. Ability to locate key words in questions and text.

Instructional Design Guidelines

1. Use simple, three to five sentence paragraphs.
2. Align reading level of passage with reading level of the learner.
3. Ask learner to read text orally to monitor decoding skills.
4. Select passage with familiar content.
5. Select passage that explicitly states information necessary for question solution.

Introductory Set

Introduce skill in simple, two to three sentence paragraphs. Questions should request only one piece of text-based information.

Generalization Set

Select passages of increasing length and syntactical complexity. Questions should require students to identify multiple pieces of information from various points in the passage. Introduce passages with level headings after students master two to three paragraph passages. Teach skills using mainstream materials.

TASK 9–19

DURING INSTRUCTION

Instructional Delivery Guidelines

1. Frame task because it is new. Alert students that task will be to find specific information in text.
2. Monitor pace carefully because this is a new skill involving connected text. Allow sufficient time to read text.
3. Ask students to read passages orally to detect miscues or other factors that may contribute to comprehension difficulties.
4. Provide decoding assistance as needed.
5. Use question-answer strategy correction procedure:
   a. Turn question into part of the answer.
   b. Identify key words in question restatement.
   c. Scan text to find key word match.
   d. Complete question.

Teaching Procedure: Identifying Information from Text

TEACHER: Textbooks have so much information that sometimes it's hard to remember everything you read. Today we're going to learn a way to find information in your science textbook. This is important because you can use this strategy in social studies textbooks, health textbooks, and many of your other textbooks.

Why is it important to have a way to help find information in your textbook? (Calls on individual student.)

COURTNEY: Because there's so much information you can't remember it all.

TEACHER: Very nice, Courtney. There is so much information.

Can you remember everything you read? (Signals.)

STUDENTS: No, you can't remember everything.

TEACHER: You can't remember everything so there are things you can do to help you find the answers.

Reading the passage over again slowly is one way you could find the answer, but it's not the quickest way. Today we'll learn a quicker way to find information.

TEACHER: Now let's review what we already know about answering questions.

(Teacher reviews procedure for turning question into part of the answer.)

Turning the question into part of the answer is the first step.

The second step is finding the key words.

Everyone, the question is "Tell one way that Montreal and Quebec are alike." Write the beginning part of the answer on your paper. (Teacher scans papers.)

OK, when I signal read the first part of your answer. (Signals.)

STUDENTS: "One way Montreal and Quebec are alike is . . ."

TEACHER: Exactly right. Now let's find one way Montreal and Canada are alike.

To find specific information in the text, you scan the text.

Scanning means looking for key words that will help you answer the question.

Does scanning mean you read every word carefully, or just look for key words? (Signals.)

STUDENTS: Just look for key words.

TEACHER: That's right, you scan the text looking for specific words that are in the question.

Remember, to help find the part, find the key words in the question and then find those same key words in text.

(Students have previously been taught key word identification skill.)

TEACHER: We learned about key words last week.

Key words tell us the important part to look for. They tell you the part that is special about the question.

Let's practice finding the key word in this part of the answer.

"One way Montreal and Quebec are alike is . . ."

TEACHER: The question is asking how Montreal and Quebec are alike. The key words you need to find in the text are Montreal and Quebec. Now let's scan to find Montreal and Quebec in the text. You follow along with your eyes as I find them. Say stop when I come to Montreal or Quebec.

CANADA

Canada is our neighbor to the north. The country is bigger than the United States. Most Canadians speak English or French. Today most French-speaking Canadians live in Montreal or Quebec.[9]

(Demonstrates scanning procedure with text on overhead projector.)

STUDENTS: Stop.

TEACHER: Great, now we've found the part where Montreal and Quebec are found in the text. Let's see if the answer to the question is in the part.

TEACHER: "One way that Montreal and Quebec are alike is . . ." Read the sentence with Montreal and Quebec to see if the answer is in that sentence. Underline the answer when you find it.

(Allows sufficient time for students to find answer, then presents following choice-responses.)

TEACHER: "One way that Montreal and Quebec are alike is . . ."

Listen as I read the choices:

A. They are languages.
B. French-speaking Canadians live there.

Write A or B on your card, and when I signal, hold up your answer. (Signals.)

(All students display B.)

---

[9]From *Teaching reading comprehension series,* Level D, DLM, Teaching Resources, 1983, p. 39. Reprinted by permission.

TEACHER: Excellent. The answer is B. To find the answer, you found the key words in the question, then found those same words in the passage, and then read that part to find the specific answer to the question. Let's try another one.

Provide multiple examples of single-paragraph passages with explicit matches between key word questions and key word passages. Once this skill is mastered, introduce passages where answers must be derived from multiple sources in the text. As students develop skill in identifying correct responses, shift to production response tasks, either written or oral. Incrementally increase length of passages as students develop proficiency in strategy. Schedule passages with headings that coincide with their introduction in mainstream texts.

TASK 9–20

AFTER INSTRUCTION

Analyze Errors and Make Instructional Decisions

Possible error types are:

1. Unable to find key words in question.
   Instructional decision: Reteach key word identification skills.
2. Unable to scan and locate key words in text.
   Instructional decision: Reteach skill in simpler, shorter passage.
3. Inability to transform information in text to answer question.
   Instructional decision: Provide instruction in transforming question into part of answer. Use passages in which questions and answers use same syntactical format. Provide choice-response options.

SUMMARY

Informational or expository prose is the primary instructional medium used to communicate information in general education content area classes. Quite frequently, students with academic learning problems experience considerable difficulty when asked to learn from informational text. In this chapter, we described the features of informational prose and the potential hazards they pose for low-performing students. Failure to learn from informational prose was analyzed as an interactive condition that involves the reader, task, text, and strategies. To analyze failure, features of these four components were identified and discussed according to their potential impact on learner comprehension and recall.

Also included in the chapter were three mechanisms for addressing the comprehension deficits of students with academic learning problems. First, selected pre-, during-, and post-reading instructional interventions for enhancing content area learning from textbook prose were reviewed. Guidelines from the generic instructional set were highlighted to provide a model for designing instruction and simplifying informational prose. Delivery procedures were reviewed as applied to textbook prose. Finally, the design and delivery procedures for simplifying informational prose were coordinated and illustrated in instructional formats.

APPLICATION ITEMS

Select a passage that has accompanying comprehension questions from a content-area text to complete the following items:

1. Identify text-based features of this passage that contribute to potential comprehension difficulties of students with academic learning problems. List a positive feature of this text that might enhance a student's ability to comprehend the content.

2. Identify the objective of the lesson. Evaluate the passage according to the following features of the generic instructional set.
   a. What is the knowledge form of the skill being taught?
   b. Is the passage appropriate for an introductory lesson with low-performing students? If yes, justify your response. If no, how can the passage be adapted for use with low performers?
   c. Assume you will need to develop the next set of passages in this skill sequence. Describe the general features of these passages (e.g., length of the passages, content, specific conventions).

3. Evaluate the comprehension questions accompanying the passage selected according to the following criteria:
   a. What response form is predominantly used?
   b. Under what conditions would this be an appropriate response form?
   c. Design two additional assessment items to measure low-performing students' comprehension of the passage.
   d. Discuss the schedule you would design to assess students' comprehension of this passage.

4. You are a teacher of fourth-grade students who have decoding and comprehension problems. From the pre-, during-, and post-reading activities discussed in the chapter, select a procedure for each stage of reading that would be appropriate to use with the passage you selected. Explain the rationale for your selections. Provide a brief description of how you would implement each procedure. Specify the examples you would include in the teaching sequence.

REFERENCES

Adams, A., Carnine, D., & Gersten, R. (1982). Instructional strategies for studying content area texts in the intermediate grades. *Reading Research Quarterly, 28,* 27–55.

Alexander, D. (1985). The effect of study skill training on learning disabled students' retelling of expository material. *Journal of Applied Behavior Analysis, 18,* 263–267.

Archer, A. L., & Gleason, M. M. (1989). *Skills for school success.* Boston: Curriculum Associates.

Armbruster, B. B. (1984). The problems of "inconsiderate text." In G. G. Duffy, L. R. Roehler, & J. Mason (Eds.), *Comprehension instruction: Perspectives and suggestions* (pp. 202–217). New York: Longman.

Armbruster, B. B., & Anderson, T. H. (1988). On selecting "considerate" content area textbooks. *Remedial and Special Education, 9,* 47–52.

Armbruster, B. B., & Gudbrandsen, B. (1986). Reading comprehension instruction in social studies programs. *Reading Research Quarterly, 21,* 36–48.

Baker, L., & Brown, A. L. (1984). Metacognitive skills and reading. In P. D. Pearson (Ed.), *Handbook of reading research* (pp. 353–394). New York: Longman.

Brown, A. L., & Palinscar, A. S. (1982). Inducing strategic behavior from texts by means of informed self-control training. *Topics in Learning and Learning Disabilities, 2,* 1–17.

Carnine, D., & Darch, C. (1986). Teaching content area material to learning disabled students. *Exceptional Children, 53,* 240–246.

Carnine, D., Silbert, J., & Kameenui, E. (1990). *Direct instruction reading* (2nd ed.). Columbus, OH: Merrill Publishing Company.

Chall, J. S. (1983). *Stages of reading development.* New York: Academic Press.

Cook, L. K., & Mayer, R. E. (1983). Reading strategy training for meaningful learning from prose. In M. Pressley & J. R. Levin (Eds.), *Cognitive process research: Educational applications* (pp. 87–131). New York: Springer-Verlag.

Cunningham, P. M. & Cunningham, J. M. (1987). Content area reading-writing lessons. *The Reading Teacher, 40,* 506–513.

Durkin, D. (1978–1979). What classroom observations reveal about reading comprehension instruction. *Reading Research Quarterly, 14,* 481–533.

Gersten, R., & Carnine, D. (1986, April). Direct instruction in reading comprehension. *Educational Leadership,* 70–78.

Graves, A. W. (1986). Effects of direct instruction and metacomprehension training on finding main ideas. *Learning Disabilities Research, 1,* 90–100.

Jenkins, J. R., Heliotis, J. D., Stein, M. L., & Haynes, M. C. (1987). Improving reading comprehension by using paragraph restatements. *Exceptional Children, 54,* 54–59.

Kameenui, E. J., Simmons, D. C., & Darch, C. B. (1987). LD children's comprehension of selected textual features: Effects of proximity of information. *Learning Disability Quarterly, 10,* 237–248.

Manzo, A. V. (1970). Reading and questioning: The ReQuest procedure. *Reading Improvement, 7,* 80–83.

Moore, D. W., & Readence, J. E. (1980). A meta-analysis of the effect of graphic organizers on learning from text. In M. L. Kamil & A. J. Moe (Eds.), *Perspectives in reading research and instruction* (pp. 213–217). Twenty-ninth Yearbook of The National Reading Conference.

Moore, D. W., & Readence, J. E. (1984). A quantitative and qualitative review of graphic organizer research. *Journal of Educational Research, 78,* 11–17.

Nicholson, T. (1984). You get lost when you gotta blimmin' watch the damn words: The low progress reader in the junior high school. *Topics in Learning and Learning Disabilities, 3,* 16–27.

Palinscar, A. S. (1986). Metacognitive strategy instruction. *Exceptional Children, 53,* 118–124.

Rowe, M. B. (1987, Spring). Wait time: Slowing down may be a way of speeding up. *American Educator,* 38–43.

Schumaker, J. B., Deshler, D. D., Alley, G. R., Warner, N. W., & Denton, P. H. (1982). Multipass: A learning strategy for improving reading comprehension. *Learning Disability Quarterly, 5,* 295–304.

Singer, H. (1978). Active comprehension from answering to asking questions. *Reading Teacher, 31,* 901–908.

Smiley, S. S., Oakley, D. D., Worthen, D., Campione, J. C., & Brown, A. L. (1977). Recall of thematically relevant material by adolescent good and poor readers as a function of written versus oral presentation. *Journal of Educational Psychology, 69,* 381–387.

Sternberg, R. J. (1984). What should intelligence tests test? Implications of a triarchic theory of intelligence for intelligence testing. *Educational Researcher, 13*, 5–15.

Torgesen, J. K. (1982). The learning disabled child as an inactive learner: Educational implications. *Topics in Learning and Learning Disabilities, 2*, 45–52.

Valencia, S. W., & Pearson, P. D. (1988). Principles for classroom comprehension assessment. *Remedial and Special Education, 9*, 26–35.

Williams, J. P. (1986). Teaching children to identify the main idea of expository texts. *Exceptional Children, 53*, 163–168.

Wong, B., & Wong, R. (1986). Study behavior as a function of metacognitive knowledge about critical task variables: An investigation of above average, average, and learning disabled readers. *Learning Disabilities Research, 1*, 101–111.

APPENDIX A

Comprehension Tasks Classified by Response Form, Response Modality, and Comprehension Type

TASK 9–21
Name three jobs the Japanese held in the 1880s on the West Coast.

Response Form: Production.

Response Modality: Oral comprehension.

Comprehension Type: Literal/acquisition

TASK 9–22
The _____ industry is important in New England.
citrus   cotton   textile

Response Form: Choice.

Response Modality: Written.

Comprehension Type: Literal/acquisition.

TASK 9–23
Conduct an experiment to determine whether a lighter or darker area makes a difference in temperature.

Response Form: Production.

Response Modality: Oral, written, and motor.

Comprehension Type: Application/integration.

TASK 9–24
Given the information you just read about the planet Mars, compare conditions there with the conditions on Earth.

Response Form: Production.

Response Modality: Oral or written.

Comprehension Type: Integration.

APPENDIX B

Classification of Content Area Text Comprehension Skills by Knowledge Form

COMPREHENSION TASK 9–25
Recognizing Relations of Information in Text

Knowledge Form: Cognitive strategy.

Comprehension Tool: Visual display/graphic organizers.

Component Skills

1. Identifying key information in passage.
2. Knowledge of relationship between concepts.
3. Organizational knowledge.

Instructional Procedure

1. Ask student to read a short, simple passage in its entirety.
2. Present graphic organizer, a piece at a time, highlighting critical information and focusing on relationships between information.
3. Review cumulatively all information presented.
4. Lead student in rehearsing information in display, noting relations between concepts.
5. Present blank organizer to assess recall. Walk student through organizer, a step at a time, verbally rehearsing the information.
6. Lead student in placing information into visual organizer.
7. Ask student to review information independently.
8. Test student by having student verbally reconstruct information in organizer.
9. Repeat step 1 with new text.
10. Practice on additional paragraphs.

Once the student develops proficiency at recalling information at the simple passage level, the student may proceed to more complex passages. The same instructional procedure is followed.

COMPREHENSION TASK 9–26
Comprehension Monitoring

Knowledge Form: Cognitive strategy.

Component Skills

1. Self-appraisal knowledge.
2. Self-monitoring knowledge.
3. Main idea/topic sentence knowledge.
4. Decoding fluency.

Instructional Tool: Adjunct question/self-interrogation.

Instructional Procedure

1. State objective of task to have student recognize a failure to understand what is read.
2. Require student to read simple, three to four sentence paragraph.
3. Model monitoring procedure by overt self-questioning: "Do I understand what I just read? What was the main thing that happened?"[10]
4. Ask student to read another simple paragraph.
5. Lead student in evaluating comprehension through overt self-questioning procedure.
6. Test student by requesting specific information from text.
7. Practice on additional passage.
8. Introduce multiple-paragraph passages upon mastery at single-paragraph level.
9. Model self-questioning procedure after each paragraph.
10. Lead student on additional multiple-paragraph passages.
11. Assess comprehension through specific questions.
12. Introduce covert self-questioning procedure once student masters overt self-questioning.
13. Assess comprehension on a number of paragraphs.
14. Practice on multiple paragraphs.

APPENDIX C

Range of Examples for Content Area Prose

TASK 9–27
Locating Specific Information from Text

Knowledge Form: Cognitive strategy.

Examples: Paragraphs and multiple-paragraph passages.

---

[10]Adapted from Graves (1986) comprehension monitoring procedure.

Limited Set

1. Three-sentence paragraph of appropriate reading level for student.
2. Relatively familiar content.
3. Factual information question explicitly answered in text.

Expanded Set

1. Multi-sentence paragraphs.
2. Multiple paragraph passages.
3. Factual information questions implicitly answered in text.

COMPREHENSION TASK 9–28
Using Graphic Organizers to Facilitate Comprehension of Informational Prose

Knowledge Form: Cognitive strategy.

Examples

1. Selected expository passages.
2. Simple graphic organizers containing no more than six to eight cells.
3. Teaching script.

Limited Set

1. Brief passages with easily identified concepts.
2. Well-structured and coherent text.
3. Variety of content.

Expanded Set

Passages of longer length containing no more than 12–16 important concepts.

APPENDIX D

Sequence of Examples for Content Area Textbook Prose

COMPREHENSION TASK 9–29
Pronouncing and Defining Pivotal Vocabulary Terms

Knowledge Form: Cognitive strategy.

Sequence of Examples

First Teaching Sequence
1. One-paragraph passages.
2. One pivotal vocabulary term accompanied by pronunciation guide.
3. Term defined in context.

Second Teaching Sequence
1. One-paragraph passages.
2. One pivotal vocabulary term accompanied by pronunciation guide only.
3. Term defined only in glossary.

Third Teaching Sequence
1. Multiple-paragraph passages.
2. Multiple pivotal vocabulary terms accompanied by pronunciation guides.
3. Some terms defined in context; others defined only in glossary.

The following passage could be used in the initial teaching sequence:

> Some animals' colors allow them to camouflage (kam-ö-fläzh) themselves in their environment. Polar bears and crocodiles, for example, blend quite well in their surroundings. Can you think of other animals that use camouflage?

COMPREHENSION TASK 9–30
Self-Study Strategy

Knowledge Form: Cognitive strategy.

Sequence of Examples:

First Teaching Sequence
1. Three passages.
2. Two or three divisional headings in each passage.
3. 20–40 word paragraphs.
4. Selections from a range of content areas.

Second Teaching Sequence
1. Three passages.
2. Four to six divisional headings in each passage.
3. 30–60 word paragraphs.
4. Selections from a range of mainstream content area texts.

APPENDIX E

Text for Graphic Organizer

Fossil Fuels

Our main energy resources today are fossil fuels. Fossil fuels have energy from plants and animals that lived millions of years ago. From where did the energy in the plants and animals come? As the organisms died and began to decay, they became buried in the Earth. Heat and pressure caused the decaying organisms to change into coal, petroleum, and natural gas. Coal, petroleum, and natural gas are fossil fuels. When fossil fuels are burned, the energy in them is released.[11]

[11]From *Accent on science*, Grade 6 (1985), p. 107. Columbus, OH: Merrill Publishing Company. Copyright 1985 by Merrill Publishing Company. Reprinted by permission.

Sample Graphic Organizer

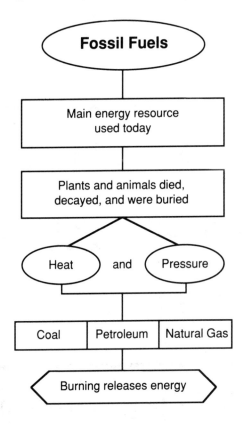

C H A P T E R

TEN

Designing Instructional Strategies for Teaching Mathematics: Facts, Concepts, and Operations

This chapter was coauthored by Eric Jones, Bowling Green State University

Chapter Objectives

Upon successful completion of this chapter, you will be able to:

1. DESCRIBE the two primary approaches to mathematics instruction.
2. IDENTIFY features of mathematics skills and conventional programs that pose predictable problems for low performers.
3. APPLY the generic instructional set to the design of mathematics instruction.
4. APPLY the before, during, and after instructional phases to mathematics instruction.
5. DEMONSTRATE design and delivery procedures in mathematics teaching formats.
6. IDENTIFY guidelines for modifying conventional mathematics curricula and instruction.

APPROACHES TO MATHEMATICS LEARNING

A fundamental goal of instruction in the elementary grades is to equip students with the basic skills to solve quantitative problems in everyday life. The results of the 1982 National Assessment of Educational Progress (cited in Carpenter, Matthews, Lindquist, & Silver, 1984) clearly indicate that too many students in the elementary grades fail to acquire sufficient skills in the operations and applications of mathematics. For low-achieving students, the problem is severe and pervasive. The mathematical skills a student acquires will depend largely on the prior skills that have been taught. Becoming proficient in mathematics depends on the sequential mastery of hierarchies of skills; failure to learn specific math skills jeopardizes the acquisition of subsequent math skills.

Mathematics experts agree that the teaching of basic math skills involves (1) progression through sequences of skills that become increasingly more complex and abstract, (2) concrete applications of abstract representations of quantitative relationships, (3) drill and practice, and (4) applications of previously taught skills to the solution of higher-level skills that have not been taught. There is, however, considerable disagreement among math educators regarding the role of the teacher and the emphasis given to instruction. Some educators argue that the teacher should be nondirective and act primarily as a facilitator of the pupils' discoveries of principles and solutions. This approach is commonly referred to as the discovery approach. The opposite of the discovery approach is the direct instruction approach.

Discovery Approach

The discovery approach to mathematics instruction emerged in the early 1960s with the development of programs frequently referred to as "new math." To some extent, the modern math movement resulted in the realization that young children could be taught math skills that were more complex than had previously been presented in the traditional curricula—but even that effect was limited. None of the new math programs have survived. The reasons for the failure of the new math are complex. In part, the failure of the new math movement was due to the fundamental ignorance of reformers regarding the culture of schools and of the change process in cultural institutions (Sarason, 1971). Other reasons for the failure of the movement are related to critical flaws in the logical bases of the discovery learning approach.

Thus, it is important to examine these flaws critically. We will consider three issues: (1) the basic rationale for discovery learning, (2) the problem of error rate, and (3) the difficulties in specifying objectives. For more extensive critiques of the assumptions of the discovery learning approach, see Ausubel (1968) and Keislar and Shulman (1966).

Rationale for Discovery Learning

Advocates of the discovery approach argue that students will reach the greatest understandings and appreciations of the subject matter if they are permitted to discover the relationships and solutions for themselves, rather than be directed by the teacher (e.g., Bruner, 1961; Rogers, 1969). They consider it superior to direct instruction because students (1) will learn more, (2) will understand the problem-solving process more thoroughly, (3) will be intrinsically motivated and enjoy the task of learning more, and (4) will become better able to generalize their knowledge and skills more broadly compared to students who learn in teacher-directed instructional programs.

Despite impressive claims for the discovery approach, when it is applied to the instruction of slow learners, two important criticisms emerge. First, learners must engage in substantial amounts of unstructured trial-and-error activities. Second, it is difficult to identify and measure progress toward academic goals in discovery teaching.

Discovery Learning and Error Rate

There are two apparent differences between the discovery approach to instruction and the direct or expository approach (Glaser, 1966). First, discovery requires that the student be presented examples of a concept or rule. The student examines the relationships between the examples and determines the general concept or rule. Second, teachers using the discovery approach impose minimal structure on the instructional sequence. Glaser observes:

> This kind of sequence, of necessity, allows the student to pursue blind alleys and find negative instances; and consequently, he makes some wrong moves or incorrect responses in the process of learning. Discovery implies a low probability of making a successful response. Such being the case, errors have a high probability of occurrence. (p. 15)

Given that high rates of errors would be virtually assured in the unstructured learning situation, it is predictable that students with learning handicaps will not persevere in the task and may actually try to avoid the situation altogether. Furthermore, the discovery approach is inefficient. Children with learning handicaps are capable of learning meaningful concepts, principles, and skills more quickly and without being subjected to the frustrations that will accompany a process that involves such predictably high error rates.

Difficulties in Specifying Objectives

Proponents of the discovery approach contend that the discovery approach results in greater learning than the direct approach. Their argument, however, is difficult to defend. They argue that students who participate in discovery learning programs simply learn more than students who receive teacher-directed instruction. Unfortunately, empirical research fails to support assumptions that participation in a discovery process results in either mastery of concepts and skills or the acquisition of more skills and concepts than had been intended by the instructor. Certainly, students learn something in discovery programs, but it is difficult to determine what they learn. The ambiguity of what has been learned through discovery learning is directly related to the lack of specification of what should be learned before participation in a discovery activity (Ausubel, 1968; Keislar & Shulman, 1966; Scandura, 1968).

The second claim for the superiority of discovery learning is that it results in more learning because it facilitates later learning of new knowledge and skills (e.g., Bruner, 1961). The claim that the generalization of learning is efficiently promoted through discovery learning activities is limited. It is logically impossible to account for generalization of previously learned skills without being able to identify the skills and without determining whether the skills were learned. Furthermore, no empirical evidence from the research on learning and instruction supports Bruner's claim.

In summary, it is apparent that although discovery learning is intriguing, it is difficult to observe or demonstrate. Keislar and Shulman (1966) stated that their exhaustive reviews of the literature led to the inescapable conclusion that the term *discovery learning* is far too ambiguous and far too imprecise to be meaningfully used by educators or researchers. Kendler (1966, p. 176) considered that the term *discovery* had outlived its usefulness and had become a "nine-letter dirty word."

Direct Instruction

In teacher-directed instruction, the teacher provides the student with the rule first and then follows up with a set of exemplars of the rule. The deductive rule-example sequence of instruction is more efficient than the discovery approach. If the rule is clear and the examples and nonexamples are carefully chosen, direct instruction can be virtually errorless. To appreciate this point, consider the following example from Scandura (1968). First, examine the following sets of numbers and consider the relationship between the quantities in brackets and the quantity following the arrow:

(4 3 1) → 3   (7 3 3) → 4
(9 2 4) → 5   (8 6 2) → 6

Then determine the quantities that should follow (4 9 3) and (5 0 2). If you took the time to examine the different possible relationships, you probably induced that the answers were 1 and 3 respectively. You're probably feeling clever about your accomplishment. Doubtless you would have learned the solution to the last two problems more quickly if you were told the solution rule, "The third number in the bracket subtracted from the first number in the bracket will equal the number outside the bracket," and had not been left to your own devices to induce the rule. A well-phrased rule-example presentation of the direct approach will result in more rapid learning of underlying rules compared to the example-rule presentation of the discovery approach.

Teacher-directed presentations *can* be more efficient than student-centered approaches. We are not, however, going to argue that expository instruction is *always* efficient. If it is poorly or haphazardly implemented, it can lead to many errors and much frustration. On the other hand, systematic, well-controlled, teacher-led instructional programs will contribute to the greatest student learning (Anderson, St. Pierre, Proper, & Stebbens, 1978; Gersten, 1985; Stevens & Rosenshine, 1981). It is not sufficient that the instructional program be teacher led. The teacher must keep careful control of the details of both the presentation and the instructional sequence.

DEVELOPING MATHEMATICS CURRICULA FOR STUDENTS WITH LEARNING PROBLEMS

In this section we will discuss the importance of a well-articulated scope and sequence of math skills, call attention to the particular areas of the skill hierarchies where students with learning handicaps frequently encounter difficulties, and illustrate the application of the generic instructional set to the design of instructional procedures for several math skills.

Scope and Sequence of Mathematics Skills

A first step in the design of an instructional sequence is to clarify the sequences of skills and preskills within the mathematics curriculum. Such sequences should include clear indications of the relationships between the target skill, subskills, and related skills from different domains. The hierarchy of skills and necessary preskills is fairly clear in mathematics. Thus, it is easier to plan curricula for math than for subjects such as reading where the hierarchies are less clear. We can be certain that a student will not be able to solve computational multiplication problems or use multiplication in applied problem solving if basic count-by and addition skills have not already been mastered. Similarly, a student will not be able to analyze and apply decimal fractions adequately unless skills in the analysis and interpretation of regular fractions have been mastered.

The task of preparing and implementing instructional programs is time consuming, but it is particularly necessary when working with low-performing students. Average and high-achieving students tend to succeed despite deficiencies in basic skills curricula. However, commercial programs often fail to specify guidelines for the efficient instruction of students with learning difficulties. Teachers must be skilled in the evaluation and modification of commercially available math programs and the design of effective instructional mathematics formats.

Hierarchies of Math Skills

Beginning math skills can be divided into four basic categories: (1) math-related language and vocabulary, (2) numeration skills, (3) computation skills, and (4) problem-solving skills (see Figure 10–1). The categories are interrelated. Efficient mastery of some skills in one category are facilitated by mastery of skills from another category. For example, fluency in count-by series, a numeration skill, facilitates the rapid acquisition of computational skills in multiplication (Carnine, 1980a). In other cases, it is essential that the

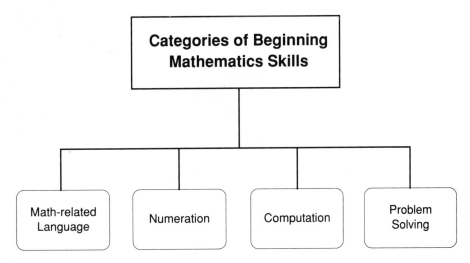

FIGURE 10–1
Beginning mathematics skills categories

skills from one area be taught as preskills to the mastery of skills from another area. For example, most division problems result in quotients that contain remainders. Adequate comprehension of the answers obtained from computing division problems depends on previous mastery of rudimentary skills in fraction analysis.

The skills hierarchies of math-related language, numeration, computation, and problem-solving skills are interwoven. However, separating math skills into four hierarchies and examining their relationships to one another is important to the design of efficient instructional programs. We do, however, consider it more productive to integrate skills related to (1) the analysis and computation of fractions and decimals and (2) the application of quantitative skills to the solution of measurement, time, or money problems that should be included in the hierarchies of numeration, computation, and problem-solving. There are two reasons why we prefer to limit the number of hierarchies to four. First, the skills required to solve problems involving fractions, decimals, measurement, money, or time can be readily identified as skills from the areas of numeration, computation, or problem-solving. Thus, there is no compelling logic for separating them. The second reason is that if sets of skills such as working with fractions or counting money are considered separate from the major emphases of instruction, they are apt to be given less emphasis than the skills such as counting or computing that are generally recognized as important. The odds that instruction in those skills will be slighted are likely to increase if we place them in separate categories. On the other hand, if skills involving fractions and decimals, money, time, and measurement are recognized subskills in the hierarchies of math-related language and vocabulary, numeration, computation, and problem-solving skills, they are less apt to be ignored.

The hierarchies of basic math skills and knowledge are presented in Appendix A. This hierarchy is based on one developed by Silbert, Carnine, and Stein (1981) and on our review of several basal math programs. The skills are listed according to their major categories of skill hierarchies, and in the order they would generally be found in basal math programs. The relationships between skills hierarchies are not detailed. The relationships can, however, be determined by the numbering of the preskills. The numbering represents the cross-referencing of skills that are taught in a program at approximately the same points. The numbers are not decimal fractions of a grade level. They merely indicate sequence and serve to help reference skills across domains.

The detail of the hierarchies is not exhaustive, but it is sufficiently comprehensive to facilitate (1) evaluation of the comprehensiveness of the program, (2) identification of important preskills for major objectives, (3) selection and ordering of instructional examples, (4) selection of efficient and transferable instructional strategies, and (5) distribution of practice and review activities.

Criteria for Evaluating Math Curricula

Basal math programs have two basic problems when instruction of students with learning handicaps is considered. First, the skill hierarchies of basal math programs are often insufficiently detailed, and, second, specific preskills that are critical to the mastery of major objectives are ignored. Ignoring certain preskills will frequently result in the failure of students with learning problems. Consider the example in Figure 10–2.

FIGURE 10–2
Subtraction problems with zeros
in minuend

$$
\begin{array}{rrr}
390 & 4030 & 6400 \\
-278 & -3489 & -6297 \\
\end{array}
$$

Subtraction problems such as the ones presented in Figure 10–2 contain zeros in the minuend and require regrouping. Such problems frequently present difficulties for low-achieving students. Preskills in place value should be directly addressed and direct training of regrouping with zeros given before the child is expected to perform the entire task independently.

Virtually any scope and sequence of math skills will indicate that as one progresses through the skills hierarchies the tasks become increasingly complex. One means of increasing the probability that a student will correctly apply previously learned skills of knowledge is to schedule transfer exercises where the application of the skills is explicitly taught. A well-detailed instructional hierarchy will be useful in deciding the most opportune time to introduce the review exercises. For example, the understanding of computational division will depend on the student developing basic skills in fraction analysis. First, the reading and writing of fractions and the translation of graphic representations of fractions should be introduced before the student encounters division problems that have remainders in their quotients. Next, the introduction of division problems involving quotients with remainders should be scheduled. Exercises in reading and writing fractions should be reintroduced. Finally, the conceptual relationship between the representation of fractions and the operation of division should be directly taught.

In this section, the divisions of skills within mathematics curricula and the interdependencies of skills within the mathematical hierarchies were described. Also illustrated were properties of language, numeration, computation, problem-solving examples, and instructional features that pose predictable difficulties for naive learners. In the ensuing sections, we address these curriculum-based and instructionally based problems by applying the generic instructional set.

DESIGNING MATH INSTRUCTION: APPLYING THE GENERIC INSTRUCTIONAL SET

The generic instructional set constitutes the minimum requirements that must be considered in designing instruction for the prevention and remediation of academic learning problems. To apply the generic instructional set, we must determine the knowledge form of the task, scrutinize the selection and sequence of examples, and fashion test and practice examples that assess, reinforce, and extend a learner's knowledge. In combination with the procedures of framing, preteaching, think time, signals, pacing, firming, and corrections, the generic instructional set supplies the pedagogical scaffolding for instruction that reduces a learner's risk of academic failure. This is accomplished by identifying and controlling instructional factors that traditionally receive minimal consideration.

Step 1: Determining the Knowledge Form

As we have advocated throughout the text, the form of knowledge to be communicated specifies the parameters for how that information should be taught. To classify mathematics tasks according to knowledge forms, it is necessary to identify the component form or forms of the tasks to determine how those component forms are integrated into specific mathematics skills. Mathematics skills cover the gamut of knowledge forms. Therefore, the first step in designing mathematics instruction entails categorizing the particular task according to one of the following forms of knowledge:

Classifications of Knowledge Forms

1. Verbal associations
   a. Simple facts
   b. Verbal chains
   c. Discriminations
2. Concepts
3. Rule relationships
4. Cognitive strategies

As was illustrated in the section on scope and sequence of mathematics skills, there are literally dozens of skills a learner must master in the mathematics curriculum. In the following section, we categorize selected mathematics skills according to knowledge form (e.g., concepts, rule relationships) rather than skill area (e.g., addition, fractions). This organizational tack is designed to illustrate the range of mathematics skills that cluster within the same knowledge form. By knowing that basic addition and subtraction facts fall within the same knowledge form as numeral and symbol identification, we also know that these skills are taught using a similar instructional format. This information allows us to focus our instructional repertoire on a highly functional group of instructional procedures and to focus on the details of teaching. Following the classification of skills, instructional procedures for selected skills within the same knowledge form are outlined to demonstrate how determining knowledge forms translates into instructional decisions. The instructional procedures in this section are not fully detailed but are designed instead to exemplify the instructional samenesses that exist across mathematics skills of similar knowledge form.

Mathematics Skills Classified as Verbal Associations

Verbal associations consist of simple facts, verbal chains, and discriminations. Examples of mathematics skills classified as verbal associations are illustrated in Table 10–1.

In all three cases, a correct response is based on a single, well-defined piece of information. Therefore, the model, lead, check/test format provides the framework for instructional design. Likewise, correction procedures are based on a similar process where the teacher demonstrates the information, leads the learner in practicing the information, then tests the learner's acquisition of the newly taught information. In the following section, the form of knowledge is specified along with details for designing mathematics instruction.

Coin identification represents a mathematics skill that is classified as verbal association.

TABLE 10–1
Mathematics skills classified as verbal associations

Knowledge Form	Example Skills
Simple facts	Numeral identification: 2, 15, 7, 100 Symbol identification: $=$, $+$, $<$, $>$, %, \$. Basic facts: $3 + 5 = 8$, $5 - 2 = 3$, $4 \times 4 = 16$, $12 \div 3 = 4$ Measurement: 12 in. $=$ 1 ft., 16 oz. $=$ 1 lb. Money: coin identification
Verbal chains	Rote counting: (1, 2, 3, 4, . . . 100) Interval counting: (2, 4, 6, 8, 10, . . . ; 5, 10, 15, 20, . . .)
Discriminations	Symbol identification: $+$, $-$, $=$, $\times$, $\div$ Numeral identification: 3, 8, 6, 9 Shapes: oval, circle Fractions: proper, improper Numeral identification: 10, 100; 2, 1/2 Money: coin identification Time: hour, half hour, quarter hour

Simple Facts

TASK 10–1
Numeration

Examples: 2, 5, 19, 100.

Knowledge Form: Verbal association—simple fact.

Instructional Task: Orally producing numeral names.

Instructional Procedure

1. Model ("This number is 2").
2. Lead.
3. Test.
4. Practice.
5. Review.

Correction Procedure: Repeat steps 1–3.

TASK 10–2
Basic Facts

Examples

$5 + 5 = 10$
$4 - 2 = 2$
$7 \times 7 = 49$
$56 \div 7 = 8$

Instructional Task: Orally producing basic facts in addition.

Instructional Procedure

1. Model ("5 + 5 = 10").
2. Lead.
3. Test.
4. Practice.
5. Review.

Correction Procedure: Repeat steps 1–3.

TASK 10–3
Labeling Components in Computational Problems

Example: sum, quotient, remainder, product.

Knowledge Form: Verbal association—simple facts.

Instructional Task: Identifying the names of specific components of computational problems (e.g., sum, remainder, product, etc.).

Instructional Procedure

1. Model ("This is the remainder").
2. Lead.
3. Test.
4. Practice.
5. Review.

Correction Procedure: Repeat steps 1–3.

Verbal Chains

TASK 10–4
Rote Counting by Ones

Example: Counting forward from 1 to 10.

Knowledge Form: Verbal association.

Instructional Skills: Orally stating the numbers in sequence but without reference to objects.

Instructional Procedure

1. Model ("Listen, my turn to count by ones. I'll start at 1 and stop at 10. 1, 2, 3, . . . 10").
2. Lead.
3. Test.
4. Practice.
5. Review.

Correction Procedure

1. Model difficult part.
2. Lead learner on difficult chunk.
3. Test learner on difficult chunk.
4. Integrate chunk into whole sequence.

Discriminations

MONEY TASK 10–5
Identifying Different Coins

        Examples: nickel, dime, penny, quarter.

        Knowledge Form: Verbal association.

        Instructional Task: Discriminating a newly introduced coin (nickel) from known coins and stimuli.

        Preskills: Basic fact knowledge of individual coin names.

Instructional Procedure

1. Model ("This coin is a nickel").
2. Lead.
3. Test.
4. Practice.
5. Review.

Correction Procedure

1. Repeat model of coin.
2. Lead learner on difficult task.
3. Repeat test example.
4. Remove similar examples from sequence.

Mathematics Skills Classified as Concepts

Concepts are objects, actions, events, or situations that belong to a class of objects, actions, events, or situations. Concepts are concepts because of a particular attribute shared by all members of that class. Determining whether a mathematics skill is a concept requires identifying that particular attribute and demonstrating it through examples that clearly communicate the intended information and rule out possible misinterpretations. By demonstrating the sameness through a select set of examples, concept teaching allows students to generalize to a set of untaught examples, making concept instruction much more efficient yet complex than verbal association instruction. As indicated in Chapter 6, often those unique features of concepts are easier to demonstrate through concrete, visual examples than through verbal abstractions. In the following section, example concepts relevant to mathematics learning are detailed.

Knowledge Form	Example Skills
Concept of shape	Circle
	Square
	Rectangle
	Parallelogram
	Angles

Knowledge Form	Example Skills
Concept of quantity	Greater than
	Less than
	Equal
	Whole
	Part
Concept of position	First
	Last
	Bottom
	Top
	2nd, 3rd, 4th, . . .

TASK 10–6
Naming Geometric Shapes

Examples: circle, trapezoid, equilateral triangles.

Knowledge Form: Concepts.

Instructional Task: Discrimination between examples and nonexamples of specific shapes.

Instructional Procedure

1. Model range of positive and negative examples ("This is an equilateral triangle; this is not an equilateral triangle").
2. Test on taught and untaught examples.
3. Practice.
4. Review.

Correction Procedure

1. Repeat steps 1–4.
2. If error persists, present demonstration sequence before retesting.
3. If problem is discrimination error, remove similar stimuli from testing sequence until learner is firm on response.

LANGUAGE TASK 10–7
Describing Relationships Between Objects and Groups of Objects

Examples: more, less, equal, greater than, less than, larger, smaller.

Knowledge Form: Concepts.

Instructional Task: Discrimination between examples and nonexamples of stimuli that possess the relative attributes of greater than, less than, equal to, and so on.

Instructional Procedure

1. Model range of positive and negative examples ("Watch, I'm going to show you greater than or not greater than").
2. Test on taught and untaught examples.
3. Practice.
4. Review.

Correction Procedure

1. Repeat steps 1–4.
2. If error persists, present the demonstration sequence again before retesting.
3. If problem is discrimination error, remove minimally different stimuli from testing sequence until learner is firm on response.

Mathematics Skills Classified As Rule Relationships

Mathematics rules, like all other academic rules, are based on the relationship or connection between two pieces of information. These two pieces of information may include facts, discriminations, and concepts.

In Chapter 6, the two critical pieces of the rule relationship were identified as knowledge chunks, the first knowledge chunk serving as the basis of the prediction for the second knowledge chunk. For example, consider the following mathematics rule: *"If the first number after the decimal is 5 or greater, you round to the next whole number."* By knowing the first knowledge chunk (italicized component), you can determine whether the example fits the criterion of the rule relationship.

Many rule relationships in mathematics form the basis of higher level cognitive strategies; therefore, it is essential that students' knowledge of these rules is firm and fluent. In the following section, a sample of mathematics skills are classified as rule relationships. Finally, instructional specifications for two mathematics rule relationships are provided.

Knowledge Form	Example Skills
Rule relationships	Regrouping in subtraction
	Regrouping in addition
	Commutative property of addition
	Commutative property of multiplication
	Prime number rule
	Rounding off rule
	Equality rule
	Expanded notation

Selected Mathematics Rule Relationships

1. Subtraction of multi-digit numbers requiring regrouping: "When the bottom number is greater than the top number, you have to regroup."
2. Telling time: "When the long hand is on the 12, it is o'clock."

3. Addition of multi-digit numbers requiring regrouping: "If the sum of the numbers in the column is 10 or more, you have to regroup."
4. Multiplication of numbers with decimals: "When you multiply a number by 10, you move the decimal one place to the right."
5. Division of multi-digit numbers: "If the remainder is bigger than the divisor (point to number), the digit in the quotient needs to be bigger."[1]
6. Commutative rule of addition: "When you add the same numbers, changing the order of the numbers does not change the sum."
7. Commutative rule of multiplication: "When you multiply the same numbers, changing the order of the numbers does not change the product."

SUBTRACTION TASK 10–8
Regrouping in Multi-digit Subtraction Problems

Examples

$$\begin{array}{r} 26 \\ -19 \end{array} \qquad \begin{array}{r} 32 \\ -18 \end{array} \qquad \begin{array}{r} 83 \\ -74 \end{array}$$

Knowledge Form: Rule relationship:
"If the bottom number is more than the top number, you have to regroup."

Component Skills

1. Discrimination of ones and tens columns.
2. Discrimination of bottom and top number.
3. Discrimination of more than and less than.
4. Simple fact: Symbol identification.
5. Simple fact: Numeral identification.
6. Simple fact: Basic facts knowledge.

Instructional Procedure

1. Model critical feature of first knowledge chunk. ("Listen and watch, I'll tell you if the bottom number is more than the top number").
2. Check/test.
3. Link second knowledge chunk with first knowledge chunk ("Will I have to regroup?, How do I know?").
4. Check/test.

Correction Procedure: Use the first knowledge chunk as the basis for correction procedure ("Is the bottom number more than the top number?").

---

[1]Rule adapted from Silbert, Carnine and Stein (1981). *Direct instruction mathematics.*

TASK 10–9
Rapid Computation of Basic Facts Through Application of Commutative Law

Examples: $3 + 2 = 5$, $2 + 3 = 5$.

Knowledge Form: Rule relationship:
"When adding the same two numbers, changing the order of the numbers does not change the sum."

Component Skills

1. Discrimination of position.
2. Discrimination of operation: addition, subtraction.
3. Simple fact: Mastery of basic facts.
4. Concept: Knowledge of term *sum.*

Instructional Procedure

1. Model critical features of first knowledge chunk ("Listen and watch, I'll tell you if I am adding the same two numbers").
2. Test students on knowledge of first knowledge chunk.
3. Link second knowledge with first knowledge chunk ("Will the sums be the same? How do I know?").
4. Check/test.

Correction Procedure: Use first knowledge chunk as basis for correction procedure ("Are you adding the same two numbers? So what do you know about the sums?").

Mathematics Skills Classified as Cognitive Strategies

The fourth and final class of knowledge forms is cognitive strategies. Many of the skills in mathematics curricula are classified as cognitive strategies. Mastery of these strategies equips learners with skills that generalize to a wide range of mathematical problems. In the ensuing section, we identify selected mathematical cognitive strategies.

Knowledge Form	Example Skills
Cognitive strategy	Telling time
	Solving story problems
	Solving problems involving:

1. measurement
2. money
3. fractions
4. decimals

Complex operations involving multi-digit factors:

1. addition
2. subtraction
3. multiplication
4. division

Cognitive strategies in mathematics include the skill of telling time.

TASK 10–10
Addition of Multi-digit Numbers with Regrouping in More Than One Column

Examples

```
  695      453
+ 128    + 357
─────    ─────
  823      810
```

Knowledge Form: Cognitive strategy.

Component Skills

1. Rule relationship: "When more than one column requires regrouping, sums are regrouped consecutively."
2. Rule relationship: "When the sum of the numbers in a column is more than 9, you have to regroup."
3. Discrimination: Determine consecutively whether column totals require regrouping.
4. Discrimination: Identify the ones, tens, and hundreds columns.
5. Simple fact: Determine proper column alignment.
6. Simple fact: Basic fact knowledge.

Instructional Procedure

1. Review regrouping rule.
2. Model new rule relationship: "When more than one column requires regrouping, the columns are regrouped consecutively."
3. Lead students in this component only.
4. Test on this component only.
5. Complete problem solution.
6. Test on problem solution.
7. Practice on additional examples.
8. Review.

Correction Procedure: Determine whether error is related to knowledge of rule relationship, procedural error, or fact error.

DIVISION TASK 10–11
Dividing Multi-digit Dividends by Single-digit Divisors with Remainders

Example:
$$4\overline{)393} \quad 5\overline{)761}$$

Component Skills

1. Rule relationship: "If the remainder is larger than the divisor, use a larger number in the quotient."
2. Rule relationship: "When the divisor is larger than the first number in the dividend, use the first two numbers in the dividend."
3. Discrimination: One- or two-digit dividends.
4. Simple fact: Placement quotient in proper alignment with the dividend.
5. Simple fact: Mastery of basic division, multiplication, and subtraction facts.

Instructional Procedure

1. Review rule for determining whether to use one- or two-digit dividend.
2. Test knowledge of dividing two-digit dividends by one-digit divisors with no remainders.
3. Model new rule relationship: "If the remainder is larger than the divisor, use a larger number in the quotient."
4. Lead students in this component only.
5. Test on this component only.
6. Complete problem solution.
7. Test on problem solution.
8. Practice on additional examples.
9. Review.

Correction Procedure: Determine whether error is related to knowledge of rule relationship, procedural error, or fact error.

TASK 10–12
Word Problem Solving Involving Multiplication (Read or Listen to a Verbal Problem and Apply the Appropriate Arithmetic Operation to the Solution.)

Example: Vicki has 4 boxes of books to sell. Each box contains 12 books. How many books does she have to sell?

Knowledge Form: Cognitive strategy.

Component Skills

1. Rule relationship: "If you are adding the same number more than twice, you multiply."
2. Discrimination: Determine whether the story problem indicates that one of the quantities is dealt with repeatedly.
3. Discrimination: Determine which quantity of the solution is missing.
4. Concept: Comprehension of verbs related to comparison and classification.
5. Simple fact: Mastery of basic facts.

Instructional Procedure

1. Review rule for determining whether problem involves multiplication operation.
2. Identify factors to be used in problem solution.
3. Convert word problem to numeric equation.
4. Complete problem solution.

Correction Procedure

1. Determine whether error was due to component form error, fact error, or procedural error.
2. If error is due to component form error (e.g., rule relationship), model additional examples of that component form only.
3. If error is due to procedural error (i.e., difficulty in coordinating steps in strategy) reteach portion of sequence where procedure breaks down and reintegrate in entire sequence.
4. If problem is due to fact error, model fact and schedule fact practice.

Summary of Knowledge Form Analysis

Classifying mathematics skills by knowledge form involves more than assigning a label to a particular task. To classify a mathematics skill as a verbal association, concept, rule relationship, or cognitive strategy, a detailed analysis of the skill must be conducted where all the component forms in the skill are identified and sequenced in a format that communicates the information to be learned. As illustrated in the previous examples, the instructional design formats for some mathematics skills are relatively simple, consisting of only one component form. Others such as rule relationships and cognitive strategies are complex. Successful application of these complex routines is contingent on the learners' mastery of prerequisite knowledge forms and on their ability to recall, sequence, and implement all the necessary component forms in the instructional procedure.

Completing the instructional design.   Determining the knowledge form is a critical task for setting up the generic instructional set. Thus, we allocated considerable attention to determining the knowledge forms of mathematics skills in the previous section. In this portion of the chapter, we will complete our analysis of mathematics instruction by applying the remaining features of the generic instructional set. The four remaining guidelines include:

Step 2: Determining the range of examples.

Step 3: Sequencing examples.

Step 4: Selecting test examples.

Step 5: Designing and scheduling practice examples.

The critical features of these steps have been reviewed repeatedly in previous chapters. Therefore, our discussion of steps 2 through 5 concentrates on specific features and concerns of designing mathematics instruction.

Step 2: Determining the Range of Examples

Some mathematics skills have a restricted number of members in a set, while other skills seemingly have an infinite number of examples. To determine the range of examples of a task, we refer to the knowledge form of the task. The guidelines in Table 10–2 may be used for determining the range of examples in mathematics tasks:

With the exception of verbal associations, which have a restricted set of examples, an adequate range of examples must be provided to allow the learner to generalize the concept, rule, or strategy to untaught examples.

Step 3: Sequencing Examples

As with decoding examples, the visual similarity between examples can seriously complicate the learning of verbal associations such as mathematical symbols (e.g., $<$, $>$) and numerals (e.g., 6, 9). With simple facts, visually similar examples should be separated to avoid mislearning. However, when teaching concept acquisition, sequencing examples according to similarity and minimal differences serves a critical function. Examples that

TABLE 10–2
Guidelines to determine range of examples

Knowledge Form	Range of Examples
Verbal association	Narrow range
Concepts	Narrow to wide range depending on the concept
Rule relationships	Wide range, but depends on the learner's preskills
Cognitive strategies	Wide range, but depends on the learner's preskills

use similar rules or strategies should be sequenced in close proximity to demonstrate the generality of the rule or strategy. Consistent with other academic areas, mathematics tasks that are easy for the learner should be juxtaposed with more difficult tasks to provide opportunities for success. The following guidelines are offered for sequencing mathematics examples:

1. Separate visually or auditorily similar simple facts in introductory exercises; similar examples should be included in discrimination exercises after the learner is firm on each independent fact.
2. Strategically sequence sets of examples and nonexamples of concepts in juxtapositions where the differences become increasingly more subtle to convey distinctive features.
3. Cluster examples requiring the application of rule relationships or cognitive strategies to demonstrate the generalizability of the procedure.
4. Schedule easier examples early in the sequence. More difficult examples (e.g., problems involving multiple steps or operations, numbers with zeros, problems with extraneous information) should be introduced after the learner is proficient with easier examples.

Step 4: Selecting Test Examples

Test examples must assess the learner's ability to retain, discriminate, and transfer new information. For example, if subtraction of two-digit numbers has been the focus of recent instruction, test examples should assess the learner's performance on two-digit subtraction tasks as well as the retention of skills taught earlier in the instructional year. Too often, unit tests only assess knowledge of one recently introduced skill and fail to determine whether the learner is able to select the appropriate operation when two problem types are included. Finally, to ensure accurate diagnosis of the problem, examples selected for testing must parallel the format used in instructional conditions. Guidelines for designing test examples include the following:

1. Assess learner's knowledge of mathematics skill immediately after skill is introduced with similar problem formats.
2. Withhold inclusion of discrimination examples of similar simple facts until the learner demonstrates mastery of facts in isolation.
3. Include items that assess the newly introduced skill as well as those that measure previously introduced skills.
4. Design tests of concepts, rule relationships, and cognitive strategies in which at least half of the items assess generalization skills.

Step 5: Designing and Scheduling Practice Examples

A primary consideration when structuring practice exercises is selecting the examples according to the learner's mastery of prerequisite skills. As stated earlier, proficiency on a given math skill (e.g., telling time) often depends on prior mastery of other skills (e.g., counting by fives and counting from a number). Furthermore, tasks involving cognitive strategies and rules should not include basic facts on which the learner is not firm, nor should independent exercises include examples of tasks unless the learner demonstrated at least 80% accuracy in guided practice activities. These factors must be considered in the selection of examples for practice.

Initial practice exercises should be conducted under teacher-supervised conditions and scheduled frequently throughout the day and over the course of the week. As the learner becomes more facile with the skill, independent practice exercises may increase and the schedule of practice may be distributed over longer periods of time and for shorter time increments.

Finally, the knowledge of the task should be considered when scheduling practice activities. Basic facts are generally unmotivating. Thus, lengthy renditions of the fact practice can become quite punishing. Verbal association practice activities should be relatively brief in duration and distributed throughout the day. The third-grade teacher who carries multiplication flash cards in a pocket just in case the lunch line is moving slowly or there is a wait at the restroom is a judicious manager of practice time. Basic facts can be reviewed quickly and corrected easily and, therefore, are ideal tasks to fill in empty time slots. On the other hand, more intricate skills involving rule relationships and cognitive strategies are not as easily demonstrated or corrected and will need to be reserved for more structured contexts. Here are some guidelines for developing and scheduling practice examples:

1. Schedule multiple practice sessions of relatively brief duration (1–2 minutes for verbal associations; 3–5 minutes for rule relationships and cognitive strategies) for newly introduced skills.
2. Increase the length of practice sessions with the proficiency of the learner.
3. Introduce items as independent practice activities only after the learner exhibits 80% accuracy under supervised practice conditions.

Applying Instructional Design and Delivery Guidelines

In the remainder of this chapter, we demonstrate how the generic instructional set can be used as the framework for mathematics instruction for low-performing students. The instructional formats that follow incorporate the procedures of preteaching, framing, think time, signals, pacing, corrective feedback, and firming. Both the design and delivery components are developed within the before, during, and after phases of instruction to establish the rudimentary sequence of instructional decisions and activities that must be addressed in the prevention and remediation of mathematical learning problems.

INSTRUCTIONAL FORMATS FOR MATHEMATICS SKILLS

ADDITION TASK 10–13
Orally Producing Solutions to One-digit Plus One-digit Addition Facts

BEFORE INSTRUCTION

Task Status: New.

Target Skills: 2 + 2, 3 + 2, 4 + 2, 5 + 2, 6 + 2.

Preskills

1. Ability to recognize numerals.
2. Ability to identify and name plus and equals symbols.
3. Ability to follow left to right progression.

Instructional Design Guidelines

Knowledge Form: Discriminations and simple facts.

Range: 5 new +2 facts are being introduced. However, if the learner errs on any individual fact, no new facts will be introduced until the incorrect fact has been correctly identified on two successive trials.

Sequence: +2 facts are introduced in ascending order (see sequence that follows).

Test Examples

Introductory Set: 2 + 2, 3 + 2, 4 + 2, 5 + 2, 6 + 2.

Expanded Set: Same facts presented in random order.

Discrimination Examples: 2 + 1, 3 + 1, 4 + 1, 5 + 1, 6 + 1.

Sequence for Discrimination Set: 2 + 2, 3 + 2, 2 + 1, 4 + 2, 4 + 1, 5 + 1, 5 + 2, 6 + 2, 6 + 1, 4 + 1, 2 + 2.

Generalization Set: Application to written worksheets.

Practice Examples

1. All new facts.
2. All previous facts on which learner was not firm.
3. Juxtaposed review facts.

TASK 10–14

DURING INSTRUCTION

Instructional Delivery Guidelines

1. Presentation format: Model, lead, check/test.
2. Framing: Frame explicitly because the task is new.
3. Preteaching: On discrimination exercises, remind students that old and new facts are included.
4. Pacing: Tasks should be presented at moderate pace.

5. Think time: Because task is new, allow 3-second think time.
6. Signals: Facts are presented either on board or on flash cards. Teach student to respond when you touch under the fact.
7. Correction procedure: Model, lead, test.
8. Firming: Repeat the presentation of any facts that were in error immediately after correction. Firm any erred facts throughout lesson and at the end of session. Review all new information at end of lesson.

Teaching Procedure for +2 Addition Facts

Introductory Set

TEACHER: OK, everyone, I need your attention.
    Today, we're going to learn +2 facts.
    We will use these facts many times so it is important that we learn to answer these facts quickly and correctly.
    How do we need to answer these facts? (Calls on individual student.)
ALEXANDER: Quickly and correctly.
TEACHER: Nice listening, Alexander.
    Now I need your eyes on the board.
    First I'll read the problem (places hand under problem), then I'll say the answer (touches where the answer will be). Remember, first I'll read the problem, then I'll say the answer. I'll say the answer when I touch under the problem. When will I say the answer? (Calls on individual student.)
PENNY: When you touch under the problem.
TEACHER: Right, I'll say the answer when I touch under the problem.
    Listen and watch carefully. My turn to answer this problem.

(MODEL)

TEACHER (presents $2 + 2 = \Box$ problem on board):
    $2 + 2 =$ how many? (Teacher touches under first part of the problem, waits 2–3 seconds, and touches under box.) 4.
    (Teacher writes the answer in the box, then erases it.)
    $2 + 2 = \boxed{4}$. (Repeats.)
    Your turn to do it with me.

(LEAD)

TEACHER AND STUDENTS: $2 + 2 = \Box$ (waits 3 seconds, signals) 4.
TEACHER: Again, all together.
TEACHER AND STUDENTS: $2 + 2 = \Box$ (waits 3 seconds, signals) 4.

(CHECK/TEST)

TEACHER: Now by yourselves. Get ready.
    (Teacher uses hand to pace problem presentation.)
STUDENTS: $2 + 2 = \boxed{4}$.

(INDIVIDUAL TEST OF STUDENTS)

TEACHER: Great answering, class. Sharon, your turn to answer by yourself.

SHARON: 2 + 2 = $\boxed{4}$.

TEACHER: Exactly, Sharon, 2 + 2 = $\boxed{4}$. (Calls on other individuals who need additional practice.)

LYLE: 2 + 2 = $\square$ (hesitates, doesn't respond).

(CORRECTION PROCEDURE)

TEACHER: 2 + 2 = $\boxed{4}$.
    Together, everyone.
    2 + 2 = $\boxed{4}$.
    Now by yourself, Lyle.

LYLE: 2 + 2 = $\boxed{4}$.

TEACHER: Wonderful, that's exactly right, 2 + 2 = 4.

Expanded Set: Introduce next member of +2 set. Cumulatively review all members of set introduced after the presentation of each new fact.

Cumulative Test:

1. Assess knowledge of +2 facts in ascending sequence.
2. Assess knowledge of +2 facts in random sequence.

Discrimination Teaching Sequence: +2 and +1 facts are presented on chalkboard in random order—see discrimination sequence.)

TEACHER: OK, class, some of these problems are the new +2 facts, others are facts we've learned earlier. Pay close attention, because some of them look alike. (Teacher points to 2 + 2 fact.) Everyone, when I touch, read the first part of the problem, then wait for my signal to answer. Ready?
    (Teacher proceeds through randomly ordered problems.)

TASK 10–15

AFTER INSTRUCTION

Analyze Errors and Make Instructional Modifications

1. Were students able to correctly answer all five new facts? If not, reduce the number of new facts presented in the next instructional set.
2. Were students' answers correct but not within the 3-second period? If so, schedule frequent firming periods throughout the day.
3. Were there specific facts that were consistently missed? Did the error occur in introductory sessions? If so, include that fact in the new instructional set.
4. Did the introduction of the discrimination problems increase the number of errors? If so, firm introductory set and then present the discrimination set again.

Instructional Format for the Commutative Property of Multiplication

---

TASK 10-16
When Multiplying the Same Numbers, Changing the Order of the Numbers Does Not Change the Product

---

BEFORE INSTRUCTION

Task Status: New.

Example Target Skills: $5 \times 2 = 10, 2 \times 5 = 10$.

Preskills

1. Concept of order.
2. Simple fact of product.
3. Numeral recognition.
4. Symbol discrimination ($\times$, $\div$).
5. Knowledge of first multiplication fact in each fact pair.
6. Discriminating whether two numbers are same.

Teacher Wording

"The answer to this fact is the same. How do I know? Because when you multiply the same numbers, changing the order of the numbers does not change the product."

Instructional Design Guidelines

Range
Limited only by the number of basic facts familiar to the learner. First fact in fact pair should be known; second fact has not been introduced. Include a range of facts with different multiplicands.

Sequence
1. Separate facts that are potentially confusing for the learner.
2. Introduce rule in context of easy, familiar facts.
3. Juxtapose positive (multiplication; same factor problem) and negative examples (division facts; different factor problems).
4. Introduce facts to parallel order of introduction in multiplication sequence.

Test Examples
Introductory set: $5 \times 2, 2 \times 5, 5 \times 3, 3 \times 5, 5 \times 4, 4 \times 5$.
Expanded set: Additional examples of known facts.
Discrimination set: Any new multiplication facts known by the learner. Juxtapose division facts using the same numerals.

$$3 \times 4, 4 \times 3$$
$$5 \times 3, 3 \times 5$$

$$4 \times 2, 4 \div 2$$
$$5 \times 2, 2 \times 5$$
$$4 \times 2, 2 \times 4$$
$$6 \div 2, 6 \div 3$$

Practice Examples:
1. All examples incorrectly identified in test examples.
2. Additional examples not taught in the introductory set.

TASK 10–17

DURING INSTRUCTION

Instructional Delivery Guidelines

1. Framing: Stress need to attend to operation sign and numbers in the problem.
2. Pacing and think time: Correct answer only requires discrimination of operation symbol and numbers; therefore, maintain a moderate pace. Allow a maximum of 3 seconds once task is presented.
3. Signals: Use group responses since answer to task is consistent across examples (same or not the same).
4. Corrections: Use rule relationship to correct errors. Restate rule, than ask about pivotal concept, "Are you multiplying the same numbers? So what do you know about the product?" If error persists, reteach rule relationship beginning with the first example.
5. Firming: Because mastery of this rule will reduce the total number of basic facts that need to be taught, the rule should be reviewed and practiced with the introduction of new multiplication facts.

Teaching Format for Commutative Property of Multiplication

Framing
TEACHER: OK, it's time to get started. I need everyone's attention.
Today we're gong to learn a rule about multiplication facts.
What are we going to learn?
EDWINA: A rule about multiplication.
TEACHER: That's right, the rule is about multiplication. This rule is about the order of numbers in the multiplication problem. What is the rule about?
EDWINA: The rule is about the order of numbers in the multiplication problem.
TEACHER: Very good. The rule is about the order of numbers in the multiplication problem. The facts look a lot alike, so it's very important that you look carefully at the problems on the board.

TEACHER: Listen to the rule about multiplication problems. When you multiply the same numbers, changing the order of the numbers does not change the product. Listen again. When you multiply the same numbers, changing the order of numbers does not change the product.

Examples	Teacher Wording	Student Response
1. $5 \times 2 = 10$	Get ready to answer the fact. (Signals.)	(Answers fact.)
5×2 2×5	Look at these problems. I'm going to tell you if products are the same or not the same.	(Attends.)
	The products are the same. How do I know? Because I am multiplying the same numbers. We know that $5 \times 2 = 10$.	
$2 \times 5 =$	Get ready to tell me the answer for this fact. (Signals.)	10.
2. $5 \times 3 =$	Get ready to answer the fact. (Signals.) That's right, $5 \times 3 = 15$.	15.
5×3 3×5	Look at these facts. I'm going to tell you if answers are the same or not the same.	(Attends.)
	The answers are the same. How do I know? Because I am multiplying the same numbers.	
$3 \times 5 =$	Get ready to tell me the answer. (Signals.)	15.
3. $6 \div 2 =$	Get ready to answer the fact. (Signals.) That's right, $6 \div 2 = 3$.	3.
$6 \div 2$ $2 \div 6$	Look at these facts. I'm going to tell you if answers are the same or not the same.	(Attends.)
	The answers are not the same. How do I know? Because I am not multiplying the numbers. I am dividing.	
4. $5 \times 4 =$	Get ready to answer the fact. (Signals.) That's right, $5 \times 4 = 20$.	20.
5. 5×4 2×4	Look at these facts. I'm going to tell you if answers are the same or not the same.	(Attends.)
	The answers are not the same. How do I know? Because I am not multiplying the same numbers.	

Model an additional example where two numbers are not the same and where two operations ($\times$, $\div$) are not the same.

Text Examples

6. 5×4 4×5	Here are two facts. It's your turn. Tell me if the answers are the same or not the same. (Signals for group response.)	The same.
	How do you know?	Because you are multiplying the same numbers.

Continue with additional positive and negative examples. Negative examples may differ according to two features: (1) multiplication or division operation and (2) whether the two numbers are the same. For low performers, it may be necessary to create two teaching sequences: one where students are taught to discriminate between multiplication and division symbols and another where students focus on the attribute of using the same numbers.

Correction Procedure: Use same example, identifying observed component of the rule, "We are multiplying the same numbers. So what do we know about the answers to the facts?" If error persists, repeat first example.

Generalization Tasks: Extend application of rule to additional problems.

TASK 10–18

AFTER INSTRUCTION

Analyze Errors and Make Instructional Modifications

1. Determine whether errors were due to component part, procedural, or fact errors.
2. Component part errors: Teach separate pieces of rule, "Are the same numbers being multiplied?" Distinguish if error is due to operation, discrimination error, or same number discrimination error. If learner is not firm on component parts, schedule separate teacher sequences for these components.
3. Procedural errors: Model additional examples, highlighting sequence of procedures.
4. Fact errors: Fact errors can be detected early in the sequence; therefore, if the learner is not firm on the fact, introduce another fact on which the learner is firm and provide additional practice on erred fact at another time.

Instructional Format for Solving Classification Word Problems Involving Addition or Subtraction

WORD PROBLEM-SOLVING TASK 10–19
Classification Word Problem Solving Involving Addition or Subtraction

BEFORE INSTRUCTION

Task Status: New.

Knowledge Form: Cognitive strategy.

Example Problems

1. Jill has 2 dolls and 3 cars.
   How many toys does she have?
2. Mrs. Griffin has 6 children; 4 are girls.
   How many are boys?
3. Ed ate 2 doughnuts in the morning and 3 cupcakes in the afternoon.
   How many pieces of food did he eat in all?

Preskills

1. Knowledge of addition and subtraction basic facts.
2. Fact family knowledge.
3. Vocabulary knowledge.
4. Knowledge of rule relationship: "When the total number is given, you subtract."
5. Knowledge of rule relationship: "When the total number is not given, you add."
6. Concept knowledge of addition and subtraction.
7. Ability to write mathematical equations.
8. Language classification skills.

Instructional Design Guidelines

Range
1. Problems should only contain operations involving known facts and fact family relationships.
2. Both addition and subtraction problems should be included in sequences.
3. Problems should include a variety of classifications to demonstrate generality of strategy.
4. Initial problems should contain only one operation.
5. Examples should be within learner's independent reading level.
6. Terminology within word problems should be familiar to learner.
7. Syntactic format of problem should be simple. Avoid using passive voice and negation.
8. Introductory problems should contain minimal amounts of distracting or extraneous information.

Sequence
1. Word problems may be introduced once the learner is firm on basic facts in problem.
2. Problems involving small numbers should be introduced prior to problems using large numbers.
3. Addition and subtraction problems should be juxtaposed.

Test Examples
1. Initial test items should assess students' acquisition of strategy.
2. Generalization items should be restricted to classes and fact family relationships known to learner.

Practice Activities
Word problem solving is a complex cognitive activity; therefore, extensive and frequent guided practice periods will need to be scheduled prior to independent practice activities.

TASK 10–20

DURING INSTRUCTION

Instructional Delivery Guidelines

1. Framing: An explicit framing procedure will be needed because students must attend to multiple factors.
2. Preteaching: Students will need to be cued to attend to the discriminations required in determining the type of operation to perform.
3. Pacing: The pace of initial instructional exercises will be slow because of the number of components involved in problem solution.
4. Think time: Allow sufficient think time to process all steps in strategy.
5. Signals: Signals can be used to prompt component part as well as solution responses.
6. Corrections: There are many possible sources of errors in cognitive strategies. These error types may be classified as fact errors, component skill errors, or procedural errors. Use the strategy as the source of the correction. Determine where the solution breaks down and reteach that component. Next, reintegrate that component within strategic sequence. (See more explicit correction procedures in after instruction component.)

Framing Format for Classification of Word Problem Solutions

TEACHER: OK, everyone, let's get started. Today, we're going to learn how to solve word problems. What kind of problems are we going to solve? (Signals for group response.)

STUDENTS: Word problems.

TEACHER: Right, word problems. Word problems are different from the other kinds of problems because they use words and numbers.

TEACHER: What two things do word problems use?

STUDENTS: Word and numbers.

TEACHER: Right. Words and numbers. In word problems, first you have to figure out what the number problem is. Remember that in word problems, first you have to figure out what the number problem is.

What is the first thing you need to figure out? (Calls on individual student.)

KEVIN: What the problem is.

TEACHER: Very nice. First you figure out what the number problem is.

The following instructional format for teaching classification word problem solving skills (Figure 10–3) is from Silbert, Carnine, and Stein (1981, 265–267). In this approach to verbal math problem solving, the sequence of instructional activities is (1) to teach students to use the fact family preskill to determine the missing number in the fact family, and (2) to apply the fact family strategy to more complex addition and subtraction story problems. Students have been previously taught the fact family strategy. In the following sequence, the strategy for teaching language classification skills is taught. Finally, fact family and classification knowledge are integrated in the strategy for solving story problems.

Day	Task 10–21 Language Training Problems	Task 10–22 Structured Board Problems	Task 10–23 Structured Worksheet Problems	Task 10–24 Less Structured Worksheet Problems
1-3	4-6			
4-6		6		
7-10			6	4
11-13				8
14-accurate				6-8

Task 10–21: Language Training

TEACHER	STUDENTS
1. "I'LL SAY A BIG CLASS, PEOPLE. TELL ME SMALL GROUPS IN THAT CLASS OF PEOPLE." Call on individual students. Accept reasonable answers: boys, girls, children, men, women, etc.	
2. Repeat step 1 with vehicles, tools, animals, containers.	
3. "I'LL SAY TWO SMALL GROUPS. YOU SAY WHAT WE WOULD CALL THE BIG GROUP IF WE PUT THE SMALL GROUPS TOGETHER. MEN, WOMEN. WHAT WOULD WE CALL THE BIG GROUP?" Repeat step 3 with: cup, glass; trucks, cars; lions, tigers; roses, tulips	"People"
4. "I'LL SAY SOME GROUPS. YOU TELL ME THE BIGGEST GROUP. LISTEN. CATS, ANIMALS, DOGS. WHAT IS THE BIGGEST GROUP?" Repeat step 4 with hammer, saw, tool; vehicle, car, truck; men, women, people; children, girls, boys.	"Animals"

Task 10—22:   Structured Board Presentation

1. "IF THE BIG NUMBER IS GIVEN, WHAT DO YOU DO?"	"Subtract"
"IF THE BIG NUMBER IS NOT GIVEN, WHAT DO YOU DO?"	"Add"
2. "LISTEN: THERE ARE 8 CHILDREN; 3 ARE BOYS. HOW MANY ARE GIRLS? LISTEN AGAIN." Repeat story. "THE PROBLEM TALKS ABOUT CHILDREN, BOYS AND GIRLS. WHICH IS THE BIG GROUP, CHILDREN, BOYS OR GIRLS?"	"Children"
"CHILDREN IS THE BIG GROUP. I WRITE CHILDREN OVER THE BIG BOX."	

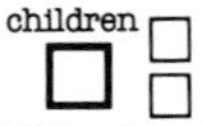

children ☐
☐ ☐

3. "LISTEN." Repeat problem. "CHILDREN IS THE BIG GROUP. DOES THE PROBLEM TELL HOW MANY CHILDREN?"	"Yes"
"SO THE BIG NUMBER IS GIVEN. WHAT IS THE BIG NUMBER?"	"8"
Write 8 in big box:	

children ☐
8 ☐

FIGURE 10–3

Format for teaching classification word problems

4. "THE BIG NUMBER IS GIVEN. SO WHAT DO YOU
DO TO WORK THE PROBLEM?"   "Subtract"
"I START WITH 8 CHILDREN AND SUBTRACT 3
BOYS TO FIND HOW MANY GIRLS." Write 8 - 3.
"TELL ME THE ANSWER." Pause, signal.   "5"
"YES, IF THERE ARE 8 CHILDREN AND 3 OF THE
CHILDREN ARE BOYS, HOW MANY ARE GIRLS?"   "5"
Repeat steps 1 - 4 with five more problems.

Task 10–23:   Structured Worksheet

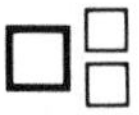

a. Jill has 5 hammers and 4 saws.
How many tools does she have?

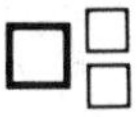

b. Bill has 7 friends; 2 of the friends are girls.
How many of the friends are boys?

1. "IF THE BIG NUMBER IS GIVEN, WHAT DO YOU DO?"   "Subtract"
"IF THE BIG NUMBER IS NOT GIVEN, WHAT DO YOU DO?"   "Add"

2. "READ PROBLEM a."

3. "WHAT IS THE BIG GROUP, HAMMERS, SAWS, OR
TOOLS?"   "Tools"
"WRITE TOOLS OVER THE BIG BOX."   Students write tools over big box.

4. "NOW READ THE PROBLEM TO YOURSELVES AND
GET READY TO TELL ME IF THE BIG NUMBER IS GIVEN.
(pause) IS THE BIG NUMBER GIVEN OR NOT GIVEN?"   "Not given"

TO CORRECT: "WHAT IS THE BIG GROUP? DOES THE
PROBLEM TELL HOW MANY TOOLS?"

"WRITE N.G. IN THE BIG BOX."   Students write n.g. in big box.

5. "THE BIG NUMBER IS NOT GIVEN SO HOW DO YOU
WORK THE PROBLEM?"   "Add"
"SAY THE PROBLEM YOU ARE GOING TO WRITE."   "5 + 4"

6. "WRITE THE PROBLEM AND WORK IT." Pause.

7. "HOW MANY TOOLS?"   "9"
"YES, IF SHE HAS 5 HAMMERS AND 4 SAWS, SHE HAS
9 TOOLS IN ALL. WRITE 9 TOOLS."

Repeat steps 1 - 7 with remaining problems.

Task 10–24:   Less-structured Worksheet
Give students worksheet as in Part C.

1. "TOUCH PROBLEM a."

2. "READ THE PROBLEM."

3. "WHAT IS THE NAME OF THE BIG GROUP?" Pause,
signal. "WRITE THAT OVER THE BIG BOX."

TO CORRECT: "IS THE BIG GROUP DOGS, CATS, OR
PETS? YES, PETS."

4. "IS THE BIG NUMBER GIVEN OR NOT GIVEN?"
Pause, signal.

TO CORRECT: "WHAT IS THE BIG GROUP? DOES
THE PROBLEM TELL HOW MANY?"

"WHAT DO YOU WRITE IN THE BIG BOX? WRITE
IT."

5. "WHAT TYPE OF PROBLEM IS IT?"

6. "WRITE THE EQUATION AND WORK IT."

FIGURE 10–3
Continued

From *Direct instruction mathematics* (pp. 265–267) by J. Silbert, D. Carnine, and M. Stein, 1981. Columbus, OH: Merrill Publishing Company. Copyright 1981 by Merrill Publishing Company. Adapted by permission.

TASK 10–25

AFTER INSTRUCTION

Analyze Errors and Make Instructional Modifications

As discussed previously, cognitive strategies involve the systematic application and organization of multiple facts, discriminations, concepts, and rule relationships. Sources of word problem failure may reside in any of the following components.

Possible Fact Errors

1. Unfamiliar mathematics facts.
2. Unfamiliar words in problem.

Correction Procedure: Model fact and provide practice. Preteach difficult vocabulary.

Possible Component Skill Errors

Rule application error. "If the total number is given you subtract. If the total number is not given you add."

Correction Procedure: Reteach rule in context of easy problem. Model additional examples and schedule several guided practice examples.

Possible Procedural Error

Learner skips steps in strategy or fails to implement steps in proper sequence.

Correction Procedure: Chunk instruction into smaller segments. Cumulatively review each step with the addition of each new chunk.

In this section, we illustrated the application of the generic instructional design and delivery procedures to selected mathematics skills. In these exercises only the skill was specified. The instructional designer was required to survey the features of the skill and to structure instructional wording, examples, and sequences that communicate the necessary information. Teacher-generated instructional sequences are clearly the most labor-intensive exercises. Although tailoring instructional sequences and presentations may require a great deal of a teacher's time and may seem tedious, the effort allows for control over critical instructional variables. Left unattended, those variables often contribute to learning failure. In the following section, procedures for designing new math programs and modifying existing curricula according to critical instructional variables are reviewed.

CURRICULUM-BASED DEFICIENCIES AND PREDICTABLE PROBLEMS OF STUDENTS WITH ACADEMIC LEARNING PROBLEMS

Students with learning difficulties have predictable problems with some skills in the instructional hierarchies. As discussed in previous chapters, low-achieving students are often casualties of curricula that assume too much and teach too little. Difficulties are related to the learners' fragile preskills and the subsequent failure of the curriculum to explicitly address those skills. Figure 10–4 diagrams the four major skill domains in which low-performing students are apt to require carefully planned and sequenced instruction. In the next section, we will discuss some of the predictable learning problems from each skill domain.

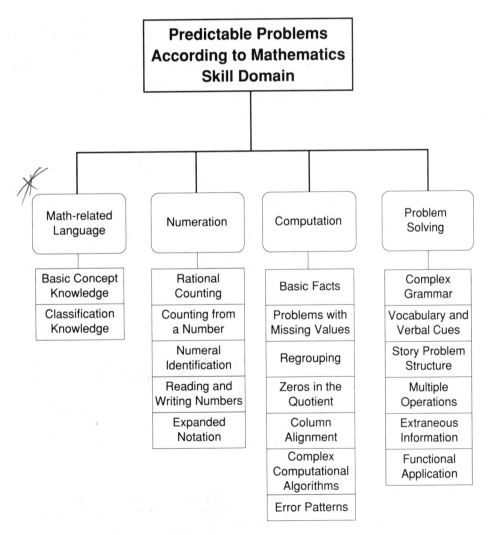

FIGURE 10–4
Predictable problems in mathematics skill domains

Math-related Language

Language skills are just as important to the mastery of mathematical skills as they are to the mastery of reading, listening, writing or speaking skills. It is, however, unusual to encounter a commercial math program that deals extensively with the development of math-related vocabulary. Most programs merely provide passing attention to concepts such as *equality, before, after,* and *every.* Many students will acquire adequate comprehension of the math-related language skills from the activities provided in their language arts and math curricula, but low-achieving students need direct and extensive training in language concepts.

Basic Concepts

Many of the concepts discussed in Chapter 6 are applicable to mathematics. For example, the positional concepts of *first, second,* and *third, left* and *right,* and *top* and *bottom* are critical prerequisites to place value instruction and multi-digit computations. Quantitative concepts such as *all, greater than, less than, more,* and *equal* are fundamental to many mathematics tasks. Rather than risking failure by assuming that students understand these basic concepts, teachers should directly teach and test the acquisition of these concepts before their application.

Classifications

Immature students and students with learning difficulties frequently have trouble combining sets of objects that are related by a subordinate/superordinate relationship. For example, when confronted with a problem such as, "Mary has 5 gerbils and 2 kittens. How many pets does she have?" some children will have difficulties combining the two subordinate classes of pets (gerbils and kittens) into the superordinate classification (pets). Research on children's difficulties in solving story problems (Kilpatrick, 1969, 1978) suggests that explicit attention should be given to the teaching of classifications. With immature learners, it may be necessary to allocate extra time to the instruction of language comprehension skills.

Numeration

The domain of numeration skills includes counting and numeral identification. Although more mature and capable students learn both types of numeration skills swiftly, naive learners frequently have difficulties. Research on the difficulties that learners with handicaps have mastering these skills indicates that counting and symbol recognition should be taught as separate skills (Spradlin, Cotter, Stevens, & Friedman, 1974). Instruction will be most efficient if the tasks are not carelessly intermingled.

Rational Counting

Students with learning handicaps may experience difficulties learning rational counting skills. These difficulties can be addressed through the design of instruction. For example, there is a tendency to offer instruction in rational counting (i.e., the counting of objects) before rudimentary skills in rote counting (i.e., saying the names of numbers in sequence without reference to objects) have been developed. Silbert, Carnine, and Stein (1981) suggest that instruction in rational counting should begin after the student is able to rote count from 1 to 10.

A common problem of students is that they may fail to count an object in a set, or they might count an object more than once. In part, the prevention of this problem should involve initial arrangements of the objects into arrays to limit confusion. For example, two arrays of the same number of objects are shown in Figure 10–5. Students who are learning to count are likely to be more accurate counting the objects in array A than in array B. The arrangement of the objects in A is less confusing. It may also be helpful for the student to learn to move each object out of the array as it is counted. The teacher should model the counting procedure and, if necessary, the movement of the objects. In some cases, it may be necessary to physically guide some students through the association of objects and numerical labels.

A common recommendation of curriculum designers is to provide students with a great deal of practice in counting "manipulatives" or real objects (e.g., Reidesel, 1985). While the use of manipulatives frequently facilitates learning in the early stages of acquisition, it may be inadvisable to use them beyond the point at which they make demonstrable improvements to the student's comprehension and accuracy of counting (Carpenter & Moser, 1984; De Corte, Verschaffel & De Win, 1985; Spradlin et al., 1974).

Counting from a Number

Rational counting from a number is an important preskill for computations, telling time, and measurement. It is impractical to expect students to carry around a pocket full of manipulatives or a paper and pencil. They will, however, have their fingers to count in the event that they need to perform a computation problem and have either forgotten or not adequately learned a basic fact. Performing computations by counting fingers from a large number is more efficient than if the student counts up from one (Silbert, Carnine, & Stein, 1981). To count up from a larger number a student (1) begins by holding out the same number of fingers as indicated by the smaller number, (2) says the larger number, and then (3) counts off the extended fingers and stops. A frequent mistake is made by saying the large number while counting a finger, which results in a consistent error of one less than the correct answer.

FIGURE 10–5
Arrays of objects and accurate counting

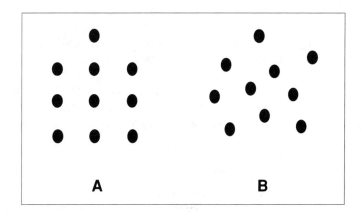

A   B

Numeral Identification

Virtually every teacher has observed the confusion that many students experience distinguishing between *b* and *d*. In numeral identification there is a similar problem with the discrimination between 6 and 9. Silbert, Carnine, & Stein (1981) suggest avoiding this problem not by teaching numeral recognition in ordinal sequence (i.e., 1, 2, 3, ... 8, 9, 10). Instruction for the discrimination between numerals 6 and 9 should not be attempted until the student can recognize five or six intervening numerals (e.g., 1, 5, 8, 2, 4, 7).

Reading and Writing Numbers 11–19

The writing of the teen numbers can also result in a predictable error pattern. The student who says 35 and writes the numbers 3 and 5 can apply the same strategy to any number from 20 to 99 and write the numeral correctly. Applying that strategy to the writing of teen numbers will produce a set of errors. For example, if told to write the number 15 some students will say "fif" (and write 5) "teen" (and write 1). The student must memorize these exceptions just as they must memorize irregular words. To make that memorization as efficient as possible, the teacher should use the model-lead-check/test procedure.

Expanded Notation

Writing and reading a number in expanded notation (e.g., 437 = 400 + 30 + 7) facilitates the processes of carrying and regrouping in computational algorithms. Because computational algorithms can be mechanical, we recommend that the task of writing and reading multi-digit numbers in expanded notation be directly taught before it is taught in computational problems requiring regrouping or carrying.

Computation

Much classroom time is devoted to teaching students to add, subtract, multiply, and divide, and justifiably so. During their school careers, students are expected to calculate many arithmetic computations accurately and rapidly. Computation is, however, an abstract endeavor. Practice on applications and problem-solving activities may facilitate comprehension of the abstract operations, but infusing large doses of application and problem-solving activities into math curricula will not be sufficient to overcome the difficulties that low performers have in developing computational fluency. Merely drilling the students on computations is not an efficient use of instructional time either; the proper design of the drill can significantly impact computational accuracy and fluency. The rate at which students develop fluent computational skills can be substantially influenced by (1) teaching the relationships between basic facts and operations, (2) strategically separating commonly confused facts, and (3) frequently firming and practicing fragile skills.

Basic Facts

Some children learn the relationships between basic facts without a great deal of instruction. Children with learning difficulties generally do not learn fact relationships on their own (Myers & Thorton, 1977; Rathmell, 1978; Thorton, 1978). For example, Carpenter & Moser (1984) note that by mid-third grade almost 20% of the students do not use their knowledge of basic facts to solve addition problems, if manipulatives are available. Instead they use counting strategies—including the primitive strategy of counting up from one. Slightly more than 20% of the third-grade students still rely on counting strategies to solve subtraction facts. The most optimistic view of the Carpenter and Moser finding is that there are substantial increases at each grade in the numbers of students who memorize the basic facts, but it is unacceptable to have such a large proportion of mid-third graders still lacking proficiency in basic addition and subtraction facts. Analysis of the relationships between basic facts and operations should be used to guide the selection and presentation of basic facts.

The learning and retention of basic facts is facilitated by teaching computations according to their relationships to each other, instead of according to the sizes of their factors (Cook & Dossey, 1982; Steinberg, 1985; Thorton, 1978). Sequencing facts according to their relationships to each other reduces the number of facts that must be learned through sheer memorization. Thus, sequencing the instruction of basic facts by relationships (e.g., for addition: doubles series $2 + 2, 3 + 3, 4 + 4$; plus one facts $4 + 1, 5 + 1$; doubles plus one $6 + 7, 4 + 5$; and reciprocals) is superior to factor size sequences (e.g., plus one facts, plus two facts, plus three facts). Given the easily defined relationships among basic facts and the superiority of presentations based on relationships between facts, it is difficult to understand why publishers of math curricula arrange their basic facts instruction according to factor sizes. Teaching rules, principles, and relationships for basic fact mastery will result in greater efficiency of learning, and is thus worth the extra attention required for instructional design (Baroody, 1984).

Problems with Missing Values

The tasks of learning the relationships between operations (e.g., $5 + 3 = 8$; $8 - 3 = 5$) and the solution of problems with missing values (e.g., $5 + \underline{\hspace{1cm}} = 8$, or $\underline{\hspace{1cm}} - 3 = 5$) are related and should be dealt with directly. Because knowledge of reciprocal relationships in inverse operations will contribute to the understanding of the computational mastery, we suggest that it be directly addressed in instruction.

One approach to illustrating the inverse relationships of operations is through instruction on fact families (e.g., $5 + 4 = 9, 4 + 5 = 9, 9 - 4 = 5, 9 - 5 = 4$) and problems with missing values (e.g., $4 + \underline{\hspace{1cm}} = 9$). Hiebert (1982) found that both the type and location of the missing quantity were related to the difficulty of the problem. Missing factor problems were harder to solve than problems with missing answers. Problems with the answer positioned to the extreme left were harder to solve than problems with the answer on the right side. Teachers could minimize the difficulties associated with variations in problem orientation and location of the missing values if they based their instruction on sequences of examples that had missing values and solution quantities equally distributed across positions and problem orientations (Hiebert, 1982).

One approach for the presentation of the concept of inverse operations is illustrated in Figure 10–6. In that method, the instructor presents a set of cards with the numbers and operation signs of a fact family printed on them. A blank card is used to indicate the missing value. The quantities and operation symbols are then manipulated before the students. This dynamic presentation of the relationships between operations may be more efficient than the static juxtapositions (cf. Carnine, 1980b).

Regrouping

Several points need to be considered when teaching low-achieving students to solve problems involving regrouping. First, after the process of regrouping has been learned, students should be required to solve mixed sets of problems, some of which require regrouping and others that do not. If low-achieving students are not given opportunities to practice discriminating between regrouping and non-regrouping problems, they are apt to make the common mistake of applying regrouping in problems that do not require it.

A second consideration is that zeros in one of the factors will present difficulties for some students. Special attention in the selection and presentation of examples may be required. Consider the following problems:

1.	504	2.	400	3.	30
	−247		−346		×28

The zeros in subtraction problems will contribute to errors for two reasons. First, for problems like example 1, naive students will likely have difficulties because it appears that in regrouping they will be reducing a zero in the tens place to nine. To them, that maneuver is contra-intuitive. For problems like example 2, students' difficulties are

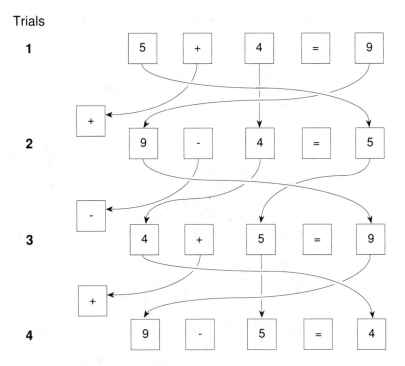

FIGURE 10–6
Dynamic presentation of a fact family

compounded because the process of regrouping with zeros must be done in sequence and all of the values in the minuend will be affected. Regrouping multi-digit multiplication problems with zeros, such as example 3, is apt to contribute to errors in the alignment of values in the sub-products.

Regrouping errors in problems that contain zeros in the factors are both frequent and predictable. The following two steps will reduce the probability of many of the errors. First, present problems with zeros after the student has demonstrated proficiency in regrouping without zeros (Silbert, Carnine, & Stein, 1981). When the student demonstrates proficiency with each problem type independently, the problems with zeros will be integrated with problems that do not contain zeros in the factors. Teachers who use basal math programs as the basis for their math curricula should be particularly cautious when introducing this skill. Many commercial math programs do not systematically approach the task of teaching problems that contain zeros. Second, rename several columns at once before computing the answers for each column of a multi-digit subtraction problem (Cacha, 1975).

Zeros in the Quotient

Many students will encounter difficulty when confronted with division problems where there is a zero in the quotient (e.g., $5\overline{)4535}$). Students are likely to omit the zero in the quotient and thus report a quotient of 97 instead of 907. It is possible to avoid unnecessary difficulties in division. The introduction of problems with zeros in the quotients should be delayed until students have developed facility with problems that do not contain zeros. The teacher should then provide specific instruction on the use of zero as a place holder.

Column Alignment

Students with learning difficulties frequently misalign columns and consequently make errors. This problem frequently occurs when students are presented complex computations such as 7 + 34. Some students will align from the left $\begin{array}{r} 34 \\ +7 \\ \hline \end{array}$ instead of from the right $\begin{array}{r} 34 \\ +\ 7 \\ \hline \end{array}$ and thus make an error. Errors in column alignment indicate that the student has not mastered place value concepts. Additional training in writing problems in expanded notation will help remediate the problem. A plan to remedy errors in alignment should also include exercises in writing vertical equations. Silbert, Carnine, & Stein (1981) recommend having the student write the larger number first and then use that numeral to align the other numbers in the problem.

Complex Computational Algorithms

The task of learning to compute problems when factors contain different numbers of digits (e.g., 478 × 57; 48 + 5; or 621 − 72) is an important step in any of the four basic operations. It is particularly important to teach the computation of complex addition facts. Addition of two-by-one digit facts is a preskill for long-column addition. Low-achieving students frequently will need specific training on those facts before introducing long-column addition problems.

Error Patterns

Low-achieving students rarely respond at random to computational arithmetic problems. Their error patterns may be obscure, but they are generally not random. Roberts (1968) analyzed many of the common, as well as rare, errors that students make in computational math. He identified four categories of errors. First, some errors are the result of applying the wrong operation to the solution. In some cases the wrong operation will be applied to only part of the problem. For example, a student may report that $457 \times 40 = 1807$. The error is a result of subtracting 0 from 7 and then multiplying 45 by 4. A second error pattern is the obvious computational error. Roberts refers to the third category of error patterns as the defective algorithm. Errors in regrouping or column alignment are examples of defective algorithm (or procedural) errors. It may, at first, appear that the student has made a computational or fact error, but the error is really due to failure to follow through on the necessary steps of the algorithm. The fourth category of computational errors, the random response, is rarely encountered.

Problem Solving

The fourth category of skills in mathematics curricula is problem-solving. One of the most persistent problems in mathematics instruction is that many students do not learn to apply their computational skills in verbal problem-solving situations (Ashlock & Herman, 1970; Carpenter, Matthews, Lindquist, & Silver, 1984; Kameenui & Griffin, 1989; Silver & Thompson, 1984). In this section, we review some of the variables identified in a growing body of literature that indicates the direct and systematic manipulation of several variables of instructional design will improve word problem-solving performance.

Verbal math problem-solving tasks require the student to correctly determine the appropriate operation or operations for the solution. Five variables that affect the student's ability to identify the correct operation are (1) complex grammar, (2) vocabulary and verbal cues, (3) story problem structure, (4) multiple operations, and (5) extraneous information. With so many variables to consider, designing an instructional sequence for problem solving can become complex. The complexity of problem-solving is inadequately dealt with in many published curricula; therefore, teachers will have to take a greater role in the development and tailoring of instructional activities.

Complex Grammar

Whether the student has to acquire information by reading the problem (Wheeler & McNutt, 1983) or by listening to oral presentations of the problems (Larsen, Parker, & Trenholme, 1978), it is clear that problems with simple sentence structures are the easiest to comprehend. Problems with complex interrogative sentences or compound sentences are the most difficult. Simplifying the structure of story problems may also contribute to higher levels of achievement (De Corte, Verschaffel, & De Win, 1985).

Vocabulary and Verbal Cues

Obviously, it is important that students are able to read the words and that the vocabulary of the problem is comprehensible. Fortunately, the vocabularies used in the story problems of commercial math programs are usually familiar to the students who are expected to solve the problems. Some students will, however, need additional language training to solve story problems.

Another problem related to readability is the frequent presence of verbal cues. Unfortunately, story problems are frequently written in such a manner that verbal cues are included. To the extent that the students depend on the cues rather than reading the problems, verbal cues will hinder progress (Nesher, 1976; Wright, 1968). It is difficult to avoid the use of key words, but it is necessary to design problem-solving curricula that do not teach misrules. From the time that problem-solving exercises are begun, the examples should contain few, if any, key words. As the students become more proficient, problems with so-called key words may be introduced. Eventually, examples of story problems that contain key words that function as distractors should be introduced. These problems should also be paired against problems that do not use key words as distractors. Unless care is taken in constructing instructional examples that require the development and use of students' knowledge of action verbs, comparative relationships, and classifications, it is likely that too many students will attempt to use potentially misleading keyword strategies.

Story Problem Structure

Consistent relationships have been found between problem structure and the difficulties students have solving story problems (e.g., De Corte, Verschaffel, & De Win, 1985; Jerman & Mirman, 1974; Jones, Krouse, Feroene, & Saferstein, 1985; Kilpatrick, 1969; Wilson, 1967). Silbert, Carnine, and Stein (1981) proposed a classification that acknowledges the differences in problem structure. They identified four basic structures of addition/subtraction problems and two types of multiplication/division problems. Examples of each of the different structures of story problems are presented in Table 10–3. Simple action problems can be readily translated into arithmetic sentences, because the direction of action is readily apparent. Complex action problems depict an action, but the direction of the action is more difficult to determine than in simple action problems. Classification problems are based on subordinate and superordinate classifications of objects or events. Comparison problems depict the comparison of objects or events. Multiplication/division

TABLE 10–3
Examples of four different types of story problems

Type of Problem	Example
Simple action	Mary had 6 oranges. She shared 4 with her friends. How many does she have now?
Classification	19 dogs were put into the pound. 4 of them were black. How many were not black?
Complex action	Linda hiked 4 miles in the afternoon. She also biked 7 miles that morning. How many miles did she travel that day?
Comparison	Ellen's backpack weighs 14 pounds. It is 5 pounds heavier than Jack's pack. How much does Jack's pack weigh?

problems are separated into types that contain key words (e.g., *each, every, split up, divide*) that indicate that groups are being dealt with repeatedly.

Few commercial math programs consider problem structure when selecting or sequencing instructional examples. Jones et al. (1985) compared the effects of providing instruction on the four different structures of addition/subtraction story problems identified by Silbert, Carnine, and Stein (1981) in sequenced and mixed presentations. Students who received training on the different types of problems presented in sequence made significantly greater gains and were able to solve significantly more problems on the post-test compared to the students who received training on mixed assortments of the problem structures.

De Corte, Verschaffel, and De Win (1985) examined children's solutions to three different wordings of story problems. When students were given access to manipulatives and allowed to develop their own strategies, they observed that (1) children tended to develop different solution strategies to each of the different wordings, (2) ambiguities in the wording of problems were related to higher proportions of incorrect solutions, and (3) rewording problems to remove some of the ambiguity resulted in improved performances. It is instructive to consider which children did not respond to the rewording of the story problems. The researchers did not describe the students whose performances did not improve as a result of rewording the story problems. For low-achieving students, rewording problems is not an entirely sufficient educational intervention. It may be necessary to combine the rewording tactic with carefully designed strategy training and preskill instruction.

Much of the research on the teaching of math problem-solving strategies has been influenced by the work of George Polya (1965a, 1965b, 1973). Polya's method is a description of an heuristic, or theoretical description of the process of determining *what information is given* and *what information is needed*. Studies of the effects of training students to apply the Polya method to the solution of story problems (e.g., Bassler, Beers, & Richardson, 1975; Blankenship & Lovitt, 1976; Wilson, 1967) have reported improved performances with the application procedures based upon Polya's model. Silver and Thompson (1984) commented, however, that although the Polya model has been useful in suggesting procedures for organizing instruction for problem-solving skills, the model is abstract and is deficient as a description of actual problem-solving behavior. It is unclear whether students, particularly low-achieving students, use the abstract strategies as described by Polya (1973). None of the studies has systematically examined the effectiveness of the model across different problem structures.

The curriculum for remedial math instruction developed by Engelmann and Carnine (1981), and described by Silbert, Carnine, and Stein (1981), is based on (1) the presentation of a careful selection and sequencing of simple action, classification, complex action, and comparison story problems, and (2) the explicit teaching of a generalizable problem-solving strategy. Darch, Carnine, and Gersten (1983) evaluated the effectiveness of a direct instruction problem-solving curriculum by teaching low-achieving students to solve multiplication and division story problems. Their comparison of the direct instruction strategy with a Polya-type approach revealed that (1) significantly greater proportions of students who received the direct instruction strategy reached criterion compared to students who received the Polya-type treatment, (2) extended practice had a significant effect on the maintenance of skills for students who received training in the generalizable strategy described by Silbert, Carnine, and Stein (1981), but (3) extended practice did not promote higher levels of performance or maintenance for students who received the comparison training. Problem-solving instruction that is based on carefully chosen examples and explicitly taught generalizable strategies is likely to result in significantly higher levels of achievement than instruction that is based upon either the application of an heuristic strategy (Darch, Carnine, & Gersten, 1983) or the selection and modification of examples (cf. De Corte, Verschaffel, & De Win, 1985).

Multiple Operations

Most examples of math story problems are simply stated problems that may be solved with a one-step computation. It is important to prepare students to solve the more difficult multi-operation story problems. Training on multi-step/multi-operation story problems should begin after students demonstrate reasonable proficiency with one-step story problems. Inexperienced students or students with learning difficulties will need instruction in the application of the problem-solving strategy. Low-achieving students will need to be guided through a carefully sequenced set of problems. A plan to teach multi-step story problems should include problems with two-step/same operation solutions, two-step/different operations, and multi-step/different operations solutions.

Extraneous Information

In everyday life, math problems rarely occur as simple two- or three-sentence tidy little problems. They occur in the presence of extraneous information that can distract or mislead. The skill of determining which information is needed and which is extraneous is one of the most critical problem-solving skills. It is also one of the most difficult skills to acquire (Arter & Clinton, 1974; Blankenship & Lovitt, 1976; Carpenter, Corbitt, Kepner, Lindquist, & Reys, 1980; Carpenter et al., 1984; Englert, Culatta, & Horton, 1987; Goodstein, Bessant, Thibodeau, Vitello, & Vlahakos, 1972; Goodstein, Cawley, Gordon, & Helfgott, 1971; Thibodeau, 1974). The skill is difficult for nonhandicapped students to acquire (Carpenter et al., 1984), but students with learning handicaps have even more difficulty (Englert, Culatta, & Horn, 1987; Goodstein et al., 1971; Goodstein et al., 1972).

Several writers have offered guidelines for the systematic development of skills in solving story problems containing irrelevant information. Goodstein (1974) suggested that visual aids be used to facilitate comprehension of the problem-solving situation. As students began to develop greater proficiency in problem-solving, the visual aids would be faded out. The procedures he described are based on the procedures developed for the Project M.A.T.H. curriculum (*Mathematics Activities for Teaching the Handicapped,* Cawley, Goodstein, Fitzmaurice, Lepore, Sedlak, & Althaus, 1976–1977). The use of visual aids to teach basic problem-solving skills may be well advised. Many of the problems in everyday life have a concrete context that can be represented (and frequently is represented) with visual arrangements. Verbally presented story problems are, on the other hand, abstractions of the event. The abstraction of the events of the problem-solving situation may contribute to the difficulty low-achieving students experience. Thus, it appears that there should be no substantial reason against the systematic use of visual problem-solving aids. As long as the student is not permitted to become dependent on the visual aids, the cues may serve as resources in the design of curricula.

Englert, Culatta, and Horn (1987) observed that students respond differently to different types of extraneous information. Problems with irrelevant numerical information were significantly more difficult than either problems with irrelevant verbal information or problems without irrelevant information. They also observed that the location of the irrelevant information in the story problem was related to the difficulties students have solving the problems.

Functional Applications

Functional applications are a special set of problem solving skills. The term refers to any math skills that are necessary for successfully meeting the demands of vocational, social, recreational, and daily living activities (Schwartz & Budd, 1981). Time, money, and measurement are only a sample of the possible applications of math skills. These skills are of general importance in daily living and are frequently addressed in traditional curricula.

An important point to consider in developing instruction for functional applications of quantitative skills and knowledge is that the activities must indeed be application activities. Although functional math activities are important examples to use as bases for the application of skills to form other hierarchies, it is pointless to introduce activities in functional math (either as goals or as examples) until the students demonstrate proficiency on necessary preskills from other areas.

MODIFYING MATHEMATICS CURRICULUM PROGRAMS

Because the mere presentation of tasks is clearly insufficient for many students to acquire the desired levels of skill mastery, it is apparent that what is learned in a curriculum-dependent subject such as mathematics will also depend upon *how well* the skills in the curriculum are taught. Although some curricula are clearly better than others and may need little modification, the adaptation of math curricula is an important and inescapable responsibility—and a vital skill—for teachers of low-achieving students.

Carroll's (1963) model for school learning will be the basis for our discussion of program modification. Carroll proposed his Model of School Learning, which is based on five elements that can be used to predict the rate at which a student would be expected to learn any given skill. He described the first element, *aptitude,* as the amount of time it takes an individual to learn a given skill under ideal learning conditions. His second element, *ability to understand instruction,* referred to the interaction between general ability and level of achievement. It is certainly reasonable to consider that ability to learn could be measured in terms of the degree to which a student has mastered relevant preskills of the target skill (Slavin, 1984). *Quality of instruction,* the third element of Carroll's model, is defined in terms of how rapidly and efficiently the tasks can be learned from a given organization and presentation. Fourth, the *opportunity for learning* refers to the time allocated to the learning of a given task. The final element of the model is *perseverance,* or the amount of time the learner spends actively engaged in the learning of the skill.

A basic premise of this book is that the primary reason for the failures of a great many children is the inadequacy of the instruction they receive. In the terms of Carroll's

(1963) model, failure is not due to low aptitude. Aptitude is defined in terms of the amount of time necessary to learn a task under ideal instructional conditions. There is ample evidence that the instructional conditions that many failing students endure are far from ideal. Under better instructional conditions, they could learn more.

The improvement of instructional programs begins with an examination of goals for instruction and the selection of programs that will be most adequate in helping the remedial student meet those goals. Three elements of Carroll's (1963) model are particularly important and should be scrutinized when decisions are to be made about the selection or modification of an instructional program (Slavin, 1984). The elements are quality of instruction, perseverance, and time or opportunity to learn. These elements are under the control of the teacher and thus are alterable.

Quality of Instruction

Although only after the instructional program has taken place can we speak with most certainty about its quality, we can make some reasonable predictions about its quality before and during the delivery of instruction. As stated earlier, programs that have a well-described scope and sequence and well-designed instructional strategies are predictably superior quality programs.

Scope and Sequence

The appropriate point to begin assaying a prospective course of instruction is with an examination of the scope and sequence of skills hierarchies. First, obtain and review a reasonably detailed scope and sequence such as the one provided in Appendix A of this chapter and use it as a standard to compare the program in question. Second, review the instructional activities. Third, determine if the objectives are appropriate. The objective of a given activity should be consistent with the objectives stated in the publisher's scope and sequence charts.

Three major problems with commercial curricula are insufficient scope and sequence, poorly sequenced skills hierarchies, and inclusion of superfluous objectives or activities. Most basal math programs are reasonably comprehensive. That is, the major objectives are addressed, and orderly sequences of skills leading to their accomplishment are set forth. Unfortunately, the specific skills hierarchies of basal math programs are frequently inadequately detailed, incomplete, or insufficiently integrated. For example, few published curricula actually break down instruction on regrouping in subtraction to deal specifically with the predictable problems that some students will have in solving problems with zeros in the minuends. Problem-solving hierarchies are incompletely dealt with, and very few basal math programs systematically approach the task of dealing with irrelevant information.

The general handling of problem-solving sequences also provides a prime example of inadequate integration of skills hierarchies (Cawley, Fitzmaurice, Shaw, Kahn, & Bates, 1978; 1979). Superfluous or irrelevant goals are rarely listed in the publisher's scope and sequence charts. They are not, however, particularly hard to spot, and become readily apparent when the teacher asks the question, "What objective does this activity serve?" For example, an irrelevant item that is frequently in evidence in commercial curricula is the equation puzzle (see Figure 10–7). Apparently, the objective in the equation puzzle is to develop proficiency in the identification and completion of equations embedded in a matrix of extraneous numerals. Clearly, this is a skill that does not contribute to any meaningful objective except, perhaps, to keep students occupied until it is their time for group work with the teacher. The same objective (i.e., keeping the student occupied) is also addressed by the large amount of coloring required in some basal programs.

Some teachers use supplemental programs to teach specific skills they perceive are not addressed adequately in the basal math programs. Specific skill programs do not claim to be comprehensive. They are marketed to provide instruction on specific skills such as computation, fractions or measurement. As Silbert, Carnine, and Stein (1981) observe, some of these programs are well constructed. Others are merely collections of worksheets and are generally not referenced to a more comprehensive program. Thus, they are not particularly useful, even as practice activities. They address only a limited range of skills. Teachers who use specific skills programs should prepare additional instructional activities to integrate the programs into the overall program.

Specification of Strategies

Commercial curricula and skills programs are often deficient in both instructions provided to teachers and specification of problem-solving strategies to be learned by students. Instructions to teachers are often vague; such imprecise directions allow for a wide variety of possible implementations of the instructional program. Vague instructions are particularly difficult when the purpose of instruction is to facilitate the communication of a problem-solving strategy to the student. Publishers can improve the quality of instruction by providing detailed instructions, but if instructions are not detailed, the teacher should, as part of preparing for instruction, flesh out the lesson plan so that important problem-solving skills can be efficiently communicated.

Improvements in the quality of instruction will occur with the selection and development of efficient learning strategies for the student. It is not unusual for commercial programs to suggest several tactics that a student might apply in learning basic math skills. Presumably, if the student fails to learn a skill adequately by using one strategy, other strategies can be brought into play. There are, however, no data to support the notion that applying multiple strategies contributes to greater levels of achievement than the application of a single, well-designed and generalizable learning strategy. Evaluations of direct instruction indicate that individualization of instruction does not entail the use of multiple teaching strategies or the acquisition of multiple learning strategies (Gersten, 1985). There is, on the other hand, evidence that the use of wide ranges of diverse instructional options and resources is negatively associated with student achievement (Baker, Herman, & Yeh, 1981). Individualization is best considered in terms of (1) levels

FIGURE 10–7
Equation matrix—Circle the numbers that make an addition fact

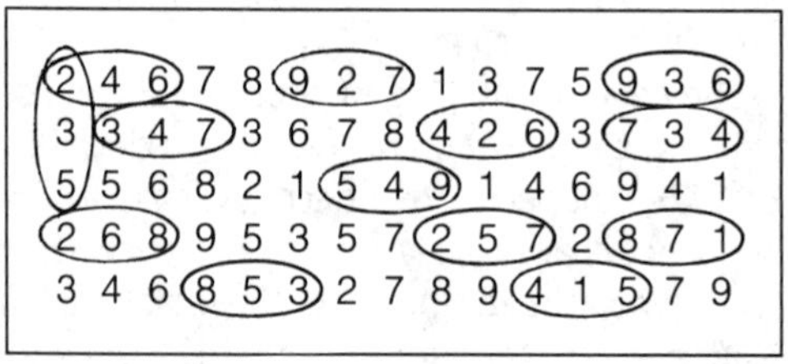

of preskill achievement, (2) timing of corrections, (3) reinforcement procedures, and (4) the amount of practice necessary for mastery (Becker & Carnine, 1981).

Silbert, Carnine, and Stein (1981) recommend the use of two criteria in the selection or development of learning strategies: (1) the efficiency of the strategy and (2) the relationship between the strategy under consideration and the strategies that are generally taught in the regular classroom. The first consideration is of fundamental importance. Remedial students need to learn more skills in less time to achieve normal levels of achievement. To accomplish that goal, they will have to learn the most efficient strategies. If they are to retain the skills they acquire, they must also learn strategies that will be supported by their environment. Occasionally, it will be necessary to make a trade-off between the efficiency of acquisition and the likelihood that a newly acquired skill will be supported outside the training situation. For example, we do not recommend the introduction of low-stress algorithms (see Figure 10–8) to students who have computational difficulties. Very few teachers are fluent in the use of low-stress algorithms. Furthermore, it is unlikely that the use of low-stress algorithms will be supported outside the initial training setting. It is better to teach the procedure most commonly used outside the remedial instruction program.

Example Selections

Three common deficiencies in commercial curricula are (1) a lack of sufficient amounts of instructional and practice examples, (2) inadequate distribution of practice activities, and (3) poor instructional and practice examples. Teachers must assume some of the responsibility for the production of additional examples. These examples should, however, be carefully selected and sequenced to serve as the basis for the application of a strategy. Successful application of the skill should be possible, and successful solution of the problem should depend on the application of the learning strategy. Instructional and practice examples should match the student's skills. The instructional and practice examples should not allow for a correct solution by the application of some unintended strategy, nor should the solution require the use of skills that are not in the student's repertoire. Unnecessary errors occur when the student is required to perform skills that have not been previously mastered.

Poorly chosen sets of instructional examples can contribute to the failure of students to attend to the critical aspects of a task. Thus, it may appear that a skill is being

FIGURE 10–8

Low-stress algorithms and traditional multiplication algorithms

```
   798          798
 ×  25        ×  25
 ------       ------
    40         3990
   450         1596
  3500        ------
   160        19950
  1800
 14000
 ------
 19950
```

learned when, in fact, it is not. In such cases, it is difficult to determine that skills are not being learned because the students give correct answers. Poorly selected sets of examples contribute to the failure to learn intended concepts, as shown in the domains of computation and problem-solving. For instance, some computational exercises are composed entirely of problems requiring regrouping, and correct completion of such exercises would appear to indicate that the student has mastered the desired skill. If, however, the exercise contained a number of computations that did not require regrouping, a correspondingly lower percentage of correct responses might be observed. Part of the task of regrouping requires that the student learn to discriminate between problems that require regrouping and problems that do not. If the student can solve all the problems in the exercise without making this discrimination, the selection of examples is faulty. Under such conditions, we cannot claim that the intended learning has taken place.

A similar and common instance of poorly arranged instructional examples is in the area of problem solving. It is ill advised to allow students to depend on key word strategies to solve story problems. Students who rely on key words tend not to read the problems. They will make high rates of errors on problems that do not contain key words or contain key words that are used as distractors. A related problem is the number size in story problems. All 100 basic facts in addition and multiplication comprise one-digit-by-one-digit numbers, but 45 of the basic subtraction facts and 58 of the basic division facts comprise two-digit-by-one digit problems. For students whose computational skills are limited to solution of basic facts, there is a danger that poorly selected sets of story problems will contribute to their learning the erroneous strategy, "When you see a two-digit number in the story problem you will subtract (or divide)." Such an ill-conceived strategy is dysfunctional; it is also predictable and avoidable. In illustrations from both computations and problem-solving, it is possible for the student to fail to learn the intended skills and knowledge without making a large number of errors on the training exercises. Features of the examples that are irrelevant to the correct solution of the tasks are frequently associated with the relevant features. Too often the irrelevant features become misleading cues.

Sometimes it is difficult to identify faulty sets of instructional examples. Vargas (1984) suggests four questions to guide the detection of these problems:

1. Are irrelevant cues that give away the answers present in the set of examples or the presentation (charts, pictures, etc.)?
2. Do the highlighting and physical layout give away the answers and make it unnecessary for the student to examine the problems and consider the demands of the tasks?
3. Are students able to solve story problems without reading them?
4. Do all the examples in a set have the same solution, thus making it unnecessary to attend closely to the discrimination between problems or selection of the appropriate strategies?

If irrelevant features are carefully balanced across positive and negative examples of the concept, they will not contribute to the learning of misrules. For example, students will not depend on number size as a cue in beginning problem solving if the proportions of both one-by-one-digit and two-by-one-digit problems are equally represented in both addition and subtraction story problems.

The quality of instruction can be substantially improved by identifying the student's level of preskill achievement. Commercial curricula can provide adequate instructional experiences if students are placed in appropriate levels of those curricula. Determining the appropriate level of instruction involves (1) examining the student's performance, (2) referencing performance to a well-defined hierarchy of skills and knowledge, and (3) developing appropriate goals. Instruction will be of the highest quality if the student's response to instruction and progress toward goals are continuously evaluated (see Chapter 2).

Perseverance

If students are to learn and practice using the skills and knowledge, they will need incentives to do so. Students may not persevere through math instruction for several reasons. Some possibilities are that they may be bored, threatened, generally unsuccessful, or enticed by alternative activities. The longer a child fails in mathematics, the more likely one or all of these possibilities may be realized. Students with long histories of frustration, anxiety, and failure are apt to be more resistant to remediation than those with shorter histories. Clearly, developing a student's perseverance will depend in part on the prevailing reinforcement conditions and on the schedule and design of instruction. If tasks that are easier are juxtaposed with more difficult skills, the student is likely to persevere through the more difficult portions of the sequence.

Perseverance will also be greatly influenced by the quality of instruction. When instruction focuses primarily on increasing self-esteem or self-concept without directly addressing basic competence, it will not be successful for promoting academic achievement or affective growth (Prawat, 1985). The results of the national Follow-Through study, which examined the effectiveness of programs with potential special education students, indicate that students in the systematic, teacher-led instructional programs had significantly higher levels of affective growth, compared to students in the less-structured student-led programs. There is no necessary reason for direct teacher-led instruction to be boring and dull. If it is well designed and skillfully orchestrated, teacher-led instruction will hold the interest of the students.

Opportunity to Learn

The third alterable element of a curriculum is the amount of time devoted to instruction in the given skill areas. Comparisons between second-grade classrooms that participated in the Beginning Teacher Evaluation Study, a California-based research project that studied teacher behavior and student achievement, revealed a wide variation in the average amounts of time allocated to math instruction (Fisher, Berliner, Filby, Marliave, Cahen, & Dishaw, 1980). One class allocated an average of 25 minutes per day, while another allocated an average of 60 minutes per day. In some specific areas the variations were sensational. For example, in one second-grade class, the average student received only 9 minutes of instruction associated with money for the entire year. In another second-grade class, the average student received 315 minutes of instruction in the area of money for the year. Not surprisingly, Fisher et al. (1980) observed that the amount of time allocated to instruction was positively correlated with achievement.

Publishers of curricula rarely indicate the amount of time that should be allocated to instruction in any given skill. Inferences about the amounts of time necessary can be made from the amount of emphasis devoted to instruction in the given skills area. The amount of time allocated to instruction should be related to the student's need for instruction, but there are fixed limits on the amount of time available for teachers to allocate. If clock time is considered a fixed asset, then the most significant source of additional instructional time will come from improving the quality of instruction and increasing the students' levels of active engagement or perseverance during instruction.

SUMMARY

In this chapter, students' mathematical deficiencies were analyzed in relation to alterable variables; that is, according to the instructional factors over which teachers have jurisdiction and expertise. To frame this analysis, the primary approaches to mathematics instruction (discovery learning and direct instruction) were contrasted and the advantages for teacher-directed instruction were discussed. A hierarchical sequence of mathematics skills was proposed for evaluating the order of skills introduction, and also as a means of measuring the learner's mastery of sequentially related skills. Basic math skills were classified into four major domains: (1) mathematics-related vocabulary and language, (2) numeration, (3) computations, and (4) problem solving. Relationships between the strands of skills were set forth to illustrate the interdependency of skills within the mathematics curriculum. Next, the generic instructional set was applied to selected mathematics skills demonstrating the importance of knowledge forms, example selection and sequence, as well as test and practice examples for designing mathematics instruction. The before, during, and after paradigm provided the structure for organizing the essential pieces of information into teaching formats. Educators were alerted to the properties of mathematics skills and instruction that pose problems for low performers and to the alternative instructional design and delivery procedures that can be employed to minimize learning difficulties in the mathematics content area. Finally, guidelines were proposed for evaluating and modifying extant mathematics programs.

APPLICATION ITEMS

1. Use the hierarchies from Appendix A to develop sequences to assess the addition and subtraction skills of a low-achieving third-grade student, and multiplication and division skills of a low-achieving fifth-grade student.

2. If a student makes the following pattern of errors on practice exercises, what should the teacher do?

47	68	6529
+ 3	+ 38	+3109
41	151	9611

3. Specify the instructional sequence and wording of problems that a teacher would use to teach a student how to solve division problems with decimals in the divisor. Assume that the student can already solve multi-digit division problems.

4. Outline the arrangement of basic facts, for each operation, that would contribute to the most effective mastery of basic computations.

5. Assume that a student can already solve simple single-operation story problems. Identify and sequence the component knowledge forms that are needed to solve the following problem:

> Andy needs $50. He worked 5 hours on Thursday for $4 an hour. On Friday he worked for 2 hours at $5 an hour. Next week he can work for 10 hours at $4 an hour. How many hours does he need to work next week to have $50 in total?

REFERENCES

Anderson, R. B., St. Pierre, R., Proper, E., & Stebbins, L. (1978). Pardon us, but what was the question again?: A response to the critique of the Follow Through Evaluation. *Harvard Educational Review, 48,* 161–170.

Arter, J. A., & Clinton, L. (1974). Time and error consequences of irrelevant data and question placement in arithmetic word problems, II: Fourth graders. *Journal of Educational Research, 68,* 28–31.

Ashlock, R. B., & Herman, W. L. (Eds.). (1970). *Current research in elementary school mathematics.* New York: Macmillan.

Ausubel, D. P. (1968). *Educational psychology: A cognitive view.* New York: Holt, Rinehart & Winston.

Baker, E. L., Herman, J. L., & Yeh, J. P. (1981). Fun and games: Their contribution to basic skills instruction in elementary school. *American Educational Research Journal, 18,* 83–92.

Baroody, A. J. (1984). Children's difficulties in subtraction: Some causes and questions. *Journal for Research in Mathematics Education, 15,* 203–213.

Bassler, O. C., Beers, M. I., & Richardson, L. I. (1975). Comparison of two instructional strategies for teaching the solution of verbal problems. *Journal for Research in Mathematics Education, 6,* 170–177.

Becker, W. C., & Carnine, D. W. (1981). Direct instruction: A behavior theory model for comprehensive educational intervention with the disadvantaged. In S. W. Bijou & R. Ruiz (Eds.), *Behavior modification: Contributions to education* (pp. 145–210). Hillsdale, NJ: Erlbaum.

Blankenship, C. S., & Lovitt, T. C. (1976). Story problems: Merely confusing or downright befuddling? *Journal for Research in Mathematics Education, 7,* 290–298.

Bruner, J. S. (1961). The act of discovery. *Harvard Educational Review, 31,* 21–32.

Cacha, F. B. (1975). Subtraction: Regrouping with flexibility. *Arithmetic Teacher, 22,* 402–404.

Carnine, D. (1980a). Preteaching versus concurrent teaching of the component skills of a multiplication algorithm. *Journal for Research in Mathematics Education, 11,* 375–379.

Carnine, D. (1980b). Relationships between stimulus variation and the formation of misconceptions. *Journal of Educational Research, 74,* 106–110.

Carpenter, T. P., Corbitt, M. K., Kepner, H. S., Jr., Lindquist, M. M., & Reys, R. E. (1980). Solving verbal problems: Results and implications from the national assessment. *Arithmetic Teacher, 28,* 8–12.

Carpenter, T. P., Matthews, W., Lindquist, M. M., & Silver, E. A. (1984). Achievement in mathematics: Results from the national assessment. *Elementary School Journal, 84,* 485–495.

Carpenter, T. P., & Moser, J. M. (1984). The acquisition of addition and subtraction concepts in grades one through three. *Journal for Research in Mathematical Education, 15,* 179–202.

Carroll, J. B. (1963). A model of school learning. *Teachers College Record, 64,* 723–733.

Cawley, J. F., Fitzmaurice, A. M., Shaw, R. A., Kahn, H., & Bates, H., III (1978). Mathematics and learning disabled youth: The upper grade levels. *Learning Disability Quarterly, 1,* 37–52.

Cawley, J. F., Fitzmaurice, A. M., Shaw, R. A., Kahn, H., & Bates, H., III (1979). LD youth and mathematics: A review of characteristics. *Learning Disability Quarterly, 2,* 29–44.

Cawley, J. F., Goodstein, H. A., Fitzmaurice, A. M., Lepore, A. V., Sedlak, R., & Althaus, V. (1976–1977). *Project MATH,* Levels I, II, III, and IV. Tulsa, OK: Educational Development Corp.

Cook, C. J., & Dossey, J. A. (1982). Basic fact thinking strategies for multiplication-revisited. *Journal for Research in Mathematics Education, 13,* 163–171.

Darch, C., Carnine, D., & Gersten, R. (1983). *An evaluation and analysis of a direct instruction approach to teaching math problem solving.* Paper presented at the annual conference of the American Educational Research Association, Montreal.

De Corte, E., Verschaffel, L., & De Win, L. (1985). Influence of rewording verbal problems on children's problem representations and solutions. *Journal of Educational Psychology, 77,* 460–470.

Engelmann, S., & Carnine, D. (1981). *Corrective mathematics.* Chicago: Science Research Associates.

Englert, C. S., Culatta, B. E., & Horn, D. G. (1987). Influence of irrelevant information in addition word problems on problem solving. *Learning Disability Quarterly, 10,* 29–36.

Fisher, C. W., Berliner, D. C., Filby, N. N., Marliave, R., Cahen, L. S., & Dishaw, M. M. (1980). Teaching behaviors, academic learning time and student achievement: An overview. In C. Denham and A. Lieberman (Eds.), *Time to learn.* Washington, D.C.: USOE/GIE.

Gersten, R. (1985). Direct instruction with special education students: A review of evaluation research. *Journal of Special Education, 19,* 41–58.

Glaser, R. (1966). Variables in discovery learning. In L. S. Shulman & E. R. Keislar (Eds.), *Learning by discovery: A critical appraisal* (pp. 13–29). Chicago: Rand-McNally.

Goodstein, H. A. (1974). Solving the verbal mathematics problem: Visual aids + teacher planning = the answer. *Teaching Exceptional Children, 6,* 178–182.

Goodstein, H. A., Bessant, H., Thibodeau, G., Vitello, S., & Vlahakos, I. (1972). The effect of three variables on the verbal problem solving of educable mentally handicapped children. *American Journal of Mental Deficiency, 76,* 703–709.

Goodstein, H. A., Cawley, J. F., Gordon, S., & Helfgott, J. (1971). Verbal problem solving among educable mentally retarded children. *American Journal of Mental Deficiency, 76,* 238–241.

Hiebert, J. (1982). The position of the unknown set and children's solutions of verbal arithmetic problems. *Journal for Research in Mathematical Education, 13,* 341–349.

Jerman, M. E., & Mirman, S. (1974). Linguistic and computational variables in problem solving in elementary mathematics. *Educational Studies in Mathematics, 5,* 317–362.

Jones, E. D., Krouse, J. P., Feroene, D., and Saferstein, C. A. (1985). A comparison of concurrent and sequential instruction of four types of verbal math problems. *Remedial and Special Education, 6,* 25–31.

Kameenui, E. J., & Griffin, C. C. (1989). A national crisis in verbal problem solving in mathematics: A proposal for examining the role of basal mathematics programs. *Elementary School Journal, 5,* 575–594.

Keislar, E. R., & Shulman, L. S. (1966). The problem of discovery: Conference in retrospect. In L. S. Shulman & E. R. Keislar (Eds.), *Learning by discovery: A critical appraisal* (pp. 181–199). Chicago: Rand-McNally.

Kendler, H. H. (1966). Reflections on the conference. In L. S. Shulman & E. R. Keislar (Eds.), *Learning by discovery: A critical appraisal* (pp. 171–176). Chicago: Rand-McNally.

Kilpatrick, J. (1969). Problem solving in mathematics. *Review of Educational Research, 39,* 523–534.

Kilpatrick, J. (1978). Research on problem solving in mathematics. *School Science and Mathematics, 78,* 189–192.

Larsen, S. C., Parker, R. M., & Trenholme, B. (1978). The effects of syntactic complexity upon arithmetic performance. *Learning Disability Quarterly, 1,* 80–85.

Myers, A., & Thorton, C. (1977). The learning disabled child—learning the basic facts. *Arithmetic Teacher, 25,* 46–50.

Nesher, P. (1976). Three determinants of difficulty in verbal arithmetic problems. *Educational Studies in Mathematics, 7,* 369–388.

Polya, G. (1965a). *Mathematical discovery: On understanding, learning, and teaching problem solving, Vol. 1.* New York: Wiley.

Polya, G. (1965b). *Mathematical discovery: On understanding, learning, and teaching problem solving, Vol. 2.* New York: Wiley.

Polya, G. (1973). *How to solve it* (3rd ed.). Princeton, NJ: Princeton University Press.

Prawat, R. S. (1985). Affective versus cognitive goal orientations in elementary teachers. *American Educational Research Journal, 22,* 587–604.

Rathmell, E. C. (1978). Using thinking strategies to learn the basic facts. In M. Suydan (Ed.), *1978 Yearbook of the National Council of Teachers in Mathematics.* Reston, VA: National Council of Teachers of Mathematics.

Reidesel, C. A. (1985). *Teaching elementary school mathematics* (4th ed.). Englewood Cliffs, NJ: Prentice-Hall.

Roberts, G. H. (1968). The failure strategies of third grade arithmetic pupils. *Arithmetic Teacher, 15,* 442–446.

Rogers, C. (1969). *Freedom to learn* (2nd ed.). Columbus, OH: Merrill Publishing Company.

Sarason, S. (1971). *The culture of the school and the problem of change.* Boston: Allyn & Bacon.

Scandura, J. M. (1968). Research in psychomathematics (research in the emerging discipline of psychomathematics). *Mathematics Teacher, 61,* 581–591.

Schwartz, S. E., & Budd, D. (1981). Mathematics for handicapped learners: A functional approach for adolescents. *Focus on Exceptional Children, 13,* 1–12.

Silbert, J., Carnine, D., & Stein, M. (1981). *Direct instruction mathematics.* Columbus, OH: Merrill Publishing Company.

Silver, E. A., & Thompson, A. G. (1984). Research perspectives on problem solving in elementary school mathematics. *Elementary School Journal, 84,* 529–545.

Slavin, R. E. (1984). Component building: A strategy for research-based instructional improvement. *Elementary School Journal, 84,* 255–269.

Spradlin, E. E., Cotter, V. W., Stevens, C., & Friedman, M. (1974). Performance of mentally retarded children on pre-arithmetic tasks. *American Journal of Mental Deficiency, 78,* 397–403.

Stokes, T. F., & Baer, D. M. (1977). An implicit technology of generalization. *Journal of Applied Behavior Analysis, 10,* 349–367.

Steinberg, R. M. (1985). Instruction on derived facts strategies in addition and subtraction. *Journal for Research in Mathematics Education, 16,* 337–355.

Stevens, R., & Rosenshine, B. (1981). Advances in research on teaching. *Exceptional Education Quarterly, 1,* 1–10.

Thibodeau, G. P. (1974). Manipulation of numerical presentation in verbal problems and its effect on verbal problem solving among EMH children. *Education and Training of the Mentally Retarded, 9,* 9–14.

Thorton, C. A. (1978). Emphasizing thinking strategies in basic fact instruction. *Journal for Research in Mathematics Education, 9,* 215–227.

Vargas, J. S. (1984). What are your exercises teaching? An analysis of stimulus control in instructional materials. In W. L. Heward, T. E. Heron, D. S. Hill, & J. Trap-Porter (Eds.). *Focus on behavior analysis in education* (pp. 126–141). Columbus, OH: Merrill Publishing Company.

Wheeler, L. J., & McNutt, G. (1983). The effect of syntax on low-achieving students' abilities to solve mathematical word problems. *Journal of Special Education, 17,* 309–315.

Wilson, J. W. (1967). The role of structure in verbal problem solving. *Arithmetic Teacher, 14,* 486–497.

Wright, J. P. (1968). A study of children's performance on verbally stated problems containing word clues and omitting them. *Dissertation Abstracts, 29,* 1770B.

APPENDIX A

Hierarchies of Numeration, Computation and Problem-Solving Skills[2]

Math Related Language and Vocabulary Skills

K   characteristics of objects (e.g., round, triangle).
K   relationships between things (e.g., near/far, different) and relationships between groups of objects (e.g., equal, bigger/smaller, more/less).
K   terms associated with mathematical operations (e.g., sum, multiplier, fraction, numerator).
K   mathematical operations (e.g., add, subtract, multiply, divide).
K   classifications of subordinate/superordinate categories (e.g., dogs, cats, and pets; coins, bills and money).

Note: Training in math related vocabularies and language will begin in kindergarten and proceed throughout the entire curriculum.

Numeration Skills

Counting

K   rote counting by 1s to 30.
K   rational counting of objects in one and two groups (cardinal and ordinal numbers).
K   rote counting from a number by 1s to 100.
K   skip counting by 10s.
K   rote and rational counting backward from 20.
K   skip counting by 100s.
1   skip counting by 2s and 5s.
2   rote and rational counting by 1s from a number through 999.
2.3   skip counting by 3s, 4s, 6s, 7s, 8s, and 9s.
2.3   rote and rational counting by 1s from a number through 1,000,000.

Symbol Identification and Place Value

K   reading and writing numerals 1–10.
K   writing the number of objects in a set.
1.1   reading and writing teen numbers and numbers 20–100.
1.3   column alignment of two-digit numbers.
1.4   expanded notation.
1.6   column alignment of combinations of one, two, and three digit numbers.

Note: The above skills should be acquired with numbers up to 999. For larger numbers recycle through the same sequence.

---

[2]Adapted from *Direct instruction mathematics* (pp. 49–52) by J. Silbert, D. Carnine, and M. Stein, 1981, Columbus, OH: Merrill Publishing Company. Copyright 1981 by Merrill Publishing Company. Adapted by permission.

Fraction Analysis
1.1   state the fraction that is represented in a diagram or other concrete representation.
1.1   represent in concrete form a numerically stated or written fraction.
1.1   determine whether a fraction is equal to, greater than, or less than one.
2.0   read and write mixed numbers (e.g., 4 1/2).

Computational Skills

Addition
K   addition by counting all the members of both sets.
K.1   addition by stating the number of members in the larger set and counting members in the other set from that number.
1   missing addend problems.
1   column and horizontal addition of basic facts.
1.5   addition of 2 by 1 digit facts (no renaming).
2.1   addition of 3 and 4 one digit addends.
2.2   addition of 2 by 2, 2 by 3, and 3 by 3 digit facts (no renaming).
2.5   addition with renaming in the 10s place.
2.5   adding fractions with like denominators.
3   adding fractions with unlike denominators.
3.2   adding mixed number fractions with like denominators.
3.2   adding with renaming in the 100s place.
4.3   addition of multidigit problems with 3 or more addends.

Subtraction
K   subtraction with concrete and semi-concrete objects.
1   column and horizontal subtraction of basic facts.
1.2   subtraction with missing subtrahend.
1.6   subtraction of a one or two digit number from a two digit number (no renaming).
2.2   subtraction of a one or two digit number from a two digit number (with renaming).
2.2   subtraction of a one, two, or three digit number from a three digit number (renaming in the ones and tens columns and discrimination of whether or not renaming is required).
2.5   subtracting fractions with like denominators.
3   subtracting fractions with unlike denominators.
3.2   subtracting mixed number fractions.
3.3   tens minus 1 facts.
4   subtraction of one, two, and three digit numbers from three digit numbers with zeros in the 1s and/or 10s places.
4.3   subtraction of single and multidigit numbers from minuends of 1000 or larger (following the same basic considerations described above for renaming and renaming with zeros).

Multiplication
2.2   multiplication of one digit basic facts in column and horizontal orientation.
2.3   multiplying fractions.
2.3   missing factor multiplication.
2.4   multiplication of fractions with like and unlike fractions.
3.2   one digit factor by two digit factor multiplication (no carrying).
3.3   one digit factor by two digit factor multiplication (carrying).
3.4   one digit factor by two or three digit factor multiplication.
4.2   one digit factor by two, three, or four factor multiplication with zeros in the 1s, 10s, or 100s places of the multiplicand.

4.3   multiply fractions by whole numbers.
4.4   two factor by two factor multiplication.
4.5   two or three factor by three factor multiplication.
5.1   two factor by three factor multiplication.
5.2   three factor by three factor multiplication.
5.3   multiplication of multidigit multiplicands by multidigit multipliers with zeros in the 1s, 10s, and 100s places.

Division
3.1   division of basic facts (in the algorithm and with the ÷ sign).
3.3   division with one digit divisors with and without remainders in the answers.
3.4   division with missing values.
4.1   problems with two or three digit dividends divided by one digit divisors (no remainders).
4.2   problems with two or three digit dividends divided by one digit divisors (with remainders and without remainders).
4.3   rewriting improper fractions (e.g., 12/3 or 17/4) to whole and mixed numbers.
4.4   conversion of remainders to fractions.
4.5   division where quotients are carried out to decimal values.
4.7   conversion of fractions into decimal values.
4.8   division of multidigit dividends by multidigit divisors.
5.3   dividing fractions.

Problem-solving

Story Problems (discrimination of appropriate operations)
1   addition and subtraction problems where the direction of *action can be readily translated* into an arithmetic algorithm.
1.2   addition and subtraction of problems where the direction of *action cannot be readily translated*.
2.1   addition and subtraction of problems with multiple and/or hierarchical *classifications* of objects (e.g., 5 cats, 2 dogs, how many pets?).
2.3   addition and subtraction problems involving the *comparisons* of quantities.
3.2   multiplication story problems with the words *each* and *every*.
3.3   multiplication story problems without the words *each* and *every*.
3.5   division story problems containing key words that indicate partitioning into equal groups (e.g., divide, share split up, etc.).
3.8   division story problems containing key words that indicate partitioning into equal groups (e.g., divide, share split up, etc.).
3.9   story problems with large numbers.
3.8   story problems with extraneous verbal information.
3.9   story problems with extraneous quantitative information.
4.4   multistep problems without extraneous information.
5.1   multistep problems with extraneous information.

Telling Time (applications of numeration and computation skills)
Preskills
K   mastery of the concepts of before and after.
2.2   knowledge of numbers of minutes in an hour.
2.2   discrimination between minute and hour hands.
2.2   counting by 5s and counting by 1s from a number.

Reading an analogue clock face
2.3   look at an analogue clock face and state time as minutes after an hour.
2.4   state time by stating the hour first.
2.4   state time as quarter past, quarter 'til, and half past an hour.
2.4   write the time in standard form with a colon and state time given on a digital clock face.
3.2   state time as minutes before a given hour.

Money (applications of numeration skills)
Preskills
1   counting from a number by 1s, 5s, 10s, or 25s from a number.
2.2   skip counting by 1s, 5s, 10s, and 25s.

Coin values
2.1   state the name and value of a single coin.
2.2   count up the value of a set of coins of the same denomination.
2.3   count up the value of a set of coins of mixed denominations.
3   count up the value of a set of coins of mixed denominations and paper currency.
3.2   read and write dollar and cents notations as decimal fractions.
4.5   determining whether or not there is enough money to make a purchase.

Measurement (English Standard Units)
Length
2.1   state the number of inches in a foot.
2.1   state the number of feet in a yard.
3.5   given a one foot ruler, yard stick, and/or tape measure determine the length of an object in whole inches, feet or yards.
4   given a one foot ruler, yard stick, and/or tape measure determine the length of an object in mixed units of length (e.g., feet and inches, feet and yards, yards and inches).
4   given a one foot ruler, yard stick, and/or tape measure determine the length of an object in whole and fractional units (e.g., 3 and 1/2 inches).

Weight
2.2   state the number of ounces in a pound.
2.2   state the number of pounds in a ton.
2.3   determine the weight of an object in whole ounces, pounds, and tons.
2.3   determine the weight of an object in mixed units of weight (e.g., pounds and ounces, tons and pounds).

Liquid capacity
2.3   state the number of ounces in a cup, the number of cups in a pint, the number of pints in a quart, and the number of quarts in a gallon.
2.3   determine the volume of a measure in whole ounces, cups, pints, quarts and gallons.
2.3   determine the volume of a measure in mixed units of volume (e.g., ounces and pints, quarts and cups, gallons and quarts).

Measurement (Metric Units)
Use the same skills progression as with English Standard Units.

Application of Units of Measurement in Computations
4.4   computation of measures of mixed units (e.g., feet and inches) without regrouping.
4.5   computations of measures of mixed units with regrouping.

Conversions Between English Standard and Metric Units

CHAPTER
ELEVEN

Designing Instructional Strategies
for Teaching Expressive Writing

Chapter Objectives

Upon successful completion of this chapter, you will be able to:

1. RECOGNIZE the complexity of expressive writing tasks.
2. IDENTIFY instructional factors that influence expressive writing performance.
3. COMPARE and CONTRAST the predominant methods of writing instruction.
4. LIST the hierarchy of skills necessary for expressive writing.
5. APPLY features of the generic instructional set in the design of expressive writing instruction.
6. APPLY the before, during, and after framework to expressive writing instruction.

EXPRESSIVE WRITING: THE PROBLEM

The scene is a fourth-grade class on the first day of school. After introductions and a review of classroom procedures and rules, the teacher makes the following assignment:

> Class, I want you to write a three-page paper. The title of the paper should be *How I Spent My Summer Vacation*. Remember to use good writing skills. Be creative. You will have 30 minutes to complete your paper. Any questions?

A few students eagerly begin to write, others sit idly pondering what to write, the remainder have somewhat puzzled looks on their faces. One student raises a hand and asks, "Does spelling count?" while another looks for a pencil with an eraser. At the end of the 30-minute period, the teacher collects the papers, which vary in length from two sentences to three pages and in legibility from quite readable to some semblance of English orthography. The teacher evaluates the papers, emphasizing spelling, punctuation, and capitalization, and returns them to the students with a few cryptic notes such as "Watch your spelling" and "Make sure you use complete sentences."

Clearly, this is a worst-case scenario of writing instruction; a case where students are asked to perform a complex task with no instruction. Nonetheless, this practice has prevailed over time and is certainly not restricted to fourth-grade classrooms. Fortunately, educators are learning more about writing skills and are using this knowledge to improve instruction in expressive writing. Interest in writing and ways of promoting writing skill has grown dramatically within the past few years. This chapter highlights these recent findings, identifies the intricacies and difficulties of expressive writing, and presents methods to teach expressive writing skills to low-performing students.

Undoubtedly, we have all experienced anxieties analogous to those created by the first-day-of-school writing task. The act of committing ideas to paper is often laborious, threatening, and problematic for many individuals. Scardamalia and Bereiter (1986) noted that writing difficulty "is not a matter of a minority . . . but rather a matter of the majority" (p. 778). If writing is such a difficult undertaking for academically successful individuals, imagine the reactions and difficulties of the student with low achievement.

From the low performer to the university graduate student, written expression is the most complex of language skills. In the hierarchy of language skills, it is the last to develop in the sequence of listening, speaking, reading, and writing. As a fundamental means of communicating information in the academic areas, it cannot be ignored.

Defining Expressive Writing

In this chapter, we use the term **expressive writing** to refer to text the learner composes. The composition unit may be as small as a phrase or as extensive as a research paper. Some reserve the term for activities in which the writer relates personal experiences or creates prose to express emotions and opinions. We define expressive writing as any writing activity that involves the generation, organization, selection, and transcription of ideas and information. It may be as simple as writing a sentence to describe what is happening in a picture or as complex as composing an essay conveying one's opinions on capital punishment.

As depicted in Figure 11–1, expressive writing involves multiple skills that begin with the copying and correcting of text and progress to writing simple sentences, a paragraph of text, and finally multi-paragraph prose.

It also includes the mechanical components of writing, such as using correct capitalization and punctuation, that historically have dominated writing instruction. However, expressive writing is much more comprehensive and goes beyond simple copying or applying grammatical rules.

For decades, teachers have questioned whether writing can be taught. Our premise is that expressive writing is a set of skills that can be taught and learned much like any other academic skill. Writing skills are teachable and not an innate gift endowed to a select group of individuals whose surnames are Hemingway or Dickens. Undeniably, our instructional methods may not transform *all* nonwriters to poet laureates. However, the answer to whether writing can be taught is an emphatic and enthusiastic yes!

Teachers are responsible for helping learners to acquire and master writing skills, enabling them to satisfy academic and social uses of written language. For students to learn how to write, they will need explicit instruction. An important principle of this text is that for academically at-risk and low-performing students *teaching* how must precede *learning* how. Simply assigning a writing topic in no way assures that students will learn how to write; *they must be taught*. To frame the design and delivery of expressive writing instruction, we will first examine the state of writing instruction.

Instructional Explanations for Writing Deficits

Writing involves a host of skills, any one of which could create problems for low performers. Writing on the topic "What I Would Do If I Found $100" requires the composer to generate ideas, transform ideas into words, write, spell, punctuate, capitalize, space, indent, follow grammatical rules, use appropriate plural and possessive word forms, structure sentences within paragraphs, use consistent tenses, organize and link paragraphs, evaluate, and revise the composition. Obviously, the demands and difficulties vary according to the task. However, even simple sentences require the coordination and mastery of multiple skills.

Researchers and practitioners offer a number of plausible factors to explain the difficulties people experience on written expression tasks (Isaacson, 1987; Scardamalia & Bereiter, 1986; Shanahan, 1980). In keeping with the assumptions of this text, we will focus on the instructional variables that teachers can control to impact students' writing

FIGURE 11–1
Progression of expressive writing skills

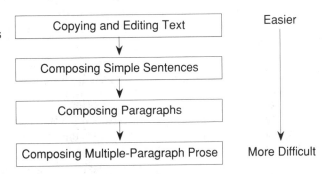

skills. Specifically, we confine our discussion to problems in current instructional practices. This component draws heavily on the work of Stephen Isaacson (1987), and we encourage readers to consult his work for a more comprehensive review.

Writing tasks require the orchestration of a host of skills that eventually result in a permanent product, a product that displays to the audience the thoughts and competencies of the writer. Although students are frequently asked to write, only within the last decade has writing competency received substantive attention (Scardamalia & Bereiter, 1986). As a result of this increased focus, emerging evidence indicates that learners' writing deficiencies can be addressed through instruction. Because writing research and instruction is in its infancy, the findings are not definitive, but they do shed light on a critical skill that students often lack and teachers seldom teach.

Teachers Are Not Taught How to Teach Writing

An undisputed finding of educational researchers is that students receive minimal instruction in how to write. This condition stems partly from teachers' inadequate preparation at the preservice level. Shanahan (1980) reported that recent studies of teacher preparation programs indicate only 5% offer courses in writing instruction. Furthermore, basal programs offer teachers little direction and few strategy suggestions (Isaacson, 1987).

The instructional void in educational curricula results in part from a lack of information about how best to teach writing. Given this lack of instructional direction, teachers' attempts to teach writing by letting children write is certainly understandable. The predominant models of writing instruction offer conflicting methods of teaching writing, leaving teachers without clear procedures to undertake this complex task. Because of this lack of training, the following explanation for writing deficiencies will come as no surprise.

Minimal Attention to Explicit Writing Instruction

Although reading, mathematics, and spelling skills are established components of the academic curriculum, systematic and explicit writing instruction rarely is. Students receive writing tasks such as "Write an ending to the story" or "Write a report about elephants," but these assignments are seldom prefaced by instruction. Students ostensibly learn expressive writing skills through repeated practice rather than direct instruction. Applebee (1984) noted that "writing is more likely to be assessed than taught" (p. 194), and the instruction that does occur is in the form of teaching basic mechanical conventions such as punctuation or capitalization. Clearly, this approach contributes to students' writing difficulties.

Minimal Time Allocated to Writing Tasks

A related factor that presumably affects students' writing skills is their opportunity to write. Under ideal conditions, students would be taught writing skills and then provided opportunities to practice those skills under teacher supervision. Such conditions are not commonplace in either special or regular classrooms. Leinhardt, Zigmond, and Cooley (1980) found that students with learning disabilities in self-contained classrooms spend less than 10 minutes per day composing. British children spend an average of 9 1/2 hours per week composing; U.S. children only 1 1/2 hours per week (cf. Isaacson, 1987). Obviously, there is a significant discrepancy between the importance of writing skills and the time allocated those skills in the instructional environment. Researchers suggest scheduling writing activities daily rather than using them as filler activities when there is "extra" time on Friday afternoons. Writing instruction and practice must assume an established position in the academic curriculum if we are to address the writing deficiencies of low-performing students.

Scheduling opportunities to write, however, is necessary but insufficient to correct students' expressive writing difficulties. Merely letting students write without providing instruction will not correct fundamental skill-based deficits. Admittedly, skills do improve with practice. Practice allows you to run farther than you did the first time on the track, to speak more fluently than you did during your first group presentation, to answer math facts more rapidly than you did during the previous trial. However, any learning that occurs from practice is reactive. Students perform the skill and, if fortunate, learn from feedback. This is an inefficient and costly sequence for students with low achievement who need to narrow the gap between where they are functioning academically and where they should be functioning. A more cost-efficient and profitable sequence teaches learners writing conventions, rules, and strategies before asking them to apply these principles in practice. The desirable instructional sequence couples explicit instruction with increased opportunities to write.

Once students receive fundamental writing instruction, writing practice is a logical and necessary requirement. However, just "getting students to write" is apt to be a problem because of their aversive experiences with writing. Educational researchers are currently studying the potential of the computer as a means of increasing students' opportunity to practice writing and simultaneously making the writing task more motivating.

"Computers appear to have the potential for fostering higher-order abilities in composing . . ." (Scardamalia & Bereiter, 1986, p. 797). Computers presumably make the laborious tasks of correcting spelling, punctuation, capitalization, and formatting errors more palatable. Higher-level structural, organizational, and content changes would also apparently be less-demanding when performed on the computer. Emerging evidence documents some of the advantages of having unskilled writers compose on microcomputer word processors.

Vacc (1987) found that adolescents with mild mental handicaps wrote significantly longer letters and made more revisions when writing letters on the computer instead of writing by hand. However, overall, holistic evaluation ratings did not differ between computer-written and handwritten letters. Although results suggest that computer-produced products are superior to conventional handwritten letters on some measures, regardless of what tool is used to compose the text, we reiterate the importance of teaching prior to practicing expressive writing tasks.

Writing Instruction Is Introduced Too Late in the Curriculum

An additional instructional factor that influences expressive writing skills involves *when* writing instruction is introduced in the curriculum (Isaacson, 1987; Shanahan, 1980). Typically, writing instruction is reserved until students are proficient readers. Researchers indicate that the "traditional approach to curriculum design and instruction where students receive several years of reading instruction preceding the introduction of writing is unnecessarily inefficient" (Shanahan & Lomax, 1986, p. 123). The delay of writing instruction can deter writing skills (Juel, 1988; Shanahan & Lomax, 1986) because students fail to benefit from coordinated reading and writing activities.

Emerging evidence indicates the reciprocal relationship between reading and writing (Shanahan & Lomax, 1986). That is, reading and writing are interactive skills that tend to build on each other. Reading skills such as word analysis and familiarity with story structures complement students' spelling and story writing. Conversely, writing skills including vocabulary diversity and grammatical syntax also relate to improved reading comprehension (Shanahan & Lomax, 1986).

Programs that withhold writing instruction until learners master the bulk of reading skills fail to capitalize on the shared benefits available from a combined reading-writing curriculum. Based on these findings, teachers should initiate writing instruction as soon as students are capable of reading short units of connected text at the sentence level.

Relationship Between Reading and Writing Performance

The previous sections addressed instructional factors that account for students' writing deficits. However, any discussion of writing performance is incomplete if it fails to acknowledge the relationship between a student's reading and writing performance. This information is even more valuable if it provides instructional direction. We discuss the relationship between reading and writing to point out the possible impact of reading instruction on writing performance.

A high correlation exists between a student's reading and writing ability. That is, students who are good readers are usually also good writers, and vice versa. Although there are a few exceptions, the rule generally holds true.

In a longitudinal study, Juel (1988) examined the reading and writing development of children as they progressed from first through fourth grades. Some of her specific interests were whether poor writers remain poor writers, what skills poor writers lack, and what factors keep poor writers from improving. Her research findings indicate that poor writing ability in the first grade is significantly related to poor fourth-grade writing skills; however, this relationship tends to strengthen in second and third grades. In other words, the probability of remaining a poor writer increases with grade level. The instructional factors previously discussed in this chapter undoubtedly have a bearing on this relationship. If low-performing students receive little instruction and little time to practice, it is doubtful their skills will change.

From her findings, Juel (1988) characterized the deficits of 21 less-skilled writers. Seven poor writers had good spelling but poor expression of ideas. Seven poor writers had good expression of ideas but poor spelling. The remaining seven had both poor spelling and poor expression of ideas. She concluded that lower-level skills such as spelling directly influence children's willingness to write and ultimately their quality and quantity of writing.

Obviously, expressive writing involves much more than spelling and the mechanical features of handwriting and capitalization. However, when these features deviate so greatly from acceptable ranges, they can obscure the message of the composition. Furthermore, when mechanical skills have not reached an automatic level, they consume excessive cognitive resources, leaving little for generating ideas and composing organized products. Juel (1988) noted that in earlier grades, spelling deficits make it "just too difficult to write a story" (p. 15) because of the effort expended on lower-level tasks.

Finally, Juel (1988) examined factors that keep poor writers from improving, and we have already discussed some plausible instructional explanations for this situation. Juel examined the relationship between reading and writing, and with few exceptions found that poor readers become poor writers. Of the 21 students identified as poor readers, 17 were also poor writers. The majority could neither write good stories nor tell good stories. Poor writers wrote descriptive text rather than text that followed a narrative storyline.

The findings of this study also reinforce the need to establish decoding skills early in children's academic careers. The majority of poor readers who in turn became poor writers lacked phonemic skills such as segmenting and soundblending as well as phonics skills. Although it seems a circuitous route to improve writing, bolstering students' reading skills appears to be a means of enhancing writing skills. As we discussed in Chapter 7, students who do not read well learn fewer words through reading, encounter fewer concepts, and are less motivated to read (Stanovich, 1986). These deficiencies culminate in what Juel (1988) describes as a vicious cycle where students' reading and writing skills become more and more discrepant from those of their average-achieving peers. The findings of recent research confirm the effect that decoding deficits have on reading comprehension and point to their influence on students' writing skills as well.

Summary of Writing Instruction Inadequacies

A number of factors can explain students' lack of expressive writing skills. Teachers are not adequately prepared to teach writing. Students are not given sufficient opportunities to practice writing. Furthermore, writing is introduced too late in the academic curriculum. Despite these possible explanations, no factor has generated more controversy and attention than the actual procedures of how to teach writing. In the next section, we discuss the two prevailing methods for teaching written expression.

THEORETICAL MODELS OF WRITING

Historically, two models have dominated methods of teaching writing: product-based and process-based instruction. The controversies of these two models parallel those of the code-based and meaning-based models of reading. Although the ultimate instructional objective of both writing methods is to create writers who are able to express themselves clearly and effectively, the teaching procedures promoted in each model differ greatly.

Product Approach to Writing Instruction

The product approach to writing prevailed in the classroom until the last decade (Newcomer, Nodine, & Barenbaum, 1988) and focused primarily on grammar, spelling, capitalization, punctuation, and handwriting. Although a popular alternative to this approach exists, traces of the product approach linger in today's classrooms. The new wave of writing instruction was in large part precipitated by the inadequacies of the product-based approach. In the following analysis, Newcomer, Nodine, and Barenbaum (1988) describe the procedures and deficiencies of the product method:

> The product approach was based on the notion that students learn to write from reading and analyzing published texts and noting their stylistic and organization features. Having read the work of others, students were given assignments to write similar types of compositions. Those compositions, or products, were critiqued by teachers; errors—usually in mechanics—were marked and grades were assigned. Usually, the initial writing effort was regarded as the final draft. Instructional feedback was minimal during writing and no opportunities for revision were provided. (pp. 560–561)

The product approach exposes learners to multiple examples of sentences, paragraphs, poetry, and other prose formats. From this exposure, students are supposed to extract the critical features and apply them in their own writing products. For students with low achievement, exposure is not an efficient or sufficient means of effecting changes in writing skills. Average and above-average students are somehow able to benefit from being immersed in writing examples and receiving feedback. They may note the same-nesses and differences, the good points and bad points in the examples, and transfer this information to their own writing. It is doubtful low-performers will see the do's and don't's without more direct instruction.

Isaacson's (1987) analysis of writing products documented a range of differences between skilled and unskilled writers. He categorized writing skills according to five components common to the majority of writing tasks. The characteristics of skilled and unskilled writers are presented in Table 11–1. Not surprisingly, less-skilled writers exhibited difficulties in each of the five areas. These five components are presented in Figure 11–2.

The following writing samples in Figure 11–3 are products of an average-achieving student and a student identified as learning disabled, both enrolled in a fourth-grade classroom. The assignment was to read a passage in 3 minutes and to write about the passage for a specified time. Although the students were not required to generate original ideas, the products illustrate obvious differences in the students' writing skills.

Inspection of the products reveals they differ substantially in a number of component skill areas. Even though neither of the writers' products was flawless, the surface-level analysis of the products corroborates Isaacson's (1987) summary of findings.

First, the quantity written in the same amount of time by the less-skilled writer is substantially less than that of the skilled writer. The contents of the products vary according to completeness and detail, with the skilled writer including a sufficient amount of information for the reader to follow the storyline. Sentence length and complexity, vocabulary, as well as mechanical features such as spelling, handwriting legibility, and grammatical usage also confirm the difficulties posed by the task and instructional needs of the student.

A number of factors could account for differences in the students' products. First, the recall task itself may have favored the average-achieving student. It is quite probable the reading comprehension of the average-achiever exceeded that of the student with the learning disability. On the other hand, the task did not require the writers to generate

TABLE 11–1

The writing product of skilled and unskilled writers

Component	Unskilled Writer	Skilled Writer
Fluency	Writes few words in allocated times. Writes incomplete sentences.	Writes many words in allocated time. Writes complete sentences.
Syntax	Writes in simple S-V or S-V-O sentences.	Writes in longer, complex sentences with embedded clauses and phrases.
Vocabulary	Uses high-frequency words. Uses favored words repetitiously.	Uses mature words. Avoids repeating favorite words.
Content	Shows disregard of audience. Includes irrelevant information. Has poor organization and structure.	Uses style appropriate to topic and audience. Keeps to topic with good cohesion from sentence to sentence and overall. Produces compositions that have good beginning, logical development, and clear conclusion.
Conventions	Spells many words incorrectly. Omits punctuation or uses incorrectly. Writes illegibly. Errs in use of verb inflections and/or choice of pronouns.	Spells adequately. Uses correct punctuation. Writes legibly. Presents reasonably neat paper. Uses correct verb endings and pronouns.

From "Effective Instruction in Written Language" by S. L. Isaacson, 1987, *Focus on Exceptional Children, 19,* p. 4. Copyright 1987 by Love Publishing Company. Reprinted by permission.

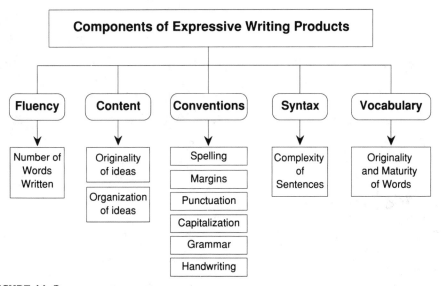

FIGURE 11–2

Components of expressive writing products

427

Product of Student of Average Achievement

Once there were 3 sons there father wanted to know witch one was the bravest, So he called his advisers, His advisers called the kings sons to the oak tree, They said "Witch ever son is the bravest and can do the best trick is the strongest, The people of the castle gathered round, The first son jumped with his horse and made a hole then he jumped back through the hole, The second son jumped over the tree and

Product of Student With Learning Disability

Cheif made the sons get on their horses and rid to the oak tree and when they they got to the oaktree do a trick. The cheif didn't no whech one was the most clever. The cheif went to a metteing.

FIGURE 11–3
Writing products of a student of average achievement and a student with a learning disability

original information but rather to recall and record. This structure would tend to favor the writing product of students who have difficulty coming up with ideas.

Experts generally agree the product approach to writing instruction is outmoded and fails to provide a comprehensive picture of the student's skills. We contend that the fundamental flaw with this method is its failure to *teach* writing. Although many examples may be provided in the product approach, there is a missing link in this model— *systematic* and *explicit* instruction. Prior to writing, students should be taught rather than exposed to expressive writing tasks. The write-evaluate-review sequence is simply an unacceptable method for students with academic learning difficulties.

Process Approach to Writing Instruction

Within recent years, a popular alternative to the product-based method of writing instruction has emerged (Newcomer, Nodine, & Barenbaum, 1988). The shift to the process approach grew largely from the inadequacies of the product approach (Hume, 1983). Teachers and researchers wanted to know more about the procedures the writer employs to develop a written product.

The process-based approach stresses the writing process and emphasizes three basic, interactive writing stages: prewriting (planning), writing (translating), and rewriting (revising) (Hayes & Flower, 1980). During the **planning phase**, students generate ideas about topics, organize these ideas, activate background knowledge, and essentially develop the framework for the composition. This phase includes the preparatory efforts the writer makes to get the thoughts ready for paper. In the **translating phase**, the writer converts this information into text or written language. Students are encouraged to think of this as the drafting stage, a first attempt to translate ideas into text. In the **rewriting phase**, writers modify their original draft, making changes in content as well as correcting spelling and grammatical errors as the product is put into final form.

The process is the general steps the writer uses to create the written product. Hayes and Flower (1980) stress that the writer is not bound to follow the three steps rigidly but may enter different phases as demanded by the writing task. For example, ideas may be developed during the transcribing phase or while editing. According to this theory, the writer may return to other phases as needed.

In the process approach, the teacher assumes the role of facilitator: conferring with the writer, discussing, questioning, suggesting, and responding. Rather than recording concerns and comments on the final product, the teacher works the student through the composition. For example, the teacher might say, "You have some good ideas for your story on dogs. Is there anything else you think is important to include?"

Advocates promote the process-based approach as a tool for self-expression. Not surprisingly, the processes skilled writers use to express themselves differ from those of less-skilled writers. Isaacson (1987) summarized these process differences in Table 11–2.

The writing process is admittedly an important phase of writing skills development that is far superior to the "give them a topic and let them write practice." When these processes are taught, students learn strategies for attacking this complex task of writing. Unfortunately, like most writing skills, the process of how to write is seldom taught in the academic curriculum.

TABLE 11–2
The writing process of skilled and unskilled writers

Stage	Unskilled Writer	Skilled Writer
Planning	Does not participate in prewriting discussions.	Explores and discusses topic.
	Spends little time thinking about topic before beginning composition.	Spends time considering what will be written and how it will be expressed.
	Makes no plans or notes.	Jots notes; draws diagrams or pictures.
Transcribing	Writes informally in imitation of speech.	Writes in style learned from models of composition.
	Is preoccupied with technical matters of spelling and punctuation.	Keeps audience in mind while writing.
	Stops only briefly and infrequently.	Stops frequently to reread. Takes long thought pauses.
Revising	Does not review or rewrite.	Reviews frequently.
	Looks only for surface errors (spelling, punctuation).	Makes content revisions, as well as spelling and punctuation corrections.
	Rewrites only to make a neat copy in ink.	Keeps audience in mind while rewriting.

From "Effective Instruction in Written Language" by S. L. Isaacson, 1987, *Focus on Exceptional Children, 19*, p. 6. Copyright 1987 by Love Publishing Company. Reprinted by permission.

However, even if we teach students how to plan, draft, revise and edit, the success of this writing process rests on the assumption that students have fundamental writing skills. The majority of research examining the efficacy of the process approach has not involved students of low academic achievement; therefore, process approach advocates must proceed with caution when making instructional recommendations for writing instruction (Newcomer, Nodine, & Barenbaum, 1988).

We contend that the tension between writing methods is unnecessary. Just as the controversy over the code-based and meaning-based approach divides the reading community, the same tension exists among writing researchers and teachers of writing. Expressive writing is more than the sum of its parts. It is more than processes and products. Good writers need basic writing skills.

A SKILLS ANALYSIS OF EXPRESSIVE WRITING

This chapter offers a skill-based analysis and approach to expressive writing instruction. This approach teaches a set of basic skills and systematically develops these skills for advanced exercises and applications. To ensure that students learn and maintain this foundation of basic writing skills, we rely on specific instructional design principles to govern expressive writing instruction. Specifically, we apply the before, during, and after phases as the instructional framework and couple this with the specific steps of the generic instructional set used throughout the text.

The conceptual framework and specific skills analysis draw from two writing programs: (1) the Expressive Writing I program by Englemann and Silbert (1985) and (2) Action Express Paragraph and Story Writers by Howe and Kameenui (1983). Both programs endorse the skill-based approach to beginning expressive writing instruction rather than the process-based alternative. We consider this emphasis most appropriate for children with academic learning problems or unskilled writers in the beginning stage of expressive writing instruction. Engelmann and Silbert (1985) provide the rationale for a skill-based approach to expressive writing instruction:

> Teachers understand that teaching reading to beginners involves a careful sequence of steps. No teacher would expect the beginning reader to tackle fifth-grade material because this material requires too many reading skills. Paradoxically, teachers often fail to recognize that expressive writing is like reading. Writing involves a series of skills and implies a sequence of activities, starting with those that are basic to all expressive writing. (p. 1)

A skill-based approach to expressive writing focuses first on the writing of the basic sentence.

We agree the foundation of writing instruction is teaching students to express their thoughts clearly in basic sentences. In our analysis of expressive writing, the basic sentence serves as the primary building block. Basic sentences are simple declarative statements that name someone or something and tell more. As students master basic sentence writing, they extend expressive writing skills to paragraph and story writing.

Our analysis of writing is in keeping with Hayes and Flower's (1980) three phases of writing—the planning phase, the writing phase, and the editing phase. However, the sequence in which we teach these phases differs. Our instructional emphasis focuses first on the writing and editing phases. Once beginning writers master the mechanics of writing and editing, the process of planning is introduced and developed. In short, our analysis provides students the skills of writing, then teaches them to rely on those skills when engaging in the process of planning more complex written products such as narrative and descriptive paragraph writing. In the sequence of writing instruction, we introduce the student-initiated planning phase last because initial phases are teacher-directed. This sequence of phases does not require the traditional planning process discussed by Hayes and Flower (1980) because the teacher defines the specific task requirements. As instructional sequences progress, writing tasks become more complex and rely more on student-directed and student-generated activities than on teacher-directed tasks. By this point in students' writing development, they possess the basic skills that will allow them to engage in the process of writing creatively and expressively.

Scope and Sequence of Beginning Writing Skills

A skills analysis of expressive writing, like the analysis of other complex academic skills (e.g., decoding, reading comprehension, mathematics), requires a scope and sequence. Because expressive writing is one of the most complex cognitive operations, the scope and sequence of skills is likely to be extensive. Expressive writing involves multiple strands of complex cognitive and motoric skills, all of which must be executed spontaneously, simultaneously, and intelligently. As Isaacson (1987) noted, the task of expressing one's thoughts in words can be very difficult for low performers and naive writers. Clearly, the complexity of expressive writing makes identifying a scope and sequence of skills a difficult and somewhat elusive task. It is not surprising that teachers begin expressive writing by requiring naive writers to use their imaginations to write a story.

We contend a story-writing task places an unfair burden on beginning or unskilled writers. It requires them to "write in acceptable sentences, capitalize and punctuate appropriately, possibly create a variety of 'interesting sentences,' follow rules of grammar and verb-noun agreement, use consistent tenses, organize paragraphs appropriately, and display imagination or creativity" (Engelmann & Silbert, 1985, pp. 1–2). Obviously, such tasks require the mastery of a wide range of skills, many of which have yet to be taught in writing programs. Each of these skills requires deliberate demonstration, careful explanation, extensive practice, and sustained attention over time. In short, the teaching of expressive writing skills commands the careful consideration of design of instruction principles.

The proposed scope and sequence of skills for expressive writing is for beginning writing instruction only and is not comprehensive. It does not address more complex and advanced writing forms such as descriptive or argumentative writing forms. This scope and sequence merges skills proposed by Engelmann and Silbert (1985) and Gleason (1988) and consists of four major strands. We list the major strands and the component skills within each of these core writing skill areas:

1. Mechanics of writing.
   a. Copying sentences accurately.
   b. Capitalizing the first word in a sentence.
   c. Ending a telling sentence with a period.
   d. Ending an asking sentence with a question mark.
   e. Indenting the first word of a paragraph.
2. Writing simple sentences.
   a. Identifying a sentence as naming somebody or something and telling more about the person or thing.
   b. Selecting sentences that name somebody or something and tell more about the person or thing depicted in the picture.
   c. Completing sentences that name somebody or something and tell more about the person or thing depicted in a picture or series of pictures.
   d. Generating sentences that tell the "main thing" that happened in a picture or series of pictures.
   e. Generating sentences that name somebody or something and tell more about the person or thing without use of pictures.
   f. Combining simple sentences to create more complex sentences.
3. Writing paragraphs.
   a. Identifying a paragraph as naming a topic and telling more about the topic depicted in a picture.
   b. Identifying the topic of a paragraph as the "main thing" the paragraph tells about as depicted in a picture or series of pictures.
   c. Completing paragraphs that refer to pictures.
   d. Generating paragraphs that report on an individual in an illustration.
   e. Generating paragraphs that tell about a series of things an individual did in a sequence of pictures.
   f. Generating paragraphs that interpret what must have happened between pictures in a sequence.
   g. Generating paragraphs without reference to pictures.
4. Editing.
   a. Identifying sentences that do not report on what a picture shows.
   b. Correcting mistakes in capitalization and punctuation.
   c. Identifying sentences in a paragraph that do not tell about a specified topic.
   d. Correcting run-on sentences.
   e. Correcting sentences with present-tense verbs by changing them to past-tense and writing all sentences in past-tense.
   f. Correcting inappropriate noun-verb relationships and inappropriate pronouns.

The four instructional strands (mechanics of writing, writing simple sentences, writing paragraphs, and editing) comprise the core skills of a beginning expressive writing program. Naturally, expressive writing in its most advanced state involves many other skills not identified in the previous scope and sequence. This chapter focuses only on skills necessary to teach beginning expressive writing. In the next section, we provide a rationale for the component skills of this scope and sequence. We also explain the range of instructional formats and instructional tools to teach these skills.

Scope and Sequence Rationale

Use of pictures.   The proposed scope and sequence for teaching beginning expressive writing has two unique instructional features. First, on beginning tasks, writers report on events depicted in a picture rather than events or ideas generated in their imaginations. Pictures provide an instructional tool that allows teachers to control and monitor what students are writing. Because the content of writing is restricted to vocabulary and events related to the picture, teachers can more readily evaluate the accuracy and adequacy of the information students write. For example, the sentence-writing task that follows requires students to write a sentence about the picture.

Write a sentence that names the person in the picture and tells more about the person.

Relying on pictures in the beginning stages of teaching writing is in stark contrast to tasks that encourage students to use their memory and imagination as the primary vehicles to teach writing. Tasks such as "Write about your summer vacation" require much of the writer. Analyzing failure in less-structured tasks is virtually impossible because of the multiple demands placed on the writer. When students fail to write products of sufficient length or quality, it is difficult to determine whether the problem is due to lack of knowledge of the content, insufficient task knowledge, or the mechanical demands of the assignment. Pictures in beginning writing assignments control the complexity of the writing task by limiting the requirements placed on the learner. We should note, however, that pictures are a tool for beginning writing instruction and should be gradually faded as students develop writing proficiency. Progressively, less-structured task sources such as starter sentences and general topics are scheduled, but only after students master basic writing skills under structured conditions using pictures.

Task formats.   The second feature of the scope and sequence is the task format. Specifically, the initial task formats for beginning writing instruction are highly teacher-directed. In beginning exercises, teachers structure, model, and direct each instructional activity. Initial sequences begin with simple task formats and progress to more complex types that provide less structure and place greater demands on the writer. For example, beginning writing tasks require students merely to *select* complete, simple sentences. This selection task requires students to discriminate sentences that do and do not follow the rule for a simple sentence. Students are taught the rule, "A simple sentence names someone or something, then tells more about that person or thing." Once students master this selection format involving the discrimination of positive and negative examples of simple sentences, a sentence completion task is introduced. In completion task formats, the writer *completes* a sentence either by naming a person or thing or by telling more about a person or thing already named in a sentence. Following the mastery of sentence completion writing tasks, the writer *generates* or produces complete simple sentences based on events depicted in a picture or series of pictures. Eventually, the instructional format of a writing task (e.g., teacher-directed tasks consisting of selection responses) and the instructional tools (e.g., single pictures vs. a sequence of pictures) are changed to allow the beginning writer more independence and ownership in the writing product (e.g., no teacher assistance and no pictures).

Example tasks occurring in the beginning phases of noun-verb agreement instruction illustrate the sentence completion task requirements:

The dog _____ in the house. (was were)

The dog and the cat _____ in the house. (was were)

In this task, the writer *selects* the correct verb. In subsequent, more advanced editing task formats, the writer identifies errors of noun-verb agreement in paragraphs, then later *generates* sentences incorporating noun-verb agreement in paragraphs.

Introducing simple tasks before complex tasks and using pictures are instructional tools that reduce writing demands and facilitate performance feedback. They are instructional design features—the same types of features used throughout this text. Similarly, instructional sequences that require students to master simple sentence construction before generating paragraphs illustrate the importance of instructional design in expressive writing. The proposed scope and sequence of writing skills adheres to these fundamental principles. Table 11–3 summarizes selected design features used to structure expressive writing instruction with unskilled writers. This table also specifies how these features must vary with the skill level of the writer.

In addition to addressing these task and learner requirements, a well-designed writing program must be comprehensive—teaching the major core skills of sentence writing, mechanics and editing. In other words, exercises involving sentence writing are taught in conjunction with editing and mechanical skills. This melding of writing skills allows teachers to address the isolated skills while illustrating the cohesiveness and relationship of these component skills to the overall writing product. A typical 30-minute lesson should include activities in each of the core skill areas with the exception of paragraph writing. Paragraph writing skills are introduced only after students are able to generate acceptable simple sentences. The content of each lesson necessarily varies with the learner. General guidelines for structuring a writing lesson follow in Table 11–4.

The sample lesson is unlike a traditional beginning writing lesson because it does not involve a sustained period of "creative writing" during which students write freely. Instead, this lesson integrates skills from three of the four major skills strands into a cohesive lesson. Naturally, 5 and 10 minutes of instruction and practice in each skill area

TABLE 11–3
Design features of expressive writing instruction

Variables	Beginning Writing Instruction	Advanced Writing Instruction
Degree of Teacher Guidance	Extensive ⟶⟶⟶⟶⟶⟶⟶⟶⟶⟶ Minimal (Fade as students demonstrate skill mastery)	
Instructional Tools	Single picture ⟶ Multiple pictures ⟶ Topic sentence ⟶ Topic	
Task Format	Selection response ⟶ Completion response ⟶ Generation response	
Writing Product	Words ⟶ Sentences ⟶ Paragraphs	

is not very significant when considered within one lesson. However, the development of these individual component skills on a daily basis and sustained over a period of 50 to 60 lessons *is* significant. Daily instruction that provides the beginning writer continuous modeling and practice on a set of complex skills allows unskilled and naive writers to become experienced, successful, and creative.

Advanced lessons should also incorporate multiple strands of writing skills and build on the skills developed early in the writing program. These lessons should include greater concentrations of complex paragraph writing and editing tasks than earlier lessons. Instructional tasks should also be less teacher-directed, involve more student-

TABLE 11–4
Activities and time allocations for beginning expressive writing lesson

Tasks	Core Writing Area	Specific Writing Skill	Time Allocation
Task 1	Writing simple sentences	Identifying a sentence as naming somebody or something and telling more about the person or thing (review task)	5–8 minutes
Task 2	Mechanics of writing	Copying sentences (review task)	5–8 minutes
Task 3	Writing simple sentences	Review of 1–2 examples from Task 1 Selecting sentences that name somebody or something and tell more about the person or thing depicted in the picture	8–10 minutes
Task 4	Editing	Identifying and correcting capitalization errors in simple sentences that name somebody and tell more	5–8 minutes
Task 5	Review	Summary of writing, editing, and mechanics tasks	3–5 minutes

generated writing, and rely less on picture-based writing products. In addition, advanced lessons should involve fewer separate tasks (e.g., three individual tasks) and engage students in increasingly longer periods of writing activity. By later writing lessons, basic mechanical skills are in place, thus creating more time for sustained instruction and writing practice. An example that specifies the time, skill, and task requirements of advanced writing lessons follows in Table 11–5.

Although tasks in advanced writing lessons are more complex and require more time than those in simpler lessons, they rely heavily on skills developed in earlier lessons. For instance, in more complex tasks students still need to apply and monitor lower-level mechanical skills such as capitalization and punctuation while also adhering to the rules for constructing simple sentences.

Writing researchers as well as program developers recommend teaching students to use self-monitoring checklists to evaluate and edit their writing products. After completing the writing exercise, the writer checks the product for the specific criteria on the checklist. Items on the checklist vary according to the specific skill being taught. Beginning skills checklists will necessarily be more focused and restricted than lists for advanced writing products. A sample checklist for a beginning paragraph writing lesson might contain the following items:[1]

1. Does each sentence begin with a capital?   Yes   No
   (If no, correct the ones that do not.)

2. Does each telling sentence end with a period?   Yes   No
   (If no, correct the ones that do not.)

3. Does each asking sentence end with a question mark?   Yes   No
   (If no, correct the ones that do not.)

4. Is the first word of the paragraph indented?   Yes   No
   (If no, correct.)

5. Does each sentence tell more about the person in the picture?   Yes   No
   (If no, find the ones that do not and either remove them or change them
   to report on the person.)

6. Does the order of the sentences make sense?   Yes   No
   (If no, reorder the sentences.)

7. Does the paragraph have run-on sentences?   Yes   No
   (If yes, correct.)

Checklist statements serve as important reminders of the features of good writing. Their systematic use in beginning writing instruction prompts students to internalize these rules and features over time. In more advanced writing lessons, teachers can phase out the checklist statements or provide minimal cues to prompt students to edit their work.

Much like reading, expressive writing is a cumulative skill. Advanced applications such as creative story writing depend on the acquisition and automaticity of lower-level skills. If students do not have basic simple sentence-generation skills, it is unlikely their paragraphs and essays will pass minimal acceptable standards. In the next section, we discuss how to foster students' beginning writing skills by applying the generic instructional set to expressive writing instruction.

---

[1]Adapted from *Expressive Writing I: Teacher Presentation Book* (p. 7) by S. Engelmann and J. Silbert, 1985, Chicago: Science Research Associates. Copyright 1985 by SRA. Adapted by permission.

TABLE 11–5
Activities and time allocations for advanced expressive writing lesson

Tasks	Core Writing Area	Specific Writing Skill	Time Allocation
Task 1	Writing paragraphs	Review of critical rules for writing paragraphs	3–5 minutes
Task 2	Writing paragraphs	Writing a sequence of 2–3 paragraphs from a topic sentence (e.g., transportation today is very different from 20 years ago)	25–30 minutes
Task 3	Editing paragraphs according to specified criteria	Correcting run-on sentences Checking verb tense Correcting mechanical errors in punctuation and capitalization	5–8 minutes

USING THE GENERIC INSTRUCTIONAL SET IN EXPRESSIVE WRITING

The skills analysis of beginning expressive writing presented so far in this chapter can also be framed within the generic instructional set. The generic instructional set alerts the teacher to the minimum requirements of a beginning writing lesson. In the next section, we identify each component of the generic instructional set and describe its application to designing expressive writing teaching sequences.

Knowledge Form

As we noted earlier, expressive writing is a complex cognitive and motoric operation because it involves the written communication or expression of ideas. Teaching students how to express these ideas in written form requires various forms of knowledge ranging from discriminations to rule relationships to cognitive strategies. The knowledge form varies with the specific writing skill. For example, the construction of simple sentences can be taught through a rule relationship: "A simple sentence names somebody or something, then tells more about that person or thing." This rule relationship specifies the connection between the critical features of a simple sentence; a sentence must (1) name somebody or something, then (2) tell more about that person or thing. Paragraph writing, on the other hand, is a cognitive strategy involving a principal rule relationship ("A paragraph is made of simple sentences that name a main topic and tell more about it") as well as rules governing the mechanical and organizational components of paragraphs. The primary rule specifies the connection between the critical features of a paragraph; a paragraph consists of (1) simple sentences that (2) name a topic and (3) tell more about that topic. Clearly, paragraph writing is a complicated skill.

Explicitly teaching the rule relationships for simple sentences and paragraphs before having students write clarifies the writing process and also makes it easier to determine the sources of difficulty. Through this teach-test sequence, checks can be made to determine whether students understand the features of the rule or strategy prior to compounding the task with actual writing requirements. These critical features are anchoring concepts that allow the naive writer to determine whether the written product meets the basic criteria of a sentence or paragraph. The absence of these features signals that the written product is not a sentence or a paragraph. For example, the statement "A dog" is not a sentence because it names something but does not tell more about that thing. The statement "Sat in the corner" is not a sentence because it does not name somebody or something.

Writing skills also involve less complex knowledge forms such as discriminations, simple facts, and basic concepts. Copying sentences is a motor task in which the writer compares and discriminates the accuracy of the product against the original text. Changing the present tense form of an irregular verb to its past tense form is a simple fact. No rule or strategy is available that would allow the writer to derive the correct past tense of irregular verb forms (run—ran). Therefore, presenting the verb as a simple fact, "The past tense of *run* is *ran*," is the most direct and precise method to teach irregular verb forms. When teaching this simple fact, the teacher presents the fact, uses the present form in context, "The children run in the park," then models the past tense in context, "The children ran in the park." Only irregular verb forms are taught as simple facts. Present/past tense conversions of regular verbs are best taught through rule relationships.

Rule relationships are the predominant knowledge form of expressive writing skills. For example, the mechanical components of writing, such as capitalization, punctuation, and indentation, all entail rule relationships. Simple sentence generation is also taught through a rule relationship: "A sentence names somebody or something and tells more about that person or thing." Clearly, this rule is limited by its simplicity. It does not discuss the grammatical constraints that sentences must have subjects and predicates; neither does it specify that a sentence must express a complete thought. The language of this rule was selected because it is manageable and understandable for naive and low-performing students. We demonstrate the sophisticated requirements for sentence writing through examples. From the modeling of multiple examples and a range of sentences, students induce the critical features of sentences.

As in all other academic skills, the knowledge form establishes the basis for teaching. The following examples identify selected component skills of the four major writing strands and classify the knowledge form of each.

Component Writing Skills Classified by Knowledge Form

WRITING TASK 11–1
Copying Sentences Accurately

Writing Strand: Mechanics.

Knowledge Form: Discrimination—motor task.

Component Skills

1. Fine motor skills to coordinate and execute handwriting.
2. Ability to discriminate accurate from inaccurate copying.

Instructional Procedures

1. Identify correct copy.
2. Identify incorrect copy.
3. Model discrimination of correct and incorrect copy.
4. Lead learner in discrimination exercise.
5. Test learner on discrimination exercise.

WRITING TASK 11–2
Generating a Sentence About a Picture

Writing Strand: Writing simple sentences.

Knowledge Form: Rule relationship
"A sentence names somebody or something and tells more about that person or thing."

Component Skills

1. Selecting a sentence from a group of sentences that tell about a picture.
2. Completing the missing component of the sentence (either naming the person or thing or telling more about the person or thing).
3. Using proper writing mechanics and conventions: capitalization, punctuation, spelling, handwriting.

Instructional Procedures

1. State rule relationship and repeat it.
2. Review selection procedure, identifying sentence that tells about the picture.
3. Review sentence completion task, having students practice completing both components of sentence.
4. Model procedure for generating a sentence from picture.
5. Have student verbally generate the person or thing in the picture.
6. Have student verbally generate the "tells more" part of the sentence.
7. Request students to record the sentence on paper.
8. Evaluate the sentence by applying components of the rule relationship.
9. Repeat with additional pictures.

WRITING TASK 11–3
Correcting Mistakes in Capitalization

Writing Strand: Editing.

Knowledge Form: Rule relationship
"The first word in a sentence begins with a capital letter."

Component Skills

1. Identifying first word of sentence.
2. Discriminating capital from lowercase letters.
3. Identifying sentence units.

Instructional Procedures

1. Model rule relationship in five or six positive and negative examples.
2. Lead learner in applying rule to sentences.
3. Model an additional example of sentence.
4. Repeat step 2.
5. Test learner on capitalizing first word in sentence on at least three or four additional sentences.
6. Provide additional practice.

The previous examples of beginning writing skills are not exhaustive. Rather, they represent the range of skills and associated knowledge forms needed to design beginning expressive writing instruction.

Range of Examples

Expressive writing, like decoding, reading comprehension, and mathematics skills, is best taught through examples. Teaching students about the mechanics of writing or about simple sentences and paragraphs requires many examples of each of these skills. Although we propose teaching simple sentences through a rule relationship, we still present students positive and negative examples of simple sentences. Through examples, students acquire the critical information about sentences, paragraphs, editing, and mechanics of writing.

The range of examples for each of the four major strands of writing skills varies from skill to skill. For some component skills, such as paragraph writing, the range of examples is extensive. Paragraphs can be short, comprising simple sentences with straightforward messages. Paragraphs can also be lengthy, with complex sentences and highly abstract and philosophical messages. In contrast, teaching students the component skill of capitalizing the first word in a sentence involves a limited set of examples. Specifically, either the first word is capitalized or it isn't; a wide range of examples is not needed to communicate this fact to the naive writer.

The examples for each component writing skill can also vary according to the instructional format. For example, when students are taught to construct simple sentences, the instructional formats can range from sentence selection examples (students complete one part of a sentence), to sentence generation examples (students produce a complete sentence on their own). These same instructional formats can be used with paragraph writing and other editing skills, such as changing present-tense verbs to past-tense verbs. The degree of skill knowledge required of sentence selection formats is less than that required for sentence generation formats. As a result, sentence selection examples are easier and should be introduced before more difficult sentence generation formats.

In addition to varying the degree of skill knowledge required of students to complete a writing task, the teacher can also vary the context in which a skill is introduced. Skills can be introduced alone (in isolation) or in the context of other skills (embedded). For example, verb-tense forms, such as changing the present-tense form of a verb to its past-tense form, can be presented in isolation ("*Is* tells what is happening, *was* tells what happened"). This same skill can be presented within the context of sentences (" 'The dog *is* barking' tells what is happening. 'The dog *was* barking' tells what happened"). Similarly, simple sentences can be taught in isolation or within the context of complex paragraphs and passages.

As a general rule, present the range of examples of writing skills in easy, highly structured, teacher-directed examples before presenting difficult, student-generated examples. For example, introduce simple sentences in a sentence selection instructional format before using more complex sentences in a sentence generation instructional format. We also recommend teaching writing skills in isolation first, before embedding them in more complex instructional contexts.

Following is a selected list of writing tasks and the range of examples for each skill. Also indicated are the writing strand and the knowledge form of each skill.

WRITING TASK 11–4
Capitalizing the First Word in a Sentence

Writing Strand: Mechanics of writing.

Knowledge Form: Rule relationship.

Limited Set

Series of five to six separate, simple sentences:
the boy went to the movie.
bill did not like his lunch.
after school, Sally had skating practice.

Advanced Set

1. Student-generated sentences.
2. Sentences presented in paragraph form.

WRITING TASK 11–5
Ending an Asking Sentence with a Question Mark

Writing Strand: Mechanics of writing.

Knowledge Form: Rule relationship.

Limited Set: Set of five to six unpunctuated asking sentences.

Advanced Set: Student-generated asking sentences.

Discrimination Set: Set of sentences, mixture of asking and telling sentences.

WRITING TASK 11–6
Completing Simple Sentences Based on a Picture

Writing Strand: Writing simple sentences.

Knowledge Form: Rule relationship.

Limited Set: Examples of 8–10 complete and incomplete sentences that tell about the picture (discrimination task).

Advanced Set

1. Set of partly completed sentences requiring student to complete by naming either the person or the thing in the picture.
2. Set of partly completed sentences requiring student to complete by telling more about the person or thing in the picture.
3. Mixed set of partly completed sentences requiring student to complete by naming person or thing or by telling more about the person or thing.

WRITING TASK 11–7
Generating a Paragraph As a Set of Simple Sentences That Tell More About One Person or Thing Without Pictures

Writing Strand: Writing simple paragraphs.

Knowledge Form: Cognitive strategy.

Limited Set

1. A picture with one sentence telling the main thing that happened in the picture. Students generate at least two more sentences that tell about the picture.
2. Two or three additional pictures with sentences that tell the main thing that happened.

Advanced Set

1. A topic sentence with no picture, students generate paragraph.
2. Two or three additional topic sentences.

Sequence of Examples

The general guidelines for placing the examples of a particular skill in a proper sequence are very similar to the guidelines described previously for other academic skills. We recommend two general sequencing guidelines. First, present easy examples before more difficult examples of a writing skill. Easy examples do not require the learner to rely greatly on previously acquired writing skills or general background knowledge. For example, generating a paragraph about a given topic without any teacher assistance requires extensive background knowledge of the topic as well as a great deal of skill knowledge about constructing a paragraph. In contrast, requiring students merely to write two sentences that tell more about an individual already named in a picture does not demand much background knowledge about a topic or skill knowledge about paragraph writing. Easy examples should also be presented in teacher-directed instructional formats that provide students explicit assistance in completing a specific writing task. Furthermore, selection and completion tasks should be taught before generation tasks.

Once easy examples have been presented, introduce examples requiring students to apply specific skill knowledge. The new examples should require students to rely on the new skill knowledge and involve less teacher support and less explicit assistance. A set of sequencing guidelines developed by Gleason (1988) for expanding simple sentences to make them more interesting and sophisticated follows. These sequencing guidelines represent general guidelines to follow when developing examples of expressive writing skills:

1. Present a picture that focuses on one noun. The teacher and students brainstorm by identifying all adjectives that could describe that noun—for example, adjectives that describe a kitten that looks soft, cuddly, and tiny in the picture.
2. Present a kernel sentence, which is a basic sentence unit such as "The kitten sat in the basket." Require students to expand the sentence to include selected adjectives named in step 1. For example, "The soft, cuddly kitten sat in the basket."
3. Present a picture and require students to write a kernel sentence about the picture. Then require students to improve upon the sentence by embellishing it with adjectives.
4. Present a picture of someone in action. Require students to brainstorm all verbs that could be used to describe the person's activity. For example, "The boy walked" (skipped, hurried, or rushed).
5. Present a kernel sentence, such as, "The boy walked down the street." Require students to expand the sentence by changing the verb to one named in step 4. For example, "The boy rushed down the street."
6. Present a picture and require students to write a kernel sentence about the picture. Then require students to improve upon the sentence by embellishing it with adjectives and changing the verb to a more descriptive verb.

The guidelines developed by Gleason (1988) for embellishing simple sentences are in concert with the two general guidelines specified earlier. First, easy examples requiring little skill and background knowledge are presented before more difficult examples. Second, the easy examples are followed by more difficult examples that build on new skill knowledge acquired by students. The new examples also involve less teacher assistance (see step 6).

Test and Practice Examples

The remaining components of the generic instructional set pertain to the selection of test and practice examples. Because we have detailed procedures for selecting and scheduling test and practice examples in the previous six chapters (e.g., see Chapter 8), we will not repeat those details here. The general guidelines for designing any testing and practice sequence apply to those for beginning expressive writing skills. In general, the testing sequence should follow directly from the teaching sequence. In other words, align the testing examples with the kinds of examples presented during instruction. Similarly, use testing formats similar to those used during instruction. For example, after the teacher models two sentences that involve identifying the part of the sentence that "tells more," students should perform the same task on a different set of sentences. This testing sequence is, in part, a discrimination testing sequence requiring students to differentiate between the part of the sentence that tells more and the part that doesn't. The testing sequence should also assess generalization by including novel sentences similar in format to those used in instruction but not explicitly taught. In a sense, the testing sequence evaluates students' ability to acquire, discriminate, and generalize a newly taught writing skill. The proposed scope and sequence of beginning writing skills coupled with the explicit teacher assistance and support in the initial stages make the testing of skills more consistent and representative of students' knowledge.

Expressive writing skills, like many other complex cognitive skills, require extensive and sustained practice over time. This practice is necessary because of the many component skills that must be kept at a high criterion level of performance for consolidation and execution in the skill known as expressive writing. To establish these skills, schedule practice frequently and for small chunks of time during the early stages of teaching writing.

Furthermore, once component skills are taught, they must be used and folded into new, more complex skills. For example, once students learn to capitalize the first word of a sentence presented in isolation, they should practice this editing skill in the context of new, more complex skills, such as writing simple sentences. Once students master the skill of writing simple sentences in isolation, they must practice this skill within the context of the new, more complex skill of writing paragraphs. During the more advanced stages of writing instruction, brief practice sessions on component skills shouldn't be necessary. Schedule less frequent but longer independent practice sessions to allow students practice on the most complex skill taught to date. For example, if paragraph writing is the most recently taught complex skill, then allocate the greatest amount of practice and instructional time to this skill. However, continue practice on other recently introduced component skills (e.g., punctuation and capitalization).

During the initial stages of writing instruction, the teacher should monitor students frequently and provide feedback immediately. During latter stages, teacher feedback and monitoring are less structured and less frequent, thereby giving students more responsibility for monitoring their writing tasks and performance.

EXAMPLES OF BEGINNING EXPRESSIVE WRITING SKILLS

In this section, we present examples of selected beginning expressive writing skills. As in other chapters, we present skills within the before, during, and after phases of instruction. For each selected expressive writing skill, we specify the writing task, the knowledge form, examples of the writing task, and instructional procedures for the writing task. In each case, we present actual examples of the specific writing task the teacher presents to students, the response form required of students, and the teacher wording for each writing task. The examples illustrate the range of details necessary to design beginning writing tasks. In many cases, the examples can be tailored to the instructional needs of less naive or sophisticated learners.

WRITING TASK 11–8
Writing Simple Sentences Using Pictures

BEFORE INSTRUCTION

Task Status: New.

Preskills

1. Ability to discriminate missing part of something.
2. Ability to perform handwriting requirements of task.
3. Basic skills in spelling, capitalization, and other mechanical skills of writing.

Instructional Design Guidelines

The instructional design to teach sentence writing involves three response forms: *selection responses, completion responses,* and *generation responses.* Introduce the formats consecutively. That is, once students master selection responses, progress to tasks involving completion and then generation formats. The following instructional design recommendations illustrate the change of response forms across stages of sentence writing. Therefore, there will be introductory sets whenever response formats change.

Introductory Set (Sentence Selection Task)

1. Use single pictures that clearly depict actions, events, or characteristics of person or thing.
2. Accompany each picture with four or five statements. Include both positive and negative examples of simple sentences. Negative examples (sentences that do not satisfy rule criteria) should be obvious.

3. Provide practice on a minimum of five to six additional pictures. Model two or three examples; test on additional three or four items.

Introductory Set (Completion Task)

Provide seven or eight incomplete statements. Vary missing component of sentences—some sentences name the person or thing and others tell more about the person or thing.

Introductory Set (Generation Task)

Provide pictures that depict simple, single events, situations, or characteristics.

Generalization Set (Generation Task)

Provide practice on additional pictures.

TASK 11–9

DURING INSTRUCTION

Instructional Delivery Guidelines

1. Frame the task and response requirements because they are new.
2. Move students through the sentence selection tasks at a moderate pace.
3. Allow more time for generation tasks because the requirements are significantly greater than selection or completion responses.
4. Require learner to follow along as examples are presented.
5. Have students respond in unison on initial examples because the task requires a single, easily identified correct response.
6. Check for student understanding and review/reteach as necessary before introducing new response form.

General Instructional Procedures

The procedures depend on the examples and response forms selected (e.g., sentence selection, sentence completion, sentence generation). In all examples, the teacher requires students to apply and follow the rule.

1. Require students to select, complete, or generate a simple sentence. The rule should be applied to each sentence to determine whether the sentence is acceptable.
2. Model rule: "Is this a simple sentence? Yes. How do I know? It names a person in the picture and tells more about that person."
3. Lead student during the application of the rule.
4. Test students on selected examples.
5. Provide practice and review of sentence writing.

Specific Instructional Procedures for Sentence Selection

TEACHER: Today we're going to learn about simple sentences.

Simple sentences are important because they help you write about people and things.

What are we going to learn about?

STUDENTS: Simple sentences.

TEACHER: Exactly, listen carefully to the rule about simple sentences.

(Points to rule written on board.)

A simple sentence names somebody or something and tells more about that person or thing.

Listen again. A simple sentence names somebody or something and tells more about that person or thing.

A simple sentence must have two parts. It must name somebody or something and it must tell more about that person or thing. What is one thing a simple sentence does?

STUDENTS: It names somebody or something.

TEACHER: What is the other thing a simple sentence does?

STUDENTS: It must tell more about that person or thing.

TEACHER: That's right.

A simple sentence names somebody or something and tells more about the person or thing.

TEACHER: Listen and watch as I read about this picture. You follow along.

1. The boy sat in the tree.   A
2. Sat in the tree
3. The dog
4. The dog waited for the boy.

(Models simple selection procedure with one picture. Reads each sentence or sentence part. After each, tells the students whether it is a simple sentence or not a simple sentence and why.)

"The boy sat in the tree." That's a simple sentence. How do I know? Because it names the boy and tells more about the boy—he sat in the tree.

"Sat in the tree." That is not a simple sentence. It does not name somebody or something.

"The dog." That is not a simple sentence. It names something but it does not tell more about the thing.

"The dog waited for the boy." That's a simple sentence. It names something—the dog—and tells more about the dog—it waited for the boy.

Now let's look at another picture. (Teacher presents picture and set of statements.)

1. On a log   B
2. The man sat on a log.
3. The boy roasted a hot dog.
4. The moon smiled.

Illustrations © 1983, the Stoelting Co., 620 Wheat Lane, Wood Dale, Illinois 60191. All rights reserved. Reproduced by permission.

I'll read the sentences below the picture, you follow along to find the simple sentence with me. Remember, what two things must a simple sentence do?

STUDENTS: It must name somebody or something and it must tell more about the person or thing.

TEACHER: Great, listen while I read. Then you tell me whether it is a simple sentence or not a simple sentence.

(Teacher reads first sentence.) "On a log." Is that a simple sentence? (Pauses and gives think time, signals for group response.)

STUDENTS: No.

TEACHER: Right. Why isn't it a simple sentence?

STUDENTS: Because it doesn't name somebody or something.

Correction Procedure

If the child responds incorrectly, model the answer. Listen, that is not a simple sentence. It doesn't name a person or thing and tell more about that person or thing. Listen. "On a log." Is that a simple sentence? (Child responds.) How do you know? (Child responds.

The teacher may want to model a new set of examples for the learner before continuing the testing sequence.) Teacher continues through the remaining examples, checking student's understanding using the rule for simple sentences.

TEACHER: I'll read the next sentence, you follow along.
    "The man sat on a log." Is that a simple sentence? (Provides think time, calls for group response.)
STUDENTS: Yes.
TEACHER: How do you know?
STUDENTS: Because it names somebody and tells more about that person.

Teacher asks students to identify the person and the part that tells more. Teacher provides three or four more structured examples, then tests students on selecting simple sentences.

1. A bee was buzzing.   C
2. The singer played the guitar.
3. The small crowd
4. The crowd was small.

1. The man was fishing.   D
2. The boat
3. A big leak
4. The boat had a big leak.

See Appendixes A and B for example sentence completion and generation tasks.

TASK 11–10

AFTER INSTRUCTION

Analyze Errors and Make Instructional Decisions

1. If consistent errors occur, determine whether the students understand the separate rule components: names somebody or something and tells more about the person or

thing. Some students may require instruction on the separate parts before combining the parts into the rule.

2. If inconsistent errors occur, reteach rule and schedule frequent practice on the rule application using additional examples.

3. If students demonstrate mastery of this skill, introduce sentence completion stage of simple sentence writing. The sentence completion and sentence generation instructional components follow the same general procedures to teach simple sentence selection. Instruction is always based on the rule. The teacher models the first few examples, then monitors student responses to questions to determine the number of additional examples to present. In all instances of a new task, teacher prompting and modeling is extensive in the initial phases and withdrawn as students demonstrate proficiency with the task. (See Appendixes A and B.)

WRITING TASK 11–11
Completing Paragraphs about Pictures—Topic Sentence Provided

BEFORE INSTRUCTION

Task Status: New.

Knowledge Form: Cognitive strategy.

Preskills

1. Ability to read a short paragraph and identify the topic of the paragraph and the parts of the paragraph that tell more about the topic.
2. Ability to follow mechanical conventions of writing (e.g., indentation, punctuation, capitalization).
3. Ability to write simple sentences.

Instructional Design Guidelines

The instructional design to teach paragraph writing involves three response forms: selection responses, completion responses, and generation responses. The following sequence represents the completion stage of paragraph writing. Before introducing this sequence, students should be able to select the topic of the paragraphs and identify parts that tell more about the topic. The next step in the paragraph writing sequence, paragraph generation instruction, can be introduced after students consistently complete paragraphs from topic sentences. An example setup for teaching paragraph topic selection and paragraph generation is provided to demonstrate the general procedure.

Paragraph Completion Design Guidelines

1. Use single pictures with easily identified topics and supporting information.
2. Accompany each picture with a topic sentence.
3. Include a minimum of five pictures for each teaching sequence (two modeled, three test examples).

Introductory Set: Use single pictures with an accompanying topic sentence.

Generalization Set: Use sequences of pictures that require student to summarize critical information in several pictures.

TASK 11–12

DURING INSTRUCTION

Instructional Delivery Guidelines

1. Frame task carefully. This is a new response form and a more complex task than previous topic selection activities.
2. Review critical rule for paragraph writing—"Paragraphs are made of simple sentences that name a topic and tell more about it."
3. Inform students of other rules for writing paragraphs that will be introduced in later sessions (i.e., mechanical and organizational rules for paragraph writing).
4. Use the rule as the correction procedure. Model the example, then test the student on the same example as well as on additional untaught examples.
5. Monitor pace because this is a complex, multiple-step task.
6. Provide sufficient think/work time to complete task.
7. Require students to provide answers orally before recording them on paper on initial practice tasks.

Teaching Procedure

Modeled Example

TEACHER: Today we're going to learn to complete paragraphs. You have already practiced how to find the topic of a paragraph and find sentences in the paragraph that tell more about it. Let's review the rule for a paragraph.

A paragraph is made of simple sentences that name a topic and tell more about it. Let's practice this rule in a paragraph. (Teacher has students practice finding the topic and determining whether the sentences tell more.)

Paragraph Reading and Topic Selection Examples

TEACHER: Look at the picture. Each sentence in this paragraph names a person or thing and tells more. Some sentences will tell more about Jack. Some sentences will tell more about the fish. I'll read each sentence of the paragraph, then we'll choose the best topic of the paragraph. Remember, the topic is the main thing the paragraph tells about.

Jack saw a big fish. The fish was the biggest he had seen all day. Jack swam toward the fish. He thought of spearing the fish. The fish looked at him. Jack looked at the fish.

Teacher calls on students to identify the topic of the paragraph. As each student volunteers a topic, the teacher applies the rule by asking each student, "How do you know that's the topic of the paragraph?" The student responds: "Because it's the main thing the paragraph tells about." The teacher requires students to read a set of statements on their own and select the statement that represents the best topic for the paragraph.

1. Jack thought about spearing a big fish.
2. The big fish swam away.
3. Jack is a good diver.

TEACHER: Great. "Jack thought about spearing a big fish" is the best topic sentence. We know that paragraphs name a topic and tell more about the topic. In the paragraph about Jack, the topic sentence and the simple sentences that told more were given.

This time only the topic sentence is going to be provided. We must complete the paragraph by adding sentences that tell more about the topic.

What are we going to add to the topic sentences to make a paragraph?

STUDENTS: Simple sentences that tell more.

TEACHER: Correct. Everyone look at the picture of the boy and the dog. Listen as I read the topic sentence. "Jerry ran from the dog."[2]

Jerry ran from the dog. He _____

_____

_____

TEACHER: Look at the picture. Write a paragraph on what Jerry did. Copy the sentence that tells the main thing Jerry did. Then make up at least two more sentences that tell more about what he did. Begin each new sentence with *he*.

(Teacher models adding the sentences to the topic sentence. Teacher models an additional example, completing sentences based on topic sentence.)

This time, you are going to think of the sentences that tell more about the picture. Look at the picture and follow along as I read the topic sentence.

Reading comprehension series, Level D DLM, Teaching Resources, 1983, p. 16. Reprinted by permission.

---

[2]Based on a lesson from *Expressive Writing I: Student Workbook* (p. 35) by S. Engelmann and J. Silbert, 1985, Chicago: Science Research Associates. Copyright 1985 by SRA.

TEACHER: Look at the picture. Complete the paragraph about what Natalie and Nathaniel did. Copy the sentence that tells the main thing they did. Next, make up at least two sentences that tell more about what they did.

Natalie and Nathaniel were playing baseball. Natalie _____

_____

Nathaniel _____

_____

Correction Procedure:

If the child cannot generate sentences that tell more, prompt student by asking, "Can you tell more about what Natalie is doing? Can you tell more about what Nathaniel is doing?" If student fails to provide additional information, model simple sentences that tell more.

Provide practice on two or three more paragraph completion tasks. Once students master paragraph completion tasks, introduce paragraph generation tasks.

Paragraph Generation Procedures

The design for paragraph generation training follows the same format as sentence selection and completion exercises. Two examples follow illustrating the general procedures for paragraph generation. Steps of the generic instructional set and before, during, and after phases of instruction should be added to complete this teaching sequence.

Paragraph Generation Examples

fished   motorboat   sat   fishpole

buoy   held   water

TEACHER: Look at the picture. Write a paragraph that reports on Bruno. Begin your paragraph with a sentence that tells the main thing Bruno did. Then write at least three more sentences that tell more about what he did.

TEACHER: Look at the pictures. Copy the best title sentence. Then write a paragraph that reports on what happened. Write sentences that tell the main thing each numbered person or thing did.

John woke up.

The dog had a nightmare.

The dog howled.

TASK 11–13

AFTER INSTRUCTION

Analyze Errors and Make Instructional Decisions

Problems in paragraph completion tasks may stem from multiple sources. Therefore, it is important to analyze student performance carefully to isolate particular components that may require additional instruction and practice. Be careful to evaluate student performance only on tasks that have been taught. For example, if rules for indenting paragraphs or capitalization have not been taught, do not assess paragraph writing for that component. As a rule, restrict initial feedback to the critical rule for writing paragraphs—paragraphs are made of simple sentences that name a topic and tell more about it.

1. If the problem is due to an inability to generate sentences about the topic, select additional pictures with familiar content. Model the procedure and provide practice.
2. If the problem is due to an inability to apply the simple sentence rule, reteach simple sentence writing and provide additional practice.
3. If the problem is due to an inability to restrict sentences to those that tell more about the topic, provide additional practice in sentence selection tasks. Model the procedure with several examples before testing the learner.

WRITING TASK 11–14
Editing—Correcting Mistakes in Capitalization and Punctuation in Paragraphs

Task Status:　New.

Preskills

1. Ability to discriminate capital and lowercase letters.
2. Ability to discriminate punctuated from unpunctuated sentences.
3. Ability to perform handwriting requirements of task.
4. Knowledge of concepts *beginning* and *end.*
5. Knowledge of concept *telling sentence.*
6. Ability to capitalize and punctuate simple sentences presented in isolated format.

Knowledge Form:　Rule relationship
"A correct telling sentence begins with a capital and ends with a period."

Instructional Design Guidelines

1. Review capitalization and punctuation editing in simple sentences.
2. Introduce prompted paragraph pairs first. Prompted paragraph pairs include one model paragraph that is correctly punctuated and capitalized; the other paragraph is incorrectly punctuated and capitalized.
3. Introduce unprompted paragraphs (no correct model provided) after students are able to correct paragraphs with prompted examples.
4. Select simple paragraphs containing three to five sentences.
5. Include sentences of simple syntactical format.
6. Select passages of appropriate reading level for student.

Introductory Set

Use prompted paragraph pairs containing three to five sentences. Sentences should not be complex in syntactical construction. In initial unprompted paragraphs, all first word capitalization and ending punctuation should be missing.

Generalization Set

Require learner to edit paragraphs without provision of prompted model. Maintain similar paragraph length and complexity.

TASK 11–15

DURING INSTRUCTION ════════════════════════════

Instructional Delivery Guidelines

1. Frame task by alerting students to pay close attention to the paragraph. Inform students they will be asked to identify missing capitalization and punctuation and to fix the mistakes.
2. Review critical rule for sentence punctuation and capitalization: Telling sentences begin with a capital and end with a period.
3. Maintain a brisk pace because task is mechanical in nature.
4. Correct mistakes by referring to rule. Isolate particular error and emphasize that component of the rule.
5. Make frequent checks to monitor student understanding of task.
6. Require students to provide answers orally on initial examples. This minimizes excessive erasures.

Teaching Procedure[3]

Students are given two paragraphs. The paragraphs are identical, except that one is capitalized and punctuated correctly, the other is missing all initial capitalization and ending punctuation.

CORRECT
Paragraph 1

> My best friend ran in a ten mile race yesterday morning. People from all over came to run in that race. Six hundred people started the race. Only two hundred people finished the race. My friend came in second. I was very proud of her.

INCORRECT
Paragraph 2

> my best friend ran in a ten mile race yesterday morning   people from all over came to run in that race   six hundred people started the race   only two hundred people finished the race   my friend came in second   i was very proud of her.

TEACHER: We've been learning to think of sentences to write in paragraphs. There are also other things we need to know about paragraphs. When you write paragraphs, you must capitalize the first word in the sentence and end each telling sentence with a period. Remember, capitalize the first word and end the telling sentence with a period.

What two things must we do to each telling sentence in a paragraph?

STUDENTS: Capitalize the first word and end it with a period.

TEACHER: Great. Let's look at paragraph 1. It is written correctly. (Shows student copy of paragraph.)

(Students read each sentence in the paragraph and apply the rule.)

Let's read the first sentence in the paragraph. "My best friend ran in a ten mile race yesterday morning." Let's check to see whether the sentence follows the rule.

Does the first word begin with a capital?

Does the sentence end with a period?

This sentence is correct. Let's look at the first sentence in the bottom paragraph. Everybody read the sentence with me. What two things are wrong with the sentence? (Calls on students.)

The first word is not capitalized and it does not end with a period. Watch me as I fix that sentence. (Models correction procedure—crosses out lowercase m and makes a capital M; adds a period to the end of the sentence.)

Everyone, make those corrections on your paper.

---

[3]From *Expressive Writing I, Teacher Presentation Book* (pp. 30–31) by S. Engelmann and J. Silbert, 1985, Chicago: Science Research Associates. Copyright 1985 by SRA. Reprinted by permission.

Now, let's go back to the top paragraph. (Teacher continues the comparison-correction process with another example, then has students correct the remaining sentences on their own.)

(Teacher evaluates remaining sentences in paragraph.)

After students demonstrate the ability to edit and correct errors when prompted paragraphs are provided, eliminate the prompted model. An example unprompted model follows:

a young boy threw a ball   the ball went over his friend's head it rolled into the street   a big truck ran over the ball   the truck driver gave the boys a new ball   they thanked the truck driver[4]

When using these examples, the teacher models several example sentences before asking students to edit and correct the remaining sentences in the paragraph.

TASK 11–16

AFTER INSTRUCTION

Analyze Errors and Make Instructional Decisions

After the prompted paragraph pairs task, evaluate whether students are able to identify and correct errors.

1. If students are able to identify errors and make appropriate corrections when a prompted model is available, introduce unprompted tasks.
2. If students are unable to apply the rule for correct sentences with the provision of a model, break the task into component parts. Identify the component that is problematic for the learner (i.e., capitalization, punctuation) and reteach. Provide additional practice and do not introduce unprompted paragraphs until student masters editing with prompts.
3. If editing and correcting problems surface when no prompted models are provided, break the task into smaller parts. Review capitalization and punctuation in single sentences, then combine into larger units.

---

[4]From *Expressive Writing I, Teacher Presentation Book* (p. 76) by S. Engelmann and J. Silbert, 1985, Chicago: Science Research Associates. Copyright 1985 by SRA. Reprinted by permission.

SUMMARY

This chapter addressed the complex and often elusive task of expressive writing. Instructional factors relating to students' problems with expressive writing tasks were reviewed along with two primary approaches to writing instruction: the product approach and the process approach. For students with academic learning problems, we recommended a skills-based approach to expressive writing instruction. This approach focuses on a scope and sequence of basic skills that students establish and develop through instruction and practice. To teach expressive writing skills, we recommend applying steps of the generic instructional set and integrating these steps in instructional sequences using the before, during, and after instruction paradigm.

APPLICATION ITEMS

1. For each expressive writing skill listed below, identify the component *writing* skills required to execute the task successfully:
   a. Writing a paragraph describing a person's appearance.
   b. Writing a letter to a friend.
   c. Writing answers to a set of social studies questions.

2. The teacher describes Leslie's writing as "unexciting." Leslie either uses no describing words or uses the same words repeatedly. Design a teaching strategy using steps of the generic instructional set to teach "using describing words." Identify the knowledge form, the range of examples, the sequence of examples, the testing sequence, and the practice examples.

3. Figure 11–3 (p. 428) shows the writing product of a student identified as learning disabled. Use this writing sample to complete the following items:
   a. Evaluate the written product according to the major writing strands and component skills within each strand. Based on the sample, identify the skills deficits of the learner, categorizing them according to writing strand, specific writing skills, and order in which they would be taught.
   b. Identify the first skill in each strand you would teach.
   c. Construct an instructional lesson framework (see p. 436). Be sure to specify the core writing strand, specific writing skill, sequence of skills introduction within the lesson, and time allocated per skill.
   d. Select one of these skills and design the instructional sets you would use to introduce the skill. Also, describe the test and practice examples you would use.

4. Your group of eighth-grade junior high students do not have basic paragraph writing skills. Using the generic instructional set as the instructional framework, discuss whether and how the passages, tasks, and instruction would vary from those you would use to teach paragraph writing skills to fourth graders.

REFERENCES

Applebee, A. N. (1984). *Contexts for learning to write: Studies of secondary school instruction.* Norwood, NJ: Ablex.

Engelmann, S., & Silbert, J. (1985). *Expressive writing I.* Chicago: Science Research Associates.

Gleason, M. (1988). Teaching basic writing skills to children with learning disabilities. Unpublished manuscript, University of Oregon.

Hayes, J. R., & Flower, L. S. (1980). Identifying the organization of writing processes. In L. W. Gregg & E. R. Steinberg (Eds.), *Cognitive processes in writing* (pp. 3–30). Hillsdale, NJ: Erlbaum.

Howe, D., & Kameenui, E. J. (1983). *Action express: Paragraph and story writers.* Chicago: Stoelting.

Hume, A. (1983). Putting writing research into practice. *Elementary School Journal, 84,* 3–18.

Isaacson, S. (1987). Effective instruction in written language. *Focus on Exceptional Children, 19,* 1–12.

Juel, C. (1988, April). *Learning to read and write: A longitudinal study of fifty-four children from first through fourth grade.* Paper presented at the meeting of the American Educational Research Association, New Orleans.

Leinhardt, G., Zigmond, N., & Cooley, W. (1980, April). *Reading instruction and its effects.* Paper presented at the annual meeting of the American Educational Research Association, Boston.

Newcomer, P., Nodine, B., & Barenbaum, E. (1988). Teaching writing to exceptional children: Reactions and recommendations. *Exceptional Children, 54,* 559–564.

Scardamalia, M., & Bereiter, C. (1986). Research on written composition. In M. C. Wittrock (Ed.), *Handbook of research on education* (3rd ed., pp. 778–803). New York: Macmillan.

Shanahan, T. (1980). Impact of writing instruction on learning to read. *Reading World, May,* 357–368.

Shanahan, T., & Lomax, T. (1986). An analysis and comparison of theoretical models of the reading-writing relationship. *Journal of Educational Psychology, 78,* 116–123.

Stanovich, K. E. (1986). Matthew effects in reading: Some consequences of individual differences in the acquisition of literacy. *Reading Research Quarterly, 21,* 360–406.

Vacc, N. N. (1987). Word processor versus handwriting: A comparative study of writing samples produced by mildly mentally handicapped students. *Exceptional Children, 54,* 156–165.

APPENDIX A

Sentence Completion Examples

1. _____ ran around the fire.
2. The man sat _____ .
3. _____ was high in the sky.

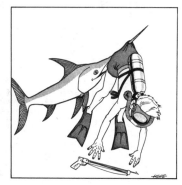

1. The swordfish _____ .
2. _____ fell from the boy's hands.
3. _____ had an air tank and mask.

1. _____ had a striped shirt.
2. _____ knelt while painting.
3. _____ held his paint can.

1. _____ watched as the woman swam.
2. The woman swam away from _____ .
3. The fin was _____ .

APPENDIX B

Sentence Generation Examples

Task 1   TEACHER: Write sentences that tell the main thing each person did.

Task 2   TEACHER: Write sentences that tell the main thing that happened in each picture.

crawling	nasty	stepped
fell	sidewalk	stomped
insect	sign	store

PART IV

Strategies for Classroom Management

C H A P T E R

TWELVE

Designing Classroom Management Strategies Within the Context of Instruction

Chapter Objectives

Upon successful completion of this chapter, you will be able to:

1. DESCRIBE how behavior is viewed as information.
2. EXPLAIN how understanding a problem influences how a teacher solves the problem.
3. DESCRIBE the assumptions about the learner that are important to designing classroom management strategies.
4. DEVELOP a strategy for defining what is expected of children beginning with the first day of school.
5. DEVELOP a 180-day management plan based on instruction.
6. EXPLAIN why punishment is considered a transition tool.
7. DEVELOP a set of instructional and reinforcement strategies for managing the classroom.

CONCEPTUALIZING CLASSROOM MANAGEMENT AS INSTRUCTION

No other aspect of teaching cuts at the gentle voice of the teacher's soul as sharply as negative interactions with students about their behavior. Behavior management problems are not simply problems of reinforcement and punishment that can be addressed exclusively through the language of behavior modification, assertive discipline, reality therapy, or transactional analysis. Behavior management problems in particular, and classroom management problems in general, must be viewed in a broader context. In this chapter, we examine these problems within the context of instruction.

Behavior as Information: Managing Behavioral Information

In a comprehensive review of classroom organization and management, Doyle (1986) states, "Broadly speaking, classroom teaching has two major task structures organized around the problems of (a) learning and (b) order" (p. 395). The tasks related to learning and order, as Doyle observes, are "closely intertwined," as many of the tasks exist simultaneously and are complementary. Doyle defines order to mean "that within acceptable limits the students are *following the program of action necessary for a particular classroom event to be realized in the situation*" (p. 396, original emphasis). In our analysis of classroom management, the problems of learning and order are best addressed through instruction. If we accept Doyle's definition of order, then the "program of action necessary for a particular classroom event to be realized" is a program of instruction—a teaching program whereby the teacher provides students with the information they need to succeed (e.g., how to behave during small group reading) *before* the problems of order and learning occur.

We state throughout this text that teaching is the communication and interpretation of information. However, when we think of managing a child's behavior in the classroom, we do not think of it as teaching. Instead, we think of it as management—something a teacher must do to establish "order" and to get "control" of a child or situation. However, when a child misbehaves or acts in an unacceptable manner, that child is giving the teacher information about many things: the child's immediate needs, the demands of the instructional task, the social context of the instruction, the clarity of the teacher's directions (Colvin & Sugai, 1988). For example, after being asked three times by the teacher to complete the math assignment, a fourth-grade student finally throws the pencil at the wall, pushes the books off the desk, and starts mumbling. This behavior might be viewed as a tantrum and the child considered overly sensitive, emotional, rude, and disruptive. However, these behaviors can also be thought of as information. This child is communicating to the teacher that the math task is difficult, and this sets the occasion for disruptive behavior.

The information to be interpreted and communicated is signaled by the child's behavior. A child's actions, movements, twitches, and overt impulses are not neutral, isolated, and independent events. For that matter, neither are those of the teacher. A student's or teacher's behavior takes place in a social context and is interpreted by those in the context at that time. Those very actions, movements, twitches, and impulses are assigned labels such as appropriate, out-of-line, naughty, cute, wild, and intelligent. In fact, the very same set of actions may be construed by some as appropriate and by others as highly inappropriate. Those actions may be judged as acceptable at one time and unacceptable at another. Sometimes a behavior is judged inappropriate despite a child's genuine insistence, "I didn't do anything."

Obviously, one of the teacher's unavoidable responsibilities in managing the classroom is to judge children's behavior. Human beings make judgments about people all the time—how they look or don't look, how they act or fail to act. In the case of the classroom teacher and school officials, many of these judgments form the basis of significant decisions that are translated into actions affecting the academic and social futures of children. Needless to say, how a child's behavior is judged by the teacher, principal, parents, and other students is no trivial matter. In this section, we describe ways of thinking about behavior management problems within the context of instruction that should provide teachers a set of decision rules for interpreting a child's behavior as information.

Interpreting a child's behavior is not the only task facing a teacher. The teacher must also define and communicate the goals and expectations of the classroom to children. The teacher must teach children how to act (or not act), react, move, respond, anticipate, acknowledge, and gesture. Later in this chapter, we specify the instructional procedures for managing children's behavior. Our orientation in this section on classroom management is on the *instructional process* for managing behavior and not simply on the management process for merely reinforcing, punishing, or shaping behavior. We do not see behavior management as a set of teaching conditions and activities distinct from instruction. When teachers teach, they also manage behavior through actions. If teaching and managing are viewed as one, the overall process of teaching is likely to be more coherent, more reinforcing, and more sustaining for teachers and students in the long run.

Understanding and Acting on a Problem: An Elusive Relationship

In Chapter 1, we proposed a set of assumptions specific to three prominent variables of instruction: the teacher, the learner, and the content or skill to be taught. We argued that these provided teachers with a kind of personal charter—a set of beliefs that influenced how a teacher went about making sense of the world and the ever-changing posture of events in it. As Schwartz and Lacey (1982) point out, this "quest for understanding is so regular a part of life that we may hardly notice it" (p. 2). These authors also note, "How we understand an event can have a dramatic impact on what we do about it" (p. 2). The relationship between understanding something and acting on it, as Schwartz and Lacey point out, is an important one and strikes at the heart of the assumptions we are about to examine. The teacher's understanding of why a child misbehaves serves as a critical basis for how the teacher acts toward the child. In the next section, we describe an example of how understanding a problem leads to a solution.

An Instructional Problem

A puzzling and often insidious behavior that teachers confront is lying. Typically, a teacher responds to the problem *after* a child is caught or reported lying. A common and understandable response is that the problem is a psychological insecurity or a character flaw. Lies are not tolerated and are generally punished, and they are thought to be difficult to predict and prevent. Rarely is lying thought of as an instructional problem. However, a child who lies lacks information about lying in much the same way a child who makes a mistake lacks information about a concept or fact. Instead of viewing lying as requiring punishment, the teacher can treat it as an instructional problem and teach the child about lying and not lying. The teacher structures opportunities for the child who shows a tendency to lie to practice telling the truth. For example, in a one-to-one teaching situation, the following teaching sequence is used to teach telling the truth.

TEACHER: OK, Jennifer. I'm going to ask you some questions that may seem silly, but I want you to answer the best you can. How are you going to answer my questions?

JENNIFER: The best I can.

TEACHER: Very good. Where do I want you to look when we work together and I am talking?

JENNIFER: At you.

TEACHER: Yes, thank you. Listen, I want you to get the green pencil that's on my desk.

(Jennifer walks to the teacher's desk, picks up the green pencil, and returns to the table where the teacher is waiting. Jennifer hands the pencil to the teacher.)

TEACHER: Thank you, Jennifer. I want you to tell me what you just did.

JENNIFER: Well, I walked over and got you the pencil that you asked me to get off your desk.

TEACHER: Yes, that's exactly what you did. Thanks for telling me exactly what you did. Do you know what it's called when you tell someone exactly what you did?

JENNIFER: No, not really. You just tell them what you did.

TEACHER: Well, when you tell someone exactly what you did, you tell the truth. You just told me the truth. What did you just tell me?

JENNIFER: The truth.

TEACHER: And what was the truth that you told me?

JENNIFER: What I did. I got the pencil from your desk.

TEACHER: Did you pick up a cup from my desk?

JENNIFER: No.

TEACHER: Did you tell me that you picked up a cup from my desk?

JENNIFER: No.

TEACHER: OK, good, Jennifer. When you tell me exactly what you did, you tell me the truth. What day is it today, Jennifer?

JENNIFER: Monday.

TEACHER: Yes, and tell me what Steve is doing. (Teacher points to a child who is sharpening his pencil.)

JENNIFER: He's sharpening his pencil . . . and now he's sitting down at his desk.

TEACHER: Excellent. What is it called when you tell me exactly what Steve is doing?

JENNIFER: The truth.

TEACHER: So, did you tell me the truth about what day it is and what Steve did?

JENNIFER: Yes.

TEACHER: You sure did. You told me the truth, you didn't lie.

This sequence describes the beginning of an instructional strategy designed to inform the learner about the concept of lying. The strategy is based on the assumption that for a child to perform successfully in the school environment, the child must first be taught the information needed to succeed. In this case, the child must know about telling the truth to succeed in the classroom. Often, adults assume that children understand basic social concepts such as telling the truth when in fact they don't. It is the teacher's responsibility to make sure that the child has the prerequisite knowledge needed to respond to classroom and school expectations.

The teaching sequence described is incomplete and will require a greater number and range of positive and negative examples of telling the truth. The teaching sequence will also require further practice in which Jennifer is placed in unsupervised situations that make telling the truth more difficult. Although the examples given appear less than problematic (e.g., picking up the pencil, naming the day, and describing a child's actions), they are intended to provide Jennifer easy, unambiguous examples of telling the truth that could be verified by the teacher. These easy examples provide Jennifer a clear communication of what is involved in telling the truth. More practice on easy examples will be followed by more difficult examples in which the teacher stages a situation requiring Jennifer to report the truth even though it can't be directly observed but is still verifiable by the teacher.

Once satisfied that Jennifer fully understands telling the truth and has had sufficient practice in discriminating between positive and negative examples of the concept, the teacher can rule out that Jennifer simply doesn't have the information necessary to succeed. At this point, the problem is not a "can't" problem—Jennifer can't tell the truth because she lacks the information necessary to know when truth telling ends and lying begins. The teacher is now in a position to treat the problem as a "won't" problem—Jennifer won't tell the truth because the context and conditions of lying are too strong and reinforcing for her at this time. In this context, the teacher can determine the punishing consequences for lying, because punishment is appropriate and necessary. However, it must be understood that punishment refers to decreasing a behavior. We will discuss this can't/won't distinction and the use of punishment more completely later in the chapter.

In the example of Jennifer, the way a teacher responds to a child's lying depends on the teacher's understanding of the problem. The actions we take as teachers are always largely determined by the understanding we have of a particular problem or situation.

Assumptions Before Actions: A Foundation for Behaving Intelligently

As in Chapter 1, we stake our analysis of classroom management upon a set of assumptions about the learner. Before the nuts and bolts of instructional strategies can be put into place and tightened, a broader framework of teacher beliefs and assumptions must be established. This framework provides the teacher with a foundation for managing children within the broader context of instruction. The assumptions presented here are about the learner and the context of instruction. By holding to these assumptions, teachers should identify behavior problems in ways that translate directly into instructional remedies.

Assumption 1: A child's inappropriate behavior is not random or evil.

This may seem like a peculiar assumption for a teacher to make. We are not sticking our heads in the sand and pretending that children's actions are always good and well-intentioned. Children sometimes do act in ways that seem evil (e.g., repeated aggression), and many inappropriate behaviors appear to be by chance. The assumption that inappropriate behaviors are not random suggests they must have a purpose. In the context of the school, classroom, and instruction, this assumption compels the teacher to search for a cause of the problem. The assumption boldly acknowledges that the behaviors are repeatable, and in spite of their seeming disorderliness, they are, in fact, orderly and often predictable. Were the teacher to accept the explanation that a problem occurs by chance and is driven by demons in the child, there is nothing the teacher could do about it.

By engaging in a problem-solving mindset to explain how and why things happen, the teacher is less likely to dismiss a problem as weird or evil and outside the teacher's control. The teacher will be led to "the discovery of lawful regularities in nature" (Schwartz & Lacey, 1982, p. 11), no matter how peculiar or evil a behavior may appear to be. This search for causality is not a blind leap of faith but is based on other assumptions about the workings of human nature and the environment. The teacher won't find the cause of all problems, but the search provides a starting point.

Assumption 2: Inappropriate behaviors are learned and predictable.

This assumption is critical to shaping and changing the context of instruction and is derived from behavior theory, which has at least two central features. First, the primary focus of behavior theory is on the behavior and the environment. The focus is not on what B. F. Skinner (1971) referred to as the "autonomous inner man" (p. 15) or on internal events within the individual. Outside environmental events significantly influence how and why human beings behave the way they do. Secondly, behavior theory is based on the familiar Skinnerian chant: Behavior is a function of consequences. Schwartz and Lacey (1982) state that "behavior theorists expect that the major burden of explaining human action will be carried by a small set of environmental events, events which we typically call rewards and punishments. The central thesis of behavior theory is that virtually all significant voluntary human actions can be understood in terms of their past relations to rewards and punishments" (p. 15).

This assumption compels teachers to look at the child's behavior—the child's actions, movements, and overt impulses—as the basis for making decisions about what to do about the problem behavior. The teacher acts to influence the child's behavior by manipulating some aspect of the teaching environment (e.g., the curriculum materials, the specific task, the level of teacher direction, the physical location of the child).

The tenets of behavior theory strike some educators as hostile and coercive because they are often construed to mean that human behavior is precisely controlled and can be predicted with unparalleled precision in all instances. Moreover, the tools of behavior theory are often seen as controlling human behavior and limiting individual freedom. Although behavior theorists have made significant strides in understanding and explaining human behavior, these advances do not suggest that all behaviors are absolutely predictable and precisely controlled. The assumption requires teachers to look first for the "regularities to human action." Once "these regularities are discovered and properly formulated," they can serve as a way of accounting for "human action in the past" and predicting "human action in the future" (Schwartz & Lacey, 1982, p. 12).

The reliance on behavior theory alone is still not adequate for successful classroom management. We argue that behavior theory falls short primarily because of its focus on what happens *after* a behavior or a class of behaviors occur; its essential tenet is that behavior is a function of consequences. We contend the proper focus should be on what happens *before* behavior occurs, and this requires that the teacher establish a classroom environment that makes clear how students should behave appropriately before they behave inappropriately.

As noted earlier in this text, if teachers believe that problem behavior is inherent in the child and unpredictable, they are in the hopeless position of having no problem-solving strategy for making sense of difficult behavior problems. Recognizing that behaviors are both learned and predictable empowers the teacher.

Assumption 3: A learner's inappropriate behavior is the learner's best effort to be intelligent.

In Chapter 1, we stated this assumption about the learner—an assumption that is even more applicable in the context of classroom management. This assumption says that inappropriate behaviors (e.g., hitting, biting, screaming, soiling, tearing, and breaking) are smart for the learner, because they benefit the learner in some way. Even if we were to decide that some inappropriate behaviors were deviant, unintelligent, and disgusting, what would such an understanding imply for the teacher? Does it suggest that the teacher treat the learner with less respect? Is the child's uniqueness and individuality worth less if the behaviors are judged unintelligent or repulsive? Certainly not.

This assumption applies to serious, noncompliant behavior problems and to what we refer to as the "nickel and dime" behaviors—the behaviors that tend to annoy and aggravate most teachers in the course of 180 school days of teaching. We argue that the most difficult feature of classroom management is managing the little behaviors that surface repeatedly in a school day. These nickel and dime behaviors include the brief interruptions, the frequent questions of what to do next, the constant reminders of what not to do next, the whispers during large group work, the incidental whining, the intentional tattling on other students, and so on. These nickel and dime behaviors are smart for learners because they place the teacher in a reminding, if not nagging, mode that gives children instant, albeit negative, attention. The teacher's behaviors also communicate to learners that they need not attend to the teacher the first time around because the teacher will invariably provide them the information when requested the second, third, or fourth time.

> **Assumption 4:** There is no place for ridicule or humiliation of children in the process of managing behaviors.

The demands on teachers and school officials are immense, and they sometimes create stressful situations that result in teachers making poor decisions about managing inappropriate behaviors. In times of great fatigue, agitation, and stress, the system breaks down. Some argue that the system breaks down more than we admit and that incidents in which children are punished unnecessarily and unfairly are not rare. This failure is due to a feature in the system that serves as both its strength and its weakness: School officials are human—peculiar creatures who are less than perfect. Indeed, teachers and children understand this condition of imperfection. But the issue is not one of perfection, for parents and children do not expect teachers, principals and other school officials to be perfect. However, they do expect (and rightly so) that children, more than just being treated with respect, will not be ridiculed or humiliated, regardless of the circumstances.

The teacher's responsibility is to arrange and manage the classroom environment in ways that reduce the likelihood of the system breaking down. The teacher must become familiar with the conditions that test the teacher's management, as when a child swears and yells at a teacher. These situations can trigger a negative response in which the teacher lashes out verbally or physically at a student. But in most cases, these potentially explosive situations can be seen in advance and are preventable. Once these conditions are identified, precautions must be taken to avoid them, prevent them, or respond to them in a way that does not ridicule or humiliate children.

> **Assumption 5:** The teacher's mere presence influences how children behave.

If the teacher accepts the four assumptions we have described, then this assumption follows naturally. It is based on the premise that a child's behavior is influenced by the environment. The driving force of the classroom environment is the teacher, and what the teacher does or says and how the teacher moves in the classroom and school environment communicate to children what is or is not important. The teacher doesn't really have a choice in deciding whether to influence a child's behavior. The teacher's mere presence in the environment influences the child's behavior. The teacher cannot stop in the middle of the classroom and say, "I'm not going to influence how the class is behaving." By virtue of the teacher's physical presence in the classroom, children's actions, attitudes, and thoughts are influenced negatively or positively.

The decision facing the teacher is not whether to influence how children behave, but deciding what actions, attitudes, and thoughts to influence more readily and consistently. By accepting the premise that the teacher is always shaping what children do and how they do it, the teacher is mindful of how children's behaviors are influenced. The teacher's constant awareness should lead to a positive self-questioning in which the teacher is seeking what is best for children.

GENERAL PROCEDURES FOR PREVENTING MANAGEMENT PROBLEMS

The assumptions we described will help guide the teacher's actions in the daily work with children. The teacher operates as a problem solver, and children's behaviors are viewed as intelligent and learned, not random and evil. The teacher solves problems by observing the child's behavior and the environmental events that influence it. The teacher is mindful of influencing children. Although these assumptions anchor the teacher to a personal charter for thinking about classroom management, they do not provide the teacher with the procedural details to prevent and respond to management problems. In this section, we describe six general prevention strategies that serve as the foundation for the classroom management plan with instruction as its centerpiece.

Specifying Expectations: Upfront From Day 1

Beginning with the first minute of school, the teacher must clarify expectations of how students will behave. As Doyle states, "From the perspective of classroom order, the early class sessions of a school year are of critical importance" (1986, p. 409). Doyle goes on to cite Bagley, who admonished teachers over 75 years ago by noting that "the only way absolutely to insure a school against waste is to make the very first day thoroughly rigorous in all its details" (1907, p. 22). Effective classroom management begins with the teacher communicating clearly and unambiguously what is expected of children, and this must continue throughout the first week. Periodic reviews should be scheduled frequently in the first 2 months of school (e.g., systematic review every Monday and after holidays). Unless this is done, the teacher will be faced with significant difficulties simply because children will not know what is expected of them. This pivotal point makes classroom management an instructional process and not a behavior management process. By specifying exactly what is appropriate or acceptable behavior, the teacher teaches children a concept they may not know. The concept is that of the *teacher's expectations*. It isn't fair to test children on a concept or piece of knowledge that they don't know and then penalize them for not knowing it. However, once children have the new information, the teacher is in a position to reinforce and strengthen this new learning.

Often, teachers assume students already know what appropriate classroom and school behavior is. In fact, one of the most serious mistakes that teachers make is assuming that children already know "how to behave" in school and that what is known implicitly by students need not be made explicit by the teacher. Children of all ages certainly do attend the first day of school with much knowledge about what is or is not acceptable school behavior. However, what is important to the process of order and learning is what children gain from the teacher's *own* communication about what is acceptable in the classroom and behavior. On the first day of school, the teacher must communicate both the information about appropriate student behavior and *positive* authority as teacher, adult, and professional educator.

The early communication of expectations eliminates second-guessing by children about the teacher's intentions and their own responsibility in the classroom. This beginning-of-the-year communication creates for children a stable, predictable environment in which they know what to expect at school. To ensure clear communication of classroom expectations, we rely on the following instructional procedures: rule teaching, preteaching, and framing. We use these strategies in the before and during phases of instruction. We have described the details of these teaching procedures in previous chapters.

Before we engage in rule teaching, preteaching, and framing, we must decide *what* we want to communicate to students. What do we mean by the teacher's expectations? What should the teacher communicate to students about acceptable or unacceptable behavior? How does the teacher decide on these values? What guides the teacher in what to expect of children in the classroom and school environment? The answers to these questions are not absolute but vary from teacher to teacher. Many answers are already prescribed by state administrative rules. Parental influences and concerns also shape the atmosphere and goals of schools. Although we do not have prescriptive answers, we do offer a few guidelines. We suggest that teachers decide what it is they expect of students by thinking about it long *before* the first day of school. Reflection upon the following questions may be helpful:

1. What do I want my classroom to be like?
   Do I want it highly organized with everything in place most of the time?
   Do I want it quiet most of the time?
   Do I want children to be active and interactive with each other most of the time?
   Do I need to have things quiet, or can I tolerate a great deal of activity?
2. How do I want children to treat me as a person?
   Is it acceptable for children to take issue with me and correct me when I am wrong?
   Is it acceptable for children to raise their voices to me even when they are right and I am wrong?
   Is it important for children to always, no matter what the circumstances, respond to me in a courteous manner?
   Do I feel that hitting a child is ever acceptable? (We never consider corporal punishment appropriate.)
3. How do I want children to treat one another?
   Is it acceptable for children to speak roughly or rudely to one another?
   Is it acceptable for children to laugh at one another's mistakes?
   Do I want children to be kind to one another and speak to one another with gentle voices?
4. What kind of information or values do I want to communicate to students about being an adult, an educator, a woman or a man in today's society?
   Do I want to demonstrate a strong work ethic in which hard work is seen as important and necessary to success?
   Do I want children to know that making mistakes is natural to the process of learning?

> Do I want children to respect the process of asking questions, no matter how silly or stupid the questions seem to be, and do I want to encourage children to ask questions?
> 5. How do I want children to remember me when the last day of school ends and I am no longer part of their daily lives?
> What image do I want children to have of me when they think of me?
> What feeling do I want children to have when they think of me in their later years?

There are no right answers to these questions. The answers are personal to each teacher and are shaped by a teacher's teaching and life experiences. The answers, nevertheless, should reflect the teacher's genuine attempt to provide students with the best educational context possible. Teachers should on the first day of school communicate, in their own words, the following message or promise to students:

> Hi. My name is Mr. Learner. I'm really pleased you are here. I want to welcome you to Bright Elementary School and to classroom number 12. Before we talk about school rules, classroom rules, hallway rules, bathroom rules, and rule rules, I want to tell you something about what I am thinking. We will spend a great deal of important time together. During that time, I'll ask you to do many things—read, write, talk, listen, calculate, think, feel, and so on. Sometimes our work will be hard and tiring, and we may feel grouchy. Sometimes we'll disagree. But most of the time, I hope class will be fun and enjoyable. I want to make you a promise—I will give you my best teaching. I hope you will give me your best effort.

When teachers make their expectations known to children, they are engaged in the process of instruction, not management. Once children are given the information, the teacher must provide the practice necessary with any new concept. It would be inadequate for the teacher merely to state or demonstrate these expectations on one occasion. Teaching children what is expected of them involves a complete teaching sequence in which children are given many examples and many opportunities to practice the information.

By not teaching children classroom expectations at the beginning of the school year, the teacher is unwittingly placed in what we refer to as the punishment/instruction dilemma. The dilemma occurs when the teacher is caught in a situation that calls for an immediate response to a child's inappropriate behavior. The perplexed teacher doesn't know whether to punish or give the child more information. For example, the teacher states, "I've told you a thousand times to quit monkeying around. What do I need to do? What's your problem?" The questions reveal a doubt as to whether the child has the information to act appropriately. Perhaps the child wasn't informed adequately about classroom expectations.

This and all classroom situations require teaching—providing children with clear, consistent examples of what is expected of them from the first day of school.

Management As a 180-Day Schedule

The teacher must view classroom management as a 180-day process that begins on day 1 and ends on the last day of the school year. The teacher will need a 180-day classroom management plan—a general blueprint that specifies the management strategies the teacher will use week by week for 36 weeks. This plan causes the teacher to think about managing behaviors not only in September, when the novelty of school is most pronounced, but also in the long haul of the winter months when the potential for fatigue is greatest. A 180-day management plan prompts the teacher to consider how management strategies should change over the course of nine months.

The 180-day plan that we recommend is best conceptualized as a three-phase plan, each phase with 3-month segments, as shown in Table 12–1.

The 60-day plan presented in the table describes the primary strategies the teacher will use in managing the classroom on a weekly basis in the first 3 months of school.

The strategies used in the first 2 months of a fourth-grade classroom are different than the management strategies used in the sixth and seventh months (i.e., February–March) of school. In the beginning of the school year, the management process is an instructional one in which the teacher emphasizes what is acceptable and unacceptable classroom behavior. The primary focus is on demonstrating, reinforcing, and reviewing what is expected. Punishment is minimal, because problems are viewed as information

TABLE 12–1
Management plan: First three months

First Month			
	Week 1	**Week 2**	**Week 3**	**Week 4**
Teach rules				
Preteaching				
Framing				
R+ rules*				
Instruction				

Second Month			
	Week 1	**Week 2**	**Week 3**	**Week 4**
Review rules				
Preteaching				
Framing				
General R+*				
Instruction				
Ignoring				

Third Month			
	Week 1	**Week 2**	**Week 3**	**Week 4**
Preteaching				
Framing				
R+ academics*				
Instruction				
Ignoring				
High criterion				
Monitoring				

*R+ : Reinforcement

problems ("can't" problems), not effort problems ("won't" problems). After the first month of teaching, the teacher shifts to using a consistent punishment procedure such as ignoring, coupled with various activity and social reinforcers.

During the latter part of the school year, the emphasis shifts to independence, self-evaluation, and self-monitoring, and children play a more significant role in directing and evaluating their own classroom and school behavior. The assumption at this point is that children are fully aware of the teacher's expectations and need few reminders. Children, in effect, have mastered the skills of how to behave in the school environment, and the teacher shifts the responsibility of management to the students.

By thinking about classroom management as a 180-day plan, the teacher visualizes a bigger picture of how the year should unfold. This puts the teacher in a preventive mode of thinking about the long haul and how children should behave not only in September, but also in February and May. The teacher is architect and carpenter in the design and construction of this plan. The teacher is also tenant and must live with the plan, but perhaps the most important feature of this 180-day plan is a psychological one. If teachers think about this classroom management plan as a kind of physical conditioning program like training for a marathon, the most difficult part of the training is in the beginning, when the runner is in the worst shape and has every reason to stop the unrewarding endeavor. However, with enough persistence, well-planned exercises, and sound nutrition, the runner reaches a level of acceptable performance. Once this level is reached, maintaining the runner's optimal level of performance is a matter of sustained practice. If the runner fails to maintain this peak conditioning, the price for starting over from the beginning is high. Certainly it is easier for the athlete to maintain the peak condition than it is to start again from the beginning.

The teacher, like the runner, must establish a conditioning program for the class-room. The teacher must work hard in the beginning to establish the conditions for acceptable academic and social interactions in the classroom. Once established, the teacher maintains the conditions. Like the athlete, the teacher knows that it is easier to maintain a good, steady training program than it is to start over.

Management Through Reinforcement

An important strategy for classroom management is reinforcement, which we define as the actions or events that increase or strengthen a behavior or class of behaviors. In contrast, punishment refers to the actions or events that decrease or weaken a behavior or class of behaviors. The teacher must set up the classroom to consistently reinforce (i.e., increase or strengthen) selected behaviors rather than consistently punish (i.e., weaken or decrease) those behaviors.

If reinforcement is a valuable management strategy, then the teacher must have something in place to reinforce, which is why we recommend that teachers clarify their expectations on the first day. Once the teacher establishes what is expected through instruction, reinforcement takes place to increase and strengthen those behaviors the teacher values. Effective classroom management is built on sound instruction and rein-forcement: The teacher teaches the information children need to succeed and reinforces that information by reinforcing children's behavior.

After expectations are established, reinforcement increases or strengthens desired behaviors.

The primary management strategy is to give children information about what is appropriate and strengthen that information over time. Success depends on the clarity and consistency with which the information is communicated. To appreciate the importance of reinforcement in classroom management, we examine its advantage over punishment. Sprick (1981) notes that reinforcement has at least three advantages over punishment. Reinforcement procedures can be used (1) to "teach a new skill and encourage its use," (2) to "teach the student to behave even when the teacher is not present," and (3) to "foster positive feelings" (p. 2). A careful examination of these advantages suggests that when reinforcement occurs, new skills, independence, and positive feelings result. But what actually happens in the process of reinforcement? Do new skills and good feelings surface like magic?

Reinforcement is not magical, and doesn't simply happen because children, teachers, administrators, and parents want it to. New skills, independent learning, and positive feelings do not come about by chance. The essential elements in the process of reinforcement are the actions of the teacher, principal, or parent. Those actions provide the learner with information that connects with what the learner already knows to create new skills, positive feelings, or independence of thought and spirit. Oddly enough, reinforcement is as much a process of information exchange as is teaching. The teacher acts and the learner interprets the actions and increases some new and old ways of behaving. In turn, the learner continues to act in ways that increase the teacher's actions, the teacher reciprocates in kind, and the cycle of reinforcement, interaction, instruction, and cooperative learning is underway.

Punishment As a Transition Tool

The word *punishment* is often associated with a negative interpretation. Some people refuse to use the word, and in the extreme it suggests a harsh process in which children are either verbally or physically coerced to obey an authority. Typically, punishment is associated with fear, robbing of dignity, and forcing children to "behave" in accordance with social standards. As Becker (1986) points out, "Probably no area of behavioral psychology has generated more emotion, confusion, and misunderstanding than the topic of punishment" (p. 51). The negative interpretation of punishment is far removed from the definition of punishment.

When we use the word *punishment* in this text, we are simply referring to weakening or decreasing the future occurrence of a response (e.g., a hit) or a class of responses (e.g., hitting). It is incorrect to associate punishment automatically with a set of negative procedures such as yelling, spanking, and harsh verbal reprimands. Similarly, it is incorrect to associate smiles, hugs, candy and other "warm fuzzies" exclusively with reinforcement. Punishment and reinforcement are not defined by the actions of teachers or school administrators, but by the reactions of children. Specifically, we cannot determine if an action (e.g., a smiley face or a stern look) is reinforcing or punishing until we examine student responses to that action. If the responses *increase* in the future, the action can be considered reinforcing. If the responses *decrease* in the future, the action can be considered punishing. A smiley face is only a reinforcer if, after given to a child for staying on task for 5 minutes, it increases the child's on-task behavior in the future. Sitting in the hall is only a punisher if, after it has been given to a child for *not* staying on task for 5 minutes, it decreases the child's off-task behavior. Teachers have often encountered situations in which seating a child in the hall has resulted in increasing a problem behavior. At the same time, liberally awarded smiley faces have resulted in decreasing an appropriate behavior.

It is important for teachers to understand the correct definitions of punishment and reinforcement to appreciate the scope of punishment *and* reinforcement procedures. By holding to incorrect definitions of these terms, teachers assume some things to be reinforcers or punishers that are not. More importantly, the consequence of treating something as a reinforcer when in fact it is a punisher is destructive. This could undermine the teacher's, as well as the child's, integrity. Depending on the age, personal history, and personality of the child, these effects can be long lasting.

If we look at the advantages of reinforcement cited by Sprick (1981), we also find the disadvantages of punishment. The most important feature to understand about punishment is that it *does not teach* and should not be used as a tool to teach. Punishment, if used correctly, can be a powerful tool for decreasing and stopping a misbehavior. However, it does not provide the learner with information about the behavior that *is* appropriate. Stopping an inappropriate behavior is only one part of a management program, and it should be a very small part of that program. The teacher and child alike must have a behavior that replaces the misbehavior. Punishment can be a transition tool to move a child quickly from the negative context of a misbehavior to the positive context of an appropriate behavior. But the movement must be swift, and punishment should never be used as a steady diet.

The use of punishment as a transition recognizes that punishment is powerful. If a teacher uses it incorrectly and indiscriminately, then punishment becomes abusive, ineffective, and unethical. If a teacher uses it correctly and discriminately, then it is a powerful transition tool. The teacher intends for punishment to decrease or stop the target behavior. If the behavior doesn't stop or decrease as expected, the strategy used is not punishing. In some cases, the target behavior will get worse before it gets better, but the teacher can usually predict this. In general, if a punishment strategy isn't working, either the teacher has selected it inappropriately or the teacher is implementing it incorrectly. Punishment as a transition tool is depicted in Figure 12–1, which suggests the small and transitory role of punishment and the primary roles of instruction and reinforcement.

The final feature of punishment is that it should never be used in isolation and independent of an established plan of instruction and reinforcement. Punishment is a transition tool, not a collection of procedures that stand alone. Because of the potentially negative effects of punishment, the teacher must take great care to choose punishment that is indeed appropriate and necessary. Before any punishment is used, we recommend that teachers ask, "Have I examined every aspect of the instructional program?" Such a question requires the teacher to scrutinize critically all three phases of instructional dimensions listed in Chapter 4 on designing a generic instructional set. By examining these before, during, and after instruction dimensions, the teacher should be alerted to

FIGURE 12–1
Punishment as a transition tool

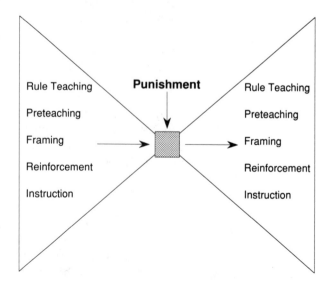

potential instructional problems that require instructional solutions, not behavior management ones. The teacher should also answer the following questions:

1. Is the behavior problem a chronic (day after day) problem or just a one-time occurrence?
2. Is the behavior problem specific to a particular person, or does it involve more than one person?
3. Is the behavior problem specific to a particular instructional task? Form of response? Problem type?
4. Is the behavior problem specific to a particular time of day? Setting?
5. Is the behavior problem specific to a particular sequence of events?
6. Does the behavior problem interfere directly and frequently with instruction?
7. Is the child aware of the behavior problem?
8. Is the behavior problem specific to the teacher?
9. Does the behavior problem occur within the teacher's control?
10. Is the behavior problem so severe and disruptive that it is beyond the control and discretion of the teacher?

The purpose of these questions is to ensure that punishment is not used prematurely without first examining the full context of the behavior problem. The questions will help the teacher arrive at a clear understanding of the behavior problem. The teacher may realize that punishment is not appropriate or necessary, for the teacher should avoid punishment and use other ways to address the problem whenever possible. If punishment is necessary, then the teacher must have full knowledge of its tools.

Behaving Now for Later

Perhaps the most elusive and confusing aspect of punishment and reinforcement is its effect on both the present and the future. In other words, when a teacher responds to a child for whatever reason, the teacher is in effect behaving for now as well as for later. What the teacher does now in response to a "good" or "bad" behavior could affect the behavior both now and in the future. It could also have no effect on the child's behavior. What is most difficult for teachers is the dilemma of knowing that what may appear to be the best way to stop an inappropriate behavior *now* (e.g., sternly grabbing a child and sitting the child down), may be a poor way to decrease that behavior in the future. Often what stops a behavior now only serves to increase that behavior later.

Teachers, in effect, must constantly operate on two levels of awareness. On one level, the teacher must examine a situation and problem solve to meet the immediate demands of the instructional context. "What should I do now?" At the same time, the teacher must make a guess as to how the present actions will affect the target behavior in the future. The teacher will usually answer the second question first: "How will what I do now affect this behavior down the road?" The answers to these questions can only be derived from the teacher's interactions with individual students over the course of the school year. What is deemed a best response for one child may not be appropriate for another. Although we have a good idea of what generally works as punishers and reinforcers for children, in the final analysis, what works for each child must be determined individually.

Management and the Language of Consistency

The classroom is an environment filled with influences that compete constantly for a child's time, attention, and favor (Paine, Radicchi, Rosellini, Deutchman, & Darch, 1983). These competing influences include the behavior of other children, the temperature of the classroom, the proximity of a child's desk to socially influential peers, nonacademic activities such as recess, morning announcements by the principal, social interactions between classmates, family-related problems, and so forth. The competing influences are the real challenge to the teacher. In meeting this challenge, one of the first tests of sound management is the teacher's consistency in responding to misbehaviors. For example, Alberto calls out an answer during small group reading and the teacher calls on him to answer the question. Alberto, who already answered correctly, repeats his answer and is praised. Two minutes later, Alberto calls out again, but this time the teacher reprimands him for not raising his hand. In another situation, the teacher tells Irene that late assignments are "simply unacceptable." Two days later, Irene turns in an assignment one day late. Because of Irene's novel topic selection and clever analysis, the teacher accepts the assignment and presents it to the class as model writing for all eighth graders studying the short stories of O. Henry.

By responding to problems inconsistently, the teacher confuses children by giving them mixed signals as to what behavior is acceptable and what isn't. Is it all right to call out answers during reading group today if they are correct? Are late assignments acceptable if the writing is clever and well constructed? For low performers, this unpredictability is especially distressing, because it communicates that the environment (the classroom) is not stable and that anything can happen at any time without any warning. Acceptable performance becomes, in some cases, a roll of the dice.

However, the teacher's inconsistency in responding to misbehavior creates a more significant problem that is not obvious to the teacher at first glance. The problem is the integrity of language and the trust that children place in the communication of ideas, knowledge, and truth. When a child learns that what a teacher or adult says doesn't really matter, the general rule communicated to the learner is that language is meaningless; words in the hands of certain authorities are stripped of their power to inform, persuade, and enlighten. Words become empty threats and unclear expectations, and they need not be attended to or trusted. Children learn that people say what they don't mean and mean what they don't say.

We are overstating the case here, but with reasonable justification. Teachers have no more powerful tool than words—the communication of ideas, information, and experience. The words are given meaning by the teacher's actions—what the teacher does to support what is said. When actions are not consistent with words, the same words in the future are deemed meaningless. The easiest and fastest way for a teacher to undermine classroom management and sound instruction is to reinforce or punish behaviors inconsistently.

We consider it imperative that teachers implement a management program consistently. Often teachers select punishment strategies (e.g., ignoring children who yell out answers in group) that they know will be difficult to carry out consistently each day. Rather than abandon the strategy at the beginning in favor of a strategy they know they can implement, teachers continue to use punishment strategies begrudgingly, inconsistently, and unsuccessfully. This dilemma can be avoided if teachers take the time *before the school year begins* to examine management strategies thoroughly and select those that are most agreeable to them. For example, if a teacher expects to have a difficult time ignoring a variety of "nickel and dime" behaviors (e.g., calling out during class, tattling), then the teacher should *not* use ignoring as a primary strategy for managing those behaviors—at least not until the teacher has mastered the skill of ignoring. The teacher will want to choose another punishment strategy for decreasing those behaviors.

It makes no sense for teachers to choose punishment strategies they know will be personally difficult to implement consistently. Teachers must come to know what they can tolerate, what they can physically and emotionally handle, what bugs them, what they consider simply unacceptable before they can determine what strategies to select and use as part of their 180-day classroom management plans.

The Task-Tantrum Relationship

The last general strategy we propose deals again with the relationship between management and instruction. The strategy is perhaps better thought of as a problem-solving framework than as an explicit strategy because it is designed to encourage teachers to think about the variation between a child's performance and the focus, task, skill, or content of the performance. We are concerned with examining the relationship between the requirements of a task and the child's actual performance on it. The most important examination must take place *before* the performance because many "behavior problems" surface most intensely during task performance. Teachers frequently select tasks that are difficult along several task dimensions, such as the form of response required of the learner (e.g., oral, written), the length of the task, the number of steps to be completed, and the sequence of the tasks. Sensitivity to the dimensions of a particular task or series of tasks can avoid many problems.

One of the most challenging situations for a teacher is working with a student who is highly verbal and quick to engage the teacher in a discussion about the task or about events at home. This student is quick to note that the task is "easy" and a waste of valuable time. What the teacher learns after a minute of working with this child is that the task is not easy, and the student verbalizes throughout the instruction. The verbalizations interfere with the lesson by luring the teacher into justifying the task or by trapping the teacher in a cycle of reminding the student not to interrupt.

Teachers often begin instruction by providing these students with the very oral tasks that create the excessive verbalizations and behavior problems. Oral tasks set the occasion for a high rate of verbalizations that are both on- and off-task. The oral task also makes it difficult for the teacher to control the rate and nature of the child's responses, because the student responds spontaneously and unpredictably. The only control of the verbalizations the teacher has is to prevent the child from talking.

The solution to this dilemma is a manageable one, but more importantly, an instructional one. Rather than initially giving the child a task that requires an oral response, the teacher should begin the lesson with a task that requires a written or manipulative (e.g., pointing, touching) response, as in a paper and pencil task. The task should not involve a new response but require the child to use known skills and responses. Depending on the age and level of the child, the task will have a varying number of written responses that include expressive writing, cursive writing that practices the mechanics of writing, matching responses, working math operations, and so on.

This change in dimensions of the task is an instructional change, not a management one. It also demonstrates the intimate relationship between the requirements of a task and the child's behavior. Teachers must understand this relationship and appreciate how task selection and variation can create behavior problems. Behavior problems can often be prevented by simply varying dimensions of the task. In fact, we argue that this approach of carefully matching selected task dimensions with learner performance variables is the best classroom management strategy, because it is both preventive and instructional; it stops a problem before it occurs by providing children with the information they need to succeed. In short, by critically examining the dimensions of tasks, teachers are in a better position to prevent failure.

The Contexts of Classroom Management and Instruction

In this chapter, we have described an instructional framework for thinking about behavior problems and classroom management. A graphic depiction of this framework is given in Figure 12–2.

Instruction and classroom management can be thought of as a series of three concentric circles (Colvin, 1982). At the center of these circles is the behavior or classroom management problem. The problem can be a serious one, or it can be a small, rather insignificant one. Regardless of the severity and intensity of the problem, it is "treated" within the broader context of classroom management and instruction, wherein behavior problems are a subset of classroom management problems. Classroom management problems are in turn viewed as a subset of instructional problems. Because behavior problems are a result of problems with instruction, they serve to signal bigger problems in instruction and are best addressed by examining initially the context of instruction.

FIGURE 12–2
Classroom management and the context of instruction

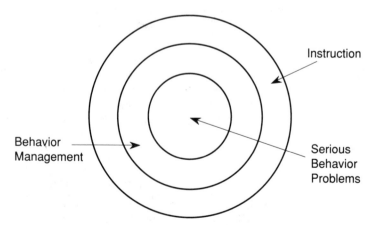

Instruction

Behavior Management

Serious Behavior Problems

What is required in examining the context of instruction as the primary means of correcting behavior problems? Throughout this text, we have been detailing the requirements of instruction in reading, language, mathematics, reading comprehension, and expressive writing. The instructional requirements in each of these skill areas are complex. The requirements include conducting an instructional assessment that informs the teacher of the learner's potential to respond successfully to selected task requirements; framing tasks adequately so that the learner is clear on when and how to respond; varying the sequence of tasks by including new, difficult tasks with familiar, less difficult tasks; pacing the task presentation and teacher talk at an appropriate rate. The list of instructional requirements goes on and on.

By conceiving of management as instruction, the natural consequence for teachers is that the solutions they must consider are complex instructional ones. Classroom management is often laborious. It is not a process of quick fixes, magic tricks, and exotic "b-mod" (behavior modification) programs of reinforcers and punishers. It is not a matter of being "tough," of not smiling until December, or of showing children who's the boss. Classroom management is a process of instruction—a process of communication, social interactions, and information exchanges. More importantly, it is not a neutral process but a value-laden one in which teachers communicate what is valued by them and the public. The teacher is in a position to influence how children care about themselves and others, and how they share their thoughts. The teacher helps shape a child's self-questioning, social criticism, empathy, motivation, and sense of what is right and wrong. The teacher's social and personal significance to children is profound. The teacher's approach to classroom management has a significant impact on children as well.

SUMMARY

In this chapter, we provided a general framework for classroom management that considers classroom management as instruction. Classroom or behavior management is not a process of merely using reinforcers and punishers to control behavior. Instead, reinforcement and punishment procedures are viewed as tools for communicating information, especially teacher expectations.

Good classroom management maintains several assumptions. A child's inappropriate behavior is learned, predictable, and intelligent. Children are always treated with respect. The teacher's mere presence influences how children behave. These assumptions serve as the anchor points for the teacher's understanding of behavior problems, and the teacher's understanding of problems influences the actions taken to solve the problems.

In this chapter, we described six general management strategies, which include (1) specifying teacher expectations from the first day of school, (2) designing a classroom management plan for the entire school year, (3) managing through instruction and reinforcement, (4) using punishment only as a transition tool, (5) responding to problems consistently, and (6) coordinating selected dimensions of tasks with learner variables. These strategies are designed to promote instruction, which is maximized through reinforcement. Punishment typically interferes with instruction by limiting children's access to instruction and is therefore given only a transitional role. The most important feature of the classroom management analysis offered in this chapter is instruction. By viewing classroom management as instruction, the teacher's role as the primary agent of instruction is maintained. The teacher is not split between being a manager of instruction at one time and a manager of behavior problems at another. Instruction is the proper centerpiece of the teacher's responsibilities.

REFERENCES

Bagley, W. C. (1907). *Classroom management: Its principles and techniques.* New York: Academic Press.

Becker, W. C. (1986). *Applied psychology for teachers* (rev. ed.). Chicago: Science Research Associates.

Colvin, G. T. (1982). *Managing serious behavior problems.* Paper presented at a meeting of Special Education Faculty, University of Montana, Missoula, MT.

Colvin, G. T., & Sugai, G. M. (1988). Proactive strategies for managing social behavior problems: An instructional approach. *Education and Treatment of Children, 11*(4), 341–348.

Doyle, W. (1986). Classroom organization and management. In M. C. Wittrock (Ed.), *Handbook of research on teaching* (3rd ed., pp. 392–431). New York: Macmillan.

Paine, S. C., Radicchi, J., Rosellini, L. C., Deutchman, L., & Darch, C. B. (1983). *Structuring your classroom for academic success.* Champaign, IL: Research Press.

Schwartz, B., & Lacey, H. (1982). *Behaviorism, science, and human nature.* New York: Norton.

Skinner, B. F. (1971). *Beyond freedom and dignity.* New York: Knopf.

Sprick, R. S. (1981). *The solution book.* Chicago: Science Research Associates.

Name Index

Abelson, R., 251
Adams, A., 5, 322
Alexander, D., 322
Algozzine, B., 5, 13, 23
Alley, G. R., 322
Allington, R. L., 11, 258, 262
Althaus, V., 403
Anderson, R. B., 362
Anderson. R. C., 11, 203, 250, 251, 252, 258
Anderson. T. H., 256, 312
Applebee, A. N., 422
Archer, A. L., 322, 323
Armbruster, B. B., 60, 256, 260, 310, 311, 312, 314
Arter, J. A., 200, 403
Ashlock, R. B., 400
Au, K. H., 250, 252, 254
Ausubel, D. P., 360, 361

Baer, D. 64
Bagley, W. C., 475
Baker, E. L., 406
Baker, L., 314
Barenbaum, E., 425, 426, 429, 430

Baroody, A. J., 397
Bassler, O. C., 402
Bateman, B. D., 5
Bates, H. III, 405
Baumann, J. F., 252, 253, 256
Baer, D. M., 417
Beck, J., 60
Beck, I. L., 60
Becker, W. C., 5, 61, 62, 65, 105, 407, 481
Beers, M. I., 402
Bereiter, C., 420, 421, 422, 423
Berliner, D., 105, 409
Bessant, H., 403
Bickel, D. D., 5
Bickel, W. E., 5
Biddle, B. J., 105
Biemiller, A., 11
Blankenship, C. S., 402, 403
Bloom, B. S., 65
Bond, G., 203
Bourne, L. E., Jr., 66
Bradley, L., 207
Briggs, L. J., 65
Brophy, J., 11, 89, 97, 105, 254

Brown, A. L., 80, 260, 311, 314, 320
Bruner, J. S., 65, 66, 82, 108, 360, 361
Bryant, P. E., 207
Budd, D., 404
Burkes, A., 60

Cacha, F. B., 399
Cahen, L. S., 409
Calfee, J. S., 262
Campbell, J., 16, 88
Campione, J. C., 311
Carnine, D. W., 5, 15, 16, 62, 66, 73, 74, 75, 76,
         78, 82, 91, 105, 108, 127, 152, 153,
         154, 158, 160, 162, 203, 208, 209, 224,
         252, 253, 256, 319, 321, 322, 351, 363,
         364, 389, 395, 396, 397, 398, 399, 401,
         402, 403, 406, 407
Carpenter, T. P., 360, 395, 397, 400, 403
Carroll, J. B., 11, 404, 405
Cawley, J. F., 403, 405
Chall, J. S., 201, 203, 262, 306
Christensen, D. L., 66, 72, 108, 148
Christenson, S. L., 89
Clark, D. C., 66, 154
Clinton, L., 403
Clymer, T., 212, 214
Cochiarella, M. J., 16, 66, 108
Cohen, R. L., 262
Colvin, G. T., 14, 468, 486
Cook, L. K., 313, 324, 397
Cooley, W., 422
Corbitt, M. K., 403
Cotter, V. W., 394, 395
Culatta, B. E., 403, 404
Cunningham, J. M., 252, 317, 318
Cunningham, P. M., 317, 318

Darch, C., 5, 311, 351, 402, 403, 484
De Corte, E., 395, 400, 401, 402, 403
Deno, S. L., 25
Denton, P. H., 322
Deshler, D. D., 322
Deutchman, L., 484
De Win, L., 395, 400, 401, 402, 403
Dishaw, M. M., 409
Dixon, R. C., 252
Dossey, J. A., 397
Doyle, W., 468, 475
Duncan, M. J., 105
DuncanMalone, L., 60

Durkin, D., 60, 252, 253, 262, 333
Dykstra, R., 203

Echols, C. H., 260
Ehrl, L. C., 207, 209
Elementary School Journal, 60
Engelmann, S., 5, 14, 16, 66, 73, 75, 76, 78, 82, 91,
         108, 127, 152, 153, 154, 158, 160, 162,
         431, 432, 433
Englert, C. S., 5, 89, 235, 403, 404

Feroene, D., 401, 402
Field ing, G. D., 5
Filby, N. N., 409
Fisher, C. W., 409
Fitzhenry-Coor, I., 257
Fitzmaurice, A. M., 403, 405
Flavell, J. H., 260
Flood, J., 254
Flower, L. S., 429, 432
Forness, S. R., 200
Fox, B., 208
Frayer, D. A., 66, 160
Freebody, P., 252
Freschi, R., 252
Friedman, M., 394, 395
Fuchs, L. S., 25

Gage, N. L., 10
Gagne, R. M., 16, 61, 65, 66, 68, 70, 72, 75, 79, 80,
         82, 108, 148, 160
Gallagher, J. J., 22
Gallimore, R., 80
Gersten, R., 5, 322, 351, 362, 402, 403, 406
Ghatala, E. S., 66, 160
Gildea, P. M., 158
Gilhool, T. K., 4
Glaser, R., 361
Gleason, M. M., 322, 323, 444, 445
Glenn, C. G., 256
Goldman, S. R., 217
Goldstein, S., 66
Golinkoff, R. M., 210
Good, T. L., 11, 89, 97, 105, 254
Goodman, K., 62
Goodstein, H. A., 403
Gordon, S., 403
Gough, P. B., 201
Gould, S. J., 22
Graves, A. W., 321

Griffin, C. C., 400
Grossen, B., 5
Gudrandsen, B., 60, 314
Gurney, D. E., 256

Hallahan, D. P., 5
Hayes, D. A., 251
Hayes, J. R., 429, 432
Haynes, M. C., 314, 320, 346
Helfgott, J., 403
Heliotis, J. D., 314, 320, 346
Herman, J. L., 406
Herman, W. L., 400
Herr, C., 5
Hiebert, E. H., 203, 258, 397
Hogaboam, T. W., 217
Horn, D. G., 403, 404
Howe, D., 431
Howell, D., 257
Huitt, W., 105
Hume, A., 429
Hunter, M., 105

Idol, L., 256
Isaacson, S., 421, 422, 423, 426, 429, 432

Jenkins, J. R., 200, 252, 262, 263, 314, 320, 346
Jerman, M. E., 401
Jitendra, A., 60, 154, 158
Johnson, D. D., 257, 258
Jones, E. D., 401, 402
Joyce, B. R., 105
Juel, C., 203, 207, 424, 425

Kahn, H., 405
Kameenui, E. J., 5, 60, 62, 74, 154, 158, 200, 203,
        209, 252, 253, 256, 258, 260, 268, 311,
        319, 321, 400, 431
Kauffman, J. M., 5
Kavale, K. A., 200
Keislar, E. R., 360, 361, 362
Kelly, B., 5
Kendler, H. H., 362
Kepner, H. S., 403
Kilpatrick, J., 394, 401
Kinder, D., 256
Klausmeier, H. J., 66, 160
Klix, F., 72
Krouse, J. P., 401, 402
Kuhn, T. S., 79

LaBerge, D., 64
Lacey, H., 13, 15, 469, 472, 473
Lapp, D., 254
Larsen, S. C., 400
Leinhardt, G., 422
Lepore, A. V., 403
Lesgold, A. M., 203
Lewis, R. B., 200
Lewkowicz, N. K., 207, 208
Lindquist, M. M., 360, 400, 403
Link, W. E., 66
Lomax, T., 424
Lovitt, T. C., 402, 403

Maheady, L., 5, 13
Manzo, A. V., 320
Markle, S. M., 66, 108, 160
Marliave, R., 409
Mason, J. M., 250, 254
Matthews, W., 360, 400, 403
Mayer, R. E., 313, 324
McCaslin, E., 60
McConaughy, S. H., 256, 257
McGreal, T. L., 105
McKeown, G., 60
McKeown, M. G., 60
McNeil, J. D., 250
McNutt, G., 400
Merrill, M. D., 160
Merrill, P. F., 66
Miller, G. A., 158
Mirman, S., 401
Moore, D. W., 324
Mosenthal, P., 23, 250
Moser, J. M., 395, 397
Murphy, J., 105
Myers, A., 397

Nagy, W. E., 11
Nesher, P., 401
Newcomer, P., 425, 426, 429, 430
Nezworski, T., 257
Nicholson, T., 306
Nodine, B., 425, 426, 429, 430

Oakley, D. D., 311
Omanson, R. C., 60
Ortony, A., 251
Osborn, J. R., 262

Paine, S. C., 484
Palincsar, A., 80, 320
Pany, D., 252, 263
Paris, S. G., 80, 260, 261, 263
Park, Ok-Choon, 66, 75, 108
Parker, R. M., 400
Pearson, P. D., 24, 51, 250, 252, 257, 258, 313
Perfetti, C., 204, 217, 252
Piontkowski, D., 262
Polsgrove, L., 5
Polya, G., 402
Prawat, R. S., 409
Prehm, H., 6
Proper, E., 362

Radicchi, J., 484
Rathmell, E. C., 397
Readence, J. E., 324
Reid, E., 215, 216
Reidesel, C. A., 395
Reith, H. L., 5
Resnick, L., 203
Reys, R. E., 403
Richardson, L. I., 402
Roberts, G. H., 400
Rogers, C., 360
Rosellini, L. C., 484
Rosenshine, B. V., 5, 11, 89, 105, 362
Ross, A. O., 6, 13
Routh, K., 208
Rowe, M. B., 336
Rumelhart, D., 251

Saferstein, C. A., 401, 402
Samuels, S. J., 64, 250
Sarason, S., 360
Scardamalla, M., 420, 421, 422, 423
Scandura, J. M., 361, 362
Schallert, D. L., 258
Schank, R., 251
Schulman, L. S., 360, 361, 362
Schumaker, J. B., 322
Schwartz, B., 13, 15, 469, 472, 473
Schwartz, S. E., 404
Schworm, R., 212, 213
Scott, J. A., 203, 258
Sedlak, R., 403
Segars, J., 105
Semmel, M. I., 5
Shanahan, T., 421, 422, 423, 424

Shannon, P., 62, 256, 258
Shaw, R. A., 405
Shulman, L. S., 360, 361, 362
Silbert, J., 5, 74, 105, 203, 209, 252, 319, 321,
    364, 389, 395, 396, 399, 401, 402, 403,
    406, 407, 431, 432, 433
Silver, E. A., 360, 400, 402, 403
Simmons, D., 5, 200, 260, 311
Singer, H., 320
Skinner, B. F., 472
Slavin, R. E., 404, 405
Smiley, S. S., 311
Snow, C. E., 262
Spear, L. D., 203, 262
Spector, J., 262
Spiegel, D. L., 254
Spradlin, E. E., 394, 395
Sprick, R., 14, 105, 480, 481
Squires, D., 105
St. Pierre, R., 362
Stahl, S., 252
Stanovich, K. E., 12, 148, 203, 204, 217, 254, 263
Stebbens, L., 362
Stein, M., 5, 105, 256, 257, 262, 314, 320, 346,
    364, 389, 395, 396, 399, 401, 402, 403,
    406, 407
Steinberg, R. M., 397
Sternberg, R. J., 203, 262, 352
Stevens, C., 394, 395
Stevens, R., 11, 89, 105
Stokes, T. F., 417
Strange, M., 258
Sugai, G. M., 468

Tennyson, R. D., 16, 66, 72, 75, 108, 148, 160
Tharp, R. G., 80
Thibodeau, G. P., 403
Thompson, A. G., 400, 402
Thorton, C. A., 397
Throne, J. M., 4
Tiemann, P. W., 66, 75, 160
Tierney, R. J., 251, 252, 258
Torgesen, J. K., 352
Trabasso, T., 257
Trenholme, B., 400

Vacc, N. N., 423
Valencia, S. W., 24, 51, 313
Van der Westhuizen, G., 80, 260, 261, 263
Vargas, J. S., 408

Verschaffel, L., 395, 400, 401, 402, 403
Vitello, S., 403
Vlahakos, I., 403
Vuicich, G., 253

Warner, N. W., 322
Wasik, B. A., 80, 260, 261, 263
Watson, J. D., 79
Weil, M., 105
Wesson, C., 232
Wheeler, L. J., 400
Wilce, L. S., 209
Wilkinson, I. A. G., 203, 258
Williams, J. P. 5, 203, 204, 320

Williams, P., 160
Wilson, C. R., 252
Wilson, J. W., 401, 402
Wilson, R., 232
Wong, B. Y. L., 263, 311
Wong, R., 263, 311
Woodward, J. P., 5
Worthen, D., 311
Wright, J. P., 401

Yeh, J. P., 406
Ysseldyke, J. E., 23, 89

Zigmond, N., 422

Subject Index

Adjunct questions, 319
Affixes, 216
Anaphora, 253
Assessment
  comparison of assessment types, 26
  curriculum-based. *See* Curriculum-based
      measurement
  definition of, 22
  instructional. *See* Instructional assessment
  normative-referenced, 24, 26
  traditional, 24, 26
Assumptions of instruction
  content, 16–17
  learner, 12–16
  model of, 9
  teacher, 8–12
Auditory segmenting, 207–208
  instructional format for, 236–238
Auditory soundblending, 207–208

Background knowledge
  in narrative comprehension, 250–252, 255
  in textbook prose comprehension, 314, 317
Base word, 215–216

Basic facts, 368
Behavior management. *See* Classroom management
Bundles of knowledge, 120–122

Change-up task, 37–39
Classroom management
  assumptions of, 471–475
  contexts of instruction in, 486–487
  language of consistency in, 484–485
  prevention procedures for, 475–487
  relationship to instruction, 468–471
Clause constructions, 275
Code-based reading instruction, 201–202
Cognitive strategies
  definitions of, 70–72, 78–81
  examples of, 80–81
  instructional requirements and implications for,
     81
  overview of, 71
Column alignment, 399
Component skills
  identification of, 62
  knowledge and relationship to reading
     comprehension, 252–253, 255

Comprehension. *See* Narrative text comprehension
      instruction; Textbook prose,
      comprehension skills required of
Concepts
   classes and examples of, 4–76, 153
   definitions of, 70, 74–76, 148
   instructional requirements and implications of,
      74–76
   overview of, 71
Concept teaching
   design features of, 151
   expansion of generic instructional set to, 148–149
      adding examples, 148
      nonexamples, 148–149
      teacher wording, 149, 156–157
   instructional formats for
      comparative concepts, 164–169, 185–186
         design features of, 168
      noun concepts, 173–177
         design features of, 179–180
      positional concepts, 169–173
         design features of, 173
   using the generic instructional set for, 152
      knowledge form, 152–153
      practice schedules, 164
      range of examples
         minimally different pairs, 160–162
         negative examples, 160, 163
         positive examples, 158–159
      selecting materials and examples for, 155–157
      teacher wording, 156–157
      testing examples, 162–164
Content area text. *See* Textbook prose
Content framing, 317–318
Contexts of learning, 23
Contextual analysis
   description of, 216–218
   instructional format for, 242–244
   skills in, figure, 217
Correction procedures
   examples of
      decoding, 234–235
      narrative comprehension, 279–280
      textbook prose comprehension, 337–338
      verbal chains, 134
   during instruction phase, 99–100
Corrective feedback, 234
Criterion level of performance, 103
Critical reading skills, sequence of examples for
      teaching, 275

Cumulative retell, 321–322, 331
Curriculum-based measurement, 24–25
Curriculum compression, 11–12
Curriculum deficiencies. *See* Mathematics curricula
Cycle of instruction, 88–89. *See also* Phases of
      instruction

Decoding
   definition of, 204–205
   textbook prose comprehension, 252
Decoding instruction
   component skills in, 206. *See also* Contextual
         analysis; Phonic analysis skills; Structural
         analysis
   delivery procedures for, 231–235
   instructional formats for, 237–244
   model of, 205
   using the generic instructional set
      knowledge form, 218–221
      practice schedule, 230
      range of examples, 221–223
      sequence of examples, 224–227
      test examples, 227–230
Delayed retesting, 38–40
   examples of, 40–42
      CVC words, 41
      elementary level, 42
      primary level, 40
Delivery of instruction, 60
Design of instruction
   comparison to delivery of instruction, 60
   explanation of 5–6
   phases of. *See* Phases of instruction
   relationship to disability, 6
Direct instruction in mathematics, 362
Disability, 6
Discovery learning approach in mathematics,
      360–362
Discriminations
   application of the generic instructional set to,
      136–137
   definitions of, 68, 136
   guidelines for designing sequences for teaching,
      144–145
   instructional format for, 137–140, 142–143
   overview of, 71
   sequence for testing, 142–143

Examples, concrete, 149–152. *See also* Generic
      instructional set

Expanded notation, 396
Expository text
    determining main idea of passage, 293
    explanation of, 258–259. *See also* Textbook
        prose
Expressive writing
    definition of, 420–421
    examples of, 428
    hierarchy of skills, 421
    scope and sequence of skills, 432–434
Expressive writing instruction
    approaches to, 425–430
        skills analysis, 430–438. *See also* Process
            approach to writing; Product approach to
            writing
    design features of, 436
    instructional formats for
        editing mechanical errors, 457–460
        writing paragraphs, 451–456
        writing simple sentences, 446–451
    task formats, 434–435
        for advanced writing exercises, 438
        for beginning writing exercises, 436
    using the generic instructional set
        knowledge form, 438–441
        practice schedule, 445–446
        range of examples, 441–444
        sequence of examples, 444–445
        test examples, 445–446

Facilitative questioning strategy, 266, 295–296
Firming cycle
    definition of, 93, 235
    examples of
        in decoding, 236
        in narrative prose comprehension, 280
        in simple facts, 127
        in textbook prose instruction, 338
Framing
    definition of, 231
    examples of
        in concept teaching, 170, 175
        in decoding, 231–232
        in narrative comprehension, 277–278
        in textbook comprehension, 334
        in verbal chains, 134
    instructional procedures for, 97
    purpose of, 96
    use of, in classroom management, 476, 478

Functional inadequacy
    model of, 17
    relationship to disability, 6

Generic design features. *See* Generic instructional set
Generic instructional set
    basic components of, 108–109, 120. *See also*
            Cognitive strategies; Concepts; Rule
            relationships; Verbal associations
    practice schedule, 112–114, 122
    range of examples, 109–110, 120
    sequence of examples, 110, 120
    test examples, 110–112, 120–122
    model of, 113, 123
    overview of, 108–114, 137
Graphic organizers
    description of, 324
    examples of, 335, 341, 357
    instructional formats for using, 339–342

Inferences, ranges of examples for teaching,
        270–271. *See also* Narrative text
        comprehension instruction
Instructional assessment
    advantages of, 27
    applications in, 44–52
        arithmetic computation, 47–49
        beginning decoding, 44
        reading comprehension, 49–52
    dimensions of, 27–36. *See also* Response
        dimensions; Task dimensions
    explanation of, 22, 24–27
    limitations of, 27
    procedural flowchart, 45
    techniques of, 36–42
        figure of, 37. *See also* Change-up task; Delayed
            retesting; Instructional prompting; Task
            variation and sequencing
    withdrawing, 52
Instructional cycle. *See* Cycle of instruction
Instructional design. *See* Design of instruction
Instructional features
    active, 106–107
    generic design. *See* Generic instructional set
    static, 106–107
Instructional interaction, 7–17
    model of, 9
    relationship to functional inadequacy, 17
Instructional prompting, 40–42
    examples of

Instructional prompting, *continued*
    in alphabetizing, 43
    in decoding, 43
Instructional technology. *See* Technology of
    instruction
Interaction. *See* Instructional interaction
Irregular-word reading
    description of, 211–212
    guidelines for teaching, 212
    instructional format for, 240–241

Knowledge forms, 59, 65–83
    Bloom's taxonomy, 65–66
    categories of, 68–83
    Gagne's categories, 67
    summary of, 71
    taxonomy of, 58, 67–72
        figures, 69, 121. *See also* Cognitive strategies;
        Concepts; Rule relationships; Verbal
        associations

Letter combinations
    description of, 212–213
    guidelines for teaching, 212–213
    major sounds, 212–213
Literal comprehension skills, 253, 266, 270–271.
    See also Narrative text comprehension
    instruction

Main idea
    knowledge form of, 266
    range of examples for teaching, 268. *See also*
        Narrative text comprehension instruction
Mathematics curricula
    modifying, 404–410
    problems of, 364–365, 393–404, 407–408
Mathematics instruction
    instructional formats
        for addition facts, 380–383
        for commutative property of multiplication,
            384–387
        for solving classification word problems,
            387–392
    using the generic instructional set
        knowledge form, 366–378
        practice examples, 379–380
        range of examples, 378
        sequence of examples, 378–379
        test examples, 379

Mathematics skills
    basic facts, 396–397
    column alignment, 399
    complex algorithms, 399, 407
    computation, 363, 393, 396–400, 412–413
    expanded notation, 396
    functional applications, 404, 413–414
    language, 363, 393–394, 411
    missing values, 397–398
    multiple operations, 403
    numeral identification, 396
    numeration, 363, 394–396
    problem-solving, 363, 400–404, 413–414
    rational counting, 394–395
    regrouping, 398–399
    scope and sequence of, 363–365, 411–414
Meaning-based reading instruction, 202
Metacognition, 260–261. *See also* Self-monitoring
Motivation, relationship of, to reading
        comprehension, 254–255
Multisyllabic words, 216

Narrative comprehension strategies
    examples of, 266–300
    relationship to phases of instruction, 264
Narrative comprehension tasks
    description of, 259–260
    features of, 261
Narrative text
    features of, 256
    types of
        scriptally implicit, 258
        textually explicit, 257
        textually implicit, 257
Narrative text comprehension instruction
    components of, 250–263
        figure, 251
    instructional formats for
        inferential comprehension, 297–300
        literal comprehension, 294–300
        main idea using pictures, 281–288
        main idea of a passage, 288–294
    instructional strategies
        before reading, 263–275
        during reading, 275–280
    using the generic instructional set, 263–275
        knowledge form, 263–267
        practice schedule, 273–275
        range of examples, 268–270
        sequence of examples, 270–273

Narrative test comprehension instruction, *continued*
  guidelines for, 272–273
  test examples, 273, 276
    guidelines for designing, 276
Nonsymbolic operations and task, 14–15, 61–65
Numeral identification, 396

Pacing
  definition of, 97–98, 232
  in narrative comprehension, 278
  in textbook comprehension, 335–336
Paragraph restatements
  description of, 319–320
  instructional format for, 342–346
  procedures for teaching, 320
Paragraph writing checklist, 437. *See also*
    Expressive writing instruction
Passive voice construction, 268–269
Phases of instruction
  after instruction
    adapting/modifying instruction, 103
    assessing instruction, 102–103
    managing instruction, 104
    reflecting on instruction, 105
    summary of critical features, 101–102, 106
    transferring instruction, 104–105
  before instruction
    adapting/modifying instruction, 93–94
    defining instruction, 90–91
    designing instruction, 91–93
    managing instruction, 93
    summary of critical features, 89–90, 94
  during instruction
    adapting/modifying instruction, 99–100
    delivering instruction, 97–99
    managing instruction, 95–96
    model of, 88–89
    summary of critical features, 95, 101
Phonemic awareness, 207–208. *See also* Auditory
    segmenting; Auditory soundblending.
Phonemic segmenting. *See* Auditory segmenting.
Phonic analysis skills, 206–214
  components of, 206
Prediction confirmation. *See* Text confirmation
    activities, 323
Prediction generation, 316–317
Preteaching
  definition of, 92, 232
  examples of
    in decoding, 232–233

in general, 92–93
  in narrative comprehension, 278
  in textbook comprehension, 335–336
  use of, in classroom management, 476, 478
Problem structure in mathematical problem solving,
    401–403
Process approach to writing
  deficits of less-skilled writers, 430
  description of, 429–430
Product approach to writing
  deficits of less-skilled writers, 427, 425–429
  description of, 426
Punishment as a transition tool, 481–483

Question generation, 320

Rational counting, 394–395
Reading comprehension. *See* Narrative text
    comprehension instruction; Textbook prose
Reading instruction for low-performing students,
    203–204. *See also* Code-based reading
    instruction; Decoding; Meaning-based
    reading instruction; Narrative text
    comprehension instruction; Textbook prose
Regrouping, 398–399
Regular-word reading
  description of, 209
  guidelines for teaching
    according to word complexity, 210–211
    sounding-out, 209–210
    whole-word, 209–210
  instructional format for, 238–239
Reinforcement in classroom management, 478–481
Response dimensions, 31–36
  format, 31–34
    examples of, 33–34
    figure of, 32
  modality, 32, 33–36
    examples of, 36
    types of, 32
Response format. *See* Response dimensions
Response modality. *See* Response dimensions
Rule relationships
  definitions of, 70, 76–77, 180
  examples of, 76–77, 180–181
  instructional requirements and implications of,
    76–78
  overview of, 71
  teaching
    instructional formats for, 187–188, 189–190

Rule relationships, *continued*
    using the generic instructional set for, 182–185
    procedures for breaking rules into chunks,
       182–183
Rules teaching in classroom management, 476, 478

Scope and sequence
    of beginning writing skills, 432–434
    of decoding skills, 206
    of mathematics skills, 405–406, 411–414
Self-monitoring
    checklist for expressive wirting, 437
    comprehension procedure for, 320–321,
       329–330
Self-study strategy, 322
Semantics, 216, 252
Signaling
    description of, 98, 233
    in textbook prose comprehension, 336–337
Simple facts
    application of generic instructional set to, 122–128
    correction procedures for, 126
    definition of, 68, 122
    instructional formats for teaching, 127–128
    overview of, 71
    testing sequence for, 125–126
Sound-symbol associations, 208–209
    classification of
       continuous sounds, 209
       stop sounds, 209
    guidelines for teaching, 208–209
Special education litigation, 4–5
Special rule words
    description of, 213
    examples of, 213–214
Story grammar, 256–257
Story problems, 401. *See* Mathematics skills,
       problem solving
Structural analysis
    description of, 215–216
    figure of skills in, 206, 215
Symbolic operations and tasks, 14–15, 61–67
    design of, 63–67
Syntax, 216–217, 252

Task
    features of expository tasks, 313–314
       examples of, 313–314
    relationship to narrative comprehension,
       259–260, 261

Task dimensions, 28–31, 36, 260, 261
    competency, 28–29, 31
    domain, 29–31
    examples of, 31
    figure, 29
    schedule, 29–31
Task-tantrum relationship, 485–486
Task variation and sequencing, 37–38
Taxonomy of knowledge. *See* Knowledge forms,
       taxonomy of
Technology of instruction, 4–5
Testing
    for acquisition, 276
    for discrimination, 276–277
    for generalization, 277
    for retention, 276
Text
    relationship of, to reading comprehension, 256,
       307
    types of, 256–259. *See also* Narrative text;
       Textbook prose
Textbook prose
    comprehension skills required by, 315
    description of, 306
    instructional formats
       for locating information from text, 346–349
       for using graphic organizers, 339–342
       for using paragraph restatements, 342–346
    instructional strategies for, 316–324, 325
       after reading, 322–324
       during reading, 318–322
       pre-reading, 316–318
       summary of, 325
    task-based factors that influence comprehension
       of, 308, 313–314, 352–353
    text-based factors that influence comprehension
       of, 307–313
       appropriateness, 310–311, 312
       coherence, 310–311, 312
       concepts, 308
       conventions, 309–310
       structure, 310–311, 312
    using the generic instructional set
       knowledge form, 326–328, 353–354
       practice schedule, 333
       range of examples, 328–330, 354–355
       sequence of examples, 330–332, 355–356
       test examples, 332–333
Text confirmation activities, 323
Text synthesis activities, 323–324

Think time
    definition and purpose of, 98–99, 233
        in decoding, 233
        in narrative comprehension, 279
        in textbook comprehension, 336

Verbal associations
    defined, 68
    instructional requirements and implications, 73–74
    types of, 68. *See also* Discriminations; Simple
        facts; Verbal chains

Verbal chains
    application of generic instructional set, 128–130
    correction procedure for, 134
    defined, 68, 128
    examples of, 73
    instructional format for teaching, 130–131
    overview of, 71
Visual displays. *See* Graphic organizers
Vocabulary instruction
    knowledge form of, 267
    sequence of examples for, 274